Commodity
& Propriety

Commodity & Propriety

~

COMPETING VISIONS OF
PROPERTY IN AMERICAN
LEGAL THOUGHT
1776–1970

Gregory S. Alexander

THE UNIVERSITY OF CHICAGO PRESS
CHICAGO & LONDON

Gregory S. Alexander is professor of law at Cornell Law School.

The University of Chicago Press, Chicago 60637
The University of Chicago Press, Ltd., London

© 1997 by The University of Chicago
All rights reserved. Published 1997
Printed in the United States of America

06 05 04 03 02 01 00 99 98 97 1 2 3 4 5

ISBN: 0-226-01353-7

Library of Congress Cataloging-in-Publication Data

Alexander, Gregory S., 1948–
    Commodity and propriety : competing visions of property in
American legal thought, 1776–1970 / Gregory S. Alexander.
        p.   cm.
    Includes index.
    ISBN 0-226-01353-7 (alk. paper)
    1. Property—Social aspects—United States—History.   2. Property—
United States—History.   3. Civil society—United States—History.
I. Title.
KF562.A43   1997
330.1′7—dc21   97-16784
                                                                                    CIP

To Kim

Contents

Acknowledgments

Writing acknowledgments is an act of celebration. It celebrates not only the book's completion but also the fact that so many people contributed to its production. Like all other authors, I have been the beneficiary of the help and support of many people, and I am genuinely happy to acknowledge them here. In the long course of this book's gestation, several colleagues and friends, at Cornell and elsewhere, have generously read various portions of the manuscript at different stages: Paul Carrington, Theodore Eisenberg, the late Alan Freeman, Hendrik Hartog, James Henretta, Barbara Holden-Smith, Paul Hyams, Isaac Kramnick, James Krier, Sheri Lynn Johnson, Elizabeth Mensch, Frank Michelman, Russell Osgood, Carol Rose, Bernard Rudden, Andrew Rutten, Steven Shiffrin, Robert Steinfeld, and Katherine Stone all read and commented on various chapters. Alfred Konefsky, John Henry Schlegel, and William Treanor were particularly profligate with their time, reading several chapters and offering invaluable advice.

Various chapters were presented at several workshops: American University (AA), Boston University, the University of Chicago, Cornell, the University of Michigan, and SUNY, Buffalo. I am sincerely grateful to those institutions for inviting me and to the participants in the workshops for their insightful comments and suggestions.

Institutional support was indispensable to the book's completion. Dean Russell Osgood was continually encouraging and provided a research leave and other financial support. The staff of the Cornell Law Library could not have been more helpful. I am especially grateful to Claire Germain, the Edward Cornell Law Librarian, and John Hasko, Associate Law Librarian. My secretary, Karen Wilson, helped me through many aspects of the book's production. Superb research assistance was provided by Eve Newman and Jennifer Zimmerman.

Acknowledgments

Working with the staff at the University of Chicago Press has been a genuine pleasure. John Tryneski has been as enthusiastic an editor as any author could hope for. My copyeditor, Robert Caceres, has been considerate, patient, and insightful.

Finally, there is my wife and best friend, Kim. No author has been more indebted to any one person than I am to her. For her intelligence, wisdom, encouragement, and boundless love, I am inexpressibly grateful.

Introduction

THE AIM OF THIS BOOK is to correct a widely shared misconception about the historical meaning and role of property in American law. For too long now, legal scholars, judges, historians, and political theorists have tended to accept uncritically the claim that there has been a single tradition of property throughout American history. Property, according to this mistaken view, has served one core purpose and has had a single constant meaning throughout American history: to define in material terms the legal and political sphere within which individuals are free to pursue their own private agendas and satisfy their own preferences, free from governmental coercion or other forms of external interference. Property, according to this understanding, is the foundation for the categorical separation of the realms of the private and public, individual and collectivity, the market and the polity.

The economic expression of this preference-satisfying conception of property is *market commodity*. Property satisfies individual preferences most effectively through the process of market exchange, or what lawyers call *market alienability*. The exchange function of property is so important in American society that property is often thought to be synonymous with the idea of market commodity.

The basic argument of this book is that this commodity theory of property is only half right. Property-as-commodity is one-half of a dialectic that American legal writing has continuously expressed from the nation's beginning to the recent past. The other half of the dialectic is a conception that, following the lead of Carol Rose, I will call "property as propriety."[1] According to this view, property is the material foundation for creating and maintaining the proper social order, the private basis for the public good. This tradition, whose roots can be traced back to Aristotle, has continuously understood the individual human as an inherently

1

social being, inevitably dependent on others not only to thrive but even just to survive. This irreducible interdependency means that individuals owe one another obligations, not by virtue of consent alone but as an inherent incident of the human condition. This view of human nature provides the basis for the political-legal principle in proprietarian thought that when individuals fail to meet their precontractual social obligations, the state may legitimately compel them to act for the good of the entire community.

The concept of the common weal, moreover, was understood to have substantive meaning. The common law maxim *salus populi suprema est lex* (the welfare of the people is the supreme law) had real content.[2] The public good was not understood as simply whatever the market produces, for the market was viewed as a realm in which individuals were too vulnerable to the temptation to act out of narrow self-interest rather than, as proprietarian principles required, for the purpose of maintaining the properly ordered society.

Just what the proper social order is has been an enormously controversial issue throughout American history. The existence of different substantive conceptions of the proper social order means that there have been multiple versions of the proprietarian conception of property in American legal thought. Not only over time but also at any single moment, American legal writers have held sometimes radically different notions of the public good and its implications for property. All of these understandings of property share, however, a commitment to the basic idea that the core purpose of property is not to satisfy individual preferences or to increase wealth but to fulfill some prior normative vision of how society and the polity that governs it should be structured.

It may be surprising to most readers that individual liberty seems to have no place within this dialectic. After all, it is a commonplace of liberal political theory that liberty and property are intimately intertwined. As Michael Kammen noted in his Curti Lectures, "Liberty and property . . . have usually been understood as complementary values: deprive or deny one, and the other is instantly in jeopardy."[3] Indeed, guaranteeing individual liberty, or autonomy, is often thought to constitute *the* core substantive role of property rights. Where, then, does liberty fit within the dialectic of commodity and propriety?

The answer is that it is part of both sides. Liberty, both generally and in its specific relationship to property, is an ambiguous concept. It may mean either immunity of the private realm from public interference (freedom *from*) or personal autonomy as a precondition for effective citizenship (freedom *to*).[4] The first is commonly associated with the name of John Locke, the second with James Harrington; the first, or "negative," meaning of liberty coalesces with the commodity theory of property, while liberty in its civic sense is closely connected with property-as-propriety.

Negative liberty and property-as-commodity share three important normative commitments: first, the moral and political priority of the individual over the community; second, the subjectivity of values (values as preferences); and, third, the market as the primary mechanism for mediating individual preferences within society. The configuration linking positive liberty with property-as-propriety is more complex and less familiar to modern readers. At its core, however, is the idea that the proper society is more than just whatever emerges from market relations. The properly ordered society may coincide with the market society, but the two are not identical. The market view of society is essentially empty. It can and historically has yielded many different sorts of society. The proprietarian, by contrast, is always committed to some particular substantive view of how society should be ordered. This is why the distinction between the proprietarian and commodity conceptions of property cannot be dissolved simply by saying that the commodity conception, too, is "proper" because it emerges from the market.

The commodity and propriety conceptions of property, together with their associated conceptions of individual liberty, are ideal types. Few, if any, American legal writers were consistently and exclusively committed to one or the other. Not only did both ways of looking at property occur simultaneously throughout American history (though with varying degrees of influence), but individual texts often exhibited aspects of both conceptions.

Both conceptions, moreover, were complex and mutable. The changes in their meanings were synchronic as well as diachronic. The consequence of this complexity is that terms such as "liberty" often seemed to wander from one side of the dialectic to the other. These occasions sometimes were the result of self-contradiction, but more frequently they resulted from some variation in the term's meaning. Used by themselves, terms like "liberty" have a habit of meaning different things in different situations, and this is even more true when the term is part of a broader, more complex conceptual configuration.[5] In its relation to property, the

complexity of the meaning of "liberty" is best examined through the dialectic of commodity and propriety.

~

While the idea of property as commodity is familiar to the point of banality, the other half of the dialectic rings oddly in modern ears. Demonstrating that property-as-propriety *was* (and continues to be) a part of American legal thought will be the major burden of this book. As inhabitants
of a modern, marketized society, we are so used to thinking of property
as market commodity that it seems difficult to imagine that property
might be intended to benefit anyone other than the owner. We are limited
not only by the pervasiveness of market exchange in virtually every sector
of modern life but also by the fact that the very notion of the public good
seems anachronistic to modern sensibilities. That notion was more than
familiar to our predecessors, however; it was an article of faith. So, too,
was the idea that privately owned property is intended to serve the public
good.

To many American lawyers in the generation of the Founders, the
public good was whatever maintained a social structure within which
each person and each institution had a proper role and position. The
modern idea of a fluid society in which individuals readily move, either
geographically or, more important, in the social hierarchy, was anathema
to this mentality, which the Founders' generation inherited from premodern sources. The proper social order was by and large a static one. The
public good was best served if everyone fulfilled a role in the natural
hierarchy.

Property was central to this plan of social stability. It anchored the
citizen to his (for in this premodern vision, the citizen-freeholder could
only be a man) rightful place in the proper social hierarchy. Property, of
which the only important form was the freehold estate in land, was more
than wealth; it was authority, or at least a source of authority. Far from
being looked on as a market commodity, land was, as Gordon Wood has
put it, "a means of maintaining one's gentility and independence from
the caprices of the market."[6]

The American Revolution effected some change in this proprietarian
vision but did not eliminate it altogether from American legal thought
or writing.[7] A revised version of the proprietarian conception continued
to be very much in evidence in the post-Revolutionary and Constitutional
periods. The Revolutionary ideology of civic republicanism reshaped the

old premodern understanding, to be sure, purging it of its most conspicuously hierarchical and aristocratic aspects. It is a mistake to suppose, however, that the civic republican understanding of property itself was neither
hierarchical nor proprietarian. Nothing could be further from the truth.
Republican property had its own hierarchy. Married women were legally
incapacitated as autonomous property owners. Enslaved African Americans were nonowners in most respects. White males stood at the top of the
property-owning hierarchy, and it was they to whom republican ideology
looked to create and perpetuate the proper social order and the proper
polity.

This is not to suggest that the idea of property as governance and order
was the only way of thinking about property available to American lawyers
in the eighteenth century. The opposing idea of property as commodity
had always had some presence in eighteenth-century American legal discourse. It became increasingly conspicuous in the Constitutional era, as
lawyers debated which interests merited special protection under the Constitution and what form of protection was appropriate. With the tremendous economic and social changes that characterized the decades after
the War of 1812, the market seemed to Americans ever more important
in their daily lives, and legal rhetoric reflected this growing market consciousness. This trend in legal writing about property hardly abated in the
second half of the nineteenth century, characterized as it was by increasing
accumulation and concentration of capital in the hands of a relatively
small number of business firms. The idea of property as wealth loomed
large in legal consciousness during this period, and it threatened to mo-
nopolize legal thought just as much as Standard Oil Company monopolized the oil industry. The threat never became reality, however. The old
idea of property as propriety, although clearly weaker now than the commodity conception, still competed for attention.

The story is largely the same in the twentieth century. The language
of the market has dominated American legal discourse about property,
but the vision of property as the basis of proper order and the common
good has remained viable. From the Progressive era through the New
Deal and, later, the Great Society, property has undergone profound
changes, both as a social institution and as a legal concept.[8] But through
all of these changes, one feature of American legal thought and writing
about property has remained constant: its dialectical character.

The story that this book tells about property, then, is one of continuity.
The sense in which I see American legal thought about property as contin-

uous, however, differs importantly from the sense of continuity that pervades the conventional historiography. The dominant view sees American legal thinking about property as continuous in a monist sense. American legal writers have held only one understanding of property—market property—throughout the nation's history. According to this view, there have never been any serious external ideological challenges to the monopoly hold of that conception on American legal writers. Nor has American legal writing about property reflected any tensions, ambiguities, or paradoxes in the idea of market, or commodified, property. The whole course of property's intellectual development in legal discourse has been smooth, internally coherent, and uniform.

This monist perspective has had very different ideological implications for different historians. For centrist or center-right scholars, it is a legitimating story. It is no coincidence that this conventional historical wisdom about property in American legal thought strongly echoes themes that we now associate with the so-called consensualist historians of the 1950s, notably Louis Hartz and Edward S. Corwin. Hartz's famous book *The Liberal Tradition in America* argued that since its founding America has consistently had a single political tradition—liberalism.[9] Corwin told a similar story about America's constitutional past. American constitutionalism, Corwin argued in several books and articles,[10] originated in an ancient tradition of higher law principles. Those principles turned out to be familiarly liberal—vested rights, judicial review, and due process— and the tradition was liberalism's basic division of the world into private right and public power.

For historians on the Left, the monist story is the basis for critique of the American legal system. A recent example of this genre is Jennifer Nedelsky's book, *Private Property and the Limits of American Constitutionalism*.[11] As Professor Nedelsky tells it, American constitutional history from 1787 to 1937 has been one long story of property being privileged over all other interests and values. Property, moreover, has meant the same thing to lawyers throughout these years: market property, property as commodity, property as the wall between private preference and the public weal. "[T]here were not," she contends, "two competing ideologies or rhetorics of property. The dominant image prevailed of property as a fundamental American value, a basic individual right secure against encroachment, even by the powers of government."[12] In her view, market property's privileged position in the constitutional hierarchy has undermined American democracy. The implication is clear: property must be knocked off its throne so that a new, more democratic political order can be created.[13]

While the primary aims of this book are descriptive and analytical, it does have implications for current political issues. The discovery that American legal thought and writing has understood property in a proprietarian sense as well as in a market sense means that there is no basis for historically privileging one conception over the other. Those commentators on the political Right who have argued that any and every government action that interferes with the ability of property owners to use their property for the exclusive purpose of satisfying private desires offends a timeless and singular American tradition[14] are quite simply wrong. Similarly, those on the political Left who attack American legal thought about property as historically committed to a single, Lockean tradition are wrong. There is no single American traditional meaning of property in American legal thought. Rather, there have been multiple meanings and multiple traditions of property throughout our history.

Nevertheless, if one had to choose between these two views, Professor Nedelsky's would have the better argument. The very fact that so many people do think that the market idea of property has monopolized American legal thought gives it greater credibility and legitimacy in our political environment. This was recently made apparent in the United States Supreme Court's decision in *Lucas v. South Carolina Coastal Commission*.[15] In that case, the Court overturned the South Carolina legislature's determination about when an environmental regulation that did not provide compensation for affected landowners was appropriately in the public interest. In his opinion for the Court, Justice Antonin Scalia relied on the supposed existence of a singular American tradition concerning the protection of private property. Had Justice Scalia been more historically informed, he would have understood that the legislature's determination itself was part of another American tradition concerning the appropriate use of land—one that can be traced back to eighteenth-century republican roots.

Thus one aim of this book is to make it more difficult for scholars and judges to indulge in historical pretensions such as Justice Scalia's in *Lucas*.

◁◇▷

What accounts for the existence and continuity of the dialectic between the market and proprietarian conceptions of property? Historical phenomena, including intellectual phenomena, rarely lend themselves to simple explanations. In general, I have tried to steer a middle course between idealist and materialist explanations. Indeed, I regard that as a false choice. In this sense, the historiographical commitment of this book departs from more materialist approaches such as the Wisconsin school of the great Willard Hurst and his progeny and, on the other side, the structuralist legal histories sometimes associated with the early Critical Legal Studies movement.

My general view of the relationship between economic and intellectual-cultural factors can be summarized this way: Throughout American history, particular changes in economic circumstances created conditions that cultural and intellectual elites regarded as dilemmas, or "predicaments," as I prefer to call them. The most influential legal writings of given historical periods were responses by legal elites to these predicaments. They were attempts to resolve (or some cases, dissolve) those predicaments. Elite legal writers were, after all, lawyers, and as such they were trained to attend to concrete problems. Their legal training predisposed them to be primarily concerned with the concrete political and economic conditions within which legal doctrine and legal rules operate. This is not to say that legal ideas lack any degree of autonomy; rather, as lawyers, legal intellectuals (including those of the late twentieth century) have tended to be highly responsive to particular political and economic circumstances in developing their ideas.

While multiple factors doubtless influenced the development of American legal thinking and writing about property, two factors seem especially important in explaining the dialectical character of American legal discourse about property. First, the proprietarian conception was a well-established tradition in European legal-political thought, and eighteenth-century American legal intellectuals were the heirs of that tradition. The most obvious expression of that tradition in the eighteenth century was the civic republican ideology.

Ideology was not the only factor that influenced how eighteenth-century American lawyers understood property. Social practices and institutions reinforced the ideological underpinnings of the proprietarian understanding of property. The American colonies themselves began as property-based arrangements that were overtly proprietarian in character. The founding charters were sources of political authority to the colonial trustees as much as they were conveyances of land, and it was expected that the founders and trustees would exercise their authority and property rights for the purpose of creating a properly ordered society. James Oglethorpe and the original Trustees of Georgia, for example, intended that their new colony would be "as much a beacon to the rest of the world as the New England Puritans had intended Massachusetts Bay to be a century before."[16] To achieve that goal, they created a social hierarchy only somewhat less rigid than their Puritan counterparts, forbidding Roman Catholics, African slaves, and even lawyers from the colony on the ground that these groups threatened good government.[17]

The founding charters of the American colonies were not the only instance in which the significance of ownership of property was that it defined the scope of authority for governing. The European practice of endowing cities with land ownership and vesting the authority of managing that property in municipal corporations provided the model for municipal governance in colonial American cities like New York.[18] Similarly, enterprises were commonly created on the basis of grants that were simultaneously sources of governing authority and transfers of exclusive property rights.

The existence of private authority based on monopoly property interests in seventeenth- and eighteenth-century America should not lead to the conclusion that the state was inactive in assuring that property was used in the interest of maintaining the proper order. Thanks to the "commonwealth studies" of the Handlins, Harry Scheiber, Willard Hurst, Leonard Levy, and, more recently, the "common regulation" work of William Novak,[19] we now know just how heavily regulated property was in pre-nineteenth-century America. All of this state regulatory activity reflected the proprietarian understanding that certain activities and certain resources should not be left to regulation by the market, for the market could not assure that the proper social order would be maintained. State regulation, moreover, was not understood as a response to particular interests engaging in what economists call "rent seeking." Rather, it was, as William Novak has expressed it, "a moral exercise for the promotion of public happiness in the good society." Novak goes on to specify the core features of this proprietarian conception of state regulation: "(1) an adherence to the common law as an experiential yet flexible source of value and guidance; (2) an overriding concern with common, rather than private goods and interests; and (3) a commitment to the commonwealth as the guarantor of public happiness and the general welfare."[20] Here again we see the core proprietarian ideas that the primary purpose of property is to maintain the proper social order and that the market cannot be relied on to create that order.

The second causal factor is less strictly intellectual than cultural. The dialectic between these two understandings of property involves the relationship between property and modernity (as distinguished from modern*ism*)[21] in American law and American society. More precisely, it is about how elite American legal writers reacted to the emergence and gradual expansion of the modern cultural conception of property. The persistence of the proprietarian conception in American legal writing after the Revolution was, I argue, a discursive means of responding to the newly ascendant modern world and its culture.

"Modernity" is a notoriously slippery term. Unfortunately, it has no substitute that is any more precise in specifying its meaning as a particular culture. Without attempting a complete account of modernity, we may cite two features that characterize modern society and culture: first, the market as the dominant mechanism for structuring the social order, and, second, the belief in human progress through human will.

Few historians or social theorists would doubt that market society and market property are essential elements of the culture of modernity. Simon Schama's characterization of modernity as a culture in which "capital replaces custom as the arbiter of social values, where professionals rather than amateurs run institutions of law and government, and where commerce and industry rather than land lead economic growth"[22] captures the centrality of the market and commodification to modernity. In the modern society relationships are largely structured through market transactions. The key bases of premodern society—custom, kinship, local authority—are gradually replaced by or at least subordinated to less personalized exchange transactions. Property has a distinct meaning in modern culture. As Hendrik Hartog has pointed out, one of the defining characteristics of modernity is that it is a culture "where property is characterized by the relationship between a person and peculiarly economic resources, a world where land itself has been largely reduced to a commodity."[23]

A second defining characteristic of social and cultural modernity is a commitment to progress through individual human agency. The modern outlook is optimistic about the prospects for society's future. The belief in social progress, the belief that societies always have it within their power constantly to improve their lot, is an article of faith in modern consciousness.[24] The idea of progress itself, of course, is hardly unique to secular modern culture. Christianity, for example, has always strongly relied on a belief in progress. But one of the crucial differences between modern and premodern culture is the precise meaning that its *mentalité* attaches to progress. The basis of premodern Anglo-American Christian millenialism was not a belief in progressive improvement but in providence.[25] History *was* directional, not in terms of a progression from want to wealth, though, but from humanity's fall to its redemption. The modern idea of progress did more than merely secularize this belief. While retaining its linear understanding of history (a matter that I explore in some detail in chapter 2), modern culture transformed the very meaning of progress. From the modernist perspective, social change is desirable precisely because it is equated with improvement in the material conditions of society, here and now. Progress, moreover, is neither inevitable nor teleological. It occurs to the extent that human effort brings it about, and there has no inherent limitation. As the late Christopher Lasch explained, "The [modern] idea of progress . . . owes its appeal . . . to the seemingly . . . realistic expectation that the expansion of productive forces can continue indefinitely."[26]

These two characteristics—the dominance of market relations in society and the belief in the possibility of endless material progress through the exercise of individual will—are closely linked in modernity. Modern culture *is,* primarily, market culture because it is one in which individuals realize their authority through commodity-exchange relationships. Material progress is the result of the actions of autonomous individual actors realizing their full potential in market transactions. Individual autonomy to act in the marketplace has always been a core ideological precept of modern culture. Modernity's heroic figure is the self-governing economic agent, the man (for depictions of this hero have usually been gendered in modern culture) of energy and action, freeing himself of artificial constraints on his ability to realize his full potential through market transactions. As T. J. Jackson Lears has pointed out, "From the [modern] view, the autonomous self was a Promethean figure, conquering fate through sheer force of will."[27] The Promethean experience is one of personal liberation. The story of Prometheus is one of release of energy when Prometheus frees himself from the chains with which Zeus had shackled him to a rock as punishment for stealing the fire of creativity from the gods and giving it to humans. Writ large, this mythic vision depicts individual will as a reservoir of great energy whose release from the restraints of an oppressive and hierarchical authority benefits society as a whole as well as the individual.

This is the vision that underlay modern legal culture's perception of the role of property. The modern vision is especially evident in connection with enterprise property, but it applied to family property as well. It is evident in the familiar interpretation of the historical development of Anglo-American property law as the steady expansion of individual freedom of ownership, especially freedom of transferability. According to this story, marketability of property progressively increased as courts cast off first feudal, then mercantilist restraints. That self-perception of American property law as breaking with the past and liberating individuals dates as far back as the decades before the Revolution, when legislative reforms, like Jefferson's in Virginia, self-consciously purged American property law of its most conspicuous "feudal" entanglements.[28]

The same vision underlay antebellum nineteenth-century statements of public policy concerning property. Willard Hurst summarized that vision in his characteristically lucid way. Mid-nineteenth-century public policy, Hurst wrote, reflected the perception that "[h]uman nature is creative, and its meaning lies largely in the expression of its creative capacity; hence it is socially desirable that there be broad opportunity for the release of creative human energy."[29] The classic judicial expression of this "release of energy" vision, as Hurst noted,[30] was Chief Justice Roger Taney's opinion for the Court in the *Charles River Bridge* case,[31] but there were countless other expressions of the same outlook in more mundane legal texts throughout the nineteenth century.

While the "release of energy" vision represented the dominant legal outlook toward market property, a less optimistic reaction to modernity has also been present in the legal discourse of property. From the nation's very beginning, various legal writers have expressed anxiety about modernity and specifically about the market idea of property. The immediate reasons for their anxiety changed over time as social and economic conditions changed, and even during the same periods not all of these writers expressed identical concerns. Still, throughout these writings there emerged a recurrent theme that the market mentality would corrode the traditions, habits, and values that, in the writers' views, constituted the core of the republic.

The most coherent expressions of that view drew directly from the civic republican tradition of sentiment that American Revolutionaries had inherited from seventeenth-century English Whigs. It would be grossly anachronistic, of course, to describe the entire civic tradition as anti-modern. The American incarnation of civic republicanism, however, can be meaningfully understood as, at least in part, a response to modernity. The core ideas of civic thought—the priority of virtue (individual and collective) over self-interest, the fear of corruption, the need for stability, property as a material foundation of civic virtue—easily lent themselves to being put into the service of expressing doubts about the benefits of a society where the market was the final arbiter of values. The intellectual leaders of the American Revolution were, Professor Pocock has taught us, "involved in a complex relation both with English and Renaissance cultural history and with a tradition of thought which had from its beginnings confronted political man with his own history and was, by the time of the Revolution, being used to express an early form of the quarrel with modernity."[32]

This is not to say that the American legal writers who used republican rhetoric were clearly anti-market or anti-commerce. Without getting into a defense of Pocock and other historians associated with his interpretation, it must be said that some of the Pocockian school's critics have been too quick to attribute to him the claim that Thomas Jefferson was opposed to commerce, markets, and economic progress.[33] Jefferson was no American Luddite. No one possessing the interest in and accomplishments at science and engineering that Jefferson did could be opposed to technological development. Nor was he an unwavering champion of social tradition. No one who wrote that "the earth belongs in usufruct to the living"[34] could be eager to preserve the dead hand of the past. What Pocock's study underscored (although his own rhetoric did not make entirely clear) was that many American lawyers and political leaders of Jefferson's generation inherited the English Whigs' view that a nation whose political economy and whose culture became entirely devoted to the creation of wealth— modernity in that sense, later expressed as Hamilton's "commercial empire"—could not also be a nation whose primary public value was civic virtue. There was no room in a culture devoted to private wealth for a substantive vision of the proper social order with property as its keystone.

The same anxiety was evident in the legal discourse of subsequent generations. As modernity changed American society in increasingly profound respects throughout the nineteenth century, some legal intellectuals continued to articulate a conception of property as the foundation for preserving the social order. They did not so much express a "dread of modernity"[35] as they did a concern with the question whether the idea of proper social order could be accommodated within modern market culture. To be sure, some expressions of this mentality were more nostalgic, more "anti-modern," than others. Still, elite legal writers rarely were in a position to oppose modernity *tout court* and certainly were not in a position to oppose capitalism as such. What they did oppose was an open-ended form of social transformation, a culture in which an unconstrained market was the ultimate determinant of social values and the social structure. What they wanted to maintain was a social order in which every person occupied his or her proper place and in which property was used to promote the good of the entire community.

Precisely because there were different substantive conceptions of what the proper social order was, it is more accurate to speak of multiple proprietarian visions than a single legal idea of property-as-propriety that endured throughout American history. Stated in terms of a distinction well known to philosophers, while property-as-propriety was a single *concept,* the substantive meaning of that concept has been contested over time, creating multiple *conceptions* of that concept.[36]

For the same reason, I have chosen to refer to multiple "dialectics." American lawyers writing within the proprietarian tradition have reacted to the rise of the market understanding of property by offering different substantive visions of the proper social order at different times. The social vision of pro-slavery Southern legal writers in the antebellum nineteenth century, for example, differed in fundamental respects from that of eighteenth-century republicans, and these differences produced different responses to market property, both as a concept and an institution. The terms of the dialectics changed as the social, political, and economic conditions of modernity changed. These dialectics were conceptual and discursive responses to the predicaments of modernity that the legal cultures of different periods identified as central to them. As the identities of these predicament changed, so did the particular dialectics.

The predicaments themselves changed for reasons that were both exogenous and endogenous to legal thought and culture. The exogenous sources of change include social, economic and political developments, such as the emergence of large-scale industrial enterprises and shifts in the balance of power of particular political groups. Legal thought about property, however, did not develop solely in a responsive fashion. It was not strictly epiphenomenal to social, political, and economic forces. Tracing its development also requires paying attention to the processes of internal conceptual change. Ambiguities and paradoxical aspects of the conceptual elements of one period sowed the seeds for change, if not destruction, of that period's articulation of their predicament and their discursive responses to that predicament.

This is a study of legal thought in the broad sense of that term. It is not primarily a history of doctrinal development, although I do not entirely ignore doctrine. My focus is on how legal intellectuals have constructed the core meanings of property as a social, political, and economic concept and institution rather than as a strictly legal concept. The writers, including judges, whose texts are the subject of this study were consciously concerned with the relationship between property as a legal concept and institution and the nonlegal worlds in which legal property is embedded.

My view is that legal culture, while obviously distinctive in certain respects and to some degree autonomous, is not a black box. In constructing meanings of fundamental legal concepts like property, legal intellectuals draw on cultural and intellectual sources that are not strictly legal. Legal intellectuals are participants in what Alfred Konefsky has called "cultural nexus[es]," which he defines as "complex relationships with other social elites."[37] Those other elites include nonlegal intellectuals and other leading figures of the period's culture. Cultural nexuses are an important means of transmission of ideas and values between legal and nonlegal elites.

This book traces legal thought and legal writing through a very long time frame—the bulk of our nation's history. I have divided that extended time frame into four main periods: the civic republican period, 1776–1800; the commercial republican period, 1800–1860; the industrial period, 1870–1917; and the late modern period, 1917–1970. I refer to these periods as "cultures." More accurately, they are stages in the development of a single legal culture, that of modernity, rather than separate and discrete cultures themselves. Insofar as the major institutions and concepts of modern society and culture were in place in the United States by the end of the Revolutionary War, American society and culture, including its legal culture, have been modern since the nation's founding. But while American legal culture after the Revolution has always been modern, it has not been unchanged. Applied to legal culture as well as the culture and society more generally, modernity is not a static phenomenon. My periodization represents an attempt to identify and emphasize the critical ways in which modern legal culture, particularly in its relationship to property, has changed while retaining its basically modern character.

At the beginning of each of the four parts, I have included a short prologue. The purpose of these prologues is to describe the relationship between elite legal writers and the rest of the profession. To what extent do elite legal texts such as James Kent's *Commentaries on American Law* reflect the ideas and understandings of the non-elite portion of the bar and to what extent did they help shape those ideas and understandings? My view is that elite legal writings historically have not been created in a vacuum, isolated from the consciousness of the rest of the profession. While the sociology of the American legal profession certainly has changed—in some respects radically—since the late eighteenth century, the profession has always had a considerable degree of cohesiveness. At least since the late eighteenth century, legal elites have been sufficiently connected with the activities of the legal profession as a whole to enable them to have had access to the attitudes, ideas, and understandings of non-elite lawyers. To a considerable degree, this connection ("fusion" would be far too strong a term) resulted from the process of professionalization of lawyers that had begun prior to the late eighteenth century and continued in the early nineteenth century.[38] Nevertheless, the relationship between elite legal writers and the majority of the profession has changed over time. These changes need to be noted in interpreting the legal discourse of property during different periods.

Americans often assume that their cultural symbols have a single historical meaning, only one tradition. Put somewhat differently, they suppose that every symbol is associated with only one story about our past.[39] That assumption allows ideological constituencies to lay claim to these symbols as privileging their own particular political visions for the future. The historical reality behind our greatest cultural symbols, however, is seldom that neat. Throughout American history, different Americans have attached very different, sometimes contradictory, messages to the nation's core symbols and used the same symbol to tell very different stories. The American flag is one example. That symbol can be and has been used to tell both a story of a historical struggle against tyranny and a story of imperialist and racist oppression, to pick only two of the many stories that one could plausibly associate with Old Glory. Historical reality embraces both of these stories. Neither trumps the other. Both are parts of our national tradition.

Private property is another such symbol. Property has been a powerful cultural symbol throughout American history. It has signified more than one message, more than one tradition for Americans. One of those traditions is a commitment to allowing individuals to satisfy their personal preferences and to increase their wealth through market exchange. No one would doubt that commodification has been one of our (to borrow a phrase from Margaret Jane Radin) "cultural commitments of property."[40] But it has not been our only commitment. Another has been to the idea of property as the foundation for the proper social order—the proprietarian tradition.

The existence of both of these cultural commitments in legal thought throughout our history means that in debates over public control of private property no one can legitimately rely on history as exclusively endorsing their own political agenda. Whether one wishes government to exercise less power over the use of private property or, on the other hand, favors strengthening the public dimension of property through regulation, taxation, or other means, the case must be made on its own substantive merits. Historical "tradition" provides no shortcut to any political end concerning the role of private property. There is no single past to which we can return.

PART ONE

The Civic Republican Culture,
1776–1800

Legal Writing in the Civic Republican Era

L EGAL WRITING IN THE late eighteenth century was strikingly different from what it is today. Largely concerned with the broad issues of the time, it seems to modern eyes distinctly nonlegal. Unlike most writing that lawyers produce today, it was not primarily intended to serve the needs of the legal profession as a discrete social group. Little of it was highly technical or intelligible only to other lawyers.

For guidance, American practitioners had to turn to English texts, if they were available. There were no American-written manuals on technical topics like replevin or contingent remainders. Americans did not even produce a general treatise on American Law until James Kent's *Commentaries on American Law* first appeared in 1826. The legal discourse that did focus on technical legal issues connected those issues with the fundamental political issues of the day, such as the dismantling of "aristocracy" and getting rid of all vestiges of feudalism. No American legal texts published in the last quarter of the eighteenth century were strictly doctrinal, written for the purpose of summarizing or clarifying the law. It was not until the nineteenth century that American lawyers produced practice manuals, doctrinal treatises, and similar professionally oriented texts.

We cannot explain this absence of professional legal literature on the lack of any non-American models that were available to American lawyers at the time. English legal writers had produced monographs that were strictly doctrinal and highly technical as early as the seventeenth century. These were early versions of what we think of today as legal treatises.[1] Most were on narrow topics, such as contingent remainders[2] and distresses and ejectments.[3] While these texts would not have been available to ordinary American lawyers of the late eighteenth century, they certainly were available to the highly literate portion of the American bar. The personal libraries of men like Madison and Jefferson were filled with books, including legal texts, published in Europe and not widely available in America. Elite American lawyers at that time were doubtless familiar with a more strictly legal form of legal writing, yet they chose not to pursue that form. Why not?

The explanation that historians most commonly offer points to the unprofessional character of the American bar in the years after the Revolution. (By "unprofessional," I refer not to the quality of their work, but to the sense of cohesiveness and collective identity that we associate with social practices of professions.[4]) The picture that historians have given us of lawyers in the late eighteenth century depicts the American bar as disorganized and disreputable. According to Perry Miller's influential account, the legal profession in 1790 was in a "chaotic condition."[5] Lawyers, Miller told us, had little social or economic power until the nineteenth century. In the post-Revolutionary era, there was widespread hostility to lawyers and to law in general but especially the common law. Both lawyers and the common law were considered to be un-American vestiges of English hierarchy and oppression. Facing such antipathy, the conventional account goes, American lawyers had all they could do to keep any role for themselves at all. There was simply no opportunity for them to engage in professional activities like technical legal writing.

Putting aside the broader issue of whether public hostility to lawyers was so pronounced, compared, at least, with that found in any other period,[6] I want to suggest an alternative explanation for the unprofessional character of American legal discourse during the last quarter of the eighteenth century. American legal writing of the post-Revolutionary and Constitutional periods, I want to argue, was overwhelmingly nontechnical and in that sense nonlegal because of the image that lawyers, especially at the elite level, held of law and of themselves. Committed to the tenets of civic republicanism[7] but increasingly anxious about the feasibility of creating a virtuous republic, elite lawyers of all political persuasions after the Revolution came to view law as the social agency best suited for transcending a polity based on narrow interests. As a concomitant of that conception of law, they regarded themselves as the sole group in American society capable of creating and then leading a republican government.

The reigning ideology of civic republicanism required that public leaders be virtuous, meaning that leaders be free from self-interest and capable of acting in the interests of the common good. The central dilemma confronting those who set about to realize the republican ideal was identifying a group of citizens who possessed the requisite independence. There was little dissent from the view that "men of learning, leisure and easy circumstances . . . if they are endowed with wisdom, virtue & humanity, are much fitter for every part of the business of government, than the ordinary class of people."[8] But who met the requisite criteria? The problem was that America had no genuine leisure class. Very few Americans possessed sufficient personal wealth to allow them to refrain from working so that they could single-mindedly pursue civic virtue.

The solution was to conceive of lawyers as learned professionals whose work transcended the marketplace.[9] Justifying the role of lawyers as the preeminent voice in the republic, Alexander Hamilton argued that lawyers "truly form no distinct interest in society."[10] They "will feel a neutrality to the rivalships between the different branches of industry, be likely to prove an impartial arbiter between them, ready to promote the interests of either, so far as it shall appear to [them] conducive to the general interests of society."[11] Legal training was regarded as desirable precisely because it was, in the view of the post-Revolutionary era American lawyers, the best preparation for a public life. Law, Thomas Jefferson wrote, "qualifies a man to be useful to himself, to his neighbors, and to the public. It is the most certain stepping stone to preferment in the political line."[12]

To a considerable extent lawyers fulfilled this self-image. Whatever the overall position of the legal profession during the Revolutionary and post-Revolutionary periods, it is clear that lawyers dominated the ranks of the political leaders who forged the new nation. The overwhelming majority of leaders among the generation of Founding Fathers—Jefferson, Madison, Jay, Hamilton, John Adams, to cite only the most famous—were lawyers. Nearly half of the signers of the Declaration of Independence and three-fifths of the delegates to the Constitutional Convention were lawyers.[13] At lower levels as well, lawyers were the largest force in politics.

Lawyers' political influence did not end with holding public office. In post-Revolutionary America, the leading orators and public speakers were lawyers, replacing ministers as the nation's primary public spokesmen.[14] As Robert Gordon has pointed out, in the late eighteenth century lawyers "were rapidly becoming the primary medium of America's public discourse and indeed its 'civic religion.'"[15]

This self-image influenced the character of legal writing. Elite lawyers viewed legal writing as a form of public discourse. The intended audience for nearly all public legal discourse included lawyers certainly, but it was not confined to lawyers. Legal writers sought to reach a broader range of citizens, men (for citizenship was strongly gendered at the time) who were educated, high-minded, and civic-oriented. The writing that elite American lawyers produced in the Revolutionary through Constitutional eras was as much political as it was legal, if not more so. "Political," moreover, must be understood in a very broad sense that may be almost unrecognizable to us today. Thus a text as seemingly apolitical as Thomas Jefferson's *Notes on the State of Virginia,* first published in 1785, had a profoundly political subtext. The book was a kind of manual on the necessary concrete conditions—social, economic, and even geographical—for a people to be virtuous citizens.

The distinction between what was political and what was legal in public discourse, which seems so transparent to us now, was much less clear to the late eighteenth-century American lawyer. The legal and the political interpenetrated each other in public discourse to an extent unknown in our culture. A particularly clear example of that is John Adams's essay *A Dissertation on the Canon and the Feudal Law.* As I discuss in chapter 2, Adams focuses on two legal regimes—the canon law of the Roman Catholic church and the feudal law of medieval England—as metaphors for political tyranny. The essay does not discuss technical legal aspects of either legal system, nor does it provide a neutral systematic account of the historical origins and development of either system. Rather, it describes in grand terms the historical dialectic of politics within which Adams wanted to situate for his audience the American struggle for republican autonomy. It was a dialectic in which "tyranny," "corruption," and "ignorance" were pitted against "liberty," "virtue," and "knowledge." This was the dominant rhetoric of elite legal writers during the years of the early republic.

Such a civic mode of legal writing was possible only in a legal culture that viewed law and legal practice as above self-interest. Legal skills, particularly discursive skills, were not regarded as commodities for sale in the marketplace. Rather, they were to be deployed for the public welfare. It was that self-image that led Tocqueville, some thirty years later when the character of legal practice and legal writing had already changed, to describe American lawyers as "arbiters between the citizens, . . . directing the blind passions of the litigants toward the objective."[16] However much the reality of late eighteenth-century legal practice deviated from this self-image, and doubtless the degree of deviance was considerable, elite lawyers took this self-image seriously. Shaped by this self-image, they produced a form of legal writing that has all but disappeared.

The succeeding chapters in part 1 focus on the leading American legal texts that discussed property in the revolutionary and constitutional eras. Chapter 1 is devoted to Thomas Jefferson's writing on property. Jefferson was the most important exemplar of the civic republican conception of property in American history, and his writings, including private letters, essays, and legislative proposals, were enormously influential. Chapter 2 examines the leading legal texts that struggle with the question of the relationship between past and present, the English tradition of property and property in the new American republic. Texts like Adams's *Dissertation on the Canon and the Feudal Law* and Jefferson's *A Summary View of the Rights of British America* created a set of discursive dialectics that defined for Americans the relation between the past and present of property. Chapter 3 traces the decline of the civic republican conception of property during the constitutional period. Texts like *The Federalist Papers,* James Madison's famous 1792 essay on property, and Noah Webster's less famous but influential essay, "An Examination of the Leading Principles of the Federal Constitution," defined a conception of property that rhetorically remained rooted in the republican tradition but that substantively broke from it in important respects.

ONE

Thomas Jefferson and the Civic Conception of Property

RECOVERING FROM AN ILLNESS that had incapacitated him during the first week of September in 1789, Thomas Jefferson, then serving as ambassador to France, drafted a letter to James Madison setting forth a political and legal doctrine remarkable for its boldness and simplicity. "The question," Jefferson began, "whether one generation of men has a right to bind another, seems never to have been started either on this or our side of the water. Yet it is a question of such consequences as not only to merit decision, but place also, among the fundamental principles of every government."[1] Turning directly to the answer to this "fundamental" question, Jefferson continued, "I set out on this ground, which I suppose to be self evident, 'that the earth belongs in usufruct to the living': that the dead have neither powers nor rights over it."

This letter is a central text in the Jeffersonian canon; it represents, as Herbert Sloan has observed, "a summa, a profession of faith that tells us what mattered most to Jefferson at a significant moment in his life."[2] It was his expression of the widely known doctrine of "political relativism": each generation has the right to be free from the burdens assumed by the past generation and the concomitant duty to respect the same right of its successor. At one level the doctrine is an answer, albeit a remarkable one, to an aspect of the larger problem of intergenerational justice familiar to modern political theorists and lawyers: what rights and duties, if any, do generations owe to each other?[3] Jefferson's endorsement of the rights of the present generation was hardly original. It was a theme common among mid- to late eighteenth-century political writers influenced by republican ideology. As Sloan states, "The dead hand [of the past] had few if any defenders among the enlightened and was under assault everywhere in prerevolutionary Europe."[4]

Still, there *was* originality to Jefferson's articulation of the doctrine, as he himself (uncharacteristically) claimed.[5] Jefferson asserted a principle of political economy the extent of whose dynamism few of his contemporaries were prepared to accept—i.e., each generation is free to create its own social order and is under no constraints from actions taken by past generations. Jefferson went so far as to suggest that all constitutions and laws naturally expire and must be either reenacted or revised at the end of nineteen years (a period he calculated to be the life expectancy of any single generation).

At a fundamental level, Jefferson's letter may be seen as an attempt to define for the republican legal and political culture the proper relationship between property and society. He unambiguously asserted that specific property rights are strictly social creations, even while admitting the general principle that the earth belongs to the living is grounded in the laws of nature and, therefore, is by definition presocial and prepolitical. So, upon the death of the owner of land, Jefferson stated, "[T]he child, the legatee, or the creditor takes it, not by any natural right, but by the law of a society of which they are members, and to which they are subject."[6]

This assertion—that society creates property rights and ought continually to control them—separated Jefferson's doctrine from the Lockean tradition of thought regarding the origin and character of property rights.[7] The very idea of property rights being *usufructuary* (a term borrowed from classical Roman law) placed a considerable distance between the Jeffersonian and the Lockean conceptions of property. Usufructuary interests confer only a lifetime right to use;[8] they confer none of the individual sovereignty over resources that fee simple ownership is thought to do in the Lockean tradition. Such a notion of ownership presupposes an integration of individual and society, private and public.

The conception of property embedded in Jefferson's doctrine asserts not only the social character of property rights but their political character as well. Property was valued not as an end in itself but as a foundation for republican government. Each generation had to be free to redefine property because the specific configuration of property rights depended upon the political demands of the republic and the maintenance of virtue.

The doctrine that the earth belongs to the living, then, represents an attempt to create a public meaning of property in the new nation in terms of time. Through the use of naturalistic metaphor, it figuratively depicted American property. More precisely, it depicted *republican* American property, for the doctrine emanated from the ideology of civic republicanism: freed from the past, dynamic, nonstatic.

But defining the meaning of republican American property in those terms prompted a series of questions about our relationship to the past that Jefferson did not answer.[9] If we were to be liberated from the past, as the doctrine suggests, from exactly what experiences were we free? Did our rejection of the past commit us to embracing an unlimited future, and with it, change, at the expense of stability, as Jefferson's linkage between social time and natural time suggested?

At the root of the concern with time was an anxiety about the type of polity we were creating and the relationship between the individual and that polity. The republican ideology to which Jefferson was so firmly attached seemingly required a stable polity and a stable institution of property to serve as the central devices for creating the appropriate political and social order. If political dynamism was the American destiny, was there any hope for creating and maintaining the new nation as a virtuous republic, committed to the public good rather than to personal interest?

Jefferson's doctrine of political relativism both contradicted and affirmed the requirements of republican politics. Jefferson did not develop his doctrine as a fatalistic response to the inevitable dependence of the republic on the will of each generation, nor did he merely restate the familiar political principle that legislatures cannot bind all future legislatures. His doctrine affirmatively embraced each generation's exercise of its power to transgress settled practices and to recreate political institutions.[10] That power is seemingly compatible with republicanism to the extent that republicanism seeks to develop individuals' political personality. But insofar as republicanism includes a political vision of maintaining traditions and other sources that maintain good order, then it undermines republican tenets to celebrate the power to "destabilize"[11] existing social practices, institutions, and traditions.

The political relativism doctrine potentially poses an even deeper dilemma. It can be extended to affirm the power of each individual to call into question the legitimacy of existing institutions and practices. That power promotes individual autonomy in the republican sense by seeking continually to assure that political authority was not unequally distributed and that each citizen remains an equal participant. It also can be made consistent with the other aspect of republican social thought, community, if we depict the dissenting individual as affirming union with the polity. But that interpretation misreads the dissenter's message. It is the very condition of being embedded in widely shared practices and institutions that the empowered dissenter fears. In promoting republican autonomy, the Jeffersonian doctrine undermines republican social union. In this respect its implications epitomized the social dilemma of republican thought while its explicit message epitomized the temporal dilemma.[12]

The Intellectual Universe of Civic Republicanism

"Republicanism," as Gordon Wood has explained,[13] "meant more for Americans [of the revolutionary generation] than simply the elimination of a king and the institution of an elective system." The core of American republican thought during the eighteenth century was the idea that private "interests" could and should be subordinated to the common welfare of the polity. This idea originated in classical Greek political writing, particularly that of Aristotle, and underwent periodic revivals and modification in Renaissance Florence and again in seventeenth-century England.[14] By the time of the American Revolution it animated nearly all political and legal writing. "By 1776 the Revolution came to represent a final attempt . . . by many Americans to realize the traditional Commonwealth ideal of a corporate society, in which the common good would be the only objective of government."[15]

The holistic conception of society made the notion of the public good as the central objective of political life intelligible. Society was thought of as a homogeneous body whose members were organically linked together. The common good, then, was not merely what the consensus of society's individual members wished but a substantive conception of the moral good that transcended individual interests. This understanding of society did not exclude the concept of individual liberty, but it did require a public conception of liberty. The central dilemma of American politics was not thought to be the protection of individual freedoms against collective encroachment, but rather, the protection of the public rights of the people against aristocratic privileges and power. Because of society's homogeneous character, protecting the political liberty of the collective people necessarily protected individual liberty.

The fundamental challenge to realizing this ideal was maintaining a particular moral character among the citizenry. The republic required citizens to constantly practice "virtue," which may be defined as the willingness of the citizen to subordinate his or her individual wants for the well-being of the entire polity. American republicans were well aware of how extraordinary this demand was and how fragile the requirement of virtue made the republic.

Eighteenth-century American republican discourse was dominated by a dialectic between "virtue" and "corruption." Indeed, virtue was understood as being constantly threatened by "corruption." Political writing was preoccupied with the question of the sources of corruption and the necessary social, economic, and political conditions for virtue to thrive. The civic republican ideology posited that virtue, public and private, required the existence of certain social conditions. Jefferson articulated this "sociology of virtue," as J. G. A. Pocock has called it, through an opposition between the "aristocracy of wealth" and the "aristocracy of virtue and talent."[16] That dichotomy was a trope that was in turn part of a cluster of oppositions that characterized the entire structure of civic republican discourse. The most important of these tropic oppositions included:

virtue	vs.	corruption
equality	vs.	privilege
leisure	vs.	luxury
independence	vs.	servility
liberty	vs.	wealth

Property occupied a central place in that discussion. Its role, however, was neither straightforward nor strictly functional. Rather it was dialectical and symbolic.

The Dialectics of Property in Civic Republican Discourse

The role of property in civic republican discourse differs from the more familiar understanding of the function of property supplied by the political theory that C. B. Macpherson called "possessive individualism."[17] Though property plays a prominent role in both theories, the two ideologies attach strikingly different functions to it. From the perspective of possessive individualism, property is the basis for the categorical separation of private life from the public sphere. It is the central mechanism by which autonomous individuals shield themselves from the potential of collective tyranny. The private realm, in possessive individualist thought, inevitably reduces to property and consolidated ownership.[18]

Civic republicanism, both in revolutionary American thought and in its earlier Harringtonian version, did not categorically separate public and private life. Lacking a categorical opposition between polity and individual, it did not assign a negative role to property. At least protection against governmental action was not the exclusive, or even the primary, role of property in American civic republicanism. Instead, republicans conceived of property as necessary to facilitate a publicly active, self-governing citizenry. Republicans believed that ownership of property provides the necessary foundation for virtue, enabling citizens to pursue the common welfare. J. G. A. Pocock has succinctly stated the republican function of property: "The citizen possessed property in order to be autonomous and autonomy was necessary for him to develop virtue or goodness as an actor within the political, social and natural realm or order. He did not possess it in order to engage in trade, exchange or profit; indeed, these activities were hardly compatible with the activity of citizenship."[19] Property was valued "as a means of anchoring the individual in the structure of power and virtue and liberating him to practice these activities."[20]

Individuals who do not own property are forced to devote their attention to providing for their own personal welfare, exposing them to corrupting influences and distracting them from the public good. John Adams expressed the concern that people who do not own property will be vulnerable to corruption, asking rhetorically, "Is it not . . . true that men in general, in every society, who are wholly destitute of property, are . . . too dependent on other men to have a will of their own? . . . Such is the frailty of the human heart, that very few men who have no property, have any judgment of their own."[21]

American civic republicans, then, understood property within the framework of a conflict between "autonomy" and "dependency." Autonomy is a necessary condition for virtue, while dependency undermines it. Jefferson expressed the civic republican meaning of dependency in his *Notes on the State of Virginia,* stating, "Dependence begets subservience and venality, suffocates the germ of virtue, and prepares fit tools for the designs of ambition."[22]

Static vs. Dynamic Property

The republican image of property as the foundation of political, social, and moral order was by itself ambiguous. It failed, for example, to specify what *type* of property was necessary to perform this function, or whether any particular type of property at all was required. Could the republic survive if property were dynamic and continually free to change forms as social and economic conditions changed, or did it have to be static, maintaining a certain type? Related to this question was an uncertainty concerning the character of property as *mobile* or *immobile.* While a dynamic conception of property would as a practical matter involve a high degree of mobility, in order for property to remain static its mobility would likely have to be restricted. These two meanings of republican property were not simply different, they were contradictory. The static meaning implied an apparently greater degree of control over property to maintain its preferred form and fixity. On the surface the dynamic meaning required little or no social control of property. Only collective restrictions to maintain its fluidity would be necessary.

These two meanings of property were both republican in the sense that they were different readings of the commitments to republic, civic virtue, and the common good. Jefferson's writing on the benefits of cultivated land owned in fee simple and worked by citizen-owners—the republic as constituted by the "fee simple empire"—is often taken to represent the paradigm of republican property. The same interpretation defines the Jeffersonian conflict as one between landed and commercial forms of property. The concept of "commerce" did play, as this interpretation suggests, a crucial role in American republican discourse, just as it did in the discourse of English republicans. But Jefferson's commitment to fee simple ownership of land did not represent a rejection of commerce. The opposition, rather, was between agricultural property and industrial property, i.e., cultivation of land, which he assumed to have a commercial dimension, and manufacturing. "Those who labor in the earth" *were* the "chosen people of God," insofar as they were not exposed to the corrupting influence of manufacturing.[23] As "[d]ependence begets subservience," manufacturing begets dependence. "[T]he class of artificers," he observed, "[are] the panders of vice and the instruments by which the liberties of a country are generally overturned."[24] The form property takes in a society thus provides the test for the society's viability as a republic. Reinforcing this view, he stated in the *Notes:*

> [G]enerally speaking, the proportion which the aggregate of the other classes of citizens bears in any State to that of its husbandmen, is the proportion of its unsound to its healthy parts, and is a good enough barometer whereby to measure its degree of corruption. While we have land to labor, then, let us never wish to see our citizens occupied at a workbench, or twirling a distaff.[25]

Later in the *Notes* he stated:

> Our interest will be to throw open the doors of commerce, and to knock off all its shackles, giving perfect freedom to all persons for the vent of whatever they may chose to bring into our parts, and asking the same in theirs. . . . [I]t might be better for us to abandon

the ocean altogether, that being the element whereon we shall be principally exposed to jostle with other nations; to leave to otheres to bring what we shall want, and to carry what we can spare. This would make us invulnerable to Europe, by offering none of our property to their prize, and would turn all our citizens to the cultivation of the earth.[26]

Here, then, we have, not an opposition between land and commerce, but a dialectic between static and dynamic property. On the one hand, the republic may be fatally threatened if property can be transformed from an agricultural into an industrial form. On the other hand, throwing open our doors to commerce represented the embracing of a form of economic dynamism that complemented the political dynamism that he later espoused so forcefully.[27] Moreover, to the extent that Jefferson's thinking remained consistent over the years and that his earlier statements on economic dynamism anticipated the doctrine of political relativism, how could that doctrine be reconciled with the need to maintain property in an agricultural mode, whose very stasis implies intergenerational control? Under the doctrine of political relativism, would not each generation be free to cast off past generations' commitment to any particular form of property and decide for itself what type of property best suited its own needs?

The Dilemma of Unequal Distribution

The ambiguity of the meaning of republican property for stasis or change also affected the related questions of the mobility and distribution of property. Jefferson and others viewed the unequal distribution of property, specifically land, as incompatible with republicanism. Writing from Fountainbleau in 1785, Jefferson observed that the high degree of concentration of French land in the hands of the aristocracy was the source of the high degree of unemployment, as French landowners left their lands uncultivated for hunting. He then reiterated a view that he propounded throughout his career:[28]

> I am conscious that an equal degree of property is impracticable. But the consequences of this enormous inequality producing so much misery to the bulk of mankind, legislators cannot invent too many devices for subdividing property, only taking care to let their subdivisions go hand in hand with the natural affections of the human mind.

The dilemma he faced was how to prevent the unequal distribution of land from undermining republican virtue while pragmatically acknowledging the "natural affections of the human mind" that were embodied in the concept of individual ownership. John Adams, citing Harrington's dictum that power always follows property, expressed the recurrent anxiety about the consequences for republican virtue in terms of a need to maintain a balance of property in order to maintain a balance of power:

> The only possible way . . . of preserving the balance of power on the side of equal liberty and public virtue is to make the acquisition of land easy to every member of society; to make a division of land into small quantities, so that the multitude may be possessed of landed estates.[29]

Jefferson's solution was similar but more complete. He proposed equal distribution when the state is compelled to distribute land and when land is inherited, but protection of existing property rights against governmental *re*distribution.[30] This accommodationist strategy underlay, for example, his well-known reforms of Virginia inheritance law, including the abolition of primogeniture in favor of partible inheritance and the abolition of entail.[31] The strategy was for the state to take advantage of the abundance of uncultivated land in the American West and insure that every able-bodied citizen be given a relatively small parcel of land.[32] Cultivating this land would make the citizen self-sustaining and independent, and the state would then protect the personal autonomy secured through ownership.

But that strategy was incomplete. It failed to insure that autonomous owners would not exercise their right to transfer land (a right clearly part of the extant common-law conception of ownership and which Jefferson never questioned) in such a way as to undermine the scheme for maintaining republican virtue treating land as a commodity. The real thrust of the static conception of republican property, which asserted the dependence of the republic upon an ideal type of property (i.e., land) and an ideal form of property holding (i.e., fee simple ownership), was to prevent land from, as these republicans saw it, degenerating into a mere commodity.

It was not the rise of commerce alone but the potential for commerce to transform the sociology of property that aroused the Jeffersonian anxiety. The social transformation would change the meaning of freehold land from that of the stable foundation for republican politics to a fluid item of commerce. Further, property would no longer mean a moral and political component of society, an aspect of virtuous personality, but rather would represent a mere artifact of private life. So transformed, property might become a solvent that dissolves the political bonds of the community.

Restated in modern terms, the anxiety was that property, reduced to mere commodity, would mediate social relations. Individuals would relate to each other as abstract economic actors—buyers or sellers in the marketplace—rather than as concrete, multidimensional human beings. In this respect the civic republican critique of commodified property anticipated the modern theme that connects highly mobile forms of property with the phenomenon of alienation in social relations. Although the concept of alienation did not flower until the next century, its seed was planted well before then. It exists in all theories that define the role of property in terms of self-development and self-governance realized through union with others.[33]

What prompted the Jeffersonian anxiety was the rapid development of intangible forms of property, especially credit.[34] These interests, which were based on nothing more real than a hope, seemingly were indistinguishable from the "expectancies" that the common law long had held not to be property. Jefferson feared that treating such ephemeral interests as property would destabilize the distribution of wealth that he sought to create through legislative action. More fundamentally, it would destroy the moral personality upon which the republic depended.[35]

We must recall, though, that stability was only half of the dialectical understanding of property in American civic republicanism. The other part of that understanding was the fluidity of property that republicans sought to promote even while they feared it. Jefferson's proposal in the *Notes* to "throw open the doors of commerce"[36] suggests that what he rejected was not commerce itself but an empire of commerce in which fluid and intangible property replaced stable cultivated land. He called for a "dynamism of virtue" to counterbalance the "dynamism of commerce."[37] For virtue to be dynamic, land had to be constantly subject to circulation throughout society. His efforts to amend the law of inheritance emerged from this vision. He sought to transform land ownership into a dynamic phenomenon from the static condition that then characterized English land law, with its strict settlements, entails, and primogeniture creating a vast web of technical devices by which the heads of a few privileged families could trap large portions of land for successive generations.

While these reforms promoted what present-day property lawyers call "alienability," the meaning of that policy was ambiguous in the eighteenth century and remains controversial today. Recently, law-and-economics writers have argued that it is embedded in the logic of the market form of economic organization.[38] According to this understanding, commitment to the market as the central device for allocating economic resources necessitates a legal policy protecting the free transferability of resources. This meaning of alienability trades on a meaning of property as market commodity. Modernist critics of the economic paradigm regard that meaning as incompatible, at least in some circumstances, with the ideal of human flourishing.[39] Echoing Marx, they worry that market alienability is alienating.

While neither of these interpretations was unambiguously part of the legal consciousness of civic republicans, elements of both can be found in the late eighteenth-century legal debate. Republican writers depicted the free transferability of property simultaneously as liberating and threatening. It liberates individuals from one form of dependency (feudal hierarchy) but exposes them to another. By debasing moral personality of individuals and the polity, the free transferability policy would create a new form of dependency. Individuals would be subjects of the market, and the common welfare would be subordinated to the limitless pursuit of self-interest.

The republican anxiety over freely transferable property anticipated two related modern dilemmas.[40] The first is the problem in liberal political theory that the free transferability policy depends on the exercise of the very source of dependency that the policy is intended to avoid, namely, state power. The second is the social dilemma that commodifying all assets in the name of freedom of the market creates the risk of social exploitation within market relations.[41] Eighteenth-century republicans evaded these dilemmas, however, by defining *time* as the central question about property and property law in the new nation.

Balance and the Problem of Hierarchy Based on Property

To conflate dynamic property with market property—property as a device for regulating scarcity—would pervert the civic republic meaning that Jefferson articulated. American republicans carried forward from James Harrington the substantive idea that inequality of land distribution and social hierarchy based on a grossly uneven pattern of distribution threatened the republic because they were principal sources of corruption.[42] John Adams, for example, repeating Harrington's doctrine of balance, asserted that "power always follows property. . . . [T]he balance of power in a society, accompanies the balance of property in land." But the meanings that Harrington and eighteenth-century American republicans created for that doctrine, though similar in certain respects, differed in other, crucial ways.

For Harrington, the implication of that doctrine for popular government was enactment of the agrarian law. Its objective was to insure that "the property in lands be so diffused through the whole people that neither one landlord nor a few landlords over-balance them."[43] Harrington argued that freedom can be anchored only in an equal distribution of land, and the land acquired through inheritance, not through speculation, and owned in fee simple. The agrarian law represented a direct exercise of government power to maintain an equal distribution of land, which could not thereafter be upset through the market.[44] Adams similarly understood the doctrine of balance to mean that "[t]he only possible way . . . of preserving the balance of power on the side of equal liberty and public virtue is to make the acquisition of land easy to every member of society; to make a division of land into small quantities, so that the multitude may be possessed of landed estates."[45]

What Adams, like Jefferson, added to Harrington's formula was a dynamic of property. Harrington viewed dynamic property as a direct threat to balance; he aimed everything at stability, and thus considered partible inheritance rather than grant to be the preferred method for acquiring land. Once acquired, land was to be used for possession, not exchange. He disfavored trade in land because of its propensity to undermine balance, recreating inequality and dependency.[46]

In Adams's hands dynamic property became an antidote to inequality and hierarchy. His understanding of the dynamic of property was situated in relation to the central problems of "privilege" and "luxury." It was dynamic precisely *because* it destroyed the basis for an aristocracy of privilege and luxury. Adams sought to liberate land by removing entanglements on fee simple ownership that prevented every ordinary citizen from obtaining the parcel of land that would secure his independence. Liberating land, Adams and Jefferson thought, meant liberating the individual.

The Attack on Primogeniture and Entailments

We can see this dynamic at work in the civic republican critique of primogeniture and entailments. Inheritance was the aspect of the common law of property about which eighteenth-century American republican lawyers expressed the greatest concern. Within the law of inheritance no topics had greater importance to these writers than primogeniture and entailment of land. It seems odd to us today that even eighteenth-century American lawyers would have taken these topics seriously, let alone made them the centerpiece of their efforts to transform the common law of property in a republican direction. Several colonial legislatures abolished either or both primogeniture and entailments of land relatively early.[47] Recent scholarship indicates that even where these devices were legally recognized they were not widely utilized.[48] The significance of these institutions—and the legal writing attacking them—lies in their symbolic role rather than their functional effect.

Under the doctrine of primogeniture, when a man[49] died intestate (without a legally effective will) his lands descended to his eldest son. His personal property was distributed in equal shares to his children, including his daughters, with a portion reserved for his surviving spouse. A wealthy landowner could easily block operation of the doctrine of primogeniture, of course, merely by devising his land by will to younger sons, or to daughters for that matter. At the same time, however, the fact that a landowner had executed a will devising his land did not guarantee that the land would be divided among his children. Eighteenth-century American landowners, both in theory and in practice, enjoyed a great degree of freedom in drawing their wills, and they could exercise that freedom to produce the same pattern of distribution as primogeniture did. Moreover, from the perspective of consolidating land ownership within the family for the purpose of maintaining dynastic family power, devises were far more effective and widely used among great English landowners of the seventeenth and eighteenth centuries.

The entailment of land was the legal device that those American lawyers who despised English landed aristocracy most closely associated with the English family dynasty based on property settlements. The purpose of the entail was to keep land within the family by restricting the power of the persons to whom the testator devised land to transfer land themselves. Though this was its purpose, it was not its invariable effect, because numerous means existed for breaking entailments. In England, the much more commonly used device to preserve landed dynasties within the family was the so-called strict settlement, an elaborate arrangement for transferring land and restraining its future alienability. In England, strict settlements were enforced by Courts of Equity, but since most of the colonies had not established separate equity courts, the strict settlement was gener-

ally unavailable to American testators in the seventeenth and early eighteenth centuries, leaving the entail to be the only testamentary device for
maintaining family control of land.

Functionalist explanations are usually provided for the demise of primogeniture and the relatively uncommon use of entails. In this orthodox
view, economic conditions, in particular the abundance of land in the
colonies, distinguished the needs of wealthy American testators from their
English counterparts for legal devices designed to assure the family's foundation on large concentrations of land.[50] This tells only part of the story:
philosophical opposition also played a role. Lawyers in England and on
the Continent had heatedly debated the benefits of primogeniture since
the sixteenth century.[51] That debate yielded no consensus, and its enduring effect was to cripple the stature of primogeniture within English legal
culture even prior to the creation of an American system of inheritance.
American lawyers, then, would be bound to greet the transplantation of
primogeniture with considerable skepticism. Similarly, but with less in-
tensity, early modern English lawyers had attacked entailments of land,
arguing that the indestructibility of entails "would put a stop to commerce
and prevent the circulation of the riches of the kingdom" and that such
devices conflicted with the common law's supposedly fundamental commitment to freedom of alienation.[52] More recently still, the Scottish Enlightenment movement that influenced elite American legal writers in the
mid- to late eighteenth century had relentlessly attacked primogeniture
and especially entails as antiquated and socially harmful.[53]

Republican political theory since Harrington regarded both devices as
incompatible with republican principles. In theory, republican regimes
required partible inheritance as an aspect of the Harringtonian principle
of a balance of property.[54] This is hardly to suggest, however, that the
American critique of primogeniture and entailments was motivated solely
by a republican ideology.[55] Reinforcing the republican antipathy to these
devices were the customary inheritances practices of various groups in
the colonies[56] and American lawyers' conception of the historic common
law.[57]

Still, to American republican legal writers, primogeniture and entailments of land appeared to be the most glaring vestiges of a corrupt
past. They associated that past with English social hierarchy based on land
and viewed that social order—indeed, social hierarchy in general—with
"feudal" encrustations on the common law of property.[58] To both Adams
and Jefferson, it was precisely the feudal law of property that denied au-

tonomy to individuals, rendering them powerless and dependent. It was crucial to both republican ideology and the American common law *mentalité*, then, to repudiate primogeniture and entail, despite the fact that they were not used with great frequency. Those devices were the principal symbols of the social hierarchy that American republicans associated with "feudal" corruptions of the common law of property. Primogeniture and entailment symbolized the undesirable consequences of stability of property that required a dynamic of property to counteract. The release of land from these feudal constraints meant a release of individuals from dependency and inequality.[59]

The civic republican dynamic of property, then, was part of a dialectic with stability of property in American civic republicanism. Property—land—needed to be unencumbered for society to avoid privilege and inequality, but property also had to be stable to avoid being commodified and reduced to an object of acquisitive pursuit that would destroy republican virtue. How then would the necessary stability of property be secured? We have seen that stability meant not only that the dominant form of property in society had to remain constant, specifically that it had to be tangible agricultural property rather than industrial and intangible property, but also that its public meaning as the anchor of a virtuous civic life had to resist any metamorphosis reducing the meaning of property to that of commodity, the object of an acquisitive spirit.

These two aspects of stability affected each other because, as republicans like Jefferson understood the logic of commerce, if the public meaning of property became commodity, then its dominant social form would shift from stable fee simple ownership of land to speculative intangibles. And conversely, if intangibles came to displace cultivated land as the socially dominant form of wealth, then the public meaning of property would shift to the framework of the speculator. This would represent a change in the relational aspect of property: civic property, i.e., property as the basis for sociality and participation, would be replaced by self property, i.e., property as the basis for personal gain. Both the dialectics of stability and dynamism and of separation and union would end, as the dynamic and individuated aspects, no longer checked, would crowd out stability and sociality.

How then should this dilemma be solved? One might suppose, as Harrington evidently did,[60] that maintaining stability and sociality required collective interference with individual control over property, especially land, even beyond the initial distribution of government land to individual farmers. The legal system had to impose restraints on the transferability of land to prevent persons to whom the government had distributed land from using their land as a commodity for speculation or as the basis for family dynasties.

Jefferson acknowledged the need to restrict individual freedom of disposition to some extent (his inheritance law reforms imposed collective restraints on freedom of alienability to prevent landed dynasties, for example), but he was unwilling to abandon the principle altogether. His doctrine of political relativism had broad implications. That doctrine deviated from a Lockean understanding of individual ownership, for it effectively denied that ownership was or could be thoroughly privatized.[61] It embraced each generation's power to recreate the configuration of property rights, allowing the republican polity to limit the alienation of land to whatever extent was necessary to create the necessary conditions for republican politics.[62]

Jefferson never explicitly drew that conclusion. Part of the reason why he resisted it is that he assumed that broad collective restraints to prevent individuals from speculating in land were unnecessary. He believed that individuals would choose cultivation over manufacturing or speculation if given the choice. So long as land, owned in fee simple for cultivation, was available to them, Americans themselves would preserve the dialectic of stability and dynamism. Individuals pursued nonvirtuous modes of property and ownership in the past, he thought, because they lacked any choice. Thus in the *Notes* he observed: "In Europe the lands are either cultivated, or locked up against the cultivator. Manufacture must therefore be resorted to of necessity, not of choice, to support the surplus of the people. But we have an immensity of land courting the industry of the husbandman."[63] The virtually unlimited (as Jefferson optimistically saw it) supply of land available for cultivation placed Americans in a historically unique situation of being able to escape from the constraints that had dictated the corruption of property in Europe. Later, in a letter to John Jay, Jefferson expressed the same sense of optimism: "We have now lands enough to employ an indefinite number of people in their cultivation. Cultivators of the earth are the most valuable citizens. . . . As long therefore as they can find employment in this line, I would not convert them into mariners, artisans, or anything else."[64] Jefferson then expressed his preference in the event that any citizens were unable to live as cultivators of their own land: "I should then perhaps wish to turn them to the sea in preference to manufacturers, because comparing the character of the two classes I find the former the most valuable citizens. I consider the class of artificers as the panders of vice and the instruments by which the liberties of a country are generally overturned."[65] He also expressed uncertainty about the likelihood that his vision for the broad distribution of land would be implemented:

> It is too soon yet in our country to say that every man who cannot find employment but who can find uncultivated land, shall be at liberty to cultivate it, paying a moderate rent. But it is not too soon to provide by every means possible that as few as possible shall be without a little portion of land. The small landholders are the most precious part of a state.[66]

One can speculate about a more basic concern underlying Jefferson's unwillingness to abandon the principle of freedom of alienation. It is possible to link individual freedom of alienation with republican personal independence. The republican meaning of independence is that individual citizens are politically autonomous. While republicans traditionally argued that individuals experienced political autonomy through participation, that autonomy, understood as freedom from corruption, also required that individuals be free to choose among alternative political locales. In modern idiom, as political options "exit" might be preferable to "voice" under some circumstances.[67] Moreover, as public choice theory recognizes, political voice is more effective if local governments know that the threat of exit is maximized. Maintaining individual freedom to transfer one's property, or at least those assets that anchor to one locale, preserves personal mobility. Broad legal restrictions on the individual power to dispose of land that the government had distributed to farmers for cultivation, then, might threaten the citizen-farmers' political independence by effectively tying them to one locale and thereby weakening their political voice. Yet the problem remained that unless such restriction were imposed, individuals might exercise their freedom privately rather than publicly, that is, by using their land as an exchange commodity rather than to preserve their political autonomy.

Jefferson never directly confronted this dilemma. The two meanings of individual autonomy secured through individual ownership of property (egalitarian and hierarchical) are simultaneously present in his writings, and no attempt was made to reconcile them.

TWO

Time, History, and Property in the Republican Vision

TIME AND HISTORY were central problems in American legal writing during both the revolutionary and early national periods. More specifically, property gained meaning to American republican lawyers through their concern with time and understandings of history that reacted to that concern.

American legal attitudes towards time and the nation's place in history were deeply ambivalent. On the one hand, for American lawyers a large part of the meaning of the institutions they were creating was breaking away from the constraints of the past. Tocqueville was only reflecting a widely shared American view when he observed that in the United States "the woof of time is broken and the track of past generations is broken."[1] At the same time, however, many of the "new" legal institutions Americans had created were really English transplants, including that most unrevolutionary of institutions, the common law. American legal thinkers had to develop a vision of property that reconciled the fact of revolution (1) with the fact that there was substantial continuity between American property law and the English common law of property and (2) with the fact that the American revolution, like the English Revolution of 1688, had affirmed individual property rights. How had the American revolutionary experience altered the meaning of property so as to distinguish American property law from its English antecedents? Given that by the late eighteenth century the meaning of property in English law was already closely linked with the ideology of individual freedom, as Blackstone's *Commentaries* abundantly demonstrated, what new meaning of individual autonomy did American property law create?

American republican lawyers, including not only Jefferson but virtually everyone who wrote on the subject of property, answered with a historical understanding of property and individual freedom. Individual autonomy, they said, was secured by individual property rights because the meaning of individual liberation was negatively framed as the repudiation of "feudal tyranny," itself serving as the central metaphor for domination and hierarchy. So long as the meanings of individual autonomy and property and their relationship to each were articulated in terms of a negation, the dilemmas of individualized property rights were avoided. The historical consciousness was itself the source of intelligibility and coherence in the legal vision of securing individual autonomy through property. That is, history (in particular, the feudal past) was a trope by which property and human liberation were signified, a symbol for the past that Americans were transcending. To comprehend how reliance on history could be a move by which republican lawyers avoided confronting the dilemmas of property and autonomy, we must first sketch the historical understanding that was deeply embedded in civic republican legal consciousness.

The Ancient Constitution and the Common Law

American legal writers turned to history as the principal source from which to create meaning for their revolution and for the new nation. As practitioners of the eighteenth-century *mentalité* of reason, they believed that "the actions and affairs of men are subject to as regular and uniform laws, as other events."[2] The sources of these laws were reason and history. History itself was a repository of reason—a fund from which to discern the timeless principles of law and politics. Such principles, the revolutionaries thought, were the constituent elements of what John Adams called "the divine science of politics." They would guide Americans in their efforts to resist tyranny and protect their fundamental rights. Grounded in "reason" and discovered through history, these principles legitimized both the rejection of English political and legal institutions and the American institutions that replaced them.

Among the many paradoxes of American republican culture is the American reliance on English political and legal history as the primary historical source of meaning and legitimacy for their own institutions.[3] American Whigs of the eighteenth century saw no contradiction in their looking to English history, however, for that history was, as they interpreted it, a story of continual struggle by a people to protect their liberties against their rulers' depredations.[4] They considered their actions to constitute another chapter in the same story, an extension of the same struggle for fundamental liberties carried on by their ancestors. But they regarded the chapter that they were writing to be unlike those written by the English political actors of 1215, 1628, and 1688: they were completing the entire story. They had reached the eschatological moment of the historical process of discovering and realizing the ancient and fundamental liberties. It was the millennial chapter to which nothing would later be added.

The notion of the "ancient constitution" was necessary to creating this sense of coherence and avoiding contradiction and paradox in the American affirmation of the English common law. For the core of that conception was the belief that the ancient English constitution—the "Gothic" constitution, as it was sometimes called in order to emphasize the supposed Germanic source of Saxon liberties—transcended not only time but also place. Its integrity was not confined to any particular nation or culture.

The conception of the common law as "the ancient constitution" animated the eighteenth-century American historical consciousness. The common law stood at the center of the Whig science of politics and history. Robert Ferguson has summarized the role of this historical understanding of the common law and its role in the Whig ideology:

> The Whig vision of history . . . assumed an ancient constitution, which through immemorial common law, guaranteed the rights of Englishmen in perpetuity. The virtues of that ancient constitution had been undermined by the incursions and usurpations of William the Conqueror and his kingly heirs, transforming all of English history into one long struggle for the recovery of lost liberties. In this view the Glorious Revolution of 1688 had been "the triumph of the Common law and lawyers over the king."[5]

This historical narrative chronicled the origin of the ancient constitution as linked to the common law early in Saxon times. The Saxons had developed the common law to protect certain principles of liberty, and Englishmen had continuously asserted these principles from that time through the seventeenth century. The artifice and corruption of hierarchical tyranny had occasionally undermined the Saxon liberties of the ancient constitution, but these lapses into corrupt forms of authority had always proved unstable. Eventually, Englishmen had always purified the common law and purged it of its alien elements. The Norman conquest was thus depicted as an aberration, not producing any change in the essential character of the common law.[6] To Americans of the eighteenth-century republican culture, then, the common law signified a tradition of political practice of resistance against foreign "tyranny" to protect "liberties" that were both ancient and natural. Their efforts, by cleansing the common law of the corruptions which the English Crown and inherited aristocracy had introduced into it, represented the continuation of this historical teleology.

The historical stories that inhabit cultures, if they are successful, achieve the level of myth. The narrative of the common law and its connection to the ancient constitution had acquired that character well before its telling by the American Whigs, dating back, in different versions, to the histories of Coke and, later, Hale. But it was not a myth lacking paradox. As Coke told the story,[7] the law that judges declare is unwritten and immemorial, embodying the wisdom of generations gained through experience—what Coke called "artificial reason." The customary nature of that law allowed it constantly to adapt to new situations. Therein lies the paradox. Adaptation suggests a historicist conception of the common law, meaning that it comprehends that law as historically contingent, not fundamental. But Coke's mission was to affirm the timeless character of the common law in order to firmly and finally ground its legitimate and superior authority (and therefore that of its discoverers, the common law judges) against the contentions of the Crown. Legitimating the political claims of the present by depicting them as continuous with the politics of the past would work only if that past was itself depicted as temporally transcendental. To interpret the past as an adaptation to a particular set of circumstances would undermine the strategic interpretation of timelessness. What enabled the story with which Coke is so closely associated to succeed was the notion of the common law as custom. That discursive formulation of the common law itself signified in an intelligible way the temporally ambiguous character of the common law. For custom reconciles itself with the future through adaptation, while simultaneously embracing the past as having no identifiable source point. As custom, then, the common law transcended the limits on legitimacy set by time by looking both toward past and future, making it, in Selden's famous allusion, the English Janus.

English Transformation of the Myth of the Ancient Constitution

American revolutionaries could hardly be expected simply to transplant the mythology of English lawyers and adopt it as their own. Nevertheless continuity does exist between the telling of the stories by English and American lawyers, making the American version a variation rather than an entirely original or indigenous myth. To some extent the change paralleled in the American version itself reflected changes that had occurred in the English telling of the story between the sixteenth and eighteenth centuries. The eighteenth-century version differed from its predecessor most notably by replacing "custom" with "reason" as the source of both the coherence and legitimacy of the ancient constitution, the former having lost intelligibility under the rise of ideas about sovereignty. English liberties were indeed ancient, but they were grounded in reason. The role of history was one of confirmation, not derivation.

The other notable difference between the sixteenth- and eighteenth-century versions of the story was the acknowledgment of feudalism and the accommodation of the Norman conquest within the common law's linear development. Seventeenth-century historians, in particular Sir Henry Spelman, had made it impossible to deny the facts that there had been a conquest and that feudalism existed as a foreign element in the English past. But while eighteenth-century lawyers could no longer depict the history of the common law as entirely smooth or continuous, they could—and did—minimize the discontinuity that feudalism represented in the story. Of the eighteenth-century English historians who accommodated the feudal past with the common law's historical preservation of "Saxon liberty," Blackstone was especially successful in reducing the ideological significance of the feudal past by portraying it as "a mere interruption of the true course of the national life."[8]

More so than any other single historical work of its time Blackstone's *Commentaries on the Laws of England* was responsible for articulating the entire spectrum of symbolic vocabulary through which both English and American lawyers interpreted the relationship between the common law and time. He combined, without any sense of incompatibility, Coke's notion of the common law as ancient and immemorial[9] with Hale's theory of adaptive evolution (as well as with Hale's outline).[10] That is, he simultaneously acknowledged and denied the historicist character of the common law.

Blackstone's historical vision oscillated between two incompatible theories of historical development: cyclical and linear. Like Hale but unlike Coke, he acknowledged the reality of the common law's feudal past but resolved the problem it created for common law mythology in contradictory ways. Describing the common law's "successive mutations at different periods of time,"[11] he portrayed the common law as having come full circle, with the fifth and present stage constituting "the complete restitution of English liberty, for the first time, since its total abolition at the conquest."[12] At the same time, Blackstone chronicled[13] the story of the linear progress of the common law after the fall into feudal "despotism," with each successive stage representing improvement in the condition of English liberty. The linear metaphor also stressed the fact that modern England exemplified the commercial stage in social, legal, and political development, a stage whose superiority over all prior history is indicated by its simplicity and refinement.[14]

What was consistent in these two versions was the figurative use of feudalism. The *Commentaries* developed feudalism into a symbol for the theme that departures from English liberty were only aberrational corruptions. That theme was forcefully signified by Blackstone's repeated opposition between "servility" and "liberty." One of the ironies of the historical rendering of the common law during the late eighteenth century is the fact the Blackstonian symbology closely paralleled the tropes of American political and legal discourse, in particular the opposition between "feudalism" and "liberty,"[15] even while the English and American symbol-systems signified conflicting political objectives. No single American text of that time illustrates this irony more emphatically than John Adams's famous essay, *A Dissertation on the Canon and Feudal Law.*[16] Written at about the same time as the *Commentaries,* the *Dissertation* chronicled essentially the same historical tale as Blackstone's work did. Yet while Blackstone's message was to confirm the rationality and justice of the extant English regime, Adams's was precisely the opposite.

The Historical Symbology of Tyranny: Adams's *A Dissertation on the Canon and the Feudal Law*

To the modern reader, Adams's *Dissertation* appears odd in several respects. Why would an American republican lawyer, writing political tracts for newspapers to argue the case for revolution, be interested in the canon law of the Roman Catholic church or the English feudal law of centuries past? For that matter, why would anyone bother to juxtapose the canon law with the feudal law? The sense of oddness disappears, however, if we recognize Adams's use of the topics as figurative rather than literal. Feudal law and canon law were symbols for different aspects of tyranny that Americans had, for the first time in history, the opportunity, indeed the destiny, to overthrow. One civil, the other ecclesiastical, they were symbols for the past that was to be transcended in the American republic.

"Since the promulgation of Christianity," Adams began, "the greatest two systems of tyranny . . . are the *cannon* [*sic*] and the *feudal* law."[17] The former was "framed by the Romish clergy for the aggrandisement of their own order," while the latter was "originally a code of laws for a vast army in a perpetual encampment."[18] Adams continued that the "grandees" of the two systems had created a "confederacy" and that "as long as this confederacy lasted, and the people were held in ignorance, Liberty, and with her, Knowledge, and Virtue, too, seem to have deserted the earth."[19] "[T]he struggle between the people and the confederacy" began with the Reformation. Adams defined that struggle in terms of the opposition of liberty, knowledge, and virtue against tyranny, ignorance, and corruption. That opposition was the basis for nothing less than the meaning of America itself. "It was this great struggle, that peopled America. It was not religion *alone,* as is commonly supposed; but it was a love of a *universal Liberty,* and an hatred, a dread, an horror of the informal confederacy . . . that projected, conducted, and accomplished the settlement of America."[20]

Adams is here defining the teleology of America—one that is eschatological. The American experience is seen as a singular moment in history, the point in time toward which all other moments have aimed but never reached. It is not a matter of returning to some ancient constitution that had temporarily been corrupted; rather, the vision is linear and progressive. The very reason for our existence as a nation was finally and conclusively to establish liberty as the victor over tyranny. Because we had been created without a feudal past and without an ecclesiastical government, we had succeeded where no other nation had.[21] Adams's America was the epiphany of liberty, and what made that experience possible was America's escape from the past, its victory over time.

But while the American political and legal regime might be unique in history, its success—the ultimate success of liberty over tyranny—was not guaranteed. Liberty was not self-executing. There yet remained a threat to the American system as the culmination of the historical struggle. The sources of that threat remained what they had always been—the feudal and the canon laws:

There seems to be a direct and formal design on foot, to enslave all America. This however must be done by degrees. The first step that is intended seems to be an entire subversion of the whole system of our Fathers, by an introduction of the cannon and feudal law, into America. The cannon and feudal systems, tho' greatly mutilated in

England, are not yet destroy'd. Like the temples and palaces, in which the great contrivers of them, once worship'd and inhabited, they exist in ruins; and much of the domineering spirit of them remains.[22]

From Adams's transcendental perspective, then, it was possible to see the English common law as *foreign* to American law, and not as its parent, with all of the sense of authority and greater wisdom that that image would imply. It was necessary, therefore, for Americans to undertake positive steps to insure that the canon and feudal laws acquired no foothold here.

The law of property was clearly a part of the necessary design. Although Adams did not discuss property in detail in the *Dissertation,* he explicitly underscored its role in resisting feudal intrusions. In doing so, he used a distinction that was a basic part of the figurative vocabulary of English and American eighteenth-century common law historiography: the distinction between "feudal" and "allodial" land, that is, land "held" by one who occupied a subordinated position in a hierarchy of ownership versus land autonomously "owned" by one person, free of all hierarchical entanglements. The distinction signified the Whig distinction between "servility" and "liberty," translated in the context of land ownership. The association between the feudal regime, in particular property, and personal dependence was so strong in the American republican legal discourse that merely to characterize something as "feudal" was itself sufficient to indicate condemnation.[23]

Adams did not assert that land ownership in America had always been allodial. Given the royal chartering of the colonies, he could hardly do so. Yet he was still able to deny that feudal property had ever existed here. He explained this historically unique *tertium quid:*

> To have holden their lands, allodially, or for any man to have been the sovereign lord and proprietor of the ground he occupied, would have constituted a government, too nearly like a commonwealth. They [the Puritans] were contented therefore to hold their lands of their King, as their sovereign Lord, and to him they were willing to render homage: but to no mesne [i.e., intermediate] or subordinate Lords. . . . In all this, they were so strenuous, that they have ever transmitted to their posterity, a very general contempt and detestation of holdings by quit rents [i.e., a rent paid in lieu of a required feudal service[24]]: As they have also an hereditary ardor for liberty . . .[25]

Here again, Adams metaphorically communicated the correlative messages of America's escape from time and its destiny with liberty. Ironically, Adams's thesis prefigured Louis Hartz's now-rejected view that America was born liberal.[26] From the very outset of their experience Americans had escaped the past, which was associated with "feudal" tyranny and corruption. The original regime of property in America had illustrated this unique achievement.

To American republican lawyers, then, feudalism and feudal property were the dominant symbols for the past that was rejected or, rather, transcended. But what was the alternative that American republicans were affirming? The symbolic opposite of feudal property was "allodial" land. Why was this seemingly technical and obsolete concept from the English common law meaningful to American republican lawyers? What did it signify to them? We gain an appreciation for the seriousness with which American lawyers took the concept of allodial land and some idea of its symbolic function from Jefferson's widely circulated pamphlet, *A Summary View of the Rights of British America*.[27]

The Dialectic of Allodial vs. Feudal Land

Intended to justify colonial complaints against English tyrannical practices, *A Summary View* also set out Jefferson's historical understanding of the development of the common law regarding property. That understanding by and large followed the American variation on the English myth that Blackstone and others had popularized, with one important change. Unlike Adams, Jefferson did not deny that feudal property had ever been introduced into the American colonies. He conceded that it had but then argued that the introduction of the feudal tenures into colonial law "at a very early period of our settlement" had been "an error in the nature of our landholdings." The historically accurate account, Jefferson contended, was that the general rule of the common law even after the conquest was the Saxon regime of "Allodial" land, held "in absolute dominion, disencumbered with any superior." Feudal tenures were "but exceptions out of the Saxon laws of possession," and the latter "still form the basis or groundwork of the common law, to prevail wheresoever the exceptions have not taken place." But why had not those exceptions correctly become part of colonial law, and why were feudal tenures nevertheless in fact introduced here? In a truly ingenious move, Jefferson simultaneously resolved both paradoxes and laid the historical foundation for colonial claims against the crown:

America was not conquered by William the Norman, nor it's [*sic*] lands surrendered to him or any of his successors. Possessions there are undoubtedly of the Allodial nature. Our ancestors, however, who migrated hither, were laborers, not lawyers. The fictitious principle that all lands belong originally to the king, they were early persuaded to believe real, and accordingly took grants of the own lands from the crown. And while the crown continued to grant for small sums and reasonable rents, there was no inducement to arrest the error and lay it open to the public view. But his majesty has lately taken on him to advance the terms of purchase and of holding to the double of what they were, by which means the acquisition of lands being rendered difficult, the population of our country is likely to be checked. It is time therefore for us . . . to declare that [his majesty] has no right to grant lands of himself.[28]

Jefferson further developed the idea of allodial land in an extraordinary exchange of correspondence with Edmund Pendleton two years after publication of *A Summary View*. His discussion here reveals the central symbolic function of the concept of allodial property. That function was to signify the role of property in realizing the republican vision of individual autonomy, which was personal independence serving a political, civic function.

In a missing letter to Pendleton, Jefferson made two proposals regarding the disposition of Virginia land. He urged that all Virginia land, including land already held by individuals who owed tenurial obligations to the state, should be allodial in character. The immediate and obvious effect of purging land of this vestige of feudal land law would have been to wipe out the remaining tenurial obligations that landholders owned to the state. A less obvious, but to Jefferson equally important, effect would have been symbolically to replace hierarchical land*holding* with autonomous land*ownership*.

Jefferson also proposed that the government sell all unsettled lands, which it owned, in fee simple. By the end of the eighteenth century the general view behind this proposal became the land policy of both the federal government and some municipalities as well. The Northwest Ordinance of 1787, for example, can be understood as implementing the Jeffersonian land policy.[29] Similarly, New York City embarked on a program of disposing of its public land in Manhattan through unrestricted grants in fee simple absolute.[30]

Writing to respond to these two proposals, Pendleton was frank: "I have [been] beating my brain about your old Opinion that our Land tenure should be merely Allodial, and a New Opinion frequently mentioned during the last convention, that the unappropriated Lands should be sold for the benefit of the commonwealth."[31] Pendleton raised two objections to both proposals. The first concerned the terms of the original Virginia charter. It entitled every newly arrived settler to 50 acres of land to be held in so-called socage tenure[32] in exchange for the annual payment of a modest annual fee, known as quitrent. Pendleton argued that both proposals would unfairly put new settlers in a comparatively better position than existing settlers. Second, Jefferson's plan would disadvantage the poor, "who would not be able to bid against the others" (i.e., the "men of property") for the unappropriated land.

In response, Jefferson reiterated his historical theory that the English common law that had been transplanted to the colonies, when correctly understood, provided for allodial ownership. Whether any American land may have been converted into feudal land by legislation or by the terms of grants was a matter of speculation, but even if any land had been so changed "we have it in our power to make it what it ought to be for the public good."[33] Jefferson left little doubt which regime of ownership he considered as comporting with the public good:

> [W]as not a separation of the property from the perpetual use of lands [i.e., feudal tenure] a mere fiction? Is not it's [*sic*] history well known, and the purpose for which it was introduced, to wit, the establishment of a military system of defence? Was it not afterwards made an engine of immense oppression? Is it wanting with us for the purpose of military defence? May not its other legal effects . . . be performed in other more simple ways? Has it not been the practice of all other nations to hold their lands as their personal estate in absolute dominion? Are we not the better for what we have hitherto abolished of the feudal system? Has not every restitution of the antient [*sic*] Saxon laws had happy effects? Is it not better now that we return at once into that happy system of our ancestors, the wisest and most perfect ever yet devised by the wit of man, as it stood before the 8th century?[34]

The effect of Jefferson's historical chronicle was much the same as Adams's. Both stories strongly affirmed the themes of America as breaking with the past and the historical priority of "allodial" over "feudal" property in America. Feudal property signified "tyranny" and the corruption of "virtue," which in turn was understood in terms of the question of hierarchical social relationships. Allodial land signified "liberty" and "virtue." The stories were structured by a dialectic in which "feudal" and "allodial" land were symbols for opposed political, social, and legal ideals.

But this dialectic ignored important ambiguities. The positive meaning of "allodial" property was less clear than its negative meaning, i.e., the rejection of formal social hierarchies and personal dependency. If allodial property signified personal autonomy and equality, or at least a nonhierarchical society, did that imply anything like a commitment to radical egalitarianism in the distribution of land or even abandonment of the common law conception of privatized ownership?[35] Adams did not address these matters in the *Dissertation* itself, but a partial response may be found in his *Fragmentary Notes* for the *Dissertation*. He wrote: "Property monopolized or in the Possession of a few is a curse to Mankind. We should preserve not an Absolute Equality.—this is unnecessary, but preserve all from extreme Poverty, and all others from extravagant Riches."[36] If this statement seems unclear, Adams's views on property distribution and property rights, as we shall see shortly, later became clearer. Jefferson's views on the distribution of land and on the configuration of property rights were, as we have already discussed, even more fraught with ambiguity. In the correspondence with Pendleton at least, he made it clear that he contemplated distribution of small parcels of land to all settlers, not by selling unappropriated land but merely by allowing settlers to do what they were bound to do anyway, that is, appropriate western lands.[37]

Uncertainty over the essential character of property remained. We have already seen that American republicans, including Jefferson, the most conspicuously "agrarian" among them, were deeply ambivalent about the character that property ought to take. Did their conception of allodial property imply an embrace of dynamic property as a means of eliminating the material basis for a possible American recreation of formal hierarchies? Or was their anxiety rooted elsewhere?

The real source of republican anxiety was not feudal property, including tenures, entails, and the like, but commercial property, or more accurately, "commodified" property. Republicans associated commodified property with personal dependency; it created social as well as economic hierarchies that replaced the old "feudal" hierarchies. What is striking, then, about the "feudal vs. allodial" property discourse is that this dichotomy overlooks the form of property with which American civic republicans, like their English counterparts, were most preoccupied, namely, commodified property.

We have in fact, then, three, not two, forms of property in the symbology of American civic republicanism—"feudal," "allodial," and "commercial"—and two dichotomies, not one—"feudal vs. allodial" and "feudal vs. commercial." Each form signified a particular mode of historically understood social life. That is, each occupied a position within a temporal line, a stage of social development.

To say that American civic republican lawyers arranged these modes of social life historically does not indicate, however, *how* they were arranged. We have already seen that two different arrangements of history were available in eighteenth-century Anglo-American historiography (cyclical and linear) and that it was possible to confuse the two, leading some (such as Blackstone) to an oscillate inconclusively between the two. To American republicans, this inconclusiveness was not simply the result of sloppiness or inattention. Rather it signaled a deep anxiety about commerce, specifically its attendant changes on the form of property, and an ambivalence about social change in the new republic.

Historicizing Property: Predicament and Responses

Commerce and time were inextricably linked together in legal writing, and their meanings were mutually dependent. They were metaphors for each other. Anxieties about one were articulated through the other. Commodified property—the outcome of commerce—represented modernity. Civic republicans were anxious about modernity because the very idea of social change seemed directly to threaten the stability that was so necessary to virtue. For civic republicans, as for many individuals today, it was easy to see social change as a force whose natural effect was to undermine basic principles. This attitude was at the core of the dialectic of dynamism and stability. But republicans worried about modernity also because they associated it specifically with commerce and commodified property, the form of property that civic republicans considered to be fundamentally incompatible with republican tenets.

The Predicament of Time and Republican Property

Republican attitudes toward time and its relationship to property, then, were complex. In relation to the past, time posed one problem—the existence of feudal property in the common law, representing personal dependency. That threat to the republican vision led to the related themes of breaking with the past and creating a dynamic of property that would prevent the recreation of feudal hierarchies. It is from this point of view that American property lawyers could regard legislative reforms that effected little practical change as crucially important.

No features of the old common law of property better illustrate this point than the abolition of entailments and primogeniture.[38] Neither device had much practical significance in American legal practice by the mid-eighteenth century.[39] However, they symbolized the connection between what was thought of as "feudal" property and social hierarchy. American lawyers viewed these feudal restraints on alienation as the foundations on which English aristocrats had constructed their family dynasties. Viewed through the lens of the "feudal" past, in which inalienability of property was a principal basis for creating and maintaining a social hierarchy, it is easy, merely by reversing the association, to link the alienability of property with social equality.

In relation to the future, however, time posed another problem—the loss of stability, without which virtue could not be maintained, brought about by the rise of commodified property. J. G. A. Pocock has established the role of public credit, whose growth was part of the so-called Financial Revolution of the first half of the eighteenth century,[40] in the emergence of intangible and highly mobile forms of wealth as property.[41] Land has always enjoyed a certain mystique for its function of anchoring social and political relations, and it of course had long been subject to exchange, but enough of its mystique remained in eighteenth-century English understandings to have prevented it from being treated as a commodity. The "new property" of the eighteenth century—marketable shares of public debt[42]—was obviously unlike the paradigmatic form of property (land), not only its intangibility but in the popular perception that its character as property depended on its exchangeability. The fluidity of marketable interests in public debt helped to create an understanding, in popular thought, of other forms of property, including land,[43] as dynamic, and that understanding, in turn, affected the legal understanding of property and pushed it toward the status of commodity. Courts, first in England and later in the United States, gradually came to regard property interests as protectible because of their value, derived from exchange.[44]

American civic republicans were faced with corruption when it looked to the past and with uncertainty when it looked to a future in which the corrupting forces of manufacturing and commodification might be victorious. They could hardly avoid experiencing a sense of anxiety: "Here are the origins of American historical pessimism."[45]

Responses to Historicism

This predicament might have been avoided simply by denying the identification of time with change and contingency. The old common law mentality did so through the understanding of the common law either as the ancient (or "Gothic") constitution or as embodying the principles of an immanent natural and timeless order. The central claim of this understanding was that the common law and all of its associated institutions (property being the most significant) was not contingent but had remained constant through time.[46] Adams's strategy in his *Dissertation* comes close to adopting this response, but for a crucial difference: He does not so much as deny time than escape from it. Jefferson and Adams shared with virtually all American republicans—indeed all Americans at that time (and still perhaps today)—a deep-seated belief in the historical uniqueness of the new society and its institutions. For Jefferson, that belief meant that the material circumstances of America were unique. The virtually unlimited amount of land here permitted the creation of a fee-simple empire. For Adams, the historical novelty was the fact that America and all of its social institutions, including property, were from the very outset created free from the taint of the old world, the world of the feudal and the canon laws. American law was unique in never having been part of the *ancien régime*. Still, neither Jefferson nor Adams denied change wrought by time. Neither directly confronted the possibility of the historical contingency of our institutions, but, significantly, neither denied it.

Adams's response to time differed from Jefferson's in yet another respect. Adams drew on the Christian millennialist tradition to define a relationship between the new American society and time. This tradition underlay Adams's vision of America as escaping secular time: America was the millennium realized, and with its arrival America was the culmination of secular history. In contrast, Jefferson's religious skepticism made the Christian millennium idea unacceptable to him, and lacking that concept, the only meaning of time and history available to him was a secular one.[47]

For several reasons, denial of contingency as a consequence of time was not an available response to the predicament of time for well-read American legal writers in the late eighteenth century. Increasingly sophisticated critiques of historicist chroniclers of the common law's feudal past eroded the static conception of the common law, indeed of all social institutions. By the second half of the eighteenth century, that conception largely had disappeared in English and colonial American legal writing.[48] While many legal writers did continue to discuss the ancient constitution, that reference was no more than a "fragmented survival,"[49] that is, a rhetoric whose original meaning had lost virtually all of its original coherence. The public meaning of time had changed from continuity to contingency.

American lawyers inherited from English civic humanist sources extending back to Harrington[50] a public meaning of time that unambiguously acknowledged the inevitability of change in all societies. That meaning was expressed in a well-defined theory of social development. Societies were thought of as organic and developmental, rather than mechanistic and static.[51] To articulate the pattern of social development civic republicans turned again to metaphor, interpreting society in terms of what they believed they best understood, themselves. As humans developed, so did societies. That metaphor defined the pattern by which all societies changed. The pattern was one of birth, growth, decay, and death. Individual societies, like individual humans, did not continuously develop in a linear direction. They flourished for a time but eventually deteriorated.[52]

For republicans, the consequence of this cyclical theory was deeply troubling. It implied that the virtuous polity gradually decayed as society passed through a cyclical series of changes. The actual histories of past republics, of which eighteenth-century American republicans were well aware, reinforced this message. The republics of Sparta and Rome and the Renaissance Italian republics had all not only failed to elude change but had passed through the cycle of decay precisely as the theory posited.

Moving from the macro to the micro level, from entire societies to particular institutions, the message was equally worrisome. Property, as the foundation of society and personality, was at the center of this cycle of change. In all known societies property had changed form over time, originating in a natural state in which ownership anchored personal autonomy, but thereafter being transformed into increasingly corrupt forms which replaced autonomy with dependence and hierarchy.

It is just this matrix of historical change that explains both the prominence and the ambiguous meanings of the dichotomy between allodial and feudal land. For the cyclical theory of social change, and with it, the sociology of property, was simultaneously the source of optimism and pessimism. Indeed, what emerges perhaps most clearly from the discussions of the allodial/feudal dichotomy, and the cyclical theory generally, is a dialectic of optimism and pessimism, which is built into the very image of the cycle. While that image encouraged the notion of the restoration of "Saxon liberty" associated with allodial land by abolishing all vestiges of feudal property (again, the movement to eliminate the entail and primogeniture looms large here), the logic of the cycle dictated that forms of property and society that are marked by a high degree of personal autonomy must eventually succumb to decay and dependence. With the experience of European nations whose economies had already been transformed by manufacturing, credit, and the rise of mobile and intangible forms of property serving as examples of how the seemingly inexorable logic of social change produced dependence and corruption, Americans could well wonder whether they could escape the same fate.

We have already seen that one response to this predicament that republican American lawyers made was to assert, with more hope than conviction, an escape from history. This was clearly Jefferson's response, articulated repeatedly from *A Summary View* through *Notes on the State of Virginia* and later correspondence. The scheme of land distribution, made possible by the vast extent of the West, was an expression of the hope to escape history as it had been known until now. The unique conditions of the American experience, for which, of course, the West was and remained such an incredibly powerfully symbol, as writers like Henry Nash Smith, Leo Marx, and Ernest Tuveson[53] have told, seemed to Jefferson to make it possible to redefine the pattern of historical development and to break the cycle in which decay, corruption, and dependence ultimately prevailed. Social progress need not always lead to decay. In America, the dynamic of land—the fee-simple empire—might maintain virtue and personal autonomy, even in the presence of commerce. Societies, Jefferson had claimed in the *Notes,* resorted to manufacturing only by reason of necessity. The vast expanse of land in America held out the promise for the first time in known history of breaking the historical authority of necessity.

But as we have also seen, this was no more than a hope. Jefferson was well aware that the uniqueness of the American experience might be only temporary, reducing it to a "Rousseauian moment."[54] Eventually the land will all be settled, and the safety valve will close. At that moment—the "Machiavellian moment" when time, secularly understood, confronts virtue and personal autonomy—the cycle must resume and "allodial" property give way to "feudal" property, autonomy to dependency and hierarchy.

The Embrace of Modernity: The Scottish Historical Thesis and the Transformation of Property, Liberty, and Time in American Republicanism

There was another response to the predicament that history, understood as "public time,"[55] posed for society in general and property in particular. This response, as we have learned from recent scholarship, was developed by eighteenth-century Scottish social theorists, including David Hume, Adam Smith, John Millar, Adam Ferguson, William Robertson, and for lawyers the most significant member of the circle, Lord Kames.[56] The central achievement of these Scottish Enlightenment social theorists was to develop an alternate interpretation of commerce and its effect on society to the interpretation that originated within a civic humanist framework. If the ultimate message of civic humanism's interpretation was pessimism about time and commerce, Scottish social theory was one that encouraged optimism about the future and the effects of social change, particularly about the rise of commercial society.

From Politics to Society

The two interpretations differ in their emphasis on the fundamental object of historical study. While civic humanism focused on politics as such, the Scottish interpretation shifted attention to society.[57] This shift is reflected most obviously in the difference between the categories of their historical typologies. The dominant civic republican categories had been monarchy, aristocracy, democracy, and republic. The Scottish Enlightenment categories lack any such political dimension. The central dichotomy is feudal versus commercial, and this dichotomy is situated within a time line whose categories—hunting, pastoral, agriculture, and commercial—are all categories of the intellectual paradigm that later became known as "political economy" but whose public meaning was social and economic. These categories do not signify alternative types of polity but, rather, differing modes of social behavior.

Focusing on a shift from the political to the social risks distorting the extent to which the civic republican and Scottish Enlightenment interpretations of time differed. The two understandings in fact were locked together in various and complicated ways. For one thing, writers in the two groups did not understand their work to constitute a rhetoric that competed with the rhetoric of civic humanism. If Scottish historical social theory was a theory of *civil*, as distinguished from *civic*, humanism, it was nevertheless consistent with civic republicanism to the extent that it was, above all, a theory of humanism. Both interpretations shared a overriding concern with the human personality. Civic republicans and Scottish social theorists differed over which aspect of that personality should be emphasized, political or social, or, more accurately, over the meaning of the human personality, not over the paramount importance of the nature of human personality.[58] Moreover, Hume, Smith, Ferguson, Robertson, and Kames all shared with civic republicans the understanding of time as change. Insisting that the study of history and society must be scientific and adhering to the historiographical advances made in the preceding century by Spelman and Hale, the Scottish historical writers were hardly more likely than Harringtonian civic republicans to reject the insights gained in the preceding century by the critics of the ancient constitution myth.

What separated the two paradigms was their reactions to that understanding of time. This difference was inextricably related to the difference over the nature of personality, for the effect of, if not the incentive for, shifting attention from the political to the social was to make it possible to welcome social change in general and commercial culture and commercial values in particular. To see why this is so, we need first to consider the theory of social development to which virtually every writer associated with the social-historical-comparative branch of the Scottish Enlightenment subscribed, the so-called four-stages theory.[59]

The "Four-Stages" Theory

Inspired by the example of Montesquieu's highly particularistic study of legal change in *The Spirit of Laws,* scholars in Scotland and in France, whose civil law system greatly influenced Scottish social theorists,[60] looked for what Montesquieu had not unambiguously provided: a pattern of legal change, applicable to all societies, from primitive origins to full maturity. Apparently simultaneously,[61] both groups articulated the theory that societies progress through four stages: hunting, pastoral, agricultural, and commercial.[62] One of most significant themes of this progressive theory was the linkage between property regimes, division of labor, and social wealth. Division of labor was seen both as a consequence and a determinant of the system of property. According to the dominant version of the story, especially that told by its less sophisticated chroniclers, in the early stages of societies labor tasks were simple because the forms of, and rights in, property were rudimentary, and the rudimentary regime of property in turn created no need for greater division of labor. For a variety of reasons (which sometimes were weakly articulated, if at all) more complex forms of property and more complex property rights emerged. Private ownership of land, for example, initially appeared at the third, agricultural, stage, according to Adam Smith. Labor tasks increasingly became specialized so that by the time the final stage, commercial society, was reached, a substantial division of labor existed. And the arrival of that stage profoundly increased the aggregate amount of social wealth.[63]

The Scottish writers regarded their history as scientific, or as they called it, "philosophical," in the sense that it purported to describe an immutable pattern of social development, but they were hardly objective about the story they told. They depicted their social transformation as the development of "civilization." "Civilization" was later, especially in the nineteenth century, to become "progress," but it had much the same meaning in the late eighteenth century. All of the contributors to this story left no doubt that each stage represented a progressively higher mode of social development. Adam Smith, for example, characterized the hunting stage as the "lowest and rudest state of society," while modern commercial society was said to be characterized by the "polish," "taste," and "manners" of a refined society.

Here we have the theme, with which Montesquieu's and Hume's names are usually associated, of commerce as a moderating, socializing phenomenon—*le doux commerce,* as Montesquieu called it,[64] or "mildness," in Hume's terms. Far from being a source of instability, the Scottish writers understood commerce to have a softening effect on manners and a stabilizing effect on social behavior within all of the various types of government.[65] Far from constituting a threat to the public good, commerce promoted the common welfare by stimulating the individual initiative and industry that was understood as indispensable to the moral personality that itself was indispensable to the maintenance of a virtuous republic. And far from undermining individual autonomy, the dynamism and fluidity of commercial society prevents the recreation of feudal hierarchies in which status determined all and ownership of property secured personal independence in fact only for one person, the king.[66]

Toward a Rapprochement between Commerce and Virtue

The meaning of commerce that Scottish writers developed made it possible for American political and legal writers to link it with virtue,[67] and thus overcome the civic humanist understanding that the two were rival rhetorics. Cultivated freehold land and the commercial market would no longer be seen as rival symbols for the agency that would liberate America from the past and liberate individuals from domination, which the past itself signified. Indeed, the reworking of what commerce meant was at the core of a general process of redefinition of principal republican terms (i.e., "virtue," "corruption," and "luxury") that was the basis for the broader redefinition of American republicanism from its civic form to a commercial form.[68] As we will see below, however, while redefinitions of important terms in the republican vocabulary eliminated virtue and commerce as constituting a dialectic, they did not eliminate the more basic dialectic altogether. The premodern, republican dialectic of temporality, metaphorically expressing the modern dialectic of sociality, continued to be articulated by later Federalist writers like Noah Webster. "Redefinition," then, did not produce a "transformation."

The classical conception of virtue that American civic republicans, influenced by the cyclical understanding of history, had commonly articulated by invoking the name of Sparta, was gradually replaced by a more "modern" public meaning. This redefinition associated virtue with individual productivity rather than with self-abnegation or austerity, and is best understood as the result of a critique that occurred within republican culture rather than as evidence of a victory won by an antagonistic external ideology.

Civic republicans early on expressed skepticism about the plausibility of individuals practicing self-denial in the long run. They, like John Adams,[69] shared much of the outlook on human nature that animated the critiques of classical virtue carried on in England, Scotland, and France, an outlook that asserted the primacy of private passion for personal gain as fundamental to the human personality. Most American civic republicans, including Jefferson, realized that the rise of commerce could not altogether be stopped and that the emergence of commerce in America indicated at least some appetite for private gain.

The redefinition was driven internally also in the sense that the oscillation between the cyclical and linear visions of history both reflected and stimulated uncertainty and ambivalence about the classical meaning of virtue. The association of virtue with Sparta was a metaphorical articulation that was intelligible only to the extent that history was understood as cyclical, so that in time the American republic could be seen as the restoration of a *polis* even older than that of the ancient constitution. But the continual reappearance of a linear vision of history, often blended with cyclical rhetoric, made such a belief tenuous and fraught with ambiguity. Redefining the meaning of virtue as individual productivity clarified the direction of history as continuously linear and provided grounds for overcoming anxieties about the implications of modernity. Virtue was no longer associated with the past (represented by Sparta) but with the future. This was the basis for reconciling virtue with time.

This theory of social, economic, and legal development was a code, and it is not difficult to detect a message of optimism in it. The code signaled three claims: the inexorability of society's embeddedness in time, the inexorability of change that follows from the movement of time, and the beneficial consequences of that change. The structure of the theory itself created a basis for embracing time and its companion, modernity. The theory always depicted social development as a movement from past to future: society is constantly moving away from, escaping as it were, the past. Since the past signified rudeness, barbarity, hierarchy, and dependency, the constant development of societies away from it signified continual social improvement.

The Scottish social theorists themselves did not indulge in unqualified optimism, however. Too perceptive not to understand the full implications of their theory, they appreciated the fact that their logic provided no basis for viewing commercial society as a terminus. Their theory, that is, was not teleological, only evolutionary. Commercial society was no millennium, Christian or otherwise, to the Scottish writers. The process of change that leads from primitive to commercial society could easily lead to social degeneration. Lord Kames expressed this view in stating, "[T]his [commercial] state is never permanent: great opulence opens a wide door to indolence, sensuality, corruption, prostitution, perdition."[70]

This logic, which seemed to the Scots so clearly confirmed by the experience of the Greek and Roman empires, suggested, then, that the historical pattern of social change was cyclical.[71] J. G. A. Pocock has pointed out that virtue remained very much present within the Scottish paradigm of human personality; not, of course, as the focus of its admiration, but as the aspect of personality that is, unavoidably but regrettably nevertheless, lost with the emergence of specialization and diversification in commercial society. They foresaw the possibility of what we call atomized society as an unintended consequence of the subordination of politics in the commercial stage, and they regarded that possibility with dread.[72]

The progressive theory of social development affected the American republican meaning of property in several ways. First, it replaced the simple feudal/allodial dichotomy with a more complex array of property forms, associated with each stage of social development. Second, by uncoupling personality from any specific form of property, it eliminated the grounds for pessimism about historical change.[73] Historicizing the forms of property in terms of morally neutral stages of production meant that the change in the form of ownership from ownership of allodial land to ownership of newer forms of property, especially those that were intangible and highly mobile, did not necessarily corrupt individual or social moral personality. Indeed, the theory historicized moral personality as well, showing that rather than being lost in the past it had simply adapted to new circumstances. Third, it implied that time and history favored individuated ownership. Both Montesquieu and the Scottish historical social theorists had claimed that ownership that is strongly public existed only in precommercial stages. Precommercial societies at first lacked any concept of ownership at all, and when a concept of ownership did develop it was predominantly communal. Even where individuated ownership did exist in precommercial societies, a wide variety of communal use-interests encumbered the individual owner's freedom to do with his property as he pleased. By contrast, the defining characteristic of ownership in commercial society was the drastic reduction of such communal entanglements, thereby consolidating the individual owner's control of his own assets.

The message of this progressive theory of history, then, indicated by its virtual abandonment of the feudal/allodial dichotomy and the dialectic between cyclical and progressive theories of social evolution, was that the Harringtonian vision of property and individual autonomy as morally coherent only as serving the active civic life of each citizen was not so much wrong as it was fated. The Scottish writers historicized the Harringtonian vision. The upshot of their account of social development was that the classical Republican interpretation of property was fated by the logic of history to disappear with the passing of precommercial society. In this respect the Scottish progressive historical theory of property and society was an early, though somewhat softened, version of necessitarian arguments for individuated ownership that became increasingly prominent in the nineteenth century and that remain prominent in legal writing today.[74] Changes in social conditions, the thesis implied (and modern scholars explicitly assert), necessitate changes in forms of ownership. More to the point, individuation of control over items of property takes precedence over more socialized forms of ownership not as a matter of social choice or of ideology, but as a matter of historical inevitability. In the dialectic of sociality, the separation theme outweighed the social union theme.

The Multiple Meanings of Individual Liberty
and Its Relation to Property

The conception of individual autonomy that operates in this conception of property is no longer that of the civic republican notion of self-sufficiency as a precondition for virtuous politics. The Scottish historical social theorists did not define individual liberty as the condition in which the citizen is liberated from distractions so that he is able actively to participate in the affairs of the polity for the well-being of all. Rather, it meant freedom from constraints on the ability, through individual initiative, to pursue one's own conception of the good. That is, it was a kind of prototype for what political philosophers today call "negative liberty." To be sure, like the idea of negative liberty, the Scottish conception of individual liberty shared with the civic republican understanding of individual liberty a strongly social dimension. Individual autonomy still meant having the capacity to engage with others from a position of independence. But its objective of sociability had shifted away from the purpose of governance that was central to the civic republican understanding to the purpose of satisfaction of personal ends.

This redefinition of individual autonomy and its relationship to property influenced American writers, particularly during the years after the Revolution. The need to respond to what appeared to many American republicans in the late eighteenth century to be the inevitability of the triumph of commerce prompted this shift in meaning. It was also prompted, of course, by the political struggle over the federal Constitution. The story that the Scottish historians told seemed to confirm to their American readers all that they were witnessing around them (just as it confirmed what the Scots thought they were witnessing with their own economic and political changes). There is a kind of collective adaptive preference,[75] a response to avoid cognitive dissonance—the psychological frustration of attempting to change seemingly inevitable conditions—at work in both cases.

Changes (or perceived changes) in economic and political circumstances, and psychological reactions to those changes, only partly explain the shifts in the meaning of individual liberty and property. It is dangerously easy to exaggerate the extent to which there *was* a redefinition and to say, using our own vocabulary, that it was all public in the mid-eighteenth century and thereafter all private. That, of course, is a caricature. The meanings of liberty and property throughout the eighteenth century combined elements of both the public and private. Liberty was highly ambiguous, and its very ambiguity facilitated interpretive shifts. The redefinition, then, was due as much to endogenous factors as to exogenous changes.

To make this point more concrete, consider the meaning of individual liberty in relation to virtue, the concept with which liberty was inextricably connected in republican discourse. Recent historiography tends to interpret the civic republican term "virtue" as the equivalent of altruism, i.e., an abnegation of self-interest for the sake of others' welfare.[76] This interpretation is understandable in view of such republican rhetoric as Benjamin Rush's in this statement: "Every man in a republic is public property. His time and talents—his youth—his manhood—his old age— nay more, life, all belong to his country."[77]

Lance Banning has pointed out, however, that what American civic republicans contemplated was "vigorous assertions of the self within a context of communal consciousness and a willingness to live by the community's decisions."[78] Virtue meant acting on the basis of self-interest, as opposed to self-absorption. This meaning of virtue in turn affected the meaning of liberty. Virtue required that citizens live in liberty. If acting virtuously meant acting according to one's self-interest, then liberty must mean negative freedom. Individuals must be freed from external constraints, including political constraints, inhibiting their pursuit of individual wants.

There is obviously a strong tension, if not a contradiction, between this private aspect of virtue and liberty and the public obligation to accommodate one's interests with the needs and decisions of the community. The Revolutionaries had sought to resolve the dialectic of self and other, separation and union, through their thesis that once hierarchy was abolished by, for example, purging the common law of property of its feudal corruptions, individuals' permanent interests would merge with the public interest. As republicans later grew increasingly skeptical about this thesis, the tension inherent in the early republican conceptions of virtue and liberty became more apparent. Realizing that the original American understanding of those concepts was unworkable prompted a reworking of their meaning.

Just as it would be wrong to ignore the private aspect of virtue and liberty in early American republican discourse, so it would be misleading to suppose that the thrust of the configuration of liberty and property that emerged in the late eighteenth century was strictly negative. Separation perhaps was being given greater weight after 1787, but the relational (civic) theme of property had by no means disappeared. There remained a dialectic. For Federalists like Madison, Wilson, and Webster, the meaning of individual liberty was not confined to freedom from governmental oppression but included the expectation that one would use one's abilities in active participation in public life. Property was crucial in this conception of individual liberty. To those trained in the common law especially, property strongly symbolized stability and assured the conditions that were necessary for the exercise of one's skills in the public sphere.[79] To these Federalists, moreover, the public sphere was not confined to governance, but included commerce. Extending the theme of *le doux commerce*,[80] these writers regarded commerce as beneficial in part because of its socializing consequences. To be free to engage in commerce was to participate in public life.

James Madison's famous 1792 essay on property presents what is perhaps the clearest example of this attempt to connect private activity and public life through the configuration of individual liberty and property. There he explicitly contended that the term "property" has two meanings: it simultaneously embraces a private, Blackstonian conception and a public, if not civic, conception.[81] The private meaning is the familiar legal conception of property as "that dominion which one man claims and exercises over the external things of the world, in exclusion of every other individual." Madison emphasized that a second, "juster" meaning must be added to this common-law understanding, in which property "embraces every thing to which a man may attach a value and have a right."[82] The first meaning includes a man's "land," "merchandize," and "money." The second sense extends the meaning of property to include a person's opinions and "the free communicating of them." It also includes "the free use of [one's] faculties and the free choice of the objects on which to employ them." This second meaning encompasses what we today would think of as "civil" rights.

Madison's essay had several objectives, the first of which was to ensure the greatest possible protection for the personal rights of the less propertied. He perceived these rights to be threatened by measures like Hamilton's plan for a national bank and sought to elevate them to the status of "property."[83] Madison was also indicating that property, in both senses, contemplates *activity*. Activity, the property of exercising one's "faculties," connects property with individual liberty and individuals with society.

Thus another part of Madison's message was that property is not atomizing but socializing. The individual liberty interest that is associated property, moreover, does not mean that individuals are isolated from the larger society and polity. Rather it means that they are freed from constraints on their becoming involved in the broader community through the full use of their abilities. The private and exclusive aspect of the configuration of property and liberty, therefore, complements the public aspect by enabling individual activity.

Summarizing the discussion up to this point, we have identified in the late eighteenth century certain redefinitions within the American republican cultural code in which property and time are interconnected at the center. These code redefinitions signaled the emergence of a cultural understanding of property that departed in several crucial respects from the meaning that civic republicans created, while simultaneously retaining much of the rhetoric of civic republicanism. Individual autonomy and property remained closely linked in the emerging code, but the linkage was increasingly understood as oriented toward a private realm of activity, that is, outside the arena of governance.

We have also seen that these redefinitions responded to the predicament that time posed for the coherence of civic republicanism's conception of property. Specifically, they permitted republicans to embrace modernity rather than to fear it. With respect to property, it enabled American republican lawyers increasingly to accept with approval, or at least without unqualified anxiety, emerging forms of property in American society. In particular, historicizing property facilitated acceptance of emerging intangible and speculative economic interests as property.

The Triumph of Imaginary Property

The implication from Blackstone's account of the law of property as having to do with rights as to "things"[84] meant that English common law confined property to tangible assets (land being the most obvious example). In spite of this, intangible interests were hardly unknown to the eighteenth-century common law of property. As English and American common lawyers then knew it, property included a variety of future possessory interests (called "remainders," "reversions," and "executory interests"), some of which provided the interest-holder with only the slightest possibility of ever becoming entitled to take possession of assets. It also included a category of interests that common lawyers called "incorporeal hereditaments,"[85] which were mostly what modern property lawyers would call "easements" and "profits in land" but which also included such remnants of feudal land law as "advowsons"[86] and "tithes." These legal forms were thoroughly assimilated into the common-law fabric as "things," despite legal awareness, as Blackstone stated, that "[t]heir existence is merely in idea and abstracted contemplation."[87]

By the late eighteenth century, economic changes facilitated by legal changes had introduced new sorts of intangible and speculative interests that were more important, both quantitatively and qualitatively, than the old intangible interests had been. Changes in commercial practices and in public finance had made transferable paper forms of property, including promissory notes, banknotes, and certificates of public debt, increasingly important forms of wealth in the last decade of the eighteenth century. Changes in the law regarding commercial paper during the second half of the eighteenth century enabled negotiable paper to succeed over the traditional legal strictures against the assignment of "choses in action."[88]

Meanwhile, in the realm of public finance, masses of public securities, such as loan certificates issued by Congress, appeared on the market and were heavily traded by speculators.[89] This was happening even before the 1790 adoption of Alexander Hamilton's plan for strengthening public credit by funding the enormous public debt. The Hamiltonian funding plan, which included issuance of new federal securities in exchange for old public securities and creation of a Bank of the United States, strengthened confidence in public credit and decisively established liquid forms of property as central to the economy.[90]

All of these debt instruments, governmental and nongovernmental, represented property that was based on nothing more than promises, hopes, and expectations. American opponents of Hamilton's plan to create monetized public debt, echoing the arguments raised earlier in the eighteenth century by opponents of Walpole's scheme for saving public credit in England,[91] pointed to just this fact in their efforts to stem the shift from the form of property that was, it seemed to many skeptics, literally "real property"—land—to a form of property that was represented by pieces of paper but that rested on nothing more real than imagination. Today, lawyers take for granted the notion of basing property on expectations.[92] To many eighteenth-century common lawyers, expectation as the basis of property seemed both unnatural and politically dangerous. At the same time, throughout Anglo-American legal doctrine prior to the boom in public credit and paper property, pockets of such thinking about the basis of property and what sorts of interests could be property could be found. We have already noted that future interests in landed estates were nothing more than expectations but were deemed to be property nevertheless. And while courts classified the inheritance interest in an expectant heir during the ancestor's lifetime as a "mere expectancy" (even if the ancestor were mentally incompetent and legally incapable of making a valid will), English Courts of Equity accorded to such interests many of the same characteristics as property interests, strictly so called, the most important of these being alienability.[93] All of these legal changes reflected a gradual and general shift in legal understanding of what could be the subject of property, from assets that were tangible and stable to assets that were intangible, speculative, and highly fluid.

It is not hard to discern a basic compatibility between the emerging code of property and time that we have been examining and the outlook of those American lawyers and political writers who unambiguously rejected republicanism of all types, such as Hamilton.[94] Hamilton and other (though certainly not all) Federalists did more than simply shift the meaning of virtue to something more compatible with commercialism; they explicitly rejected it as both implausible and unnecessary. We can say, then, that in doing so, they radically altered the vocabulary of politics, law, and property from that of the Jeffersonian civic republican culture. But in saying this, we must be careful not to overlook the degree of continuity that accompanied change. To appreciate how much continuity accompanied conceptual change we need to examine the dialectic that emerged in the American political and legal writing of the late eighteenth century. In doing so, we will find reason to reconsider the conventional wisdom that the post-Constitutional era, specifically the 1790s, marked a dramatic transformation in American political-legal discourse.

THREE

Descent and Dissent from the Civic Meaning of Property

The American Critique of Civic Discourse

THE MEANING OF MANY political and legal concepts changed during the Constitutional era, and an especially important change concerned the keystone of the entire civic republican structure: virtue. Throughout this era political and legal writers on both sides of the Atlantic critiqued the concept of virtue, which resulted in the shifting of its meaning away from the one it had to the American revolutionaries.

The principal situs for the American critique was *The Federalist Papers,* but even among Federalists there were substantial differences concerning the role and the meaning of virtue. The critique of virtue did not originate, at least not entirely, in American writings. Gerald Stourzh, Garry Wills, Stanley Elkins, and Eric McKitrick have thoroughly documented the extent of Hume's influence on Hamilton, especially his economic thinking.[1] Crucial elements of Hamilton's and Madison's essays were derived from Hobbes and Mandeville as well as from Hume. The entire discursive structure through which the critique was conducted was inherited (although the American critics transformed it) from Machiavelli, Rousseau, and, more immediately to the Founders, Montesquieu.

The most important feature of this discursive structure was an elaborate metaphorical opposition between "virtue" and "passion." Classical republican writings depicted "passion" as threatening "virtue" and with it "the public good." These were code words. "Passion" signified not merely self-interest but self-aggrandizement as well. "Virtue" signified commitment to others, that is, the "public good." The conflict between passion and virtue, then, can be translated into the modern conflict between self-interest and community.

Montesquieu and Rousseau attempted to mediate the opposition between virtue and passion by locating passion in the public sphere, that

is, passion for the public good. This move dissolved the opposition between virtue and passion, because they had defined virtue itself as passion
for the public good—an interpretation that particularly influenced John
Adams. More than any other American republican, Adams systematically
worked through the ambiguous meaning of virtue. He wrote in 1776:
"There must be a positive Passion for the public good . . . established in
the Minds of the People, or there can be no Republican Government, nor
any real liberty; and this public Passion must be superior to all private
Passions."[2]

By 1787, however, Adams had substantially lowered his sights. Virtue
now seemed to him to be "merely a negative quality: the absence only of
ambition and avarice."[3] In expressing a decidedly less robust understanding of virtue, Adams joined the company of other American writers whose
early faith in virtue had weakened since the early Revolutionary years.
William Vans Murray was especially direct in articulating these doubts,
observing that if virtue were "of so delicate a nature, as to suffer extinction
by the prevalence of those luxurious habits to which all national improvements lead—it certainly is a principle of too whimsical a nature to be
relied on."[4] Even earlier, during debate over the Massachusetts Constitutional Conventional of 1778, Theophilus Parsons had expressed skepticism about the human capacity to sustain virtue: "It may be said, the
virtuous American would blast with indignation the man, who should
offer him a bribe. Let it now be admitted as a fact. We ask, will that always
be the case? The most virtuous states have become vicious."[5]

Alexander Hamilton and the Commodificationist Outlook

Virtue and passion increasingly became opposed terms. It was expected
that passion would be the ultimate victor in the war with virtue. The
critique of virtue asserted the primacy of the passion over virtue on both
ontological and political grounds. Ontologically, selfishness was assumed
to be fundamental to human nature, virtue to be artificial, forced, or
utopian. Politically, the paradox of selfish behavior producing political
well-being was increasingly articulated.

Hamilton forcefully asserted both grounds in a full-scale attack on the
civic conception of virtue. In the New York Ratifying Convention, for
example, he left no room for doubt concerning his hard-boiled outlook
on human nature, stating: "Men will pursue their interests. It is as easy
to change human nature, as to oppose the strong current of the selfish
passions."[6] Similarly, his political theory clearly showed the influence of

the critiques of Hume, Hobbes, and Mandeville. Again at the New York Ratifying Convention, he echoed Mandeville's notorious formula of private vices, public benefits: "Look through the rich and the poor of the community; the learned and the ignorant. Where does virtue predominate? The difference indeed consists, not in the quantity but kind of vices, which are incident to the various classes; and here the advantage of character belongs to the wealthy. Their vices are probably more favorable to the prosperity of the state, than those of the indigent; and partake less of moral depravity."[7]

Hamilton was not the sole author of the redefinition of virtue, but he was its most influential contributor. The redefinition had profound consequences for the public meaning of commerce and, concomitantly, property. The civic republican sociology of virtue posited that it was possible only under Spartan conditions; what was required, Montesquieu had argued, was a "mediocrity of fortunes."[8] While this did not imply an "extreme equality," civic republicanism did insist that both ends of the economic spectrum, great wealth and poverty, were incompatible with virtue. The whole purpose of property was to serve the public good by establishing the stable conditions for virtuous citizenship.

Hamilton did nothing less than stand this analysis on its head. He argued that concern for the public good would be "a graceful appendage of wealth," rather than the other way around. Public-spiritedness was, in his view, a by-product of private gain rather than its rival. Hamilton considered the vision of maintaining only modest disparities in wealth altogether futile. His repudiation of the civic republican meaning of property in favor of a commercial meaning of property was complete and unambiguous. He stated, for example, "The difference of property is already among us. Commerce and industry will increase the disparity."[9] The following statement is even more striking:

> As riches increase and accumulate in few hands; as luxury prevails in society; virtue will be in a greater degree considered as only a graceful appendage to wealth, and the tendency of things will be to depart from the republican standard. This is the real disposition of human nature.[10]

Hamilton sought to reverse the meaning of virtually every crucial concept in American civic republicanism. Great wealth, "luxury," and social and economic hierarchy were all accepted, if not positively embraced, while "virtue" was subordinated to the creation of social wealth: the Shining City on a Hill was on its way to being defined as the capital of the Empire of Commerce.

More than any other single American before him, Hamilton was responsible for the emergence in American political-legal writing of a commodified, wealth-creating understanding of property as a clear alternative to the civic conception that Jefferson held. This did not mean, however, that Hamilton repudiated the notion that property played a role in creating and maintaining the proper social order. Hamilton had a very clear vision of what the properly ordered society was, and property played a central role in establishing that society. While he rejected the civic conception of property, then, he was strongly committed to an understanding of property that one can accurately call *proprietarian.*

Private property's role, in Hamilton's vision, was not to secure political independence, but to create the properly ordered society. That society was what Stanley Elkins and Eric McKitrick have aptly called a "mercantile utopia,"[11] a society of great wealth and power whose life blood was the class of enterprising merchants. Rather than republican Rome or classical Sparta, his model was more likely to be contemporary Great Britain, the wealthiest, most commercially developed, and militarily most powerful nation on Earth. Yet Britain did not provide an entirely complete or accurate model for Hamilton, for he wanted none of the vestiges of feudal society to inhibit the entrepreneurial strivings of merchants. There was, in fact, no precedent for the kind of society that Hamilton wanted the United States to become.

Merchants were the proper elite in Hamilton's vision. He looked to them to create enormous wealth for the young nation by exploiting the nation's vast resources through trade and industry. A society whose ideal member was the industrious merchant-entrepreneur was the proper society not simply because it was prosperous, though that was hardly unimportant to Hamilton, but also because its members possessed the morally correct and, one may say, virtuous temperament. Drawing inspiration directly from Hume, Adam Smith, and other Scottish Enlightenment writers,[12] Hamilton developed an understanding of what Elkins and McKitrick, speaking of Hume, have called "a sociology of economic development."[13] Applied to Hamilton, that description is apt as far as it goes, but it obscures a dimension of Hamilton's thought that must be placed foremost if we are to appreciate what Hamilton shared with his Jeffersonian colleagues. That dimension was a strong concern with encouraging certain traits of character that Hamilton thought proper. These traits—

energy, ambition, creativity, innovation—*were* proper not simply because
they were essential to a nation's economic development but also because
they were intrinsically virtuous.

It would be wrong to depict Hamilton's thought as amoral, or even
purely instrumental. The economic instrumentalism is there, and it is very
prominent, but Hamilton considered these character traits important not
solely because it led to material prosperity, but because they were intrinsically proper. "[T]o cherish and stimulate the activity of the human mind"
was intrinsically good, he wrote in the *Report on Manufactures.*[14] Commercial enterprise, as the ultimate expression of this sort of proper character, was virtuous, though not in a civic sense. Its virtues were more of
the private sort, enhancing self-development and personal fulfillment.

A commodity understanding of property would fit naturally enough
within this vision of the proper social order. To discover Hamilton's conception of property, though, we will have proceed indirectly by examining
his writings on public finance and industrial development, for Hamilton
did not develop a theory of property as such. His theories of public finance
and government support of business depended on an unarticulated understanding of property that can comfortably be called "property-as-
commodity." For Hamilton, property was strictly a means to wealth; it
did not matter what form property took so long as it was effective in
creating wealth.

Within Hamilton's theories of public finance and economic development, government was a positive, indeed an indispensable force for the
success of the merchant class.[15] This is not to say that Hamilton was a
mercantilist, as some historians have claimed.[16] One can hardly claim that
every economic theory that urges an active governmental role in promoting economic development is mercantilist, or else many aspects of recent
neoclassical economic theory, not mention all varieties of Keynesian economics could be described as such. The truth is that the debate over Hamilton's status as a mercantilist or laissez-fairist is a nonstarter, for, as Clinton Rossiter noted,[17] Hamilton was pragmatic and eclectic, picking and
choosing what seemed to him most likely to work. He was absolutely
convinced in the indispensable role of government policies and institutions to create the conditions necessary for the national economy to develop at a robust rate. Nowhere was that conviction more evident than
in his plan for a funded public debt, which he articulated in his 1790
Report on the Public Credit.

In the *Report,* the immediate question that Hamilton, the new Secretary of the Treasury, addressed was how the new federal government should handle the multiple levels of public debt that had grown up during the long Revolutionary War. To Hamilton, that question could not be separated from the more long-term question what plan of public finance would create the strong public credit that would be required in order to provide capital for manufacturing and industry. Hamilton's solution to the problem of the massive public debt was to fund it, that is, refinance it with a firm commitment to discharge it in the future through taxation. The refinancing would occur through the relatively simple process of issuing new government securities on uniform terms in exchange for the old securities that the government had issued in the past under fluctuating terms. The key to the plan was the taxing power, which guaranteed the security and stability of the public securities. Hamilton's insight, which he gained from his close study of England's Financial Revolution, was that the government's taxation power could be capitalized to obtain the large pool of capital needed for financing the nation's economic transformation.[18] With the taxation power behind them, the new securities possessed considerable liquidity and could be used as capital to finance the economic ventures of the entrepreneurial class.

This was pure commodity thought. Hamilton consciously set out to transform the national economy, indeed the nation's basic character, by transforming public securities from a special form of debt used for limited and specific purposes into fungible capital. In the *Report on Public Credit*, he explained that the funded debt would serve "most of the purposes of money" and as "capital" that would stimulate trade and manufacturing.[19] Hamilton realized that the funded debt was not, strictly speaking, capital itself, but functioned indirectly to create capital. In his famous 1791 *Report on Manufactures,* he wrote that "though a funded debt is not in the first instance an absolute increase of Capital, or an augmentation of real wealth; yet by serving as a New power in the operation of industry, it has with certain bounds a tendency to increase the real wealth of a Community."[20]

The debt would perform this capital-creating function because the securities that represented it would be freely transferable. To be sure, Hamilton did not want the securities to be used for speculation, but his objection to speculation of the public securities was crucially different from Jefferson's objection to speculation in land. While Jefferson's eye was on avoiding the corruption of civic virtue, Hamilton's eye was on maintaining investor confidence. He was eager for the securities to become attractive investments, especially to foreign investors, and he was well aware of past experiences in which speculation had undermined markets and triggered their total collapse. But avoiding speculation is one thing; avoiding transferability is another. Transferability of the new public securities was indispensable to the plan's success. The securities were not valued for some inherent quality but on the basis of their opportunity cost. Like all commodities, it must, as Hamilton fully appreciated, be changeable and exchangeable for its economic value to the holder and, therefore, its contribution to social wealth, to be maximized.

Continuity with the Civic Meaning

Federalist writings did not constitute a simple, uncomplicated dissent from the Jeffersonian understanding of property, polity, and society. They also signified an intellectual descent from, or continuity with, the Jeffersonian vision. We have already seen how Hamilton's own social thought shared with Jefferson's a proprietarian character. Other Federalist writing displayed an even stronger sense of continuity. Many Federalists in the Constitutional and post-Constitutional years continued to use not only much of the civic republican rhetoric of the Revolutionary years, but the Jeffersonian meanings of that language as well. At a deeper level, this late eighteenth-century Federalist discourse continued some of the same dialectical themes that animated civic republican texts, but with somewhat altered meanings than those dialectical themes held for Jefferson and his followers.

The Dialectic of Dynamism vs. Stability Redux

The dominant dialectic, as we saw earlier, was stability versus dynamism. The civic republican texts depicted stability and dynamism as simultaneously necessary and contradictory. One aspect of individual autonomy, the dimension that saw liberty as realized through involvement in public life, required stability. The other aspect of autonomy, which connected personal liberty with social and, to some extent, economic equality, required dynamism. Connecting dynamism with virtue, civic republicans saw a dynamism of virtue as the force that would prevent the creation of aristocracy through unequal wealth. The metaphorical distinction between two regimes of property, allodial and feudal, which dominated legal writing on property, was the rhetorical formulation of this dialectic that was most common in American legal texts throughout this period and during the early nineteenth century as well.

In one sense, Federalist writings from 1787 throughout the 1790s approached the theme of stability and dynamism from a perspective that was in tension with that of civic republicans. For if civic republican ideology was inclined to favor stability over dynamism, accepting dynamism grudgingly and with skepticism, Federalism tilted the balance in favor of dynamism in the context of the uses of property. Hamilton's empire of commerce was nothing less than the consequence of the dominance of dynamic, wealth-creating property. The core purpose of property, he thought, was to serve the creation of wealth. That purpose would best be achieved by systematic governmental policy initiatives aimed at developing the United States as a predominately commercial and industrial nation.[21] Among the actions that he contemplated for government was the creation of new forms of property, including intangible property created through credit transactions generally and specifically through those of the national government and its agencies, such as the Bank of the United States.

At the same time, however, dynamism as a general stance was the proverbial two-edged sword. It mattered a great deal what sort of dynamism one had in mind. The Federalists, of course, were hardly likely to favor political dynamism, at least if we associate political dynamism with radical democracy or the sort of localism that encouraged political variation.[22] Nor were they likely to favor social dynamism. They never doubted the existence of a natural elite which, because of its superior intelligence, education, and practical judgment, ought to be the ruling class.[23]

The dynamism that animated Federalist writings was an economic dynamism, which in turn required a dynamic concept of property. But even that form of dynamism was a source of ambivalence. One aspect of economic dynamism is ever-expanding commercial activity that generated greater amounts of wealth. In twentieth-century economic jargon, this aspect is "allocative efficiency." Economic dynamism has another meaning that is in tension with the wealth-creating understanding. This is a dynamism in the distribution of social wealth. Such a meaning of dynamism very quickly becomes an ideology of egalitarianism, or as the neo-Harringtonians called it, "levelling." Egalitarian sentiments, of course, do not easily coexist with a commitment to political rule by a natural elite, and so it is hardly surprising to find the rhetoric of stability shadowing the rhetoric of dynamism in Federalist texts.

No single text by a Federalist legal writer better illustrates this continuation of the dialectic of dynamism and stability than Noah Webster's essay, written in 1787, urging adoption of the new Constitution, *An Examination of the Leading Principles of the Federal Constitution.*[24] Equally important, it indicates a fundamental change in American legal thought. The earlier sense of anxiety about the effect of a free alienability policy on social relations was entirely absent from Webster's essay. The commodity *mentalité* had eclipsed the discourse of civic personality.

Change and Continuity: Noah Webster and the Emerging Commercial Republican Meaning of Property

Webster sounded many of the themes that characterized Federalist writing about property and politics, society and individual. Attempting to deflect anti-Federalist arguments that the new Constitution would destroy popular power in favor of Congressional power, that is, replace democracy with aristocracy, Webster used property as the instrument for accommodating republican (and anti-Federalist) notions of individual autonomy and equality within a hierarchical society and polity. The key to realizing this accommodation of conflicting visions was the policy of unfettered circulation of property within society. Webster's defense of the Federalist scheme, premised on property, provided a clear expression of the legal policy of alienability conjoined with freedom of ownership. His essay not only sounded many of the themes that dominated eighteenth-century American legal and political writing about property but also anticipated themes that would increasingly dominate legal discourse in the nineteenth and twentieth centuries. In a very real sense, then, Webster's essay was Janus-faced.[25]

Webster began his argument affirming the democracy of property in this passage from the longer essay:

> [T]he power of the people has increased in an exact proportion to their acquisition of property. Wherever the right of primogeniture is established, property must accumulate and remain in families. Thus the landed property in England will never be sufficiently distributed, to give the powers of government wholly into the hands of the people. But to assist the struggle for liberty, commerce has interposed, and in conjunction with manufacturers, thrown a vast weight of property into the democratic scale. Wherever we cast our eyes, we see this truth, that *property* is the basis of *power;* and this, being established as a cardinal point, directs us to the means of preserving

our freedom. Make laws . . . destroying and barring entailments; leave real estates to revolve from hand to hand, as time and accident may direct; and no family influence can be acquired and established for a series of generations—no man can obtain dominion over a large territory—the laborious and saving, who are generally the best citizens will possess each his share of property and power, and thus the balance of wealth and power will continue where it is, in the *body of the people.*[26]

This passage expresses an astonishingly wide variety of themes, extending from those of Jefferson and Harrington to themes of the Scottish Enlightenment writers and Hamilton. Webster's basic premise, that power follows property, was, of course, a recurrent theme in the civic republican tradition. Harrington had fully developed the connection between polity and property, and his theme was picked up by American civic republicans like John Adams. Webster, moreover, developed this premise along figurative lines that echoed Adams's *Dissertation on the Canon and the Feudal Law.* Like Adams, Webster used history to affirm the meaning of the new nation and its regime of property. Feudal property was the mirror image of what we were to become. Webster's use of entailments and primogeniture was entirely symbolic, for by this time those devices had been eliminated virtually everywhere. What is notable is the seriousness with which Webster discussed the need to abolish entail and primogeniture, suggesting that they continued to act as powerful symbols long after any threat that the English society of landed aristocracy would be recreated in America had dissipated. Webster, doubtless fully aware this, appreciated that their very irrelevance made them all the more useful as symbols by which to discuss the form of aristocracy that *was* taken seriously at this time—the one that many Americans believed the Federalists sought to create through the Constitution. Webster's basic objective in writing this essay was to defend the Federalist social order, one based on unrestrained commerce. His strategy was to develop a variation on the familiar theme of history as progressive, a variation that situated the Federalist order at the opposite end of the spectrum from aristocracy.

Webster pointed out that property can distribute power in two ways, hierarchically or democratically. Representing these two paths were, on the one hand, primogeniture and entailments, which, signified aristocracy, and on the other hand, commerce, which represented freedom and democracy. By associating freedom with commerce, Webster crucially shifted from a Harringtonian and Adamic framework to one whose roots exist in the Scottish Enlightenment tradition and whose development was the project of Federalist writers.

The Federalists claimed that commerce and manufacturing, where it prevailed, had thrown the weight of property in favor of democracy and away from aristocracy. The understanding of liberty and freedom that operates barely beneath the surface here is not solely the negative meaning of anti-aristocracy or anti-English but an association of liberty and freedom with private activity. Commerce instrumentally promotes freedom, rather than jeopardizes it, as civic republicans thought, because the meaning of freedom—and with it, property—has shifted from the Harringtonian notion of activity within and for the public realm to activity within and for one's own sphere. Individuals are free when they "revolve" land "from hand to hand, as time and accident may direct." Webster here unmistakably affirmed the dynamic understanding of property. But the dynamic activity he depicted was that of autonomous economic actors rather than civically connected citizens. Even less compatible with his social order are the ideas of persons as socially interdependent and market alienation of property as problematic for social relations. Earlier republican writing anticipated aspects of these modern ideas, but they were entirely absent from Webster's text.

In one sense, the privatization of freedom and property constituted a repudiation of the civic republican ideology, but it is important again to stress the point that the meaning of property that Webster was creating here did carry forward cultural beliefs that were fundamental to Jeffersonians. The repudiation of family dynasties based on property tied up through entailments and primogeniture, the endorsement of individual ownership of limited amounts of land, even the depiction of "the laborious and the saving" as the best citizens, a characterization that was congenial to nonrepublicans like Hamilton—all were familiar Jeffersonian themes. Webster's objective was to create a meaning of property that integrated a vestige (but only as a "fragmented survival") of the old republican understanding of property as political and social with the newer understanding of property as private. Property, rendered dynamic for private gain, was the path to realizing the vision of a democratic society.

That this integrated public/private meaning of property animated Webster's essay becomes even clearer when we examine the rest of his argument. He continued:

A general and tolerably equal distribution of landed property is the whole basis of national freedom: the system of the great Montesquieu will ever be erroneous, till the words *property or lands in fee simple* are substituted for *virtue,* throughout his *Spirit of Laws.*

Virtue, patriotism, or love of country, never was and never will be, till men's natures are changed, a fixed, permanent principle and support of government. But in an agricultural country, a general possession of land in fee simple, may be rendered perpetual, and the inequalities introduced by commerce, are too fluctuating to endanger government. An equality of property, with a necessity of alienation, constantly operating to destroy combinations of powerful families, is the very *soul of a republic*—While this continues, the people will inevitably possess both *power* and *freedom;* when this is lost, power departs, liberty expires, and a commonwealth will inevitably assume some other form.

Gordon Wood has interpreted rhetoric such as this as indicating a widespread loss of faith in virtue which in turn signaled the demise of classical republicanism in American thought.[27] In response, J. G. A. Pocock has rightly pointed out that Webster was adopting a directly Harringtonian—and, needless to mention, Jeffersonian—position that "a material foundation was necessary to ensure virtue and equality" and that land owned in fee simple was such a foundation.[28] Webster here was quite deliberately resuming the Harringtonian tradition of identifying property of a particular type and employing an overtly common-law vocabulary to prescribe ownership of a particular kind as foundational for both equality and freedom.

Webster's primary objective, it must be emphasized, was to respond to the charge that Federalist politics were hierarchical and would reinforce an American aristocracy that already had begun to take the place of the hated English aristocracy. Appropriating the Jeffersonian critique of landed aristocracy was strategically well suited to this purpose. This is not to say that his endorsement of a relatively wide distribution of fee simple ownership of land was disingenuous. Rather it is to insist that change accompanied continuity in the Jeffersonian rhetoric of property among different practitioners of that rhetoric. Jefferson and Webster wrote with different needs in mind: Jefferson sought a path to maintaining a vestige of the civic republican vision in a society that with growing evidence was moving toward commercialization and modernity; Webster sought some way to connect a political regime designed for modernity with the nation's premodern revolutionary culture.

One of the most noteworthy aspects of the essay is Webster's use of the symbolic language of stability and dynamism that pervaded virtually all of the civic republican discourse about property. He continually moves back and forth between stability and dynamism, in one sense continuing a dialectic with which civic republicans (including, as we have seen, Jefferson) would have been familiar, but in a more profound sense shifting the meaning of the figurative language of stasis and flux from that understood within the civic republican system of signification. This process illustrates again how the ambiguity of that vocabulary permitted, indeed encouraged, innovation that led to transformation.

Let us notice, first of all, how Webster juxtaposed stability and instability in the following passage to minimize the threat that commerce posed to republican government and republican ideals: "[In] an agricultural country, a general possession of land in fee simple, may be rendered perpetual, and the inequalities introduced by commerce, are too fluctuating to endanger government." He was anxious to insist that stability not assume the public meaning of inequality. Stability can coexist with equality through ownership of land in fee simple. But the crucial step linking land ownership with stable equality, supplied in the next sentence, is a *dynamic* regime of ownership: "An equality of property, with a necessity of alienation, constantly operating to destroy combinations of powerful families, is the very *soul of a republic.*" Land, with its obvious physical immobility, is easily associated with stability, but, as Webster subtly reminded his American readers, the meaning of stability by itself is ambiguous. After all, English social and political hierarchy rested on a foundation of stable ownership of land. Linking stability of land ownership with equality requires the mutually reinforcing measures of limiting, as much as possible, the estate in which land ownership exists to the fee simple and protecting the free and full alienability of land. Together these two measures create a dynamic of land ownership. Webster here drew attention to a central paradox: dynamism is necessary to achieve stability. Equality and freedom can be secured only through a regime of land ownership based on a dynamic of alienation of unencumbered property interests. It is the legal policy of alienability, then, that Webster saw as the crucial mechanism by which property will be the foundation for individual freedom and equality rather than hierarchy and aristocracy.

Webster's emphasis on the importance of alienability of property indicates a shift toward a more privatized meaning of freedom and more formalized meaning of equality than those terms had within civic republican discourse. Alienability of property expressed a vision of marketized social relations, not a vision of property as the foundation for citizens to participate in the creation of public life. It certainly did not express a vision of equality in fact. The purpose of property was to enable people to create their own lives and pursue their own conceptions of the good. "Freely transferable property" was a metaphor for opportunity, not for entitlement. Removing restraints on the alienability of land gives people access to property, through market transactions, but it does not insure that all social distinctions will be eliminated.[29] It secures individual freedom in the sense that status and property are formally uncoupled.

The choice between feudal property and alienable property that Webster continually posed indicates his understanding of individual freedom as formal and negative. Feudal property, which he described in terms of entailments and primogeniture locking up land, locked individuals within a formal hierarchy. Webster continually defined the freedom that property would secure in the new order as the mirror image of the regime of formal hierarchy based on privileged holdings of land. Stable freedom and stable equality would exist by liberating land from all of the feudal entanglements, leaving the "pure" form of ownership, the freely alienable fee simple, as the dominant estate in land. It is the juxtaposition of feudal and alienable property as the only available alternatives that made it intelligible for him to assert, "The power of entailing estates is more dangerous to liberty and republican government, than all the constitutions that can be written on paper, or even than a standing army."[30]

Webster's dichotomy between feudal and alienable land obviously resembled the older and more familiar feudal/allodial dichotomy, but this is only a surface resemblance. The feudal/alienable dichotomy transformed the feudal/allodial distinction in the sense that the meaning of "allodial" had never expressly emphasized alienability. Transferability, of course, was implicit in the idea of allodial land, but it was not its defining characteristic. Allodial land had signified a natural order that was perverted by an unnatural political regime that made land the basis for domination of the many by the few. It had also represented an indigenous order that had been suppressed by a foreign influence.

Alienability was not central to these civic messages. But it was central to the Federalist message. Federalists regarded the idea of the human personality as civic to be dangerously wrong-headed. A strong policy of alienability of property encouraged individual freedom by advancing a wedge between public and private life. Webster made no attempt to connect the alienability policy with political independence or self-governance. His understanding of individual liberty was liberal and negative rather than positive and civic. He associated the policy of alienability with the principle of freedom to alienate, and he equated collective, or regulatory, restraints with the old feudal restraints. Both forms of restraints were objectionable because they equally cut back on the transferability of property. He never considered that this policy might require sacrificing the principle of individual freedom to alienate. Rather he saw them as mutually reinforcing. It is significant that Webster's account of the alternative regimes of property did not mention the civic republican scheme of allodial land that is used to anchor public citizenship. Having confined the available alternatives to feudal hierarchy and domination and alienable land, the correct choice was a foregone conclusion. Alienable property, in Webster's code, represents the polar opposite of feudal property, its mirror image realized. Thus, Webster indicated, the new social order, based on alienable property, constitutes the triumph of equality and individual freedom over hierarchy, and simultaneously, the present and future over past.

We have a final sense, then, in which Webster's essay extended the dialectics that were evident in Jeffersonian discourse. It deviated from the civic understanding in that it did not define the role of property and alienability in terms of self-governance or political participation. Indeed it paid scant attention to the problem of the social character of property. Webster's essay betrayed no hint of anxiety about the effect of individual control or free transferability of property on social relations. If the civic discourse about property and alienability had anticipated the modern concept of alienation, that awareness was absent in the emerging legal discourse that would later characterize nineteenth-century American legal writing about property.

At the same time, Webster's essay continued aspects of the American civic discourse. Webster, like Jefferson, Adams, and American republican legal writers, explicitly connected property, individual freedom, and time. The promise of realizing individual freedom through property depended, for him as for them, on escaping the past. The path to liberation, from the past and what he and other American writers associated with it, lay for Webster in stability.

Stability as the key to America's escape from history was a final meaning that Webster created for the dialectic of stability and dynamism. He connects America's historical uniqueness with the theme of stability in this passage:

> The English writers on law and government consider Magna Charta, trial by juries, the Habeas Corpus act, and the liberty of the press, as the bulwarks of freedom. All this is well. But in no government of consequence in Europe, is freedom established on its true and immoveable foundation. The property is too much accumulated, and the accumulations too well-guarded, to admit the *true principle of republics.* . . . . But in America, and here alone, we have gone at once to the fountain of liberty, and raised the people to their true dignity. Let the lands be possessed by the people in fee simple, let the foundations be kept pure, and the streams will be pure of course. . . . . All other [free] nations have wrested *property* and *freedom* from *barons* and *tyrants; we* begin our empire with full possession of property and all its attending rights.[31]

The vision that Webster articulated here was the liberal conception of ownership as consolidated control in individual hands. This conception, of course, was not new. Blackstone had articulated it in his widely known definition of common-law ownership as "that sole and despotic dominion which one man claims and exercises over the external things of the world, in total exclusion of the right of any other individual in the universe."[32]

It is no coincidence that Webster would articulate this conception in a metaphorical vocabulary that Blackstone's definition lacked. The fee simple interest was more readily expressed as the "pure" fountain in the eighteenth-century American context of vast wilderness and, equally important, as a widely shared self-image of historical uniqueness. Webster and most American lawyers understood that the Blackstonian conception of ownership was a myth in the context of English society. Indeed, they considered that ownership based on individual autonomy and equality had not in fact existed anywhere in history. The common law, in developing the concept of the fee simple absolute, may have articulated that ideal, but no legal system had actually implemented it. Because the common-law conception of ownership as the fee simple absolute had not existed previously anywhere, it had not fulfilled its promise of individual liberation. That conception remained only a part of English legal mythology. In America, for the first time in history, the promise was fulfilled, and the ideal made reality.

We may detect a continuation of the theme of millennialism in Webster's pronouncement that that meaning of property has at last been realized. In tone, if not in all substantive respects, Webster's essay resembles Adams's earlier *A Dissertation on the Canon and the Feudal Law* and even his later *Defence of the Constitutions of the United States of America.*[33] Like Adams's essays—indeed like most eighteenth-century American political writing[34]—Webster was articulating the sacred history of the New World, a teleology whose destined moment is the founding of the American republic. Like many other American lawyers at the time, Webster defined that teleology within the framework of property. Webster was announcing in the passage just quoted the arrival of the fee simple empire. But, departing from Adams's millennialist vision, Webster not only completely secularized the millennium (dropping all Biblical allusions) but also depicted it as occurring within the dynamic of individual economic activity. The fee simple empire was no longer described as an empire of citizen-farmers; to Webster, it had become an empire of landowners who use land as the subject matter of economic transactions.

Webster's essay, then, exemplifies the paradox of ideological change occurring through continuity. He continued to define the meaning of property in figural language and extended virtually all of the important figurative devices from civic republican discourse, including (1) the juxtaposition of property with time, (2) the dichotomy of forms of property, and (3) their correspondence with two historical visions of social order, one hierarchical and oppressive, the other democratic and liberating. But in using individual ownership of property as the basis for his attempt to defend the Federalist program against the charge of creating a new aristocratic social order, he shifted the meaning of the civic republican vocabulary in crucial respects, helping to create the cultural language of what has been called "commercial republicanism."[35]

The thrust of Webster's argument for individual ownership of freely alienable property as the only stable foundation for the individual freedom was to locate property in the realm of individual economic activity. The concomitant effect of this identification of individual liberation from domination and hierarchy with alienable property was more clearly to establish individual activity with the unrestrained market as the dominant metaphor by which American lawyers understood the central meaning of property and its relationship to the political ideal of individual freedom. The public and private dimensions of property had become more distinct from each other than they had been in civic republican discourse. The dialectic had not ended, but it had shifted.

PART TWO

The Commercial Republican Culture, 1800–1860

Legal Writing in the Commercial Republican Era

B Y MID-CENTURY, the idea of legal practice and legal discourse as activities that transcended ordinary work had all but disappeared. In its place was a decidedly more utilitarian perception of the lawyer's appropriate activities. "To the mass of practitioners," wrote an anonymous author in the influential legal journal *The American Law Register,* "the law is not, except on some rare occasions, an intellectual pursuit. . . . We are clever men of business, as a mass, and no more."[1] The image that lawyers put forward increasingly after 1830 was the lawyer as an apolitical technician. Elite lawyers, concerned with shaping the profession's image to conform with the rising egalitarian public sentiment of the Jacksonian era, consciously set about redefining the lawyer, "transforming him," as Maxwell Bloomfield has observed, "from a designing cryptopolitician into a benevolently neutral technocrat."[2]

This redefinition of the legal profession's self-image manifested itself in several ways. One was a general decline of emphasis on a liberal background in favor of technical legal training. Great learning, anchored in the classics, was no longer seen as a prerequisite to a successful legal practice, except to older lawyers who clung to an antiquated self-image. Robert Ferguson has explained how what he calls the "configuration of literature and law" that was so prevalent in the early Republic broke down after the War of 1812. Lawyers and legal writers were no longer expected to be men of letters; they were expected to be informed about and technically proficient in the increasingly complex world of legal rules and institutions.

Another way the redefinition was manifested was the divorce of legal discourse from political discourse and practice. The ideal of the republican lawyer as civic spokesman generally declined. Elite lawyers no longer regarded political office as the pinnacle of their professional lives. As one writer observed, "It is well known that men of the highest eminence in our profession are seldom members of legislative assemblies in this country, and, when they are, their influence is comparatively small."[3] The legal heroes of the Revolutionary era generation, the Thomas Jeffersons, John Adamses, and Alexander Hamiltons, were no longer the appropriate role models for a generation of lawyers concerned with establishing their technical competence. The great lawyer-statesmen of the antebellum period—Olympian figures like Daniel Webster—seemed all the more remarkable because they were so atypical.[4] They were anachronisms, a vanishing breed in a changed environment.

Even those elite legal writers who did continue to preach the old republican ideal revised that ideal to make it apolitical. The crucial distinction that these lawyers drew was between "civicness" and politics: The lawyer's highest calling was civic life, but civic life (the life devoted to serving the commonwealth) was not politics. No one was clearer about that distinction that Rufus Choate, whose reputation and influence within the bar matched that of his publicly better-known contemporary, Webster. "[B]etter than any other," Choate stated, "[the legal] profession enables [the lawyer] to *serve the State*. . . . I make haste to say that it is not at all because the legal profession may be thought peculiarly adapted to fit a man for what is technically called 'public life,' and to afford him a ready, too ready an introduction to it. . . . It is not the jurist turned statesman whom I mean to hold up to you as useful to the republic . . . , it is the jurist as jurist; it is the jurist remaining jurist; it is the bench, the magistracy, the bar,—the profession as a profession, and in its professional character,—a class, a body, of which I mean exclusively to speak."[5] Law was one profession, politics another, Choate and others argued, and politics was not the only way, or even the best way, in which the lawyer could serve the state. Law itself, redefined as technical and apolitical, was a civic endeavor.

Several factors contributed to this redefinition of the image of legal practice and legal writing. The most important factor was the prevalence of anti-elitist attitudes during the Jacksonian era. The pretensions of elite lawyers as the American version of an aristocracy, the image that Tocqueville was celebrating even as lawyers were dismantling it, was hardly likely to resonate well with the American public at a time when any form of social hierarchy seemed undemocratic and un-American. The emphasis on technical competence allowed lawyers, as Maxwell Bloomfield has put it, "to rationalize their elite status in American society on grounds that made some sense even to radical democrats."[6] The argument was that legal services were fundamentally no different than those of any other skilled craft. They required special training, but the profession, like other specialized occupations, was open to anyone willing to work hard and diligently. Legal services, moreover, contributed to building a growing and strong society just as other crafts did. Emphasizing the character of legal practice as work in this way allowed legal writers, or at least so their elite ranks thought, to reconcile the profession's exclusiveness (which, paradoxically, the focus on law's technicality reinforced) with the demands of a growing middle class for an open society.

A second factor that contributed to the redefinition of the profession's self-image was the increased complexity of law and, therefore, of law practice. Measured in a variety of ways, American law was considerably more complicated by the mid-nineteenth century than it had been at the close of the eighteenth century. The sheer amount of law for lawyers to master, particularly with the appearance of official reports of judicial decisions, had mushroomed. The first official state court reports did not appear until 1804.[7] By 1847, case reports existed for all of the states.[8] Not only was there more law, but its content was more complex. As American society became increasingly commercialized, economic transactions grew more sophisticated, requiring, in turn, a more complex body of law regulating those transactions. These social and economic changes made legal practice in the nineteenth century far more demanding than it had been in the post-Revolutionary years. It is easy to understand the following observation of one practitioner comparing the situation of the practicing lawyer in 1840 with his predecessor at the turn of the century: "The labor of a lawyer was easy [in 1800] compared with that of the present day. There were few books of authority to be examined and cited; there were no volumes of reports scattered as now . . . upon his path, and the standard of legal acquirement was moderate. A good voice, a fluid utterance, and a discussion of general principles answered every demand."[9]

The reimaging of legal practice as apolitical and technical had three important consequences for legal writing. First, it contributed to the development of the American legal treatise. Kent's *Commentaries,* along with the treatises of Joseph Story,[10] are commonly identified as the beginnings of the tradition of legal treatises in the United States.[11] Recently, however, John Langbein has convincingly argued that Kent's work belongs to a different tradition of legal writing, one that is now defunct—the so-called institutes of national law.[12] The distinguishing characteristics of work in that tradition were comprehensiveness, self-consciously national definition, didacticism, and systemicism. Kent's *Commentaries* possessed all of these attributes. The most important for my purposes is the second. As Langbein notes, the central aim of that work was to "giv[e] character and definition to the law of a newly self-conscious nation."[13] In that sense, the *Commentaries* can be said to have had an overtly political dimension, a dimension that makes it plausible and illuminating to connect the work with the older republican form of legal discourse.

Story's treatises were a different matter. Unlike Kent's *Commentaries,* they were true treatises. Although titled "commentaries," they were intended to be objective and exhaustive treatments of discrete areas of law. Story was primarily concerned with presenting an organized summary of American law on diverse topics, primarily commercial in nature, rather than, as Kent had been, to establish the identity of American law as *American* law. As Kent Newmyer has stated, Story "wrote in response to the pressing needs of the working lawyer who had to bring vast quantities of unorganized case and statute law to bear on the novel problems of a new age."[14] The character of discourse in Story's treatises and those that closely followed his, notably Simon Greenleaf's *Treatise on the Law of Evidence* and Theodore Sedgwick's *Treatise on the Measure of Damages,* was more technical than that in Kent's *Commentaries.* This is not to say that there was no strictly doctrinal material in the *Commentaries* or that the work lacked an outlook that we can call pro-professional. Large portions of it were highly technical and clearly were intended to aid the practicing lawyer. But that was not its dominant objective. It was, however, Story's. It was his work, not Kent's, then, that represented the real beginning of the modern legal treatise.

The second major consequence of the redefinition of legal practice and legal writing was the rise of professional legal periodicals.[15] Between 1810 and 1870, the number of journals devoted exclusively to law rose from 1 to 17. In fact, more than 50 law journals were introduced between 1830 and 1870, but many of them failed after a few months of publication. Unlike the older law magazines, the post-1830 journals were aimed strictly at the practicing lawyer and were "rigorously utilitarian."[16] They eschewed broad or theoretical subjects in favor of topics that assisted the common practitioner, ranging from summaries of recent court decisions to office organization. Reading through them, it is striking how closely they resemble the standard practitioner's magazine of today. Virtually nothing in them is directed at the lawyer as a member of the broader educated community or as spokesman for the civic republic. Instead they are pitched, as one journal characterized itself, at the "*workingmen* of the profession."[17]

The third significant effect of the revision of legal discourse was the decline of the oratorical tradition. The older self-image of lawyering had emphasized oral forms of legal rhetoric far more than written discourse.[18] The legendary lawyers of the eighteenth and early nineteenth centuries, men like Daniel Webster and Rufus Choate, *were* legends because of their oral skills, not their skills in writing briefs or drafting complex legal instruments. Great courtroom speeches, public addresses, lyceum lectures— these were the favored occasions of high legal rhetoric. On these occasions the great orators really strutted their stuff. They were more likely to draw on the Bible, Shakespeare, or Greek and Roman classical literature for support than they were to cite legal precedents. Their performances were more theater than legal argument.

By the mid-nineteenth century, the oratorical tradition was on the wane. It never fully disappeared, of course. Public fame for lawyers continued to rest largely on talent at courtroom oratory. (It still does today.) Men like Horace Binney and Charles Sumner took over for the generation of Webster and Choate. But things had clearly changed. Detailed knowledge of the law had replaced rhetorical flourish and literary allusion as the basis on which court cases were usually won.[19] Moreover, professional success no longer depended on a life in the courtroom, even if public fame did. Increasingly, the lawyers who enjoyed the largest reputations within the profession seldom saw the inside of a courtroom. They represented the new breed of lawyer—the law-office lawyer, who specialized in transactions, rather than litigation. These lawyers had little use for writing that was pitched at a high level of abstraction or that framed legal questions as matters of political or moral principle. The mode of legal writing that was the grist for their mills was highly technical, tightly focused, and assiduously apolitical.

The chapters that comprise this part will focus on the legal discourse discussing the dominant themes of property law in the first half of the nineteenth century. Chapter 4 examines the discourse of legislative reform of property law, focusing on the important New York Revised Statutes of 1828–1836, which was the single most important attempt systematically to streamline and substantively simplify American property law prior to the Civil War. Chapter 5 turns to the property law sections of James Kent's *Commentaries*. Kent was critical of the New York legislative reform project, both generally and in its details. His remarks, coupled with the Revisers' Commentary, constituted a dialectic concerning both the substance of property law and the broader issue of legislative versus judicial law. Chapter 6 returns to the subject of legislative reform of property law by examining the revision of married women's rights as property owners. Chapter 7 turns from private law to public law, discussing the development of the vested rights doctrine, which was the centerpiece of constitutional protection of property in the early nineteenth century. Finally, chapter 8 examines a distinctly regional property legal discourse in the antebellum era, Southern legal texts on slavery. It focuses particularly on Thomas Reade Rootes Cobb's essays on slavery, the leading attempts by a Southern lawyer systematically to rationalize the use of human beings as objects of property.

"Liberality" vs. "Technicality": Statutory Revision of Land Law in the Jacksonian Age

DESPITE EFFORTS BY JEFFERSON and others to purge American property law of its most arcane and most aristocratic (and one may say, most English) aspects, it remained highly technical, especially that part dealing with land. Only lawyers specifically trained in the common law's labyrinths of estates, conveyances, mortgages, and trusts could practice in the area with any degree of confidence. For laypersons, the law regulating land transactions was literally incomprehensible; only the ignorant or the informed risk-taker would engage in even routine land transactions without legal assistance. The risk they ran was that a court would later declare as void and unenforceable an otherwise clear and unambiguous legal document for transferring an interest in land because, say, it provided that Robert Bridges transferred his land to William Surrency "absolutely," rather than, as the law required, "and his heirs."[1]

This inaccessibility of the law regulating land transfers to the general public was hardly compatible with the participatory vision of Jeffersonians. It was no less incompatible with the commercial empire vision of Hamiltonians, for land law's technicality impeded the market-fluidity of land as the economy's most important commodity. The ideology of commercial republicanism was founded on this shared commitment to enhanced marketability of land. It dominated legal and political thought through most of the first half of the nineteenth century and connected political and legal rhetoric of the antebellum period with that of the post-Revolutionary era.

At the same time, neither Jefferson's nor Hamilton's ideological descendants within the legal profession were prepared to accept the consequences of making land law completely accessible to the public. Radical democratization of American land law would have virtually eliminated the lawyer's role in land transactions—a result not even the most fervent democrat in the legal profession would accept. Some role for lawyers and courts in land transaction had to be preserved, not only for purely self-interested reasons but also because virtually all lawyers, regardless of political persuasion, genuinely believed that lay people needed their services. Legal rules were needed to guide the conduct of participants in land transactions and to help courts resolve disputes that inevitably would arise. Although there was room for improvement, legal rules inevitably would involve a certain degree of technicality, with the consequence that land law could not and should not be totally purged of technicality.

This simultaneous desire to simplify land law and to preserve its lawlike character created a legal dialectic between "liberality" and "technicality" that pervaded antebellum legal writing about property. The principal locus of this dialectic was the debates that surrounded efforts to revise property law through legislation that would replace the common law. Statutory revisions of property law were enacted in several states between 1820 and 1850 and actively considered in even more. By far the most important of these revisions, however, were the New York Revised Statutes of 1828 and 1830. They were the model for legislative reform of property law throughout the rest of the country and represented, in Lawrence Friedman's words, "a summing up of a full generation of reform."[2]

The dialectic between liberality and technicality cannot be reduced to a dialogue between two discrete and opposing legal-political ideologies. There were two such ideologies throughout the first half of the nineteenth century, to be sure. But with respect to the issue of democratization through simplification of property law, these ideological positions were not cleanly defined by the antinomy between liberality and technicality. No one endorsed liberality or technicality exclusively; it was, rather, a matter of degree and, to some extent, what the specific question was.

In the legal discourse of antebellum America, liberality was not itself a distinct ideology. It was a sentiment, or disposition, that was compatible with more than one political-legal ideology. Most obviously, perhaps, it was quite compatible with the commercial republican ideology reflected in such constitutional era texts as Noah Webster's *Examination of the Leading Principles of the Federal Constitution.*[3] Indeed, many of the Revisers' Notes to the New York Revised Statutes expressed a slightly updated version of the commercial republican argument that Webster and others had made just a few decades earlier: the policy of alienability was the key to assuring the conditions for genuine citizenship, for by making land freely alienable, we realize the democratic aspirations of the new nation.

This argument, and the antebellum sentiment of liberality generally, is compatible also with many aspects of economic liberalism. Liberality's comfortable relationship with these two ideologies is no accident, of course, since commercial republicanism represented the partial assimilation of liberal ideas into the matrix of republican discourse.

The debates also revealed the genuinely dialectical character of the discourse of antebellum legal writing about property. That discourse was internally heterogeneous at all times. Liberality and technicality were always simultaneously present in the discourse. Neither vanquished the other; there was no "triumph" of liberality. Moreover, legal writers during the first half of the nineteenth century understood the two dispositions as irreducibly opposed, that is, as antinomic. Technicality and liberality were mutually dependent parts of a whole; one could not exist without the other. Each acquired its meaning in relation to the other, and the meanings of both evolved as a result of their interpenetration.

The liberality-versus-technicality dialectic represents a continuation of the post-Revolutionary dialectic of stability and dynamism, even while it represents a shift in legal discourse about property. The two dialectics were continuous in several respects. First, at the most literal level, the discourse of liberality and technicality did not entirely supplant the late eighteenth-century discourse of time, continuity, and change. Throughout pre–Civil War legal writings about property the language of temporality was blended with the language of liberality and technicality. The problem of time and what to do about the vestiges of "feudal" English land law remained very much a dilemma for antebellum American lawyers and was prominently discussed in legal writing.[4]

Second, once the issue of marketability of property was established as the dominant background issue in property law, it was easy to understand "liberality" and "technicality" as transliterations of "dynamism" and "stability," respectively. A liberalized property regime was one in which property of all forms was freely marketable and dynamic in the eighteenth-century sense of that term. Easy fluidity of property in turn resulted in a sacrifice of stability. Conversely, a technical property regime preserved the regime's stability, both legally and socially, while concomitantly rendering that regime less dynamic because property was less mobile.

Third, and more fundamentally, the liberality/technicality dialectic was the successive metaphorical expression of the dialectic of sociality that underlay the American civic republican discourse of time, stability, and dynamism. Liberality and technicality could simultaneously be seen as associated with opposing social visions. The positive side of liberality, of course, was its promise to end (at least for white males) the severe constraints that a hierarchical social order founded largely on property arrangements created for social and economic mobility. But a liberalized property regime, had a potentially dark side as well: the loss of a world in which social relations were face-to-face, in which individuals actively labored for the well-being of the communities to which they felt they belonged, and in which self-sufficiency and economic autonomy allowed individuals fully to develop their personalities.

That these concerns resemble the critiques of modernity that emerged much later is no coincidence. Anxieties about the social consequences of a fully liberalized economy and property regime were, in fact, early manifestations of an anxiety about modernity and its effect on social relations. It is conventional to interpret the legal discourse and doctrinal developments of the first half of the nineteenth century as expressing the liberated spirit of the New Capitalist Man.[5] While such a spirit certainly is evident in antebellum political and legal rhetoric,[6] it was by no means the only sentiment evident. Dialectically situated with the optimism over the Market Revolution was deep ambivalence about the new and quite evident society developing in many parts of the country and nostalgia for, to paraphrase Peter Laslett's expression,[7] the world the nineteenth-century Americans had lost.[8] What they had lost, or at least were in the process of losing, was a premodern culture in which property played a very different role than it was ordained to play as a result of the Market Revolution and its attendant social and economic changes. The language of liberality and technicality, so often presented in an uneasy coexistence in antebellum legal texts, metaphorically expressed this dual sense of regret for loss of the past and optimism about the effects of present and future change.

This ambivalence about modernity and premodernity is evident in legal discussions over the social implications of technicality and liberality. On the one hand, technicality in property law connoted social hierarchy and privilege. It also suggested order, security, and regularity, all of which were indispensable conditions for maintenance of republican government. No one who wrote about legal technicality was prepared to purge property law of all traces of its technicality, then. The articulated question was which of property law's technical aspects can be reconciled with republican politics. That question evidenced a deeper question that many lawyers and other social elites felt: what elements of the old property law were necessary to preserve a connection with a premodern culture with which they were not at all entirely prepared to part. The debates over the statutory revision of property law in New York in the 1820s and 1830s provide a window through which we can glimpse these cultural as well as legal dilemmas.

The Political Culture of the Reform Era: Jacksonian Republicanism

The New York statutory revision of property law was part of a general cultural attack on privilege and hierarchy that is associated with what conventionally is referred to as Jacksonian Democracy.[9] The Jacksonian political culture is better understood through the lens of the concept of republicanism than as a democratic movement for several reasons, three of which may be mentioned here. First, much of the decline of the social aristocracy, at least in New York, preceded Jackson's ascendancy.[10] Second, Jacksonian Democracy was decidedly undemocratic in many crucial respects. For one thing, Jackson's leadership did not produce direct popular democracy, and, indeed, neither Jackson nor his followers thought direct popular democracy desirable. Few, if any, Jacksonians questioned the identity between democracy and representative democracy. Jacksonianism also lacked of a true class focus. American politics between 1828 and 1840 cannot be characterized as a conflict between the rich, privileged few and the common majority: many Jacksonians were wealthy, and some even were descendants of aristocratic families. Jacksonians seldom advocated a radically egalitarian distribution of wealth. Lastly, a profound sense in which Jacksonianism was undemocratic is found in its acceptance of exclusion of African Americans, Indians, and women from political participation and other incidents of citizenship.

A third objection to an interpretation of Jacksonian ideology that focuses on democratization is that it obscures the role that republican ideas continued to exert on American political culture after Jefferson's presidency. While historians have been right to criticize the traditional view that a straight line of descent can be traced from Jefferson to Jackson,[11] it would be equally wrong to assert that there was no ideological connection between what Marvin Meyers calls the "Jacksonian persuasion" and the tradition of civic republicanism.

While American republicanism had always been somewhat ambiguous in meaning, its ambiguities had become manifest by the beginning of the nineteenth century, even as its leading political figure, Thomas Jefferson, assumed the presidency. Republicans might continue to oppose Hamilton's specific policies, but not all of them continued to share Jefferson's opposition to a political economy based on manufacturing rather than agriculture. To many, manufacturing no longer seemed incompatible with virtue, and economic growth was not inevitably associated with corruption. Noah Webster's 1787 essay, in which he argued that commerce and manufacturing "had thrown a vast weight of property into the democratic scale,"[12] was an early indication that the sociology of virtue was clearly changing.

The ambiguities of the emergent commercial republicanism became more pronounced after 1815, when, as Charles Sellers has put it, "postwar boom galavanized [*sic*] the market culture into market revolution."[13] A new caste of republican emerged, especially in the emerging commercial centers of the Northeast—the entrepreneurial republican. No longer opposed to the private pursuit of wealth through entrepreneurial activities, this new species of republican had a conception of the proper relationship between government and the market that was fundamentally different from that which Jefferson contemplated. In their view, government should serve the market, rather than subordinating the market to government. Entrepreneurial republicans favored government aid to enterprise through corporate charters, tax exemptions, monopolies for favored enterprises, use of state credit to amass capital that financed tremendous changes in transportation, and government policies that facilitated development of the corporate form of economic organization (the primary means of accumulating mobile capital). Much of the legal profession shared this desire to advance entrepreneurial activity. Indeed, as seminal studies by Willard Hurst, Lawrence Friedman, Harry Scheiber, and Morton Horwitz have demonstrated, throughout the Antebellum period judges (especially those in the Northeast where entrepreneurial activity was greatest) molded legal doctrine to the clear advantage of entrepreneurs.[14] The upshot was that Republicans, the descendants of Thomas Jefferson's Democratic-Republican Party, had not only co-opted much of Hamilton's pro-development vision but had pushed farther than he had ever imagined.

Entrepreneurial republicanism was by no means universally accepted, however. Many social groups, certainly those who were not benefited by the economic transformation that was occurring after 1815, were skeptical or downright hostile to the new entrepreneurial outlook, and held beliefs and attitudes that were also republican. Chief among these attitudes and beliefs, which they, with considerable justification, regarded as more faithful to the ideology of the "Old Republic," were (1) a loathing of "aristocracy" and a renunciation of special "privileges," especially those conferred by government; (2) a view of entrepreneurs as sources of "corruption"; and (3) a fear of "instability" and a conviction that institutions associated with entrepreneurial activity inevitably bred instability. These attitudes and beliefs formed the basis for a Jacksonian republican political economy that was very much at odds with the political economy of entrepreneurial Republicans.

Crucial to the Jacksonians' political economy were the issues of credit, fluid paper money, and banks. All three issues acutely raised the concerns with "aristocracy," "privilege," "corruption," and "instability." To Jacksonians, credit was a privilege available only to the "aristocratic" few and a source of corruption, as those seeking credit sacrifice their independence to gain favor with lenders. The attack on a market economy (in which payments were made via highly fluid paper money, rather than in specie) was related to the opposition to credit-based commerce. As the nation experienced booms and busts, Jacksonians attacked the paper money system as a principal source of economic instability. Overriding all of these concerns, however, was the bank issue. Jacksonian opposition to creation of a Second National Bank, or the "Monster Bank," as they called it, became the major symbol of Jacksonian republicanism.[15] It represented the entire constellation of Jacksonian attitudes—aversion to privilege, aristocracy, instability, and corruption. Jacksonians regarded it as the major source of economic instability despite the fact that the Bank, especially after Nicholas Biddle assumed its leadership, was the primary source of sound currency in the country. They considered it to be the creation of an aristocratic plutocracy, the heir of the Hamiltonian vision, and the source of corruption.

These reactions reflected a deep-seated anxiety about the fundamental economic and social transformation that these developments both created and symbolized. The Jacksonians' hatred of the Bank and their concerns about credit and paper money was underlain by their sense that these institutions represented a new culture with its own form of social relations in market transactions—impersonal, intangible, and nonreciprocal.[16] It was not the market as such that underlay this new culture, but the commodification of the economy. Credit, fluid paper money, and the Bank all symbolized an emerging understanding of the form of property as intangible and institutional, rather than tangible and personal; this understanding also saw the role of property as creating wealth, rather than as providing the material foundation for subsistence and, through it, genuine political citizenship. Anxieties over the changing form and role of property in the emerging modern culture were evident in the debates surrounding efforts to simplify and codify the law of property.

The Codification Debates

Among the forces that Jacksonian republicans held responsible for this turn to what we now call the "culture of modernity" were the legal system and the legal profession. In particular, Jacksonians, and their ideological predecessors, attacked the common law as the source of much of what they viewed as the corruption of the republic.[17] Their ideological attack on the common law and judicial power engendered debates over whether legislatures should reform and codify the common law. These debates lasted roughly from 1820 to 1850.

American legal historians have devoted a great deal of attention to what they have conventionally called the "codification movement."[18] More recently, historians like Robert Gordon and Charles Cook have convincingly reinterpreted this legal activity, reducing it from a grand movement to a discourse, or series of debates, that occurred primarily within the legal profession and, even then, primarily among elite legal writers.[19] Yet, although the debates themselves were largely limited to the legal mandarinate, the discourse resonated with many of the central themes of Jacksonian republicanism, particularly the anxieties about the emerging culture of modernity.

In several senses the antebellum law reform and codification debates added nothing new to American legal discourse. Statutory reforms aimed at ridding the common law of elements that seemed un-American or, more to the point, un-republican, had occurred well before the 1820s. Jefferson's work revising Virginia's inheritance law[20] was only the most conspicuous example. Indeed, some of the tangible results of Antebellum legal reform efforts, including provisions in New York's statutory revision of property law, merely reiterated Jefferson's own work, as well as that of others.[21]

Nor did American law reform originate from republican-inspired changes in the late eighteenth century. It grew out of a strand of Anglo-American popular thought that was deeply suspicious of lawyers and objected especially to the common law. In America, this attitude predated the Revolutionary era[22] and, in England, it can be traced at least as far back as the Puritan Revolution.[23] Many of the issues raised in these earlier debates were the same as those raised in the antebellum American debates:

making law more accessible to ordinary lay people, reducing the discretionary role of judges, and, notably, simplifying land law by purging it of its "feudal" and "technical" elements.

The Ambiguity of Legal "Science"

Legal reform expressed a vision of law's transformation into "legal science." The notion of law as science did not originate in nineteenth-century American legal thought.[24] In the seventeenth and eighteenth centuries, leading English legal writers like Sir Matthew Hale and Lord Mansfield had held basically the same vision, and that vision was the animus for their own efforts to reform the common law. As Perry Miller showed, however, the idea of law as science dominated all of antebellum elite American legal writing.[25] Virtually every elite legal writer would have agreed with the conception of law that James Gould clearly stated in explaining his plan for the Litchfield Law School: "The object . . . is to teach the law—the *common* law, especially—not as a collection of *insulated positive rules . . .* but as a *system of connected, rational principles:* for, such the common law unquestionably is. . . ."[26]

The understanding of law as science became almost universally accepted among the legal elite in part because it fit so neatly with the by-then dominant vision of teleological legal development. As discussed in chapter 2,[27] by 1800 virtually all lawyers agreed that, in societies like the United States, law and government developed progressively from feudalism toward the final stage of evolution, commercial republicanism. The validating consequence of this process was that it progressively enhanced both social wealth and individual liberty. As a crucial step in this direction, the society's legal system had to be purged of legal rules that were vestiges of earlier stages of social development and that were incompatible with individual freedom and increased social wealth.

The problem with the scientific conception of law was that its implications for codification were ambiguous. Legal science meant different things to different groups. To many Jacksonians, particularly those who were anti-lawyer, it meant throwing most of the common law away and replacing it with new legislative codes that demystified the law and made it directly accessible to ordinary people.[28] Hardly surprisingly, this was not the reaction of most lawyers. A few, however, did urge the abandonment of the "undemocratic" common law with a statutory code. One prominent spokesman for this view in the legal profession was Robert Rantoul, a leading Massachusetts lawyer who represented the "radical" strand of Jacksonianism.[29] "Statutes," Rantoul argued, "enacted by the legislature, speak the public voice."[30] Unlike the common law, which gave judges despotic power, a code would be "a positive and unbending text."[31]

Most lawyers understood legal science to mean rather less than replacing the common law with a statutory code having new content. For one thing, within the legal profession a long tradition, dating back to Bacon, Hale, and Mansfield, favored systematizing the common law and giving it a rational structure along the lines of the Roman and continental civilian legal systems. These lawyers did not think that a code as such was necessary to make the law more scientific. What was needed was a two-step reform effort, consisting of (1) a procedural effort to develop a more rational and descriptive classification scheme, and (2) a modest degree of substantive law reform aimed at eliminating the most antiquated elements of the common law. Indeed many lawyers, including those associated with the Federalist and, later, Whig parties, continued to regard the common law and equity as the repository of wisdom accumulated over centuries of experience. It was, to be sure, exceedingly complex, but complexity was the price of adaptability. The unfulfilled task was to make it more systematic. This would be done by inductively distilling from the vast quantity of judicial decisions in various fields general principles and then deducing from these principles particular rules.[32] Only those possessing specialized study and experience in law, of course, could hope to undertake such a task.

The view held by the most prominent members of the profession—men like Joseph Story, Luther Cushing, Charles Sumner, and James Kent—was that the common law could indeed be made more scientific and that aspects of it were amenable to codification. Their approach to the codification question reflected their Whig ideology. Modest reform, both procedural and substantive, was needed to make the law more systematic and more adaptable to changing economic circumstances, and codification was a useful technique of implementing substantive reforms in some areas of law. At the same time, though, these men regarded codification for the purpose of entirely replacing the common law or displacing the power of the judiciary as not only not required to make law more scientific, but it was seriously dangerous. A crucial part of their conception of legal science was the view that the process of defining legal rights must remain primarily entrusted to lawyers, particularly the most highly educated, and to judges.[33]

This conception of legal science enabled this group of elite lawyers to mediate the related dialectics of liberality/technicality and dynamism/stability. Legal science, they considered, increased the legal system's ability to adapt to new circumstances. The processes of enlightened common-law adjudication, treatise writing, and modest legislative codification would liberalize the law where it needed to be liberalized and, through liberalization, make it more dynamic than the rigid English common law. At the same time, this conception of legal science did not permit so great a degree of liberalization that it threatened the social order (or, one cannot help but notice, their own positions of power). Indeed, their three-step view of legal science would, they thought, enhance social order by making the law clearer, more systematically organized, and more substantively rational. As legal science promoted stability, so it preserved a role for legal technicality. This group of elite legal writers viewed technicality, or at least some degree of it, as legitimate because it was instrumental to promoting legal and social stability.

While the discourse about law reform that occurred between 1820 and 1850 was continuous with earlier legal discourses about law reform, it differed from prior discussions about revising or codifying the common law in one important respect: The Antebellum legal discourse about law reform reflected an anxiety about the growing commodification of property, both as a legal concept and as a social institution, and more generally about the culture of modernity that the commodification phenomenon reflected. The context in which this anxiety is most apparent is the legislative reform of property law, especially that in New York.

The Political Background to the New York Statutory Revision

Legislative law reform was by no means unprecedented in New York prior to the 1820s. New York had revised its statutes twice during the colonial period and after the Revolution, in 1786, 1801, and 1813.[34] The three postindependence revisions appear to have been nothing more than attempts to consolidate the existing statutes and amendments. They made no attempt at systematic rearrangement and were not obviously animated by a commitment to legal science. More important, they made no significant substantive changes and certainly were not the result of any sort of attempted democratization of law. The 1828–1830 revision differed from these prior attempts at legal housecleaning in both respects. It clearly represented a conscious attempt to make the law of property more scientifically intelligible, and it owed its genesis to the ideology of democratization, although the rhetoric of democratization greatly outpaced the revision's actual effects.

The immediate catalyst for the revision was the adoption of a new state constitution following the constitutional convention of 1821. Dixon Ryan Fox has characterized the convention as the public event which in New York marked the passage from republican aristocracy to prudent democracy.[35] That characterization may overstate the consequences of the new constitution, but one cannot gainsay the convention's preoccupation with issues of democratization. Nowhere was this more evident than on questions involving suffrage. The convention rejected attempts by Kent and other standard-bearers for the Old Federalism to limit the franchise through property requirements. Kent's support for the selective franchise itself reflected an anxiety about the social and economic transformation that was already evident in New York. His nostalgia (and it *was* nostalgia) was not for an aristocratic social order of the type that existed in England but for the social vision of the Old Republic: America as the "plain and simple republics of farmers."[36] What Kent and other Old Federalists feared was, as Marvin Meyers has put it, "the imminent coming of anonymous democracy, detached from soil, neighborhood, custom, tradition—detached above all from the guiding influence of wise stewards."[37]

The influence of pro-democratic sentiment on the constitutional convention was evident from other issues as well. Chief among these was the existence of a system of equity in American jurisprudence. Equity was even less popular than the common law among democratization advocates. Echoing Blackstone, the great defender of the common law, these advocates argued that equity conferred on judges unbridled discretion and made judges pure legislators.[38] Equity's lack of a jury strongly contributed to this perception, as did its apparent lack of legal formality. But there was more to the opposition to equity than these procedural characteristics. Equity was the source of legal forms and arrangements, like the trust, that seemed to many democrats to serve the interests only of the wealthy. Preventing the recreation of an English-like aristocracy in America required that these legal forms and arrangements be abolished. As we will see,[39] this line of thought strongly influenced the statutory revisers' handling of several aspects of property law, especially those that concerned family property settlements.

Other important actions of the convention reflected the same sentiment of democratization. The convention abolished both the Council of

Revision and the Council of Appointment. These two bodies substantially limited the power of the legislature, conferring, in the case of the Council of Revision, legislative power on the Chancellor and the highest judges of the state and, in the case of the Council of Appointment, the governor and four leading senators. Both bodies were widely perceived as tools of an entrenched cadre of political leaders (Chancellor Kent among them) that routinely frustrated the will of the people.[40] The same opposition to perceived aristocratic oligarchy led to the adoption of nominating conventions as the means for selecting political candidates, replacing the congressional caucus, which the public widely reviled.[41]

Supporters of popular democracy did not succeed in using the occasion of the 1821 constitutional convention to secure all of their objectives, but they did succeed in creating substantial momentum for democratization that led subsequently to additional political reforms. By 1826, constitutional amendments had been passed establishing universal suffrage, except for African Americans, and popular election for presidents and justices of the peace.[42] Lee Benson dates the election of 1824, which saw the defeat of Martin Van Buren's powerful faction of nonradical Republicans, the so-called Albany Regency, as the event marking the arrival of "populistic democracy" in New York.[43] This prevailing political sentiment, together with the need to reconcile existing statutes with the new constitution, provided the impetus for a new, more ambitious statutory revision.

The first attempt to initiate a new statutory revision was made in 1823 by Governor Joseph C. Yates, a faithful servant of the Albany Regency whom Regency leaders later dumped for politically expedient reasons. The legislature failed to act immediately, because, according to Jabez Hammond, it "possessed little talent."[44]

Following Yates's call for legislative revision again in 1824, the legislature, preoccupied with the coming elections in the divisive atmosphere that prevailed,[45] put off action until just before adjournment. "Not wishing to leave the appointment of the revisors to their successors,"[46] the legislators appointed Chancellor Kent, Erastus Root, and Benjamin Franklin Butler (who, somewhat ironically, had written to Van Buren urging that Governor Yates not be renominated as the party's candidate for Governor in the 1824 election) as revisers. Kent, who had only recently retired as Chancellor, declined, explaining that he would have preferred to work as sole reviser.[47] As the distinguished Federalist Chancellor, Kent could not have been eager to serve as an equal with Butler, the 29-year-old rising star in the Albany Regency. As correspondence among the eventual revisers reveals, though, Kent cast a great shadow over the entire project despite his nominal noninvolvement. Kent was replaced by John Duer. Following a disagreement over the basic conception of the project between Root and his two younger colleagues, Root resigned and was replaced by Henry Wheaton, the reporter for the U.S. Supreme Court. Wheaton was appointed to a diplomatic post shortly thereafter, however, and was replaced by John C. Spencer. Little work had been done on the project by the time of Wheaton's resignation, so the revision was almost entirely the work of Butler, Duer, and Spencer.

The Revisers

Butler owed his appointment as reviser to a powerful political mentor, Martin Van Buren, who had been a close personal friend of his father. He had learned his law as Van Buren's apprentice and was closely associated with him. After admission to the bar in 1817, he became Van Buren's law partner. In 1821, the same year in which Van Buren was elected to the U.S. Senate, Butler was appointed district attorney of Albany County. Following his work on the statutory revision, he served in various Cabinet positions, as Attorney General and Secretary of War under Van Buren and Attorney General under Jackson. He was offered the same position in the Polk administration. Butler also founded, in 1835, the New York University School of Law.

John Duer's family was also politically well connected. His father, William Duer, had been a member of the Continental Congress, an Assistant to the Secretary of the Treasury, Alexander Hamilton, and had a sullied reputation as an entrepreneur and stock speculator.[48] John Duer had established a reputation for himself as one of the leading litigators in the state by the time he was appointed reviser. Duer had learned his law in Alexander Hamilton's office and under Hamilton's influence became a Federalist. Van Buren, eager to build coalitions between Federalists and Bucktail Republicans, provided crucial political support for Duer's ambitions.[49] He had served as a delegate to the 1821 constitutional convention where he played a prominent role. Duer later served as justice and chief justice in the Superior Court in New York.

Like Duer and Butler, John C. Spencer was the beneficiary of substantial political connections. His father, Ambrose Spencer, had served successively as Attorney General of New York State, Justice of the New York Supreme Court, and Chief Justice. He worked as private secretary to Governor Daniel Tompkins and later became an ally of DeWitt Clinton.

Elected to the U.S. House of Representatives, he chaired a committee investigating the United States Bank and prepared a report attacking the Bank on many of the same grounds that Jackson would later raise. He was later elected Speaker of the New York State Assembly and New York State Senator, the position that he held at the time of his appointment as reviser. Subsequent to his work on the New York statutory revision, he served as Secretary of War under President Tyler.

The Revisers' Conception of the Project

It is no coincidence that several of the revisers were among the cadre of lawyers who largely controlled the 1821 constitutional convention, for both the legislature and the governor envisioned the revised code as an extension of the political work of the convention.[50] The legislature authorized the revisers to "to alter the phraseology of the laws of this state, passed prior to the adoption of the present constitution, which may require such alterations by reason of provisions of the said constitution, or by reason of any acts of the legislature which have been passed in consequence of the adoption of the said constitution."[51] It would strain credulity to interpret this authorization as a signal for the revisers to undertake a codification effort; the legislature aimed at something quite less ambitious and controversial. Other political forces, however, did urge that the revision be a codification that would minimize the importance of the common law and democratize law. In 1825, Governor DeWitt Clinton, who succeeded Yates, told the legislature that the revision should create a code that "prevented judicial legislation, which is fundamentally at war with the genius of representative government."[52]

Butler and Duer were sensitive to such pro-codification sentiments. Their response to the legislature, while carefully avoiding the word "codification," unambiguously suggested that they contemplated a project more ambitious than that which the legislature had authorized. They stated that "our law should be comprised under appropriate titles; and that these titles should be classified in their natural order; and more especially . . . various provisions of each statute should be arranged in the clearest most scientific method, which the nature of the subject will permit."[53] What Butler and Duer were proposing to the legislature, then, was a scientific rearrangement of the law, inspired by Bacon's conception of a systematic digest.[54] Along with their report to the legislature, they enclosed as samples of what they proposed to do two model statutes, one on the judiciary system and one on Chancery. As Bernard Rudden has aptly noted, "when compared with the existing English-based morass," these models were sure to please.[55]

What they were careful not to propose—indeed took pains to deny[56]—was the creation of a code. Butler and Duer were politically astute men, and their ears were close to the ground. While they recognized that some politically powerful forces, including Governor Clinton, supported the idea of a code, they were keenly aware that the overwhelming majority of the bar was aligned against it. These men were themselves part of the legal elite and had represented the interests of wealthy individuals. Moreover, even among the less wealthy portions of the lay population, the idea of a code carried a good deal of political baggage, including the nativist notion that a code was an alien idea, incompatible with American traditions and culture.

At the same time, Duer's and Butler's political and ideological allegiances made it unlikely that they would have been content with the modest project that the legislature had first defined for them. Especially with respect to property law, too many vestiges of the "aristocratic" English system remained part of the law of New York, even if only formally, to satisfy the rising sentiment of democratization.

Impetus for a more ambitious revision had also come from England, where, besides Bentham, more legally influential advocates of law reform such as Brougham and Romilly had strenuously called for thorough substantive reform of English law.[57] Indeed, as English writers themselves noted,[58] there was considerable irony in the fact that English efforts at land law reform had been more successful than efforts in America. English law reformers could not understand why the new nation had not taken advantage of its unique opportunity to create a more rational and modern system of property law. The work of James Humphreys had a particular influence on the New York revisers. They had read Humphreys's *Observations on the Actual State of the English Laws of Real Property with the Outlines of a Code* soon after its publication in 1826 and expressly referred to it in their report to the legislature of March 15, 1826.[59] It is worth dwelling on Humphreys's plan in some detail because both its general conception and particulars clearly influenced the New York project.[60]

Humphreys's project embraced a modernist conception of property, according to which land is understood as a commodity, i.e., a marketable good no different than all other marketable goods. "[B]oth good policy and express laws require that land should be *commercial* or, in another word, alienable. Indeed, to be assured of this we need only remark that a purchaser scarcely buys but he improves."[61] Humphreys simply assumed that the legal function of land was economic, to increase wealth. He implicitly rejected the premodernist conception of land as the foundation of proper social and political order, an expression of one's position in a formal social hierarchy and, concomitantly, of political power.

Land's solely economic meaning led Humphreys to draw two conclusions: first, a modern land law regime should retain the system of estates, despite that system's distinctly premodern origins. Within the culture of modernity, the estates system could be adapted to serve a function very different than the noneconomic function it performed in the premodern culture. Its new purpose was to resolve the problems of how to arrange ownership of income streams, capitalized income, and discounted capital and how to facilitate the expeditious transfer of income-producing assets. He argued that the existing English law of property contained three principal obstacles to resolving these problems—tenure, uses, and bare trusts. These legal forms, Humphreys argued, "do not fix, they do not regulate, but merely obscure the only essential purposes of property, namely enjoyment, transmission, and legal liability."[62] Here again, Humphreys reasserted, or rather assumed, that property serves only the economic functions of satisfying personal wants and increasing social wealth. He never considered that it might also serve the social and political functions that premoderns had understood land to serve.

This shift from a social-political vision to an exclusively economic vision is reinforced by Humphreys's illustrations of his basic point: personal property, which he understood to include stock and other securities, "forms an aggregate far exceeding descendible land in produce and value. There we discover no traces of tenure, or of uses, and little of merely formal trusts."[63] Humphreys was signaling that the reign of land as the dominant form of property had ended, replaced by the modern reign of intangible and ephemeral forms of property. As Bernard Rudden has pointed out, the emphasis on stocks and company shares as the more important form of property was a crucial move, albeit a curiously timed one since 1826 saw the collapse of stock values from the boom of 1825.[64]

Although the New York revision departed from Humphreys's proposed code in several details, largely owing to differences between American and English property rules, the same basic conception of property drove the New York project. Like Humphreys, the American revisers sought to replace a political conception of property with a basically economic one. It is crucial to understand, though, that the Americans were motivated by politics. Both the revisers and critics of the revision (like James Kent) viewed the economic, commodified conception as more democratic, and therefore more American, than the premodern political-social conception. Commodifying property freed it of its premodern role as the foundation for social hierarchy and family position. Liberated from that role, property, including expanding newer forms of wealth like company stock, would be available to a much wider spectrum of the population.

The Substance of the Revision

The revised statutes effected three basic substantive changes in New York property law: abolition of tenure; simplification of the system of estates, especially future interests and rules regulating future interests; and severe restriction of trusts. The first of these was primarily symbolic in significance; the latter two were genuinely innovative.

Abolition of Tenure

In direct language strikingly uncharacteristic of legislation (then and now alike), the statutes wiped out the feudal doctrine of tenure in one move:

> All lands within this state are declared to be allodial, so that, subject only to the liability to escheat, the entire and absolute property is vested in the owners, according to the nature of their respective estates; and all feudal tenures, of every description, with all their incidents are abolished.[65]

This provision effected no genuine change in New York law, but it did have symbolic significance. The basis for the feudal system of tenure was the idea that all land is held, directly or indirectly, by the Crown. The theory of tenure, which provided the foundation for the feudal structure of society, was based on dependent land holding—the Crown permitted individuals to hold, not own, land in return for services rendered. Feudal lawyers spun from this theory an incredibly complicated system of various types of tenure. Some gave tenants more security than others, but the basic idea behind all of them was the same: no landholder was legally autonomous.

Legal historians have debated whether the English concept of land tenure was transplanted to America. Whether or not it was, New York had certainly abolished it in 1787, as part of the republican-inspired legislative reform of land law.[66] As a result, New Yorkers owned land allodially, i.e., not holding it of someone else. The purpose of the revised statutes' redundant declaration was symbolic and exemplary. It was perhaps the perfect exemplar of the vision of transforming property law from a state of "technicality" to one of "liberality." This vision, more than any other, was at the heart of the revisers' project.

"Liberality" in Antebellum Legal Discourse

The term "liberality" was quite ambiguous, even within legal discourse. In the eighteenth century, reflecting the influence of civic republican ideas, it was used to indicate freedom from servility and social and economic dependency.[67] It retained much of this meaning in antebellum discourse, and this was evident in the context of abolition of land tenures. There, it was used to signify the repudiation of "feudalism." Few legal concepts were as closely associated with feudalism as land tenures. No one thought that America was then or had ever been a feudal society, of course. "Feudalism" in antebellum legal discourse figuratively expressed formal social hierarchy, just as it had in late eighteenth-century American legal discourse. Purging land law of its "feudal" vestiges was meant to eliminate the formal conditions of social servility. By the time of the New York statutory revision project, its meaning had evolved to reflect the ambition of making law and society more "democratic." What it meant to make law more democratic was itself highly ambiguous. At a minimum, though, it meant making it more accessible, at least to lawyers. More severe critics focused on the law's inaccessibility to the ordinary layperson.

Another respect in which antebellum legal reformers viewed "liberality" as closely related to democratization was through their elimination of legal rules that frustrated the intentions of individual owners. "Intentionality" was an extremely strong theme running through antebellum American legal writing about property. There was a strong sense that property rules ought to be created to fulfill private intentions but that the existing law frustrated that goal. Critics of property law had good reason to hold this view. The common law of property was filled with such intent-frustrating rules as the Rule in Shelley's Case, the Rule against Perpetuities, and the Doctrine of Worthier Title. These rules were fairly easily avoided by skilled—and, therefore, expensive—conveyancers and estate planners, but they were booby traps for the average practitioner, who may have heard of them but was not expert in their details. For the layperson who wished to save some money by self-preparing what seemed a relatively simple legal transaction, these rules could utterly ruin the dispositive plan in a deed or a will. Reforming property rules so that they gave effect to the intended meaning of fairly straightforward words was an obvious way to make law reflect rather than impede popular will and in that sense make it more democratic.

This connection between intent-effectuating rules and democracy was not always explicitly drawn, but was nevertheless apparent slightly below the surface. One locus for this connection concerns the question courts confronted when construing terms whose lay meaning differed from their technical legal meaning; which should apply? American courts, following the English courts' lead, utilized an established rule of construction to favor the legal meaning. Criticism of this rule began to appear early in the nineteenth century and became more prominent thereafter. In his book, *Law Miscellanies,* Hugh Henry Brackenridge, a leading Jeffersonian legal writer of the early nineteenth century,[68] directly attacked the conventional rule:

> I would just reverse this rule; viz. that a devisor shall *not be presumed* to use a word in a technical sense, unless it can be collected from the whole of the will, that he did mean so to use it.
>
> We all know who are the usual *scriveners,* or drawers up of last wills and testaments in Pennsylvania; the school-master of the neighbourhood; a commissioned justice of the peace, or some one that has been about the courts and has some reputation for clerkship. The school-master has his Clerks' Assistant . . . or some book of *bad precedents,* from which he picks terms without distinguishing the use: the justice in like manner, or other person, little learned in the law, and yet affecting much. The terms, *heir, issue, begotten,* etc., get in, or the arrangement of the words, by *implication* is such as to be construed to mean what in fact never was intended.[69]

Brackenridge's point was not difficult to grasp: courts ought to construe language in wills and other legal instruments transferring property according to the meaning that the person who drafted the instrument likely intended, especially bearing in mind the legal sophistication of the drafter. In a society in which most instruments were not drafted by lawyers, construing terms according to their technical meaning further aggravated the hostility that ordinary lay people held toward law, especially property law.

Brackenridge later extended his attack on technicality in the construction of wills, arguing that the conventional rules of construction in fact contradicted each other. As Brackenridge correctly noted, the English common law included two rules governing construction of wills. One, as we have just seen, provided that courts must give technical legal terms their technical meaning. The other was that courts must construe terms in such a way as to enforce the intention of the individual owner. Apologists for the common law like Blackstone argued that the two concepts, technicality and intentionality, were entirely compatible. The best known expression of this conventional view was Blackstone's argument in a famous English case, *Perrin v. Blake.*[70] Blackstone there made the following claim:

> The great maxim in construction of devises is that the testator's intention must be fully observed, "served so are as the same is consistent with the established rule of law; *and no farther."*—If it did not go so far, it would be an infringement of that liberty of disposing of a man's own property, which is the most powerful incentive to honest industry, and is therefore essential to a free and commercial country:—if it went *farther*, every man would make a law for himself; the metes and boundaries of property would be vague and indeterminate, which must end in its total insecurity.[71]

Brackenridge would have none this; he flatly rejected the conventional wisdom. Technicality and intentionality could not be reconciled because they are mutually exclusive concepts:

> There has been no point of law upon which I have been more dissatisfied with the decisions of the English judges than with regard to the *construction* of last wills and testaments. The rule which they have laid down, and their reasoning upon it, or application of it, is so inconsistent and contradictory, that I have been at a loss to know what to make of it. According to one, the *technical* term is to govern; according to another, the *intention* is to govern; or the construction is to be a *compound* of both. . . . *Intention* or *technical term must govern; there cannot be a compound of both.*

Brackenridge did not hesitate from expressing his view about which concept should control judges:

> *Intention* with me should be absolute; and I would fetter it with nothing deducible from art or science of which I could not suppose the person writing to have a correct knowledge.[72]

In addition to promoting accessibility and effectuating individual owners' intentions, a third sense of the term "liberality" was used in relation to property law. Extending the ideas of late eighteenth-century commercial republicans like Noah Webster, antebellum lawyers understood "liberality" to mean freedom from legal impediments to the easy alienability, or transferability, of property. They viewed alienability of property and democracy as related to instrumentality: making property more alienable made law more democratic insofar as it was easier for ordinary people to obtain property. Conversely, many "technical" aspects of property law made it much more difficult for people to acquire property, with the result that they had little opportunity to escape conditions of economic servility.

No one, certainly not the New York revisers, thought that declaring (again) that the system of land tenures was dead would itself liberalize property law in the senses just outlined. The revisers did think, though, that that system was the best symbol of what they aimed to throw out that they could choose. With their goal clearly communicated through this figurative means, they moved on to more substantive matters.

Revision of the System of Estates and Restraints on Alienation

The law of estates was then (and, alas, remains today) one of the most needlessly complicated areas in all of American law. The system of estates in early nineteenth-century New York by and large was the same that had existed in England for centuries, with some notable departures such as New York's abolition of entails. Few areas of property law were more ripe for substantive change.

An obvious, and important, example of the revisers' general approach to estates law is the abolition of the Rule in Shelley's Case. The revisers shared none of the fondness for this old relic of the common law that Kent and others had expressed. In their view there was no "other motive for preserving it . . . except that it may remain as one of the subjects on which the ingenuity of the bar is to be exercised at the expense of suitors."[73] The Rule, which still exists today in a few states, basically provides that if a landowner transfers his land by deed or will to one person (let us call him A) for life, and the deed or will further states that on A's death possession goes to A's "heirs," the interest following the life estate (called a remainder) is not in fact transferred to A's heirs, as one would suppose and as the original owner obviously intended, but instead is transferred to A, the life tenant.[74] The effect of the Rule is to frustrate the owner's intention by preventing the land from passing to the intended beneficiaries.[75] Moreover, the Rule spawned a vast body of refinements that made it was one of the most complex rules in land law. It was precisely the sort of "technical" rule that the revisers could abolish without much threat of opposition.

There is considerable disagreement about the reason why the English judges developed the Rule. The conventional view is that they did so to end feudal tax evasion when feudalism remained only as a fiscal policy. Whether or not that was the original motive, it obviously had no relationship to nineteenth-century American conditions. Nevertheless, other consequences of the Rule, not intended by the English judges, might justify retaining it. The reason most often given today for continuing the Rule is that it promotes the alienability of land by freeing land of a contingent remainder in unascertained persons and instead placing it in the hands of one individual, the present possessor. The revisers were surely aware of this argument, for it was precisely the argument that Blackstone had made in the Rule's defense in the famous *Perrin* litigation.

> I own myself of the opinion, that those constructions of law, which tend to facilitate the sale of property in a free and commercial country, and which make it more liable to the debts of the visible owner, which derives a greater credit from that ownership;—such constructions, I say, are founded upon principles of public policy altogether as open and as enlarged, as those which favor the accumulation of estates in private families, by fettering inheritances till the full age of posterity now unborn, and which may be born for half a century.[76]

The emphasis on making land more available to creditors is worth noting. The *Perrin* litigation occurred at a time when a credit economy was firmly taking root in England. Part of the reason for the rise of the policy of alienability in late eighteenth-century English legal consciousness was to facilitate the growth of a credit economy. A corollary of the alienability policy was the emergence of the modernist view that land is a market commodity, replacing the premodern understanding of land as the essential material foundation for a proper social order. Blackstone assumed that the implication of commodification for the Rule in Shelley's Case was clear: the Rule had to be retained. The curiosity, then, is why the New York revisers, who otherwise shared Blackstone's commitment to the alienability policy and the commodified conception of property, failed to refer to this argument.

Despite Blackstone's assurance, commodification had ambiguous implications for the Rule. From one point of view, it made perfectly good sense to conclude as Blackstone did that the Rule was consonant with a commodified conception of land insofar as it made land more readily available to creditors. On the other hand, the commodified conception of property was not strictly an economic idea; more fundamentally, it was part of a broader social vision. The Rule in Shelley's Case was associated with a very different social order than that which the revisers wished to encourage, and the rejection of that social order may well have seemed to require that the property code of modern society be purged of all remnants of the premodern social order. From this perspective, it would have been anomalous for the revisers, who boldly asserted their intention to modernize property law, to retain a rule that was generally associated in American legal consciousness with the English feudal social order.

Certainly the best-known change that the revisers made in the law of estates was their adoption of the so-called two-lives rule against suspending the power to transfer property. By the beginning of the nineteenth century, alienability had become the overriding topic of concern to American property lawyers. As Lawrence Friedman has stated, "The dominant theme of American land law was that land should be freely bought and sold."[77] No single issue was more important to alienability than the treatment of privately imposed restraints on alienation. The revisers' approach to this issue was to attempt to substitute a rule against suspension of the power of alienation for the infamous common-law Rule against Perpetuities. The Rule against Perpetuities is quite possibly the most complicated and misunderstood rule in all of property law. It is aimed at the problem of remoteness of vesting, i.e., future interests that remain for too long a time subject to a condition that must be fulfilled in order for the owner of the interest to be entitled to take possession of the affected land. It provides that a contingent future interest is invalid from its inception if there is any possibility that the contingency will remain unresolved more than twenty-one years[78] after the deaths of everyone who was alive when the interest was created.

The use of an unlimited number of lives, which the Rule then permitted, had recently led to several well-known abuses in England. In one case, *Thellusson v. Woodford*,[79] the court had upheld a trust created by an eccentric man to disinherit his family so that his £800,000 fortune would accumulate for the lives of all of his then-living descendants. This trust aroused such opposition in England that five years before the case was decided, Parliament enacted a statute, known as the Thellusson Act,[80] that severely restricted such accumulations. James Humphreys had proposed using the Thellusson Act as a model for a new rule against perpetuities. His rule would have restricted inalienable gifts to a period measured by the actual lives of the donees.[81] The New York revisers acknowledged the strong influence of Humphreys's proposal on their thinking,[82] although they did not adopt it entirely.

The revisers' initial draft forbade the suspension of "the absolute power of alienation" for longer than "a life or lives in being." For reasons that are not clear, they decided to relax this restriction somewhat. The report of September 2, 1828, instructs the reader to strike out "a life or" and substitute "not more than two." Thus began the famous two-lives rule against suspension of the power of alienation.

The revisers presented the new rule as a substitute for the Rule against Perpetuities, but it was not one. While both the common-law Rule against Perpetuities and the rule against suspension of alienation aim at enhancing the transferability of land, they approach that objective in very different ways. The two-lives suspension rule attempts to make land more marketable by striking down future interests that remain unassignable for more than the permitted two-lives period. Although another provision of the revised statute declared that all "expectant estates," i.e., future interests, are fully transferable,[83] a future interest is practically assignable only if all of the owners of the interest are ascertainable. If one or more owners of an interest is unascertained and, therefore, unable to consent, the interest cannot be assigned. So, the suspension rule applies only to interests that contingent because they are held by unborn or unascertained persons. By contrast, the Rule against Perpetuities attempts to make land more marketable by striking down future interests that may remain contingent too long. It sweeps more broadly than the suspension rule, applying not just to interests that are contingent because they are held by unborn or unascertained persons but to all contingent interests.

In truth, though, neither rule promotes the alienability of land very effectively. Neither rule limits the duration of future interests, and both rules only indirectly restrict the number of future interests that can be created. The suspension rule really was a rather moderate measure; it did not represent a radical restriction on the power of property owners to restrain the subsequent alienability of land they had transferred to others.

Four

Restrictions on the Uses of Trusts

Perhaps the most far-reaching changes that the Revised Statutes made concerned uses and trusts. The trusts provisions began dramatically: they abolished all trusts except those expressly allowed in subsequent provisions. The revisers swept aside all "passive" trusts and permitted only "active" trusts, i.e., trusts in which the trustee was "clothed with some actual power of disposition or management, which cannot be properly exercised without giving him the legal estate and actual possession."[84] They recognized that active trusts were often "indispensable to the proper enjoyment and management of property," but they argued that "the creation of trusts is always in a greater or less degree the source of inconvenience and expense, by embarrassing the title, and requiring the frequent aid of a court of equity."[85] Consequently, it was necessary to limit the types and duration of active trusts as much as possible.[86] This change, they felt, would "sweep away an immense mass of useless refinements and distinctions; w[ould] relieve the law of real property, to a great extent, from its abstruseness and uncertainty, and render it, as a system, intelligible and consistent."[87]

The statutes permitted trusts to be created only for four quite limited purposes:

1. To sell lands for the benefit of creditors;
2. To sell, mortgage or lease lands, for the benefit of legatees [i.e., beneficiaries under wills], or the purpose of satisfying any charge thereon;
3. To receive the rents and profits of lands, and apply them to the use of any person, during the life of such person, or for any shorter period . . . ;
4. To receive the rents and profits of lands, and to accumulate the same, for the purposes and within the limits prescribed in the first Article of this Title [i.e., for the benefit of minors].[88]

A trust created for any other purpose would, "if directing or authorizing the performance of any act which may lawfully be performed under a power [i.e., a power of appointment, a legal device by which an individual other than an owner may transfer ownership to another person]," be valid as a "power in trust." That is, no trust would be created, but, subject to other complex provisions regulating the creation and use of powers of appointment, the arrangement would create a valid power in which the power-holder would be bound by a legal duty to exercise the power in a way consistent with the original owner's intentions, rather than having discretion not to exercise the power.[89]

As the revisers acknowledged, this change was "an extensive" and "perhaps . . . an alarming innovation."[90] It eliminated all intentional trusts of personal property precisely at the time when, due to general changes in dominant forms of social wealth, the subject matter of trusts was shifting from land to intangible assets such as financial instruments. That change alone would have dramatically altered patterns of family property settlements. The four purposes allowed for trusts of land effectively blocked the use of trusts as the means for creating long-term trusts, which was the staple of property settlements for wealthy families. The upshot, clearly intended by the revisers, was to confine trusts to so-called caretaker trusts,[91] i.e., relatively short-term trusts created to protect an specific individual or group, such as minors. Indeed, the revisers explicitly stated that trust purposes should be confined "to receive the rents and profits of lands, and to apply them to the education of a minor, the separate use of a married woman, or the support of a lunatic or spendthrift."[92]

This narrow conception of the permissible purposes of trusts led to one of the striking innovations in all of the provisions on property: the statutory creation of all trusts as "spendthrift trusts." A spendthrift trust is one in which the beneficiary's interest is both nonassignable and immune from creditor attachment. The beneficiary is assured of receiving the future stream of income that the trust property produces, regardless of his actions. English and American property rules generally forbade restraints on alienation of legal (i.e., nontrust) interests. While there are indications that prior to the nineteenth century English equity judges were more permissive than common law courts concerning restraints on the alienability of beneficiaries' interests in caretaker trusts,[93] English equity in the early nineteenth century unambiguously moved against all such restraints in an attempt to make common-law and equity rules entirely consistent in full pursuit of the alienability policy.[94] The revisers acted seemingly in direct contradiction to this policy.

The revisers were willing to compromise their stand on alienability in this limited context because of their protectionist attitude toward the likely classes of trust beneficiaries. They anticipated that, given the restriction on the types of express trusts that could be created, trust beneficiaries for the most part would only be persons who were economically dependent on the settlor and who would likely be vulnerable to the vagaries of the market or their own ill-considered actions. When the revisers stated that trust income should be used for "the education of a minor, the separate use of a married woman, or the support of a lunatic or spendthrift," they reflected the consciousness of elite white males in a highly patriarchal society. In that consciousness, married women could seriously be classified along with "spendthrifts" and "lunatics."[95] Like these two categories of persons, married women were considered unable to care for themselves, or certainly at least for their financial and economic interests. Although the legal status of married women as property owners began to change in the 1820s and especially after 1830, a paternalistic outlook toward married women still dominated among legal elites at the time of the New York statutory revision.[96]

The statutory creation of trusts as spendthrift trusts indicates, then, the limits of the commodification conception of property as of 1830. Here was an important point of continuity with culture of premodernity. The legal policy of alienability, despite its enormous appeal generally, still was considered to be inappropriate to particular social spheres. The market's realm of legitimacy in legal consciousness, though expanding, was far from universal. Property continued to play social and political, i.e., non-economic, functions well into the nineteenth century. As we will see,[97] the source of this continuing limit to the market and commodified property was social boundaries that elite lawyers established for democratization itself.

The Limits of Liberality: The Nonradical Character of the Statutory Property Rules

The New York revisers never addressed the criticism that seems so obvious to us today: making property more alienable does not insure that it will be democratically distributed. While they certainly understood that property and democracy were closely—and problematically—related, their solution was the decidedly nonradical one of moving toward formal rather than substantive equality. The nonradical character of the New York revision becomes especially apparent if we compare its approach with the radically egalitarian program offered by the Thomas Skidmore.

Skidmore, a self-made intellectual who had worked as a machinist, teacher, and inventor (but not as a lawyer), wrote his biting tract, *The Rights of Man to Property!*[98] at the same time the New York statutory revision was completed. Anticipating Marx, Skidmore used the labor theory of value to mount a radical critique of private ownership of property. "[A]s long as property is unequal, or rather, as long as it is so enormously unequal," he argued, "those who possess it *will* live on the labor of others."[99] He called on labor and the poor to "rip all up, and make a full and General Division" of property.[100] Surveying the present scene, he attacked a wide variety of social institutions as antithetical to genuine democracy, among them private banks, chartered monopolies and corporations, private ownership of manufacturing firms, and, of great importance to Skidmore, chattel slavery. Skidmore's vision, however, was not some sort of protocommunist state. He did not advocate total abolition of private ownership of the means of production or complete elimination of differences in wealth. His aim rather was to eliminate the main sources of exploitative privilege and permanent economic subordination. For Skidmore, the institution whose abolition was most vital to achieving a genuinely democratic property regime was *inheritance.* He proposed confiscating a person's property on death and redistributing it equally among all persons who had just reached the age of majority.

The contrast between Skidmore's bold proposal to abolish inheritance and the New York revision of the inheritance system indicates not only the comparative tameness of the statutory reforms but, more generally, the limits of liberality. The liberality critique of property law never questioned the basic structure of property law. Its immediate goals were to enhance the intelligibility of property rules to the legal profession and, to a lesser extent, to the general population, and to expand the alienability of property. Its more profound effect was to facilitate the acceptance of the modernist conception of property within legal consciousness. That conception, with its emphasis on commodification, was incompatible with views like Skidmore's on social exploitation.

Ultimately, the limited scope of criticism and change of the existing property system that occurred under the rubric of liberality was a consequence of legal reformers' own elite professional consciousness. Liberality and technicality were concepts within the vocabulary of the legal elite, not that of radical lay critics like Skidmore. In truth, liberality, as the New York revisers meant the term, was not opposed to technicality but was an aspect of technicality, for the changes that they made and justified under the heading of liberality were largely technical and not fundamental. Inheritance of property remained largely intact. The system of estates, by which the wealthiest members of society could perpetuate the power that comes with accumulated property within their families for several generations, was retained, with only relatively minor alterations. Individual power to impede the free movement of land and other forms of wealth was only slightly curtailed. Liberality was hardly revolutionary in its impact on legal practices; it was never meant to be. Much less visibly, though, the discourse of liberality did have consequences that, if not revolutionary, were far from merely technical. It speeded the triumph in legal thought of the modern over the premodern conception of property.

FIVE

James Kent and the Ambivalent Romance of Commerce

REPUTATIONS, ONCE ACQUIRED, are notoriously hard to shake. Perhaps no figure in American legal history illustrates this observation more clearly than James Kent. Variously characterized by historians as conservative,[1] a "flinty conservative,"[2] an "ultra-conservati[ve],"[3] a "Tory,"[4] someone who was "[s]trongly supportive of property ownership,"[5] Kent is widely, if not universally, seen as an indomitable antidemocrat and staunch defender of the status quo in an age of tremendous social, political, and economic change. If conservatism is defined in relation to legal reform, then that characterization of Kent seems justified. No American legal figure spoke and wrote so forcefully or articulately about the dangers of the various reform measures that dominated the attention of New York state after 1820, including the 1828–30 statutory revision of property law.

Kent can also aptly be characterized as conservative in relation to his views about democracy. His vigorous opposition during the 1821 New York Constitutional Convention to proposals to extend the suffrage are well known[6] and provide much of the basis for his current reputation as political retrograde. His views were those of an Old Federalist and stood in stark opposition to the rising spirit of popular democracy in the Jacksonian era. Like Adams, Kent believed that the ideal polity was, to borrow Marvin Meyers's typically lucid description, "an informally stratified republic, where a wholesome freeholder population chose leaders from among their well-born, well-trained, well-off neighbors—leaders who would maintain the rights and interests of the whole community, with a special regard for property rights."[7] This vision was especially solicitous of property rights because property was the basis for this proper social and political order. Kent's notion of a proper order was not identical, however, with classical republican order. It lacked civic republicanism's moral epistemology. Kent, as we shall see, repudiated virtue as the core political value, and consequently did not assign to property the political role of providing the necessary material conditions for autonomous and virtuous citizenship.

Kent's *Commentaries on American Law* were the single most sustained discussion of property law by any American writer at the time. The first edition was published between 1826 and 1830. That he regarded property as the central concept and institution in the entire legal system is suggested by the extraordinary amount of attention he devoted to property law in the *Commentaries;* he devoted more attention to property, both personal and real, than to any other single topic. Altogether, the property portions occupied nearly two-thirds of the four volumes, half of volume 2 and two-thirds of volume 3 on the law of personal property and the remaining third of volume 3 and all of volume 4 on real property law.

This chapter will analyze Kent's discursive treatment of property, focusing primarily, though not exclusively, on his *Commentaries.* The goal is not to provide an exhaustive analysis of Kent's entire contribution to developing American property law in all of the professional capacities in which he served over a long life—practitioner, judge, teacher, and scholar. Rather, the focus will be more limited: to examine his contribution to the development and acceptance of the commodified conception of property in American legal consciousness. Though he interacted with only a fraction of the antebellum legal profession, namely, elite old Federalist mandarins like Joseph Story, Daniel Webster, and Simon Greenleaf, Kent's writings, especially the *Commentaries,* had a much wider influence. The *Commentaries* were the most influential legal text on property, indeed, on all of private law, in the antebellum American legal profession.[8]

The *Commentaries,* like Kent's judicial opinions, certainly reveal a strong concern for protecting property. However, to say that Kent favored property rights is not very revealing. One could hardly expect Kent to express sentiments antagonistic or even indifferent toward protecting individual ownership interests. Saying that one supported legal protection of property rights was virtually as obligatory as declaring one's commitment to the Constitution. Understanding Kent's attitude toward property requires an inquiry into his conceptual and normative views regarding the role of property in the emerging modern American culture. Did he take the legitimate purpose or purposes of property to be the premodern civic understanding of property as the material foundation of a virtuous polity, the classical liberal understanding of property as guarantor of individual liberty and limited government, or the modern instrumental understanding of property as a means for promoting economic development and the creation of wealth? How did he react to the increasingly dominant commodity conception of property and its effect on American culture? To what extent, if any, did he, as one of the most elite members of the legal profession in the antebellum nineteenth century, contribute to the facilitation and legitimization of the modern conception of property as commodity in American society?

Kent is an especially appropriate figure through whom to examine elite legal attitudes toward the modern conception of property and to define the role they played in constructing the modern, commodified conception as the dominant understanding of property in American legal consciousness and, in turn, the dominant form of property in American society. As the author of the widely used *Commentaries* and one of the most distinguished judges in the country, he was one of a small handful of figures who literally shaped legal thought and legal practice throughout much of the first half of the nineteenth century. Beyond being a highly prominent figure in the legal profession, though, Kent, more than any other legal writer of his time, articulated an understanding of property that was compatible with the enormous changes in the American economy and society that had occurred in the half-century since the nation's founding.

The most important contribution of the understanding of property that emerges from the *Commentaries* was to shift American legal consciousness in a way that accommodated these external changes, as the eighteenth-century conception could not. These economic and social changes were not wholly external to legal thought, however. By accommodating these changes within legal consciousness, Kent's conception of property in turn facilitated the process of further changes in economic and social institutions and practices, such as the development of the modern corporation. Thought and action cannot be defined in simplistic cause and effect relations. They interpenetrate each other to such an extent that cause and effect must remain ambiguous. The conception of property that Kent articulated was both a response to and a cause of the economic and social changes that marked the market revolution.

It is reasonable to ask how exemplary Kent's views on property were among ordinary (i.e., non-elite) members of the antebellum American bar. One can only speculate, of course, for we have little record of the thinking of non-elites, who had no occasion to develop or express in writing their systematic views. To the extent that we can extrapolate from the writings of elite lawyers, Kent stands well within the mainstream of antebellum legal thought, though it would be too much to describe him as exemplary of the entire profession. His views certainly reflected those of Old Federalists, men who wished to preserve the traditional social hierarchy and who, during the 1830s, felt deeply threatened by Jacksonian democracy. At the same time, the gap between Kent's views and those lawyers who were reform-minded was not impossibly wide. In fact, Kent himself provided several bridges between the two shores.

Kent's treatment of property in the *Commentaries* signaled the end of political virtue as the central concept in American legal discourse about property. His conception of property was not only nonagrarian but, more important, noncivic. His vision represented a clear rejection of the Jeffersonian understanding of the most valuable form of property as land, owned in freehold by citizen-farmers, and the dominant role of property as the necessary material condition for creating and maintaining a virtuous republic. While land remained an extremely important form of property, he by no means shuddered at the prospect of other forms of property, especially imaginary forms such as credit and franchises, eventually replacing freehold land as the consequence of the market revolution. This recognition of and willingness to accept, even embrace, a shift in the dominant forms of property resulted from a distinctly non-Jeffersonian understanding of property's role in society. Property's central function was, to Kent, to facilitate commerce. Above all, Kent stressed the importance of the legal policy of alienability. Property of all forms must remain freely transferable so that the "spirit of commerce," as he repeatedly called it, would prevail. Kent's stress on alienability as the crucial characteristic of ownership for American property law to protect laid the foundation for a more thoroughly commodified understanding of property, an understanding in which the eighteenth-century dialectic of virtue and corruption was utterly absent.

To say that Kent's *Commentaries* signaled the end of the virtue/corruption dialectic is not to say that his discussion of property was nondialectical. By rejecting virtue as the central property, Kent moved toward an uncoupling of property from the public sphere, but that uncoupling was not complete. The discourse of the *Commentaries* reflected the same dialectic of "liberality" and "technicality" that was so evident in legal writings supporting the New York statutory revision of property law. Kent's discussion of these concepts, however, was not just a response to the predicament that law was increasingly inaccessible to ordinary people. The terms "liberality" and "technicality" metaphorically expressed two clusters of dialectically related economic and political values. They were dialectical responses to deeper intellectual and ideological predicaments arising from the profound political, economic, and social changes that America went through between 1815 and 1860. These predicaments centered around the basic question whether primacy should be given to preserving the stability and power distribution of the existing order, perceived as natural, or to promoting social, economic, and political change through legal policies. Property was the central concept through which this question was posed again and again. Virtually all of the important antebellum property cases involved the predicament of security of the natural order versus economic and social change. Over and over, from the mill acts of the early nineteenth century[9] to the U.S. Supreme Court cases involving legislative destructions of state-created property interests,[10] courts were required to determine whether to protect existing ownership interests or to permit those interests to be destabilized in the interest of promoting economic development. For Kent, as for most elite American lawyers, conflicts between existing property rights and new entrepreneurial property interests posed a basic tension between their premodern concern with security and natural order, on the one hand, and their modern desire to facilitate the release of individual energy in the marketplace, on the other.

Kent's understanding of individual freedom in America was primarily market freedom: the "American Adam"[11] unbound from the shackles of the feudal order and free at last creatively to express himself in the marketplace. Freedom meant the existence of a historically unique opportunity for men (more accurately, for some men—the opportunity did not extend to African-American men, just as it did not to African-American or European-American women) to use their energies, skills, and talents in an active, robust market for the purpose of fulfilling their own goals and creating their own wealth. This vision of a new kind of heroic man, the precursor of the Horatio Alger heroes in the marketplace who would appear in popular literature forty years later, required an expansive interpretation of property as a commodity. Commodified property, released from the shackles of an antiquated legal and social order, was the American individual's tool for forging his way through the market wilderness, clearing, building, creating. At the same time, though, unrestricted freedom of individual to compete in the marketplace threatened the stability of the social order and the security of one's possession and one's economic and social position, premodern values that Kent cherished at least as much as he did individual freedom. These values required that the market's domain be limited and that property not allowed to become thoroughly commodified.

Kent treated these two visions in a genuinely dialectical fashion, not simply as a duality or an antinomy. Throughout the *Commentaries,* the juxtaposition of the rhetoric of stability and order with the rhetoric of market freedom and activity suggests that he understood both sets of values as interdependent parts of a whole. Each derived meaning from the other and interpenetrated the other. The dialectical movement between the two sets of values in turn clarified and even shifted the meaning of both. Of course, Kent made no attempt to resolve this dialectic through any sort of grand synthesis emerged from this dialectic, however. Most of the *Commentaries* consists of technical dissections of cases, doctrines, statutes, and such, exemplary of the sort of professional legal writing that first developed in the antebellum period. The most obvious reason for not resolving this dialectic is that he did not structure his discussion of property primarily on the basis of this or any other dialectic. Indeed, on the surface, most the discussion of property in the *Commentaries* seems largely devoid of all theory.

A deeper reason is that Kent seemed unable to commit himself entirely to either vision. His reaction to the market revolution and the effect it had on the changing role of property in American society may be best described as ambivalent.[12] The period between the end of the War of 1812 and the beginning of the Civil War, unquestionably a period of unprecedented growth and change, is often seen as one in which unbounded optimism (save for the glitches caused by the Panics of 1837 and 1843) and a blind faith in progress and economic development were universally shared. Kent's treatment of property suggests that this was not the case. Fear and enthusiasm were simultaneously present in his discussions of legal changes such as statutory revision of property law and growth of corporate franchises as a form of entrepreneurial property. Kent's experience was no aberration; a sense of regret and fear as reactions to economic growth and prosperity was widespread throughout American society.[13]

Nor should we shrug off Kent's qualms as the anxieties of an old Federalist whose sun was now in Jacksonian eclipse. Politics and class interest are relevant in explaining his reaction, but they do not provide a complete explanation. Kent was neither an apologist for the capitalist class that benefited from economic development nor an unreconstructed sentimentalist about the old agrarian social order. His discussion of property in the *Commentaries* reveal that even as he participated in developing and legitimizing the commodified conception of property, he was mindful of what society was losing as the premodern understanding of property diminished in legal consciousness. Kent *was* an ardent proponent of strong property rights, but he was far from being an unequivocal champion of property, conceived of strictly as a commodity for increasing personal and social wealth. Even as he celebrated the triumph of the legal policy of alienability, the foundation for the dynamic, entrepreneurial form of property, he lamented legal changes that facilitated entrepreneurial activity.

Kent legitimized a commodified view of property in terms that partially reconciled the modern conception of property with the civic tradition of the Founders' generation. This is what made the *Commentaries* the single crucial legal text on property written before the Civil War: it enabled the profession to come to terms with the market revolution while simultaneously preserving some connection with the older republican tradition. Although he clearly favored economic development, he did not couch his arguments regarding free alienability solely on the basis of economic benefits. Rather, he combined economic (or, more accurately, quasi-economic) arguments with moral-political-historical theory that echoed republican themes of the preceding generation.

Formative Influences

Kent was a member of an influential group of elite lawyers whose careers bridged the gap between the civic republican period to the Market Revolution. Born a half generation later than the Founders, Kent's circle, which included the first group of professional legal writers (men like Joseph Story, Nathan Dane, and Peter DuPonceau), was too young at the time of the Federal Constitutional Convention to have influenced it but old enough to have been influenced by it. Kent was both, to paraphrase the subtitle of Kent Newmyer's biography of Story, one of the last statesmen of the old republic[14] and one of the first spokesmen of the commercial empire.

Kent's early connections with political leaders from the generation of the Founding Fathers were crucial to his career and were decidedly Federalist. They began almost immediately after his graduation from Yale College in 1781, when he entered into a legal apprenticeship in Poughkeepsie, New York, with Egbert Benson, a prominent member of the bar who was then the state attorney general.[15] Benson's neighbor at the time was John Jay, one of the authors of the Federalist Papers, future governor of New York, and first Chief Justice of the United States.[16] The opportunity to meet Jay proved extremely beneficial to Kent, as Jay subsequently became his sponsor for various positions, including his appointment as the first professor of law at Columbia College[17] and as a judge.[18] In addition to Jay, Kent, through Benson, became acquainted with other leading Federalists, including George Washington, Alexander Hamilton, Aaron Burr, and George Clinton.[19]

Hamilton exerted a particularly strong influence on Kent. Although Hamilton was only seven years his senior, Kent seems to have regarded him as a professional and intellectual mentor.[20] Kent probably would have embraced the Federalist pro-development position even if he had never met Hamilton, but it is clear that his vision of the central role of commerce for the well-being of the polity was distinctly Hamiltonian. Early in his career, he avidly supported Hamilton's bank and funding programs against the attacks of the Republican George Clinton. Kent wrote that Hamilton's plan was not only constitutional and economically sound but "essential to the prosperity of the nation."[21] He never wavered in his support of the national bank when that idea became the political litmus test for Jacksonians. In the first volume of the *Commentaries,* published in 1826, he endorsed the bank as "a convenient, a useful and essential instrument in the prosecution of the fiscal operations of the government."[22] Like Hamilton, Kent also thought that states as well as the federal government should charter banks. Indeed, at the time that Hamilton's plan was being debated in Congress, Kent was one of the leaders in the New York legislature of a successful plan to charter New York's first state bank, the Bank of New York.[23] He wrote to his brother-in-law that the state bank was necessary to "control the influence of a National Bank as a State government to control the influence of the general government."[24]

Kent did not acquire all of his economic views solely from Hamilton, nor did he agree with all of Hamilton's positions. An astonishingly well-read person, Kent early on read through virtually all of the important texts on political economy that ushered in modern, commodificationist conception of property, especially the works of the eighteenth-century Scottish Enlightenment. He was familiar with Gerard de Malynes's *Con-*

suetudo; vel, Mercatoria, J. R. McCulloch's *Dictionary of Commerce . . . and Commercial Navigation,* Hume's *Political Essays,* Sir James Steuart's *An Inquiry into the Principles of Political Oeconomy,* and Adam Smith's *Wealth of Nations.*[25] Smith's views had an especially strong impression on him, and where Smith's position deviated from Hamilton's, Kent was more apt to follow Smith. Commenting on Hamilton's proposal to increase domestic manufacturing through high import duties, for instance, Kent stated that "if the liberal system of Adam Smith had been generally adopted, it would have carried forward nations, with accelerated motion, in the career of prosperity and greatness."[26] Kent accepted the Scottish Enlightenment writers' four-stage theory of social and legal evolution as a profound truth. That theory was an important source of his romance of commerce, so strongly depicted in the *Commentaries.* Like Smith and the other eighteenth-century Scottish political economists, Kent regarded the commercial age and the commercial "spirit" as constituting the highest stage of the progressive evolution of societies.

Kent's romantic views of commerce did not stem solely from his reading of the Scottish writers or his relationship with Hamilton. His experience in practice and in the business world reinforced Hamilton's and Smith's influences. Kent's time as a practicing lawyer was limited and not terribly successful,[27] but it exposed him to activities that constituted the core of commercial life in the early republic—debt collection, land transactions, and marine insurance litigation.[28] He also had first-hand experience with the world of commerce, participating in land speculations, investments in various enterprises, bank receivership, and even as a trustee of a corporation established for the purpose of building a railroad across the Panama Isthmus.[29] All of these experiences left him with a strong conviction of the centrality of commerce to human progress and the consequent need to encourage enterprise, decidedly non-Jeffersonian notions. At the same time, though, we must remember that Kent's formative years were spent in the revolutionary and constitutional periods when the political language of civic republicanism provided a common vocabulary that crossed party lines.

The Character of the Commentaries

The genesis of Kent's *Commentaries* is a familiar story. The work began as a reworked transcription of lectures that he delivered as professor of law during a second teaching stint at Columbia between 1824 and 1826, when he ended his teaching career for good.[30] Kent had been forced to retire as Chancellor in 1823 on his sixtieth birthday[31] and was anxious to find some other position.[32]

The *Commentaries* retained the character of their origin. The contents, for example, were labeled "lectures," rather than "chapters." Kent seems to have regarded the *Commentaries* as a direct extension of his Columbia lectures, stating in the preface to the first volume that it was intended for the benefit of students and "junior members of the profession."[33] That Kent would be sympathetic with the difficulties of learning the law is hardly surprising. On more than one occasion he recalled the frustration he experienced as a law-office apprentice trying to learn the law by reading it. In a letter to Simeon Baldwin, a Yale College classmate and lifelong friend, he stated that law "is a field which is uninteresting and boundless. . . . The study is so encumbered with voluminous rubbish and the baggage of folios that it requires uncommon assiduity and patience to manage so unwieldy a work."[34] Countless other lawyers who shared Kent's experience would have expressed the same sentiment.[35]

Conventionally, the work is described as "the American Blackstone."[36] Doubtless, Blackstone was the model for both Kent's Columbia lectures and the *Commentaries*. As John Langbein has noted, "Blackstone supplied the inspiration for the title of Kent's *Commentaries* and for the organization."[37] Blackstone was the inevitable model for Kent for several reasons. At the most superficial level, Blackstone's *Commentaries,* like Kent's, originated as lectures delivered to law students (Blackstone was the Vinerian Professor of Law at Oxford). Related to this point, Blackstone's venture at Oxford was one of the rare examples of legal education provided in a university setting to which Kent could look in the English-speaking world. Second, from the very beginning of his interest in law, Kent had been totally enthralled with Blackstone's *Commentaries.* Professor Langbein states the point well in observing that "Kent's Damascus, his conversion to a legal career, came about through his reading of Blackstone's *Commentaries.*"[38] Late in his career, Kent recalled, "When the College [Yale] was broken up and dispersed in July 1779 by the British, I retired to a country village, and finding Blackstone's *Commentaries,* I read the 4th volume. . . . [T]he work inspired me at the age of 16 with awe, and I fondly determined to be a lawyer."[39] Third, Blackstone's *Commentaries* was the very model for the enterprise of legal science, conceived of as the rational distillation and ordering of fundamental legal principles.[40] Kent was passionately committed to the vision of law as science. His great-grandson, William Kent, accurately summarized the depth of this commitment, stating, "Mr. Kent's life had been spent in . . . inculcating into the jurisprudence of his State the grand principles of law upon the sound basis of strict scientific deduction derived from the English authorities."[41]

Kent borrowed a good deal more than the title "Commentaries" from Blackstone. He owed a considerable substantive debt to Blackstone as well. The emphasis on law as a science, the dialectic between "liberality" and "technicality," the dialectic between "feudal" and "allodial" forms of land ownership, historical setting of common law of property in a progressive evolution from dark age of feudalism to commercial stage—all of these themes appeared in Blackstone (although Blackstone did not originate them; he, too, was a borrower).

Despite Kent's considerable debt to Blackstone, Kent's *Commentaries* were not an updated and somewhat Americanized version of Blackstone's project. Some of the obvious differences included coverage,[42] classification, and materials used, although the most important difference lay in the basic ambitions of the two *Commentaries*. Kent's ambition was more than just arranging law in a systematic fashion; it was to define *American* law, that is, its distinctly national character. Blackstone had already defined the character of the common law, at least as it existed in England. Kent's challenge was somehow to make Blackstone's definition of the common law compatible with the national sovereignty and distinctiveness of the United States. Kent, moreover, had to confront the existence of local law in the various states, which was a problem that Blackstone did not have to face. Kent's stated aim was to demonstrate that the federal character of the United States did not fundamentally change the nature of the common law in America. "[T]he elementary principles of the common law," he asserted, "are the same in every state, and equally enlighten and invigorate every part of the country."[43]

The achievement of defining the national character of American law made Kent's *Commentaries* more than just a mini-code.[44] It also distinguishes the work from modern legal treatises. John Langbein persuasively argues that the work is best characterized as an "institute" of national law, a genre that had its beginnings in classical Roman law and that reached its high-water mark in the European institutes of the seventeenth and eighteenth centuries.[45] Langbein defines legal institutes according to four characteristics: being comprehensive in coverage, defining the national character of a legal system, having a didactic quality, and systematically arranging legal materials around categories and principles. Kent's work met all of these criteria. Although in fact its coverage was selective, it purported to survey all of American law. It was centrally concerned with the relationship between American law and English common law. Its didacticism is clear from its genesis as a set of university law lectures. Most important, its ambition was to define the national characteristics of the American legal system, identifying what is American about American common law. As Langbein states, "[W]hat Kent's *Commentaries* shares with the European institutes of national law is the auspicious enterprise of giving character and definition to the law of a newly self-conscious nation."[46] It was, in fact, one of the last works in this genre.

The Arrangement of Property in the Commentaries

Among the more important respects in which Kent's *Commentaries* deviated from Blackstone's example is its arrangement of the law of property. Blackstone had labeled what we call property law as "The Rights of Things."[47] The importance of the topic to him is indicated by the fact that he devoted an entire volume to it. Blackstone's labeling followed Roman precedents. Justinian's *Institutes*, for example, which clearly influenced Blackstone in many respects,[48] divided all of law into three headings: the law of persons, of things, and of actions.[49] Virtually all European legal writers had adhered to that nomenclature through Blackstone's time. Kent departed from this practice by replacing the law of "things" with "property" law, subdivided into "personal" and "real" property. The change was not trivial. It both reflected and facilitated the commodification of property in legal consciousness by replacing a term—"things"— that seemingly limited the meaning of property to tangible objects with another term—"property"—whose measure was vastly more flexible.

Blackstone's physicalist rhetoric did not in fact prevent him from recognizing as property certain intangible interests. Blackstone obviously understood that property included many interests that were not "things" literally. Indeed, much of Volume 2 of his *Commentaries* is devoted to discussing one important category of such interests—so-called incorporeal hereditaments. A common-law concept drawn from the Roman concept of *res incorporales,* incorporeal hereditaments were simply intangible property rights that were treated as land for purposes of succession to the owner's eldest son rather than to all of his children equally (i.e., primogeniture)—hence, the term "hereditament." The category included some interests that remain very important today, such as easements, as well as others, like advowsons (the right to appoint the parson of a church) and corodies (the right to room and board, usually in a monastery or other religious establishment), whose importance had diminished substantially even by Blackstone's day. Today, nobody talks about incorporeal hereditaments, but they did in the days of Blackstone and Kent. The difficulty in Blackstone's age (and for common lawyers before him) was conceptual—how such intangible interests could be property when property itself was classified as land and things. The answer was simple, if not entirely satisfactory: declare these interests to *be* things, "even if only 'in contemplation.'"[50] Legally, "things" included assets that were things literally (what we might call today "stuff") and figuratively.

Such fictions could only go so far. The reification fiction—treating intangible interests as physical things—inhibited lawyers from thinking of property as an exchange commodity. At first blush, this may seem counterintuitive. After all, we are most apt to think of interests whose primary or sole function is to serve as a medium of exchange precisely those interests that are most obviously tangible. But that reaction reflects the extent to which we are immersed in a culture of commodities and have internalized the commodified understanding of property. It was not so for common lawyers through Blackstone's time, or least not nearly as so. Property as thing was a powerful symbol of a person's proper[51] place in the social order. It publicly communicated one's role in society, as well as instrumentally enabled one to fulfill that role. This was most obviously true of land, that most fixed thing. The very fixity of land made it (and makes it, for many people today continue the old ways of understanding land) difficult to think of it as an exchange commodity, with all of the fluidity and transience that that term implies. Land's fixity made apparent to all the owner's (or, more accurately, his family's) stake in society. It literally grounded one in a particular place in the social hierarchy.

The same relationship between physicality and social order was also true of tangible things that are moveable, although the relationship is not as apparent as it is in the case of land. A person whose property consists mainly of moveables was considered poor in Blackstone's time (though surely not in ours), or at least very far from wealthy. That land was the most important form of wealth in the eighteenth century is well known. The state of being landless expressed in an unambiguous way one's standing of the proper social order, a place far removed from the great landowners. Today we suppose that the wealthy hold most of their property in tangible as well as intangible assets—art and collectibles along with securities, notes, and the like. We further take it for granted that what makes those forms of wealth matter so much is their ready fluidity, the central attribute of the commodity. In Blackstone's time, however, people did not own "things" primarily for exchange; rather, "things" constituted the physical conditions and manifestations of one's fixed role in society.

We need not determine Blackstone's understanding of property as things, or at least as noncommodities, on the basis of conjecture alone. Blackstone lived during the beginnings of the age of commodities, and he was aware of the economic changes that were creating new forms of property. He specifically addressed the emergence of intangible property that the government has directly created (e.g., creditors' shares in the principal of the public debt) as a form of moveable property. This "new species of money," as Blackstone called it, had as its only advantage "the increase of circulation by multiplying the cash of the kingdom . . . always ready to be employed in any beneficial undertaking, by means of it's [*sic*] transferrable quality."[52] Blackstone did not minimize this advantage. His volume on property (Volume 4) was, after all, a paean to the "commercial policy" (a theme that Kent was to transplant to the American law of property), and "[a] certain proportion of debt seems . . . to be very highly useful to a trading people."[53] But his anxieties lay on the surface:

> By this means [of shares in the public debt] the quantity of property in the kingdom is greatly encreased in idea, compared with former times; yet, if we coolly consider it, not at all encreased in reality. We may boast of large fortunes, and quantities of money in the funds. But where does this money exist? It exists only in name, in paper, in public faith, in parliamentary security. . . . [W]hat is the pledge which the public faith has pawned for the security of these debts? The land, the trade, and the personal industry of the subject; from which the money must arise that supplies the several taxes. In these therefore, and these only, the property of the public creditors does really and intrinsically exist.[54]

Commerce itself was an unqualified good, and with commerce came debt. But when debt instruments, used solely as the medium of financial speculation, came to occupy a place as a socially important form of property, serious risks existed for that society's well-being. With property no longer serving as the foundation for the proper social order, what else would maintain that order? What would ground authority?

One of history's many ironies is the fact that the emergence of this new and dangerous form of property and the whole commodificationist mindset of which it hinted were entirely in keeping with the evolutionary theory of property that Blackstone, or rather, the tradition that he helped to popularize, so enthusiastically endorsed. Blackstone may have wanted the meaning and purpose of property to remain constant, but he couldn't have it both ways. Property could not be both evolutionary and static. It was entirely fitting, then, that James Kent, who accepted the evolutionary thesis in its entirety, would take the next discursive step in the development of property-as-commodity by substituting "property" for reified "things."

The remainder of Kent's arrangement of property law included other innovations that further reflected changes in legal consciousness along with economic changes between Blackstone's time and antebellum America. One of the more striking differences between Kent's and Blackstone's treatment of property law is Kent's abandonment of the orthodox location of personal property. Blackstone's discussion of personal property, relegated at the end of book 2, was truncated, occupying only nine of thirty-two chapters. Nevertheless, the very fact that he discussed personal property represented an innovation, as he himself emphasized at the outset. "Our antient [*sic*] law-books," Blackstone stated, "which are founded upon the feudal provisions, do not . . . often condescend to regulate this species of property. There is not a chapter in Britton or the mirroir,[55] that can fairly be referred to this head; and the little that is found in Glanvil, Bracton, and Fleta, seems principally borrowed from the civilians."[56] Blackstone acknowledged the dependency of the character of property law on the character of a nation's economy at any given time, denying the law's complete autonomy:

> [I]n later years, since the introduction and extension of trade and commerce, which are entirely occupied in this species of property, and have greatly augmented it's [*sic*] quantity and of course it's value, we have learned to conceive different ideas of it. Our courts now regard a man's personalty in a light nearly, if not quite, equal to his realty: and have adopted a less technical mode of considering the one than the other.[57]

On the other hand, Kent treated personal property nearly as importantly as real property, and in fact greatly expanded the domain of personal property law. In Kent's hands, personal property encompassed virtually the whole of what we would call commercial law, including negotiable instruments, sales, and insurance. Kent particularly emphasized maritime law and the maritime aspects of commercial law. None of this material appeared in Blackstone, and the difference reflects not only Kent's experience in practice but the impact of commercialization of the American economy on how antebellum American lawyers conceived of property. In a sense Kent was ahead of his time, for in 1828, when the third volume of his *Commentaries* first appeared, land remained the economically dominant form of wealth in America. The days of land's reign as king were numbered, however, and Kent reoriented the law of property to keep abreast of this profound change. Still, land law remained extremely important in the American legal psyche, and Kent could hardly justify giving it short shrift. While Kent moved personal property ahead of real property and great expanded the scope of personal property law, he still devoted nearly a third of the first edition of his treatise to the law of real property. It was in this discussion that his dominant themes, especially the central role of alienability in the law of property, were first articulated.

Kent's ultimate concern in making alienability, or marketability, the cornerstone of American property law, however, was political. He was overwhelmingly preoccupied with the problematic relationship between property and democracy. Kent valued stability, or more accurately, the stability of the appropriate social order headed by an enlightened elite. Popular democracy, in whose favor public sentiment seemed to increase during the 1820s, posed, from Kent's perspective, a direct and immediate threat to stability. The predicament was how to check popular democracy in a way that was compatible with the American repudiation of aristocratic hierarchies. Given that the Revolution had committed America to a casteless (at least formally) political and social system, it was unthinkable to achieve stability by creating a land-based hierarchy of the sort that existed in England.

Kent's solution to this predicament was to try to achieve an equilibrium between property interests that promoted stability and fluid, unrestrained property. This led him in the *Commentaries* to describe and endorse a version of dynamic property that would check the excesses of democracy without being undemocratic: marketable property, or property as commodity. That vision of property, however, coexisted uneasily with the other half of Kent's equilibrium, a definition of property that checked popular democracy. The anti-democratic half of Kent's balance led to him to support judicial protection of extant property interests, "vested rights," over entrepreneurial property interests, which were the outgrowth of an understanding of property as commodity. In the end, Kent had to back away from a fully commodified conception of property, leaving his discursive treatment of American property law with a strong sense of ambivalence. The remainder of this chapter will discuss these two sides to Kent's writings on property, marketability, the dynamic, commodified half, and vested rights, the stable, nondemocratic half.

Marketability as the Core Policy

American lawyers today conventionally consider marketability, or free alienability, to be the primary instrumental policy in property law. That view owes much to the presentation of the marketability policy in the sections of real property law in Kent's *Commentaries*. Kent was by no means the first to emphasize the importance of free alienability; eighteenth-century legal writers on both sides of the Atlantic celebrated the historical expansion of free transferability under the common law.[58] Kent's contribution was to develop this theme systematically as the marketability policy and to place that policy at the very center of American property law. To accomplish this task, he deployed three sorts of arguments: historical, economic, and political.

The Historical Argument: Marketability as the Measure of Historical Progress

Kent developed his views regarding the marketability policy in the context of an extended (and somewhat scattered) historical discussion about the development of the Anglo-American property regime. Kent began his discussion of marketability by declaring that "[t]he power of alienation of property is a necessary incidence to the right [of succession]."[59] Both historically and conceptually, Kent was flat wrong. It is entirely possible to conceive of the right of succession as limited to the transmission of property at death to the owner's legal heirs but without the power of the owner to vary the course of descent by gift or devise. Indeed, that is precisely how the heritability of land developed at common law. Long before they recognized the property holder's power to disinherit his heirs, the common law courts regularly enforced the right of the holder's heirs to receive the land by inheritance.[60] (Indeed, in England, land had been regularly heritable even before the Conquest.[61]) Apparently qualifying what he meant by a "necessary incidence," Kent went on to state that the power of alienation "was dictated by mutual convenience, and mutual wants."[62] The power historically developed first, he claimed, for moveables. The free marketability of land was slower to develop. "Property in land would naturally take a faster hold of the affections, and, from the very nature of the subject, it would not be susceptible of easy transfer, nor so soon as moveable property be called into action *as an article of commerce.*"[63] It was "the genius of commerce,"[64] not natural law, that "dictated and impelled a more free and liberal circulation of property."[65]

That Kent regarded the eventual development of land as an item of commerce as a social good could hardly be doubted. It was a matter of pride for him to claim that land's character as a marketable commodity had emerged to its extent in the United States, far more so than in England, where the vestiges of landed aristocracy continued to impair the marketability of land. "In no other part of the civilized world," he boasted, "is land made such an article of commerce, and of such incessant circulation."[66]

Much of Kent's historical discussion simply repeated the historical themes that were evident throughout late eighteenth-century political-legal literature on the origins of property, especially in Blackstone.[67] Kent rehashed Blackstone's depiction of feudalism as a rational adaptation to the peculiar needs of medieval society[68] and the notion of the "natural" superiority of the allodial land regime over feudalism.[69] Moreover, like much of eighteenth-century historical writing about property, Kent's view of history equivocated between the linear and the cyclical visions. He usually depicted the development of land law as a linear and progressive evolution up from feudalism, but occasionally lapsed into cyclical rhetoric in which he described history as the restoration of the allodial regime, the historical wheel come full circle to a past Golden Age.[70]

Despite occasional lapses into cyclical historicism, which might suggest a pessimistic outlook for the republic's future, Kent's historical vision was primarily linear and optimistic. The emerging regime of land ownership in the young nation did not really represent a mere restoration of Saxon liberty (the "Gothic constitution"), and it was not seriously threatened by a lapse into feudal tyranny. The culmination of history was neither a relived feudal society based on restraints on alienation nor the mere restoration of the prefeudal land system. History was moving toward the commercial age, and the highest form of property was property (including land) used for commercial purposes.

This is why it is more accurate to say that the fundamental policy in Kent's account of property law is *marketability*. Alienability is not necessarily the same as marketability, although Kent routinely equated the two. An asset may be transferable but not subject to market exchange. The difference is crucial, for an asset, to be commodified property, must be used for exchange purposes, not merely transferable. It is the market that is focal domain in commodificationist consciousness, and it is the world of the market that Kent thought was the proper locus of property.

The historical story that Kent told continuously associated commerce with human freedom and with the release of individual energy from the restrictions of a repressive (though, again, rational for its time) legal, political, and social order. Feudal restraints on alienation, which he sometimes referred to simply as "the feudal policy," were his central means of symbolizing that order, and Kent paid a great deal of attention to the topic of restraints on alienation. Tracing what he called "the progress of the common law right of alienation from a state of servitude to freedom,"[71] Kent stated that the feudal restraint "was a violent and unnatural state of things, and contrary to the nature and value of property, and the inherent and universal love of independence."[72] Originally well adapted to the needs of feudal society, the system of restraints on alienation of land "eventually proved itself inconsistent with a civilized and pacific state of society."[73] Then, making the crucial associations of alienability with commerce, freedom, and progress, Kent declared:

> [W]herever freedom, commerce, and the arts, penetrate and shed their benign influence, the feudal fabric was gradually undermined. . . . The history of the gradual decline of the feudal restraints . . . upon alienation . . . down to the final recovery of the full and free exercise of the right of disposition, forms an interesting view of the progress of society.[74]

Kent described the commercial stage as enabling a kind of Promethean[75] liberation: individuals for the first time were free to realize their true identities, unhindered by a rigid and artificial social hierarchy. "[I]t has been the great effort of modern times to check or subdue [the feudal regime], and recover the free enjoyment and independence of allodial estates."[76] Through commerce, shackles were cast off, human energy was released, and a new, morally superior personality emerged. What made this liberation possible was the release of property from feudal restraints into commerce—the transformation of land into a commodity.

The Argument from Classical Economics

Adam Smith's classical political economy strongly influenced Kent. This influence was evident in Kent's treatment of the marketability policy. Kent thought that the American legal and political systems had substantially put Smith's theories into practice. Indeed, he said, the purposes of government that Smith outlined in *The Wealth of Nations* were "almost in so many words recognized, and declared to be the end of the union, in the preamble to the constitution of the United States."[77] The legal policy of free alienability of property was one of the most important steps toward realizing Smith's basic principle of "freedom of commerce and industry." This connection was explicitly made in Kent's discussion of entails, perpetuities, and other forms of restraints on alienation.

Kent explained the use of entails on the basis of this psychological insight: "The desire to preserve and perpetuate family influence and property is very prevalent in mankind, and is deeply seated in the human affections."[78] Kent did not condemn the propensity itself; it had, he said, many "beneficial effects." What he condemned rather were the unintended consequences of entails:

> [I]f the doctrine of entails be calculated to stimulate exertion and economy, by the hope of placing the fruits of talent and industry in the possession of a long line of lineal descendants, undisturbed by their folly or extravagance, they have a tendency, on the other hand, to destroy the excitement to action in the issue in tail, and to leave an accumulated mass of property in the hands of the idle and the vicious.[79]

Drawing on Adam Smith's observations of the effect of entailments in Scotland, Kent contended that the harmful effects were evident in Scotland, where, he asserted, fully half the country's land were locked in strict entailments. Smith and other Scottish political economists had condemned entails "as removing a very powerful incentive to persevering industry and honest ambition."[80]

Kent analyzed the problem of perpetuities on much the same reasoning. The term "perpetuity" was frustratingly vague even in Kent's time. The modern meaning of the term (contingent future interests that may vest too remotely) was not as well established in the early nineteenth century as it is today. Rather than having a technical meaning directed at one particular problem, lawyers of Kent's generation tended to apply the term to an array of property settlements that were said to be "inconvenient," including entailments. In Kent's usage, "inconvenience" became shorthand for inalienability or any impairment of property's marketability.

The Political Argument: Marketability and Inequality of Property as Republican

Kent did not rest his attack against entails and perpetuities solely on Adam Smith's classical economic theory. He often mixed the economic argument with a political argument that was certain to strike a familiar and popular chord with his American audience. Kent relied on the residual emotive force of civic republican ideology to support the marketability policy. This move is surprising in one sense because Kent otherwise had little use for republican ideology. He was not merely skeptical but quite contemptuous of virtue as the central value of politics. Human nature would not justify such a theory. Echoing the later views of John Adams, he stated in a letter to Daniel Webster, "[The] evil genius of democracy [is] to be the sport of factions. . . . All theories of government that suppose the mass of people virtuous, and able and willing to act virtuously are plainly utopian, and will remain so until the Saturnian age."[81]

Despite his repudiation of virtue as the core political value, Kent reiterated a syllogism that American legal writers had used in arguing against entails since the time of the Revolution: inalienable property was aristocratic; a landed aristocracy was un-republican; un-republican institutions were un-American; therefore, the legal policy favoring the marketability of property was mandated by the character of American politics. Any arrangement that interfered with the free marketability of property was condemned as un-American. This was true of entails:

> Entailments are recommended in monarchical governments, as a protection to the power and influence of the landed aristocracy; but such a policy has no application to republican establishments, where wealth does no form a permanent distinction, and under which every individual of every family has his equal rights, and is equally invited by the genius of the institutions, to depend upon his own merit and exertions. Every family, stripped of artificial supports, is obliged, in

this country, to repose upon the virtue of its descendants for the perpetuity of its fame.[82]

It was also true of perpetuities, which, Kent observed, "were conducive to the power and grandeur of ancient families, and gratifying to the pride of the aristocracy."[83]

Privatizing Land

Kent's attacks on "aristocratic" land arrangements as unrepublican should not mislead us about Kent's decidedly nonrepublican conception of the function of individual ownership of property. His nonrepublican understanding of property is revealed by his treatment of land as an object of commerce, rather than as the basis for agriculture to provide the material means for citizens to be independent and free from corrupting influences. The clearest evidence of this shift is Kent's casual assumption that land is, after all, a commodity like any other asset. Kent "privatized" land in the sense that he severed the tie that republicans from Harrington to Jefferson had made between individual ownership of land and civic virtue. Land's function was essentially private: the means to create wealth for individual enjoyment, not only by using it for cultivation but also by using it as a market commodity.

For much the same reason as he repudiated the civic function of land, he had no truck with ideas about substantive equality of property. He stated, "[T]he legislature have [*sic*] no right to limit the extent of the acquisition of property. . . . A state of equality as to property is impossible to be maintained, for it is against the laws of our nature."[84] He specifically and peremptorily repudiated Harrington's notion of agrarian land as the foundation for the commonwealth and Montesquieu's thesis that democracy requires laws maintaining equality and prohibiting luxury. "Such suggestions," he sniffed, "are essentially visionary, though they may not be quite as extravagant as some of the reveries of Rousseau, Condorcet, or Godwin."[85] Like his mentor, Hamilton, Kent not only did not regard accumulated wealth and political well-being as incompatible, but he considered them to be mutually reinforcing.

The civic republican understanding of great wealth as corruption was replaced by wealth's association with energy, industry, and liberty. This association was made particularly clear in his discussion of sumptuary laws, which many republicans had thought were necessary to maintain civic virtue. He declared that "[c]ivil government is not entitled . . . to regulate the use of property in the hands of the owners, by sumptuary laws, or any other visionary schemes of frugality and equality."[86] Spurning all notions of the frugal republic, Kent embraced the Hamiltonian vision of the wealthy society fueled by commerce:

> [W]e need only look to the free institutions of Britain, and her descendants, and the prosperity and freedom which they cherish and protect, to be satisfied, that the abundant returns of industry, the fruits of genius, the boundless extent of commerce, the exuberance of wealth, and the cultivation of the liberal arts, with the unfettered use of all of those blessings, are by no means incompatible with the full and perfect enjoyment of enlightened civil liberty. No such fatal union necessarily exists between prosperity and tyranny, or between wealth and national corruption, in the harmonious arrangements of Providence.[87]

What is occurring in this attack on sumptuary laws is the creation of a foundation for the strict separation of private and public spheres, with property firmly in the private camp, that was to become the orthodoxy of late nineteenth-century legal thought. The *vita activa* is no longer civically directed, and property is no longer the material basis for public values. For property to fulfill its private function of creating wealth for the satisfaction of individual desires, the law of property must have the free marketability of property as its core policy. Kent realized this, and this is why he repeatedly stressed marketability above the other major characteristics of individual ownership, use and possession.

Liberality and Technicality, Redux

One might suppose that Kent's commitment to the "commercial policy" would have led him enthusiastically to support efforts to simplify the law of real property, especially the New York statutory revision. Part of the motive for those efforts, after all, was to rid property law of the ancient and complex rules that frustrated the easy transferability of land. For all of his professed zeal for commercializing property, though, Kent was curiously skeptical about, and at times, hostile to, statutory changes of the law of property, especially land law. This skepticism was most clearly evident in his handling of the concepts of "liberality" and "technicality."

Kent was ambivalent about legislative law reform in general, especially in his later years when the forces of Jacksonian democracy pushed for

opening the political process to ordinary people. He feared that the uncontrolled and ignorant biases of the masses would unreflectedly wipe
away the accumulated wisdom of centuries of legal learning. This would
be especially true if the franchise were extended to those who were not
owners of property.[88] A decade after Kent had lost the battle to preserve
the freehold franchise, he would gloomily declare to his brother,

> My opinion is that the admission of universal suffrage [is] incompati-
> ble with government and security to property, and that the govern-
> ment and character of this country are going to ruin. This suffrage
> is too great an excitement for any political machine. It racks its to
> pieces and morals go with it.[89]

Kent was also ambivalent about the emergence of a social order that
is based increasingly on deals, speculations, and exchanges of a growing
variety of forms of wealth, all viewed as mere commodities. By the mid-
1830s, during the height of the Jacksonian fervor for democracy, he would
lament that American society was "becoming selfish, profligate, crazy. . . ."
His prescription for this social malady was the old-fashioned medicine:
"Give me the writings of Addison and Locke, and the Presbyterianism of
Dr. Ripley, Dr. Styles, and old Dr. Rodgers."[90] To be sure, Kent wrote
this at a stage in his life by which he had lost much of his youthful optimism regarding the prospects of preserving the republican polity that the
Founders had set out to create. At the same time, though, this *cri de
coeur* was not just the dyspeptic grumblings of an old conservative, but an
expression of anxiety about the emergence of a new and radically different
culture than that in which he had developed his frame of reference—the
culture of modernity in which the commodity reigned supreme. Kent's
presentation of the dialectic of liberality and technicality have to be interpreted from the perspective of his fear of modernity. The spirit of "liberality," unchecked by "technicality," might produce a crisis of legitimacy, in
which the popular understanding of the distribution of power as the outcome of raw politics rather than as the expression of an underlying natural
order.

Kent borrowed the discourse of "liberality" and "technicality," along
with the closely related dialectic between "feudal" and "allodial" land and
the historical evolutionary thesis, from eighteenth-century legal writers
on both sides of the Atlantic.[91] That discourse, however, had taken on a
somewhat different coloration by Kent's time. The codification debates
and the recent statutory revision of property law in New York strongly

influenced the meanings of "liberality" and "technicality" in the first half of the nineteenth century. Kent, who closely followed the New York revision as a might-have-been reviser, laced his discussion of the law of real property with many comments on the statutory changes. He explicitly related these comments to his overarching theme of liberality and technicality. He further connected that dialectic with two other dialectics— freedom/hierarchy and feudal policy/commercial policy. Liberality was associated with legal simplification, individual freedom, and the "commercial spirit," while technicality was aligned with hierarchy and feudalism. The entire discussion of real property in the *Commentaries,* in fact, was structured by these interrelated sets of dialectically related concepts, which Kent continuously wove into an otherwise dry treatment in a theme-and-variations fashion.

The opening to part 6, entitled "Of the Law Concerning Real Property," immediately established the themes that dominated the entire discussion of land law:

> In passing from the subject of personal to that of real property, the student will immediately perceive that the latter is governed by rules of a distinct and peculiar character. The law concerning real property forms a technical and very artificial system; and though it has felt the influence of the free and commercial spirit of modern ages, it is still very much under the control of principles derived from the feudal policy.[92]

Of course, acknowledging the artificiality of land law's rules did not necessarily mean that they were irrational or unjustifiable. Kent, in fact, went to considerable lengths to justify artificiality and technicality in law as necessary to preserve order. "Technical and artificial rules of long standing and hoary with age," Kent argued, "conduce exceedingly to certainty and fixedness in the law, and are infinitely preferable on that account to rules subject to being bent every day by loose latitudinary reasoning."[93] This argument is now familiar to the point of banality, at least to lawyers. Every first-year law student is taught that clear rules are especially important for real property law. Legal rules that were clear and whose applicability was certain and predictable were necessary so that potential exchangers could easily determine who owns what. (Economists today express this idea as "reducing information costs."[94])

Much more than his characterization of land law's ancient rules as artificial, though, Kent's contrast between technicality and what he called "the commercial spirit of modern ages" would seem to have laid the groundwork for a wholesale assault on the technicality of land law. But that proved not to be Kent's purpose. Instead, Kent's subsequent discussion revealed a deep ambivalence about the extreme technicality of the old common-law rules, continually oscillating between criticism and approval of proposals to simplify land law.

Kent's reactions to the New York Revised Statutes illustrate this ambivalence. Several of the revisers' changes made good sense to Kent because of their effect in simplifying unnecessarily complex topics. Endorsing revisions of the law of powers of appointment,[95] for example, Kent stated:

> It is impossible to make such a technical subject intelligible to any but technical men, but the article *of powers* in the revised statutes, though incapable of being understood by *ley gents* will relieve the profession and conveyancers wonderfully, and bar the introduction into this state of some of the most hidden mysteries of the science.[96]

Kent's reaction to the abolition of the Rule in Shelley's Case was more typical of his response to the project as a whole. The rule, radically boiled down, provides that if a deed or will transfers land "to A for life, then to A's heirs (or heirs of the A's body)," A, not his heirs, who were the apparently intended beneficiaries, take the interest created after the life estate.[97] The decision to abolish the rule, rather than to amend it, was a bold one. The rule was one of the grand old edifices of the common law of estates, second only perhaps to the dreaded Rule against Perpetuities, and an enormous amount of ink had been spilled explicating it. The few lawyers who had mastered must have cried to see so much learning lost in this single provision of the revised statutes. Kent was among the mourners.

The New York revisers, as we saw in chapter 4, decided to throw out the rule for two main reasons. First, it defeated the intentions of the person who transfers property "to A for life, then to A's heirs." It had become, in the revisers' view, "'purely arbitrary and technical,' and calculated to defeat the intentions of those who are ignorant of technical language."[98] Second, the product of sixteenth-century fiscal feudalism, it seemed to have lost all of its original purpose, and had consequently become a notorious vestige of an offensive hierarchical social order.

Kent made two counterarguments. First, he defended the rule as advancing the policy of making land transferable. It did this, he contended, by eliminating the ownership interests of unascertained persons (the heirs of A, a living person, are legally undetermined until A's death) who, obviously, could not consent to transfer the affected piece of land to a willing purchaser.[99]

Kent's second argument is more revealing of his underlying concern. He argued that the rule's very antiquity is evidence of its good sense. "The rule in Shelley's Case," he said, "survived all the rude assaults which it received in the controversy under *Perrin v. Blake,* and it has continued down to the present time in full vigour, with commanding authority, and with its roots struck immoveably deep in the foundations of the English law."[100] With evident sarcasm, Kent continued:

> [I]t is a question for experience to decide, whether this attainable advantage [of giving effect to the intended meaning of the words "to A's heirs"] will overbalance the inconvenience of increasing fetters upon alienation, and shaking confidence in law, by such an entire and complete renunciation of a settled rule of property, memorable for its antiquity, and for the patient cultivation and discipline which it has received.[101]

In a footnote to this last passage, Kent could not resist slumping into sheer nostalgia:

> The juridical scholar, on whom his great master, Coke, has bestowed some portion of the "gladsome light of jurisprudence," will scarcely be able to withhold an involuntary sigh, as he casts a retrospective glance over the piles of learning, devoted to destruction by an edict, as sweeping and unrelenting as the torch of Omar. He must bid adieu forever to the renowned discussions in Shelley's Case, which were so vehement and so protracted as to arouse the sceptre of the haughty Elizabeth. He may equally take leave of the multiplied specimens of profound logic, skilful criticism, and refined distinction, which pervade the varied cases in law and equity, from those of *Shelley* and *Archer,* down to the direct collision between the courts of law and equity, in the time of Lord Hardwicke. He will have no more concern with the powerful and animated discussions in *Perrin v. Blake,* which awakened all that was noble and illustrious in talent and endowment, through every precinct of Westminster Hall. He will have occasion no longer, in pursuit of the learning of that case, to tread the clear and bright paths illuminated by Sir *William Blackstone's* illustrations, or to study and admire the spirited and ingenious dissertation of Hargrave, the comprehensive and profound disquisitions of *Fearne,* the acute and analytical essay of *Preston,* the neat and orderly abridg-

ment of Cruise, and the severe and piercing criticisms of *Reeves.* What
I have, therefore, written on this subject, may be considered, so far
as my native state is concerned, as a humble monument to the memory of departed learning.[102]

This is nostalgia, to be sure, but there is more going on here than just
recherche à la temps perdu. The last line is especially revealing. What Kent
was expressing in homage to "the memory of departed learning" was regret and profound pessimism about the emergence of a participatory political and legal order, replacing the *ancien régime* in which elite lawyers
were the acknowledged wise men to whom everyone else deferred. Kent
expressed his pessimism about the passing of that order—the order that
is naturally ordained for government by the rule of law—even more
starkly in private correspondence with Joseph Story (who shared Kent's
pessimism). Kent stated, "I have no hope that this corrupt and fanatical
age can be reformed without harsh applications, and I think we are running down fast to the lowest depths of degradation."[103] A direct line connects Kent's criticism of the statutory abolition of the Rule in Shelley's
Case with that sentiment.

Members of the legal elite, like Kent and Story, owed their positions
to the existence of a conception of the rule of law as an extraordinarily
complex and fragile political-legal order. Governance through the rule-
of-law ideal, as they understood it, required the leadership of a few special
men with the necessary learning and specialized education to maintain
the delicate equilibrium among conflicting elements.[104] From this perspective, the New York revisers' decision to junk the Rule in Shelley's Case
for its excessive complexity was a perfect example of liberality as democracy gone awry. Technicality made the law inaccessible to ordinary people,
even to much of the bar, but that was a consequence of the nature of the
rule-of-law order. That the revisers could not see the benefits of so venerable a rule as Shelley's Case indicated their own inadequate understanding
of the legal order. If liberality were carried too far, as the New York Revised Statutes did, it would undermine the stability of the natural order
essential to the existence of the inherently fragile rule-of-law regime.

Kent criticized another major change in the New York Revised Statutes: the severe restriction in the types of enforceable trusts. Kent roman-
ticized equity generally throughout the *Commentaries,* allying it with liberality in the dialectic with technicality.[105] He singled out the trust as
perhaps equity's greatest triumph. The rationality of the trust institution

and the body of rules that English equity judges had developed to protect
and to regulate it were demonstrated by their capacity to adapt to extraordinary changes in social conditions in the centuries since the trust was
first recognized. "The English system of trusts is a rational and just code,
adapted to the improvements, and wealth, and wants of the nation, and
it has been gradually reared and perfected by the sage reflections of a
succession of eminent men."[106] Kent was not looking to the past in extol-
ling the virtues of the trust and trust law; he was looking to a future in
which even more extraordinary changes awaited. Time does not change
all things, though. One aspect of the past and present that would surely
never change is human nature, and this was where Kent thought the revisers made their greatest mistake. He thought that efforts to bar propertied
elites from recreating social hierarchy through family property settlements
were likely to prove futile. The centuries-old popularity of trusts used for
this purpose, he thought, exemplified this inescapable characteristic of
societies:

> The usages of a civilized people are the gradual result of their wants
> and wishes. They form the best portion of their laws; opinions and
> habits coincide; they are accommodated to circumstances; and mold
> themselves to the complicated demands of wealth and refinements.
> We cannot hope to check the enterprising spirit of gain, the pride
> of families, the anxiety of parents, the importunities of luxury, the
> fixedness of habits, the subtleties of intellect. They are incessantly
> active in engendering distinctions calculated to elude, impair, or un-
> dermine, the fairest and proudest models of legislation that can be
> matured in the closet, and ushered into the world, under the impos-
> ing forms of legislative sanction.[107]

This view of human nature underlay Kent's attack on the revision of
trust law, which was perhaps the most vigorous criticism he had of the
entire project. Narrowing the types of trusts that one could create to the
list of four that the revised statutes prescribed, Kent thought, did not trim
fat alone, but cut into the very muscle of the institution of trusts.

> The apprehension is, that the boundaries prescribed will prove too
> restricted for the future exigencies of society, and bar the jurisdiction
> of equity over many cases of trusts which ought to be protected and
> enforced, but which do not come within the enumerated list, nor
> belong strictly to the class of resulting trusts. The attempt to bring

all trusts within the narrow compass, strikes me as one of the most questionable undertakings in the whole business of the revision.[108]

The anxious tone to Kent's defense of the extant system of trusts suggests that more was at work here than merely his judgment that the attempt to limit the purposes of trusts would prove futile. One can reasonably speculate that the source of this anxiety was Kent's perception of the statutory revision as threatening the orthodox social meaning of trusts.

Perhaps no legal institution—certainly no property-related institution—was more closely associated, both functionally and symbolically, with the maintenance of the prevailing social order than the trust. We are inclined to think of the trust as something more commonly used by wealthy elites in England than in the United States, at least through the first half of the nineteenth century, and that is probably so. But trusts were hardly a rarity among wealthy American families in the antebellum period.[109] Here, as well as in England, the trust was the central legal device by which elites conserved patrimonial capital in one generation and then transferred it to the next generation. It was, moreover, the most important legal institution through which the established social hierarchy reproduced itself over time. As such, it had enormous symbolic power as well as functional importance. It symbolized the stability of the social order. Primogeniture, entails, and strict settlements, which for centuries so prominently symbolized England's land-based social hierarchy, were largely unavailable to Americans, but by the early nineteenth century the trust already performed the same symbolic purpose here. To attack the extant system of trusts, then, was to undermine the existing social order. Indeed, it was to attack the very idea of a stable social hierarchy in an out-of-control impulse to democratize American society. It was one thing to abolish primogeniture and entails, both symbols of formal aristocracy, but it was entirely a different matter to abolish or radically shrink the symbol of a social order whose existence was simply part of the nature of things. From Kent's perspective, such an action was not only likely to be futile, it was downright dangerous.

Kent's defense of the conventional regime of trusts illustrates the limits of his acceptance of the commodificationist outlook. He attached greater importance to social stability than he did to the legal policy of facilitating the transferability of property. The trust revisions, after all, were animated by policy concerns that directly reflected commodificationist thinking. The revisers repeatedly stressed their desire to eliminate the "inconveniences" of trusts to buyers and sellers of land and to creditors, emphasizing that the types of trusts they had abolished were the ones that most cluttered up land titles and defrauded creditors.[110] Kent was willing to sacrifice the "commercial policy" and to check the commodification of land to the extent necessary to maintain the social order that his generation had inherited from their eighteen-century forebears. He was eager to cast away the linkage between property and virtue on which his ancestors insisted and embrace a more privatized, certainly noncivic attitude toward property. But he had not fully internalized the *Weltanschauung* of the newly emergent entrepreneurial class, which was more than willing to suffer the social consequences of transforming property into a fully fluid, dynamic commodity.

Antebellum Statutory Law Reform Revisited: The Married Women's Property Laws

T HE SCHOLARSHIP CONCERNING the statutory reform of the law of married women's property between 1830 and 1850 is a well-plowed field. Recent historical work by Norma Basch, Marylynn Salmon, Richard Chused, Peggy Rabkin, Elizabeth Warbasse, Reva Siegel, and others[1] has established that these acts did not, as Norma Basch has put it, "create a new prototype."[2] It did not, that is, create a fundamental reconfiguration in the power or property relations between husbands and wives; it modified rather than revolutionized. The nineteenth-century legislation gave married women certain legal powers to control property that they lacked at common law, including the power of testation. To that extent, it did increase the economic power of wives within families that had capital.[3] It did not, however, end economic patriarchy as the norm for American families.

This chapter will focus on the relationship between the antebellum married women's property laws and the rising ideology of property-as-commodity. Commodification, i.e., the understanding of property's role exclusively in economic terms, provides a valuable framework within which to interpret the legislative changes made in the legal status of married women as property owners in the first half of the nineteenth century. Within that framework, several important questions concern the relationship between the statutory reforms and commodificationist ideology. First, was the statutory creation of separate property interests for married women undertaken for the purpose of protecting certain classes of persons? And if so, whom? Married women or their husbands? Second, to the extent that protectionism did underlie the married women's property acts, how did antebellum legal writers and law reformers understand legal protectionism to relate to the legal policy of free market transferability, the core of the commodified conception of property?

On the face of things, the relationship between the vision of property as commodity and antebellum marital property reforms is ambiguous. On the one hand, the married women's property laws appear to be basically consistent with the social and political values that legal writers associated with the conception of property as commodity, namely, individual self-determination and formal equality. The statutory revisions of marital property law created property rights over which married women had, at least formally, enhanced autonomous control and which they could use or transfer for their own purposes, independently of their husbands and their husbands' creditors.

On the other hand, the debates over reform of marital property law reveal that the liberation of women's property was also motivated by a protectionist outlook. That outlook could be seen as opposed to the social vision of individual self-determination that the commodificationist ideology expressed. Protectionism was more typically part of the premodern legal culture that property-as-commodity was replacing. At the root of the modern culture's understanding of commodified property were the related notions that the purpose of property is to serve the market and that in the unconstrained market all individuals would be equally free from formal social hierarchies and thereby create their own destinies. The "feudal" restraints on alienation were viewed as objectionable precisely because they interfered with the market's liberating function. To the extent that the married women's property acts were motivated by the desire to protect certain classes of people from the potentially harmful consequences of being autonomous property owners, these reforms, despite their apparently liberating thrust, seem incompatible with the commodificationism.

Legal discourse about the status of married women as property owners, then, was like the discourse surrounding other property issues in the nineteenth century: dialectical. The dialectic was between two visions of the proper relationship between wives, husbands, and property, that is, two normative understandings of how property should mediate the relationship between husbands and wives. One vision, which historically dominated the Anglo-American legal treatment of married women's property until well into the nineteenth century, was protectionist. With respect to married women as property owners, two protectionist theories were at issue in the nineteenth century: protection of wives *by* husbands (basically a marital privacy issue) and protection of wives *against* their husbands. It is this latter issue with which this chapter is concerned.

The competing vision, which was ascendant from the middle of the nineteenth century on, extended the commodity conception of property to married women. The function of property in relation to married women gradually changed from one of protection to the modern notion of enabling autonomous individuals to pursue their own desires and goals. The shift between these property conceptions rested in turn on a shift from a premodern, overtly hierarchical model of the relation between husbands and wives toward a modern model, in which the relationship is, at least formally, less hierarchical. As married women increasingly came to be viewed as formal equals to their husbands, their status as property owners changed from passive beneficiaries to active managers.

These changes did not end the dialectic with respect to women's status as property owners. The changes in legal thought and legal practice that occurred during the antebellum period did not yield complete formal equality in property rights between husbands and wives, and it certainly did not produce substantive equality between spouses, that is, how much property husbands and wives individually owned. Property was emphatically *not* degendered by the beginning of the twentieth century, and is not today.[4] To a very considerable extent legal thought and writing about women and property remains structured by the dialectic of protectionism and autonomy.

Married women's property law developed unevenly in different states in the first half of the nineteenth century. One important reason for this is the very different experiences in different states of equity, whose precedents greatly affected marital property reform. New York will be our focus for two reasons: first, as with other aspects of antebellum statutory reform of property law, New York's revisions influenced legislative changes in other states; second, reforms of other parts of property law, where New York took the lead, themselves served as catalysts for change of marital property law. A complete picture of the revision of the law of married women's property requires an understanding of how specific changes in the two stages of statutory reform were interrelated. Before describing how the modern conception of property affect marital property law in New York, it is necessary first to sketch the premodern scene.

Marital Property in Premodern Legal Culture

Feudal English law had constructed the legal meaning of marriage in terms of a metaphor that vividly expressed the subordinated role of married women in the marital property relationship: Husband and wife were said to be one person and that person was the husband.

While other overtly hierarchical concepts of feudal land law were abolished during the revolutionary period as inconsistent with the tenets of republicanism, the single-person metaphor, adopted by colonial American judges, survived. The single-person theory's justification was that it was necessary as a legal restraint on husbands from coercing their wives. Even the few republican legal writers who objected to the metaphor nevertheless accepted this justification.

The metaphor of a married couple's single identity was important not only because of its direct consequences for married women's powers, rights, and duties in property transactions, but also because of its rhetorical force. As Norma Basch has pointed out, "as a linguistic device [i]t established a way of thinking about wives and marriage." Of course, lawyers understood that the metaphor was only a fiction, and, like all legal fictions, it was riddled with exceptions and manipulated to produce acceptable results. Still, the metaphor had a powerful hold on the premodern legal and popular consciousness. It was, as Basch has aptly concluded, "a metaphor of enormous power."[5]

The single-identity theory was explained and rationalized in explicitly protectionist terms through the doctrine of coverture. Nowhere was this more clearly expressed than in Blackstone's discussion of *baron* and *feme*. "By marriage," Blackstone began, "the husband and wife are one person in law."

> [T]he very being or legal existence of the woman is suspended during the marriage, or at least is incorporated and consolidated into that of the husband: under whole wing, protection, and *cover*, she performs everything; and is therefore called in our law-french a *feme-covert;* is said to be *covert-baron,* or under the protection and influence of her husband, her baron, or lord; and her condition during her marriage is called her *coverture.*[6]

Curiously, Blackstone emphasized that marriage is nothing more than a civil contract, like other contracts. The contractual character of marriage was seen to suggest that the two parties are equals and that the terms and rights and duties of the parties under the contract are set according to the private intentions of the two individuals. Yet, the doctrine of coverture transforms the relationship between the two contracting parties from that of legal equals to a legal hierarchy. This hierarchical relationship, further-more, is set by law, with no opportunity for the parties to change it. As Hendrik Hartog has pointed out, "The point of marriage was to create a public structure of rights and duties, not alterable by the wills, goals, or desires of husbands and wives."[7]

How, then, could Blackstone characterize marriage as a contract? At least through the mid-nineteenth century, Anglo-American law consid-ered marriage to be a genuine contract, but genuine in the sense that it was consensually created by a man and a woman, not in the sense that its terms were negotiated by the parties.[8] Marriage created a public rela-tionship, the terms of which were preset by law.[9]

Coverture imposed many legal disabilities on married women. By obliterating the wife's legal existence, it imposed on married women a formal disability to own or control most property, even assets that they had brought into the marriage. All tangible personal property that the wife brought into the marriage, including furniture, jewelry, and money, became the husband's. While he did not have complete control over it, he had substantial use of it and could sell or dispose of it during his lifetime. He also had testamentary control over it (except for so-called chattels real, i.e., leases). Moreover, his creditors could attach her tangi-bles to pay off his debts. Her intangible personalty, including securities, became his only if and after he had transferred legal title to his name.

The picture was somewhat different with respect to real property. Here the single-identity metaphor was not strictly followed. The wife did not lose title to land that she owned at the time of her marriage, keeping her separate identity as a property owner to this extent. She did lose the power to manage her real property, and the husband had an absolute right to all the rents and profits during their joint lives for his own use. Importantly, though, he could not convey her land without her consent. If he trans-ferred her land without her consent, she or her representative could re-cover it after his death. By the same token, though, married women could not convey or devise land without their husbands' permission.[10] While management powers obviously conferred on husbands substantial control over their wives' land, it did not empower them unilaterally to use the land as a market commodity.

The single-identity theory imposed procedural disabilities on mar-ried women as well as subordinating their status substantively. Married women could not sue others for injury to person or property without their husbands' permission. Nor could a married women be sued in her sole name; her husband had to be named as a co-defendant. Coverture meant that husbands and wives, who were legally one person, could not contract with each other. Nor could either testify in court against the other. Married women could contract with third parties, but only for "necessaries." Husbands, who were legally obligated to maintain their wives, were liable for debts that their wives incurred for necessaries. Beyond necessaries, married women could contract with third persons only as agents for their husbands, or, as Blackstone put it, in "representation of, her lord."[11]

The inferior treatment of married women persisted even after death with respect to husbands' and wives' respective rights to their deceased spouse's property. On the wife's death, if she died with at least one surviving child, the husband had a life estate, known as curtesy, in all his wife's land. The husband's curtesy interest, in fact, was created prior to his wife's death. It was continuous as marriage through widowerhood. Moreover, curtesy extended to equitable estates that the wife held as trust beneficiary. It did not give the husband fee simple ownership; if the husband were to die without children surviving him, his wife's land reverted to her family.

By contrast, the wife's dower interest in land that her late husband owned was much less substantial. As tenant in dower, she had a life estate only in one-third of lands and tenements that he possessed during marriage. Dower did not apply to husbands' equitable trust estates. The dower right could not be barred, but the wife would lose it if she remarried. Nevertheless, dower was a positive change for the widow. It gave her, so long as she remained a widow, a degree of financial freedom that she did not enjoy during marriage. It represented a real and beneficial property interest, one that grasping husbands were trying constantly to get their wives to give up.

Important differences existed between English and American coverture law, both during the colonial period and thereafter. It is impossible to generalize about American marital property law, either as a system of formal rules or as a social practice, because the laws of the different states varied considerably, although primarily by regions rather than by states.[12] There were considerable changes in dower, for example, with some parts of the country being more favorable for women than English law and others less. Nevertheless, the basic legal institution of coverture was very much a part of American law, and for the most part the subordinated status of married women that so characteristic English common law was also true in America.[13]

Even looking just at English law, however, the picture painted thus far of married women's property interests is radically incomplete. It ignores ecclesiastical law. It ignores the variations that existed in English law in different localities. Most important, it ignores the crucial role that equitable devices played in marital property arrangements. During the seventeenth century, English equity judges avoided the restrictions that the common law imposed on married women as property owners by permitting settlors to create trusts for the separate use of married women. Wealthy fathers who wanted to protect their daughters from being financially dominated by their husbands after marriage could convey or devise property in trust to pay the income solely to their married daughters. Chancery decisions in the late eighteenth century threatened this arrangement's protective purpose. In one case, the Chancellor held that a husband's creditors could enforce against his wife's separate equitable estate a bond that she had executed to secure the husband's debts.[14] A few years later, the Chancellor enforced a wife's exercise of a power of appointment conveying to her husband's creditor the entire equitable estate that had been created for her just two weeks before she exercised the power.[15] These decisions did not reflect disapproval of the intention of using the trust as an arrangement for securing separate property interests for married women. In both cases the Chancellor expressed his sympathy with the settlor, but stated that he was bound by precedents to hold as he did.

In a fashion characteristic of lawyers for wealthy settlors, lawyers quickly avoided the impact of these decisions, however, by developing the so-called restraint on anticipation. Inserted in a trust for a married woman, this clause required that the trustee could pay income only to the intended beneficiary, depriving her of the power to transform her equitable right to a future stream of income into a fixed capital sum by transferring it to another person. This device was soon enforced by equity judges, who, as members of the same social class as the creators of these trusts, were quite sympathetic with the protective motive.[16] This sympathy was clearly indicated by the Chancellor in an 1839 case enforcing a restraint on anticipation:

> When this Court first established the separate estate, it violated the laws of property as between husband and wife; but it was thought beneficial, and it prevailed. It being once settled that a wife might enjoy separate estate as a *feme sole,* the laws of property attached to this new estate; and it was found, as part of such law, that the power

of alienation belonged to the wife, and was destructive of the security intended for it. Equity again interfered, and by another violation of the laws of property supported the validity of the prohibition against alienation. . . . Why then should not equity in this case also interfere; and if it cannot protect the wife consistently with the ordinary rules of property, extend its own rules with respect to the separate estate, so as to secure to her the enjoyment of that estate which has been so invented for her benefit?[17]

Not all equitable property arrangements for married women were so protective. English equity judges gradually permitted settlors to create trusts that gave married women some of the same powers single women enjoyed. More important, by the end of the eighteenth century it was possible to create a premarital contract for married women that did not involve a trust. Nevertheless, equity's willingness to allow married women a measure of autonomy as property owners was less an expression of the commodificationist conception of property than it was an example of the continuing force of equity's tradition of protectionism at the end of the eighteenth century.[18]

American judges adopted these English equity developments and in some cases expanded them. This was especially true in New York in the early nineteenth century. Between 1815 and 1848, New York courts enforced two types of trusts for married women: genuinely protective trusts, in which the trustee held virtually all control over trust property for the benefit of a married woman, and trusts in which the married woman, though beneficiary, had substantial control over her equitable estate.[19] While the boundary between these two types of trusts was quite fuzzy, the second proved especially influential for later legislative changes. Far more than prior equitable developments, its emergence signaled the shift from a premodern to a modern understanding of property in the context of married women's property rights.

Full recognition of the second trust type came in a famous—and pro-longed—litigation known as the *Jaques* cases. A widow named Mary Alexander had created, pursuant to a marriage settlement, a trust of all her considerable estate for herself until her marriage to John Jaques and thereafter for her own benefit, "free from the control of her husband, and at her absolute disposal." She reserved to herself and her husband a power to appoint the trust property to whomever they designated and to herself a power to appoint the property in her will. After her marriage, she exercised, with her husband's concurrence, her power of appointment by deeding all of her real estate to Robert Jaques, a brother of her husband, as trustee, directing that after her death, he should sell the land and pay one-third of the proceeds each to her husband, her relatives, and the Methodist Episcopal church.

After she died, the church alleged that during the marriage, the husband "by artful contrivances" had misappropriated most of her personalty, including valuable securities, and had used the income from her real estate for his own benefit. It was clear that John Jaques had treated her separate estate as his own, which it would have been under the law of coverture if the trust for her separate estate was not enforceable. John contended that he and his wife had agreed that he would use her separate estate to support them and that this agreement was a valid exercise of her powers under the trust. The church argued that the agreement was not enforceable because the deed of settlement did not expressly authorize this use of Mary Jaques's separate estate.

The issue was whether Mary Jaques was a *feme sole* or instead was dependent, as trust beneficiary, on the continuing concurrence of the trustee. Stated more directly, the real question was whether the trust was a shell, or a mere fictive arrangement. The New York courts, lacking any precedents of their own, turned to English chancery decisions. The English cases were not entirely clear on this question, however, and the New York courts read them differently.

Chancellor Kent took the view that the wife had only such powers over her separate estate as were expressly spelled out in the instrument. He was concerned with coercion of wives by their husbands. He believed that the policy of protection against coercion applied to a married woman with a separate estate as well as to a woman without one. The separate estate conferred on the wife only such authority as was specifically stated in the trust instrument. Applying that principle, he concluded that since the second trust did not expressly relieve the husband of his common law duty of support, the rents from that trust could not be used for the family's maintenance.[20]

The Court of Errors rejected Kent's decision as a misreading of the English cases. The court ruled that a married woman could use or dispose of her separate estate in any way she wished unless the deed of settlement expressly prohibited it.[21] The court stated the presumption was that with respect to her separate estate a married woman is considered to be a *feme sole*.

The effect of this principle (although certainly not the intent of the

Court of Errors) was substantially to enhance the separate estate as a commodified property interest that married woman could use the same as men could deal with their property. It meant that one could create—indeed one would be presumed to have created—a trust for a married woman in which the trustee was largely relegated to a nominal role and did not act as a surrogate for either the woman's husband or her father. This presumption greatly undermined the protectionist approach toward married woman as property owners. Kent had concluded that protection had been the arrangement's original rationale, but he had a good deal of trouble finding precedents supporting that interpretation.

The real significance of the *Jaques* decision was its influence on the ideology of married women's property law. Practically, the equitable separate estate had only a limited impact in American society. As a device for securing autonomy for married women, it was largely confined the wealthier classes, including professionals and merchants, and not to the laboring class. Ideologically, however, the decision was important as a signal that judicial thinking was changing on the status of married women as property owners. The old assumption that wives needed legal protection for their property against the depredations of their husbands was weakening.[22]

Still, the case did not signal a clear shift in elite legal consciousness away from the premodern protectionist ideology. The judges of the Court of Errors, who were well aware of the consequences of their decision, expressed their personal disapproval of the change in married women's status as property owners. Chief Judge Spencer asserted: "Generally speaking, the rules of the common law, which give to the common law all the wife's personal property, and the rents and profits of her real estate during coverture, are better calculated . . . to secure domestic tranquillity and happiness, than settlements securing to the wife a property separate from and independent of the control of the husband."[23]

Judge Platt's opinion for the court was even more hostile to marriage settlements. Their effect, he wrote, was to give the wife "the amphibious character of a *feme covert* and a *feme sole*." His critique of marriage settlements is worth quoting because it reflects his perception that the settlement was an institution of a modern society in which marriage had been degraded:

A wife, in the *independent enjoyment of her separate estate,* armed with distrust of her husband, and shutting out his affections and confidence, by refusing to give her own in mutual exchange, is an object of compassion and disgust. Legal chastity cannot be denied her: but there is danger, that the sacred institutions of marriage may degenerate into mere form. It is sometimes, in practice, little more than legalized prostitution; and the parties seem to have no higher object than sexual intercourse, and the sanction of legitimacy for their offspring.[24]

He could not act on his own personal feelings, however, because, as he read them, the cases had approved the use of marriage settlements. As long as there were going to be such arrangements, wives should be allowed to use her separate property freely and not be restricted by the language of the trust instrument specifically identifying a single mode of disposition. Modernity, it seemed, was here to stay, for better or worse.

The Stages of Statutory Reform

Legislative reform of married women's disabilities as property owners under the common law appeared in three stages between 1840[25] and 1880.[26] The first stage occurred largely during the 1840s, when nearly every state and territory made some kind of statutory change in its law concerning married women's property.[27] These statutes were primarily debtor-protection measures and did not attempt directly to change the status of married women as property owners from *feme covert* to *feme sole*. They protected a wife's property, usually both real and personal, from her husband's debts.

Several factors led legislatures to enact these statutes. Most important, perhaps, was the widespread and devastating economic depression throughout the nation that followed the Panic of 1837.[28] The collapse of industrial, agricultural, and commercial sectors of the economy prompted both state and federal legislatures to make many changes in laws concerning debtors' rights and banking. The general thrust of these changes was to protect debtors from attachment by their creditors. The first married women's acts operated very much like these exemption laws and fit quite comfortably with their general ideology of protecting family property.

A second contributing factor was the increasing legislative revision of other aspects of coverture law that occurred prior to 1840. Inheritance rules were changed more favorably for wives, imprisonment for debt was abolished for married women (but not for men), and land grant legislation provided benefits for widows. The changes that many states made in their probate codes illustrate the thrust of this group of statutory reforms. The new codes introduced the idea of granting widows a nonbarrable right to elect between taking what their husbands had devised to them by will or taking a fixed share, usually an intestate share, from their husbands' estates, including personalty. These elective share statutes extended the earlier practice of allowing widows to renounce their husbands' will in favor of dower. While they did not alter the balance of power between husband and wife during marriage, they did create an opportunity for the wife on her husband's death to regain some or all of the personalty that she had lost to her husband when she married.

A third factor encouraging reform of marital property law at this time was the more generalized attack on the common law and the democratic sensibility that underlay this attack. Along with future interests, fee tails, and land tenures, the common-law doctrine that husband and wife were one legal person seemed to many critics a relic of a feudal hierarchical society that was incompatible with democracy. It was one thing to consider white married women vulnerable and less competent than their husbands; it was quite another thing to maintain the fiction that married women have no separate legal identity. Besides, that legal fiction, like other legal fictions, was riddled with exceptions that one could exploit— if one could afford a clever lawyer. The marital property regime based on the single-person metaphor, then, was yet another area of law whose excessive complexity effectively meant that the overwhelming majority of people could not arrange their affairs as they wanted.

The perception of the common law of married women's property as undemocratic was even more unavoidable after Jacksonian suffrage reform took place. New York had abolished property requirements for white male adults in 1826, but extension of the franchise did not include women. This fact further isolated white women politically and made their legal inequality even more obvious to reformers. While dominant understanding of democracy did not yet require or justify giving the franchise to white women, it did seem to warrant at least abolishing the feudal single-identity fiction.

Many of the statutes that were part of this first stage of reform stated in general terms that a married woman could hold property "to her sole and separate use, as if she were a single female." Any possibility that such broad language would be used to dismantle the paternalistic coverture regime was lost when court interpreted the statutes narrowly. The pattern for a narrow reading of this language was set earlier when courts construed similar language appearing in trust instruments. Implicitly following the reasoning on which Kent had relied in the *Jaques* case, they relied on the absence of any provision in the instruments explicitly giving wives power to dispose of their separate estates to mean that married women could not contract or devise their separate estate assets. Extending this cramped interpretation, courts interpreted the statutes merely to prohibit husbands from disposing of their wives separate estates, leaving intact all of the other disabilities that coverture law imposed on married women. The effect was to make these statutes nothing more than another species of exempt-property legislation.[29]

The second stage of reform legislation established by statute the married women's separate estate. These statutes, which were passed from the 1840s through the Civil War, extended the earlier generation of reform statutes by adopting the equitable estate model. The New York statute, discussed below, is the best known of this group of statutes. Many of them, especially those enacted in the 1840s and 1850s, required the use of a trustee, indicating the continuing force of the protectionist conception. By 1860, most Northern states, following the lead of equity court decisions concerning the equitable separate estate, had eliminated the need for an intervening trustee; Southern states took longer to reach this view.[30] While this had hardly a radical change, it did clearly indicate that the future of married women's status as property owners was away from the traditional protectionist and hierarchical approach.

The third stage occurred in the late nineteenth century. The basic thrust of these statutes was to eliminate the special status of property owned by married women. Marital property law abandoned its traditional approach of immunizing married women's property from husbands and exempting the separate estate assets from the claims of creditors. Instead husbands and wives became jointly liable for purchases made for family purposes and were separately liable for individual investments.[31] These developments signaled an end—at least formally—to protectionism as the exclusive vision governing the property relations of married women.

The 1848 New York Married Women's Property Act

Passage of the 1848 New York Married Women's Property Act followed agitation for reform of marital property law in the New York legislature that continued at least since 1836. The opening salvo against the common law of marital property was fired that year by Thomas Herttell, a Democratic assemblyman who introduced a resolution for appointment of a legislative committee to report on married women's property in New York. From then until his death in 1847 he led a continuous campaign for legislative reform of married women's property law, introducing a series of bills before the New York Assembly. Herttell attempted to gain support for his first bill, filed in 1837,[32] by publishing a pamphlet that sounded virtually all of the dominant themes echoing throughout the subsequent legal debate: debtor protection, attacks on the common law as anachronistic and undemocratic, and the confusion caused by the earlier statutory revision of trusts.[33]

Herttell made one additional argument that was conspicuously absent from the legal discourse that led to enactment of the 1848 act: he argued that married women were entitled to full powers of ownership as a natural right. Women had ownership rights while they were single, and nothing about marriage justified depriving them of these rights. Analogizing the status of married women to that of African slaves,[34] Herttell argued that the common law violated natural law and constitutional principles of equal protection and due process. He asserted: "Married women, equally with males and unmarried females, possess the right of *life, liberty,* and *PROPERTY* and are equally entitled to be protected in all three."[35] This line of argument led him to advocate changes far more sweeping than those eventually adopted. These changes included enabling wives to hold legal title to assets acquired as their own wages as well as through inheritance.

Most supporters of the 1848 act rejected Herttell's natural rights argument, basing their support instead on more pragmatic arguments like debtor relief and confusion in the 1828 revision of trust law. This difference between Herttell and the majority of supporters of married women's property reform was neither trivial nor merely strategic; it was a basic ideological difference between radical egalitarians like Herttell and the centrist ideology that was behind the 1848 act.[36] Herttell's bill would have shifted away from the protectionist model of married women's property relations toward a model that was at once far more egalitarian and compatible with the commodificationist understanding of property. The 1848 act, by contrast, improved married women's formal legal status as property owners but fell far short of placing them on a par, either substantively or even merely formally, with men. Elite legal thought still viewed the social relationship between husbands and wives—and men and women generally—hierarchically. The persistent power of that model of social relations gave the protectionist conception of married women's property continuing validity even while statutory reform partially commodified married women's property.

A major concern that centrist law reformers shared with Herttell was the confusion concerning the status of the trust for married women that resulted from the trust provisions of 1828 Revised Statutes. Those provisions had numerous shortcomings. The statutes did not mention trusts of personal property as one of the types that could still be created, seemingly eliminating all trusts of personalty. This was completely contrary to the interests of fathers (and widows!) whose wealth was held in securities, debts, and the other forms of intangible personalty that were by now replacing land as the more important form of wealth. Elite lawyers, who represented these benefactors, were eager to revise the trust provisions for this reason alone, but there was more. Many lawyers interpreted the Revised Statutes to provide that when a trust or a power of appointment had been created in favor of an unmarried woman, her subsequent marriage automatically shifted the property subject to the trust or power to the woman's husband. As Herttell observed,

> the right of a female after marriage, to execute a *trust* and *power created before marriage,* is so questionable, that it is seldom hazarded and never attempted by any well informed and discreet parent, to secure the property by such means, to a daughter and her children, with a view to protect it from loss or waste through the misfortune of a good, or the misconduct of a bad husband.[37]

A third problem resulted from judicial interpretation of the 1830 amendment of the trust provisions providing that the trustee might apply the trust property to "use" of the beneficiary rather than just for her or his support and education. The courts had interpreted the amendment to mean that in the case of a married woman's trust, the trustee, not the married woman, had the power to decide whether she needed anything from pins to hosiery. That interpretation carried protectionism to an absurd extreme in the view of Herttell and centrists alike.

In a well-known book,[38] Mary Beard argued that the married woman's equitable estate made legislative reform largely unnecessary. Through this device, she reasoned, married women already had gained the ability to own property autonomously. The push for married women's property statutes occurred, she concluded, because advocates for women's rights were ignorant about the equitable estate. Whatever merits this argument may have had prior to the 1828 revision of trust law,[39] it was simply wrong after that revision. The problems in the 1828 statute left the equitable estate too uncertain a device for assuring a married woman's ability to use and control her own assets. Moreover, as Peggy Rabkin has pointed out, by converting all equitable estates (other than those expressly exempted) into legal estates, the 1828 statute undermined the project of liberating married women's property from the control of their husbands. "[S]ince the legal estate of a married woman . . . belonged to her husband, if her equitable estate were to be executed into a legal estate, she would lose her equitable estate or beneficial ownership without gaining a corresponding legal estate."[40]

Further confusion about the viability of the equitable estate for married women resulted from the fact that the New York Constitution of 1846 abolished the Court of Chancery, which previously had exclusive jurisdiction to enforce all trusts. Equity jurisdiction was transferred to the state's common law courts.[41] Equity, as a discrete legal institution, was considerably unpopular—public dislike of separate courts of equity had a long and distinguished pedigree. Chancery was an anathema to many lawyers and nonlawyers alike, especially in the wake of Jacksonian calls for democratization of the law but dating back much earlier.[42] Critics of equity courts did not deny equity's role as a law reform institution, and conceded that it was a primary source of "liberality" that ameliorated much of the common law's "technicality." Still, they considered it an elitist and undemocratic institution that served the interests only of the wealthy, who could afford its mysterious forms. As Norma Basch has aptly stated, "Probably the safest and popular argument made on behalf of reform was a democratic one, not on behalf of women relative to men, but on behalf of ordinaries relative to elites."[43] Arrangements like the trust for married women were considered antithetical to the goal of making law more accessible.

A move to clarify the effect of this change on married women's property was afoot when the delegates voted in favor of inserting a married women's property clause in the constitution. The clause constitutionalized the principle of a married woman's legal power to own property autonomously, and would have avoided, at least formally, the democratic objection of unequal access to the equitable estate device. After a heated debate in the convention, however, the delegates rescinded the vote. The convention was divided over whether the principle of autonomy of ownership for married women should be embodied in constitutional form, and, more deeply, over the continuing strength of the hierarchical model of social relations between husbands and wives.

Only two short years after the defeat of the constitutional change, the New York legislature overwhelmingly[44] adopted a married women's property statute. No new arguments appeared in the debates. Indeed, the debates over the 1848 bill were a replay of the 1846 debates. The remarkable turnaround was the result of changes in the legislature's membership: none of the constitutional provision's opponents sat in the 1848 legislature.[45]

The effect of the 1848 statute was essentially to legalize the equitable estate device. Section 1 provided that "[t]he real and personal property of any female who may hereafter marry, and which she shall own at the time of marriage, and the rents and profits thereof shall not be subject to the disposal of her husband, nor be liable for his debts, and shall continue her sole and separate property, as if she were a single female."[46] This section also specifically provided that a wife's separate property was not to be subject to her husband's debts. Section 2 took the seemingly sensible step of extending the same language to the property of women already married.[47] The constitutional validity of this retroactive change, however, was doubtful, and the provision was later declared unconstitutional.[48] Section 3 gave married women the legal ability to receive real and personal property by gift, grant, or devise for her "sole and separate use," free from claims of her husband or his creditors. The "sole and separate use" language tracked the language routinely used in equitable instruments for married women and invited courts to construe the statutory meaning on the basis of Chancery precedents. Finally, section 4 provided that all premarital contracts remained enforceable after marriage.

The act's sponsors later claimed more credit for it than it was due. "We meant," asserted George Geddes, one of the bill's leaders in the state Senate, "to strike a hard blow and if possible shake the old laws to their foundations."[49] If this was indeed the intention of the act's authors, their achievement fell far short of the mark. The act's scope was extremely limited. By prohibiting only a husband's "disposal" of his wife's separate estate, the statute left intact the other common-law restrictions on married women's autonomy.

Two restrictions were especially important. Under the statute, husbands continued to hold the power to manage their wives' property. This meant that the statute left married women who engaged in any sort of commercial or entrepreneurial activity, including running a family store or cottage business or even a family farm, formally powerless with respect to managerial control. Of course, lack of formal power did not necessarily mean that married women who ran family ventures in fact were powerless, and doubtless in many cases they were not. Still, the legal disability to manage their own assets remained.

The second restriction indicates even more clearly how far away that reform measure was from extending the commodificationist understanding to the domestic sphere. Under the statute, married women lacked legal power unilaterally to dispose of it by contract.[50] At the same time, though, husbands could not enter into contracts with respect to assets in their wives' separate estates. These assets could be sold, mortgaged, and otherwise contractually dealt with other if the couple jointly agreed. The result, while surely not making contracting separate property assets impossible, nevertheless did create something of a drag on the assets' ready marketability. Interested purchasers or lenders had to insure that if they were negotiating with only one spouse—the husband presumably—both parties consented *and* did so freely. Moreover, it was somewhat incongruous, especially at a time when concern with making assets freely marketable was increasing, to create a new class of separately owned assets and at the same time to retain impediments on their marketability. Realizing this, the legislature quickly amended the statute to permit the wife "to convey and devise real and personal property . . . as if she were unmarried."[51]

The 1849 amendment made one other important change that enhanced the autonomy of married women as property owners. Although the original statute enabled a married women separately to own property as a legal rather than an equitable estate, it did not prohibit the creation of trusts for married women. Nor did it retroactively convert existing trusts for married women into separate legal estates. Consequently, under 1848 statute, married women who were the beneficiaries of trusts actively managed by the trustee remained powerless to control their separate equitable estates. The 1849 amendment attempted to give married women a measure of control over their equitable estates by providing that a wife who was a trust beneficiary could petition a court for personal control over her trust property.[52] This did not simply convert active trusts into passive trusts, however. The court had discretion, after examining the married woman's capacity to manage and control her property, over whether to order the trustee to transfer all or part of the trust property to her. The amendment never challenged the assumption that the intervention of some third party—now a court rather than a trustee—was necessary to insure that a married woman did not act against her own best interests. The procedure may have weakened the married women's trust as a property arrangement that formalized married women's subordinated status, but it by no means signaled the death of the protectivist ideology. Even with the changes made by the 1849 amendment, the newly recognized married women's separate property interest was not a commodified property interest. While it somewhat enhanced a wife's autonomy, it was still substantially rooted in the conception of property that viewed property's purpose as maintaining a hierarchical social order.

The Antebellum Married Women's Property Reforms and the Ambiguities of Commodificationism

Despite indisputable change in the legal status of married women as property owners between 1820 and 1850, the fact remains that this change was marginal, not fundamental. Married women were not given the same legal powers of ownership as their husbands. Their separate estates could not, as their husbands' property could, be used as a commodity, a market mechanism for creating wealth and satisfying individual preferences. Given the growing strength of the commodificationist ideology, combined with the fact that lawmakers were dissatisfied with the traditional form of married women's property, the nagging question is why the function of the separate estate remained protective. Why did not the commodity ideology extend to married women? Why were legislators, who were, after all, granting greater autonomy to married women, unwilling to extend to them the same degree of autonomy over their separate assets that men had?

Some easy explanations quickly come to mind. One is that improvement in the lot of married women proceeded, as large-scale legal change usually does, in a piecemeal fashion. The antebellum married women's property acts were just the first stage in an extended story that finally culminated, by the close of the nineteenth century, in the elimination of gender difference in property relations and the triumph of commodification. The greatest improvement in the legal status of married women occurred in the second, rather than the first, half of the nineteenth century.[53] Assuming for the moment that all gender differences between men and women as property owners have now been eliminated—an assumption that strains credulity[54]—this still does not explain why there was a specific aversion to allowing married women to use or dispose of their separate estates as a commodity. The pre–Civil War wave of married women's property acts was not a tentative first step toward universalizing the conception of property as commodity; those acts represented no shift from a protective to a commodified model of property for married women. They were merely legalizing property arrangements that previously had been recognized only in Equity Courts.

Another explanation relies on the concept of power. The law reformers of 1848, almost all of whom were men, were content to keep wives in a subordinated role; commodifying married women's property would have created too great a threat to male hegemony, both within and outside of the family. Doubtless there is some merit to this explanation, perhaps a great deal of merit. America was still a patriarchal society in 1848, although not as completely as it had been a hundred years earlier. Power is the core issue in patriarchies; it can hardly be expected that men would willingly redistribute their power to women. What they, like other dominant groups whose power has been challenged, instead will do to maintain their superior position is to adopt a strategy of ameliorating the most conspicuous manifestations of that superiority while leaving the bases of power intact. From this power perspective, the 1848 act, even with the 1849 amendment, fit well with the general pattern of law reform to neutralize opposition by adopting a much diluted version of the opposition's demands.[55]

But power alone is too quick and easy an explanation. For one thing, the fact is that antebellum legislation did enhance the autonomy of married women as property owners. The further fact is that this legislation was almost entirely the work of men. Women did not assume a visible leadership role in law reform activities until around 1860, partly as a consequence of the greater attention to women's issues that resulted from the married women's property acts. To be sure, writings like Sarah Grimke's *Letters on the Equality of the Sexes*[56] appeared in the early part of the nineteenth century, which had some influence on reformers in their attacks on the common law regime. But the earliest efforts at legislative reform all came from men. It was, as Norma Basch has shown,[57] not until after the Civil War that an active, organized women's movement became an important force behind reforms of married women's property laws. Relatively few women even supported measures like Thomas Herttell's proposed married women's property act in 1837.[58]

At least as important as male power in explaining why married women's property reform did not follow the model of commodification is the change in the ideology of the family and, within it, the wife's role. The eighteenth-century American family was much more deeply patriarchal than its nineteenth-century counterpart.[59] The father controlled the family's property and was responsible for maintaining its reputation and position. The family was more than the sum of its parts; its name and honor were forms of what economists now call human capital that were passed down from generation to generation. In many respects the human capital were at least as important as land, tangibles, and other familiar forms of wealth. Individual identity was subordinated to that of the collective family. This meant that individual members were not free to pursue their own interests or create their own life plans. Their life plans were defined from the moment of their births, and the husband and father was responsible for seeing that these life plans were fulfilled as expected. It was their role to arrange apprenticeships for sons, arrange marriages and marriage settlements for daughters, and arrange for the support and maintenance of wives, whose status was that of a child in many respects.

The legal doctrine of the married couple as a single person accurately expressed the dominant social understanding of the wife's position. Wives had no independent obligations either within or outside the family. The function of the family in patriarchies is to reproduce hierarchy in the society. The family's function defines that of women: "to transmit wealth from one generation of men to the next generation of men"[60] through the process of procreation.

By 1830, this understanding had given way to a radically different conception of the family and the wife's role. A strongly patriarchal society was difficult to reconcile with the tenets of republicanism, leading to a rethinking of the role of women in the late eighteenth century. Ideology was not the sole impetus for change, though. During the first three decades of the nineteenth century the combined forces of geographic mobility that produced a much more scattered population, and economic turbulence brought about the gradual demise of institutions that were the foundation of the eighteenth-century social order. Though still a patriarchy, the nineteenth-century family was less dependent on a single figure. Rather, husbands and wives had specialized responsibilities, based on the perceived special talents of men and women. Men, still the heads of families, were the principal link between the family and the outside world. Though nineteenth-century wives often were involved to some degree with the commercial world (certainly more than their eighteenth-century counterparts), husbands had primary responsibility over economic matters. Women were in charge of hearth and home, including the nurturing and educating of children. They were regarded as the principal civilizing force in an unsettled, dynamic society, and were expected to use their special talents to cultivate moral sensibility in their children and renew moral feeling in their husbands.

The first half of the nineteenth century was the high-water mark of the ideology of a separate "women's sphere." This ideology of domesticity[61] was widely expounded in popular literature, religious sermons, and legal writings. Its popularity can be explained as a reaction to the enormous economic and social changes occurring at that time as the market revolution proceeded apace.[62] Americans were deeply ambivalent about those changes. On the one hand, the market revolution had, at some times and for some people at least, increased wealth. It had also accelerated the dismantling of the old eighteenth-century gentry-dominated social hierarchy. On the other hand, it had also ended the stability that that social order had provided. It had replaced a world of fixity with a world of flux. Even land was no longer what it had once seemed in the virtuous republic, as Ralph Waldo Emerson observed: "An orchard, good tillage, good grounds, seem a fixture, like a gold mine, or a river, to a citizen; to a large [i.e., market] farmer, not much more fixed than the state of the crop."[63]

The mid-century sense of anxiety about the market was readily understandable. The effects of the Panic of 1819 were still felt even by 1830. Not the least important of these effects was the psychological trauma as people realized that a capitalist economy produces busts as well as booms. The market no longer seemed to be predictable, the province of a hand that was rational if not visible. Incoherence and unpredictability had replaced its illusory order.

Like a disease that is indifferent to class distinctions, the fortunes of the market turned against the rich as well as the poor. Predictably, the 1819 depression had crushing effects on the working class, which was now made aware of the insecurity of wage labor. But the panic also had devastating consequences for wealthy individuals who had borrowed heavily in the economic boom that followed the War of 1812. Few debtors had the necessary specie to satisfy creditors, who were forced to participate in an accelerating process of debt liquidation by policies that the new national Bank had adopted to save itself. Businesses failed in waves throughout the country. All manner of assets sold at steeply discounted prices at sheriffs' auctions. Any remnant of the illusion that land somehow would escape commodification was dissipated as countless landowners watched estates that they considered priceless not only sold, but sold for a pittance. Even the aged Thomas Jefferson had to struggle to save his beloved "little mountain" from creditors.[64]

Deep-seated anxiety about the effects of an entrepreneurial economy was later reinforced when the Panic of 1837 followed another boom of speculation in the mid-1830s. Precipitated by another sudden change in bank policy (this time, however, from the venerable Bank of England), the 1837 depression in some ways was more devastating than the 1819 depression. Prices of internationally traded commodities, particularly cotton, collapsed around the world. Social unrest threatened political stability, and observers feared revolution.[65] The economic downturn was long-lasting as well as pervasive. After a modest improvement, the economy fell again in 1839, and the effects of this most recent reversal were felt well into the mid-1840s.

The result of these repeated swings of economic fortune was a strong psychological need for some sort of safe harbor in society, a locus of tranquillity and stability in people's lives. The family, it seemed to many, provided that "haven in a heartless world,"[66] a "refuge from the vexations and embarrassments of business," as a New England pastor put it.[67] What made the world heartless was its increasingly commodified character, for it was precisely the commodification of land and other forms of property that had made the economy and society change so fundamentally. In the sphere of the market, it seemed, the dialectic of stability and dynamism had collapsed, as incessant change swamped any semblance of genuine economic stability. But if the dialectic was lost within the discrete sphere of the economy, it could still be maintained between spheres: the family would provide the stability that was necessary to balance the market's dynamism and so equilibrate the social order.

Stability in the domestic sphere, though, required that the corrosive influence of commodification not be permitted to affect family property relations. Commodification of the married woman's separate estate was basically incompatible with the ideology of the "separate sphere." According to that ideology, women were to provide the softening influence in social relations. Their nature, unlike that of men, was to care for others, rather than the single-minded pursuit of self-interest. Marriage and motherhood were the ideal relationships within which a woman could realize her basic nature. Providing comfort and kindness to others and consistently acting according to moral principles, married women provided a model for their husbands to counteract the anti-social behavior they experienced in the market. Simultaneously, they provided to their children a living example of the moral life. So nourished by the wife and mother's disinterested love, the home was, to nineteenth-century citizens, the sole remaining outpost of virtue in American society.

Legal changes that would have allowed married women to use their separate estates as a commodity would have undermined women's disinterested nature and corrupted the family's role. In a curious reversal of eighteenth-century republican moral psychology, exponents of the cult of domesticity viewed economic dependency and virtue as complementary rather than antithetical. Dependency, they thought, was an external condition necessary for full development of a disinterested character. Economic independence would mean that wives would have the means to pursue their own goals, very likely taking them out of the domestic sphere. Market-alienability of women's property, by creating the potential of reducing the wife's dependency on her husband, represented too great a threat to maintaining the delicate equilibrium between stability and change.

Another dialectic, more important than that between stability and change, was also at stake in the question whether to create gender symmetry between men's and women's property. This was the social dialectic of independence and interdependence, alienation and connectedness, freedom and rootedness. The period between 1820 and 1850 witnessed what Robert Wiebe has aptly described as a "revolution in choices."[68] With the evisceration of the old social order by the combined forces of turbulent economic activity, revolutionary opportunities in transportation, and expansion of the nation's westernmost horizon, people had opportunities to choose their pursuits as never before. Children no longer were necessarily bound to follow the plans that their father made for them. Indeed, for many families, it was expected that children, on reaching adulthood, would set out on their own, participating, metaphorically if not literally, in the great migration. Family traditions and family honor gave way to individual life plans as the child's primary responsibility. Wives too participated in the new society of choices, particularly in their roles as mothers. As the primary agents for transmitting moral knowledge from one generation to the next, nineteenth-century mothers were considered morally independent of their husbands. Although obviously their choices were constrained, they nevertheless were expected to make choices regarding the rearing of children, management of the home, and, for those fortunate enough to have leisure time, how to use their leisure.

Of course, there were many deviations from both the old and the new family models. Some eighteenth-century children did strike out on their own, particularly those who could expect to receive nothing from a shrinking patrimony. Likewise, wives who entered the world of commerce, as wage laborers, cottage producers, farm managers, or some other commercial occupation, were by no means unheard of in eighteenth-century America. On the other end, family patterns remained intact for some nineteenth-century families, especially among the wealthy elites. But social consciousness regarding family members' roles had changed fundamentally in a way that signaled the ascendancy of individual over family and freedom over tradition.[69]

Nineteenth-century Americans who experienced this new freedom of individual choice did not regard it as an unadulterated good. There was considerable ambivalence about the world they had gained compared with the world they had lost. The world of individual choices, exercised through commodity exchange, was a world of opportunities, of dynamic development, but it was also a world without foundations, without lasting ties. The dark side of the revolution in choices was a recurrent theme of writers during the 1830s and early 1840s. In the wake of the 1837 depression, Ralph Waldo Emerson deplored the social degradation wrought by the commodificationist outlook: "The generation system of our trade . . . is a system of selfishness . . . of distrust, of concealment, of superior keenness, not of giving but of taking advantage."[70] There was perhaps no more constant a critic of the market's pathologies than James Fenimore Cooper. Clearly well out of the mainstream in some of his views, Cooper's diagnosis of the source of the country's social and moral ills was widely shared:

> Extravagant issues of paper money, inconsiderate credits that commence in Europe and extend throughout the land, and false notions as to the value of their possessions, in men who five years since had nothing, has [sic] completely destroyed the balance of things, and money has got to be so completely the end of life, that few think of it as a means. . . . All principles are swallowed up in the absorbing desire for gain—national honor, permanent security, the ordinary rules of society, law, the constitution . . . are forgotten, or are perverted.[71]

Emerson, whom Joel Porte has described as the "representative man" of Jacksonian America,[72] *was* representative because his attitudes toward the commodified society were so deeply ambivalent.[73] On the one hand, he clearly appreciated the comforts and opportunities that increased wealth made available. At the same time, he could preach that "[t]here is nothing more important in the culture of man than to resist the dangers of commerce."[74] As Quentin Anderson has observed, "[Emerson] could not for a moment bear the thought of allowing [himself] to be defined by the acquisitive activities which perforce defined most Americans in each other's eyes."[75] But if most Americans defined each other in acquisitive, individualistic terms, they could no more easily bear to define themselves completely in those terms than could Emerson. There remained a need to cling to the old values of fixed order, rootedness, and connectedness, even as evidence of those values in the external world seemed to vanish daily. In anything, the decline of the society based on those values likely strengthened this shared psychological need.

This deeply ambivalent reaction to the social changes wrought by the market and transportation revolutions[76] explains why the reform of married women's property law reached results that were so hesitant. The ideology of individual choice required some change in the law of marital property; the traditional single-person metaphor was too obviously incompatible with that ideology, with its exaltation of the triumph of the individual over the collective, to survive unaltered. The reality of women's subordination might be comfortably maintained, but symbolically, the legal denial of a wife's separate identity was too transparently hypocritical to be defended. Transforming the wife's separate estate into a commodity over which she had autonomous control, though, would have fundamentally altered the family as a locus of order, rootedness, and community. Commodities are associated with freedom, but they are also associated, in the vocabulary that was being coined at about the same time as the mid-century married women's property acts, with alienation. Individuals whose relations are mediated by commodity exchange are, to be sure, bound to each other, but, viewed from the perspective of anxiety about an unfamiliar world, the bonds are no longer those of affection. Were wives to assume a position of legal equality with the husbands as property owners, the male antebellum reformers feared (and surely some married women as well), the character of marriage itself might change as the wife's character changed. Wives would become more self-seeking and less caring, less devoted to the good of the collective family. The home would no longer serve as a sanctuary from a world in which personal relationships had been alienated by the translation of everything that has value into a commodity for exchange. The result would not simply be that the delicate balance between freedom and community would be upset, but, far more drastically, the pluralistic character of society would diminish, as the model of commodified relations became universalized.

Even if this vision of marital relations as reduced to arm's-length exchange did not become reality, the symbol of the wife as commodity owner still had to be dealt with. The symbol of the wife's control over property as subordinate to that of her husband was at the heart of the ideology of domesticity; the ideology could not survive without the legal symbol. Nonautonomous control over property did not so much symbolize an imbalance of power—although that surely was its consequence—as it did the inappropriateness of commodified property relations in the domestic sphere. That symbolic message suggests another: the continuing, if reduced, existence of the old, familiar social order. The incompleteness of married women's property law was a tether to a fading society characterized by cohesiveness, trust, and sharing.

The ascendance of the commodified conception of property to dominance in legal thought in the first half of the nineteenth century was, to be sure, greeted with optimism and encouragement. Yet it was also greeted, even by those who benefited from it, with a sense of anxiety that the social revolution it wrought might spin out of control. Nostalgia is, after all, a symptom of fear, and the antebellum property law reformers may ultimately be described as prisoners of nostalgia.

Ambiguous Entrepreneurialism: The Rise and Fall of Vested Rights in the Antebellum Era

ONE OF THE STOCK historical stories about the development of American judicial doctrines concerning property during the nineteenth century is the shift from a "vested rights" conception of property to a "dynamic" conception.[1] Indeed, virtually the entire story about judicial protection of property interests from legislative regulation throughout the nineteenth century seems to be the cyclical rise and fall of the so-called vested rights doctrine. Willard Hurst expressed the now-standard theme with his customary succinctness when he stated, "We identify no legal development more sharply with the nineteenth century than the judicial protection of vested rights."[2]

Boiled down to its basic outline, the story goes as follows. Implemented by the contract clause of the federal Constitution during the first half of the nineteenth century, the vested rights doctrine at first protected the first wave of American entrepreneurs. These men, with active government encouragement, invested in enterprises that fueled the nation's economic expansion. Later, as investment in public utilities like bridges, roads, and canals became more potentially profitable and attracted increasing amounts of private capital, courts shifted course, overriding vested rights where they conflicted with the interests of new entrants in entrepreneurial enterprises. Courts sacrificed holders of stable forms of property to protect investors in dynamic forms of property.

In the second half of the century, the story continues, courts reverted back to a strongly pro-vested rights position in order to protect entrepreneurs whose interests by now were well established. The constitutional tool for effecting this second incarnation of the vested rights doctrine was the due process clause of the fourteenth amendment, enacted after the Civil War. The key to understanding this phase of the doctrine, like the first, we are told, is a judicial desire to protect particular economic interest groups.

A different, more recent rendering of this story has challenged the dominant interest-group version. According to this interpretation, the rise and fall of the vested rights doctrine was not the product of interest-group politics, but of changes in economic theory.[3] The doctrinal shift was the result of the replacement of classical economics for preclassical, or mercantilist, policy, as the dominant paradigm in economic theory and, derivatively, in those areas of law bearing directly on economic questions. American judges came to view classical economics as the foundation on which they could construct, for the first time, a truly objective science of law.

This chapter discusses the following alternative argument: the emergence and decline of judicial protection for vested rights in the antebellum period[4] reflected a dialectic between two strands of pro-entrepreneurial discourse. One was the discourse of old Federalists like Chief Justice John Marshall and their neo-Federalist heirs like Joseph Story. These men supported legal protection of entrepreneurial activity that legislatures created by granting to private investors monopoly privileges for the construction of roads, canals, bridges, and other public improvements. Federalist-Whigs welcomed entrepreneurial activity of this sort for political as much as for economic reasons: it was, in their view, conducive to preserving the proper political order against the rising threat of popular democracy. To emphasize the fact that it was not hostile to entrepreneurialism as such, this Federalist-Whig discourse is more accurately termed "entrepreneurial republicanism."[5] Standing on the other side were Jacksonian supporters of entrepreneurial activity. The most notable judicial figure in this group was Marshall's replacement as Chief Justice, Roger Taney. These men, here termed "democratic entrepreneurs," spoke the language of equal entrepreneurial opportunity. They opposed legal protection of existing monopolistic property interests as both anti-development and undemocratic.

For all of their differences, these two groups shared two basic beliefs. Most conspicuous was their unequivocal embrace of entrepreneurial activity. Both sides favored rapid national development and population growth in the country's unsettled areas. They dreamed the same dream of unlimited economic growth and of improvements in the nation's transportation and communication systems that would enable that growth. Even Andrew Jackson himself, for all of his Jeffersonian talk about "independent farmers a[s] the basis of society and the true friends of liberty,"[6] was no unambiguous enemy of economic development. The policies for which his presidency is best known—opposition to the Second National Bank, the circulation of paper money, and most government aid to internal improvements—grew out of opposition to unequal privileges and the loss of personal liberty, not to economic progress as such.[7] Beyond Jackson and the few remaining true believers in the old Jeffersonian vision of the agrarian republic, most Americans were bitten by the bug of acquisitiveness. Looking around at his society, Francis Lieber saw an "anxiety to be equal to the wealthiest," but few of his contemporaries would have agreed with his Marx-like diagnosis of that condition as "diseased," or one that would lead to an "appalling frequency of alienation of mind."[8]

Entrepreneurialism, however, had ambiguous implications for the legal protection of property. Promoting entrepreneurial activity might mean protecting existing interests and maintaining the extant hierarchy of power. It was plausible to think this way insofar as the existing economic interests were the very source of the market revolution that had transformed American culture and society. To destabilize those interests was to threaten the institution of private property, on which entrepreneurial activity and economic growth utterly depended. This was essentially the argument that was the basis of the vested rights doctrine. Extant property rights, once they had vested, had to maintain their positions of power until they could no longer serve their appropriate function.

That interpretation, though plausible, was not inevitable. Another interpretation, at least equally plausible to the first, was available to Americans at the time. Drawing on Adam Smith's unambiguous attack on monopolies a half-century earlier,[9] one could conclude that the cause of entrepreneurial activity was best advanced by exposing established economic interests to competition. Protecting vested property interests against new entrants in a given enterprise was tantamount to maintaining a monopoly, which would rapidly choke economic growth.

Stated in the terms just described, the debate between these two views appears to boil down to the well-known debate in economic theory between preclassical and classical economists like Smith and Ricardo.[10] Alternatively, the debate can be distilled to a clash between established and rising economic interest groups.[11] Without denying that both of these interpretations have some plausibility, they can be augmented with an account that stresses their relationship to the conflict between the political theories of Federalist-Whigs and Jacksonians. That conflict provides the basis for a second common denominator of entrepreneurial republicans and democratic entrepreneurs.

That common denominator was an understanding of property as serving a social-political function as well as the strictly economic function of increasing wealth. What divided entrepreneurial republicans and democratic entrepreneurs was the identity of that social-political function. For entrepreneurial republicans (Federalist-Whigs), the vision was of property as the basis for a properly ordered society headed by a natural elite of property owners. For democratic entrepreneurs (Jacksonians), property was linked with democracy, equal opportunities, and the end of old privileges. These two interpretations indicate that the rise and fall of the antebellum vested rights doctrine, culminating in the great *Charles River Bridge* case, was not simply a clash of economic interests but a clash between two interpretations of what the emergence of an entrepreneurial society meant for the political and social order. They also indicate that although entrepreneurialism thoroughly informed the ways in which legal elites thought about property by 1850, the modern commodified understanding was not yet firmly rooted in American legal consciousness by that date.

Vested Rights as Proper Order: *Fletcher v. Peck*

The vested rights doctrine, implemented through the contract clause of the federal Constitution, was the principal doctrinal device by which Federalists on the Supreme Court promoted entrepreneurial republicanism. The doctrine first took shape in the famous Yazoo land case, *Fletcher v. Peck*.[12]

The transactional background of the case was typical of the type of entrepreneurial activity that was common at the beginning of the nineteenth century—land speculation. The Georgia legislature in 1795 statutorily authorized the governor to convey the Yazoo lands, a huge expanse of land in the western portion of Georgia, now constituting the states of Alabama and Mississippi, to four land-speculating companies. The deal was incredibly sweet: for $500,000 in specie currency, the companies received two-thirds of the territory between the Chattahoochee River, the present western boundary of Georgia, and the Mississippi, between the Tennessee and Florida borders, a total of thirty-five million acres. The sale has been called, with little exaggeration, "the greatest real estate deal in history."[13] Typical of most land speculation at that time, the sale was corrupted by bribes, mostly of cash and shares in the companies.[14] A year later, after public scandal over the bribes had broken out and a new legislature elected, the deal was rescinded. In the meantime, the four original land companies had already sold millions of acres of the Yazoo land to other speculators and individual settlors, mostly from New England. The sales earned enormous profits for the original Yazoo companies. In the most important of the sales, the New England Mississippi Land Company, whose investors included prominent Connecticut and Massachusetts politicians, bought most of the Georgia Mississippi Company's eleven million acres for $1.138 million, yielding the Georgia company a profit of nearly 650 percent on its original investment!

Some of the more legally cognizant of the New England buyers sought the legal opinion of Alexander Hamilton regarding the validity of the original sale after the legislature's rescission. Hamilton, although emphasizing that he had not had an opportunity to search the Georgia land titles, gave an opinion that was favorable to the New Englanders:

> [I]t may be safely said to be a contravention of the first principles of natural justice and social policy . . . to revoke a grant of the property regularly made for valuable consideration, under legislative authority, to the prejudice even of third persons on every supposition innocent of the alleged fraud or corruption.[15]

With this opinion in hand, two of the New England investors challenged the validity of the legislative repeal through an arranged lawsuit. John Peck nominally sold his holdings to Robert Fletcher, and per their prearrangement, Fletcher sued Peck to try title, arguing that the sale breached the contract's covenant of good title.

The case posed a conflict between the security of land titles, once created by the legislature, and the power of the legislature to correct its prior acts that were the direct result of corruption. In a very real sense this conflict translated into one between entrepreneurialism and republican virtue. From the perspective of republican theory, it would surely appear vital to the integrity of representative self-governance that one legislature have the power to correct fraudulent acts of its predecessor. Of course, correction of corrupt legislative action in this context did not necessarily mean annulling the initial sale. The dictates of corrective justice, if that were the sole concern, would have been met by affirming the transfer of title but requiring that the seller reimburse the state, as representative of the people of Georgia, for the amount of the purchase price. But republican ideology calls for more than mere corrective justice; it requires, above all else, that the integrity—the "virtue," to use the preferred term—of elected representatives and the governmental institutions that they constitute not be compromised and that, if and when they are compromised, the acts of corruption be publicly declared void, so that there remains no remaining consequences that would possibly symbolize the corruption's efficacy.

From the perspective of promoting entrepreneurial activity, land titles have to be kept clear and simple. It is especially important to the health of the market that innocent buyers be able to rely on the apparent legal soundness of titles when engaging in exchange transactions and that they not be made to bear the risk of loss that they did not create and of which they had no reasonable opportunity to learn. The concern with clarifying land titles was especially important in the context of Yazoo. The Yazoo lands were already subject to a variety of conflicting claims. Spain, the U.S. government, and at least four Indian tribes claimed title to various portions of Yazoo. These disputes alone were not enough to cool the speculation fever. People were willing to assume the risk of loss because the prospects for gaining their fortunes seemed high enough, just as people today will risk large amounts of money at the race track or on the state lottery even though the odds against their winning are extremely high. Georgia's policy of settling its frontier through favorable land sales would be seriously jeopardized, however, if subsequent purchasers who bought land from land companies with no notice of fraud were subject to losing their titles through legislative repeal of the original legislative grants. Out-of-state land speculators might be foolish enough to buy land sight unseen, but few of them would be willing to assume the risk that the state might snatch their titles away from them at any time. The marketability of land in Georgia's western territory, then, seemed to require that titles, once vested in private hands, be protected against subsequent legislative action.

In addition to the concerns with land titles, one school of economic thought also supported the Yazoo purchasers. Georgia's program of granting the rights to its western lands to a select group of land speculation companies was a product of mercantilist economic theory, an approach to encouraging economic development that most Federalist favored. Mercantilist theory, which was eventually replaced as the reigning theory by the classical economics of Adam Smith and David Ricardo, posited two basic claims: (1) economic development requires extensive and active participation by the government in entrepreneurial activities; (2) to encourage entrepreneurs to invest in some desired activity, the state must give them exclusive privileges or monopoly rights.[16] The Georgia legislation and the governor's subsequent grants illustrated both of these principles. To settle and develop its western territory, the state government did not passively rely on the workings of the market but actively encouraged investment. Beginning in the 1780s, the state had adopted an extremely liberal policy of granting lands to new settlers.[17] Successive governors tries to outdo each other in the number of acres they granted per person. This policy, combined with pervasive mania for land speculation throughout the nation, led to countless instances of fraud. Literally millions of acres of nonexistent land were sold to gullible investors, many in the North and even Europe. Nearly all of these unfortunate souls paid for ghost titles to what promotion literature made out to be a virtual paradise without ever seeing what they were supposedly buying. (This practice continues today in the sort of land promotion deals vividly depicted in the recent play *Glengarry Glen Ross.*)

The other tenet of mercantilist economics was also met. The bulk of the Yazoo lands were deeded to a few land speculation companies. These companies, in effect, held exclusive privileges to sell and settle Yazoo. The fact that they were able to earn near-monopoly profits from sales was, according to mercantilist reasoning, a necessary consequence of a policy designed to encourage risk-taking.

The conflict between these two perspectives, republican and entrepreneurial, would seem to have placed John Marshall in a quandary. Though a staunch Federalist and a lifelong opponent of Jefferson and his mode of democratic politics, Marshall, like virtually all other political leaders of his time, firmly believed in the basic tenets of republican ideology. The blatant legislative corruption behind the land deal was especially worrisome to the republican mind, as Marshall explicitly indicated:

> That corruption should find its way into the governments of our infant republics, and contaminate the very source of legislation, or that impure motives should contribute to the passage of a law, or the formation of a legislative contract, are circumstances most deeply to be deplored.[18]

There were two reasons why entrepreneurial interests took precedence for Marshall. First, like most other Federalists in the early republic, Marshall's brand of republicanism had far more in common with Hamilton's thought than it did with Jefferson's. Indeed, from the Jeffersonian perspective, Federalist encouragement of entrepreneurship was a perversion of republic ideals. Marshall and other Federalists had no confidence in the capacity of citizens to act virtuously, in the classical sense of that term. The common good was maximized through policies that appealed to self-interest rather than by expecting individuals to subordinate their self-interest to the good of others.

The second reason is that Federalist-Whigs, here termed "entrepreneurial republicans," wanted to protect entrepreneurial interests for reasons in addition to the strictly economic concern with increasing social wealth. Willard Hurst is quite correct in pointing out that the vested rights doctrine developed primarily to protect venture capital,[19] but the entrepreneurial republicans' protection of venture capital stemmed from political and social concerns as well as economic considerations. It was important to protect this capital not for its own sake but for what it represented: the proper social order, headed by a small number of men who possessed that requisite experience, intelligence, and wisdom to lead. The suppliers of venture capital in the early republic were all community and political leaders, men like Marshall, who himself engaged in land speculation.[20] Actions like the Georgia repeal statute represented the most serious threat to that order—the urge of democratic legislatures to disrupt the natural hierarchy.

The rhetoric of the repeal act itself fueled such fears of radical democracy. The repeal act was inspired by democratic hatred of arrangements that conferred privileges on the few. Fully three-quarters of the act consisted of a rambling preamble that linked the state's sovereignty to the protection of democracy. In selling the Yazoo lands to "a few individuals," the previous legislature acted contrary to the interests of

> democratical . . . government founded on equality of rights, and which is totally opposed to all proprietary grants or monopolies in favor of a few, which tend to build up that destructive aristocracy in the new, which is tumbling in the old world; and which, if permitted, must end in the annihilation of democracy and equal rights—those rights and principles of government, which our virtuous forefathers fought for and established with blood.[21]

Language such as this suggested to Marshall that what was at stake was the validity of the alleged principle that "a legislature may, by its own act, devest the vested estate of any man whatever, for reasons which shall, by itself, be deemed sufficient."[22] That asserted principle set the stage for a conflict between the republican doctrine of political relativism and the entrepreneurial requirement of secure land titles: "Is the power of the legislature competent to the annihilation of such title [that is, of a bona fide purchaser], and to a resumption of the property thus held?"[23]

Marshall's response to that question began by acknowledging the "correctness" of principle of political relativism as a general proposition: "one legislature is competent to repeal any act which a former legislature was competent to pass; and . . . one legislature cannot abridge the powers of a succeeding legislature."[24] But although that principle was valid with respect to "general legislation," it did not necessarily apply with respect to an individual who has acted in reliance on a legislative act. This was especially true where title to land has been transferred:

> [I]f an act be done under a law, a succeeding legislature cannot undo it. The past cannot be recalled by the most absolute power. Conveyances have been made, those conveyances have vested legal estates, and, if those estates may be seized by the sovereign authority, still, that they originally vested is a fact, and cannot cease to be a fact.[25]

Vitiating legislative sales of property whenever facts subsequently disclosed that the sales were tainted by corruption was incompatible with maintaining good order and stability. After all, the line between influence-peddling and corruption is exceedingly thin, if not nonexistent. One legislature could always find some evidence that the act of a prior legislature was the product of influence peddling. Screaming "corruption," it could then destroy the property interests that its predecessor had created. The scenario of legislative disruption could be extended to truly nightmarish proportions. Since the repeal act itself would doubtless have been the product of interest-group politics, the next legislature, perhaps recaptured by the ousted property owners, might undo the repeal, creating an endless circle of legislative action and repeal. Marshall was not simply splitting hairs when he asked how much and what sort of corruption would be sufficient to allow the legislature to repeal its prior act.

> Must it be direct corruption, or would interest or undue influence of any kind be sufficient? Must the vitiating cause operate on a majority, or on whatever number of members? Would the act be null, whatever might be the wish of the nation, or would its obligation or nullity depend upon the public sentiment?[26]

Maintaining the social and political order required that this sort of legislative sabotage, rationalized under the rubric of democracy, be blocked at the outset. Vested property rights were the device for securing that order. Entrepreneurial policy, understood in these terms, then, must trump the republican principle of legislative self-correction whenever legislative action created property rights.[27]

Politics and Corporations: The *Dartmouth College* Case

Having identified the contract clause as a source of constitutional protection for property interests against the excesses of democratic control, the Marshall Court extended the vested rights doctrine of *Fletcher v. Peck* to a variety of other important institutions. These included other aspects of land titles,[28] real estate taxation,[29] and bankruptcy and debtor relief.[30] Particularly important were decisions in which the Court held that the charters of private corporations were vested rights protected against legislative interference.[31] Of these the most important was the famous *Dartmouth College* case.

The case arose out of an attempt by the New Hampshire legislature to change the status of Dartmouth College to a public university. The college was established by a royal charter in 1769. The charter provided that the college should be governed by twelve trustees and their successors. The trustees were given the power to appoint and remove the president, fill vacancies on the board of trustees, and make laws and regulations for the college. In 1816 the New Hampshire legislature enacted a series of statutes changing the institution's name to Dartmouth University, substantially increasing the number of trustees, giving the governor the power to appoint the new trustees, and providing for state officials, also chosen by the governor, to oversee important decisions of the trustees. The effect of this legislation would have been to subject Dartmouth College to the political will of the legislature and elected state officials.

The legislature's attempt to amend Dartmouth's charter was the culmination of a long-running dispute between the trustees and John Wheelock, the college's president who succeeded his father, the first president and real founder of the college. The dispute initially concerned political and religious issues but later seemed to have more to do with Wheelock's imperious personality. The most recent incident before the legislature acted was the newly selected trustees' refusal to rubber-stamp Wheelock's choices for faculty positions and for the position of pastor of the local church. Wheelock took this, coupled with prior incidents in which the trustees asserted their independence, to be a personal affront to his handling of the college's affairs. Nothing short of total control over literally all aspects of the college would, it seems, have satisfied his immense ego.

It was religion and politics, though, not Wheelock's personality, that made the dispute a matter of controversy throughout New England. Colleges in the early republic were nearly always sectarian, and Dartmouth was no exception.[32] The college was associated with Congregationalism, virtually the established church of New England. The church was also closely associated with the Federalist party and so was Dartmouth. Nearly all of the trustees, for example, were staunch Federalists. Dartmouth epitomized the type of corporate institution that was common in New England during the early republic—nominally private and independent but in fact strongly allied with the New England power elite.

With the revival of the Republican party in the New Hampshire legislature after the 1810 election, Dartmouth's tilt toward the Federalist-Congregationalist axis made it a highly vulnerable target for political attacks. After attacking the trustees in a series of vitriolic pamphlets, Wheelock took his case to the legislature in 1815. His characterization of the trustees as a body of "wealthy individuals . . . supported by a rich and powerful corporation"[33] was calculated to resonate with Republican lawmakers who were Jeffersonian democrats. So, too, was his argument that the trustees' one purpose was "to complete the destruction of the original principles of the College . . . and to establish a new modified system to strengthen the interests of a party or sect, which, by extending its influences, . . . will eventually *affect the political independence of the people, and move* the springs of their government."[34] The legislature initially refused to act, but subsequent events intensified the political character of the controversy. A majority of the trustees, incensed by Wheelock's pamphlets, removed him from the presidency. The fiery arch-Republican editor of the Concord *Patriot,* Isaac Hill, launched into a series of attacks on the removal as a Federalist attempt to establish a "Law Religion" that would maintain their aristocratic control of state government.[35] Hill urged the election of a Republican governor and Republican legislature which would "correct the abuses at Dartmouth College." Those abuses, he railed, arose from the college's charter, the "last remaining relict [*sic*] of the royalty of Great Britain."[36] Hill's pleas evidently struck a chord with the electorate, which in 1816 voted in a Republican legislature and a Republican governor, William Plumer. The new governor was a strong champion of the cause of publicly controlled universities. He unequivocally endorsed the Jeffersonian principle that republican government demanded an educated citizenry and argued that state, not private, universities were the proper institutions to realize that goal. It was Plumer who introduced the bill establishing Dartmouth as a state institution.

Refusing to accede to the legislative changes in the college's charter, the trustees challenged the constitutionality of the statutes. The Supreme Court ruled in favor of the trustees, holding that the original charter was "a contract, the obligation of which cannot be impaired without violating the constitution of the United States"[37] and that the statutes amending the charter did in fact impair the contract. The bulk of Marshall's opinion for the Court was devoted, as were the concurring opinions of Justices Washington[38] and Story,[39] to the character of Dartmouth College: was it a public corporation, as the New Hampshire Supreme Court had concluded,[40] or a "private eleemosynary institution, endowed with a capacity to take property for objects unconnected with government"?[41] Inexplicably, it took Marshall nearly thirty pages to conclude that Dartmouth College was not like a political subdivision.[42]

The aspect of Marshall's opinion that deserves close attention occurs late in his discussion of public corporations. Responding to the argument that the Framers of the Constitution did not have charters of this sort in mind when they drafted the contract clause, Marshall rhetorically asked:

> Are contracts of this description of a character to excite so little interest, that we must exclude them from the provisions of the constitution, as being unworthy of the attention of those who framed the instrument? Or does public policy so imperiously demand their remaining exposed to legislative alteration, as to compel us, or rather to permit us to say, that these words, which were introduced to give stability to contracts, and which in their plain import comprehend this contract, must yet be so construed as to exclude it?[43]

The key phrases here are "legislative alteration" and "stability to contracts." For at the root of Marshall's entire opinion (and likewise Story's forty-seven page concurring opinion) is an anxiety about exposing corporations to democratic politics—disorderly and disordered.

Part of the reason for this concern was the risk that donors might be deterred from contributing property to private charities if their corporate charters were subject to legislative control.[44] But the concern went deeper than that. Marshall was eager to keep corporations immune from "the

influence of legislative bodies [because their] fluctuating policy, and repeated interferences, produced the most perplexing and injurious embarrassments."[45] What precisely were these "perplexing and injurious embarrassments"? Specifically with respect to private charitable corporations,
there is the embarrassment that the legislature would simply disregard
the donor's intent and use the donated property for whatever purpose
it thought compatible with the public's needs, as it defined them.

More broadly, Marshall's concern in *Dartmouth College* was to keep
corporations, as an institution, and their property out of the realm of
politics. While *Dartmouth College* involved charitable corporations, Marshall's reasoning could easily be extended to business corporations as well.
Indeed, in subsequent cases, Marshall never doubted that the contract
clause applied to business corporations as well as to charitable corporations.[46] Both types of corporations played, as Marshall and Story well understood, an increasingly important role in maintaining the proper social
and economic order. By the time of the Dartmouth College controversy,
corporations had already come to occupy a prominent position in the
hierarchy of powerful institutions through which the social and political
elites conducted their affairs. As an institution, they provided an unparalleled means of providing continuity of existence and purpose to a collective enterprise and of holding and managing collectively owned property
over an extended period of time. Discussing the purposes for which corporations were created, Marshall stated in *Dartmouth College:*

> Among the most important [purposes] are immortality, and, if the
> expression may be allowed, individuality; properties, by which a per-
> petual succession of many persons are considered as the same, and
> may act as a single individual. They enable a corporation to manage
> its own affairs, and to hold property without the perplexing intrica-
> cies, the hazardless and endless necessity, of perpetual conveyances
> for the purpose of transmitting it from hand to hand. It is chiefly
> for the purpose of clothing bodies of men, in succession, with these
> qualities and capacities, that corporations were invented, and are in
> use. By these means, a perpetual succession of individuals are capable
> of acting for the promotion of the particular object, like one immor-
> tal being.[47]

This analysis of the benefits of the corporate form had both an economic and a social aspect. At the level of enhancing entrepreneurial activity, this passage in some respects echoes modern economic theory. Law-

and-economics scholars have analyzed the corporate form as an institution for minimizing transaction costs,[48] and Marshall's references to the problems of "perpetual conveyances" and "perpetual succession" of owners can easily be translated into that vocabulary. Marshall obviously did not understand the benefits of the corporate form in terms of modern economics, but he did perceive that corporations were an extremely useful means of pooling capital for entrepreneurial objectives. Prior to the revolution, corporations had seldom been used for business purposes. Individuals who wanted to pool their capital and spread their risk could do so for limited and short-term ventures through partnerships and joint-stock companies, but these forms of enterprise organization were decidedly inferior means of conducting large-scale entrepreneurial activity over a long time horizon. In addition to the problems resulting from the death of one partner, these traditional institutions were limited by complex problems in transferring property and limiting each participant's liability for the enterprise's debts.

Prompted by the dominant sentiment favoring rapid economic development, state legislatures in the early nineteenth century increasingly used corporations as the vehicle for stimulating growth. Between the end of the revolution and 1801, state governments had created more than three hundred business corporations.[49] Between 1790 and 1860, the number had jumped to over 2,300, primarily in the fields of transportation, insurance, manufacturing, and banking.[50] In truth, corporations at this time *were* instrumentalities of state governments. States created them and granted them exclusive privileges, including monopoly rights of way, tax exemption, and the power of eminent domain, precisely for the purpose of performing certain public functions. In view of these entanglements with state government, the New Hampshire court's conclusion that Dartmouth, which was entangled with the New Hampshire state government in various ways, was a public corporation was entirely understandable. Marshall's fear, however, was equally well founded: if these entanglements with government were sufficient to bring corporations without the realm of politics, the advantages of the corporate form for holding and entrepreneurially using property would be placed at considerable risk. Reflecting the general Federalist outlook, Marshall regarded legislative action as the product of factions. One could not count on an equilibrium of power among different factions to provide stability for legislative policy. In *Fletcher v. Peck,* Marshall had spoken of the danger of "violent acts which might grow out of the feelings of the moment" and asserted that "[t]he restrictions on the legislative power of the states are obviously founded in this sentiment."[51] As different factions gained control of legislatures, they would exercise their control over corporate property to pursue changing goals. Capital suppliers in turn would lose confidence that their investment would continue to be used for the entrepreneurial objective that they favored and that was originally identified. Eventually, corporations would no longer be able to attract venture capital, and entrepreneurial activity would have to be conducted through more "perplexing" forms of enterprise organization.

Overlapping with this economic function of the corporation was a sociopolitical function that was at least as important a factor: the Marshall Court's eagerness to remove the corporation from the sphere of politics. From the perspective of the republican dimension of entrepreneurial republicanism, the corporation was itself a kind of mini-commonwealth. This perception was the vestigial product of eighteenth-century thinking far more than it was a harbinger of nineteenth-century social and economic thought. During the eighteenth century and into the early part of the nineteenth century, New England courts perceived the corporation as "a little commonwealth" in much the same that they had the family a century earlier.[52] This perception was by and large consistent with reality. Eighteenth-century corporations, not only in New England but throughout the nation, were little more than agencies of the state. Legislative acts created them as "Bodies Pollitick" expressly for the purpose of serving the common interest.[53] Despite the fact that by 1815, the array of activities for which corporate charters were granted had steadily widened and had spread into new sorts of enterprises having little in common with the old bodies politic, the state still continued to judge whether to grant an application for incorporation on the basis of "the primordial concept of common interests."[54] Legislative control of the old eighteenth-century corporation was so extensive that the distinction between public and private corporations that Marshall drew and that Story so extensively discussed in his concurring opinion[55] was largely meaningless. Even after the purposes of these bodies politic had begun to expand from the governance of town and municipalities to manufacturing and other entrepreneurial activities, legislatures retained the final say over virtually all important questions concerning their affairs. Legislatures controlled the details of incorporation, the corporation's internal governance, and, most important, its duration.[56] The state's involvement with the corporation was so extensive that it seemed perfectly natural to think of the corporation in the same terms as the state itself, that is, as the commonwealth.

The corporation's character and its relationship with the state had clearly changed by the first two decades of the nineteenth century. Not only did the range of activities for which legislatures created corporations expand to matters more obviously appealing to private gain, but other changes as well, including matters like the corporation's power to assess its members and limited liability of members for the corporation's debts, created an increasingly apparent split between two sorts of corporations, old and new.[57] As shareholders gained more freedom from the responsibility of the collective corporate body, so did the corporation itself seek to gain more autonomy from the legislature that created it. Gradually the new corporations, entrepreneurial in objective, wrested control over various aspects of their operations, particularly concerning issues that never arose in the context of the old "body politic" corporation, from the legislature.[58]

The most interesting aspect of this development is the paradox that the concept that was used to explain these cessions of power from the commonwealth (state) to the corporation was—the commonwealth, or public good. The contract theory that the Court adopted in *Dartmouth College* ultimately depended on the idea of the corporation, private as well as public, as commonwealth. The idea that even a private corporation, one whose dominant incentive was to maximize profits for its members, was a kind of commonwealth had apparent plausibility in the early nineteenth century. Private corporations possessed many of the powers of public government, including the power of eminent domain and the power to tax its members. Like public governments, they enjoyed monopoly privileges, conferred on them with the explicit expectation that they would use their freedom from competition to serve the public good. That expectation was crucial to the Supreme Court's explanation why corporations like Dartmouth College enjoyed immunity, albeit limited immunity,[59] from political control.

The central idea in all of the *Dartmouth College* opinions was that the state's charter of incorporation was an inviolable contract by which the legislature irrevocably bound itself not to interfere with the corporation. This idea represented, as the Handlins pointed out, an application of the old doctrine of a compact among members of the body politic to the relationship between state and corporation.[60] But what was it that the corporation gave or promised in return for the state's agreement to bind itself? Historians frequently note that Marshall's opinion slid past the legal question of what was the consideration for the state's promise? The answer, which Marshall may have taken to be utterly obvious, is that the corporation promised to use its property, which the contract clause of the Constitution was now understood to protect, for the common good. That is, while the corporation might pursue self interest, it could not act in ways that injured the public. More affirmatively, the charter of incorporation bound even the private corporation to use its property in ways that promoted the public welfare: "The objects for which a corporation is created are universally such as the government wishes to promote. They are deemed beneficial to the country; and this benefit constitutes the consideration, and, in most cases, the sole consideration of the grant."[61]

That Reverend Wheelock's institution more than met this obligation could not be doubted. What could be more compatible with the common good than, as Marshall described it, "a charity school for the instruction of Indians in the Christian religion"?[62] Meeting this obligation would be trickier for non-eleemosynary corporations, such as those created for transportation or manufacture. The public policy favoring rapid and unlimited economic expansion provided the basis for clothing even these entrepreneurial firms with the mantle of the common welfare.

The theory of incorporation as a compact by which the corporation serves the public good created a potential dilemma for removing the corporation from political control. If corporations were contractually bound to promote the public interest, then were not all corporations, regardless of the source of their property, agencies of the state and, therefore, subject to legislative control? Put differently, the compact-for-the-commonwealth theory would seem fatally to undermine the distinction between public and private corporations. Marshall's response to this dilemma was not entirely satisfying. While the corporation must serve the common good, Marshall argued, this fact alone does not give the state any exclusive right or interest in its activities.[63] The state enjoys the benefit of Dartmouth's activities along with everyone else, but no more so than the general public.

Story's explication of the distinction between public and private corporations was more complete and more expansive.[64] Elaborating on and extending the argument that he had developed earlier in *Terrett v. Taylor*, Story reasoned that the character of a corporation depended on the nature of its foundation, not its function:

[P]ublic corporations are such only as are founded by the government for public purposes, where the whole interests belong also to the government. If, therefore, the foundation be private, though under the charter of the government, the corporation is private, however extensive the uses may be to which it is devoted, either by the bounty of the founder, or the nature and objects of the institution.[65]

The shift from "function" to "foundation" was crucial; it enabled institutions like Dartmouth to explain why they are removed from political control—because their assets were provided by private individuals rather than by the government—yet continue to enjoy certain governmental powers—because they act as quasi-commonwealths for the public good. The theory was broad enough to encompass not just eleemosynary institutions like Dartmouth, but profit-seeking institutions. It is no exaggeration to say that Story's concurring opinion in *Dartmouth College* marks the doctrinal origin of the modern American business corporation.[66]

The corporation's power over its own existence was the central issue in the struggle to secure autonomy from democratic control. Marshall's opinion recognized that if the corporate charter permitted subsequent legislative modification, the contract clause did not prevent the state from controlling the corporation. Such legislative control was not uncommon prior to the decision, and the practice of including reservation clauses in corporate charters continued after the case.[67] Yet many doubted that this practice left corporations completely exposed to political control. James Kent acknowledged, in the fourth edition of his treatise, that "it has become quite the practice, in all the recent acts of incorporation for private purposes, for the legislature to reserve to themselves a power to alter, modify or repeal the charter at pleasure."[68] Expressing the view of most proponents of corporate autonomy from politics, that is to say, most entrepreneurial republicans, though, Kent stated that "it may become a matter of serious consideration in many cases, how far the exercise of such a power could be consistent with justice or policy."[69] Kent's legal argument against the unlimited power of the legislature to insert reservations clauses in corporate charters was subtle and not unpersuasive:

If the charter be considered as a compact between the government and the individual corporators, such a reservation is of no force, unless it be made part and parcel of the contract. If a charter be granted, and accepted, with that reservation, there seems to be no ground to question the validity and efficiency [efficacy?] of the reservation; and yet it is easy to perceive, that if such a clause, inserted as a *formula* in every charter and grant of the government, be sufficient to give the state an unlimited control, as its mere pleasure, of all its grants, however valuable the consideration upon which they may be founded, the great and salutary provision in the constitution of the United States, so far as concerned all grants from state governments, will become of no moment.[70]

Story expressed the same attitude. In an 1833 case, he asserted in dicta that while the reservation clause "is certainly very broad, . . . it is not without limit."[71] Other courts rapidly followed Story's and Kent's lead, holding that the Constitution limited the legislature's power to control private corporations through reservation clauses.[72] These decisions did not entirely undermine the efficacy of reservation clauses. They only limited the legislature's power to "take away the property or rights which have become vested under a legitimate exercise of the [charter]."[73] Especially after the *Charles River Bridge* decision, reservation clauses and statutes became one of the Jacksonians' principle devices for extending political control over private corporations.

Intimations of Change

The Marshall Court's contract clause jurisprudence itself was neither smooth nor continuous. Changes in the Court's attitude toward state legislation affecting contracts were apparent before the appointment of Roger Taney, Andrew Jackson's Attorney General, as Chief Justice.[74] In *Ogden v. Saunders,* a narrow majority upheld a state insolvency statute that discharged citizens of their obligations under contracts made after passage of the law.[75] Eight years earlier, the Court struck down a statute that relieved debtors of their obligations under contracts made before the statute's enactment, but Marshall's opinion in that case contained language broad enough to cover postenactment contracts as well.[76] The majority opinion reasoned that the contract clause was aimed only at retroactive legislation, which was "oppressive, unjust, and tyrannical."[77] Laws that existed at the time a contract was formed and that therefore determined the extent of the obligations created by the contract could hardly be deemed unfair.

The crucial background fact of the case was Congress's repeated inability to enact a uniform bankruptcy statute. Had the Court struck down the state law before it, then the upshot would have been, as counsel for the debtor explicitly argued, that "the country would present the extraordinary spectacle of a great commercial nation, without laws on the subject of bankruptcy."[78] Venture capitalists, on whom the hopes of national economic expansion depended, would have been left without any recourse when ventures failed, as they frequently did in those economically turbulent times.

Ogden posed a conflict between entrepreneurial policy and vested property interests. In all of the Marshall court's previous contract clause decisions, vested rights and entrepreneurialism could be seen as mutually reinforcing. For the first time, the Supreme Court signaled a preference for promoting entrepreneurial activity over protecting the economic and social order secured by property interests. In addition, the *Ogden* decision deviated from the Marshall Court's clear pattern of protecting the established order from the destabilizing force of democratic politics. From this point on, where democracy and entrepreneurial policy coalesced, that is, where legislative action undermined established property rights in the interest of entrepreneurial policy, politics would prevail over the established order. Entrepreneurial republicanism was giving way to democratic entrepreneurialism, then, even before the *Charles River Bridge* decision.

Community and Competition: The *Charles River Bridge* Case

The Charles River Bridge was constructed under the authority of a 1785 corporate charter that the Massachusetts legislature granted to a group of local businessmen for the purpose of connecting Boston and Charlestown.[79] The charter initially gave the owners the right to collect tolls for a period of forty years, but the period was later extended to seventy years. The investment was hugely profitable for the owners, due largely to the tremendous population increases of the two communities. For a total outlay of $70,000, the bridge was collecting tolls of $30,000 a year by 1828.[80] By 1814, stock in the Charles River Bridge corporation was selling at more than 600 percent over its initial price.

In 1823, a group of Charlestown merchants petitioned the legislature for a charter to build a toll-free bridge. The petition provoked howls from several quarters, including, predictably, the Charles River Bridge proprietors, who claimed that the proposed bridge would destroy their property rights. The legislature rejected this and several subsequent petitions. Finally, in 1828, prompted by an anti-monopoly propaganda campaign, the legislature granted the petition to construct the Warren Bridge. The new bridge was located only a few hundred feet away from the Charles River

Bridge, and its charter authorized the Warren Bridge corporation to charge the same toll as the Charles River Bridge but only for six years. It also provided that after the owners had recovered their costs plus 5 percent interest, the bridge would revert to the state.

When the Warren Bridge opened, the predictable effect on the older bridge occurred. The Charles River Bridge corporation's earnings revenues declined by nearly one-half within six months, as the public extolled the virtues of the new bridge.[81] By 1837, when the Supreme Court decided the case, the corporation was earning nothing on its investment.[82]

The conflict between two types of legislatively created property interests, one an established monopoly and the other a prospective competitor, could not have been more starkly posed, and it left both the Massachusetts Supreme Judicial Court and the U.S. Supreme Court unable affirmatively to reach a decision. The Massachusetts court was evenly split over whether the Charles River Bridge's charter, which was silent as to whether its owners had an exclusive privilege to operate a bridge over the Charles River, should be construed to have granted such a privilege by implication.[83] The judges dismissed the complaint in order to permit an appeal to the U.S. Supreme Court.

That the Court would hear the case was not in doubt, for the dispute over two bridges had taken on much deeper political and economic implications. Politically, the dispute represented the conflict between aristocrats and democrats. The proponents of the Warren Bridge portrayed themselves as champions of the common good and their opponents as exemplars of the old New England aristocracy, which maintained its power through state-created monopolies.[84] Economically, there could not have been a clearer example of the tension between the old view that exclusive privileges were a necessary inducement for entrepreneurs and the ascendant view that such privileges stifled economic growth and that free competition was the correct path to economic development. At a more concrete level, that conflict between two economic theories translated into whether speculators in railroad and other new technologies would be able to eliminate the monopolies enjoyed by older forms of transportation, such as canals.[85]

Between 1831 and 1837, the Supreme Court was unable to reach a decision in the case. Part of the reason for the indecision was various absences and personnel changes on the Court, including Marshall's death and replacement by Roger Taney. It also appears, though, that the Marshall Court was deadlocked by a 3–3–1 vote, with Marshall himself on the side of the Warren Bridge owners.[86] After reargument, a divided Supreme Court affirmed the validity of the statute and the power of state legislatures to grant competing corporate charters. The Warren corporation won.

It is customary to depict *Charles River Bridge* as the watershed decision that signaled the end of the Supreme Court's protection of vested property rights under the contract clause.[87] It is beyond disputing that *Charles River Bridge* did signify a change from the attitude that produced *Fletcher v. Peck* and *Dartmouth College*. But continuity accompanied change. The Marshall and Taney Courts shared a commitment to promoting and protecting entrepreneurial activity. More fundamentally, they also shared the insight that entrepreneurialism was valuable for sociopolitical reasons as much as for the strictly economic purpose of increasing wealth.

What principally separates the property thought of the two Courts is the identity of the sociopolitical role of entrepreneurial activity. While the Marshall Court understood entrepreneurial activity as a means for maintaining the proper social order and, therefore, protected only those entrepreneurial interests that were established and stable, that is, "vested," the Taney Court understood entrepreneurship as a force for undermining hierarchical privileges and opening up opportunities for the broader community. This was the crucial difference between entrepreneurial republicanism and democratic entrepreneurialism.

The two major opinions in the case, Taney's for the majority and Story's dissent, perfectly reflected the discourses of these two understandings of entrepreneurialism. Taney's opinion has been described as "brief, lucid, and to the point."[88] It was all that, but it was not without rhetoric that disclosed a deep-seated vision of how society and politics ought to be ordered and of the role of entrepreneurial property interests in that sociopolitical order. Woven into Taney's technical legal analysis of whether the Charles River bridge corporation's charter implied a right to exclude competitors is a recurrent dialectic between two sets of terms: "privilege" and "monopoly," on the one hand, and "community" and "competition," on the other. In the course of discussing the English rule of construction against implied grants, for example, Taney stated:

[I]t would present a singular spectacle, if, while the courts in England are restraining, within the strictest limits, the spirit of monopoly, and exclusive privileges in the nature of monopolies, and confining corporations to the privileges plainly given to them in their charter;

the courts of this country should be found enlarging these privileges by implication; and construing a statute more unfavorably to the public, and to the rights of the community, than would be done in a like case in an English court of justice.[89]

The rhetorical force in this passage derives from its juxtaposition of the terms "privileges" and "rights of the community." In using the term "privilege," Taney was drawing on several traditions that had coalesced in Jacksonian political-legal rhetoric. One of those traditions was the English attack on monopolies that was widely associated with the name Adam Smith. This was the basis for Taney's ironic observation that England, that hierarchical society *extraordinaire*, had lately adopted a more hostile policy toward monopolies than had the United States. Taney's assault on privilege did not draw only on liberal political economy, however, for another tradition in which "privilege" was a conspicuous target was civic republicanism, particularly its eighteenth-century American incarnation. A common theme in political-legal tracts in the revolutionary era was the attack on legally created privileges as un-American, and well into the nineteenth century Jacksonians picked up the theme. The Jacksonian interpretation of republicanism emphasized its democratic possibilities, in contrast with the Federalist-Whig interpretation that stressed its belief in a proper social and political order. Jacksonians opposed the idea that there was a proper order that the government should maintain, among other ways, by extending exclusive property privileges to the certain social groups; they believed this perverted the basic insights of civic republicanism. The core of republicanism was the opportunity of all citizens to participate in the nation's economic as well as political life, not maintaining an entrenched hierarchy.

Taney's use of the term "community" is more intriguing because of its ambiguity. He used it several times in his opinion, repeatedly referring to the "rights of the community." In a revealing passage, Taney stated that "[w]hile the rights of private property are sacredly guarded, we must not forget that the community also have rights, and that the happiness and well being of every citizen depends on their faithful preservation."[90] One possible reading of this statement is that Taney is appealing to the theme that would become increasingly common in nineteenth-century critiques of private property: that property and democracy are antithetical to each other. But that interpretation is implausible. Taney was no man of the Left, in the modern sense of being opposed to the institution of private property. To the contrary, Taney strongly supported that institution and, more particularly, its entrepreneurial form. Taney had inherited the Jeffersonian understanding of democracy as a polity of property-owning citizens. Property rights might undermine democracy, but it was not inevitable that they would do so. The key was to maintain the opportunity for those without property to gain it.

Taney did not oppose private property as such, but property that was part of an entrenched hierarchy. He drew a sharp distinction between property of the old order and property of the new order. Property of the *ancien régime* were those interests that the state had granted to a favored few, giving them exclusive privileges. That was precisely the sort of interest that the Marshall Court had protected in *Fletcher v. Peck, Dartmouth College,* and other contract clause cases, and it was also precisely the type of interest that the Charles River bridge owners were claiming here.

The old property had been the basis for a sociopolitical order that was, to Taney's way of thinking, not only rankly hierarchical but also incompatible with progress. Like the Scottish Enlightenment social theorists of the eighteenth century,[91] he rejected the civic republicans' fear of change. Taney regarded change as a positive, "progressive" force, and economic growth was, for him, a crucial aspect of social progress. Economic development, in turn, required competition, not monopolies. This was clear from his celebration of economic development as serving the public good:

> [T]he object and end of all government is to promote the happiness and prosperity of the community by which it is established. . . . And in a country like ours, free, active, and enterprising, continually advancing in numbers and wealth; new channels of communication are daily found necessary, both for travel and trade; and are essential to the comfort, convenience, and prosperity of the people.[92]

"Monopolies," understood as exclusive property interests, can be attacked from two perspectives. The first is economic theory. We have already alluded to the liberal critique of monopolies that began with Adam Smith. That theory gained in the mid-nineteenth century, as it became clearer that more private capital had become available for investment canals, roads, and other key aspects of the transportation revolution. Exclusive privileges no longer seemed as necessary a price to pay to encourage entrepreneurs to jump into these ventures.[93]

The other angle from which one can attack monopolies is politics, and this was the basis for Taney's opposition to monopolies. Taney's primary concern was with making democracy, not the market, work. Opening up the market was simply a means to democratic ends, for economic competition, from his perspective, served the interests of democracy. This is the key to understanding his repeated references to the "rights of the community." He wanted to insure that when it created entrepreneurial interests, the state did not contribute to the imbalance of power that existed under the old hierarchical order. The only way to prevent state-created property interests from serving the interests of powerful elites was for the democratically elected legislature to retain control over them. The vested rights doctrine immunized, or nearly so, such interests from politics, and Taney's repudiation of that doctrine—declaring that property rights, while "sacred," are always subordinated to the rights of the "community"—was intended to expose them to democratic politics.

Where, then, does this leave *Charles River Bridge* with respect to corporations and the conception of property as commodity? *Charles River Bridge* can be characterized as consistent with commodificationist thought to the extent that its consequence was to expose state-created franchises to competition and, in that sense, moved them into the realm of the market. But even in terms of effect, the decision only tangentially supported the commodity conception. The critical element of commodificationism is the understanding of an asset's principle function as increasing social wealth through market transfers. *Charles River Bridge* did not effect a transformation of publicly created franchises into commodities in that sense. No one suggested that corporate franchises should be freely transferable in the market, although shares in the corporation's stock were transferable. Permitting the free transfer of a corporation's franchise would effectively have ceded power to the corporation to determine who enjoys the privilege for which the corporation was created. It would also have given corporations virtually unilateral control over their existence. Despite the growing sense of the privateness of private corporations, neither of these powers could be recognized. The corporation was still regarded as created by the state to serve the state's interest. "A corporation," the leading treatise on corporations declared in 1846, "can have no legal existence out of the sovereignty by which it is created."[94] The scope of the market's domain may have been widening by mid-century with respect to other institutions, but it had not widened with respect to corporations, at least not in the sense of removing corporations from the sphere of politics.

The Court's rhetoric in *Charles River Bridge* reflected the influence of the commodity conception even less than the decision's consequences did. Taney's opinion was filled with the rhetoric of the rights of the community, not the market; of politics, not economics. Fundamentally, it signified a preoccupation with dismantling a social hierarchy supported by state-conferred exclusive entrepreneurial interests, not with wealth maximization. Entrepreneurial corporate property, Taney was declaring, might increase individual wealth, but primarily they had to serve the interests of the community as a whole.

Neither the vested rights doctrine of *Fletcher v. Peck* and *Dartmouth College* nor *Charles River Bridge,* then, was premised on the commodity conception of property. Neither reflected an attempt to move entrepreneurial interests into the sphere of the market. The Marshall Court decisions protected certain property interests as the foundation for a particular type of social order. *Charles River Bridge* symbolized an attack on that order by extending democratic control over one of its most powerful institutions. For antebellum lawyers on both sides, the ascendancy of entrepreneurial property posed a problem whose fundamental nature was social and political, not economic.

EIGHT

Commodifying Humans:
Property in the Antebellum Legal
Discourse of Slavery

ANTEBELLUM LEGAL DISCOURSE about slavery is a vast
terrain, many corners of which remain unexplored. This chapter examines only one of those corners: the impact of the ideology of commodificationism on pro-slavery legal writing in the nineteenth century. It is a
commonplace among scholars of American slavery law that the law of
slavery was characterized by an "overall property orientation."[1] Observing
that American slavery law reflected the status of the African-American
slave as chattel property does not itself tell us very much, however. The
more searching question is what conception of property underlay the
American law of slavery and, more generally, pro-slavery legal thought
and legal discourse. Did antebellum legal theorists of slavery consider this
human property primarily to be a means of creating and acquiring private
wealth, i.e., as a commodity? Or did they assign a noneconomic function
to slaves as property, a function that while not indifferent to wealth, was
more concerned with maintaining a particular substantive vision of the
proper social order?

Recent scholarship by several historians, including Eugene D. Genovese, Elizabeth Fox-Genovese, Larry Tise, and Drew Gilpin Faust, has
made clear within the past several years that pro-slavery Southern intellectuals during the period roughly between 1830 and 1860 consciously developed a distinct worldview. These historians have disagreed over the moti-
vations for the Southern intellectuals' project of developing that
worldview, with some arguing that pro-slavery ideology was the product
of an intellectual elite struggling "to establish a role for men of mind" in
a nonintellectual society,[2] and others interpreting it as the effort of a "ruling race" to explain and justify the anomaly of slavery in a liberal society,[3]
while still others explaining the ideology as a response by defenders of a

premodern social order to the emergence a modern, capitalist order in their region.[4] On the basic existence of a distinct Southern pro-slavery ideology, it now seems beyond serious question that the once-conventional interpretation of pro-slavery writing as the incoherent rantings of a racist elite obsessed by a single issue is profoundly mistaken. The Southern defenders of slavery *were,* without any question, racist, but their defense of slavery was neither one-dimensional nor was it utterly incoherent. It was the expression of an *ideology,* in the truest sense of the term.

Lawyers played a prominent role in constructing pro-slavery ideology. They were the dominant intellectual force in the South well into the nineteenth century, and their influence was clear in pro-slavery writing. Virtually all of the major antebellum Southern defenders of slavery were educated in the law. The major legal pro-slavery theorists included John C. Calhoun, Thomas Reade Rootes Cobb, Thomas Roderick Dew, George Fitzhugh, James Henry Hammond, and William Harper. Even so, their theories did not usually rely on distinctly legal arguments. There continued to be a close nexus among legal, political, economic, and social writing in the South throughout the antebellum period, so that even as late as the 1850s, Southern legal literature was less specialized than it was in the process of becoming in the North.[5] The writings of Southern theorists on slavery reflected a generalist approach. In constructing and defending pro-slavery ideology, they comfortably blended legal, moral, political, economic, and social arguments.

Antebellum Southern legal writing on slavery was neither monolithic nor static. The most notable change was the shift from a strand of Southern pro-slavery theory that accommodated the teachings of classical political economy to a strand that was in several important respects hostile to the political economic teachings of Adam Smith and David Ricardo. Southern political economists were some of the most potent minds in the pro-slavery project, but their status in the South was always marginal, even among intellectuals. Men like Thomas Cooper, Thomas R. Dew, and George Tucker represented the commercial and international outlook of the Atlantic port cities, favoring economic development above all else. A fundamental reason why they were never at the forefront of efforts to construct a credible defense of slavery was the fact that slavery posed for them an insoluble dilemma. As Eugene Genovese and Elizabeth Fox-Genovese have pointed out, within the parameters of political economic thought, "either the slave should be seen as an independent economic agent and should, accordingly, be liberated and transformed into a proletarian, free to sell his or her labor-power in conformity with the laws of the market, or the slave should be seen [solely] as a thing—a simple unit of fixed capital to be bought and sold like any other nonhuman commodity."[6] Unable to reconcile the dictates of their discipline with their region's basic institution, the Southern political economists gradually lost influence in the defense of slavery.

By the 1840s, the lead had passed to another group of writers who were unencumbered by a principled commitment to a liberal market society.[7] The latter group of writers defended slavery as part of a broader ambition and set about to construct a vision of what they considered to be the properly ordered society. Their writings not only produced a particular way of thinking about slaves as property but, more broadly, constructed a social theory that would serve as the foundation for the entire institution of Southern slavery.[8] This pro-slavery social theory represented, as Genovese and Fox-Genovese have aptly called it, "a desperate effort to project an alternate world order at once supremely reactionary and necessarily new."[9]

At bottom, the world order that the pro-slavery social theorists described was an alternative to social modernity, as mid-nineteenth-century Southern intellectuals understood it. What made modernity unacceptable to them was that it seemingly meant the market's total domination of all social relations. Modern societies, for which the North served as an emerging model, seemed to Southern social theorists to be characterized by nothing as much as the fact that the market was the sole source for defining and constituting relationships among individuals in all areas of social life. "Sole" is the important word here. The Southern social theorists' ideal society certainly was a market society in the sense that the market allocated economic resources. What set their ideal society apart from modern society was the fact that the market's influence on social life was strictly limited. Above all, pro-slavery social theorists insisted, the market could not be permitted to destabilize the existence of a social hierarchy that these intellectuals perceived as organic, moral, and proper.

Even while they embraced the premodern vision of society, Southern legal theorists of slavery had to acknowledge the reality that many aspects of commercial modernity existed within their own society. Slaves in fact did constitute an item of commercial merchandise that, while obviously not fungible with other forms of property, still functioned as a means of creating individual wealth, at least for the elite segment of Southern society. The task for pro-slavery theorists was somehow to accommodate those elements of commercial modernity within their essentially premodern vision. Their dilemma was how to preserve a premodern, hierarchical social order while at the same time acknowledging the commercial, or market, aspect of the most important form of property in their society— African-American slaves. The pro-slavery theorists' confrontation with that dilemma produced a dialectic between these two social visions and the two concomitant conceptions of property, commodified and proprietarian.

Property and the Ideal Society in Pro-Slavery Legal Ideology
The Content of Social Modernity

Southern slavery theory was primarily a social theory. The major theorists, including legal theorists, who defended slavery did so on the basis of a coherent (though utterly immoral) theory of the ideal society whose core institution was, of course, chattel slavery. That ideal society was essentially premodern and in many ways the antithesis of the modern society they saw developing in the North. Southern theorists identified that society with three characteristics that were anathema to them: (1) social leveling, that is, the denial of a natural social hierarchy; (2) the decline of inherent, that is, nonconsensual social obligations; and (3) the alienation of labor from capital. Modern society was characterized by fluidity in all aspects of social life. It destabilized traditions and natural relationships. Modernity also denied the existence of natural duties that the privileged class of society owed to the weak. Finally, it exacerbated rather than resolved the troublesome problem of the conflict between labor and capital.

Pro-slavery theorists used these three characteristics as the mirror image of the ideal social order. The defining characteristics of that social order were an organic social hierarchy based on race; the fusion of labor and capital through slavery; and recognition of paternalism as a legitimate mode of social relationship. The properly ordered society was one in which the organic social hierarchy was preserved and social relationships were not corrupted by the avaricious materialism of a completely commercialized society. Citizens did not act strictly out of self-interest, but out of a sense of responsibility to others, especially those who were naturally inferior. To be sure, the personal pursuit of wealth existed in this society. But if the properly ordered society was not a communist utopia, neither was it a modern commercialized society in which the pursuit of private wealth defined how people interacted with each other and markets defined the parameters of people's responsibility for others. The proper society that antebellum Southern social theorists defined was, in short, a version of the eighteenth-century civic republican commonwealth. As the Southern slavery theorists saw it (or at least claimed they saw it), the South was the perfect embodiment of this perfect society. The South was, they claimed, the purest instance of a premodern civic republican society that had yet been created in North America.

The foundation for this new and unsurpassed social order was slavery, the South's "peculiar institution." More precisely, the foundation was the conception of slaves as a unique form of property. Though they could be used as a commodity, slaves were not primarily valued for that function. Their core function, rather, was to anchor and maintain the stability of the proper and preordained social hierarchy. It was the preservation of that hierarchy, not the production of wealth, that was the vital interest of slaves-as-property system.

Within this social vision the commodity conception of property was highly problematic. The commodity conception is the product of a modern commercial social order that was in many ways the antithesis of what proslavery theorists valued. The social order the pro-slavery theorists contemplated was a hierarchical, paternalistic social order in which certain forms of property, most importantly slaves, functioned primarily as anchors to stabilize a social hierarchy that these theorists regarded as immanent. Within this social order slave property was valued only secondarily for its role as commercial merchandise. More important, slave property as an item of commerce could not be used in a way that threatened to transform Southern order into the fluid sort of society that existed in the bourgeois communities of the North.

Among the most influential legal texts articulating these themes were two monographs by the Georgia lawyer-politician, Thomas Reade Rootes Cobb. *Historical Sketch of Slavery* and *The Law of Negro Slavery*, both published in 1858,[10] were among the most widely cited pro-slavery texts produced in the antebellum period.[11] While it certainly did not repudiate all aspects of classical political economy, Cobb's work fits most comfortably within the social theoretic strand of pro-slavery writing. Like other Southern social theoretical work, Cobb's essays were preoccupied with the tasks of developing, defending, and propagating a vision of the proper social order, a social order that was fundamentally premodern in character. What makes his essays worth particular attention is the fact that, more than any other Southern legal writings of his time, they exemplified the preoccupation with the dilemma of reconciling the commodity status of

African-American slaves with the social vision of the South as the embodiment of the premodern republican order.

The Organic Social Hierarchy

Above all else, the ideal well-ordered society was, for Southern slavery theorists, a social hierarchy. Virtually without exception, elite Southern writers argued that society should organized on the basis of certain formal distinctions, especially race, class, and forms of property. The superiority of whites over blacks, wealthy over poor, landowners over tenants, and slaves as property over other forms of property were, they thought, natural truths, revealed both by God and by history. No greater error could be made than to try artificially to construct a society in which these distinctions were formally abolished. Yet the modern, commercial society, whose main exemplar lay just to the north, represented just that sort of false and inorganic society.

The theoretical foundation for this hierarchical society was not feudalism, as some have suggested,[12] but civic republicanism. However much the slave South in fact resembled a feudal society, nineteenth-century pro-slavery theorists were loath to accept that comparison. Their defenses of slavery repeatedly insisted that slavery was entirely compatible with, indeed best fulfilled the principles of, liberty and equality. Those are not the principles of a feudal society, but, as Southern theorists understood them, of a republican society. The ideal, properly ordered society that pro-slavery intellectuals described was, they believed, the truest form of civic republicanism that history had yet produced. Virtually every intellectually sophisticated defense of slavery after 1830 argued that Southern slave society constituted the truest republican society since the classical republican societies of ancient Greece and Rome. The trope that increasingly became the means for expressing this idea was slavery as the "cornerstone" of the "republican edifice." Slavery was, as James Henry Hammond put it in his famous "Letter to an English Abolitionist," "truly the 'cornerstone' and foundation of every well-designed and durable 'republican edifice.'"[13]

Antebellum Southern republicanism, a distinct brand of republicanism Southern theorists trumpeted as the "true republican doctrine,"[14] was in truth *conservative* republicanism. It pursued what Frank Michelman has called the "exclusionary response" to the task of realizing the political significance of property.[15] The proper practice of citizenship, in classical republican thought, requires wisdom among the citizenry, and the institutional arrangement that best insured that requisite condition was a linkage between citizenship and property ownership. The exclusionary interpretation of that linkage was to leave the distribution of property ownership determined by nonpolitical means.[16] That is, conservative republicanism, while otherwise insisting on governance through democratic participation by all citizens, removed the entire issue of who qualified as a citizen from the operation of principles of democracy.

In this sense, pro-slavery republican ideology was, as Cobb recognized, truly conservative. "Politically," Cobb wrote, "slavery is a *conservative* institution."[17] While antebellum Southern law did not formally condition citizenship on owning slaves, the slaveowner plainly was the paradigm of the proper citizen, for Cobb as for other elite Southerners. Slavery conferred on owners leisure, and, Cobb argued, "[t]he leisure . . . gives [the slaveholder] an opportunity of informing himself upon current questions of politics." This leisurely environment guarantees genuine conservatism, Cobb reasoned.

> [The slaveholder's] interest being identical with his neighbors, in preserving existing institutions, the Southern politician addresses always a body of men having a common sentiment, and not to be influenced to so great an extent by the "humbugs" of demagogues. This is an influential element in forming public opinion, and acts thus *conservatively* upon the public men of the South.[18]

The slavery theorists who drew on republican ideology argued that the slave South's version of republicanism was purer and more true to the basic tenets of classical thought than that contemplated by the Founding Fathers.[19] Even Federalist republicanism, which, as we saw earlier, was overtly hierarchical in character, had deviated from true republicanism in certain respects. Slavery was the core of Southern republicanism, but however elitist and hierarchical in fact Federalist social and political thought was—and it *was* elitist and hierarchical—it did not accept slavery, let alone place it at the center of the proper social order.

Another difference between pro-slavery republicanism and Federalist republicanism was that between a premodern and a modern social vision. Federalism was essentially an attempt to perform the impossible: reconcile social and economic modernity with the inherited traditions of republican society. Southern pro-slavery social theorists were keenly aware that the gap between the two visions was unbridgeable and they defined their social order in large part by rejecting those aspects of the social order that

Federalism had begot, the commercial society of the North, that were most distinctly modern.

Chief among these mistaken characteristics of the modern social order was the leveling of formal social distinctions, especially those based on race but also those based on social class. Southern slavery theorists hardly perceived the commercialized North as a classless society, but they did tend to view it as one that, following the principles of Federalism, had repudiated a *formal* social hierarchy. The primary basis for the North's repudiation of formal class differences, Southern intellectuals thought, was the Founding Fathers' mistaken emphasis on equality as a political value. "I repudiate," the influential politician-intellectual James Henry Hammond declared, "as ridiculously absurd, that much lauded but no-where accredited dogma of Mr. Jefferson, that 'all men are created equal.' No society has ever existed . . . without a natural variety of classes."[20]

For others who were less confident about repudiating Mr. Jefferson's principle entirely, equality was an appropriate political value, but the North had mistakenly interpreted it as requiring social leveling. The equality of all men, as the Declaration of Independence had used the term, had a very different meaning than the idea that all human beings by virtue of their very humanity possessed equal dignity and deserved equal respect. One meaning that some slavery theorists attached to equality in the context of Jefferson's document was that that it simply referred to the status of persons as a matter of positive public law of England, not as a matter of the rights of individuals between each other in private relations. This was the tact taken in John Codman Hurd's treatise *The Law of Freedom and Bondage in the United States:*

> [I]t is plain, from both the rest of the document and from history, that, if the claims of those colonies rested ultimately on the rights of private persons inhabiting their jurisdictions, it was on those rights as they existed by and in the public and political law, and as they were vested in those persons by the constitution of the empire, as hereditary and attaching to them in the character of members of existing political and civil bodies, and not in individual or relative rights as attributed by private law in social relations.[21]

Cobb's conception of equality was less technical and more consistent with the exclusionary strand of civic republican thought. Equality was demanded, Cobb argued, only among citizens, and since not all persons were fit to be citizens there was no contradiction between slavery and equality. To the contrary, slavery created a truer form of equality, understood in its correct sense.

> The mass of laborers not being recognized among citizens, every citizen feels that he belongs to an elevated class. It matters not that he is no slaveholder; he is not of the inferior race; he is a freeborn citizen; he engages in no menial occupation. The poorest meets the richest as an equal; sits at his table with him; salutes him as a neighbor; meets him in every public assembly, and stands on the same social platform. Hence, there is no war of classes. There is truthfully republican equality in the ruling class.[22]

Cobb's conception of equality was compatible not only with classical republican thought but also with the attitudes of white nonslaveholders. Slavery strengthened the Southern small property owners' sense of their own yeoman independence. Whatever other differences existed between the large plantation owner and the subsistence farmer, they shared the crucial fact that they *were* property owners, categorically distinguishing them from slaves. The nonslaveholding white owner's perception of himself as the equal of his much wealthier neighbors facilitated the acceptance of the ideology of pro-slavery republicanism among lower classes of whites as well as the elite planter class.[23]

Apart from its misguided interpretation of equality, Southern pro-slavery republicans believed that another, deeper reason why a formal class structure did not exist in the North was the existence of the market and the mode of social consciousness that it engendered. The market and its *mentalité* were at the core of Northern society. The market itself was the greatest of all levelers of formal class distinctions. A society that structured social relations on the basis of transactions for individual gain was not entirely incompatible with class differences, of course, for those with the greatest natural talents would rise to the top in such a society. But social relations within thoroughly commercialized societies were fluid, making hierarchies unstable. One could not easily maintain any formally ordained social hierarchy in such a society, for the forces of self-interest, nurtured by the market ideology, constantly corroded it and made it anachronistic.

The incompatibility of formal social hierarchies and market-structured social relations was common ground between Southern pro-slavery republicans and the Federalist forebears of the republican tradition. Where they parted company was the implication of this positive social analysis for the normative question of which sort of society was better, more moral, more humane. Southern theorists argued that the market society's apparent leveling effects made it all the more insidious, for the reality of modern market societies, as the North so vividly illustrated, was that they substituted an informal mode of social hierarchy based on individual acquisitiveness and selfishness for that natural and moral form of hierarchy based on race and class.

No Southern intellectual took this argument farther than George Fitzhugh, whose widely read books and essays advocated slavery as a desirable arrangement for white as well as black labor.[24] The North and all other modern, thoroughly commercialized societies throughout the world, Fitzhugh wrote, "inculcate selfishness and competition as the great duties of man."[25] "[A]ll government begets slavery in some form";[26] the only question is what form of slavery, what mode of social hierarchy is most humane. To Fitzhugh, there could be no doubt that the form of social dependency created in the North, which he called "slavery to capital," was vastly worse than chattel slavery. His critique of the modern commercialized society merits being quoted at length:

> The spirit of trade and commerce is universal, and it is as much the business of trade to devour the poor, as of the whales to swallow herrings. All its profits are derived from unjust exacting or "exploitation" of the common poor laboring class; for the professional and capitalist, and skillful laboring classes, manage to exact five times as much from the poor, as they pay to the tradesmen in way of profit. The poor produce everything and enjoy nothing. The people of the North are hugging to their breasts a silly delusion, in the belief that the poor can tax the rich, and thus prevent those evils that are starving and maddening the masses in Western Europe. You can't tax a rich man unless he be a slave-holder, because it does not breed or produce anything itself. Labor pays all taxes, pays the rich man's income, educates his children, pays the professional man's fees, the merchant's profits, and pays the taxes which support the Government.[27]

To provide conclusive evidence that true republics were not only openly hierarchical but were slave societies, Southern slavery theorists turned to history. Cobb's *Historical Sketch of Slavery* was typical in its appeal to the classical civilizations of Greece and Rome to demonstrate the continuity between true republicanism and the slave South. As in the South, the experiences of classical Greece and Rome revealed not only that republicanism required slavery but that equality and liberty, the very principles that Northern abolitionists stood on, required slavery. "[T]rue philosophy," Cobb wrote, "confirms the conclusions of Aristotle and Plato, that [slavery] is an element essential in a true republic, for the preservation of perfect equality among citizens, and the growth and encouragement of the spirit of liberty."[28] Equality existed among citizens under slavery because slaves were not citizens. Liberty existed under slavery because slaves were freed from the tyranny of the market. Poverty had taken the place of royalist despotism as the immediate threat to liberty in antebellum Southern slave ideology.[29] In this sense, pro-slavery theorists could depict the African American as the freest class in society. "The law," Cobb wrote, "protected [the slave's] life and his person."[30]

Slaves as Noncommodified Property: The Imperatives of Protectionism

The second defining characteristic of the properly ordered society in pro-slavery sociolegal ideology was the status of the slave as a form of property. A core tenet of pro-slavery republicanism was that slaves were a unique, noncommodified form of property. Southern self-styled republicans associated the modern, commercialized social order with the conception of all forms of property as wealth and, therefore, as fungible. The properly ordered society, as pro-slavery writers defined it, was not only a social hierarchy but a hierarchy of forms of property as well. Echoing its civic republican antecedents, Southern republican thought stressed that not all forms of property were fungible, and that property's central purpose was more than creating personal wealth. While some forms of property were fungible and were appropriately treated as commodities, the most important forms were unique and served a civic, not an economic function.

At the top of the property hierarchy stood the slave. Slaves, as a form of property, were to nineteenth-century Southern republicans what land (more specifically, fee-simple ownership in land) had been to Harringtonian republicans. As Harringtonian republicanism had regarded land as the anchor of virtuous citizenship, so pro-slavery republicans regarded slaves as the anchor of the properly ordered society. While land was clearly superior to intangible forms of property in the Southern hierarchy of property, it was nevertheless inferior in importance to slaves.

Slave property's function in pro-slavery legal and political ideology resembled that of land in Harringtonian republican ideology in a second sense as well. Like the Harringtonian fee simple estate in land, slaves had to be, at least primarily, a noncommodity, that is, an asset whose main function was not to increase private wealth by being bought and sold. Pro-slavery republicanism deviated from its Harringtonian antecedent, however, on the question why this particular form of property had to a noncommodity. Southern legal republicans like Cobb were less concerned with securing, through material means, virtuous citizenship than they were explaining and justifying slavery as a humane institution. It was precisely that imperative that led them to develop pro-slavery republicanism as an alternative (and superior) worldview in the first place. In its role as ideology that opposed commercial modernity, Southern pro-slavery theory constructed a theory of humanity and a concomitant theory of society that stressed moral duties of the strong elements of society to protect the weak. It was this ideology of protectionism that required that slave property not be reduced to mere commercial merchandise.[31]

Pro-slavery theorists constructed a theory of humanity consciously in opposition to that which underlay commercial societies, as these theorists understood them. Commercial society conceived of human beings as atomistic free agents and of society as constituted by relationship created solely on the basis of consent. Many pro-slavery legal and political theorists regarded that conception as inorganic and false. Certain social groups were naturally inferior and therefore needed protection, while others were superior. The naturally superior classes were obligated to provide protection for the inferior groups. The organically structured society that emerged from the natural relationships of dependence and protection was the slave society. Slavery was simply the institutional realization of that natural order and responsibility of the strong to protect the weak.

Pro-slavery legal writers like Cobb relied on race in defining the natural distinction between the weak and the strong. A few writers, most notably George Fitzhugh, took the theory of natural hierarchy to its logical extreme by arguing that inferior whites should be slaves along with inferior Blacks. Most, however, argued along the same lines that Cobb did. He blended racialist arguments with protectionist arguments rather than treating them as distinct bases on which to defend slavery.[32] Cobb spoke for most of his contemporaries when he stated that "[t]he negroes . . . introduced into America, were gross and stupid, lazy and superstitious."[33] African slaves were naturally fit for slavery, Cobb argued, and this fit became apparent immediately on their arrival to America:

The negroes thus imported were generally contented and happy. The lamentations placed in their mouths by sentiment poets, were for the most part without foundation in fact. In truth their situation when properly treated was improved by the change. Careless and mirthful by nature, they were eager to find a master when they reached the shore, and the cruel separations to which they were sometimes exposed, and which for the moment gave them excruciating agony, were forgotten at the sound of their rude musical instruments and in the midst of their noisy dances. The great Architect had framed them both physically and mentally to fill the sphere in which they were thrown, and His wisdom and mercy combined in constituting them thus suited to the degraded position they were destined to occupy. Hence, their submissiveness, their obedience, and their contentment.[34]

Racialist arguments explained the African's natural proclivity on the basis of a wide variety of factors, including geography and climate, as well as physical and mental characteristics. Explaining why slavery had not flourished in the North, for example, Cobb argued, "The sun is as necessary to negro perfection as it is to the cotton plant."[35] While Africans had flourished under slavery in South, emancipated slaves in the North had fallen into greater degradation. Cobb quoted extensive comments from governors and leading politicians in northern states concerning the condition and capabilities of emancipated slaves in their states. These comments, Cobb argued, all revealed the intellectual, material, and moral inferiority of the emancipated slave.[36] The experience of emancipation of black slaves in the Caribbean provided further evidence of the African's natural fitness for slavery. Emancipation in Haiti and the British West Indies, Cobb insisted, had had the effect of "gradual[ly] return[ing] to barbarism . . . a race rescued from that condition only by slavery."[37] The inexorable implication of these experiences, Cobb wrote, quoting the Northern pro-slavery clergyman Robert Baird, was "'to prove the theory of those who maintain that the negro race is by natural incapacity unfitted for self-government.'"[38] "Negroes," Cobb concluded, "are more healthy and long-lived, in a state of slavery than of freedom."[39] The contrast between the miserable status of freed slaves in Liberia and the Caribbean region and the thriving condition of enslaved Africans in the American South proved beyond any doubt, pro-slavery theorists argued, that slavery was the most beneficial condition for Africans. "In mental and moral development," Cobb asserted, "slavery, so far from retarding, has advanced the negro race."

> The intelligence of the slaves of the South compares favorably with the negro race in any country, but more especially with their native tribes. . . . [R]emove the restraining and controlling power of the master, and the negro becomes, at once, the slave of his lust, and the victim of his indolence, relapsing, with wonderful rapidity, into his pristine barbarism. Hayti and Jamaica are living witnesses to this truth; and Liberia would probably add her testimony, were it not for the fostering care of philanthropy, and the annual leaven of emancipated slaves.[40]

The only possible conclusion that one could reasonably draw from this evidence, Cobb thought, was that slavery is the natural condition of Negroes. Cobb expressed a view that was universally shared by pro-slavery writers and the overwhelming majority of the white population of the South as well when he stated that "a state of bondage, so far from doing violence to the law of [the African's] nature, develops and perfects it." He continued, "[I]n that state, he enjoys the greatest amount of happiness, and arrives at the greatest degree of perfection of which his nature is capable." The conclusion was inexorably drawn: "[N]egro slavery, as it exists in the United States, is not contrary to the law of nature."[41]

The moral implication of this natural racial hierarchy that pro-slavery legal writers like Cobb drew was that whites, as the superior race, owed a solemn duty to society to protect African Americans as the weak and vulnerable race. Protectionist theorists conceived of individuals not as autonomous agents but as inextricably—organically—linked with society.[42] Some writers went so far as to insist that the individual was subordinate to society. Society, in turn, was constituted by relationships of dependence and protection. "It is the right and the duty of the sane to take care of the insane," Hubbard Winslow wrote, "of the virtuous to restrain the vicious, of the learned to instruct the ignorant, of the wise to guide the simple, of the strong to protect the weak, of the aged to counsel the young. . . ."[43] Slavery was moral precisely insofar as it was a protective institution. It was this protective conception of the institution of slavery that was the source of the noncommodified understanding of the slave as property.[44]

The protectionist strand of pro-slavery legal ideology constituted a common theme between that ideology and the legal ideology that under-lay the law of marriage and marital property in the nonslave states of the North. As we saw in chapter 5, the antebellum married women's property reforms, which were enacted at the same time when Southern intellectuals were defending their social order as a pure system of protectionism, were motivated by a protectionist outlook. Pro-slavery legal writers did not draw attention to the fact of this common commitment. These Southern intellectuals considered their theory of society to be an oppositional ideol-ogy. This stance made it difficult for them to discern, let alone publicize that their world view was to some extent an extension rather than a repu-diation of the social order of the Northern states. The fact remains, how-ever, that with respect to the issue of protectionism the North had re-tained vestiges of the old premodern social vision. Contrary to what Southern intellectuals believed, then, its social-legal ideology was not en-tirely in conflict with the slave South's.

Protectionism operated somewhat differently in the two contexts. In the context of married women's property law in the North, the protec-tionist ideology was ambiguous with respect to the question who was the protector. Two protectionist theories were, in fact, at work here. One involved protection of married women *by* their husbands from others; the other involved protection of wives *from* their husbands. Under the first theory, husbands were their wives' protectors against creditors and other market predators. The second theory made the husband the preda-tor and looked to the legal system to protect the wife's economic well-being. In the context of black slavery in the South, there was less room for uncertainty about who was the slave's protector. The relationship between master and slave was strictly hierarchical in a way that the husband-wife relationship never was, even under the first theory of wife protection. To be sure, pro-slavery theorists recognized that slaves sometimes needed protection from their master, just as married women's property law re-formers recognized, even under the first theory of wife protection (i.e., the husband as protector rather than predator) that wives sometimes need protection from their husbands. But Southern protectionists like Cobb brushed aside incidents of abuse of slaves by their masters as the extreme exception. The rule was that masters cared deeply for their slaves and treated them as kindly and protectively as they did their own biological children (which, in some instances, they were).[45] Self-interest and affection, Cobb argued, created a special protective bond between master and slave:

> That the slave is incorporated into and becomes part of the family, that a tie is thus formed between the master and slave, almost unknown to the master and hireling . . . , that the old and infirm and thus cared for, and the young protected and reared, are indisputable facts. Interest joins with affection in promoting this unity of feeling. To the negro, it insures food, fuel, and clothing, medical attention, and in most cases religious instruction. The young child is seldom removed from the parent's protection, and beyond doubt, the institution prevents the separation of families, to an extent unknown among the laboring poor of the world. It provides him with a protector, whose interest and feeling combined in demanding such protection.[46]

The slave system did not rely on self-interest and feeling alone, Cobb pointed out, to secure protection of the slave. The law of slavery backstopped affection and self-interest to protect slaves. Legal action was especially important dealing with those relatively few instances, as Cobb depicted it, in which masters misused their power over slaves. "Statute law has done much," Cobb wrote, "to relieve the slave from this absolute dominion, and the master from this perilous power, more especially so as regards the first great right of personal security."[47]

The protectionist outlook required that slaves, though property, not be conceived as just another item of commercial merchandise. A commodified conception of slave property would have undermined the defense of slavery as a humane institution that fulfilled society's responsibility to protect its weakest members. Were the slave regarded as a mere commodity, the entire relationship between master and slave would be transformed from the personal and mutual relationship that Cobb described. The master would be transformed into a seller, and the slave into an item of property whose value cannot be expressed intrinsically but only in terms of something else. As Lewis Hyde points out, "We derive value . . . from the comparison of one thing with another. . . . [Exchange v]alue needs a difference for its expression; when there is no difference we are left with a tautology ('a yard of linen is a yard of linen')."[48] Master and slave would have to be understood as alienated, or psychologically distanced from each other, rather than as linked in a relationship of sentiment and dependency. People do not ordinarily sell objects with which they are sentimentally attached. Likewise, commodification seems incongruent with a social responsibility to protect the weak and vulnerable. A crucial aspect of that responsibility, as protectionist slave theorists defined it, was keeping slave families intact wherever possible. John Belton O'Neall, an influential judge on the South Carolina Court of Appeals, strongly disfavored breaking up slave families, and he recognized that buying and selling slaves as commodities constituted the most immediate threat to the security of slave families. In his 1848 digest *The Negro Law of South Carolina,* he suggested that an effective way of preventing the dissolution of slave families would be to limit the sale of slaves by requiring that they be sold only together with the sale of the land on which they worked.[49] This proposal had been made earlier by Byron Edwards, an intellectual leader of South Carolina's plantation class. He proposed tying slaves to land precisely to prevent them from being sold as commodity property.[50] These slavery theorists recognized that the status of slaves as exchange-property ultimately undermined the owner's protectionist responsibilities.

Even were the slave inalienable and therefore not an exchange-commodity but a use-commodity, the master-slave relationship would have to be understood as an alienated one. This was the thrust of Marx's statement at the beginning of the first volume of *Capital:* "The commodity is, first of all, an external object, a thing which through its qualities satisfies human needs of whatever kind."[51] The slave would have had worth to the owner only insofar as the slave satisfied the owner's needs. The slave's own needs would have been irrelevant, except to the extent that not meeting them would have jeopardized the owner's investment. The whole thrust of the protectionist ideology, however, was to insist that slavery fulfilled the slave's needs in the interest of humanity. That claim impelled protectionist legal writers like Cobb to emphasize the noncommodified aspect of slave property.

Slavery could fulfill its role under slave republican ideology, then, by avoiding the commodification of slave property. A core principle of that ideology was the primacy of humanitarian obligations over individual interests. A conception of slaves as mere merchandise, a commodity to be bought and sold for personal gain like any other fungible asset, would have represented precisely the reverse of this ordering of interests. Slavery legal theorists like Cobb, O'Neall, and Edwards were able to reconcile the commodification of all other forms of property, including land, with their version of republicanism, but not slave property. No other form of property so starkly posed the choice between individual interest and social responsibility to protect others.

Dissolving the Conflict between Labor and Capital

If pro-slavery sociolegal theory was a critique of the more disquieting aspects of the modern social order of thoroughly commercialized economies, then there was no greater task for antebellum Southern intellectuals to accomplish than resolving the twin problems of economic dependency and alienated social relations that they saw stemming from the wage labor system of the North. Pro-slavery legal writers like Cobb recognized that task and met it head-on. The third element of their triadic theory of the properly ordered society was the dissolution of the conflict between labor and capital, the basis of alienated social relations and social instability that they viewed as the result of the system of wage labor. The key to achieving that goal was, again, maintaining the noncommodified character of slave property.

The problem of wage dependency was closely linked with the problem posed by the organically hierarchical nature of society, but the two were not identical. The social hierarchy that Southern intellectuals identified meant that every society inevitably has subgroups of persons who are, by nature, inferior, weak, and vulnerable. Those persons are naturally unfit for self-government and, therefore, *naturally* dependent. Since the source of that form of dependency was nature rather than any human institution, no social order could eliminate it. The appropriate reaction to that problem, then, was to recognize a social duty by the strong to protect the weak.

The wage labor system created a different dilemma. Here as well, social dependency was the problem, but this form of dependency was not the result of the natural condition of society but of a particular social institution. Pro-slavery ideology was, as Eric Foner has observed, in large measure "a striking critique of northern labor relations."[52] More specifically, it was a critique of the effects of wage labor on social relations. Eugene Genovese recently has stated the point with characteristic clarity: "[The proslavery theorists] located the primary social manifestations of evil precisely in the system of free labor and celebrated slavery as an alternative to it."[53]

Pro-slavery ideologists' critique of wage labor was hardly unique. It coincided with a strikingly similar critique of wage labor that the North's first real labor movement mounted in reaction to the dramatic changes in working conditions and indeed the very meaning of work that industrialization had wrought in the North. The roots of the critique, though, originated considerably earlier, in the radical strand of eighteenth-century American republicanism associated with Thomas Paine and Thomas Skidmore.

Though important differences could be found among the various iterations of the critique of wage labor, especially the Northern and Southern versions, there was a common core. In all of its incarnations, the critique attacked wage labor as incompatible with republican principles and inimical to social stability. Both Northern advocates of the free labor theory and Southern defenders of slavery argued that wage labor created a form of economic dependency that was completely incompatible with the republican ideal of a polity comprising autonomous property-owning citizens. Moreover, they argued, the alienation of labor from capital breeds alienation in social relations and, ultimately, engenders social instability. For any society to be stable, labor must not be reduced to a commodity that is bought and sold in the marketplace. To Northern free-soilers, that meant that society should comprise petty, self-sufficient producers, family farmers, and village artisans.[54] To Southern defenders of slavery, it meant a society of slaveholders.

Aware of the Northern Free Soil response to the problem of wage labor, Southern theorists contended that slave labor was the only solution that could avert a class war between labor and capital that would destroy not only republicanism but social stability in the North. As early as 1837, John C. Calhoun identified the fusion of labor and capital as one of strongest advantages of slavery:

> There is and always has been in an advanced stage of wealth and civilization, a conflict between labor and capital. The condition of society in the South exempts us from the disorders and dangers resulting from this conflict. . . . The experience of the next generation will fully test how vastly more favorable our condition of society is to that of other sections for free and stable institutions.[55]

The pro-slavery assault on wage labor repeatedly insisted that the wage labor system threatened both republican liberty and social stability. This weaving of republican ideology with a social analysis that superficially, but only superficially, resembles elements of Marxist ideology[56] was especially strong in the following argument by the neo-Federalist South Carolina planter-writer, William Henry Trescot:[57]

There is one relation, lying at the basis of all social and political life, the shifting character of which fairly indicates the national progress in wealth and civilization—the relation of labor to capital. . . . The history of all that is great in achievement . . . proves that the best interests of humanity require, first, that labor should be subordinate to, and controlled by capital; and second, that the interests of the two should by that very dependence be as closely as possible identified. It may be safely asserted . . . that the interest of labour and capital can never be permanently or properly reconciled, except under the institution of slavery; for it stands to reason, that wherever the political theory of government recognizes the equality of capital and labor, while the great reality of society shews the one in hopeless and heartless dependence on the other, there will exist between the two a constant jealousy and bitter strife, the weaker demanding its rights with impotent cursing, or enforcing them with revolutionary fierceness.[58]

The only real solution to the conflict between labor and capital, Southern writers argued, was slave labor. The logic for slavery as the solution seemed entirely obvious: slavery transformed labor into capital. Under slavery, labor as a separate interest that was alienated from capital simply did not exist. Cobb articulated this alchemical logic in particularly clear language:

[T]here is perhaps no solution of the great problem of reconciling the interests of labor and capital, so as to protect each from the encroachments and oppressions of the other, so simple and as effective as negro slavery. By making the laborer himself capital, the conflict ceases, and the interests become identical.[59]

Trescot's analysis was more subtle and somewhat more plausible, relying less on the alchemy of slavery and more on the character of the power relationships between labor and capital. He contrasted the relationship between labor and capital in the North, where the two were horizontally related antagonists, to that in the South, where the relationship was one of vertical dependence and benefit:

At the North, the relation of labour and capital is voluntary service; at the South, it is involuntary slavery. At the North, labour and capital are equal; at the South, labour is inferior to capital. At the North, labour and capital strive; the one, to get all it can; the other, to give as little as it may—they are enemies. At the South, labour is dependent on capital, and having ceased to be rivals, they have ceased to be enemies. Can a more violent contrast be imagined?[60]

For Southerners like Calhoun, Cobb, and Trescot as much as for Northern Free-Soilers, the attack on wage labor stemmed not simply from a disagreement over economic ideology but from a more fundamental concern with modernity itself. Despite the vast differences between their respective solutions to the problem of wage labor, both groups shared the same view about what lay at the bottom of that problem. Wage labor was but a symptom of social modernity's deeper flaw: the uncontrolled expansion of the market in all realms of human existence.

The most significant effect of wage labor, Northern and Southern anti-modernist critics alike thought, was that it had transformed human labor into a commodity. That transformation fundamentally, and adversely, altered the social interaction between individuals who now stood in an employer/employee relationship. Such a relationship could not possibly be one between equals, for the whole point of wage labor was the employer's exploitation of the employee. The idea that wage labor—commodified labor—was "free labor" was sheer nonsense, in the Southern theorists' view. The wage laborer was a slave just as surely as the African laborer in the South; he and she (for wage labor's inhumanity drew no gender distinctions) were slaves of an employer who owed them no duties beyond what the terms of their contract specified.

In a broader sense, the wage laborer was, pro-slavery theorists argued, the slave of the market—"slaves to capital," as George Fitzhugh preferred to characterize free laborers.[61] The free labor system rested on the morally offensive assumptions that labor relations were a proper matter for the market to regulate and that an individual's labor was properly a resource to be treated as a fungible commodity. Those assumptions in turn reflected an even more fundamental error: the belief that the market and politics were separate and autonomous spheres of social activity. Classical political economy, as Southern pro-slavery theorists understood it, taught that the market's sphere of control had no natural boundaries , no natural limits to what could properly be treated as a commodity. Wage labor was just one more instance of the steadily expanding realm of the commodity conception that was the hallmark of modernity in social relations. Classical political economists like David Ricardo had explicitly stated that labor was nothing more or less than a commodity, and theory had been converted into practice in the industrial North. By contrast, Southern society—the properly ordered society—strictly limited the domain of the market.

The Slave as Commodity

The economic reality of the antebellum South was that slaves were by far the single most important form of property, both for individual slaveowners and in the economy generally.[62] Gavin Wright has pointed out that "even a few slaves would dominate the portfolio of all but the wealthiest capitalist or landlord."[63] Of course, not all Southern property owners were slave owners. Still, the percentages of slaveholders to the total free population were consistently high in the antebellum years. In 1830, the proportion of slaveholding families in the South's entire free population was 36 percent.[64] In some subregions of the South the percentage was even higher. In South Carolina, for example, 52 percent of white families owned at least one slave in 1850.[65] In aggregate terms, the importance of slaves relative to other forms of property becomes even clearer. By some estimates, as of 1859, slaves represented 44 percent of the South's total wealth, compared with land (including buildings), which accounted for only 25 percent.[66]

To be sure, not all white Southerners were slaveowners. Far from it. In some regions within the South, particularly the upper South and upland portions of deep South states like South Carolina and Georgia, the majority of white property owners were not slaveholders.[67] Indeed, a sizable portion of the upland white population owned no land.[68] Even within the Cotton Belt, by no means were all or even most white families slaveholders. Between 1830 and 1860, the Cotton Belt subregion of the South experienced increasing concentration of wealth and social stratification.[69] Plantations absorbed more and more land while fewer and fewer whites owned slaves.

For those who were slaveowners, slaves represented both commodity and noncommodity property. Slaveowners, that is, used their slaves for both their use-value, i.e., labor, and for their exchange-value. Even if a slaveowner retained his slaves, rather than selling them, market value remained important him.[70] It was the dominant measure of his wealth and status. In debates over reopening the slave trade, the most potent argument against introducing large numbers of new slaves into the South was that doing so would reduce the value of existing slaves. Virtually all Southern slaveholders wanted the exchange-value of their slaves to remain high. This was most obviously true of slaveholders in the upper South, who used their monopoly of slave labor to sell slaves to cotton growers in the lower South.[71,] But it was also true of these lower South planters, who used their slaves primarily for labor. In theory, reducing the market-value of the planter's slaves made him poorer only on paper, but paper wealth mattered then, as it matters now.

The fact is that the sale of slaves was more common throughout the South than historians previously have supposed. Recent scholarship has cast considerable doubt on the past assumption that slaveholders were sentimentally attached to their slaves and were reluctant to sell them. It now appears that many slaveholders actively engaged in selling their slaves, especially when slave prices rose. Unfortunately, we do not have very reliable data on either the frequency or volume of slave sales.[72] What figures we do have indicate that the annual sales rate in some parts of the South (like the low country of South Carolina) may have been as high as 3 percent of the region's slave population.[73] These data suggest that slaveowners were not as reluctant to sell their slaves as once was thought. Moreover, when slaveowners did decide to sell their slaves, they evaluated such transactions, as Robert W. Fogel has put it, "with as much shrewdness and concern for value as any western horse trader or northern manufacturer."[74]

Several institutions facilitated the marketizing of slaves. In some parts of the South the presence of a sizable number of slave-trading firms made it easier for the owner to take advantage of rising slave values.[75] These institutions, like all organized exchanges, greatly enhanced the liquidity of slaves-as-property. Moreover, many slave sales occurred through the direct mediation of legal institutions. Thomas Russell has recently established the importance of slave sales that occurred through the operation of law. Sheriffs' sales and sales by probate and equity courts, he estimates, accounted for one-half of all slave sales in South Carolina.[76] He judges that the experience of court-supervised slave sales in other states was largely the same as in South Carolina.[77]

While the reality of the slave economy was that slaves were a market commodity, the ideology of slavery resisted that fact. The Southern legal defenders of slavery barely acknowledged the existence of the lively market for slaves and indeed denigrated the merchandising of human property. Nowhere was this attitude more clearly expressed than in Cobb's comparison between slavery in North America and slavery in the West Indies. Cobb drew a distinction between slavery in the two locations as categorically different institutions. In the West Indies, he argued, "slaves were merely articles of merchandise, a commercial institution worked in large numbers, upon vast plantations, under the care of agents frequently, and for the benefit of masters whose homes were in many cases in the mother country."[78] The consequences of a system that reduced slaves to market-commodities were, as Cobb depicted, horrific. "[D]espite the [existence of] humane laws, inhuman treatment never ceased, though the government of some of the islands passed into other hands. . . ."[79] The contrast between the treatment of slaves in the West Indies and their counterparts in the American colonies could not have been greater, as Cobb described things. Slavery as an institution that did not deal in human property primarily for its exchange-value was a humane institution. Masters recognized their slaves' humanity and treated them with respect, even if not as equals.

> The [North American colonial] slave bought from the slave ship wielded his axe side by side with his master in felling the forest around his rude home. He was his companion in wild hunts through the pathless woods. A common danger made them defend a common home from the wild beast and the more cruel savage. The field cultivated by their common labor furnished to each his daily bread, of which they frequently partook at a common board. The more wealthy master generally lived in the midst of his farm. No tempting market enticed him to forget humanity in search for gain.[80]

The image that Cobb created of the relationship between master and slave in this passage is far from that between a property owner and his commodity. Indeed, it scarcely even acknowledges the master/slave dimension of the relationship. The relationship that Cobb depicted strikingly resembles that between a father and son, a true paternalistic relationship. The son is clearly the father's subordinate, but the father is the son's superior for the son's own benefit. He is wiser and more experienced than his son and is responsible for using his superior abilities to protect the son. Even while he governs him, though, the father respects his son. He does not demean or humiliate his weaker, more vulnerable companion. The two share common experiences, creating a strong sense of mutuality, respect, even affection between them.

Cobb invoked this paternalistic image precisely to reject the notion that the African-American slave was no more than commodity property to the slaveowner. Slavery in the American South was, as Cobb was so eager to demonstrate, not an economic institution (at least not primarily so) but a *social* institution. It was a social institution both in the sense of the relationship between slave and master and in the broader sense of the character of the social order of which it was a part. Both aspects of slavery's essentially social purpose were clearly evident in Cobb's discussion. Master and slave were not related to each other as owner and object.

> They stood to each other as the protector and the protected. The relation became [in the American colonies] patriarchal. . . . Such a state of society made slavery, in the Colonies, a *social institution*. It was upheld and maintained, not for gain solely, but because it had become, as it were, a part of the social system, a social necessity.[81]

But why was Cobb so eager to deny the reality that slaves *were,* to a substantial degree, commodity property? Part of the answer was the Southern apologist's anxiety to refute the dominant Northern view, raised to new heights by books like Harriet Beecher Stowe's *Uncle Tom's Cabin,* that slaveowners treated their human property in the most grossly inhuman ways. Rebutting that image was a constant concern of the pro-slavery ideologue, and it doubtless was part of Cobb's objective. A deeper concern also underlay the above passage, a concern that specifically focuses on the slave's status not just as property, but as commodity, or market, property. Cobb was anxious that his fellow Southerners, not only Northern critics, not understand African-American slaves solely as market property, or merchandise whose primary function was to create wealth. Southern slavery legal theorists like Cobb resisted that conception of the slave as part of their general resistance to the market conception of property.

Commodification and Paternalism: The Dialectic of Pro-Slavery Legal Thought

The leading Southern intellectuals were all too aware of how far reality deviated from theory, and they were too realistic to defend the institution of slavery solely on ideal grounds. They had to, and they did, acknowledge that slavery deviated from the ideal theory in certain important respects. Most important, they acknowledged, first, that slavery was an economic as well as a social, or civic, institution and, second, that slave property was important as a means of creating private wealth as well as the cornerstone in the edifice of conservative republicanism. Rather than reading pro-slavery legal writing as devoted to a single coherent sociopolitical theory, then, one gains a far more accurate understanding by reading it as constituting a dialectic whose elements are *the commodity conception of property* and *paternalism.*

The dialectic was not created simply by the recognition in Southern legal doctrine that slaves were both property and persons, although that theme acted as another dialectic that was constantly on the surface of Southern legal thought about slavery. The dialectic of commodification and paternalism ran deeper. It was a dialectic about the private and public dimensions of slave property and, more deeply still, about the private and public character of Southern slave society.

Pro-slavery's theory of the ideal society stressed the civicness of that society, exemplified by its hierarchical character. Within the proper social order, each group, each individual had a preassigned role to play. This was not a society in which individual atomistically pursued their own conceptions of the good with a collective good emerging from the satisfaction of individual preferences. Rather it was one in which the good was the realization of a hierarchical social organization that was thought of as ordained by nature and by God. Each individual was duty-bound to respect that foreordained proper order and to fulfill his or her appropriate role within it. The conception of slave property as the cornerstone of the proper social order was the highest symbolic expression of this form of civic society.

At the same time that they developed and described a civic theory of the central purpose of slave property, pro-slavery legal theorists explicitly recognized that slave property served a private, wealth-creating function as well. Cobb was not alone in acknowledging that "[t]he most desirable property for a remunerative income, is slaves." Indeed, as Cobb pointed out, slaves constituted the economic foundation of slaveholding families, the core of the planter's private patrimony. "The best property to leave to his children," he wrote, "and from which they will part with greatest reluctance, is slaves."[82]

Cobb's acknowledgment of the wealth-creating role of slave property went further than that. He conceded that slaves had replaced land as the most important form of property in the South, not only, or even primarily, in a political sense but also in an economic sense. "The most desirable property for a remunerative income, is slaves," he stated. "Hence, the planter invests his surplus income in slaves. The natural result is, that lands are a secondary consideration."[83]

It was not solely concession to reality that led Southern social-legal writers to acknowledge that slaves were an economic resource as well as the foundation for their civic order. Virtually without exception, they approved the market-exchange of slaves as a means of creating wealth. While they repudiated the most extreme pro-market, pro-economic development views of Southern political economists like T. R. Dew, J. D. B. DeBow, and Jacob Nunez Cardozo,[84] the self-styled "sociological" writers were hardly opposed to wealth or unconcerned about its creation. The purchase and sale of slaves as a valuable economic asset was simply a given. Slaveowners, whose paternalistic worldview was challenged by market transactions in slaves, may have "faced the necessity of selling slaves with sincere if effusive handwringing,"[85] but the facts remain that they did buy and sell slaves as commodities and that no social-legal theorist of slavery proposed restraining the alienation of slaves. The doctrines and institutions of Southern commercial law, including court sales,[86] accommodated slavery without making any major concessions, and legal theorists like Cobb accepted these commercial legal practices of slavery as unexceptionable. They never denied the moral or civic legitimacy as well as the legality of market uses of slave property.

The End of the Dialectic?

Acknowledging the commodity function of slaves left pro-slavery social-legal theorists with a profound dilemma. If, as they conceded, slave property was commodity as much as it was *proprietas,* could the two functions of property coexist, or would the commodity role of slave property eventually obliterate its social-political role and, with it, the South's proprietarian social order? Slavery's status as an institution that was "in, but not of, a trans-Atlantic bourgeois world"[87] was precarious enough. Southern lawyers and judges tried, with only partial success, to maintain antebellum Southern law's dualistic character—part modern and market-oriented, part premodern and paternalistic—through various mediating strategies, such as segregating the law of slavery from other, market-oriented categories of legal doctrine.[88] Were slave property, the acknowledged edifice of the nonmarketized dimension of Southern society and polity, to become thoroughly commodified, that is, perceived and valued by Southern citizens as strictly a wealth-creating asset, there would be no point in trying to maintain its legal dualism. The problem was not just whether other, clearly commodified forms of property would obliterate slave property as a noncommodified form of property, but also (and more urgently) whether the commodity aspect of slave property would drive out of social consciousness the noncommodity role of slave property. Put differently, was the market mentality imperialistic, as Gresham's law posits, or could a dialectic between the market and nonmarket functions of slave property be maintained in Southern social consciousness?

This problem, which recent political-legal scholars have referred to as the potential "domino effect" of commodification,[89] was hardly peculiar to the slave system. It is endemic to any pluralistic type of property regime that attempts simultaneously to maintain nonmarketized forms of property together with marketized property. That list includes virtually all property regimes since few, if any, purely market or nonmarket regimes have ever existed. It certainly includes the American property system since its inception, for the core of that system from the Revolution to the present has not been a purely liberal, wealth-creating conception of property but a dialectic between that conception and a competing conception, one rooted in the older tradition of property as *proprietas*. What made the antebellum Southern pro-slavery writing about property unusual was the level of its awareness of the potential problem that the commodity form might drive out the noncommodity version. The fragility of the slave system in the South by the middle of the nineteenth century made Southern intellectuals focus more closely and deliberately on the viability of such an obviously pluralistic property regime.

Most Southern social-legal writing did not provide any clear resolution to these questions, and Cobb's work was no exception.[90] Indeed, lacking anything like a systematic theory of what we call commodification, they did not directly address the dilemma in those terms. In this sense, then, it may seem the height of presentism even to raise the question. But while the language of commodification was not theirs, the anxiety that underlies the questions just framed was very much theirs. Nearly all of the leading Southern social-legal theorists of slavery were clearly anxious about the future of their paternalistic social order, and several of them speculated that the greater threats to that order were endogenous, not exogenous sources. The South's unusual dialectic between the market and the nonmarket, they feared, might be destabilized by the internal dynamics of the market society rather than by political or military action of the North.

The sense of anxiety about this possibility is evident in many of the leading texts, including Cobb's *Historical Sketch of Slavery*. It was revealed in his discussion of the effects of slave property's dominance as a form of wealth. As we saw earlier, Cobb explicitly acknowledged that slaves had replaced land as the South's primary commodity. His analysis of the social effects of slave property's rise to dominance bears close examination, not because it accurately assessed the economic consequences of substituting slaves for land but because it accurately reflected the basic sense of anxiety that pro-slavery social-legal intellectuals experienced concerning the destabilizing consequences of the premodern Southern social order's infection by the modern *mentalité* of commodification.

Cobb assumed that the emergence of slaves as the economically most significant form of property in the South would radically alter how wealthy Southerners invested their capital. Planters would substitute slaves for land as the primary, even exclusive, vehicle for creating personal wealth. Slaves would become the foundation of the wealthy class's patrimony. With land so radically devalued, the traditional hierarchy of forms of property would be profoundly altered in the Southern social order:

> No surplus [income] is left for [land's] improvement. The homestead is valued only so long as the adjacent lands are profitable for cultivation. The planter himself, having no local attachments, his children inherit none. On the contrary, he encourages in them a disposition to seek new lands. His valuable property (his slaves) are easily removed to fresh lands; much more easily than to bring the fertilizing materials to the old. The result is that they, as a class, are never settled.[91]

The concern that Cobb was expressing here was with the social and civic implications rather than the economic consequences of the substitution of slaves for land as the dominant form of wealth. His point was not that slaves were an economically bad investment, and it certainly was nothing like the modern financial insight that people ought to diversify their investments and not put all their eggs in one basket. Cobb's concern was with the future status of the South as a stable and reliably republican society. The shift from immobile land to mobile slaves as the primary form of economic attachment, he speculated, threatened to transform the South from a traditional society in which citizens are rooted, both literally and figuratively, to one in which property owners are civically, as well as physically, unconnected. In this latter sort of society, citizens are less citizens than they are autonomous, preference-maximizing agents, precisely the sort of *homo economicus* that political economists, both in the North and the South, described with admiration but that the sociological writers viewed with anxiety. As Cobb put it, "It is useless to seek to excite patriotic emotions in behalf of the land of birth, when self-interest speaks so loudly."[92]

This transformation would jeopardize the Jeffersonian vision of a virtuous citizenry anchored by fee simple ownership of land. With slave property replacing land as the economically dominant asset, the necessary conditions for civic virtue were no longer present. The paradox, then, was that under Cobb's logic, preserving the South as a premodern, republican society might require that its quintessentially premodern institution—slavery—be abolished so that the primacy of land would be reestablished. As Cobb himself acknowledged, "[W]here no slavery exists, and the planter's surplus cannot be invested in laborers, it is appropriated to the improvement or extension of his farm, the beautifying of the homestead where his fathers are buried, and where he hopes to lie."[93]

Yet Cobb, as an advocate of moral superiority of slavery, was hardly in a position to advocate its abolition. Neither was he prepared to endorse the extreme position staked out by George Fitzhugh, who explicitly advocated the abolition of market economics as the only viable means of preserving slavery.[94] For all of his concerns about the compatibility between slavery and capitalism, Cobb remained basically committed, as did most of the pro-slavery social theorists, to market economics—a republican version of market economics, to be sure, but the market nonetheless.

Cobb's unwillingness to abolish the market left him with an insoluble dilemma of which he seemed to be aware. His *Historical Sketch of Slavery* closed with a vague sense of uncertainty and unease about the future of slavery. In the end, he fell back on old racist claptrap. "So long as climate and disease," he wrote, "and the profitable planting of cotton, rice, tobacco, and cane, make the negro the only laborer inhabiting safely our Southern savannas and prairies, just so long will he remain a slave to the white man."[95] There was simply no clear resolution to the problem that Cobb and his kind could find at all acceptable. The possibility that the dialectic might end could not be denied.

PART THREE

The Industrial Culture,
1870–1917

Legal Writing in the Age of Enterprise

M ANY OF THE FEATURES of the antebellum American legal profession and of legal writing continued to be apparent after the Civil War. The decline of the configuration of law and literature continued and was virtually complete by 1870. So also was the withdrawal of mainstream legal discourse from the realm of politics. The trends toward increasing professionalization and technical complexity, both in day-to-day practice and in legal writing, also continued unabated. The image of the law as a learned liberal profession, deeply intertwined with politics, was replaced by the image of law as a business,[1] and as that self-image changed, so did the character of legal discourse.

In other respects, however, the picture had changed. Two institutional changes were particularly important. First, the postbellum period saw the emergence of the large corporate law firm. The modern law firm represented a form of legal practice quite different from anything that had preceded it. The primary locus of practice shifted from the courtroom to the office, and skills in negotiation and counseling, drafting, and financial analysis became more valuable than oratory.[2]

The second important institutional change occurring after 1870 was the appearance of the modern, university-based American law school.[3] First developed at Harvard under the leadership of its president, Charles W. Eliot, and Dean Christopher Columbus Langdell,[4] the new law school was a quite different creature from its predecessors. Among other differences, it was far more academically oriented. While university-affiliated law schools were by no means unknown earlier—indeed, among the earliest law faculties in the United States was Harvard's—their connection with the rest of the university was tenuous and shallow. Their primary ties were with the bar. Faculty tended to consist of practitioner-lecturers, and frequently taught only on a part-time basis. The main benefit that they derived from their university affiliation was the prestige of having a name like Harvard or Columbia attached to theirs. The new university law schools had pretensions of being genuinely academic in a way that the earlier law schools never did. While a few of the faculty continued to maintain a substantial law practice, law professors increasingly became full-time teachers and scholars. New institutions, like the Association of American Law Schools, were established to support the professional needs and interests of law professors. Law teaching itself had become a distinct profession.

Together, these two parallel institutional changes directly affected the character of legal discourse in the latter decades of the nineteenth century. They produced a gap between academic and practitioner legal writing, a gap that intensified in the twentieth century. Academic discourse tended to be more speculative, both in content and in tone. This was especially true of the articles that appeared in the newly established university law reviews. The first issue of the *Harvard Law Review,* the first university law review, for example, included an article entitled "Criticisms upon Henry George, Reviewed from the Stand-point of Justice."[5] By contrast, practitioner-oriented law journals, which declined in number after 1880,[6] focused on professional news or recent cases. To be sure, the bulk of law review articles was not high-theory stuff. Most of it was strictly doctrinal and, to that extent, relevant to the practicing bar. Moreover, the law reviews had pretensions of being directly useful to the bar. The student editors of the first issue of the *Harvard Law Review* wrote that they hoped the *Review* would "be serviceable to the profession at large."[7] Still, it was a far cry from articles analyzing the foundations of legal doctrines to the usual bar journal material, which ranged from trial tactics suggestions to obituaries of lawyers.

The gap between academic and practical legal writing directly contradicted the self-image of law professors. The leading legal academic writers of the late nineteenth century all thought that their work would directly benefit the bar. This professional improvement would occur as the result of their core project, which was to construct law as "legal science." The notion of law as science was itself hardly original. As early as the seventeenth century, Anglo-American lawyers have been enamored of the ideal of legal science. As we have already seen, in the early nineteenth century the idea that law could be written about and practiced as a science was a basic tenet of Federalist-Whig legal thought. In that incarnation, as in earlier versions, legal science meant nothing more than making law and legal reasoning systematic and orderly. What the late nineteenth-century legal writers meant by the idea of law as science was a conceptual ordering of all of law based on "an interlocking set of hierarchical distinction."[8] As Thomas Grey has lucidly described, this set of binary dichotomies— the core of what has come to be called "classical [American] legal thought"—"served to focus lawyers' attention on what was thought primary and essential, and what merely peripheral, in the body of legal materials."[9]

In the realm of property, a related pair of dichotomies structured much of the scholarly discussion—the distinction between rights *in rem* and rights *in personam* and the conflict between individual will and the will of the sovereign. Leading scholars like John Chipman Gray used both of these dichotomies to analyze virtually all of the law of property, as it was then defined. He contended that the distinction between personal, or *in personam*, rights and rights to things, or rights *in rem,* constituted the entire foundation of the law of property.[10] Similarly, Gray thought that the dichotomy between individual will and sovereign will unified the entire topic of restraints on alienation, a topic that, as we will see in chapter 10, was at the very core of late nineteenth-century property law.

Taken together, the classical conceptual structure was thought to embrace the entire body of American law. It was, in other words, regarded as complete and comprehensive. Preexisting legal rules, derived from established precedents and ultimately from core concepts and principles, existed for every case. And every case had a uniquely correct result.[11]

Despite the classicists' pretensions, classical legal science provided little direct benefit to the practicing bar.[12] Its virtually exclusive focus on case law made it largely irrelevant to all but a handful of practicing lawyers. At best, its attempts to organize whole areas of law into some kind of systematic order made it easier for litigators to perform legal research tasks. But the practitioner's primary locus of work was not the library or the courtroom but the business office. Little of the classicists' work aided lawyers in the growing areas of corporate finance and utility rate-making. In truth, classical legal science was of interest only to academic lawyers— and by no means all of them.

Another sort of legal science was also evident in legal writing between 1870 and 1920. This latter sort of legal science focused directly on what classical (or, we might call it, "Langdellian," after the Harvard Law School dean Christopher Columbus Langdell) legal science denied was part of law at all—public policy.[13] While Langdell and his disciplines were pursuing a value-free and autonomous conception of legal science, other writers during the period were engaged in a project of linking law with the newly emerging fields of policy science. These efforts were largely confined to public law, notably constitutional law, led by writers like Christopher Tiedemann and Thomas Cooley, municipal law, led by John Dillon, and administrative law, first developed by the University of Chicago's Ernst Freund.

Legal policy science affected property scholarship less directly than it did other fields, but its impact was still considerable. Property law as it was then defined was strictly a private law subject. Questions about the public regulation of resources and constitutional limitations on the state's power to regulate were public law issues, purged from the canon of property law as it was taught in most law schools. Still, scholars like Gray never denied the central role of public policy in property law. Indeed, Gray insisted that fundamental public policies like free alienability had to override individual intent whenever the two conflicted, even in private transactions like conveyances of land. More generally, the role of public policy in matters relating to property could hardly be ignored. The whole character of the relationship between the individual owner and the state was changing, as evidenced by increasing governmental regulation of business and the public debate over the state's expanding regulatory role in the decades after the Civil War. Academic legal writing about property became increasingly focused on those changes.

Legal policy science had more obvious relevance to certain areas of law practice than did classical legal science, but its impact, too, was limited. Cooley, Tiedemann, and Dillon produced treatises that influenced courts and were frequently cited in judicial opinions.[14] (Part of the reason for the success of Cooley's and Dillon's treatises may have been the fact that they were judges themselves.) There were, moreover, a few populist legal educators like James Woods Green, of the University of Kansas Law School, whose visions of legal education and legal writing were strongly connected with both politics and the practicing bar.[15] Still later, Roscoe Pound would call for law education and legal writing that combined law with sociology, economics, and politics. He based his plea on the need to "fit new generations of lawyers to lead the people,"[16] a vision that echoed the older self-image of the bar. Legal policy science had, as we will see in the next part, its greatest impact, both on legal scholarship and legal practice, after 1915, when it became linked with Progressive politics. But, on the whole, legal policy science never exerted a lasting, dominant influence on the American bar. Legal practice had moved too far away from the old ideal, according to which law, politics, and policy were integrally related and the practicing lawyer was genuinely a public servant. Law was now, predominately, a business, and academic legal writing had little to offer in the service of that new reality.

The two chapters that form this part examine the public law and private law sides of the debate over the relationship between individual and state in relation to property. Chapter 9 discusses the public-law aspect of the problem. It analyzes the legal discourse concerning constitutional limitations on the state regulation of property in terms of a dialectic between two competing accounts of power imbalance in America during the Age of Enterprise. Chapter 10 then turns to the private-law side of the problem. Here the central issue concerned the policy of alienability of property and the freedom of individual owners to place restrictions on future transfers of wealth, especially family wealth.

The Dilemma of Property in Public Law during the Age of Enterprise: Power and Democracy

UNTIL RECENTLY, legal historians consistently depicted the late nineteenth century—the Age of Enterprise—as the era of "laissez-faire constitutionalism."[1] According to this orthodox interpretation, constitutional doctrine protected private property interests above all else, striking down an ever-wider array of regulatory measures that interfered with freedom of the marketplace. American judges during this period, the story continues, were little more than pawns of the wealthy industrialist class. Spearheading the defense of the capitalist class's economic interests against legislative depredations was the Supreme Court of the United States. As one recent account puts it, "Armed with the due process clause of the [new] Fourteenth Amendment, the Supreme Court emerged as a champion of economic liberty and carefully scrutinized state efforts to regulate business activity."[2]

This interpretation originated in the broader story that the generation of Progressive historians told about the nineteenth century.[3] The Progressives' story,[4] with its crudely Marxist overtones, told of the continual struggle between "the people" and "the interests" that has dominated American history. The late nineteenth-century legal variant of this story describes how American judges after the Civil War initially rejected the idea of substantive due process but later adopted it during the 1880s and 1890s when grass-roots interests opposed to big business threatened to gain control of state legislatures. To protect the interests of large corporations and wealthy industrialists, the courts, particularly the Supreme Court, eventually read the ideology of laissez-faire economics into the Constitution through the fourteenth amendment's due process clause.[5] In the great battle between "the interests" and "the people," the People lost until Big Business was finally vanquished in the 1930s when a reconstituted Supreme Court sustained the New Deal. Until that final victory of democracy, laissez-faire constitutionalism reigned supreme.

The Progressives' story about laissez-faire constitutionalism would have us believe that judges in the late nineteenth century in effect constitutionalized the commodity conception of property. It supposes that when the Supreme Court interpreted the fourteenth amendment due process clause to extend substantive protection to economic interests against state regulations, it acted exclusively to promote one purpose of property: to increase private wealth.

In recent years this account has come under attack.[6] Several historians, including Michael Les Benedict, Alan Jones, Charles McCurdy, and, more recently, Howard Gillman, have persuasively argued that the men who were supposedly responsible for creating laissez-faire constitutionalism, men like Stephen J. Field, Thomas M. Cooley, and Christopher G. Tiedeman, in fact were basically hostile to big corporate interests.[7] They favored a decentralized market and old-fashioned individualism, and were influenced less by classical political economy than by the old Jacksonian worldview. These legal scholars and judges were not opposed to all instances of legislative regulation but only those regulations that favored particular social groups at the expense of others. They viewed economic regulation as permissible so long as it serve the *common* good, that is, so long as it was neutral.[8] The thrust of this recent scholarship has been to establish that the Jacksonian political ideals of liberty and equality, not the economic ideal of an unregulated market, dominated late nineteenth century American judicial thought.

But old interpretations die hard. Despite the recent revisionist scholarship, the Progressive picture of constitutional property in the late nineteenth century remains alive and well. Constitutional lawyers continue to portray the Supreme Court's property decisions as nothing more than the product of its relentlessly pro-big business bias.[9] Even as sophisticated a legal historian as Morton Horwitz continues to adhere to the old interpretive framework. Despite his own critique of Progressive historiography,[10] Horwitz continues to tell the story of warring interest groups. Less powerful and propertyless social groups like farmers, workers, debtors and the like were pitted against big and powerful corporations in a struggle over the future distribution of wealth in the American social order. The rise of laissez-faire constitutionalism in the second half of the nineteenth century, Horwitz would have us believe, was the result of an effort by supporters of the existing order, notably big business, to block legislative attempts at redistributing wealth to produce a more egalitarian order.[11]

One of the aims of this chapter is to put the old interest-group interpretation of constitutional property in the Gilded Age to bed once and for all. This is not to deny that interest groups did not exist or to claim that they exerted no influence on Supreme Court jurisprudence whatsoever. My thesis, rather, is that the Court's constitutional property cases should be interpreted within a more complex framework, one that links the constitutional debate regarding the proper domain of public law control over property during the late nineteenth century with the broader political debate over property, industrial capitalism, and the future of democracy.

The central issue in that political debate was whether capitalist accumulation could be reconciled with democracy. This problem predated the late nineteenth century, of course, but the massive changes in the structure of the nation's economy in the post–Civil War years, particularly the emerging dominance of large corporations, and the increasing efforts of state legislatures to regulate business enterprises made the problem seem all the more urgent to address.

The Supreme Court's response to the dilemma that capitalist accumulation posed for democracy between 1870 and 1905 was indirect and inconsistent. The doctrinal vehicle for its response was the new fourteenth amendment, adopted in 1868. Beginning in the 1870s, the Court set about determining the meaning of the due process clause of that amendment, and a crucial aspect of the task was redefining the constitutional parameters of government-business relations. The Court shifted positions in important ways over the next three decades, eventually settling on a position that Stephen Field had mapped out, usually in dissenting opinions, as early as 1872. Field's strategy was "to separate the public and private sectors into fixed and inviolable spheres."[12]

Despite the shift in the Court's property jurisprudence, however, one theme was constant throughout its efforts over thirty years. Its opinions consistently reflect a shared perception that the task was one of correcting an imbalance of power in the society. A consensus existed on the Court that the increasing accumulation and concentration of capital in a few private firms could be reconciled with the demands of a democratic society if—but only if—a balance of power was maintained throughout society. Hardly anyone doubted that a power imbalance existed; the question was, in whose favor was the balance skewed.

The Centrality of Power: Justice Holmes and Class Legislation

One important member of the Court who did doubt that a balance of power was possible at all was Justice Oliver Wendell Holmes. Holmes's views on the issue of "class legislation" merit special attention not because they were highly influential within the Court—they were not—but because of the way in which they reflected a deeper conception of law and society that did influence legal thinking about other issues concerning property and political economy between 1870 and 1920. That vision was that law, both judicially made and legislative, invariably expresses policy preferences and the policies it prefers are those of whatever force has power within society at a given time. Power and self-preference were, to Holmes's mind, what invariably drove law and no talk about the common good could change that fact.

Holmes's emphasis on power was starkly evident in his nonjudicial writings on class legislation. The most important essay in which he discussed the issue was his 1873 essay on the British gas-stokers' strike, appearing in the *American Law Review*.[13] Prompted by an English essay that assailed several instances of "class legislation," Holmes expressed an utterly unsentimental, Darwinian theory of legislation. It is worth quoting at some length because, in true Holmesian fashion, it so vividly articulates a powerful set of premises that would gain favor among legal and political intellectuals in time. He stated:

> The most powerful interests must be more or less reflected in legislation; which, like every other device or man or beast, must tend in the long run to aid the survival of the fittest. The objection to class legislation is not that it favors a class, but either that it fails to benefit the legislators, or that it is dangerous to them because a competing class has gained in power, or that it transcends the limits of self-preference which are imposed by sympathy. . . . [I]t is no sufficient condemnation of legislation that it favors one class at the expense of another; for much or all legislation does that; and none the less when the *bonâ fide* object is the greatest good of the greatest number. Why should the greatest number be preferred? Why not the greatest good of the most intelligent and the most highly developed? The greatest good of a minority of our generation may be the greatest good of the greatest number in the long run.[14]

The Social Darwinist cast of the passage just quoted is entirely evident.[15] In this respect there was no discontinuity between Holmes's earlier and later writings, as Mark DeWolfe Howe asserted in his unfinished biography of Holmes.[16] In his famous 1896 dissent in *Vegelahn v. Guntner,* he described organized labor as nothing more or less than part of the "free struggle for life."[17] Later still, in an essay published in 1920, Holmes stated, "[A] great fortune does not mean a corresponding consumption, but a power of command; . . . someone must exercise that command, and . . . I know of no way of finding the fit man so good as the fact of winning it in the competition of the market."[18]

As the last excerpt indicates, Holmes had no more quarrel with capital's power than he did with labor. In both cases, the struggle for power was natural and inevitable; there was no point in resisting it anywhere or in lamenting it. That one side or the other would have greater power at a given time was part of the natural order of things. The search for balance of power was fundamentally misguided and doomed.

This Darwinian, or, as J. W. Burrow has aptly suggested, "Nietzschean"[19] belief in power is the key to understanding all his views on legislation, including constitutional questions. Thus it, rather than some more principled theory about judicial restraint, explains his famous dissenting opinion in *Lochner v. New York.*[20] Less famously, it also explains, as Stephen Diamond has recently shown,[21] his views on constitutional restraints on the states' power to tax. As in the case of state labor and welfare legislation, Holmes thought that the Constitution imposed no restriction on state legislative power to tax, even if that meant that more than one state taxed the same property. The question was not one of fairness, nor of legislative wisdom (which he usually doubted); it was a matter of the "practical fact of power."[22] This perception of the character of the problem of class legislation—indeed, whether there was a problem at all—was to set him apart from other members of the Court.

The Two Narratives of Power

Two opposed interpretations of the distribution of power competed within the Court between 1870 and 1900. One interpretation was that the source of the imbalance was increasing concentration of government power. This was Field's position. What prompted this view were the changes in the state's role in business relations during the postbellum decades. To be sure, the rise of the activist, regulatory state preceded the industrial age. Government had a pervasive regulatory presence in the first half of the nineteenth century through all sectors of society,[23] including the world of the market. But its relationship with private enterprise changed as the nature of enterprise itself dramatically changed in the postbellum era. Responding in part to pressure from groups that were adversely affected by newly dominant industries, such as the railroads, state legislatures adopted a more restrictive attitude toward the freedom of enterprises to conduct their affairs as they saw fit. No longer simply encouraging industries to grow, state legislatures increasingly asserted their power to impose limits on the freedom of enterprises to use their property in whatever way they wished.

To Field and his cohort on the Court, regulatory restrictions on pricing and other important incidents of ownership seemed to exacerbate the underlying dilemma of reconciling capitalist accumulation with democracy. Echoing Jacksonian themes, Field argued that the evil of such regulation was not simply that it denied property rights but that it did so unequally. Interference with property was acceptable when it genuinely served the public interest, meaning when it was even-handed. Regulatory intrusions were undemocratic, however, when they sacrificed the many for the few, *or* the few for the many. Such legislation represented nothing more than the raw exercise of power to dominate a portion of the community.

To other members of the Court, the problem of a power imbalance did not lay in excessive government interference with business enterprise, but in the changed character of the market. Judges like Chief Justice Morrison R. Waite thought that the emergence of large-scale business enterprises presented the greater threat to democracy than did the activist state. Power was no longer widely dispersed in the market, nor was the market any longer an arena of competition among equals. With capital increasingly concentrated among a relatively few large firms, agglomerated economic power had replaced (or at least threatened to replace) the democracy of individual entrepreneurs. As the market became less competitive and less democratic, the political order could no longer rely on it to insure that businesses served the common good. The state had to intrude itself in this new and distorted market to protect the public's welfare.

Field's interpretation of the power problem and his proposed solution eventually prevailed. While the effect of that solution was to shift the constitutional meaning of property much closer to the commodity conception, that was not his objective. The more thoroughly privatized conception of property that Field and his contemporaries implemented was a means, not an end. Moreover, their conception of property explicitly acknowledged a public role for property, although considerably narrower in scope than that defined by their predecessors on the Court. They agreed that private property interests at times had to be subordinated to the public good. Laissez-faire constitutionalism, then, by no means ended the dialectical understanding of property in judicial thought.

The Coming of Industrial Capitalism

In the half-century that followed the Civil War, the nation's economy went through enormous changes that transformed the character not only of the economy but of American society. The centers of power in the economy shifted from farms and small-towns to cities, from small-scale entrepreneurs to large industrial firms. As early as 1868, Charles Francis Adam could express astonishment at the changed conditions of American life. Referring to his family, which was returning to the United States after ten years in England, he stated: "Had they been Tyrian traders of the year B.C. 1000, landing from a galley fresh from Gibraltar, they could hardly have been stranger on the shore of a world, so changed from what it had been ten years before."[24]

The shift from a largely small-scale economy to an industrial economy, spurred in the North by the Civil War, hardly abated during the postwar years. By 1873, the year of the great financial panic that ushered in a depression that persisted throughout most of the decade, the level of industrial production throughout the nation rose 75 percent above the 1865 figure.[25] In the same year the United States was second only to Great Britain in manufacturing production.[26] Expanding the time frame, the amount of capital invested in manufacturing jumped nineteenfold between 1850 and 1900.[27] By 1890, the year of Frederick Jackson Turner's announced closing of the American frontier, the value of the nation's manufactured goods exceeded that of agricultural products.[28]

Throughout the country but especially in the North and West, the trend in virtually every sector of the economy was toward concentrated ownership and large-scale production. By the end of the nineteenth century America had witnessed the emergence of the prototype for today's large industrial corporation. Two developments were crucial to the creation of the modern industrial corporation. Beginning shortly after the Civil War there gradually appeared a variety of types of financial institutions that accumulated vast sums of capital necessary for large-scale industrial production. The first of these institutions to appear was the insurance company, "the most important nonbank intermediar[y] for the mobilization and interregional transfer of capital."[29] Insurance assets, which increased twenty-fold between 1869 and 1914,[30] were crucial in the development of transportation and manufacturing industries in the North and West. Other financial intermediaries who also satisfied long-term capital needs during this period included mutual savings banks, building and loan associations, and mortgage companies. The commercial paper market also developed rapidly during this period as an interregional source of accumulated capital. It was not until the close of the nineteenth century that sale of common stock became a viable means of raising large sums.[31]

The other important development in the creation of the modern industrial corporation was the wave of consolidation that occurred in the final decades of the nineteenth century. Firms used a variety of means to grow through consolidation. These included "pools," "trusts," and, finally, outright merger. A vast wave of mergers occurred between 1897 and 1903, prompting an extended and often agitated debate, both in academic circles and the wider population, regarding the causes and effects of the rise of the giant corporation.[32]

The tremendous growth of corporate power prompted anxiety in several quarters.[33] Small entrepreneurs, labor leaders, farmers, and small-town businessmen all worried about the effects of urban corporate concentration on their futures in the unfamiliar economic order that was emerging. Compounding their anxiety, the postwar era was a time of tremendous cyclical swings in the nation's economy. Three serious economic downturns occurred between 1873 and 1900, including the deep depression that followed the Panic of 1873. Repeated and serious labor unrest added to the sense of the individual's loss of control over his economic circumstances. The railroad strike of 1877 made the Paris Commune of 1871 appear much closer to home than most Americans would have previously imagined possible.

Anxiety about social relations accompanied economic anxiety. Robert Wiebe has elegantly described how after 1877, Americans experienced a sense of loss of control over their daily lives, as their world of local "island communities" broke down and was replaced by a new bureaucratic order.[34] The change in the nature of enterprise was very much a part of this social disintegration. In addition to scrambling the hierarchy of power among social groups, the rise of the modern corporation exacerbated the problem of imbalance of political and economic power between economic institutions and the individual. Domination of the individual loomed larger as a result of the tremendous agglomeration of power by industrial combinations. The emergence of corporate power changed the nature of the basic problem of how simultaneously to respect the free-individual ideal and the commonwealth ideal.

Wealth and Class in Late Nineteenth-Century Public Discourse

The problem of capitalist accumulation and democracy was far from being a strictly legal subject of discussion. It was addressed in virtually branch of social, political, and economic discourse in the second half of the nineteenth century. Public debate over property and power was most conspicuous in the 1890s, when anxiety about corporate power and labor unrest was at its highest. The nineties was a decade of industrial concentration, depression, and labor strife, and these developments accelerated a growing sense of crisis, especially among the wealthy. But the debate began well before 1890.

Popular writings expressing anxiety about the changed character of the economy and the growing concentration of property and power in large corporations began to appear shortly after the Civil War. This issue was the central focus of three of the most widely read books of the postbellum period, Henry George's *Progress and Poverty,* Edward Bellamy's *Looking Backward,* and Henry Demarest Lloyd's *Wealth against Commonwealth.*[35] Anticipating themes that he would later develop in *Progress and Poverty,* Henry George in 1868 lamented the effects of the new form of corporations: "Capital is piled on capital to the exclusion of men of lesser means and the utter prostration of personal independence and enterprise on the part of the less successful masses."[36] George was not expressing socialist sentiments here. His fear of the consequences of the changed economic order derived instead from an abiding commitment to Jeffersonian agrarianism and Jacksonian democracy. His Single Tax proposal anticipated a utopia that was "an essentially rural republic, pastoral, small-town, run according to village values."[37] Like George, Edward Bellamy and Henry Demarest Lloyd rejected socialism as the solution to the problem of concentrated ownership of property and corporate power. While endorsing its ideal as "grand and noble,"[38] they objected to its materialist foundation and its doctrines of class conflict and revolution.

Certainly not all critics of corporate power rejected socialism or even revolution. While socialism never gained the support in the United States that it enjoyed in Europe, many leading American social critics from 1870 on circulated socialist ideas in public discussions of economics and politics. The social gospel was an especially influential version of these ideas beginning in the 1880s. Two of the most important theorists of the social gospel were the economist Richard T. Ely and the theologian Walter Rauschenbusch.[39] Both men explicitly endorsed nationalization over government regulation as the best means of dealing with corporate power. Rauschenbusch asserted, "The outside interference of government officers will prove inefficient, meddlesome, and irritating. We must come to public ownership sometime and anyone whose thinking parts are in order ought to see it by this time."[40]

Legal discourse during the age of enterprise was also preoccupied with the dilemma of corporate power and concentration of ownership. Populist lawyer-politicians like Lyman Trumbull, one-time justice of the Illinois Supreme Court and later United States Senator, warned of the dangers that "corporate monopolies" created by, as he asserted, depressing the living conditions of wage-earners:

> They see around them, in the possession of favored corporations and the pampered few, all the magnificence and luxury which accumulated wealth can bestow, while they toil and even suffer for the means, the God-given right, to live. Is it any wonder that discontent prevails among the masses, and that they act in concert in the effort to improve their condition when such a state of things exists? . . .
>
> The remedy for this growing state of things would be to restrict the formation of corporations to such as are formed for public purposes, or such as the public have an interest in. Seventy-eight per cent of the great fortunes of the United States are said to be derived from permanent monopoly privileges which ought never to have been granted.[41]

Typical of most legal criticism of corporate power at the time, Trumbull's analysis linked together several social phenomena: the growing power of private corporations; government-conferred corporate "privileges," or "monopolies"; and the accumulation of personal fortunes. Critics considered these developments to be causally related. The government made the growth of corporate power possible by granting privileges to private corporations, and corporate power in turn led to the concentration of vast wealth in the hands of a fortunate few. Even that supposedly

arch-conservative legal theorist Christopher G. Tiedeman,[42] expressed
anxieties about the growing concentration of wealth, declaring in 1886
that

> we see, more and more clearly each day, that the tendency of the
> present process of civilization is to concentrate social power into the
> hands of a few, who, unless restrained in some way, are able to dictate
> terms of employment to the masses, who must either accept them
> or remain idle; . . . at best they are barely enabled to provide for the
> more pressing wants of themselves and families, while their employ-
> ers are, at least apparently, accumulating wealth to an enormous ex-
> tent.[43]

This line of criticism intensified existing concerns about the role of class
in American law and society.

There were two opposed views in legal discourse about the question
of class. One view accepted the causal argument that Trumbull had developed and emphasized the hypocrisy of a class-based based society in a
nation whose public rhetoric celebrated even-handedness and equality.
The other view agreed that class had no legitimate role in American law or
society, but, eager to prove that the law did not play favorites, it repeatedly
assailed those instances in which legislation seemed class-based. In a famous address to the New York State Bar Association in 1895, John F.
Dillon, former state and federal judge and author of an influential treatise
on municipal corporations,[44] declared:

> The State is a commonweal. It exists for the general good, for
> rich and poor alike. It knows or ought to know no classes. . . . The
> one thing to be feared in our democratic republic, and therefore to
> be guarded against with sleepless vigilance, is class power and class
> legislation. Discriminating legislation for the benefit of the rich
> against the poor, or in favor of the poor against the rich, is equally
> wrong and dangerous. Class legislation of all and every kind is anti-
> republican and must be repressed.[45]

No one was more preoccupied with the problem of "class legislation"
or more effectively integrated a critique of that problem into a general
constitutional theory of the relationship between public power and private property than Thomas M. Cooley. Beginning as early as the 1850s,
Cooley assailed "class legislation" as being undemocratic. His theory was
most fully developed in his 1868 treatise, *Constitutional Limitations Which*

Rest upon the Legislative Power of the States of the American Union,[46] which has been described as having had "a broader circulation, greater sale, and . . . more frequently cited than any other book on American law published in the last half of the nineteenth century."[47] In it, Cooley argued not simply that government should avoid redistributing property from the rich to the poor but should not favor *any* class, rich over poor any more than poor over rich. The basis of his concern with class legislation was political and social more than it was economic. It was rooted in a vision, drawn from Jacksonian and Jeffersonian sources, of America as an egalitarian society, one in which class played no role in the government's allocation of benefits or burdens. "Equality," Cooley asserted, "of rights, privileges, and capacities unquestionably should be the aim of the law."[48]

Property as Value in the Supreme Court

The massive changes in the nature of American business enterprise dramatically affected the forms of property that dominated the nation's social and economic landscape. Land increasingly lost its role as the socially and economically dominant form of property, especially in the Northeast where urbanization and industrialization were most visible. Intangible assets rapidly proliferated throughout the nation's markets, as corporate growth and consolidation fueled the creation of various corporate debt and equity instruments. Lawyers created the corporate trust indentures, corporate debentures, preferred and common stock, no par common stock, and equipment trust certificates as innovative devices for financing corporation growth and consolidation.[49]

As a corollary to their thesis that the late nineteenth-century Supreme Court shaped constitutional doctrine to serve the interests of industrial capitalists, the Progressives argued that these changes in the forms of property compelled the Court to abandon the traditional conception of property as tangible thing in favor of the more abstract and protean conception as exchange-value.[50] This thesis was first developed by the economist John R. Commons in his influential 1924 book *Legal Foundations of Capitalism*.[51] Commons asserted that "in 1890 [in the *Minnesota Rate Case*[52]], the Supreme Court . . . made the transition and changed the definition of property from physical things having only use-value to the exchange-value of anything."[53] According to Commons's thesis, the Court's early failure to protect business enterprises as property under the due process resulted from the land-based conception of property that focused on title and possession rather than exchange-value. The force of the traditional physicalist conception was exemplified, he argued, by the *Granger Cases.*

The background leading to the *Granger Cases* reflects the sense of anxiety about the changed nature of the market and the domination of large business enterprises. After subsidizing the construction of railroad during the 1850s and throughout the Civil War, many state legislatures during the 1870s reversed their policies and began regulating railroads and utilities. Several factors contributed to this change in attitude, including rising public concerns about the rapidly growing size and predatory practices of railroad companies.[54] Various interest groups objected to different company practices, leading to different legislative responses. In the upper Midwest the interest group that objected most vociferously were farmers, who complained that the high transportation prices that railroads charged prevented them from accessing Eastern markets. Responding to pressure from a farmers' organization founded in 1867 to fight railroad "monopolies," the Patrons of Husbandry (popularly known as the "Grange"), several state legislatures enacted legislation regulating railroad rates. The constitutionality of these regulations was resolved in a group of seven cases, collectively known as the Granger Cases, that the Supreme Court decided in 1877. The Court delivered its major opinion resolving all of the cases in *Munn v. Illinois.*[55]

Commons's thesis should not be pushed too far. Unquestionably, intangible corporate property did not occupy a major role in the American market until the very end of the nineteenth century, and equally unquestionably there was a doctrinal shift in the Court's constitutional property jurisprudence between the time of *Munn* and the *Minnesota Rate Case.* But intangible forms of corporate property had appeared and been recognized as property long before the age of the modern corporation. Moreover, while constitutional property doctrine shifted, the rhetoric that Commons claimed was characteristic of the Fuller Court, the rhetoric associating property with value,[56] began to appear before the doctrinal shift signaled by the *Minnesota Rate Case.* The Waite Court had protected value as property five years earlier when it held in *Pumpelly v. Green Bay Canal Co.*[57] that total destruction of land's value by flooding from a dam constituted a compensable taking of property under the fifth amendment even though title was not affected. In a famous passage that reveals the earlier Court's ability to recognize value as property, Justice Miller stated for the majority that

[i]t would be a very curious and unsatisfactory result, if in construing a provision of constitutional law, always understood to have been adopted for protection and security to the rights of the individual as against the government, . . . it shall be held that if the government refrains from the absolute conversion of real property to the uses of the public it can destroy its *value* entirely.[58]

To the extent that a conceptual problem inhibited the Waite Court from striking down, under either the takings clause or the due process clause (whose language derived in part from the former), regulations that did not affect title, it was whether such regulations constituted "deprivations" or "takings" rather than whether they affected "property." Harry Scheiber has pointed out that "[t]he legitimate definition of a 'taking' had become the subject of diversity, confusion, and some manifest injustice so long as the Supreme Court left the separate state governments free to work out formulations of their own."[59] The exclusion of consequential damages from protection under the eminent domain clause, for example, rested on a narrow conception of a taking.[60] Justice Miller's majority opinion in *Pumpelly* expressly left open the question whether the rule that consequential damages were not a compensable deprivation of property, a rule that many state courts had followed up to that point,[61] was constitutional. It would not have been an impossible stretch of imagination for the Court to have used *Munn* as the opportunity to extend the reach of constitutional protection of property by treating rate regulation as an analogous deprivation of property without due process. Indeed, Chief Justice Waite expressly acknowledged in *Munn* that "[u]nder some circumstances" price regulation may constitute a deprivation of property without due process.[62] The decision that the rate regulation before the Court in *Munn* was not such a deprivation of property, then, did not result from the Court's inability to see that rate regulation could constitute a deprivation of property. The basis of the decision was political, not conceptual.

Quasi-Public Property: *Munn* and the *Granger Cases*

Chief Justice Waite's opinion for the seven-man majority affirmed the states' power to regulate prices only with respect to a particular type of firm, businesses that are "affected with a public interest." Waite explained the affectation doctrine on the basis of a fictitious implied grant theory:

Property does become clothed with a public interest when used in a manner to make it of public consequence, and affect the community at large. When, therefore, one devotes his property to a use in which the public has an interest, he, in effect, grants to the public an interest in that use, and must submit to be controlled by the public for the common good, to the extent of the interest he has thus created. He may withdraw his grant by discontinuing the use; but, so long as he maintains the use, he must submit to the control.[63]

The real basis of the affectation doctrine was an imbalance, as the Court saw it, of power in the marketplace. A new sort of business had recently emerged in the national economy, one whose growth "has been rapid, and that . . . is already of great importance."[64] Railroads were the quintessential example of this sort of enterprise.

Waite sensed the need to respond to the changed character of enterprise organization and of the market generally by recognizing a new legal category of enterprise that was a hybrid of private and public firms. This new category consisted of firms upon which the legislature had not extended any special privilege and were not, therefore, public in the traditional sense but which nevertheless were businesses "in which the whole public has a direct and positive interest."[65]

Waite rationalized the affectation doctrine as being merely an extension to a new situation of the long-standing common-law doctrine that common carriers are subject to legislative price regulation, but it is clear that the great Chicago grain elevators were nothing like ferries, wharves, or hackney coaches. They possessed vastly more power in the national economy than any ferry owner had ever dreamed. The Illinois constitutional convention in 1870 had asserted that grain warehouses were "public" businesses, and while Waite acknowledged that fact, he did not treat it as dispositive. It would hardly comport with constitutional rule to make businesses subject to price regulation simply on the *ipse dixit* of their legislatures. Waite might have relied on the fact that the grain elevators were indeed common carriers since they were adjuncts of the railroads,[66] but he did not do so. Instead he emphasized the power position that the Chicago grain elevators held in the nation's economy. In a crucial passage, Waite characterized the elevators as a "'virtual' monopoly":

[I]t is apparent that all the elevating facilities through which these vast productions "of seven or eight great States of the West" must pass on the way "to four or five of the States on the [eastern] sea-shore" may be a "virtual" monopoly.[67]

As a monopoly, the elevators stood "in the very 'gateway of commerce,' and [took] toll from all who pass."[68] It was the existence of this imbalance of economic power that Waite and the majority thought warranted legislative regulation.

Waite did not ignore the other side of the power equation, governmental power. The threat that the elevators would abuse their market power was, in his view, greater than the risk, which the Court conceded existed, that the legislature might abuse its political power. The reason was that for protection against abuses by legislatures the people can resort to politics itself.[69] In this sense the problems of political and economic power are asymmetrical. While those who are dominated by a politically powerful legislature have a means of redressing the imbalance, there is no comparable mechanism in the market itself for dealing with domination by an unduly powerful market agent. Balance can be restored only through politics, specifically, through legislative regulation.

The Proprietarian Conception of Property Redux

Chief Justice Waite's affectation doctrine echoed aspects of the old antebellum proprietarian conception of property. The root of that doctrine was the conviction that property's residual function was to maintain a proper social order. Businesses affected with a public interest were subject to legislative regulation insofar as their economic power threatened to disrupt or distort that social order.

The Waite Court had drawn on the old proprietarian conception four years earlier in deciding the famous *Slaughterhouse Cases*.[70] In those cases, which provided the Court with its first opportunity to construe the meaning of the new fourteenth amendment, the Court held that a Louisiana statute making a state-chartered firm the exclusive place for butchers to conduct their slaughtering operations for twenty-five years did not violate due process, equal protection, or privileges and immunities clauses of the fourteenth amendment. New Orleans butchers had attacked the statute as creating a monopoly, and that the effect of the monopoly was to deprive them of their property interest in their occupation. The Court pointed out that the statute merely required butchers to confine their slaughtering operations to one locale and to pay a reasonable compensation for the use of that place. Thus "it is not true that [the statute] deprives the butchers of the right to exercise their trade."[71]

The decision in the *Slaughterhouse Cases* that the statute did not deprive the butchers of their property without due process represented a straightforward application of the antebellum idea of regulation to protect the well-ordered society.[72] The Court justified the legislatively created exclusive privilege as a proper exercise of the state's police power. It was designed "to remove from the more densely populated part of the city, the noxious slaughter-houses, and large and offensive collections of animals necessarily incident to the slaughtering business of a large city, and to locate them where the convenience, health, and comfort of the people require that they be located."[73] Rather than altogether prohibiting butchering within the city limits or granting to the city the exclusive privilege to conduct an abattoir, which even the dissent conceded it might do, the legislature had created a corporation for this purpose. The majority opinion in effect treated that corporation as a quasi-public corporation, a precursor of the sort of business that the Court in *Munn* later explicitly recognized. Underlying both was the old proprietarian vision of property, with its monopolies and special privileges created by the legislature to preserve the proper social order.

Munn was not a mere extension of the antebellum proprietarian conception, however. It added two new ideas to that conception. First, it applied the proprietarian conception to enterprises which were not stated-created, were not incorporated, and held no legislatively created special privileges. Second, and more important, *Munn* flipped around the implications of the antebellum proprietarian conception. In the early nineteenth century Federalist jurists had relied on that conception to grant legal protection to corporate interests under the vested rights doctrine. The majority in *Munn* and the *Granger Cases* relied on it instead to justify legal regulation of prices. The impetus for this dramatic reversal was the growing fear of agglomerated economic power.

Counternarrative of Power: Field's Dissents in *Munn* and the *Slaughterhouse Cases*

Completing the legal dialectic about power in the age of enterprise, Justice Stephen Field developed a counternarrative of abuse of power in his famous and influential dissenting opinions in *Munn*, the *Granger Cases*, and in the *Slaughterhouse Cases*. That counternarrative provided the foundation for the Fuller Court's subsequent doctrinal reversal of constitutional protection of corporate property interests. Both in his dissenting opinions and his later opinions for the majority, Field conveyed a sense of fear of governmental power and domination of the individual. He frequently used the rhetoric of civic republicanism to express his anxiety about government power. Field's views also drew substantially from the writings of two strong advocates of Jacksonian democracy, Theodore Sedgwick, a political economist and author of a widely read Jacksonian tract, *Public and Private Economy (1836–39)*,[74] and Thomas M. Cooley. Field's constitutional property jurisprudence drew, then, on fragments from multiple political traditions, republican and liberal, Jeffersonian and Jacksonian as well as Lockean.

Field began developing his counternarrative of power in his dissenting opinion in the *Slaughterhouse Cases*. He scoffed at the majority's explanation of the Louisiana statute as a routine exercise of the police power. "The pretence of sanitary regulations for the grant of exclusive privileges," he wrote, "is a shallow one, which merits only this passing notice."[75] He was equally scornful of the majority's treatment of the abattoir as a quasi-public business: "The grant, with exclusive privileges, of a right thus appertaining to the government, is a very different thing from a grant, with exclusive privileges, to pursue one of the ordinary trades or callings of life, which is a right appertaining solely to the individual."[76]

This last passage sounded a theme that dominated his vision of the relationship between government and business property. Field drew a deep and sharp distinction between public and private property, one that left no room for the hybrid sort of category that Justices Waite and Miller had in mind. His motive for trying to read that distinction into the Constitution was not to protect the accumulation of wealth for its own sake, but to respond to what he perceived to be the growing threat of governmental power and domination of the individual, both in a political and an economic sense. Statutes like that before the Court represented legislative violations of the right of free labor[77] and republican equality. The Louisiana statute, he thought, was not an even-handed public welfare regulation, but a corrupt privileging of a small cadre of business interests at the expense of other butchers' equal opportunity to pursue their occupation. This was the sheerest sort of abuse of government power:

> The State may prescribe such regulations for every pursuit and calling
> of life as will promote the public health, secure the good order and
> advance the general prosperity of society, but when once prescribed,

the pursuit or calling must be free to be followed by every citizen who is within the conditions designated, and will conform to the regulations. This is the fundamental idea upon which our institutions rest, and unless adhered to in the legislation of the country our government will be a republic only in name. The fourteenth amendment, in my judgment, makes it essential to the validity of legislation of every State that this equally of right should be respected. How widely this equality has been departed from, how entirely rejected and trampled upon by the act of Louisiana, I have already shown. And it is to me a matter of profound regret that its validity is recognized by a majority of this court, for by it the right of free labor, one of the most sacred and imprescribable rights of man, is violated.[78]

Constitutional protection of private property was Field's prescription for overcoming the problem of government power. Property was the foundation of a very broadly defined private sphere within which the individual was independent, politically and economically, and free from governmental subordination. Legal doctrines like Chief Justice Waite's affectation doctrine were anathema to Field precisely because they legitimized legislatively created dependency of the individual citizen. The affectation doctrine had been used to rationalize oppressive legislation like the rate regulations at issue in *Munn* and the *Granger Cases*. That legislation, he frankly declared in his dissent in *Munn*, was "nothing less than a bold assertion of absolute power by the State to control at its discretion the property and business of the citizen, and fix the compensation he shall receive."[79] The Court's theory that owners of businesses affected with a public interest had granted the public an interest in their enterprises utterly contradicted the basic tenets of republican politics by making owners dependent on the legislature's will: "If this [the grant theory] be sound law, if there be no protection, either in the principles upon which our republican government is founded, or in the prohibitions of the Constitution against such invasions of private rights, all property and all business in the State are held at the mercy of a majority of its legislature."[80]

Cabinning Public Power

Field's position on protecting property under the fourteenth amendment due process clause remained the minority view on the Court until 1890. Two factors facilitated a doctrinal shift that led to the triumph of his vision: personnel changes on the Court and growing fears of socialism.

Beginning with Waite's death in 1888, several new appointments led to a fully reconstituted Court, one whose ideological inclinations regarding constitutional protection of economic interests were very much more in line with Field's. At the same time, a variety of circumstances made wealthy elites increasingly anxious about the specter of ascendant socialism in the United States. American capitalists did not take lightly the attacks on capitalist accumulation of property that emerged as early as the 1870s.[81] Widespread labor unrest, most dramatically represented by the Haymarket Square riot in Chicago in 1886, made the working public's discontent with the power disparities between wage-earners and the owners of corporate property. Demonstrating that such events were not isolated aberrations, events in Europe like the Paris Commune of 1871 also made wealthy elites acutely aware of the rising tide of socialist sentiment in industrialized societies. All of these were events that the defenders of the new forms of enterprise could hardly ignore. Nor could the U.S. Supreme Court overlook them.

The break in the Court's constitutional property jurisprudence first occurred in the famous *Milwaukee Road* case.[82] The Court had intimated a shift a few years earlier when it stated in dicta in the *Railroad Commission Cases*[83] that the due process clause protected even businesses affected with a public interest against "confiscatory" rate regulation.[84] *Milwaukee Road* was the first case in which the Court invalidated a state statute under the due process clause, but the violation that the court identified in that case was procedural, not substantive. The Court struck down a statute that made railroad rates that a commission had established without a hearing conclusive in judicial proceedings to enforce them. The Court reasoned that "[i]f the company is deprived of the power of charging reasonable rates for the use of its property, and such deprivation takes place in the absence of an investigation by judicial machinery, it is deprived of the lawful use of its property, and thus, in substance and effect, of the property itself, without due process of law."[85]

At the heart of the decision in *Milwaukee Road* was the concern about controlling legislative power over an enterprise's opportunity to maximize its profits. If it was unchecked, then the legislature in effect possessed the power to destroy the value of an enterprise's property by setting unreasonably low rates. At the time of *Munn* most observers agreed that if the legislature has legitimate power to control rates, that power is discretionary and not subject to judicial review.[86] No one, not even Field, questioned that the legislature had the power to set rates for railroads and comparable industries. Railroads were the clearest sort of business devoted to public use. They exercised eminent domain power and received direct government benefits, such as land, in exchange for their performing a valuable public service.[87] The question in *Milwaukee Road* was whether the legislature's power to regulate railroad rates was unchecked or was subject to some form of review for the reasonableness of its exercise.

Under one theory of the relationship railroads and the state, legislative power was unchecked. Justices Waite, Bradley, and the majority of the *Munn* Court thought that a railroad's charter empowered it to act, as Bradley later expressed, only "as an agent of the State for furnishing public accommodation."[88] Under this agency theory there was no basis for judicial or other means of review of the legislature's exercise of it power to fix rates. Railroads and comparable transport industries were entirely at the mercy of legislative will because in fact they were not private enterprises.

Field appeared at one point to concede that legislative power was unchecked, stating, "If it be admitted that the legislature has any control over the compensation, the extent of that compensation becomes a mere matter of legislative discretion."[89] Extremely anxious about ceding so much power to the legislature, though, he could not accept the agency theory of railroads. That theory, he argued, confused the distinction between a private firm with public duties and a wholly public firm.[90] The task was

> to define the limits of the power of the State over its corporations after they have expended money and incurred obligations upon the faith of the grants to them, and the rights of the corporators, so that, on the one hand, the property interests of the stockholder would be protected from practical confiscation, and, on the other hand, the people would be protected from arbitrary and extortionate charges.[91]

The Court's solution to this dilemma in *Milwaukee Road* was to require as a precondition for the rate's legal enforcement a judicial determination that it was not so unreasonably low as to be unconstitutional. That approach recognized the legitimacy of railroad (and utility) rate regulation without allowing regulators to destroy the value of property by ukase. Rate regulation—and, ultimately, the value of regulated firms' assets—was cabinned by removing it from the sphere of mere politics.

In a clear and penetrating dissenting opinion for three members of the Court,[92] Justice Bradley directly addressed the question of power. He did so in terms that echoed Waite's analysis of the power calculus in *Munn:*

> It may be that our legislatures are invested with too much power, open, as they are, to influences so dangerous to the interests of individuals, corporations and society. But such is the Constitution of our republican form of government; and we are bound to abide by it until it can be corrected in a legitimate way. If our legislatures become too arbitrary in the exercise of their powers, the people always have a remedy in their hands; they may at any time restrain them by constitutional limitations.[93]

The irony of Bradley's appeal to republicanism as a justification for the Minnesota regulation perhaps did not escape Field, who, as we saw earlier, relied on the same theory to attack the affectation doctrine in *Munn.* But, in truth, both sides could claim support from republicanism with a straight face.

Republicanism's implications for the whole issue of constitutional protection from rate regulation was irreducibly ambiguous; there simply was no "republicanly" correct position. On the one hand, one could plausibly think that protecting the public from extortionate charges by businesses that dominated the market was not only consonant with but compelled by the republican idea of equality. Moreover, judicial review of legislative determinations of the reasonableness of rate structures might be thought to be incompatible with the republican notion of individual autonomy. On the other hand, one might view the Minnesota statute as the product of legislative corruption that denied railroads republican equality and independence by subjecting their livelihoods to the whims of regulators. Republicanism's implications for the issue in *Milwaukee Road* was ambiguous because the ideal of personal autonomy, the basis for republicanism's concern with power relations between citizen and state, was itself ambiguous.

The triumph of Field's theory of rate regulation was completed in 1898 with the decision in *Smyth v. Ames.*[94] In that case a unanimous Court held unconstitutional a Nebraska statute imposing rate reductions averaging 29.5 percent on intrastate shipments.[95] In a famous passage, Justice Harlan, writing for the Court, stated

> the basis of all calculations as to the reasonableness of rates . . . must be the fair value of the property being used for the convenience of

the public. And in order to ascertain that value, the original cost of construction, the amount expended in permanent improvements, the amount and market value of its bonds and stock, the present as compared with the original cost of construction, the probable earning capacity of the property under particular rates prescribed by statute, and the sum required to meet operating expenses, are all matters for consideration, and are to be given such weight as may be just and right in each case. . . . What a company is entitled to ask is a fair return upon the value of that which it employs for the public convenience. On the other hand, what the public is entitled to demand is that no more be exacted from it for the use of a public highway than the services rendered by it are reasonably worth.[96]

Here was a response to both narratives of power, the Waite Court's scenario of huge corporations using their agglomerated market power to expropriate wealth from ordinary citizens and Field's counterscenario of government using its monopolistic political power to confiscate wealth and dominate the private sphere. Acknowledging the legitimacy of both narratives, the Court was saying that railroads were entitled to earn the equivalent of a competitive market return but were not entitled to take unlimited advantage of their legally privileged position.

The effect of the doctrinal shift from *Munn* and the *Granger Cases* to *Milwaukee Road* and *Smyth v. Ames* was to move the constitutional conception of property much closer to the commodified understanding. They did so by protecting the dimension of corporate property that matters most in the eyes of one who values property for its ability to produce private wealth: the stream of profits. They raised to a constitutional level the corporation's opportunity to realize profits for private benefit, even as to firms that were licensed to serve the public interest.

Vestige of the Commonwealth Ideal: The Public Trust Doctrine

While the effect of decisions like *Smyth v. Ames* was to move the constitutional meaning of property a good deal closer to the commodity ideology, the Court did not embrace that ideology in all respects. Members of the Court throughout the late nineteenth century, like their antebellum counterparts, recognized that private preferences at times had to be subordinated to the well-being of the community and that this required, on some occasions, subjecting individual property interests to certain forms of collective control. They agreed, moreover, that this implied more than the

Lockean proviso that owners should not use their property in ways that cause harm to others. They understood the common welfare as a collective norm, rather than as the mere aggregation of individual interests. The maxim *salus populi suprema est lex* (the welfare of the people is the supreme law) expressed that collective norm through a wide variety of rigorous public controls of property uses throughout the first half of the nineteenth century.[97] The basic idea behind that maxim retained a viable role in American legal thought even during the height of so-called laissez-faire constitutionalism.

Though they agreed that private property interests at times had to be subordinated to the public good, late nineteenth-century judges disagreed about the appropriate strategy for doing so. One branch of the Court, represented by Justices Morrison R. Waite and Samuel F. Miller, thought that the legislature had to play an active regulatory role throughout the economy. There were limits to the legislature's regulatory authority, of course, but those limits could not be predefined. The courts' job was to balance the public's interest against the property owner's interest in the particular circumstances presented. No categorical separation of public and private was possible because social and economic life had become too complex for that approach. Some degree of public interest was present in all areas of social life. How much weight should be given to the public interest all depended on the specific conditions involved in the given dispute.

The members of the Court who came to dominate its decisions after 1885, particularly Field and, later, his nephew, David J. Brewer, adopted a completely different approach to accommodating public and private. Field directly confronted the dilemma. Recognizing that property's role as serving the common good threatened to undermine the individual owner's liberty to use his property to fulfill his private wishes, Field sought to cabin the social role. Field's strategy was to define separate spheres of authority for government and private interests, guaranteeing equal treatment of the many and the few. Within the public sphere, property continued to play a civic role, serving the interests of society as a whole. Within the private sphere, however, the role of property was strictly for individual gain.

The difference between these two approaches to the task of reconciling the public's interest with the individual owner's autonomy interest should not overdrawn, however. The conventional wisdom among legal historians is that there was a sharp discontinuity between the constitutional jurisprudence of the Waite and Fuller Courts. The Waite Court, according to this view, generally took a permissive attitude toward state regulation of business enterprise, while the Fuller Court used the fourteen amendment's due process clause as a weapon against legislative interference with private property and liberty of contract. Judicial homage to liberty of contract reached its apogee in the infamous case of *Lochner v. New York.*

This conventional wisdom has led many historians to overlook the points of continuity between the two periods. While changes in the Court's personnel after 1886 and growing fears of socialism in the 1890s did produce a shift in the Court's property jurisprudence,[98] there were substantial areas of agreement between the Waite Court's and Fuller Court's views on property and its constitutional status. The Waite Court contributed important decisions that broadened the constitutional definition of property,[99] while the Fuller Court, led by that supposedly uncompromising defender of private property, Stephen J. Field, explicitly endorsed doctrines that imposed important regulatory constraints on commercial exploitation of privately owned resources. Of these constraints, the most significant was the public trust doctrine.[100]

The public trust doctrine in effect restricts the private owner's right to exploit his land for its full commercial value. It recognizes the private ownership of the affected land, but imposes an inalienable servitude on the land for the benefit of the general public. The servitude's inalienability rests on proprietarian thinking: the restriction is necessary for maintaining good social order.

The public trust doctrine has a long history, dating back at least to sixteenth-century English law.[101] In American law, it has, as Professor Rose has pointed out, "exerted a persistent hold . . . since the early nineteenth century."[102] Its most remarkable phase occurred during the late nineteenth century when the Supreme Court used it to block the commercial exploitation of certain land. This recrudescence of the doctrine demonstrated the continuing vitality of proprietarian thinking during the supposed height of laissez-fairism.

Justice Field's most important contribution to the public trust doctrine came in the famous 1892 decision in *Illinois Central Railroad v. Illinois.*[103] In that case the Illinois legislature had deeded to the Illinois Central Railroad Company the submerged lands all along Chicago's lakefront. A year later, the legislature changed its mind and revoked the grant. The question was whether the initial grant was valid. If it was, then the legislature had to pay compensation if it wanted to repeal the grant. The Court held that the grant was not valid; consequently, the contract clause of the Constitution did not prohibit the legislature from revoking its prior grant. Writing for a slim 4–3 majority, Field declared that the state held the land subject to a trust for the public's benefit and that any irrevocable transfer of such land violated the public's interest in the land. A corporation created to operate a railroad, Justice Field stated, could not be "converted into a corporation to manage and practically control the harbor . . . not simply for its own purpose as a railroad corporation, but for its own profit."[104]

This was a striking limitation on the scope of free marketability of land. The finding (conclusion, really) that a piece of land was subject to a public trust meant that it was removed from the market's domain. Justice Field in effect presumed that the public's interest in land could not coexist with the land's status as a market commodity; the commodity function, if permitted, would, or might, undermine the public interest function. The Court found that the character of the land itself made it subject to a public trust, and such a finding meant that the land could not be freely bought or sold.

What Field was trying to do in the *Illinois Central* case was not to repudiate or weaken the conception of property as market commodity but to reconcile that conception with the old notion of property as the foundation for proper order. Indeed, his ultimate objective was to strengthen the commodity conception by defining the limits of the public interest in land. It did not seem to Field either possible or desirable to deny completely any public interest in any land. Given, then, that a public interest of some sort had to be recognized, a categorical approach protected the market more than did any sort of balancing approach. So long as we know that a particular piece of land is not within the sphere subject to a public interest, then it may be freely bought and sold in unregulated markets.

This explains why Field's public-trust doctrine in *Illinois Central* did not contradict his vehement denunciation of the affectation doctrine of *Munn v. Illinois*. The affectation doctrine, like the public trust doctrine, was premised on the public nature of certain privately owned items of property. The crucial difference is that, as we saw earlier, the affectation doctrine was based on the view that certain enterprises were hybrid in character; that is, they were both public *and* private. While their "privateness" justified profit-making, their "publicness" warranted some degree of political control of the extent of monetary gain. How much public control was permissible depended on the particular circumstances. One had to balance the magnitude of the public interest involved against the private aspect of the property in question.

Field's approach was altogether different. It created a categorical separation between the public and private spheres, allowing no room for vague hybrids. If property was inherently private in character, its sole function was to facilitate individual preference-satisfaction, and there was no justification for political control over how individual owners used their property. Similarly, if property was inherently public in character, as it was in *Illinois Central* itself, it could not be used for private gain to any extent.

The crucial question that Field's theory raised was what distinguishes land that is inherently public from land that is inherently private and, therefore, commodifiable. Why was the submerged land along the Chicago lakefront different, for example, from the undeveloped Yazoo lands, which, according to *Fletcher v. Peck,* the legislature *could* grant to private corporation to be used for private gain?[105] Field's answer focused on the state's power to control navigable waterways:

> [The title to lands under Lake Michigan's navigable waters] is a title different in character from that which the State holds in lands intended for sale. It is different from the title which the United States holds in the public lands which are open to preemption and sale. It is a title held in trust for the people of the State that they may enjoy the navigation of the waters, carry on commerce over them, and have liberty of fishing therein freed from the obstruction or interference of private parties.[106]

The idea that the state holds title to submerged lands in trust for the public and that this trust title limited its capacity to dispose of the land was not new. In an important 1821 New Jersey case, *Arnold v. Mundy,*[107] which the U.S. Supreme Court later discussed but did not expressly endorse,[108] the court held that the standard doctrine applicable to land that derived from royal grants, that the Crown could not transfer trust land, applied to the legislature as well. Even though it was the people's elected body of representatives, the legislature could not "divest[ ] . . . all the citizens of their common right."[109] Field expressly (and somewhat disingenuously) relied on *Arnold* as precedent for the Court's decision to sustain the legislature's revocation of its earlier grant. He analogized the legislative grant of its trust title to an attempt to divest itself of the police power, an action that the Court had earlier held in *Stone v. Mississippi*[110] was unconstitutional. The problem with this theory was that the legislative grant in *Illinois Central* had contained an express condition that "nothing herein contained shall authorize obstructions to the Chicago harbor, or impair the public right of navigation."[111] In view of this provision, it is difficult to see how that transfer of the land alone amounted to an attempt to transfer the state's power to regulate navigation, yet that is what Field contended.[112]

However unpersuasive it may have been on the facts of *Illinois Central,* Field's theory for distinguishing the circumstances in which public control legitimately existed over property from those in which regulation unconstitutionally interfered with private property was coherent on its own terms. Public control of land legitimately existed, indeed could not be transferred to private hands, where it implicated powers that were traditionally considered governmental. Since the list of such powers that Field recognized was exceeding small, though, that theory left little room for the public trust doctrine to operate. It reduced the state's role to little more than that of a night watchman.

∽

The upshot of the doctrinal changes that the Fuller Court effected is that the center of gravity in the Supreme Court's constitutional property jurisprudence had by the end of the nineteenth century substantially shifted toward the private commodified understanding. It sanctioned capitalist accumulation, the starkest sort of property-as-wealth, for a very broad array of business enterprises, and it created a large private domain of unregulated and unregulatable market activity.

Still, for all of the gains of the commodity outlook, it had not completely eliminated all vestiges of the proprietarian tradition. The public trust doctrine was the clearest example of that tradition's survival. The idea underlying that doctrine is not maximizing individual preference-satisfaction, but fulfilling the individual owner's responsibility to the community. The responsibilities of ownership were not confined to the common law doctrine of *sic utere tuo* (use your property so as not to injure that of others).[113] At times, they required more than that; they required maintaining land, or at least certain uses of land, as a commons. While it may be possible to reconcile communal ownership with the premises of the commodity conception,[114] ideas like the public trust fit much more easily within the proprietarian tradition. No one would (or should) claim that Field or the other judges who are usually associated with laissez-faire constitutionalism were uninterested in protecting private wealth from government encroachments; plainly they were not. But that was not their exclusive concern. The ancient notions of community, commonwealth, and civic duty still had meaning to them. For all of the Court's apparent laissez-fairism, the idea that one of the roles that property should play is to maintain good social order remained alive in American constitutional thought and discourse. A dialectic between that conception and an individualistic, preference-maximizing conception of property persisted, albeit in a weakened form.

TEN

The Dilemma of Property in the Private Sphere: Alienability and Paternalism

W HILE PUBLIC LAW STRUGGLED during the late nineteenth century to define and resolve the problem of power that the enormous changes of the Age of Enterprise had wrought in politics, the economy, and society, a parallel dilemma confronted jurists and scholars concerned with defining the role and incidents of property in private law. To what extent, if at all, may individual property owners create private arrangements of property that effectively protect and immunize others from the vicissitudes of the market and their own ill-considered actions? Put differently, was the fear of and bias against protectionism, which was so evident in late nineteenth-century legal discourse about constitutionalism and regulatory matters, confined to the public sphere, or did it extend to the realm of private legal arrangements as well?

Two aspects of late nineteenth-century legal thought converged to oppose protectionist property arrangements. One was the strong sentiment against all forms of legal paternalism, which critics often treated as synonymous with socialism or even communism. Many legal commentators thought that paternalism was no more tolerable when done by private individuals than by the government.[1] In their view, allowing wealthy property owners (for these protective arrangements typically were the products of the wealthy) to create such protective arrangements was twice objectionable: it transformed property acquired through dynamic means into static wealth, protected from the market; and by legally immunizing the beneficiary's interest from being dissipated, it discouraged the development of personal virtues of independence and strength. Both transformations would mock the still-powerful Jacksonian vision of America as the land of energetic entrepreneurs whose self-reliance, hard work, and individual initiative made the American economy more virtuous than that of any other nation on Earth.

The other aspect of late nineteenth-century legal discourse that seemingly conflicted with private protective arrangements of property was the legal policy favoring the unfettered alienability, or transferability, of property. As we discussed in earlier chapters, American lawyers had long emphasized the importance of maximizing the free alienability of property in a liberal commercial society. By 1870, though, free alienability, along with liberty of contract, had become explicitly identified as one of the twin keystones of liberal private law. Virtually all of the law of real property, dealing with land, was treated as a series of variations on the theme of free alienability. Late nineteenth-century legal thought's unique contribution to the legal understanding of the alienability policy was to use that policy as the framework for an attempt to synthesize nearly all property legal doctrine. From that project's perspective, protectionist legal arrangements were completely unacceptable precisely because they were based on restrictions on the free transferability of assets that an owner had donated to beneficiaries.

The main legal device that wealthy property owners used to protect their beneficiaries from economic upheaval was the same device that the old English aristocracy had used to immunize their families and fortunes since at least the seventeenth century—the trust. There was a crucial difference, however, between the intentions of settlors of the Gilded Age and those of their earlier counterparts. The owner of old placed a specific asset, usually land, in trust for the purpose of protecting that asset. He (for the settlor was nearly always male) intended that the asset never be sold, regarding the asset itself as the material foundation of the extended family. By contrast, the creator of the new trust placed a variety of assets (sometimes land but more frequently intangible financial instruments) in trust with the express expectation that the trustee would sell them and reinvest the proceeds in more profitable investment vehicles. Within this new type of family trust, specific items of property represented investment assets, rather than, in civic republican terms, indispensable foundations for the well-being of the family as a "little commonwealth."[2] In this sense, then, the new trust represented the extension of the commodified conception to the sphere of the family in the late nineteenth century. But the fundamental purpose of the new American trust was to immunize family wealth from the effects of commodification.

The deeper issue that trusts raised regarding commodification was whether the alienability policy applied to all private property arrangements or whether exceptions would be carved out of that policy for limited protective purposes. Two conflicting conceptions of private trusts were available. One was that they were purely property arrangements and were therefore strictly subject to the policy of alienability. That conception reflected an even more pervasive extension of the commodification outlook than did the settlors' attitude toward trust assets as mere investments. The other conception saw the private trust as a property arrangement for the purpose, among others, of caring for and protecting persons whom the settlor did not consider fully capable of looking out for their own well-being. The persons whom such trusts sought to protect typically were members of the settlor's family. Influenced by the domestic sphere ideology that had developed earlier in the nineteenth century,[3] this protective conception regarded the family as a discrete realm of social life to which the commodification outlook was inappropriate.[4]

The decision whether to give effect to protective property arrangements was made even more difficult by the fact that the trusts that were the subject of debate in the Gilded Age did not fit neatly into either category. Instead, they were what Lawrence Friedman has aptly called "dynastic trusts,"[5] created more for the purpose of perpetuating the power of large personal fortunes into the future than for the care of particular individuals. These trusts immunized the beneficiaries' trust interests regardless of the individuals' competence to manage their own economic affairs and regardless of their needs. The settlor sought to protect the accumulated wealth; the beneficiaries were an afterthought. Restricting the alienability of the beneficiaries' interests, then, would primarily serve the dynastic ambitions of the wealthy.

By the end of the nineteenth century, American courts had generally ratified these dynastic trusts. In doing so, they ignored the dynastic ambitions of the owners and rationalized their decisions on the basis of the abstract principle of individual freedom of alienation. As many critics stressed, though, the effect of these decisions was to limit legal protection from the market unequally. Only those lucky enough to have been born into wealthy families enjoyed the advantages of these trusts.

"A Crime against Self": Anti-Paternalism and Personal Responsibility in Late Nineteenth-Century Legal Thought

Lately, historians have debated the prevalence of Social Darwinist ideas in late nineteenth-century American thought.[6] Revising the conventional account, usually attributed to Richard Hofstadter,[7] that depicted Social Darwinist ideas as running rampant during the Age of Enterprise, some historians have asserted, as one put it, that "Social Darwinism can now claim a dubious honor: that it has been shown not to have existed in more places than any other movement in the history of social theory."[8] But, as Dean Aviam Soifer has pointed out, anti-paternalism "was an appealing surrogate for more explicit Social Darwinist rhetoric."[9] Legal writings between 1880 and 1920 were filled with attacks on paternalism. If Social Darwinism was not a major theme in the social and legal thought of the period,[10] anti-paternalism was ubiquitous in the legal discourse of the time.

The most obvious target of these attacks were legislative measures aimed at protecting some seemingly vulnerable group. Legal writers tended to lump all such legislation together and tar it with the label of "socialism," or "communism," or both.[11] Christopher G. Tiedeman's alarmist diatribe against class legislation was typical:

> Socialism, Communism, and Anarchism are rampant throughout the civilized world. The State is called on to protect the weak against the shrewdness of the stronger, to determine what wages a workman shall receive for his labor, and how many hours daily he shall labor. Many trades and occupations are being prohibited because some are damaged incidentally by their prosecution, and many ordinary pursuits are made government monopolies. The demands of the Socialists and Communists vary in degree and in detail, and the most extreme of them insist upon the assumption by government of the paternal character altogether, abolishing all private property in land, and making the State the sole possessor of the working capital of the nation.[12]

In part, the attack on legislative paternalism was a vestige of the Jacksonian ideology of individual equality. That was especially true of commentators, like Tiedeman, who attacked any and all legislative measures that were not perceptibly and exquisitely evenhanded. Other critics of legislative paternalism (or at least what they viewed as paternalistic legislation) perverted the Jacksonian message by attacking legislation that was "populistic" and linking such legislation with the brooding threat of communism. Joseph Choate's argument against the progressive income tax in *Pollock v. Farmers' Loan & Trust Co.*[13] illustrates this sort of red-baiting assault on such legislation. "I believe," Choate told the Supreme Court, "there are private rights of property here to be protected. . . . The act of Congress which we are impugning before you is communistic in its purposes and tendencies, and is defended here upon principles as communistic, socialistic—what shall I call them—populistic as ever have been addressed to any political assembly in the world."[14] Another lawyer echoed the same theme that dependency breeds collectivism, stating, "Losing gradually their independent manhood, as they learn to rely upon the government to do for them what they should do themselves, the people drift more and more into socialistic practices."[15]

Legislative protection of vulnerable groups was not the only form of paternalism that commentators found objectionable. Many social critics considered paternalism no less offensive if it came at the hands of private individuals or groups rather than the government. Some critics carried the attack even further, treating any form of philanthropy as private paternalism. These arguments were especially revealing because what they indicated was that late nineteenth-century critics found paternalistic acts objectionable not because they sacrificed the beneficiaries' personal autonomy but because paternalism made the beneficiaries weaker. From the perspective of strengthening moral character, it does not matter whether the beneficiary consents or not to the beneficial action. Private charity weakens individual character every bit as much as government restrictions on work hours. One writer went so far as to attack New York soup kitchens, which, in his view, threatened the republican form of government because they bred dependence and weakened the moral character of workers:

> What effect is this enforced idleness having upon these suffering people? Are we not establishing a debasing and dangerous practice in teaching these hitherto useful laborers, mechanics and clerks, that it is possible for them to live in enforced idleness upon the bounty of benevolent individuals, or the State? And are we not in a sense responsible for the *chronic* pauperism that this *surface* charity is breeding among this vast and rapidly-augmenting army of mendicants? . . .
>
> I am entirely satisfied that we are, through this soup house system, degrading and pauperizing the industrial classes, to an extent that will become a positive danger to the whole community, and threatening even the stability of Republican Institutions. If you teach an army of industrial workers to live in easy idleness, will they not soon begin

to demand support as a right? and when that support is withdrawn, will not society be confronted with a clamorous army of the now "dangerous classes"?[16]

It is easy for us today to laugh at such statements as the mindless outbursts of extreme Social Darwinists, but the fact is that many commentators (legal and otherwise) in the last of the nineteenth century took such sentiments very seriously. The assault on paternalistic legislation and private property arrangements was not simply about economics; more important, it was based on a social, and for many, a moral vision, a vision that in some respect was a vestige of the eighteenth-century civic republican sociology of virtue. In other, more relevant respects, though, it was a vision appropriate to a generation whose life experience, first in war, later in commerce, had taught it that life was nothing more or less than a struggle for survival.

The vision emphasized self-interest and personal responsibility above all else. Unless your status placed you in one of the categories of persons who were deemed to be incapable of looking out for themselves—categories that erratically included Indians and African Americans, along with children and "idiots"[17]—you were responsible for the material conditions of your own life. No one owed you a duty, legal or moral, to protect you against economic misfortune or to bail you out of economic distress. If people were entitled to be protected against their own ill-considered actions or against the actions of the invisible hand, they would lack incentives to develop the personal qualities necessary for the proper moral and political personality—carefulness, determination, honesty, and above all, energy.

Some commentators additionally urged that those who were wealthy should not consume their wealth ostentatiously, echoing eighteenth-century republican assaults on "luxury."[18] For the most part, however, frugality was not part of the late nineteenth-century image of virtue. Rather, the virtuous citizen was one who earned his wealth (though not necessarily all of it), paid his own way, satisfied his debts, was honest and fair in all his dealings, commercial and otherwise, and responded to adversity by exerting himself with renewed vigor. He was, in short, the self-sufficient, productive man of integrity.[19]

The accumulation of unheard-of private fortunes during the Gilded Age provoked a public debate over whether such great wealth was socially beneficial or harmful. To many Americans, the huge personal fortunes that Robber Barons like Jay Gould and J. P. Morgan had amassed represented a perversion of American ideals. To others, they simply constituted a fair return on risk-taking entrepreneurial activity. Both sides of the debate, however, framed the question the same way. It was, as one magazine article put it, "Whether a man can render services entitling him to a fortune as great as some of ours in America[?]"[20]

Not everyone framed the matter in that way. One of the most interesting defenses of great wealth came from a man not usually counted among the apologists of the Gilded Set, Oliver Wendell Holmes, Jr. We saw earlier that Holmes viewed all aspects of life in terms of an inevitable struggle for power, so in a sense it is not surprising that he would find the desire to accumulate great personal fortune to be unexceptional. Holmes's defense of personal wealth, however, did not rest solely on his determinist outlook; nor did he recite the usual nostrums about wealth being a just reward for energy, effort, and productivity. As one would expect from one of the most unusual and subtle minds of his (or any) time, his analysis was novel and filled with insight.

Holmes began by revising the entire issue. "The real problem," he wrote, "is not who owns, but who consumes, the annual product."[21]

> The real evil of fifty-thousand-dollar balls and other manifestations of private splendor is that they tend to confirm this confusion [i.e., consumption with ownership] in the minds of the ignorant by an appeal to their imagination, and make them think that the Vanderbilts and Rockefellers swallow their incomes like Cleopatra's dissolved pearl. The same conception is at the bottom of Henry George's *Progress and Poverty*. He thinks he has finished the discussion when he shows the tendency of wealth to be owned by the landlords. He does not consider what the landlords do with it.[22]

Holmes then launches into an explanation of why the accumulation of great personal wealth serves an important social objective—satisfying the collective consumptive desires of the public.

> I conceive that economically it does not matter whether you call Rockefeller or the United States owner of all the wheat in the United States, if that wheat is annually *consumed* by the body of the people. . . .
> If then, as I believe, the ability of the ablest men under the present régime is directed toward getting the largest markets and the

largest returns, such ability is directed to the economically desirable end. . . .

It follows from what I have said that the objections to unlimited private ownership are sentimental or political, not economic. Of course, as the size of a private fortune increases, the interest of the public in the administration of it increases. If a man owned one-half of the wheat in the country and announced his intention to burn it, such an abuse of ownership would not be permitted. The crowd would kill him sooner than stand it.[23]

This passage echoes Holmes's characteristically Darwinian outlook. His dismissal of objections to great private fortunes as "sentimental," his scornful reference to "the crowd," his hard-boiled calculus of power—all of these were standard Social Darwinist stuff. What was not Darwinian and what might not have expected from Holmes was his thesis that private wealth is socially directed. By shifting the focus from ownership to consumption, Holmes was able to assert with a straight face that property is in a meaningful sense already socialized. In a 1913 speech to the Harvard Law School Association of New York, Holmes made this point even more explicitly:

[W]e need to think things instead of words—to drop ownership, money, etc., and to think of the stream of products; of wheat and cloth and railway travel. When we do, it is obvious that the many consume them; that they now as truly have substantially all there is, as if the title were in the United States, that the great body of property is socially administered now.[24]

Holmes considered ownership itself to be a largely unimportant legal relationship, and as a consequence he had little to say about it. He regarded ownership as facilitative rather than regulative. The owner did not control; he was merely a conduit between contending groups clamoring for the same product. This is why he thought that it really is of no great moment that wealth was increasingly concentrated in a few hands. "The hated capitalist," he wrote, "is simply the mediator, the prophet, the adjuster according to his divination of the future desire."[25] It was "the crowd," which "already has all there is,"[26] who had the ultimate power. Viewed from the cold light of reality rather than from sentimentality, the accumulation of huge personal fortunes was simply not a problem.

John Chipman Gray and the Social Dimension
of the Alienability Policy

If the accumulation of personal wealth was not a problem to men like Holmes, the tying up of that wealth was. Preoccupied with proving that consumption mattered far more than ownership did, Holmes had virtually nothing to say about keeping wealth freely transferable.[27] One who did directly address that issue was his close friend, John Chipman Gray. More than anyone else in his era, Gray articulated a clear and emphatic view that the free alienability of property was a social and political imperative.

Legal texts of the late nineteenth century, like those of today, greatly emphasized the centrality of the alienability policy in property law. Commentators today almost without exception explain the alienability policy in economic terms. Free transferability of property is necessary, they repeatedly state, to permit economic values to be maximized as assets move to the highest and best use.[28] To late nineteenth-century lawyers, however, alienability was important for a noneconomic reason as well. The free transferability of property is, they thought, an essential aspect of the social-political vision of personal responsibility, the gospel of the Mugwumps.[29] Restrictions on an individual's power to transfer his property, whether directly imposed by the government or by another person, tended to create personal dependency and irresponsibility. In this sense, restrictions on alienability were a piece of the larger problem of paternalism.

Beginning around 1880, in an effort to make the law more "scientific," elite legal writers consciously set out to develop unified, systematic treatments of the various branches of law.[30] The law of property, which remained highly technical and highly fragmented, resisted systematization perhaps more than any other branch, and no one tried to integrate all of it. Instead, treatise writers focused their efforts on those aspects of property law that seemed most fundamental. Among these topics, none was regarded as more fundamental than the law of restraints on alienation, and commentators produced numerous treatises on its often-arcane rules.[31]

Gray was by far the best-known of those who wrote about restraints on alienation. His attack on restraints on transferability was by far the most coherent, sustained, and widely read discussion of the entire problem in the legal literature produced between 1875 and 1920. His arguments, even when they did not persuade courts, were taken very seriously and generally reflected the thinking of other legal critics of judicial doctrines that permitted property owners to impose restraints on transferability.

Gray's general preeminence in property law during this period[32] resulted not simply from the strength of his reasoning, but at least as much from his associations within the legal profession and Boston society. A leading member of Christopher Columbus Langdell's reconstituted Harvard law faculty for an incredible forty-three years (1869–1913), Gray's professional and social connections were varied and strong. Born into a wealthy Boston family, his grandfather was reputed to be the largest ship owner and wealthiest man in New England. His older half-brother was Horace Gray, a justice of the U.S. Supreme Court. Oliver Wendell Holmes, Jr., was a longtime close friend whose views on law (and much else) Gray generally shared.[33] Indeed, Holmes, Gray, Nicholas St. Green, Melville Green, and a few others formed a small group of scholarly lawyers that frequently met to discuss ideas. Their mutual ambition to rationalize the law led to a variety of collaborative efforts, not the least of which was the founding by Gray and his law partner, John C. Ropes (whose brother had served with Holmes in the Union army during the Civil War) the influential journal, the *American Law Review*.[34] All of these men, together with a handful of other practicing lawyers and judges in Boston, constituted what Alfred Konefsky has felicitously termed a "cultural nexus,"[35] that is, a cluster of social relationships among professional elites who shared and participated in transmitting within the profession a basic social vision.

Gray was equally at home on Boston's State Street as he was in Harvard Yard. He was the only member of the new Harvard law faculty to maintain an active practice. He was co-founder, with John Ropes, of the elite Boston law firm of Ropes & Gray. In that capacity he represented some of the wealthiest and most prominent figures in Boston. The firm's early account books listing the names of clients reads like the Boston Social Register—Cushing, Dexter, Lowell, Cabot, Storrow, Weld, Sturgis, Amory, Sears, Adams, and Lawrence were just some of the firm's clients.[36] Gray had a thriving real estate and trusts and estates practice and served as personal trustee for many wealthy families.

Gray's scholarship exemplified many of the themes commonly voiced by elite property lawyers of his time. Among these themes was the conviction that the bewildering jumble of rules that constituted American property law was neither necessary nor justifiable. Gray and his peers believed that all of property law could and should be reorganized in a systematic (or "scientific," as they put it) and internally coherent way. In the introduction to the first edition of his enormously influential treatise on the complicated Rule against Perpetuities,[37] Gray articulated this grand vision for systematized legal doctrine:

> I have long thought that in the present state of legal learning a chief need is for books on special topics, chosen with a view, not to their utility as the subjects of convenient manuals, but to their place and importance in the general system of the law. When such books have been written, it will then, for the first time, be possible to treat fully the great departments of the law, or even to construct a *corpus juris*.[38]

They further believed that most, if not all of property law (broadly defined to include equitable doctrines as well as common-law rules) could be rationalized on the basis of a few core principles and policies. Paramount among these policies was the policy of maintaining the free alienability of property interests, broadly defined. The centrality of the alienability policy in the late nineteenth-century lawyer's understanding of property law explains why Gray devoted his greatest scholarly efforts to the seemingly hyper-technical areas of the Rule against Perpetuities and other rules concerning restraints on alienation.

Gray set about to reorganize all of the law in this area. In his judgment it was the fragmentation of property law doctrine that was the source of so many mistakes, as he saw them, in the crucial area of rules concerning the alienability of property:

> Such errors as have arisen in discussing restraints on alienation are largely due to the subject having been dealt with disconnectedly. If the restraint was in the form of a condition, it was treated with conditions. If it was in the form of a direction to a trustee, it was treated with trusts. Involuntary alienation, or liability for debts, has been considered without reference to voluntary transfers. It will be a gain to clear thought to bring the whole subject together.[39]

Bringing "the whole subject together" led Gray to speak of a unitary "rule against restraints on alienation," whose particular applications he set out to describe, explain, and justify. Gray divided all of the law of restraints on alienation into two categories, direct and indirect restraints (which involve what property lawyers now call "remotely vesting future interests"[40]). The latter was the province of the Rule against Perpetuities, while the former dealt with restrictions that a previous owner placed on the power of subsequent owners to transfer a property interest. It was this aspect of the law of restraints on alienation that was the locus of the most important conflict regarding the relationship between the alienability policy and the social vision of protectionism.

Gray described his treatise on the law of direct restraints, first published in 1883, as "the first attempt . . . to deal systematically with the whole of a legal doctrine, whose development is . . . in danger of being marred by too exclusive an attention to particular aspects."[41] There were three crucial differences between his treatment of the subject of direct restraints and those of his counterparts a half-century earlier. First, while Chancellor Kent and legal writers of his generation had conflated private restraints and those imposed by the government, Gray distinguished between them and focused his attention on private restraints. It was these restraints that presented the greater problem in Gray's day, as wealthy settlors sought to build their dynastic trusts on the basis of restrictions that they imposed on their beneficiaries' power to transfer the property given to them. Second, Gray, like other legal writers of his period, greatly de-emphasized the theme of technicality-versus-liberality that was so prominent in early nineteenth-century legal discourse.[42] Third, reflecting the growing dominance of positivist legal theory,[43] Gray and his contemporaries explicitly rejected the idea that restraints were invalid because they were "repugnant" to the inherent nature of property.[44] Rather than rationalizing legal rules that protected alienability on the basis of such metaphysical arguments, Gray squarely placed the issue in the realm of public policy:

> If there are any restraints on . . . free alienation, such restraints are not imposed on [property] by public policy, but by the will of those persons who have created or transferred them. It is the purpose of this essay to consider . . . with what limitations, if any, does the law say, "It is against public policy to allow restraints to be put upon transfers which public policy does not forbid."[45]

Gray's answer to the question he posed was straightforward: When a conflict arose between the legal policy of alienability and the principle of freedom of owners to dispose of their property as they wished, Gray unambiguously asserted, alienability trumped individual freedom. He thought that all rights and powers of ownership should remain consolidated in the current owner and that as property was transferred from one person to another, the power of alienation—*the* fundamental characteristic of ownership—should pass to the new owner.

Gray's argument for giving priority to alienability was social and political, not economic. The point of the alienability policy was to create the necessary conditions under which citizens would develop as independent and responsible members of the community. Alienability is apt to make property owners act responsibly, he thought. To act responsibly is to act with a future-oriented perspective.[46] Shielding an owner's assets from his own ill-considered decisions and from the claims of his creditors encourages profligate behavior. According to Gray's political sociology, individuals are more apt to behave responsibly if their subsistence depends on how they use their own property. A precondition for individual responsibility, then, is individual control, and control was at the heart of his attack on restraints on alienation of property.

The Debate over "Spendthrift" Trusts

Nowhere was Gray's passionate commitment to alienability and anti-paternalism more evident than in his reaction to the rise of the so-called spendthrift trust. As background for this controversy, it is necessary first to sketch the common law rules regarding restraints on alienation.

Well before the nineteenth century, English judges developed a set of rules regulating the validity of restraints imposed on property interests. In general, these rules made it impossible for one owner to transfer ownership to another withholding from the transferee the power of alienation. These rules were first developed with respect to so-called legal property interests, that is, property interests that were not created in the context of trusts. Early in the nineteenth century, English equity judges, who were eager to eliminate any evident conflict between the common law and the law of equity, extended the common-law prohibitions of restraints on alienation to the equitable interests of trust beneficiaries. In a famous 1811 case, *Brandon v. Robinson,*[47] the Chancellor, Lord Eldon, held that a settlor could not validly impose a direct restraint on the alienability of a trust beneficiary's life interest. In that case, a wealthy father created a trust for his son, Thomas Goom, for life, and expressly stated that his son's interest "should not be grantable, transferable, or otherwise assignable, by way of anticipation of any unreceived payment."[48] Goom subsequently went bankrupt, and a person to whom he had purportedly transferred his trust interest sued to enforce the assignment. The Chancellor ruled that the restraint was void and, therefore, the transfer was valid. The settlor could, the Chancellor conceded, make the beneficiary's interest subject to termination if he attempted to transfer it or if a creditor attempted to attach it. What the settlor could not do, however, was to give the beneficiary a property interest that would continue to pay income to the beneficiary despite the beneficiary's purported transfer of that interest or attempts by his creditors to reach that interest to satisfy his outstanding debts.

The decision in *Brandon* in effect incorporated the common-law rules concerning restraints on alienation into the law of trusts. It insured that settlors could not gain any advantage, in terms of immunizing their beneficiaries' property, by creating family property settlements in the form of trusts rather than by creating successive nontrust estates. The resulting parity between trust and common-law property doctrines was a partial fulfillment of Chancellor Eldon's general objective to assimilate equitable doctrines and common-law doctrines.[49]

American courts, which generally followed the course set in the *Brandon* decision prior to 1875,[50] abruptly changed direction. In that year, the U.S. Supreme Court expressed its approval of restraints on alienation of trust interests. Speaking for the Court, albeit in dictum, Justice Miller stated in *Nichols v. Eaton*[51]:

> Why a parent, or one who loves another, and wishes to use his own property in securing the object of his affection, as far as property can do it, from the ills of life, the vicissitudes of fortune, and even his own improvidence, or incapacity for self-protection, should not be permitted to do so, is not readily perceived.[52]

This statement was quite extraordinary. Not only did the Court repudiate well-established English trust law, which American courts usually followed, but it went out of its way explicitly to endorse the idea of trust restraints on alienation for protective, or paternalistic, purposes when it was unnecessary to do so. It did not rely merely on the argument that the court ought to give effect to donor's intent. It went beyond the seemingly neutral norm of effectuating donative preferences to consider and approve the protective purpose on substantive grounds. Not all courts were so candid, however.

The first clear decision upholding the spendthrift trust, *Broadway Bank v. Adams,*[53] illustrates how courts hid their approval of the paternalistic motive. The court purported to base its decision on the abstract principle of freedom of owners to dispose of their property as they wished. It stated:

> The founder of this trust was the absolute owner of his property. He had the entire right to dispose of it, either by way of absolute gift to his brother [the beneficiary], or by a gift with such restrictions or limitations, not repugnant to law, as he saw fit to impose. . . . His intentions ought to be carried out, unless they are against public policy.[54]

The crucial question, of course, was whether the donor's intention to deny his beneficiary the power to transfer his property interest violated public policy. The court concluded that it did not violate the policy favoring alienability. Unlike restraints on legal (i.e., nontrust) interests, restraints on equitable (trust) interests leave the trustee's legal title to the underlying trust assets unimpaired. Moreover, the beneficiary "takes the whole legal title to the accrued income at the moment it is paid to him."[55] The argument, however, begged the real question, which was why the alienability policy did not apply to equitable property interests as well as to legal interests. Unless a restraint on alienation is imposed, a trust beneficiary can assign his right to receive income to another person, either gratuitously or in return for a sum of money (presumably representing the capitalized value of the future income stream). Such interests have economic value and are marketable. Indeed, it is not uncommon for trust beneficiaries who are eager to acquire a substantial capital sum to sell their equitable interests. In the abstract, the alienability policy should extend to such marketable interests as much as it does to legal (nontrust) interests. The real basis for the decision to approve trust restraints, then, must lie elsewhere than the neutral principle of giving effect to property owners' intentions. The likely motive for the decision was a substantive reason— the judges' sympathy with the trust creator's desire to protect his family member economically. John Chipman Gray was all too aware of that motive (probably having encountered it in crafting estate plans for his wealthy Boston clients), and he made it the target of his blistering attack on the spendthrift trust doctrine.

At first glance, Gray's background makes his vehement opposition to the so-called spendthrift trust seem odd. In planning the estates of wealthy Bostonians, he doubtless represented many clients who wished to create the very sort of dynastic, indestructible family trust that he denounced.

Moreover, he himself was a product of the very social class that was most likely to create spendthrift trusts. In fact, though, his disdain for the spendthrift trust is entirely consistent with another crucial aspect of his personal history. Although the Gray family had been quite wealthy, Gray's father suffered serious financial losses during Gray's childhood. As a result Gray and his brother were forced to depend on their own energies and talents, and that experience apparently instilled in both of them a strong belief in personal achievement as the proper road to success.[56]

Gray opened his critique of the spendthrift trust by connecting that property arrangement with a broader social and political trend that he viewed with evident dread. It is worth quoting his critique at length because more than any other single text of the time, it indicates how late nineteenth-century legal theorists understood the social-political purpose of the alienability policy. Gray stated:

> The law and the social morality which had established itself in England and in the most civilized parts of the United States during the earlier part of the present century was the completion of the great change wrought under the lead of English lawyers and English philosophers by which, in English speaking countries, mediaeval feudalism had given way to the industrial and commercial states of modern times.
>
> The foundation of that system of law and morals was justice, the idea of human equality and human liberty. Everyone was free to make such agreements as he thought fit with his fellow creatures, no one could oblige any man to make any agreement that he did not wish, but if a man made an agreement, the whole force of the State was brought to bear to compel its performance. It was a system in which there was no place for privileges,—privileges for rank, or wealth, or moral weakness. The general repeal of usury laws was the crowning triumph of the system.
>
> Now things are changed. There is a strong and increasing feeling, and a feeling which has already led to many practical results, that a main object of law is not to secure liberty of contract, but to restrain it, in the interest, or supposed interest, of the weaker, or supposed weaker, against the stronger, or supposed stronger, portion of the community. Hence, for instance, laws enacted or contemplated for eight hours' labor, for weekly payment of wages by corporations, for "compulsory arbitration," etc., that is, laws intended to take away

from certain classes of the community, for their supposed good, their liberty of action and their power of contract; in other words, attempts to bring society back to an organization founded on status and not contract. To a frame of mind and a state of public sentiment like this, spendthrift trusts are most congenial. If we are all to be cared for, and have our wants supplied, without regard to our mental and moral failings, in the socialist Utopia, there is little reason why in the mean time, while waiting for that day, a father should not do for his son what the State is then to do for us all.

Of course, it would be absurd to say that the learned judges who have aided in the introduction of spendthrift trusts have been secret socialists; but it is nonetheless true, I believe, that they have been influenced, unconsciously it may well be, by those ideas which the experience of the last few years has shown to have been fermenting in the minds of the community; by that spirit, in short, of paternalism, which is the fundamental essence alike of spendthrift trusts and of socialism.[57]

Given Gray's admission that the judges who developed the spendthrift trust doctrine wholeheartedly supported the principle of individual freedom of disposition, it seems curious to characterize spendthrift trusts as "socialistic." In a very real sense, though, Gray's label captured the motive behind this institution. Once we recognize that for Gray, as for other elite lawyers of his time, the terms "socialism" and "paternalism" were synonymous, it becomes quite understandable why Gray assailed the spendthrift trust as socialistic. Its evident effect was protective, and the courts had ratified that effect. In doing so, Gray thought, the courts had violated the principle that was the foundation of the alienability—self-determination:

> The true ground [why inalienable trust interests should not be recognized] is that on which the whole law of property, legal and equitable, is based;—that inalienable rights of property are opposed to the fundamental principles of the common law; that it is against public policy that a man "should have an estate to live on, but not an estate to pay his debts with," . . . and should have the benefits of wealth without the responsibilities. The common law has recognized certain classes of persons who may be kept in pupilagge, [*sic*] viz. infants, lunatics, married women; but it has held that sane grown men must look out for themselves,—that it is not the function of the law to

join in the futile effort to save the foolish and the vicious from the consequences of their own vice and folly. It is a wholesome doctrine, fit to produce a manly race, based on sound morality and wise philosophy.[58]

Gray's attack integrated the moral theory of self-reliance, the political theory of egalitarianism, and the economic theory of unrestricted markets. Indeed, there was no real separation among these three elements in his arguments. His argument based on paying one's debtors illustrates how he blended moral, political, and economic considerations. "If there is one sentiment," he asserted, "which it would seem to part of all in authority, and particularly of all judges, to fortify, it is the duty of keeping one's promises and paying one's debts."[59] Gray then connected this moral argument with the economic argument that spendthrift trusts, by permitting, as he saw it, fraud on creditors, threatened the security of credit. He then returned to the theme of reciprocity of ownership, simultaneously drawing on history and morality:

> The current law has for centuries been in favor of removing old restraints on alienation; in favor of disallowing new ones; and especially in favor of compelling a debtor to apply to his debts all property which he could use for himself or give at his pleasure to others.[60]

Gray also drew on the political theory of egalitarianism, echoing Jacksonian democratic themes. He tied all restraints on alienation, but especially trust restraints, with privilege and class bias. Spendthrift trusts represented, Gray argued, an anachronistic throwback to feudal hierarchy:

> [I]t is hard to see the Americanism of spendthrift trusts. That grown men should be kept all of their lives in pupilage, that men not paying their debts should live in luxury on inherited wealth, are doctrines as undemocratic as can well be conceived. They are suited to the times in which the Statute De Donis [the Statute de Donis Conditionalibus, enacted in 1285, first recognized the fee tail estate, which wealthy landowners used to keep land within their families for many generations] was enacted, and the law was administered in the interest of rich and powerful families. The general introduction of spendthrift trusts would be to form a privileged class, who could indulge in every speculation, could practice every fraud, and yet, provided they kept on the safe side of the criminal law, could roll in wealth.

They would be an aristocracy, though certainly the most contempt-
ible aristocracy with which a country was ever cursed.[61]

The textual context of this passage reveals the strong connection that
Gray drew between spendthrift trusts and paternalism. In support of trust
restraints, Justice Miller in *Nichols v. Eaton* had analogized spendthrift
trusts to exemption statutes, which many states had enacted in the nineteenth century. Gray was ambivalent about these statutes, however. He
expressly disapproved of statutes that he felt exempted too much property
from the reach of creditors, but he did not categorically condemn them.
He conceded that some exemption laws could be justified "on the theory
that a man is more likely to be a useful member of society, and to pay
his debts, if he is not deprived of his tools, or of a bare subsistence."[62]

Trust restraints, however, were entirely different. Their purposes and
effect was not to provide the limited funds with which "to save poor men
from being pushed to the wall" and rendered totally useless to society,
but instead to "enable the children of rich men to live in debt and luxury
at the same time."[63] These restraints were fundamentally wrong because
they undermined the beneficiary's self-reliance and thereby eliminated
the incentive for him to become a useful, contributing member of society.
Protected from his own mistakes and from the external world of work
and debt, the trust beneficiary will fall victim to "natural dishonesty" and
become a social parasite. "The desire that property shall be kept in a man's
family, and that his descendants shall enjoy it, while their creditors shall
not"[64] is simply one aspect of the broader phenomenon of "the amiable
altruistic sentiment, to-day so fashionable."[65] Left unchecked, such "senti-
mentalism" will "dash itself in pieces against the inexorable facts of nature."[66]

From the perspective of late twentieth-century legal and culture, even
Gray's characterization of the spendthrift trust as paternalistic seems odd.
Modern critics of this property arrangement have attacked it as being
rooted in an excessively individualistic outlook and inspired by laissez-
faire ideology.[67] What explains these contradictory characterizations? In
part, the answer is that the judges who approved of the trust restraints
justified them on the basis of individual freedom of disposition. Not only
did the courts' opinions emphasize that all they were doing was giving
effect to the will of the trust creator, but they also constructed the legal
issue as involving only one potential conflict, the donor's will versus protection of creditors. Once they had shown that no such conflict in fact

existed (because creditors had ample opportunity to protect themselves from being defrauded by trust beneficiaries), there was no remaining reason to object to the donor's intent. The decision to enforce the trust restrain consequently appeared foreordained.

More deeply, the contrast between Gray's characterization of the spendthrift trust and that of modern critics reflects the difference between the two legal cultures that formed the background of the critiques. Written at the advent of Progressive regulatory reform, Gray's critique derived from a legal culture that feared that government paternalism was about to replace individual responsibility. By contrast, the cultural background for modern attacks on the spendthrift trust is the welfare state with its legitimized ethos of government protection. Protectionism involves redistributive legislative programs that identify discrete categories of persons who are thought to be vulnerable in some salient respect. Against this background the trust restraints appear reactionary. They frustrate redistributive goals by facilitating the formation and maintenance of large family dynasties, and they mock the ethos of protectionism by insulating the children of wealthy families while the rest of society is left to face the vagaries of the market. Given the gross imbalance of the distribution of wealth in modern society, it seems to today's critics absurd to justify restraints in family property arrangements on the basis of protectionism. The class bias behind the facade of protectionism, moderns contend, is as unmistakable now as it was in the seventeenth century when Chancery protected expectant heirs against the improvident sales of their inheritance interests.[68]

Nevertheless, within the context of late nineteenth-century legal thought, the spendthrift trust did represent the social vision of paternalism. Some courts acknowledged this vision and endorsed trust restraints for that very reason. In one case, for example, the court stated:

> [A] trust, however carefully guarded otherwise, would in many cases fall short of the object of its creation, if the father, in such case, has no power to provide against the schemes of designing persons, as well as the improvidence of the child itself. If the beneficiary may anticipate the income, or absolutely sell or otherwise dispose of the equitable interest, it is evident the whole object of the settlor is liable to be defeated. If, on the other hand, the author of the trust may say, as was done in this case, the net accumulations of the fund shall be paid only into the hands of the beneficiary, then it is clear the object of the trust can never be wholly defeated. Whatever the re-

verses of fortune may be, the child is provided for, and is effectually placed beyond the reach of unprincipled schemers and sharpers.

The tendency of present legislation is to soften and ameliorate, as far as practicable, the hardships and privations that follow in the wake of poverty and financial disaster. . . . The practical results of this tendency, we think, upon the whole, have been beneficial, and we are not inclined to render a decision in this case which may be regarded as a retrograde movement.[69]

An even more vivid example is drawn from a West Virginia decision of the same period:

Why should not a father having a dissolute, improvident or unfortunate son, be able to so bestow his own property as to protect that son from penury and want? Why should not a loving wife be allowed to so deposit her separate estate in the hands of a trustee so as to keep her aged, unfortunate, dissolute or improvident husband from trudging his weary way over the hill to the poor house? Why should not anyone be allowed to use his own property so as to keep the guant [*sic*] wolf of grinding poverty from the home door of those near and dear to his heart?[70]

Statements like these prompt one to ask how judges and commentators could endorse the paternalist motive that they detected in the spendthrift trust at precisely the time when anti-paternalism sentiment was at its highest. It is difficult to believe that these proponents of the spendthrift trust endorsed paternalism generally. Not only were anti-paternalist sentiments pervasively evident throughout the legal literature of this period, but state courts, who were themselves responsible for the creation of the spendthrift trust, were at the forefront of judicial attacks on social legislation (such as aid to victims of natural disasters) as overly paternalistic.[71] Rather than rejecting paternalism entirely, legal writers of the period accepted paternalism but sought to reconcile it with the dominant ethic of self-determination by confining paternalism to a limited sphere of social life.

Harmonization through Separate Spheres

Accepting both self-determination and paternalism as coexisting aspects of legal culture led most legal commentators to conclude that the two had to be isolated from each other in social life. The underlying assumption was that all of social life was (properly) divided into separate and relatively insular spheres. Since the different spheres of human activity overlapped little, if at all, the conflicting ethics of paternalism and self-determination had no occasion to compete with each other. Paternalism could be recognized as a legitimate motive without subverting the dominant ethic of self-determination.

This scheme is manifested in the vision of home and family as an area of life separate from the world of work and commerce. As discussed in chapter 5, the mid-nineteenth-century cult of domesticity posited that the family was a realm of caring, protection, and cooperation. That vision of the family and its legitimate value structure strongly persisted through the end of the nineteenth century despite increasing attacks on it from advocates of improving the status of women. The vision persisted, moreover, despite the fact that it had become an illusion for many families. More and more women, including married women and mothers, could not afford to remain at home and had joined men in the very-unprotective world of work. Legally, women were given greater independence, through married women's property acts and, eventually, the franchise, but these steps hardly constituted a revolution in actual treatment of women and did not fundamentally weaken the vision of the family as the realm of caring and protection in popular or legal consciousness.

The sense that the protectionist motive was legitimate and should be carried out was evident in legal doctrine even before the separate spheres ideology had fully developed. In England, Chancery judges had exhibited a strongly protectionist attitude throughout the eighteenth century. Nowhere was that attitude more evident than in the context of family property arrangements. A clear example was the decision to validate the married women's restraint on anticipation clause, which directed that income be paid directly to a married woman and not "be paid by anticipation." The purpose of the clause was to protect daughters who were about to marry from the "danger of parting with their property under the influence or threats of their husbands."[72] In an eighteenth-century case involving a wife's transfer to her husband of all her trust interest shortly after their wedding, the court reporter noted that the Chancellor had "a most anxious desire to find any principle of a Court of equity strong enough to protect the [trust] property against the improvident act in question."[73]

Proponents of the spendthrift trust viewed the broadening of protectionism beyond married women's trusts as a salutary elaboration of a successful episode in "social experimentation," as Maitland termed it.[74] If restraints on anticipation of married women's trust interests were an acceptable form of protectionism, what was to prevent American courts, acting in their equitable capacities, from treating all trust beneficiaries the same way? The extension seemed especially appropriate since beneficiaries of spendthrift trusts were nearly always members of the donor's family. To borrow a phrase from Maitland, "[T]he wedge was in, and it could be driven home." The social ideology that made acceptable restraints on a married woman's power to anticipate her trust interest served also to justify restraints on all private interests since, it was assumed, those interests were always held by dependents of the donor.

Although the initial cases that recognized the spendthrift trust did not explicitly draw on this rationale, commentators frequently did. The argument of one Illinois lawyer is typical:

> In Illinois a statute provides that the court appoint a conservator of a person whom a jury has declared a spendthrift. The conservator [is] to have the care and management of the ward's estate, and apply the profits thereof to the comfort of the ward and his family. . . . If a State does this for a spendthrift why should a father not be allowed to appoint a trustee, who will perform like duties for the benefit of his children? No one can know the incapacity of a child to support or protect himself, better than a parent, and certainly none should have a better right to provide against his weakness.[75]

The desire of a parent to shield and protect his children against casualties and accidents was, the writer declared, not only "natural," but "estimable."[76] Another lawyer, writing in 1902 shortly after the spendthrift trust doctrine had achieved widespread acceptance in the courts, made an even broader argument for protectionism:

> During the last half of the nineteenth century there was a noticable [*sic*] tendency in the legislation to ameliorate the condition of the unfortunate, to provide protection for the improvident and lessen the burden of the debtor class. This is illustrated by the eight hour labor laws, the laws regulating the payment of wages, and especially by the liberality and universality of the exemption laws, whereby property ranging in value from a few hundred dollars in some of the states, to five thousand dollars in Nevada, is without the reach of creditors.[77]

While courts in the earliest cases justified trust restraints on the basis of the abstract principle of freedom of disposition, a significant number

of courts in decisions after 1885 explicitly focused on the family context of spendthrift trusts. A typical example of this reasoning was the
following statement from an 1892 case: "It cannot be said that it is against
public policy for a testator to provide a support for a spendthrift child,
for the interest of the public is that such child should not become a public
burden."[78]

Besides appealing to equity's tradition of protection, the association
between private trusts and the family made it easier for courts to accept
trust restraints in two other respects. First, it meant that the common
law's traditionally solicitous attitude toward intrafamilial gifts supported
trust restraints. Judicial opinions frequently asserted that failure to enforce the trust restraint would constitute "fraud on [the father's] generosity."[79] This suggests that the courts' rhetoric emphasizing the will of the
trust creator did not reflect a blind commitment to the abstract principle
of freedom of disposition but a normative perception of trusts as an instrument of family-preserving generosity.

The second respect is that enforcing the donor's will reproduced, in
the context of trusts, the structure of power within the family. The family
property trust was (and still remains) a surrogate for the family itself.
Just as autonomy and freedom of one's children to make decisions was
considered undesirable, so was freedom of trust beneficiaries to control
their property interests. The family's hierarchical ordering, within which
the husband possessed broad discretionary control to make decisions that
affected others for their own well-being, was mirrored in the spendthrift
trust allocation of power. The beneficiaries' power was subordinated to
that of the donor and the trustee, whose duty was to carry out the donor's
wishes. In approving of restraints on the transferability of trust interests,
then, courts maintained the social image of the properly ordered family.

The Spendthrift Trust's Legacy

Some critics, Gray among them, realized that the real legacy of the spendthrift trust doctrine was not to make paternalism as such more acceptable
but to promote the trust as the central legal device for creating family
dynasties based on wealth. The spendthrift restraint's real purpose and
effect was to protect the trust entity itself. Insulated against attempts by
beneficiaries and creditors to strip it of its assets, the private family trust
could last for several generations. Perpetuating the trust meant perpetuating power, and that was the settlor's ultimate end. It is no exaggeration
to say that the spendthrift restraint, as much as any other single legal

factor, is responsible for the maintenance of the upper-class structure in modern American society. As the anthropologist George Marcus has remarked, the spendthrift restraint is the core of dynastic trusts, and dynastic trusts, in turn, are "a common denominator of upper-class family organization nationally."[80]

Marcus explains the courts' sympathetic response to the dynastic impulse on the basis of the common class identity of judges and the businessmen who created spendthrift trusts. He states: "Because it was itself a part of the tight, upper-class culture of Boston, the judiciary was well-disposed to the dynastic motive and was clearly biased toward it in deciding trust and estate cases."[81] The cultural characteristics of Boston's professional elite may well explain why the Massachusetts court was the first to hold in favor of the spendthrift trust, but culture has less power in explaining why courts in other states which lacked Boston's tight upper-class structure so readily accepted the dynastic trust. While judges in Midwestern states like Illinois and Missouri, whose class structure and culture were very different from that in Massachusetts, doubtless had close contacts with their local business elites, through professional or social ties, they were less likely to have had the almost complete sense of common identity with those elites as did their Massachusetts counterparts. The elite cultural groups in those states in the late nineteenth century were much newer and less stable than Boston's cultural elite. Moreover, politics played a very large role in the selection of judges in states like Illinois and Missouri. This made it more common for judges to be members of recent immigrant groups, such as the Irish, who were not likely to feel sympathetic toward the dynastic motives of the entrenched families of Chicago or St. Louis.

The more likely reason why American courts were willing to accept the dynastic trust was that they considered commodified property to be inappropriate in the realm of the family. Property within the family, in their view, was to be used for personal support, not as an asset to be traded or lent in commercial ventures. The courts' frequent reliance on restraints on the married woman's separate estate to justify trust restraints suggests that the same attitude was at work in both contexts. As I discussed in chapter 5, despite legislative reforms that made married women somewhat more autonomous as property owners, nineteenth-century judges regarded the function of the separate estate as primarily protective and were reluctant to permit the world of the market to intrude very far into the marital realm. That reluctance extended to the family in general.

The violent swings of the business cycle throughout the late nineteenth century made judges wary of insisting that family property be subject to market forces like investment property.[82]

The decommodification of family property was not universal, though. It was a luxury that was available only to those relatively few families who had amassed enough wealth to justify the costs of creating a family trust. For the overwhelming majority of American families, property was property, and all of it was vulnerable to the whims of a very unpredictable market.

PART FOUR

The Late Modern Culture,
1917–1970

Legal Writing in the Twentieth Century—
The Demise of Legal Autonomy

THE MAJOR DEVELOPMENT in legal scholarship during the mid- to late twentieth century was the gradual decline of legal analysis based on the premise that law is an autonomous discipline and the concomitant rise of policy-focused writing. The premise of law's autonomy had led legal academics to produce scholarship that was almost entirely devoid of any mention of politics, economics, or society. By the last quarter of the century, that sort of scholarship had all but disappeared from academic writing. Taking its place was a mode of legal writing whose primary focus was public policy and whose premise was that law is an instrument of social control.

The rise and fall of the premise of legal autonomy is a long and complex story.[1] The conventional wisdom gives virtually all of the credit to the Legal Realists of the 1920s and 1930s. The Realists certainly deserve some of the credit for knocking this understanding off its throne in the kingdom of academic legal writing, but they were not the first to attack the idea that law was an autonomous science. As we saw in the prologue to part 3, the groundwork for the Realists' critique of legal autonomy had been laid by Progressive-era figures like Oliver Wendell Holmes and Roscoe Pound. Holmes, Pound, and others had attacked the premise of legal autonomy almost as soon as it emerged as an article of faith in the newly reconstituted American law school.[2] They argued that law was nothing more or less than an instrument of social policy.

Even among the mandarins of legal orthodoxy, there were cracks in the edifice. While the curriculum of Langdell's Harvard Law School showed little awareness that law and public policy were related, the pages of the *Harvard Law Review* told a somewhat different story. Otherwise staunch Langdellians like Joseph Henry Beale occasionally published articles like "The Recognition of Cuban Belligerency,"[3] although, admittedly, titles like "Quasi-Contract, Its Nature and Scope"[4] were the more typical fare.

In the world of nonacademic legal writing, there was greater acknowledgment that law and policy are intimately related. Louis Brandeis's famous brief in *Muller v. Oregon* (1908), which extensively cited social science research to sustain the constitutionality of a statute regulating the working hours for women, was only one example of legal writing that presupposed an instrumental and policy-oriented view of law. The Progressive era was filled with an astonishing amount of law-reform activity, and much of that activity was led by members of the bar. Lawyers produced essays, lectures, legislative testimony, and other forms of writing that pressed for regulatory activism on a wide variety of fronts. Some of that legal writing explicitly drew on new policy sciences like institutionalist economics and urban sociology. All of it was premised on a vision of law as inextricably connected with politics, society, and economy.

Policy-focused Progressive legal writing created the precedent for the Legal Realists. In academic writing, what the Realists did was to extend the Progressives' premises about the nature of law into a frontal attack on legal orthodoxy, particularly the idea of legal autonomy. While historians continue to disagree about exactly what Realism was and who the Realists were,[5] no one disputes the fact that everyone associated with the rubric of "Realism" rejected the Langdellian version of legal science in favor of an explicitly instrumental, policy-based conception of law. That view of law prompted three important changes in academic legal writing. First, it led legal scholars to focus increasingly on constitutional, statutory, and regulatory law. Second, it encouraged law teachers to produce scholarship that was more interdisciplinary. Finally, it changed the character of legal scholarship that remained primarily focused on doctrine and case law. Together, these three developments constitute the real legacy of Legal Realism. We need to consider each of them in a bit more detail.

The Rise of Public Law Scholarship

The shift in focus of legal scholarship from private to public law is one of the defining characteristics of academic legal writing in the twentieth century. The immediate cause of this shift was the change in the character of law itself. The rise of the regulatory state under the Progressive-era reforms and then under the New Deal vastly increased the amount and complexity of statutory and administrative law. Faced with a vastly more active and interventionist state, legal academics could hardly cling to the illusion of Langdell's generation of legal scholars that law is confined to the common law. Public law, particularly statutes and administrative regulations, was now the increasingly dominant means of governance, and legal scholarship reflected that fact. The rise of the regulatory state brought with it a new wave of constitutional challenges, and legal scholarship reflected the growing importance of constitutional law. By 1970, doctrinal exegesis of common law cases had become the exception in academic legal writing, and normative policy analysis of public law issues the rule.

A less immediate cause of the shift from private to public law as the primary focus of scholarly attention was the emergence of the instrumental, or functional, conception of law. That conception led legal scholars to recognize that since law itself was both a principle cause of social and economic problems and the available solution to those problems, they themselves could perhaps provide solutions to society's problems. The common law, once seen the repository of timeless and objective principles, was now viewed by many scholars as the ultimate source of the maldistribution of power and wealth in early to mid-twentieth-century American society. The reformist scholars' solution was to replace the common law's regime with a more effective and just legal regime created directly through public law, specifically, legislation and administrative regulation.

The Emergence of Interdisciplinary Legal Scholarship

The second major change in legal scholarship that Realism induced was the growth of interdisciplinary legal analysis. Here again, the idea of law as an instrument of social behavior was the catalyst for change. Rather than examining bodies of cases for the purpose of deriving scientific principles, Realist legal scholars looked behind doctrinal analysis to discover the social, political, or policy bases of judicial decisions. Viewing legal analysis as a form of policy analysis led them to use the tools of other disciplines that were related to law, such as economics, political science, anthropology, and sociology, to generate insights about just exactly how law shaped society. With some notable exceptions (such as Karl Llewellyn's collaborative work with the distinguished anthropologist E. Adamson Hoebel[6]), most of this work was not very sophisticated. Part of the problem was the lack of rigor and analytical sophistication in other disciplines,[7] but another factor was the residual strength of the old Langdellian conception of law. By the latter part of the century, however, that conception had greatly weakened, and the Realists' call for interdisciplinary legal scholarship was taken much more seriously. Aided by advances in other fields, especially economics, sociology, and philosophy, legal scholars produced scholarship that was more intellectually sophisticated than their Realist forebears had generated. Funding agencies like the Russell Sage and Ford Foundations helped create law and social science programs in several law schools,[8] and an increasing number of young scholars entered the ranks of law teachers with Ph.D. degrees as well as law degrees.

Legal Doctrine as Public Policy: The Rise of Policy Analysis

Legal empiricism never gained any lasting foothold in legal scholarship, but Realism's turn to other disciplines did induce another, more enduring change in legal scholarship. Legal rules remained the center of law teachers' attention, but the character of rule-focused scholarship changed significantly. Rather than "scientifically" organizing and classifying legal rules in the way that Langdell's generation had done,[9] legal scholars now critically evaluated rules through the lens of policy analysis. As John Henry Schlegel has pointed out, "[Legal] policy analysis is the legitimate child of case law Realism practiced by [Walter Wheeler] Cook and mastered by Llewellyn, [Arthur L.] Corbin, [Grant] Gilmore, and all the heirs of Realism. . . . It is the home that Realism made for its heirs when the Realists marched to Washington to participate in public life, their only real alternative to . . . empirical science of law."[10]

As the quote from Schlegel's book suggests, legal policy science provided a new bridge between law faculties and legal practice, especially government service. It is no accident that several of the architects of the New Deal were former law professors whose writings were among the vanguard of Realist policy analysis.[11] Men like William O. Douglas, A. A. Berle, Walter Nelles, Charles Clark, and Thurman Arnold, to name only a few, first achieved their reputations as leading Realist scholars before they moved on to serve in public life at levels high enough to permit them to put their policy views into practice. Their work in government service was basically an extension of their work as legal scholars. In both spheres, what they saw themselves as doing was policy analysis.

In this respect as in others, the Realists were building on the Progressive generation's precedent of engaging in policy-focused law-reform activity. There was a difference, however, between the two generations of scholar-reformers. Unlike the Progressive law-reformers, the Realist lawyer-scholars used policy analysis in a way that was more technocratic and less morally focused. The Progressive-era reformers, men like Brandeis, Elihu Root, and C. C. Burlingham, had been raised and educated in a social and legal culture quite different from that which shaped the generation that followed them. Brandeis, Root, and Burlingham were basically nineteenth-century men, committed to the image of the good public servant. In their milieu, "goodness" had a distinctly moral overtone, so that the ideal they pursued was reminiscent of what in the civic republican tradition was called virtue.[12] In the legal culture that followed World War I and the Great Depression, belief in moral values was less characteristic than commitment to expertise. Efficacy replaced virtue as the ideal guiding the lawyer-scholars who moved between Ivy League law schools and FDR's Washington. Legal policy analysts viewed their objective as studying legal phenomena in a detached fashion, explaining those phenomena from a scientific perspective, rather than morally evaluating law.

In the second half of the twentieth century, legal policy analysis took a new direction. Still committed to the ideal of being scientific and objective, the new type of policy analysis drew on the tools of other disciplines to explain and evaluate legal phenomena.[13] Judged by volume and prestige, the most successful of these "law and" scholarship genres was the law-and-economics movement, which rapidly grew after 1960. Law-and-economics scholars like Richard A. Posner, Guido Calabresi, and Henry Manne attempted to make legal policy analysis more genuinely scientific, meaning value-free and rigorous.[14] They applied models from microeconomics to evaluate the economic efficiency of a wide variety of legal rules and institutions, and pure doctrinal scholarship declined both in quantity and in prestige. "Law and" writing proliferated as legal scholars, disillusioned about the capacity of pure doctrinal analysis to uncover the bases of judicial decisions and other legal phenomena, turned to other disciplines, such as sociology, for help. By 1970, this form of writing was becoming the dominant genre in legal scholarship, at least among the elite law faculties.

Beyond 1970

While the period studied in this book ends with 1970, it is worth looking a few years beyond that date. The turn toward technocratic, interdisciplinary, and theoretical forms of legal policy analysis produced a backlash among some legal commentators. Both within the legal academy and outside of it, one heard the complaint that interdisciplinary, "law-and" scholarship failed to serve the needs of the legal profession. This sort of work, critics have argued, has no relevance to anyone outside a small circle of inside academics. The result has been "growing disjunction" between academic writing and practitioner legal writing.[15] In an essay published a few years ago, Judge Harry Edwards of the United States Court of Appeals for the District of Columbia Circuit (and a former member of the Harvard and Michigan law faculties) articulated an opinion that others had expressed informally for several years. Judge Edwards stated:

> [M]any "elite" law faculties in the United States now have significant contingents of "impractical" scholars, who are "disdainful of the practice of law." The "impractical" scholar—that is the term I will use—produces abstract scholarship that has little relevance to concrete issues, or addresses concrete issues in a wholly theoretical way. As a consequence, it is my impression that judges, legislators, and practitioners have little use for much of the scholarship that is now produced by members of the academy.[16]

What is really at stake in the trend toward more "law and" scholarship and its critics is the ideal of legal autonomy. During the heyday of the legal autonomy ideal, the rhetoric and analytical apparatus of law professors was the same as that used by judges and practitioners because both were committed to the view that law was best studied and explained in isolation of other factors. Today, that is no longer true. While practical legal writing continues to use the vocabulary and categories of traditional legal analysis, academic legal writing has looked to various other analytical structures. These rhetorical differences reflect the fact that while in the world of the practicing lawyer (and judge) the idea of legal autonomy still dominates, in the world of the law professor it is dead.

Chapter 11 discusses the discourse of property that emerged in legal writing by Progressives and, later, by the Legal Realists. That discourse expressed the dialectic between the commodity and propriety conceptions of property in terms of the social implications of property. Texts like W. N. Hohfeld's articles on jural relations, R. T. Ely's *Property and Contract in Their Relations to the Distribution of Wealth,* and Robert L. Hale's articles on coercion and economic liberty articulated a relational conception of ownership. Chapter 12 then traces the effect of the welfare state on the legal discourse of property in post–World War II America. That discourse focused on the problems of inequality and dependency and on the appropriate role of the state in the face of those problems. Finally, a brief Epilogue sketches how the basic dialectic of commodity and propriety has continued to the present day.

ELEVEN

Socializing Property: The Influence of Progressive-Realist Legal Thought

A FTER THE BEGINNING of the twentieth century, American legal intellectuals increasingly criticized the classical Blackstonian conception of property, which depicted ownership as a "sole and despotic relationship" between a person and a thing. That conception was, they thought, both inaccurate and disingenuous:—inaccurate because it wrongly suggested it was possible for one person to have absolute freedom in the use and control of his things; disingenuous because it hid from view the political function of property. These intellectuals set out to critique the traditional Blackstonian conception and to develop an alternative conception that emphasized the social and political character of private property. The principal intellectual catalyst for this project was the political ideology of Progressivism.

It is customary to define the Progressive era as ending with World War I. That definition implies that there was a clear disjuncture between the Progressive political movement and the reformist New Deal program that Franklin D. Roosevelt initiated with his first election as President. It is as though the impulse for reform was completely moribund between 1917 and 1932 and that the New Deal reformers started on a clean slate. Neither of these implications is accurate. Many intellectual leaders of that period viewed the prewar reforms as incomplete, and after the war they argued that social and economic changes had made reform even more imperative. The Great Depression seemed to prove their arguments correct, and it created the necessary sense of urgency to renew the project of reform. The New Deal continued the agenda of Progressivism, and in this sense can be called "Progressive" as well.

The same continuity was present in legal thought. Most accounts of Legal Realism sharply distinguish that intellectual movement, which historians conventionally date in the 1920s and 1930s,[1] from sociological jurisprudence, which was closely related to early twentieth-century Progressivism. Morton Horwitz recently—and correctly—has criticized this depiction of the relationship between Progressivism and Legal Realism. He convincingly argues that "[f]or many purposes, it is best to see Legal Realism as simply a continuation of the reformist agenda of early-twentieth-century Progressivism."[2] According to Horwitz, the most important common denominator between the two political-intellectual movements was their attack on what he calls "orthodox legal thought," the crucial characteristic of which was an understanding of law as politically neutral.[3]

Horwitz's basic point was that there was more in common between legal Progressivism and Legal Realism. I will argue in this chapter that in both movements elite legal writers, joined by scholars from other disciplines who were interested in law, engaged in a common enterprise of critiquing the classical liberal conception of property. What that conception hid, they repeatedly argued, was the role that private property played in structuring social relationships. Property was best understood not from the perspective of the nonsocial relationship between persons and things but from the vantage point of how ownership affects relationships among individuals. More trenchantly, these progressive critics pressed the theme that property is power. Owners hold legally sanctioned power over nonowners in ways that affect limit the nonowners' individual autonomy and even their personal security. The task of property law, progressives concluded, is to determine when and why that power is legitimate.

The writers who pursued this project of critique and reconstruction included, in rough chronological order, the following: Richard T. Ely, Wesley Newcomb Hohfeld, Robert Hale, John R. Commons, Morris R. Cohen, Thurman Arnold, A. A. Berle, Gardiner C. Means, Myres McDougal, and David Haber. These writers did not constitute a coherent group. Indeed, they did not constitute a "group" at all, in the sense that the Bloomsbury group did, for example. Some did not even know each other; some were not contemporaries of the others. Not all of them were lawyers, and some never taught in law schools. To a considerable extent, however, they were aware of each others' work and regarded their work as building on that of those among them who came earlier. In this sense they constituted a (nonexclusive) conversational network of scholars.

Though they did not share all of the same political values, they did share the conviction that adjustments in the relationship between government and the private sphere were necessary to adapt American law and politics to changing economic and social conditions and would be adequate to achieve social and economic justice. Some, like Hohfeld, did not understand their work primarily as politically motivated, yet even the seemingly least political texts had profound implications for opening up the strongly political character of property, both as a legal concept and as an institution. All of these writers' works, in one way or another, contributed to a powerful critique of the classical liberal conception of property, which depicted the sole function of private property as securing freedom and autonomy for individuals. All of them were influential participants in an ongoing scholarly conversation about the meaning and functions of property in American law and society that continued roughly from 1913 to 1950. That conversation shaped the dominant legal understanding of property by the middle of the twentieth century. It clearly framed in American legal discourse the dialectic between two understandings of the role of property in society, one economic and private, the other political and social.

Property in the Progressive Era
The Context of the Progressive Critique: Turmoil and Reform

The period between 1890 and 1913 was a time of tremendous economic, political, and social upheaval and conflict in the United States.[4] As one historian recently observed, without exaggeration, these years "were among the most tumultuous in American history."[5] Industrial capitalism introduced unprecedented economic change, as the country experienced successive depressions and industrial corporations grew dramatically in size through combinations and consolidations. The increasing concentration of wealth and power widened the gap between the haves and have-nots and deepened feelings of resentment between opposite socioeconomic groups. In some instances, class conflict escalated into full-blown riots, and while these occasions were the exception rather than the rule, the fact that they occurred at all produced deep anxiety in many quarters.

For political and economic elites, the reasons for anxiety were especially acute. Recurrent waves of economic depression, labor unrest, and social conflict throughout the last quarter of the nineteenth century fueled the growing sense among many Americans that the old liberal political and economic order was both outmoded and unjust. For the first time in American history the unimaginable seemed possible: by the early twentieth century the Left seemed to be on the verge of becoming a serious force in American politics. As Dorothy Ross has acutely noted, "The failure of socialism to secure a permanent and substantial presence in America has made it easy to forget that its fate was still an open question in this period."[6] Leftist political groups, ranging from the Industrial Workers of the World (the "Wobblies"), which espoused a version of anarcho-syndicalism, to the much more accommodationist Populist party, gained unprecedented political clout as working people, including unprecedented numbers of immigrants, came to regard the existing distribution of wealth and power as fundamentally unjust. In retrospect, of course, there was little danger that America would be the locus of the proletarian revolution that Marx had predicted for Western Europe. None of the foundational elements of the extant order, including social and legal respect for private property, was ever seriously in jeopardy.[7] But appalling working conditions, growing concentration of economic power, and exclusion of large segments of the adult population (particularly white women and African Americans of both sexes) from the political process did produce serious social and political unrest, including labor strikes, riots, and other acts of civil disturbance on an unprecedented scale.

These social and economic conditions prompted a wide variety of reform efforts beginning in the final decade of the nineteenth century and continuing through the first several decades of the twentieth century. Historians have debated the origins and meaning of Progressive era reforms in recent years. One view is that progressivism was a conservative force initiated by business leaders to maintain the extant political and social order in the context of profound social change.[8] It is certainly true that Progressives were reformers, not revolutionaries, and that the basic thrust of their programs was to keep the political and economic order in the United States a liberal order. It is also indisputable that progressive economic reforms left the basic structure of legal relations within the economy largely intact, and in this sense progressivism was conservative.

Nevertheless, the "triumph of conservatism" thesis seems overstated. As Alan Dawley has recently shown, Progressivism "challenge[d] elites to remake the liberal state in accord with the emergent forms of social life."[9] In particular, Progressive-era reforms effected a substantial revision of economic liberalism. Government, both state and federal, increasingly occupied a far more visible role in regulating the nation's economy, altering the relationship between government and business in ways that were unimaginable just a few decades earlier. From labor relations[10] to tax policy[11] to competitive market conditions,[12] federal and state government became increasingly active in adjusting the legal rules of the market to the very different conditions that prevailed by the early twentieth century. To be sure, governments, especially state governments, had in fact regulated many aspects of economic activity well before the Progressive era, but the presuppositions of Progressive governance differed significantly from those that prevailed through most of the Gilded Age. Progressive governance made no pretense of co-existing with the joint ideologies of laissez-faire and anti-paternalism. Its ideology was frankly paternalistic and interventionist, particularly on social issues. Such measures as the "mothers' pension," workers' compensation, prohibition of child labor, regulation of women workers' hours and work condition were all pet Progressive projects, and all were promoted on the argument that government had an obligation to protect society's weaker members from its stronger members.[13]

The Critique of Classical Economics

The dramatic swings in the nation's economic fortunes during the Gilded Age, together with the sudden rise to prominence of large industrial corporations, led a new generation of economists to rethink how the market functioned and what role government should play in the market's domain. The Progressive critique of classical economics provided a model for legal scholars who initiated a critique of legal orthodoxy a decade or so after the first generation of Progressive economic scholarship appeared. Both in method and substance, the new thinking about the operation of the market and the relationship between government and business directly influenced legal thought in general and property theory in particular. Some of the legal critics had studied under Progressive political economists. Others had at least read and in some cases taught the new economists' work.[14] The economists whose work most directly influenced lawyers were Richard T. Ely, Edwin R. A. Seligman, John R. Commons, and Robert Hale.

The central insight of the Progressive critique of classical economics was that the classical model of the market no longer fit the new conditions of corporate capitalism. The classical model had posited that economic equilibrium depended solely on maintaining competition among producers. So long as a substantial number of firms competed with each other in an industry, prices would remain stable and the firms would produce efficiently. This model anticipated that the competitive market itself would maintain firms relatively small in size and that large consolidated firms were unnatural. Only minimal government interference was needed to maintain this stable state of affairs. The appearance and dramatic expansion of huge industrial firms in the American economy after 1870 increasingly placed these assumptions in doubt.

While the Sherman Anti-Trust Act (1890) reflected the persistent influence of laissez-faire assumptions that industrial concentration was unnatural and that the laws of the market would ultimately prevail,[15] younger economists in the late nineteenth century began to question the classical economic model of the competitive market. Examining the causes of the economic downturns that had occurred with bewildering frequency in many western industrialized countries, including the United States, Britain, and Germany, these economists developed a revised theory of economic behavior. Viewing classical political economy as anachronistic and unable to explain the historically unprecedented conditions of large industrial capitalism, the revisionists denied that competition was always socially beneficial or economically efficient. Increased competition among producers itself had led to overproduction and declining profit margins, thereby triggering economic downturns.[16] According to the new theory of the market, the trend toward corporate consolidation and concentration was both economically logical and socially beneficial. Large industrial corporations, the theory went, would stabilize the economy and make economic cataclysms less likely to occur.

The substantive implications of this new theory of industrial concentration for government-business relations were ambiguous, at least formally. On the one hand, as the leaders of the large corporations recognized, the theory could be used to a defend a continued government policy of deference toward corporations. One could plausibly argue (and corporate leaders did argue[17]) that attacking trusts for the purpose of maintaining competition was not only futile but counterproductive since competition was the root cause of persistent economic turbulence.

Progressives drew a different conclusion, however. They pointed out that the new theory demonstrated that the market was not always self-correcting, and that liberty of contract, the keystone in the foundation of laissez-faire, did not always increase wealth. Visible hands could and increasingly did take over the controls of the market under industrial capitalism, driving out competition in order to maintain high profit levels. How the market behaved and whether its social consequences would be positive or harmful was, at bottom, a matter of power, not of the laws of nature. The new type of industrial corporation increasingly controlled the market because its size created advantages that the old nineteenth-century corporation simply lacked. On balance, Progressives believed, the new corporations regulated the economy in socially and economically beneficial ways, but opportunities for abuse of that power clearly existed. Progressives looked to government to regulate in those areas of potential abuse. Specifically, they tended to favor regulation of oligopolistic industries, antitrust enforcement, and labor union organization. Government's function in the new marketplace, then, was as a kind of second-order regulator, regulating the large industrial corporations that were the primary regulatory institutions.[18]

Progressive political economy's methodological implications for legal theory were as important, if not more so, as its substantive implications. Methodologically, Progressive economics differed from classical economics in three main respects. First, it was committed to an empirical, or behavioral, approach to the study of economics. For those who were educated in Germany and influenced by the German historical school of social science, a historical evolutionary approach was a crucial part of their empiricism. Historical evolutionism rejected the deductive approach of classicists, who posited that the market followed certain universal laws. As Richard T. Ely put it in his autobiography, Progressive political economists of his generation accepted "the idea of [historical] relativity as opposed to absolutism and the insistence upon exact and positive knowledge."[19] Economics was, above all, a *social* science. Its domain was not an abstract or metaphysical entity known as the market, but human behavior, and there were no a priori laws of human behavior. One could meaningfully study human behavior only at particular times and in particular places.

Unlike their classical predecessors, the new generation of economists emphasized the central and irreducible role of human agency in the operation of the market. They rejected theories that minimized the role of individual volition in economic development, whether the theory came from the political Right—Adam Smith's invisible hand—or the Left—Marx's historical materialism. Nothing about the operation of the market, or any other aspect of social life for that matter, was inevitable or necessary. Necessitarian theories were not only wrong, they were also insidious, for they bred a sense of passivity and lack of responsibility among citizens.

Historical circumstances bounded the range of social and economic change that was possible, but change was both possible and, the Progressives believed, desirable.

Second, Progressive economists deliberately set out to revise their discipline and other social sciences to bring them in line with the reality of the present. They had all been profoundly affected by the late nineteenth-century changes in the character of capitalism and the social problems that those changes had engendered, including what they considered the very real threat of class conflict. The social, economic, and political upheaval of the Gilded Age made them keenly aware of the fact that the rate of historical change was rapidly increasing.[20] Their age, their culture constituted a sharp break with the past, and there was no reason to expect that the pace of change would abate. Prompted by their empiricism and historical outlook, the new generation of economists (and social scientists generally) set out to refocus attention on the actual operation of existing institutions and social practices, rather than abstract models. They sought to make their disciplines genuinely *social* sciences.

The final methodological change that Progressive social scientists made was the turn to objectivity. Increasingly after 1900, political economists and other social scientists wanted to separate the ethical from "what is" and declared that social facts, not ethical values, were the proper subject of their scientific studies. Their increasing reliance on the fact-value distinction posed a dilemma for early twentieth-century social scientists, however. Despite their professionalization, they remained keenly interested in policy matters and the political implications of their work. How could they reconcile the ideological conflicts within their ranks with their claim to value-neutrality?[21] Dorothy Ross has shown how they responded to this problem with various tactics: begging off on controversial position on the ground of "scientific modesty"; allowing provocative reformist papers to be presented at public meetings while leaving more "professional" individuals to point out the scientific flaws; and, most commonly, maintaining ideological balance, or at least the appearance of balance, in journals, professional meetings, and public discussions.[22] A politically "left" paper or presentation was always balanced by a spokesperson from the "right." In this way, although the ideological dimension of their work was acknowledged, the profession as a whole remained neutral on particular issues.

Every one of these methodological changes affected legal scholarship and legal theory. Early twentieth-century law school teachers' own aspirations to be scientific and professional led them closely to monitor developments in the social sciences.[23] While most of them continued to regard law as an autonomous discipline (it was not until the 1920s and 1930s that Realists began explicitly to treat law itself as a social science), many leading legal scholars in the first two decades of the twentieth century regarded growing professionalization and methodological changes in the social sciences as a model that legal study could and should emulate. The influences of the new social scientific method was evident in legal scholarship in many areas, but especially so in property law.

Hohfeld and the Reconceptualization of Property

No expression better captures the modern legal understanding of ownership than the metaphor of property as a "bundle of rights." That metaphor was intended to signify three key insights. First, it indicates that ownership is a complex legal relationship. Second, the metaphor illuminates the fact that the constitutive elements of that relationship are legal rights. Third, and most important, it underscores the social character of that relationship. None of these three insights, which lawyers today take for granted, was stock-in-trade within American legal thought prior to the twentieth century. While legal Progressives and their Realist descendants were not the first to make these points, they were the first to popularize them in the world of legal scholarship and legal education.

The person who is often, though erroneously,[24] credited with introducing that conception into American legal discourse is Wesley Newcomb Hohfeld.[25] Hohfeld, along with Arthur Linton Corbin and Walter Wheeler Cook, was one of the earliest and leading figures in introducing the new legal methodology at Yale. While Corbin and Cook are more commonly classified as Legal Realists[26], Hohfeld's status as a Realist has been more controversial. Some historians have argued that Hohfeld's "analytic jurisprudence was precisely the kind of abstraction that the Realists constantly complained of."[27] But this objection misunderstands the purpose of Hohfeld's critique of legal concepts like "right," "privilege," and "power" in his famous pair of articles, "Some Fundamental Legal Conceptions as Applied in Judicial Reasoning"[28] and "Fundamental Legal Conceptions as Applied in Judicial Reasoning."[29] If his objective is kept in mind, it becomes quite clear why he is properly included on lists of Realists. Hohfeld wrote those articles not simply to clarify the conceptual distinction between legal rights and legal liberties but to demonstrate why the prevailing legal understanding of those terms obscured the fact that legal recognition of rights or liberties for some people allowed them to harm others without legal redress.[30]

Hohfeld wrote the earlier article while he was still a member of the Stanford law faculty. It so impressed Corbin, perhaps the most influential member of the Yale faculty, that he convinced the Dean to offer Hohfeld a job at Yale. Hohfeld accepted and quickly established himself as Corbin's and Cook's intellectual companion. Indeed, several of Corbin's and Cook's early articles restated and applied Hohfeld's less accessible analysis.[31] The substantive insight that Cook and Corbin took from Hohfeld's work was that the fact that a person has a *privilege* to do something says nothing about whether that person has a legal *right* with respect to that action, in the sense that that person can summon state power to oppose another's interference with that action. Cook illustrated the point this way:

> Suppose A., owner and possessor of a chattel, tells B. that he may take the chattel if he can do so, but that A. will do all he can to prevent B. The permission thus given by A. to B. has as its consequence the destruction of B.'s *duty* to refrain from taking the chattel and confers upon him the *privilege* of taking it. It does not, however, give B. a *right* (in the strict sense) to take it, i.e., it does not place A. under a *duty* to let B. take it. A. accordingly commits no legal wrong in resisting B.'s efforts to take it.[32]

As Cook and Corbin understood, Hohfeld's lesson was intended to highlight and clarify the social and political dimensions of legal decisions recognizing (or not recognizing) a right or privilege in a person. The social dimension is this: each time the law protects one person's security, by recognizing in that person a right (which imposes a correlative duty on others) or a privilege (which imposes on others what Hohfeld called a "no-right," that is, a denial of access to state power to prevent the privileged action), the law unavoidably denies others corresponding security. Joseph Singer has succinctly expressed the relational dimension in this way: "Legal rights are not simply entitlements, but jural relations."[33] Duncan Kennedy and Frank Michelman have formally articulated the social aspect of Hohfeld's analysis, stating:

> Hohfeld's "correlatives" table is . . . a precise statement of what can be called the Law of Reciprocity of Entitlements and Exposures: For every legal entitlement there is an equal and opposite legal exposure.

And by an easy step we arrive also at the Law of Conservation of Exposures: The sum of legally determined exposures is a constant. . . . [J]ust insofar as some B is spared a duty, some A must suffer a no-right (and vice versa); and just insofar as some A is spared a disability, some B must suffer a liability (and vice versa).[34]

In what sense are the implication of these laws political as well as social? Hohfeld's terse and rather formal rhetoric obscured the political dimension somewhat, but his colleague and friend Corbin did not hesitate to explain in clear terms. The legal determination of what forms of interference are permitted and what are forbidden is nothing more or less than a policy determination, not a matter of neutral deductive reasoning. "The real question," Corbin stated, "in each new case always is as to the limits to be placed upon each of the parties in the 'free struggle of life.' Where the situation is a novel one, this is, of course, purely a problem of economic and social policy, conceal it how we will."[35] It was a staple of nineteenth-century analytical jurisprudence[36] that conferring a legal liberty on a person to do some act necessarily, that is, as a matter of deductive logic, meant that others were under a legal duty not to interfere with that act. Hohfeld insisted that this was not so, and that this view hid the fact that when law does impose duties on others not to interfere with another's privilege, it does so for policy (political) reasons. Both analytical accuracy and intellectual honesty require that courts acknowledge their policy choices and articulate arguments in support of those choices rather than hiding behind the veil of deductive logic.

When applied to property, Hohfeld's analysis illuminated the complex and relational character of ownership. It revealed that ownership is not the simple and nonsocial relationship between a person and a thing that Blackstone's description suggested.[37] Rather, ownership is complex and fundamentally social. "Suppose," Hohfeld stated, "that A is fee-simple owner of Blackacre."

His "legal interest" or "property" relating to the tangible object that we call *land* consists of a complex aggregate of rights (or claims), privileges, powers, and immunities. *First:* A has multiple legal rights, or claims, that *others* . . . shall *not* enter upon the land, that they shall not cause physical harm to the land, etc., such others being under respective correlative duties. *Second:* A has an indefinite number of legal privileges of entering on the land, using the land, harming the land, etc., that is, within limits fixed by law on grounds of social and economic policy, he has privileges of doing on or to the land what he pleases; and correlative to all such legal privileges are the respective legal no-rights of other persons. *Third:* A has the legal power to alienate his legal interest to another, i.e., to extinguish his complex aggregate of jural relations and create a new and similar aggregate in the other person . . . . *Fourth:* A has an indefinite number of legal immunities, using the term immunity in the very specific sense of non-liability or non-subjection to a power on the part of another person.[38]

Hohfeld was anxious to point out that thinking of ownership in this way had important practical consequences. One consequence was to refocus attention on the nonphysicalist character of ownership and on the legal consequences of adopting such a nonphysicalist understanding.[39] Hohfeld was not the first to articulate a nonphysicalist, disaggregated "bundles-of-rights" conception of property.[40] The substance of that conception, if not the metaphor, was evident in legal literature as early as 1872.[41] The question was what were the practical implications of that conception. In particular, what consequences did that conception have for the proper scope of constitutional protection of property? The answer was not obvious, for the nonphysicalist way of understanding what it means to own property could, and did, yield two politically opposite positions.

One position, as we saw earlier,[42] was that a nonphysicalist conception of ownership required broad constitutional protection under the takings clause. Legal literature in the second half of the nineteenth century increasingly reflected the idea that constitutional protection might extend to situations in which government actions interferes with the owner's interest in physical possession of her asset. Nowhere was this theory more unambiguously articulated than in an 1888 treatise, entitled *A Treatise on the Law of Eminent Domain,* by John Lewis.

> If property, then, consists, not in tangible things themselves, but in certain rights in and appurtenant to those things, it follows that, when a person is deprived of any of those rights, he is to that extent deprived of his property, and, hence, that his property may be taken, in the constitutional sense, though his title and possession remain undisturbed; and it may be laid down as a general proposition, based upon the nature of property itself, that, whenever the lawful rights of an individual to the possession, use or enjoyment of his land are

in any degree abridged or destroyed by reason of the exercise of the power of eminent domain, his property is, *pro tanto,* taken, and he is entitled to compensation.[43]

That, however, was not the implication that Hohfeld drew from the nonphysicalist conception of ownership. Hohfeld agreed that ownership was legally protected not only to allow physical possession or enjoyment but also when the owner has no intention of physically possessing or enjoying the asset. Indeed, rights or claims where the owner has no intention of possessing the asset are sometimes the economically most valuable:

> It is sometimes thought that A's rights, or claims, are created by the law for the sole purpose of guarding or protecting A's own physical user or enjoyment of the land, as if such physical user or enjoyment of the land were the only economic factor of importance. A moment's reflection, however, shows that this is a very inadequate view. Even though the land be entirely vacant and A have no intention whatever of personally using the land, his rights or claims that others shall not use it even temporarily in such ways as would not alter its physical character are, generally, of great economic significance as tending to make others compensate A in exchange for the extinguishment of his rights, or claims, or in other words, the creation of privileges of user and enjoyment.[44]

Protecting nonphysical as well as physical aspects of ownership did not necessarily mean, though, that law must protect owners from all interferences with their assets. The whole thrust of Hohfeld's analysis of property was to demonstrate that no single constituent element or set of elements was essential to ownership. Ownership was a complex set of legal relations in which individuals were interdependent. Some degree of social interference with one person's ownership interest not only did not negate ownership, it was unavoidable. Precisely because ownership *is* relational, no person can enjoy complete freedom to use, possess, enjoy, or transfer assets regarded as theirs. The real question is which interferences should be legally prohibited and which permitted. There was no analytical, or deductive answer to that question; it depended strictly on what policies society decides to promote.

Richard T. Ely and the Dialectic of Sociality

While Hohfeld's analysis of property highlighted the complex character of ownership, it did not directly address the question of how the social and individual aspects of ownership related to each other. No sociolegal scholar of Hohfeld's generation discussed that problem more comprehensively than the famous political economist Richard T. Ely. Ely directly confronted the question and answered it in an explicitly dialectical fashion.

Ely first rose to prominence in the 1880s and 1890s as an outspoken proponent of the social gospel.[45] Over and over, he reiterated his theme that economics was not a strictly positive science. Having done his graduate work in Germany under the leading figures in the German historical school of political economy,[46] Ely became imbued with the German economists' view that economics has a strong ethical dimension and that economic scholarship must maintain an ethical viewpoint. His fervent belief that all academic study—including his own subject, political economy—should always be connected with social ethics made him one of the most controversial intellectual figures on the American scene for over forty years. He was sympathetic to the ideals of socialism, but, despite the characterizations of his critics, he carefully distanced himself from it. Both politically and intellectually, Ely was at his core a reformer, not a radical. Strongly committed to the aims of the labor movement, he maintained a close affiliation with its leaders and worked on behalf of a wide variety of labor reforms.[47] He not only wrote and lectured widely on economic and political reform,[48] but he also served in several political capacities, where he attempted to put his reformist ideas, such as progressive taxation of income, into practice.

Ely's pro-labor sympathies alone would have made him a suspect figure among his fellow economists and mainstream political leaders, but academics had particular reasons for regarding him with distrust. As much as he was a political reformer, Ely was even more of a personal academic empire builder and an outspoken critic of the orthodoxy prevailing in the social sciences in the late nineteenth century. Along with John R. Commons and other so-called institutional economists,[49] he established the American Economic Association (AEA) in 1885 explicitly as an organization to attack classical economics.[50] Later, when he felt the AEA had become too much a mainstream group, he established the famous School of Economics, Political Science and History and, later still, the controversial Institute for Research in Land Economics and Public Utilities, both at the University of Wisconsin.[51]

The Institute of Land Economics was hounded from the outset by criticisms from old-line Wisconsin Progressives that it was dominated by the real estate industry and other special interest groups on whom Ely relied for financial support.[52] Ely left Wisconsin for Northwestern University in 1925 after criticism of the Institute from Senator Robert M. LaFollette and other Wisconsin Progressives, together with the hard feelings that remained following the unsuccessful attempt in 1894 by members of the Board of Regents to purge him from the Wisconsin faculty because of his support for labor's position in the Homestead and Pullman strikes and other recent labor upheavals.[53]

The unorthodoxy of Ely's views on economics made them all the more attractive to the new generation of legal scholars who were attempting to undermine the analogous (and in many ways overlapping) orthodoxy in their own field, the Legal Realists. Ely's influence on the Realists tended to be indirect. His ideas filtered through to legal scholars primarily through close associates, like Commons, who strongly influenced Realist legal writers like Karl Llewellyn. Ely's methodological ideas regarding empiricism and studying actual social practices and institutions rather than abstract models resonated with the views that Realists had about their own discipline. It was not only methodology that made Ely's work attractive to legal critics, though. Many of his substantive ideas about property clearly influenced other critics who are more commonly identified with Legal Realism, such as Robert L. Hale and Morris R. Cohen. Indeed, much of the latter two critics' ideas regarding property can be traced directly back to Ely.[54] The most distinctive aspect of Ely's discussion of property, though, is his analysis of the institution of private property as a dialectic between the individual and social dimensions. He developed his dialectical analysis most fully in his two-volume work, *Property and Contract in Their Relations to the Distribution of Wealth.*[55]

Like Hohfeld (and actually before Hohfeld), Ely explicitly rejected the Blackstonian person-thing conception of ownership in favor of a social, or relational, conception. *"The essence of property,"* Ely wrote, *"is in the relations among men arising out of their relations to things."*[56] He took it as given, moreover, that what those relations were was a matter of political decision. He dismissed the Lockean notion of prepolitical, natural property rights as something that "has long ago been totally discredited by science."[57]

Ely's major concern was working out the implications of the relational conception of ownership. While that conception meant that "there is no such thing as absolute private property,"[58] it did not mean that ownership is entirely social. The key to understanding the relational conception was to recognize that "[t]he truth is, there are two sides to private property, *the individual side and the social side.*"[59] There was nothing particularly original about that observation, although there certainly were some who would have challenged it. Ely's real contribution to the development of the relational conception was his analysis of the social and individual aspects of private property as dialectically related. The social aspect, Ely argued, is not exceptional. Rather, "it is an essential part of the institution itself. . . . It [the social aspect] is just as much a part of private property, as it exists at the present time, as the individual side is a part of it. The two necessarily go together, so that if one perishes, the other must perish."[60]

Ely seems to have regarded this dialectic as historically and culturally contingent. He thought that it was possible that the social side of property might be lost or deteriorate if it were not enforced, especially in cultures whose ideologies emphasized the individual aspect of property ownership.

> *[T]he social side of private property will fail to receive adequate recognition and development unless an active conscious effort is made to bring this about. . . .* We all know how easily the general public loses its rights, because the general public is apt to be less watchful than private individuals, and it requires a considerable development . . . in order to protect the social side of property.[61]

Ely's reasoning can be translated in terms of the now-familiar insights of rational-choice theory: while individual have incentives to maximize control over their own property, they lack incentives to monitor the use of property interests that they share in common with others. For each individual, the costs of policing the social side of property greatly exceed the individual gains, so each individual chooses to neglect the social side. As a result, aggregate social welfare diminishes unless the state, as society's agent, acts to protect the social side.

What exactly is this social aspect of property? Ely provided some obvious examples of public restrictions on private ownership of land, such as the eminent domain and tax powers.[62] He also discussed the private landowner's duties to avoid waste and nuisance. These restrictions, though, were hardly controversial. The social side of property, defined to this point, is little more than an elaboration of the Lockean proviso.

Potentially more controversial was Ely's view that the social side of private ownership was paramount to the individual side. "[I]t is the social purpose which is dominant or becomes dominant and controls the institution of private property in land," Ely wrote. "It is the social purpose, the general welfare which has been in control."[63] The primary legal device in the United States for developing and protecting the social aspect of property, Ely argued, is the police power. Ely viewed the police power as a legislative power only in form. In reality, it is a judicial power since the Constitution sets limits to the police power and vests authority to define those limits in the judiciary. In effect, then, the police power is the means by which American courts define what property is and develop its social dimension:

> *The police power is the power of the courts to interpret the concept property, and above all private property; and to establish its metes and bounds. . . . The police power shapes the development of the social side of property. It tells us what burdens the owner of property must bear without compensation. . . . [I]t is essentially the power to interpret property and especially private property and to give the concept a content at each particular period in our development which fits it to serve the general welfare.*[64]

Ely's subsequent discussion of the social aspect of property, however, quickly dashed any radical implication that that idea might have had. It is entirely clear that he in no way contemplated using it to pose any fundamental threat to the extant structure of economic power. He stated that the courts' responsibility was to maintain a "satisfactory equilibrium" between the individual and social sides of property,[65] but the equilibrium that he described clearly favored the fundamental prerogatives of the individual owner over the interests of society. In discussing the scope of regulation under the police power, Ely asserted the truism that "[r]egulation is allowed but it must be reasonable."[66] The rub is how one defines reasonableness. Ely defined it in a way that preserved what he termed the "conservative nature" of private property.[67] Ely meant "conservative" quite literally to mean conserving the institution of private property.

Ely made two basic points concerning the conservative implications of the social aspect of property. The first was that the social aspect promoted the very survival of property by permitting property to adapt to changing circumstances. Ely was eager to find a *via media* between absolute private property and socialized property. He was especially eager to demonstrate that redistributive reforms like progressive taxation, far from radically undermining private property, in fact supported it:

> It is true that we all hang together, and that you cannot attack the millionaire's palace, without threatening the widow's cottage. If you attack the millionaire's palace you make an attack upon the institution of property—using the word *attack* in a strict sense—but it does not follow that we cannot modify the institution so as to lead to a modification in the distribution of wealth, without injuring the widow's cottage. It does not follow because the millionaire pays a tax of three per cent and the widow pays a one per cent tax that the institution of property is threatened by this progressive taxation. Neither the widow's cottage is necessarily threatened thereby nor the millionaire's palace.[68]

Ely's second point was that the social aspect of property mediates conflicts between individual power and social needs. That mediating role protects the survival of the institution of private property. As social institution, property's existence depends on the welfare of society as a whole. An absolutist approach to property would be self-defeating, Ely argued, because it would threaten social welfare and society itself. "[I]f private property finds its limitations in the social well-being, then . . . a landowner may not drive people off his property to betake themselves to the sea and perish in the waves, because long before that point is reached private property will find its limitations, since society cannot think that its welfare will be found in its own destruction."[69] The social aspect acts as a check on abuses of the power that private property confers on individuals that threaten its survival. By eliminating the danger of such anti-social abuses, the social dimension blunts attacks on the very existence of property. "Unless it comes to such a pass that the institution in its very essence is injurious, there can be no general attack on private property. Invasion of the rights of private property appears the more unjustifiable if provision is made for the needs of the general public."[70]

For all of the conservative implications of Ely's conception of property, it did repudiate the social vision that saw social welfare as the product solely of individual liberty. Social welfare could not be achieved solely by protecting the individual property owner from social or government interference. Private property was not the guardian of the individual alone or even primarily; it was also guardian of society. Where individual and social interests conflicted, the social interests prevailed, and property was the institutional means of protecting society.

Property as Value, Value as Property

We saw earlier that one of the most controversial issues recurring in constitutional litigation throughout the late nineteenth century was whether rate regulation unconstitutionally deprived firms of property.[71] By the end of the century, courts, particularly the U.S. Supreme Court, had generally accepted as the test for the constitutional validity of legislatively established rates whether the rates unreasonably deprived the affected firms of the "use and income," i.e., the exchange-value of their property, quite apart from whether the rate affected "title and possession" of the firms' assets.[72] The "reasonable value" test later provoked a flurry of articles from economists and lawyers[73] when the Supreme Court explicitly adopted "reproduction cost" as the measure of value.[74] The reproduction cost standard proved to be enormously controversial in the postwar environment when inflation broke the rough correspondence that had previously existed between reproduction cost and historical cost.[75]

Even before the Court had settled on the reproduction cost standard, however, American economists extensively debated, both in legal and economic journals, how market value should be analyzed for purposes of establishing legal limits in legislative rate-making procedures.[76] They realized that by declaring that protecting property required courts to protect value, the Supreme Court had opened the door to declaring not only all rate regulation but indeed all regulation unconstitutional. As Robert L. Hale, a younger critic of legal reasonable value standard, stated in a particularly lucid and forceful expression of this insight, "The policy calling for a fair return on the value was originally adopted as a method of effectuating that policy [of not reducing property values through rate regulation]. This it succeeds in doing only if 'value' means 'exchange-value,' and if all reductions of net earnings are forbidden. But they are not."[77] Once the Court had shifted the focus of constitutional protection from physical possession and use to "value," the Pandora's box of property as inextricably rooted in contested public policy, rather than science, was open for all to see.

Among the earliest and most influential contributors to the debate about property as value was the institutional economist John R. Commons.[78] Commons contributed three important insights to this debate.[79]

The first was that in shifting the focus from what he called "use-value" to "exchange-value" American courts had fundamentally changed the legal meaning of property. The new "exchange-value" meaning of property implied that the primary function of property was economic, not political, and that there was no meaningful distinction between property and commodity.[80]

Second, "exchange-value as property" means that property not only is intangible but also is mindful of the future. Exchange-value means "the market-value expected to be obtained in exchange for the thing in any of the markets where the thing can or might be sold."[81] Commons analyzed exchange-value as composed of both what he called "encumbrances," i.e., "promises [by others] to pay, backed by government,"[82] and "opportunities," which he defined as "accessibility to markets, also enforced by government."[83] The value of these interests lay in the outcome of future behavior. "Both of them," he wrote, "lie in the future but have a value in the present. We may call them Expectancies. All value is expectancy."[84]

Commons's third insight grew out of the first two. The shift from use-value to exchange-value as the key element of property had illuminated an aspect of ownership that the old Blackstonian idea had obscured. Understood as use-value, ownership confers the power to produce, thereby increasing the supply of goods. As exchange-value, however, it creates the power to demand, restrict the supply of goods.

Hence the transition in the meaning of property from the use-value to the exchange-value of things, and therefore from the producing power that increases use-values to the bargaining power that increases exchange-values, is more than a transition—it is a reversal.[85]

Stated this way, Commons's economics seems backward. Use represents consumption, which in itself adds nothing to social wealth. Exchange increases aggregate social wealth by moving resources to the owners who value them more than others. Commons's point, however, was not really about aggregate wealth creation. His concern, rather, was with the relationship between property and power in social, particularly labor, relations. Ownership of property confers economic power over others. The meaning and effect of that power, however, has changed over time as economic institutions have evolved from feudalism to corporate liberalism. In the context of the feudal economy, in which the level of production was limited and owners supplied all the necessary factors of production, including labor, ownership did not represent power over others as much as it did power to withhold for one's own use. In a modern corporate economy, however, the power dynamic is very different because the social relations in production has fundamentally changed. A high degree of dependency characterizes the social relationships between corporate owners and those who supply labor. In this environment of interdependency, ownership represents not the power to hold for one's own use, but the power to withhold from others. Underscoring his evolutionist theory of change, Commons stated, "Just as the scales of a reptile become the feathers of the bird when the environment moves from land to air, so exclusive *holding for self* becomes *withholding from others* when the environment moves from production to marketing."[86] Taking into account increased population and demands on scarce resources, the power to withhold from others is "beyond anything known when this power was being perfected by the early common law or early business law."[87]

Commons pointed out that this power was "moral" as well as economic and that it could be immorally exercised. The moral dimension is that property ownership in itself makes some people subordinate to others. In modern democracies, in which all persons (or at least all citizens) enjoyed formal legal equality, the property relations of domination and subordination had replaced the feudal personal relations of social hierarchy. Commons argued that it was crucial for legislatures to adapt the meaning of property to fit "the new facts of power."[88] In his view this legislative responsibility is what justified recent labor reforms regulating the hours and conditions of the workplace in various industries. Such measures did nothing more than mediate the imbalance of moral power between owners and workers.[89]

The basic lesson that Commons, along with other critics, drew from the legal and economic debate over the meaning of value—and its implications for the meaning of property—was that there is no scientific or politically neutral basis upon which to decide how far regulation may legally interfere with property. "The truth which most rate bodies lack the courage to face," Robert L. Hale boldly asserted, "is, that in regulating the rates of utilities the law is trying the experiment in one limited field of turning its back on the principles which it follows elsewhere. . . . We are experimenting with a legal curb on the power of property owners."[90] Commons did not address the question of how far this experiment should be extended. The task of developing a general theory of when and why governmental regulatory interference with private ownership of property was legitimate and desirable was left to another generation of critics.

The Legal Realist Critique of Property
The Social and Economic Context of Legal Realism

World War I, which separated Progressivism and Legal Realism as intellectual movements, was, as Gabriel Kolko has observed, "the turning point in the development of the American economy."[91] Prior to the war, Americans generally felt that economic expansion was the complete antidote for all of the country's economic ills. By the 1920s, although many Americans believed that with the war behind them the country's economic prospects were bright, that sense of optimism simply was not justified. The American economy was no longer young or relatively simple. It had developed into a vastly more complex form of capitalism than anyone imagined possible even as late as 1890.

A number of serious problems accompanied this complexity. On the economic front, while firms operated more efficiently, productive efficiency was a double-edged sword. A glut of capital accumulated from wartime profits had too few outlets for investment.[92] In the postwar transition, the economy's rate of growth had slowed to its lowest level of any decade since the Civil War.[93] American corporate profits dipped during the 1920s to their lowest level in several decades, far lower than the levels that American investors had come to expect.[94] The only exception to this decline in profitability was utilities and railroads, the yield on whose stocks remained high during the decade.[95] (This was one factor contributing to the great interest during the 1920s over utility rate regulation.) The economy had not only matured, it reached a point of virtual domestic saturation.[96]

Three key aspects of the new form of capitalism created deeper, more subtle problems as well. First, the market was increasingly constituted by, and its operation controlled by, large corporations. It was no longer the province of the individual entrepreneur, the partnership, or the small family-owned firm. A rapidly growing proportion of economic activity was conducted through the corporate form. Indeed, by the mid-1920s, the large corporation appeared to be, if it was not in fact, the central institution of modern American life.[97]

Second, wealth was increasingly concentrated in a relatively small number of large corporations. The corporation's economic power could not be doubted. By 1929, the 200 largest nonfinancial firms owned 48 percent of all nonfinancial corporate assets.[98] In the transportation and public utility sectors, the concentration of wealth was especially acute.

The largest 85 firms owned 70 percent of all corporate wealth in those sectors.[99]

Third, the growth of the modern corporate system had effected a fundamental change in the character of property ownership in the business context. The traditional image of the business property owner as an individual entrepreneur who simultaneously controls the use of his assets and reaps the gains or losses of his own decisions had become anachronistic. The principal owner of business property now was a passive owner—the corporate shareholder. This new property owner did not decide how to use his assets, but left their management to a select group of corporate officers and directors over whom the shareholder had little or no effective control.

The convergence of these three developments created a predicament of power that increasingly preoccupied legal and economic intellectuals. It seemed to critics that the market was no longer a reliable mechanism for diffusing power throughout American society. As the large corporation had eclipsed the entrepreneur as the central actor in the market, and as wealth was largely in the control of a small band of managers, there was no longer any effective built-in mechanism for controlling the power whose relationship with property was more obvious under corporate capitalism than it had been under entrepreneurial capitalism. Increasingly, critics expressed concern with that power and a need for some mechanism for controlling it. This predicament of power was the dominant theme in legal discourse about property between 1920 and 1950.

From Progressivism to Realism

No great change in legal thought marked the transition from legal Progressivism to Legal Realism in general. Indeed, in some respects the only substantial difference between the two is the generational difference between their academic exponents. Perhaps the best way of looking at the relationship between Progressive legal thought and Realist thought is to view Realism as largely an extension of the project of Progressives like Ely and Commons. As we have discussed, that project itself is best understood as a reformist effort to adjust the private property/free contract legal regime to the social and economic changes associated with the rise of large-scale industrial enterprise. The project's main objective was accommodationist—to adjust the relationship between individual and social power in order to preserve the basic elements of the private property/free market regime.

333

In large measure the same was true of Legal Realism. The Realists were hardly political or legal radicals, however much their worst critics may have viewed them as such. Their recurrent substantive themes were that law and public policy were inseparable and that the public and private spheres were deeply intertwined. Those themes were not intended to lay the foundation for any fundamental transformation but rather to explain and justify the need for governmental regulation of a variety of economic activities. The Progressives, however, had already made much of the case for a regulatory state, and in this sense Legal Realism was little more than a clean-up operation, extending the critiques of economists like Ely and Commons to legal issues that Progressive economists had not addressed.

There were some differences between the two movements, of course. The most important of these was not about the substance of public policy, but about public policy's philosophical foundations. Progressivism generally lacked Legal Realism's skepticism about the rational foundations of legal, moral, and political values.[100] Progressives like Commons and Ely never questioned, as many (though not all) Realists did, the existence of rational bases for ethical and political values.[101] While Commons, Ely, and other Progressive critics rejected mid-nineteenth-century idealist and naturalist theories of rationality, they firmly believed that moral and political values could be rationally justified.[102] By contrast, one of the defining characteristics of post-1920 legal thought was the overt skepticism of any rational basis for legal, political, or moral values that Legal Realists like Jerome Frank (to cite the most obvious example) expressed. Much of the most controversial writing in the Legal Realist spirit was concerned with the problem of values.[103]

Realist writing about property, however, was not taken up with questions of rationality. Rather, Realist critiques of property reiterated the same concern that Progressives had earlier expressed regarding property and power. Their discussions of the relationship between property and power added little to what Ely and Commons had already said. Like the Progressives, the Realists of the 1920s and 1930s perceived that underlying specific legal issues like the meaning of "reasonable value" was the more fundamental question of what property means in the modern regulatory environment. Moreover, they built on the Progressives' insight that property relations were a matter of power, really only elaborating and making more explicit their predecessors' observations about the publicness of private property.

Property as Coercive Power: Robert L. Hale

The relation between property and power was most fully developed by the lawyer-economist Robert L. Hale. Hale was one of the first legal economists in American legal education. Having spent several years in corporate legal practice after graduating from Harvard Law School, he returned to his original interest in economics and took a Ph.D. from Columbia in 1918. He taught in the Columbia economics department at first and later received a joint appointment in the law school in 1922. His interests gradually shifted to legal aspects of economics, and within a few years he moved full-time to the law school where he remained until he retired from teaching in the mid-1950s.[104]

Hale's influence was greater in legal circles than among academic economists, although his work on public utility economics was respected and cited by leading economists like James C. Bonbright.[105] His work was widely cited not only by legal scholars but also by several of the most distinguished judges of the time, including Hugo Black, William O. Douglas, and Jerome Frank.[106] While the bulk of his writing concerned public utility regulation, the work for which he is best known today in legal scholarship is his 1923 article, "Coercion and Distribution in a Supposedly Non-Coercive State"[107] and, later, his article "Bargaining, Duress, and Economic Liberty."[108] That brace of articles outlined his general theory of the relationship among law, property, and power in market transactions and laid the foundation for his culminating work, *Freedom through Law,* published in 1952.[109]

Hale wanted to establish two basic points. The first was that the free market economy, like all economies, in fact was a system of coercive power. The second was that the legal system and the market, far from being separate realms, were interdependent. Taken together, these two points, Hale contended, indicated that effective policy decisions concerning resource allocation and income distribution require analysis of how the legal system itself distributes coercive power.

Hale considered the law of property to be a fundamental source of coercive economic power. He conceived the basic function of legal property rights not to be defensive, but offensive; not a means to protect oneself from unwanted interferences from others or the state, but the basis for coercing others to do something that the owner wishes. In his 1923 article on coercion and distribution Hale drew on Hohfeldian analysis explained the coercive role of ownership:

The owner can remove the legal duty under which the nonowner labors with respect to the owner's property. He may remove it, or keep it in force, at his discretion. To keep it in force may or may not have unpleasant consequences—consequences that spring from the law's creation of legal duty. To avoid these consequences, the nonowner may be willing to obey the will of the owner, provided that the obedience is not in itself more unpleasant than the consequences to be avoided. Such avoidance may take the trivial form of paying five cents for legal permission to eat a particular bag of peanuts, or it may take the more significant form of working for the owner at disagreeable toil for a slight wage. In either case, the conduct is motivated, not by any desire to do the act in question, but by a desire to escape a more disagreeable alternative.[110]

Initially, what seems odd about Hale's analysis is its conception of coercion. Why is it coercion for a person to work at an unpleasant job in order to earn enough money to buy food from another acting under coercion from the owner of the food, rather than a constrained choice? Hale's answer was that coercion *is* just the effect of one person's behavior that constrains another person's range of options. From one perspective, this sense of the term trivializes the concept of coercion, for it makes coercion ubiquitous. All choices are constrained choices simply by virtue of the fact of being made in the context of society. Every person's choices are constrained to some extent by the behavior of others, individually or collectively. Everyone is coerced, by everyone else.

But that was precisely Hale's point. He wished to establish that one could not maintain a categorical, mutually exclusive distinction between freedom and coercion. The crucial question is not, freedom or coercion, but "the *structure* of coercion (i.e., of mutually coercive capacity) and, therefore, of the *structure* of volitional freedom."[111] The crucial point for Hale was that there was nothing necessary or inevitable about the outcomes of either the market or legal processes. All legal-economic outcomes were the results of choices. The important matter on which to focus, Hale argued, is, who gets to choose?[112]

Hale was not the first to point out that allocative and distributive outcomes were the products of choices rather than the inexorable workings of the invisible hand. Commons had made the same point earlier, although less lucidly and forcefully.[113] What Hale added to this point was the further insight that one could not grant certain social practices and institutions privilege over others by characterizing them as "free" and others as "coercive." More concretely, it was pointless to try to establish market practices as being presumptively more legitimate than government regulation on the ground that government regulation coerces while market transactions do not. *Both* regulate, and *both* coerce. Hale continually emphasized that "to call an act coercive is not by any means to condemn it."[114] Clearly, some forms of coercion are illegitimate, but since coercion is ubiquitous, it can hardly be the case that all forms are illegal or improper. Arguments based on a categorical distinction between private freedom and public coercion begged the two important questions, what forms of coercion should be permitted and who gets to decide. Those questions were fundamentally issues of power, and issues of power had to be discussed and resolved openly and forthrightly.

Excursus: Is Power a Problem Only for Property-as-Commodity?

The deeper question that Hale's analysis prompts (one that he did not address) is whether a noncommodified conception of property involves the same problem of power. In treating property rights as a source of coercive market power, Hale in effect adopted the conception of property as commodity, that is, a resource whose primary function is to increase wealth through private exchange. By definition, property is a tool through which to coerce (in Hale's sense of the word) others in market transactions only to the extent that property is used for exchange purposes. But what about property for nonexchange purposes? Is property whose basic function is something other than private wealth creation also a source of coercive power? It seems highly unlikely that any noncommodified understanding of property could avoid the problem of power.

Consider the classical civic conception. According to classical republican thought, the primary role of property is to provide a secure material base for the personal independence that is the indispensable condition of virtuous citizenship. That conception implies a central concern with the proper distribution of property, for if property is distributed within the citizenry in a grossly unequal way, then a nontrivial portion of citizens will be dependent on others and, consequently, vulnerable to corruption.[115] This concern with distribution squarely raises a problem with power that is every bit as serious as that confronting property-as-commodity. For the civic conception of property the power problem does not necessarily occur in the initial distribution of property among the citizenry, for, as we saw earlier, some civic republicans believed that land was so plentiful that an amount adequate to bestow independence could be given to each citizen in fee simple. Under the assumption of virtually unlimited resources—an assumption that we now understand to be plausible only as to those few goods that are truly "public"—an initial plan of egalitarian distribution does not pose a problem of power because there is no sustained entanglement between citizen and state.[116]

The power problem occurs instead in two other instances. The first of these concerns the characteristics of ownership. Will owners be permitted to sell their property to others? If they are, then unless everyone's needs and preferences are fully sated (in which case, no subsequent transfers would occur), the same power problems that Hale identified occurs. Each owner has power over others by virtue of being entitled to withhold from others, enlisting the power of the state to enforce this entitlement, the owned thing that the other wants or needs. The only way to avoid this problem, it seems, is entirely to withhold the power to transfer from ownership. Individual owners then would lack power over others because lacking the legal ability to transfer a desired thing at all, they are not responsible for the other person's needs or desires not being met.

A double-bind problem emerges at this point, though. To prevent property from being socially coercive, the state must itself coerce property owners by withholding from them a key aspect of control over their property. To see this as coercion does not require that we presuppose that the power to transfer is an irreducible characteristic of owning property. So long as property owners want or need the power to dispose of their property, the power to withhold that ability from them is coercion in Hale's sense of the term.

This double-bind problem can be stated more broadly. From the civic perspective, the central function of ownership is to bestow independence on citizens so that they can competently practice self-government. Self-governance means that all matters of political life are subject to the will of the citizenry, and this suggests that the citizenry should always have the capacity to redo the political arrangement of property. (Recall Jefferson's doctrine of political relativism, which declares that obligations must be subject to rearrangement with the succession of each generation.) But if individual property entitlements are subject to the will of the citizenry, the precondition of independence so necessary for virtuous self-government is severely threatened. For ownership to vest independence indefeasibly, it must itself be indefeasible. That is, ownership rights must be supra-political to free owners from the will—the power—of the citizenry. The abstract definition of the civic conception of ownership, then, is caught in a double bind of power: either it recognizes the individual owner as strongly independent, thereby conferring power on him vis-à-vis the rest of the citizenry, or it gives full vent to the ideal of self-governance and thereby exposes the individual owner to the power of others to take that which was previously his.[117]

The intentionally male-gendered reference to ownership in the last sentence introduces the second instance of the civic power problem. It is well known that classical republican polities were starkly exclusionary and hierarchical. They were so because they linked self-governance with property. Civic republican thought linked the competence to practice self-governance—citizenship itself—with ownership of stable forms of property, forms that insured that citizens were truly independent.[118] The result was to exclude all women, slaves, servants, and others who lacked property ownership from participation in republican politics.[119] The conditions of modern liberal democracies, of course, ameliorate some of the reasons for classical republicanism's systematic exclusion, but they do not entirely eliminate the problem.

Liberal democracies do not formally withhold the legal capacity to own property from entire groups (although recall that this has been true for American married women only relatively recently). Nor do they formally condition the legal right to political participation on ownership of any form of property. Formally, the homeless person owning no more than the clothes on her back is as capable of self-governance as the wealthy lawyer. There is no logically compelling reason why capacity to practice virtuous politics must be predicated on property ownership, but if we were to universalize the conception of property that sees it as the material foundation for serving the civic good, it seems that we would retain some linkage between self-governance and property. Retaining liberal democracy's (formal) commitment to universal suffrage might then require some measure of property redistribution to insure that all citizens possess the material means to practice citizenship virtuously. But this step reintroduces the power problem discussed earlier in connection with redistributions of property. Collective redistributions are clearly coercive (again, in Hale's sense), even if motivated by the desire to serve the civic good. Nor can we finesse this problem by defining private ownership as being constantly subordinate to the common good, so that when redistributions occur individual owners have not lost their property because, vis-à-vis the common good, it never was theirs. That definition itself is an exercise of coercive power since it limits the individual owners' freedom by with-holding alternative uses from them.

It seems, then, that the problem of power as Hale defined it is not unique to property-as-commodity. Indeed, it occurs in every property regime so long as that regime operates in a social setting, for the problem is the consequence of the inevitable interdependency of persons in society. The only world in which the power problem does not appear is Robinson Crusoe's, at least until Friday appears.[120]

Property as Sovereignty: Morris R. Cohen

Following Hale's "Coercion and Distribution" article by just a few years and closely paralleling it was perhaps the most straightforward critique of the idea that the state plays no role in the creation or distribution of property interests. Perhaps more successfully than any other article of the period, Morris R. Cohen's famous article, "Property and Sovereignty,"[121] demolished the notion that private right and public power were categori-cally distinct from each other.

It is more accurate to label Cohen a Progressive than a Legal Realist. He matured intellectually under the influence of leading Progressive fig-ures like Herbert Croly and Walter Lippmann, who, as David Hollinger has observed, "sought to turn liberals toward the conscious, cooperative use of government power for reform."[122] He vigorously criticized aspects of Legal Realism, especially its behaviorism and its claims that moral and legal values lack rational foundations.[123] Still there was important com-mon ground between Cohen and the Realists. Most important, Cohen shared the Realists' conviction that law and politics were interconnected. He believed that laissez-faire ideology, with its insistent radical separation of the private and public spheres, was not only intellectually indefensible but morally and politically repugnant. In this respect, Cohen stood shoul-der to shoulder with Legal Realists like Hale, Walter Wheeler Cook,[124] and Jerome Frank[125] as well as Progressive economists like Commons and Ely.

Responding to the Supreme Court's decision in *Adkins v. Childrens Hospital*[126] that a federal statute setting a minimum wage for women in the District of Columbia was an unconstitutional deprivation of property without due process, Cohen set out to demolish the classical liberal as-sumption that private property is wholly distinct from and prior to governmental power. Classical liberalism defined freedom, or liberty, negatively: individual freedom from interference from the state. That definition presupposed a social ideal in which individuals act independently of each other. Within this scheme, the role of property is to protect the individual's liberty by creating for each owner a zone of autonomy. Within that zone each person was free to act as he or she wishes, free from nonpermissive encroachments by others, particularly the state. The state's sole legitimate role is to protect that zone by preventing others from unauthorized invasions.

Cohen argued that a "dispassionate scientific study" of "the nature of property, its justification, and the ultimate meaning of the policies based on it"[127] reveals "the actual fact that dominion over things is also *imperium* over our fellow human beings."[128] By the time Cohen wrote his article, this observation was well worn. Hale had written extensively on it, and before him, so had Commons and Ely. The important question was: what consequences follow from the insight that property is power, or sovereignty delegated to individuals by the state?

Cohen's initial response was hardly bold or startling. He cautioned that "the recognition that private property as a form of sovereignty is not itself an argument against it."[129] Cohen was no radical and no socialist; he was a progressive liberal who never doubted that private ownership of property was fundamentally correct. He conceded that individual labor plays a legitimate, albeit limited, role in justifying private ownership, and he acknowledged that private property has an important economic function, stating that "there is a strong *prima facie* case for the contention that more intensive cultivation of the soil and greater productiveness of industry prevail under individual ownership."[130]

Taking the familiar liberal arguments for private property for granted, Cohen argued that the question of property had to be understood dialectically. "We can only say dialectically," he emphasized, "that all other things being equal, property should be distributed with due regard to the productive needs of the community."[131] The dialectic did not apply just to the matter of distribution. It applied to all aspects of property ownership, including power to transfer, possess, and use. Private ownership confers certain negative rights to individuals owners, Cohen argued, but it is also subject to "positive duties in the public interest."[132] Cohen did not develop in detail the parameters of these positive duties and the public's correlative positive rights in privately owned property, but some legal issues that had provoked considerable debate seemed to him to fall within the core meaning of this social view of obligation. Rate regulation was among these. Cohen saw no need to resort to the affection doctrine to justify this sort of public interference with private ownership:

> Though the interests of free exchange of goods and services have never been as powerful as in the last century, governments have not abandoned the right to . . . fix the price of certain . . . services of general public importance, *e.g.,* railway rates, grain elevators and warehouse charges, etc. The excuse that this applies only to businesses affected with a public interest, is a very thin one. What large business is there in which the public has not a real interest?[133]

More generally, Cohen's point was this:

> A government which limits the right of large land-holders limits the rights of property and yet may promote real freedom. Property owners, like individuals, are members of a community and must subordinate their ambition to the larger whole of which they are a part.[134]

In effect, Cohen was trying to sketch the outline of a political and moral theory of ownership that would bracket the scope of the commodified conception of property. His real contribution was to synthesize various strands of arguments that had appeared before and explicitly to articulate that synthesis in the form of a dialectic of sociality.

A. A. Berle and Gardiner C. Means and the Problem of Corporate Property

By the time of the Great Crash of 1929, it was abundantly clear to anyone who cared to look that the shift to the large corporation as the dominant mode of doing business and with it, corporate equity and debt instruments as the dominant form of property, was now completed and irreversible. Attacks on the modern industrial corporation by critics like Edward Bellamy and Thorstein Veblen had utterly failed to slow the rapid growth of the business corporation or to weaken its enormous economic power.

The phenomenal growth of corporate power, together with the stock market's crash and the ensuing economic depression, engendered in the 1930s an intellectual milieu of skepticism about the validity of the classical theory of economic behavior.[135] That theory posited that the natural forces of market competition by themselves would force firms to supply the best products that consumers wanted at the lowest possible prices. Those that did not would decline and eventually shut down through a process of natural economic selection. The upshot of this theory was that since market equilibrium was self-maintaining, government intervention in the workings of the market was unjustified.

A central assumption of this theory was that the same person or group of persons would both supply and manage capital for a business venture. Since they would reap the gains or suffer the losses of their own decisions, self-interest would lead these persons to operate the firm as efficiently as they could. The emergence of the modern industrial corporation undermined that assumption and with it, at least in the view of critics, the coherence of the classical theory itself. Among all of the critiques of that theory and of corporate capitalism generally that appeared between 1890 and 1930, no work was more influential than A. A. Berle and Gardiner C. Means's famous book, *The Modern Corporation and Private Property*.[136]

Berle initiated the project under a grant to Columbia University from the Social Science Research Council and was the book's principal author. Means, who was a member of Columbia's economics faculty, contributed to the study primarily by collecting a substantial body of statistical data documenting the concentration of corporate ownership and the diffused distribution of stockholdings. Berle had joined the Columbia law faculty shortly after a split on that faculty had led several prominent Realists to leave. Despite the departure of important figures like William O. Douglas, Herman Oliphant, and Underhill Moore,[137] however, Legal Realism still exerted considerable influence at Columbia, largely through the presence of Karl Llewellyn and Edwin Patterson.[138] Institutional economics, championed by Robert L. Hale, also remained an important intellectual force at Columbia during the time of the Berle study. The book reflected the influence of both strands of thought.

Berle and Means developed two related claims: first, the central characteristic of the modern corporation is the separation of the control of property from its beneficial ownership; second, corporate managers and beneficial owners (i.e., shareholders) do not share the same incentives, undermining the key assumption of the classical model of the market. Berle and Means connected the two claims together in this central passage:

> It has been assumed that, if the individual is protected in the right both to use his property as he sees fit and to receive the full fruits

of its use, his desire for personal gain, for profits, can be relied on as an effective incentive to his efficient use of any industrial property he may possess.

In the quasi-public corporation, such an assumption no longer holds. [I]t is no longer the individual himself who uses his wealth. Those in control of that wealth, and therefore in a position to secure industrial efficiency and produce profits, are no longer, as owners, entitled to the bulk of such profits. Those who control the destinies of the typical modern corporation own so insignificant a fraction of the company's stock that the returns from running the corporation profitably accrue to them in only a very minor degree. The stockholders, on the other hand, to whom the profits of the corporation go, cannot be motivated by those profits to a more efficient use of the property, since they have surrendered all disposition of it to those in control of the enterprise.[139]

The implication of these claims for the economic function of property was, they thought, profound. At least in the industrial context, the role of property had fundamentally changed. Property no longer performed the economic function that classical economic theory traditionally ascribed to it. "Must we not," they asked rhetorically, "recognize that we are no longer dealing with property in the old sense? Does the traditional logic of property still apply? Because an owner who also exercises control over his wealth is protected in the full receipt of the advantages derived from it, must it *necessarily* follow that an owner who has surrendered control of his wealth should likewise be protected to the full?"[140]

For Berle and Means, the upshot of these changes in the nature of the business corporation and its concomitant effect on the function of property in the business sector was clear: "The explosion of the atom of property destroys the basis of the old assumption that the quest for profits will spur the owner of industrial property to its effective [i.e., efficient] use."[141] Large corporations could not be counted on to serve either the interests of shareholders, as the corporation's owners, or of the public generally. Since self-interest alone was inadequate, the only alternative mechanism for assuring that corporations were governed in the public interest was government regulation. Government had "to strip itself of the illusion that it might recreate the classical society of small competitors and proceed with the structural reforms needed to stabilize the economy."[142]

What made *The Modern Corporation and Private Property* so influential was not originality: virtually nothing in the book, certainly none of its major arguments, was completely new. Well-known books by Harvard economists Thomas Nixon Carver and William Z. Ripley had earlier argued that shareholders of large corporations had little, if any, meaningful power over corporate policy.[143] Before them, Thorstein Veblen had developed a similar theory of the evolution of corporate structure.[144] Still earlier, the great English economist Alfred Marshall had pointed out in 1890 that large corporations were "hampered by . . . conflicts of interest between shareholders and . . . the directors."[145]

Three factors explain the book's phenomenal success. First, unlike Veblen, Carver and other critics of the corporation, Berle and Means (primarily Means[146]) backed up their criticisms with a substantial body of statistical data. These data were intended to prove two points: that corporate wealth was concentrated in a few corporations and that ownership of corporate stock was broadly dispersed. The data effectively created the impression that a relatively small group of managers now dominated the nation's economy.

The second factor was the book's timing. The date of its first publication (1933) was ideal. After the stock market crash, the general public was quite receptive to a critical treatment of corporate power. As George Stigler and Claire Friedland have pointed out, "The 1930s was a period of accelerating movement away from a competitive, unregulated market. Reasons for distrusting such a system . . . were in demand for the new rhetoric of public policy, and Berle and Means nicely met that need."[147] Policy-oriented lawyers and social scientists were no less ready than John Q. American to hear an analysis of corporate governance that emphasized the need for external control. The crash had seemed to validate Carver's and Ripley's earlier predictions of the disastrous consequences of leaving the modern corporation unregulated. The time could not have been more ripe for a study of the modern corporation that focused on its enormous power.

The third factor was the book's functional and institutionalist approach to the study of corporations. Between 1890 and 1930, a debate raged among legal scholars over the "true" nature of the corporation. The law reviews were filled with articles, most of which were aridly conceptualist, debating whether the corporation is a "real entity" or merely an aggregation of contractual relationships.[148] By 1930, this debate had run out of intellectual steam. The philosopher John Dewey, who had considerable contact with both the law school and the economics faculties at Columbia and whose work both influenced and was influenced by them, wrote in 1926 that legal writers and courts should disconnect specific issues concerning corporations from disputes over the appropriate conceptual theory of the corporation: how law and society treat the corporation, and what powers the corporation was given, depended on political and economic choices, not on formal analysis.[149]

Heeding Dewey's advice, Berle and Means simply ignored the whole "real entity" debate. Instead, they focused on how the modern business corporation actually functioned in American society. The functional approach was perfectly suited to Berle and Means's intended audience, for the book was not directed at professional economists, or at least not the academic economic establishment. Its real target was lawyers, especially those academic lawyers who were most interested in and involved with the making of public policy—Legal Realists and their economic allies. Berle and Means's methodology effectively synthesized the institutional perspective of institutional economics and the functionalist outlook of the Legal Realists. Substantively, their analysis echoed the two dominant themes of Progressive and Realist legal-economic writers that the market was a realm of power and that economic institutions were not wholly private in character. In particular, Berle and Means's argument that large corporations were not really private institutions but actually "quasi-public" strongly reiterated and bolstered earlier arguments by Hohfeld, Hale, Ely, Commons, and others that there was no categorical distinction between the public and private in market transactions. While the economic profession was not especially interested in this line of criticism, the academic legal profession, especially its elite stratum, certainly was.

Publicly Controlling the Private Corporation

Berle and Means's most significant contribution was to sketch a theory that would provide an alternative to the affectation doctrine of *Munn v. Illinois* as the theoretical foundation for government regulation of corporate activities. As we have already seen,[150] that doctrine provided that there was no constitutional obstacle to legislative regulation of, for example, the rates that businesses charged their customers when the corporation was of the type that was "affected with a public interest." In effect, the affectation doctrine denied that such corporations were solely private. While the U.S. Supreme Court did not formally abandon that doctrine until the 1934 decision in *Nebbia v. New York*,[151] it lost virtually all intellectual credibility among lawyers well before then. It was, as the Yale Legal

Realist Walton Hamilton put it, the product of the view of a generation for whom the then-new fourteenth amendment was part of "the old constitution."[152] To a different generation, it sounded (if one was inclined to value liberty of contract above all) suspiciously hostile to property rights or (if one had taken the Realist turn) meaningless, since all businesses were in some sense affected with a public interest.[153] By 1930, its demise as a justification for legal control of corporate activities in general to insure that corporations act for the common welfare was a foregone conclusion.

Berle and Means attempted to fill the gap by advancing a novel theory. They argued that the "traditional logic of property" did not apply to the modern large corporation. Corporate power should not be exercised for the exclusive benefit of the shareholders but for the benefit of society as a whole. Shareholders are, they argued, passive property owners who have "released the community from the obligation to protect them to the full extent implied in the doctrine of strict property rights."[154] This leaves the community in a position to demand that the relationship between corporate property and the community be reconfigured in a way that recognizes that in the context of the modern industrial corporation the public/private distinction had lost much of its credibility:

> Neither the claims of ownership nor those of control can stand against the paramount interests of the community.... Rigid enforcement of property rights as a temporary protection against plundering by control would not stand in the way of modification of these rights in the interest of other groups. When a convincing system of community obligations is worked out and is generally accepted, in that moment the passive property right of today must yield before the larger interests of society. . . . It is conceivable—indeed it seems almost essential if the corporate system is to survive—that the "control" of the great corporations should develop into a purely neutral technocracy, balancing a variety of claims by various groups in the community and assigning to each a portion of the income stream on the basis of public policy rather than private cupidity.[155]

The precise content of the obligation that the corporation owes to the community remained obscure. Berle and Means never explained what the specific features of that obligation were or which constituencies are included in the notion of the "community." Rather, they vaguely called for something resembling what late twentieth-century corporate lawyers call "corporate social responsibility." But it is not entirely clear just how the Berle and Means analysis relates to the modern discourse of corporate social responsibility.

The phrase "corporate social responsibility" today may mean either of two different ideas. The first is that the officers of large, publicly held corporations should focus exclusively on the shareholders' dominant preference, which is presumed to be profit-maximization, rather than serving their own personal interests. The second meaning grows out of a quite different concern. It advocates what is sometimes called "corporate voluntarism," that is, corporate actions that sacrifice profit-maximization to pursue other social objectives.[156]

These two ideas have inconsistent implications for legal control over corporate managers. The first idea requires tighter legal control over corporate officers and directors. Corporate voluntarism, on the other hand, requires relaxing legal controls over managers, giving them greater discretion so that they can fulfill their responsibilities to the community.

These two meanings were the subject of a famous debate between Berle and the noted Harvard professor of corporate law, E. Merrick Dodd. Dodd supported the idea of corporate voluntarism, and he was unconcerned that corporate managers would exercise greater discretion in their own interests rather than the interests of social groups in addition to shareholders. He based his confidence on the theory that

> [p]ower over the lives of others tends to create on the part of those most worthy to exercise it a sense of responsibility. The managers, who along with the subordinate employees are part of the group which is contributing to the success of the enterprise by day-to-day efforts, may easily come to feel as strong a community of interest with their fellow workers as with a group of investors whose only connection with the enterprise is that they or their predecessors in interest invested money in it.[157]

Berle regarded this view as wildly naive. He simply did not think that corporate managers could be trusted to act in the interest of anyone other than themselves if they were given discretion to do so. Because of the separation of control from ownership, private property no longer performed, in the industrial setting, its disciplining role. Therefore, management powers had to be subjected to some form of legal control. One possible form is the requirement that managers act exclusively in the interest of shareholders. That approach, which Berle analogized to the controls that equity places on trustees, adopted the profit-maximization version of corporate responsibility.[158]

Berle considered strict, trustee-like controls over corporate managers to be clearly preferable to open-ended managerial discretion, if those two were the only available options. His reluctance to abandon profit-maximization as the sole objective of corporate officers and directors was rooted in social welfare considerations. Doubtless reflecting anxiety about the economic insecurity that millions of Americans were then facing during the Great Depression, he wrote, "When [corporate property] and the income stream upon which [corporate stockholders] rely are irresponsibly dealt with, a large portion of the group merely devolves upon the community; and there is presented a staggering bill for relief, old age pensions, sickness-aid, and the like."[159] Removing from shareholders their economic security so that corporate property could be used serve the interests of other groups was simply robbing Peter to pay Paul unless the government simultaneously adopts "a system . . . by which responsibility for control of national wealth and income is so apportioned and enforced that the community as a whole, or at least the great bulk of it, is properly taken care of."[160]

Berle presented his obligation-to-the-community theory as a third way, an alternative to the "managerial discretion" theory and the "strict property rights of shareholders" theory. He recognized that this theory had to be clearly developed, but he warned that "you can not abandon emphasis on 'the view that business corporations exist for the sole purpose of making profits for their stockholders' until such time as you are prepared to offer a clear and reasonably enforceable scheme of responsibilities to someone else."[161] Once the shareholders' interests were adequately taken care of, though, the community had a legitimate claim to have other groups' interests protected as well. These included "fair wages, security to employees, reasonable service to their public, and stabilization of business."[162] A program along those lines might well shift some corporate profits from shareholders to employees and other groups to whom corporations conventionally do not owe fiduciary duties, but so long as the shareholders' basic welfare needs were served, they had no legitimate basis for demanding that their profits be maximized. The corporation was, after all, a quasi-public institution, and its legal obligations had to be defined consistently with its character.

Subsequent to writing *The Modern Corporation and Private Property,* Berle's views became more obscure still. In 1954, he conceded that his dispute with Dodd "has been settled (at least for the time being) squarely in favor of Professor Dodd's contention."[163] He now considered corporate management to be free to practice social responsibility. Still later, however, he asserted that his concession was only that things had changed in fact, not that they had changed for the better. "Things being as they are," he wrote, "I am unabashed in endeavoring to seek the best use of a social and legal situation whose existence can neither be denied nor changed."[164]

Berle never got around to describing an alternative "scheme of responsibilities" for corporations. Oddly enough, he did not support proposals to reconstitute boards of directors to include representatives of employees or consumers or calls formally to redefine the goals of management.[165]

The Failures of the Realist Critiques

The Realists' critique of property as power by and large merely elaborated on a general theme that the Progressives, especially institutional economists like Ely and Commons, had already introduced into legal discourse. The Progressives were keenly aware of changes in the corporate form of enterprise and of the effects of those changes on property and power relations within the market. They were also aware that economic power easily translates into political power. Many of them believed that large industrial corporations had already achieved a position of influence in state and even the federal government that was far greater than business had ever had prior to 1870.[166] To a very considerable extent, Progressivism was a response to the perceived problem of power, economic and political, in the emerging corporate state. Realists' discussions of property added virtually nothing original to these insights.

The largest failure of Legal Realism's treatment of property was the lack of any attempt to explore alternative structures of business property that would directly address the predicament of power. The Realists' general response to the problem was legal regulation, premised on the theory that disinterested experts could best mediate the conflict between discretionary power and the public interest.[167] In this, too, the Realists followed the lead of the Progressives, who laid much of the foundation for the regulatory state generally that is generally associated with the New Deal.[168]

The Realists can hardly be faulted for anticipating that regulation would fail as a solution to the predicament of power that corporate property posed. They can more fairly be faulted, however, for failing to look to the tradition of economic republicanism as an alternative response. As we have seen, that tradition, epitomized by Jacksonian democracy, had also been preoccupied with the problem of power that corporations and corporate property posed. To be sure, the nature of the corporation had fundamentally changed between the Jacksonian period and the post–World War I era, and the problem of corporate property and power was very different from that facing antebellum nineteenth-century Americans. Nevertheless, there were enough shared concerns to make the Jacksonian republicans' response relevant to early twentieth century corporate critics. The most important of these was their common perception of the corporation as a public, or at least quasi-public, institution that affected the entire community. Unlike the Realists, Jacksonian republicans focused on structural means for assuring that that institution and the new form of property that it had introduced into the world of the market did not subvert the interests of democracy. Rather than turning to the state, a response that could only create more dependency, the Jacksonian republicans, as William Simon has observed, "appealed to a vision of an economy designed to encourage small-scale, internally-egalitarian enterprise and to protect small capital against both the state and large [corporate] capital."[169] It was not until the late twentieth century, when the failure of legal regulation to resolve the problem of power seemed obvious to both the political Right and Left, that some legal scholars began to look to that tradition as an alternative.

TWELVE

Property in the Welfare State: Postwar Legal Thought, 1945–1970

WRITING IN 1948, two Yale law professors, Myres McDougal and David Haber, took stock of the situation of property in the mid-twentieth century. "It needs no emphasis that today," they stated in the opening of their innovative Property teaching materials, "the world around, both values and property institutions are undergoing changes of ever increasing magnitude, violence, and irregularity of tempo. In the United States, after two world wars, an immense wave of prosperity, and an unparalleled depression in less than half a century, our property institutions, if not our values, are being subjected to unprecedented strain and stress."[1]

No one could seriously doubt the validity of their assertions. Events of the previous half-century *had* placed tremendous stress on property as an institution. The most obvious of these events, of course, was the Great Depression. Apart from the direct damage to millions of Americans' own property, one of the more serious by-products of the Depression undermining the extant property system was that increasing numbers of Americans now considered socialism an attractive alternative to the economic system that had produced misery for so many.[2] Throughout the 1930s, the future of private ownership of productive assets seemed doubtful to many.

The second development that posed a threat to the institution of private property as classical liberals understood it was organized labor's effort to reshape the economic system along European social-democratic lines.[3] Following World War II, whatever prospects for the success of socialism in America had previously existed were now much dimmer, especially as the reality of socialism in its Stalinist form (an association that many took to be inevitable) became more widely known. Still, there remained forces working to change the economy in ways that would have fundamentally changed property in the corporate setting. Most notably, labor union leaders like Walter Reuther and CIO president Philip Murray aggressively pursued an agenda intended to give labor a voice in setting industrial production goals, corporate investment decisions, and employment policy in key industries.[4] The labor initiative represented an attempt directly to address the problem of power and corporate property by redistributing control over the use of corporate assets from managers to employees. The initiative ultimately failed as anti-labor sentiment, most emphatically symbolized by the Taft-Hartley Act (1947), grew in the late 1940s.

The third and most important development that changed the institution of private property was the rise of the welfare state. The emergence of the prominent role of the state as direct guarantor of social welfare affected American legal thought and discourse concerning property in two opposing ways. First, it stimulated scholarship by lawyers and economists who drew on and revised classical economic theory in critiquing the welfare state in general and the status of property rights in the welfare state in particular. The most notable work in this vein was done at the University of Chicago by economists who had close ties to its law school. The most prominent figures in this group were Ronald Coase and Harold Demsetz. Both men were hostile to the welfare state and its effects on property rights. Their work implicitly adopted a commodified conception of property in an effort to prove that less, not more, government involvement with the market is the path to social welfare. By 1970, their scholarship had already contributed to the advancement of a commodified conception of property in American legal thought.

The other prominent response to the welfare state in legal writing was by those who welcomed welfarism but worried about its consequences for individual autonomy. Legal scholars like Charles Reich sought to protect the personal security of welfare recipients from government oppression by arguing that welfare benefits and other forms of wealth that derived directly from the government *are* property rather than largesse. Their analysis of welfare benefits as property implicitly rejected the commodified conception of property. By 1970, these two responses to the welfare state had emerged clearly enough to indicate that legal thought about property in the late twentieth century was unmistakably dialectical.

The Development of Public Welfare, 1850–1970

The origins of the welfare state in the United States certainly preceded the 1930s, but the welfare state as we now know it first took shape under

Franklin Roosevelt's New Deal policies. Prior to the New Deal, government in general played a very limited role in assisting the poor and protecting economically disadvantaged groups. Poor laws and debtor relief existed but not in the form or on the magnitude of the public relief programs created in the 1930s and especially after 1937. In the nineteenth century, relief of the poor was primarily a matter of private charity and to a lesser extent a local and state government concern. The role of the federal government was virtually nonexistent. The federal attitude was nowhere better expressed than in President Franklin Pierce's 1854 veto of a bill to provide federal relief for the indigent insane (whose author was the influential welfare advocate, Dorothea Dix): "I cannot find any authority in the Constitution for making the Federal Government the great almoner of public charity throughout the United States."[5] In truth, Pierce's opposition to federal social welfare legislation was not based strictly on legal considerations. It was part and parcel of a general ideological opposition to any significant governmental effort to reduce poverty.

Classical liberal economists, both English and American, taught that poverty was the natural condition of the wage-earner. "Poor laws," trying to change the inevitable, were doomed to fail, they asserted. Moreover, by interfering with the natural right of people to accumulate and own property, the poor laws were morally wrong as well.[6] These ideological objections to public welfare were particularly persuasive in the United States, where seemingly unlimited opportunity and abundance made poverty inexplicable on any basis other than personal failure. Crudely describing the so-called culture of poverty in 1897, the influential economist Francis Walker stated, "[P]auperism is largely voluntary. . . . Those who are paupers are so far more from character than from condition. They have the pauper trait; they bear the pauper brand."[7]

The ideological grounds for opposing public welfare began to weaken in the early decades of the twentieth century. Several factors contributed to the gradual relaxing of hostility to governmental efforts to aid the disadvantaged: the growing professionalization of social workers;[8] industrialization of the economy, which appeared to change the causes of unemployment and poverty in ways that made the individual seem less responsible, less failed; and the "gospel of prevention," which provided a leading role for government as the best mechanism for preventing, not simply alleviating, poverty.[9] Still, government's role in welfare assistance remained limited and sporadic through the first several decades of the twentieth century. As of 1929, the federal government spent no money on public relief except for Indian wards, veterans, seamen, and a few institutions.[10] At the state level, the picture was hardly more encouraging. In 1930, no state provided unemployment insurance, and most state spending on welfare went to construction and maintenance of custodial institutions like almshouses.[11] Several states went so far as to disenfranchise anyone who received public assistance.[12] The one area in which public welfare was commonly accepted by 1930 was in family assistance. Championed as efforts to preserve the family, so-called widows' pension and mothers' aid laws, which were the foundation for the Aid to Dependent Children program in the 1935 Social Security Act.[13] While public welfare for women and children, as the deserving poor, was acceptable, other forms of public assistance remained tainted by old nineteenth-century attitudes.

The New Deal ushered in a different attitude toward public welfare. While the New Deal programs themselves did not in fact fundamentally alter the nation's economic or social structure (nor were they intended to),[14] they eventually laid the foundation for a new premise underlying welfare programs. The new assumption was that government has the primary, not simply residual, responsibility for the economic security of its citizens.[15] Although this "statist" premise was most conspicuous in the 1960s programs of Lyndon Johnson, it was apparent both earlier, in parts of the New Deal, and even later in the Nixon and Reagan years. As Alan Brinkley has pointed out, "[T]he New Deal was not only an effort to deal with the particular problems of the 1930s; it was also a process of building government institutions where none existed, of choosing among various prescriptions for an expanded American state."[16] The prescriptions that the Roosevelt administrations chose gave the federal government a wider role in economic life than it had previously had, although certainly nothing close to the dominant, or "socialist," role that conservative (i.e., classical liberal) critics charged.

The New Deal provided two important contributions to the true welfare state that emerged in the 1960s. First, it created the four-part structure that constituted much of the social welfare state over the next forty years: general relief, funded by state and local governments; work relief, funded by the federal government; categorical assistance for the needy over sixty-five, blind people, and dependent children; and social insurance providing pensions to retired workers and temporary unemployment compensation.[17]

The New Deal's second contribution was ideological. It repudiated the old ideological tenet that poverty was a cultural problem and replaced it with the understanding of poverty as an economic problem.[18] The change was crucial, for it paved the way for the view that public welfare is a right. Much of the credit for this ideological change belongs to a segment of the social work profession that rejected the profession's traditional ideology of "condescending moralism."[19] Charlotte Towle, a prominent exponent of this branch of the profession, expressed its basic commitment in her influential book, *Common Human Needs:* "We place a great deal of emphasis on the individual's *right* to assistance in the belief that it dignifies, that it frees him from humiliation, and that it leaves him unshackled by feelings of personal obligation to the agency."[20] This attitude dominated the Federal Bureau of Public Assistance, the predecessor of the current Social Security Administration, as early as 1935.[21] It was also evident in the first Social Security Act (1935), which included a provision expressly recognizing a right to a hearing on a claim of wrongful denial of welfare benefits.[22]

The New Deal, then, was the first sustained reaction by the federal government to widespread public anxiety about economic security following a national economic depression. Yet while it laid the foundation for the modern American welfare state, the welfare state that it created was crude and rudimentary, certainly nothing like the welfare state that exists today. The idea of the federal government as the source of an economic "safety net" for all citizens—the core of modern American domestic policy—was hardly conceived, let alone accepted as policy, by the end of the New Deal.

If the modern American welfare state was not the creation of the New Deal, it was hardly the product of the period between the end of World War II and 1960. Concerning public welfare policy, that period is best described as one of "benign neglect."[23] To be sure, existing welfare programs continued, and Congress even added several programs.[24] Moreover, Congress amended certain programs, especially Aid For Dependent Children and old age, survivors, and disability insurance, that considerably liberalized benefits.[25] Even with these changes, though, neither social insurance nor welfare programs made a dent in reducing poverty within any single socioeconomic category, let alone the entire population. What was completely absent in government policy between 1945 and 1960 was a commitment to eliminate national poverty through a commitment of government resources.

Several factors contributed to this pervasive neglect among policy makers. One was the widespread perception that after the war, with the prosperity that the postwar era had brought to millions of Americans, poverty simply did not exist, or at least that it was limited to small, isolated communities.[26] Perhaps the most striking expression of this perception was Harvard economist J. K. Galbraith's best-selling book *The Affluent Society.*[27] Galbraith, incredibly, claimed that poverty was a uniquely "minority problem" that existed only in areas like Appalachia. The claim was wildly inaccurate, but it was widely shared among policy makers and policy analysts. Most analysts believed, in James Patterson's words, that the poverty that remained after the war would "wither away." That was not Galbraith's view, but the main message that he intended his book to convey—that poverty and unemployment stemmed from structural problems in the economy—was largely lost on readers.[28]

Related to the perception that poverty did not exist was another key factor in the postwar decline of government welfare efforts—a deeply conservative political climate. The combination of McCarthyism and the Red Scare, leading to deep distrust of any government policy that vaguely smelled of socialism, and a conservative political coalition in Congress made any sort of large-scale federal welfare campaign virtually unthinkable. Added to those obvious factors was an intellectual environment that was decidedly unsympathetic to public anti-poverty programs. Between 1945 and 1960, leading social scientists, reflecting a pervasive attitude,[29] emphasized the classless, consensual character of the United States. "As far as the bulk of Western society is concerned," the noted sociologist Robert Nisbet declared in 1959, "and especially in the United States, the conception of class is largely obsolete."[30] Another group of social scientists, the conservative functionalists, acknowledged the continuing existence of economic stratification and class distinctions, but they dismissed it as a problem that could never be solved. As James Patterson has pointed out, "[c]onservative functionalism . . . was matter-of-fact if not complacent about poverty and economic inequality."[31]

A very different attitude emerged in the 1960s. There is no clear consensus regarding the reasons for the change in attitude and public policy regarding welfare in the early 1960s.[32] One theory emphasizes the role of the great migration of African Americans from impoverished rural areas in the South to the cities of the North in search of jobs and racial equality. The migration,[33] the argument goes, led to a dramatic increase in the number of people receiving public assistance, as the newly displaced citizens were unable to find the jobs in an economy that had less and less need for unskilled labor.[34] Challenging this explanation, Frances Piven and Richard Cloward have argued that the increase in the relief roles was "a political response to political disorder."[35] Governments increased the amount of public assistance, Piven and Cloward contend, in order to mollify discontented northern urban Blacks, who now constituted a significant political force.[36]

Whether the dynamic was strictly demographic or political, it is clear that the increase in public assistance in the early 1960s *was* dramatic[37] and that it focused public attention on the problem of poverty. Books and articles about poverty in America began to appear almost as soon as the decade began. Among these, by far the most influential was Michael Harrington's *The Other America.* Harrington argued that what made it possible to perceive America as "the affluent society" was the fact that most poverty in the United States was invisible:

> The other America, the America of poverty, is hidden today in a way that it never was before. Its millions are socially invisible to us. No wonder that so many misinterpreted Galbraith's title and assumed that "the affluent society" meant that everyone had a decent standard of life. The misinterpretation was true as far as the actual day-to-day lives of two-thirds of the nation were concerned.[38]

Harrington's book and other writing on American poverty paid dividends in government policy. President Kennedy conceived of the so-called War on Poverty initiative after reading Harrington and other critics of American welfare policy.[39] Even before the War on Poverty was launched, federal spending on welfare was significantly increased through legislation like the 1962 Public Welfare Amendments to the Social Security Act.[40]

The centerpiece of the War on Poverty, which Lyndon Johnson announced in 1964, was the Equal Opportunity Act. That Act was at once ambitious and stingy. Its explicit aim was to end poverty (which, of course, it utterly failed to do), but the Act itself increased federal welfare spending only by a modest amount.[41] Like much else of the federal approach to welfare during these years, its announced aim was, as Sar Levitan has characterized it, "to restructure society by giving the poor a chance to design and administer antipoverty programs."[42] The truth is, though, that the federal welfare programs of the Great Society were far more intrusive and paternalistic than they had ever been before.[43]

The social welfare system developed into its present form primarily between 1965 and 1975.[44] The crucial development in this maturation was a gradual movement from programs that relied heavily on insurance principles, according to which benefits depended on level to one's contributions, to a more eclectic approach that blended programs funded from general revenues with wage contribution-based programs. The upshot of this shift in funding principles was that the line between social insurance and public assistance increasingly became blurred.[45] As one policy analyst succinctly put it, "Entitlement to income security has become less individually earned and more a social right of citizenship."[46] That change in expectation—the conception of welfare benefits as entitlements—was the central predicament of property for American legal scholars in the postwar period.

Property in the Welfare State
Institutional Changes in Property

Welfarism as a state policy fundamentally changed private property, both as a social institution and as a legal concept. As an institution, property in the welfare state was more obviously public than it had been throughout the nineteenth century. Three characteristics defined the mid-twentieth century American welfare state:

> (1) a vast increase in the range and detail of government regulation of privately owned economic enterprise; (2) the direct furnishing of services by government to individual members of the national community—unemployment and retirement benefits, family allowances, low-cost housing, medical care, and the like; and (3) increasing government ownership and operation of industries and businesses which, at an earlier time, were or would have been operated for profit by individuals or private corporations.[47]

All three of these characteristics overtly shifted the character of property from the private to the public realm. Welfare benefit programs, of which Social Security (first created in 1935) was the prototype, had the effect of identifying the government as the direct source not simply of "services" but wealth for increasing numbers of Americans. To be sure, during the 1930s, Social Security played only a limited role in providing income through its retirement and unemployment insurance programs.[48] Still, even during these early years its effect was to challenge the classical liberal principle that people should acquire property only through private means—creation, or more commonly, or market exchange. The government was now a third source of wealth for millions of Americans.

A related institutional change was that regulation increasingly weakened the prerogatives of private property, particularly business property. Most New Dealers were strongly committed to an "aggressively statist" approach to the economy for the purpose of protecting consumers and workers. New Deal policy makers considered these two groups to be particularly ill-served by unregulated corporate capitalism, and they pushed for legislation that sought to protect vulnerable groups by imposing mandatory contractual terms and creating new regulatory regimes for certain industries.[49] Legislation like the Communications Act (1934), the Railroad Retirement Act (1934), the Fair Labor Standards Act (1937), the Public Utilities Holding Company Act of 1935 (the Wheeler-Rayburn law), and, above all, the Wagner Act (1935) altered many of the prerogatives of private property ownership for employers and business owners, although they were far from producing the radical revision of property relations that many opponents feared they would.[50]

The social legislation of the 1960s, especially the Great Society programs, deepened this institutional change in property. State as well as federal legislation greatly extended the range of property relationships that were subject to government regulation. Housing is a particularly striking example. The relationship between landlords and their tenants, which traditionally was subject to minimal legal regulation, underwent a massive legal change during the 1960s.[51] Federal legislation like the Fair Housing Act of 1968 prohibited discrimination in the private housing market on the basis of race, religion, gender, and national origin.[52] At the state level, many states, prompted by court decisions, enacted statutes creating a "warranty of habitability" that guaranteed tenants the right to live in safe and livable conditions. These statutes reversed the traditional legal rule that allocated to tenants the responsibility for the care and condition of rental housing. The most important aspect of this new "warranty" was that it was nonwaivable; landlords and tenants could not bargain around the new warranty even if they were so inclined. The overall effect of these and other changes was to remove landlord and tenant relations, especially in the residential context, from the realm of private ordering to the domain of public regulation. The new regulatory regime withdrew from landlords many of the traditional prerogatives of property ownership.

Changes in the Idea of Property in the Welfare State

The welfare state affected ideas and attitudes toward property at least as much as it did the institution of property. For Americans, the emergence of the modern welfare state created a legitimacy crisis concerning property in a way that it never did for Europeans, whose legal-political-economic orders had shifted to welfarism considerably earlier. European legal and nonlegal thought regarding property was explicitly dialectical even before the appearance of the modern welfare state. Legal concepts such as "social obligation of ownership" (*soziale Pflichtigkeit*), today enshrined in the German Basic Law[53] but much older in origin, expressed the extant popular understanding that private property rights were not trumps.

Americans lacked the same tradition of consciousness about the dialectic character of property. Prior to the New Deal, although American legal and popular thought about property in fact was dialectical, most Americans denied that there was a dialectic between property as commodity and property as the foundation for civic order. The ideology of individual autonomy blurred the civic half of the dialectic. While American lawyers today recognize that there is no inherent contradiction between the institution of private property and a regulated economy, that point was much less clear to self-styled defenders of private property at the time of the New Deal. Those who associated private property with unregulated markets viewed the growth of the federal government's regulatory apparatus under the New Deal as signaling the end of private property. It was not, of course; it was only the end of private property as they knew it.

The most fundamental effect of the social welfare programs on the idea of property was that they undermined the commodity conception. Various types of property which traditionally were regarded as market assets came to be seen as serving other, nonmarket functions. On those occasions when free market transferability seemed to threatened these functions, the law changed to protect the noncommodified aspects of property arrangements.

Landlord-and-tenant law again provides a clear example. The "revolution," as it has been called,[54] in the law regulating landlord-tenant relations was based on the implicit premise that residential housing should not be treated solely as a market asset, subject to being bought or sold on whatever terms the parties want. At least as important as the economic function is a political-moral function: residential housing is one of the crucial material conditions that determine whether and how people will flourish personally and as citizens.[55] Courts and legal scholars explained the legal changes creating new rights for tenants as based on a shift from antiquated feudal property law to contract law, but that account was very misleading. The new tenants' rights rules were not entirely consistent with contract law and certainly were not contractarian in the sense of reflecting a commitment to private ordering. The real basis for the overall doctrinal shift was a change in how the legal culture perceived the character of residential housing. Margaret Jane Radin has articulated the new perception that underlies legal protection of the tenant's interest in this way:

> A tenancy, no less than a single-family house, is the sort of property interest in which a person becomes self-invested; and after the self-investment has taken place, retention of the interest becomes a priority claim over curtailment of merely fungible interests of others. To pursue the parallel with home ownership, there the owner's interest is personal and the mortgagee's interest is fungible. That is why it seems right to safeguard the owner from losing her home even if it means some curtailment of the mortgagee's interest.[56]

That is, while the landlord's interest, like the mortgage lender's is (usually) strictly financial—a commodity—the tenant's property interest is primarily personal and only secondarily financial. Tenants enter into leases primarily to have a home, a place in which to belong, not as an investment. Protecting that personal interest means treating it as at least somewhat outside the domain of market ordering, in which the rights and duties of the two sides are set through the process of bargaining. The new landlord-tenant rules replaced bargaining with legally imposed terms regulating the relationship precisely to protect the tenant's noncommodity interest from the possibly corrosive effects of the market.

Welfare programs that created government benefits for the poor, the elderly, and the disadvantaged also made the commodity character of property problematic but in a different way. A critical aspect of commodity ownership is that it liberates the individual owner from dependency on the state, or at least it minimizes the degree to which the owner is subject to state control. Under fully commodified ownership, owners are free to decide how to use or sell their property so that they may satisfy their preferences as they see fit. Recipients of government benefits generally lack that degree of autonomous control over the wealth that the state transfers to them. The benefits may be subject to various state-imposed conditions and restrictions, but even where they are not, the welfare recipient is still beholden to the state. The most vivid manifestation of that personal insecurity is that the government may (and in some cases, has) terminate the program and, therefore, the benefits, altogether. That degree of personal insecurity is, at least theoretically, inconsistent with commodity ownership.

Scholars responded to this predicament generally in two ways. Classical liberals, who regarded the minimal state as the only political regime that is compatible with individual freedom, argued that the welfare state had to be dismantled. Beginning in the 1940s, classical liberals like Friedrich Hayek mounted a strong campaign against all forms of government economic planning, in which they included most welfare programs, as undermining the rule of law. The rule of law ideal presupposed, they argued, hard-and-fast rules that minimize the degree of central discretion and intervention. Welfare programs rely on an approach of "administrative coercion and discrimination"[57] that contradicts that requirement.

Welfare rights advocates responded to the traditional liberal critique by propertizing welfare benefits. In effect, these scholars conceded the basic premise of the Hayekian argument, that a discretionary welfare regime jeopardizes the rule-of-law ideal and individual freedom, but they rejected the conclusion that the welfare state had to be sacrificed to protect individual liberty. These reformist liberals, of whom the Yale law professor Charles Reich was the most prominent legal scholar, tried to accommodate the welfare state with the rule of law by doctrinally transforming welfare benefits from largess into legally protected property.

These two responses defined the parameters of political-legal discourse about property in the welfare state for much of the mid- to late-twentieth century. As we will see, they created a dialectic about the commodity conception of property that was apparent and increasingly contentious by the last quarter of the century.

The Dilemma of the Rule of Law in the Welfare State

No book attacking the whole idea of the welfare state was more influential in the postwar period than Friedrich Hayek's *The Road to Serfdom*, first published in 1944. Hayek did not write for a legal audience; indeed, he did not write for an American audience. He wrote the book during the war years while he was teaching at the University of London, intending it, he stated, to be "a warning to the socialist intelligentsia of England."[58] Still, he considered its lessons to be equally relevant to his unexpected American audience. Nor, in his view, did the passage of time and the dwindling influence of socialism, strictly so called, diminish that relevance. In the foreword to the first American paperback edition, published in 1956, he suggested that "although hot socialism is probably a thing of the past, some of its conceptions have penetrated far too deeply into the whole structure of current thought to justify complacency." He cautioned that the "hodgepodge of ill-assembled and often inconsistent ideals which under the name of the Welfare State has largely replaced socialism as the goal of the reformers needs very careful sorting-out if its results are not to be very similar to those of full-fledged socialism."[59]

Hayek articulated the core principle of his attack on government economic intervention at the beginning of the book's most crucial chapter, entitled "Planning and the Rule of Law": "Nothing distinguishes more clearly conditions in a free country from those in a country under arbitrary government than the observance in the former of the great principles known as the Rule of Law."[60] The "essential point," Hayek asserted, was that "the discretion left to the executive organs wielding coercive power should be reduced as much as possible."[61] Minimizing official discretion requires, he contended, strict adherence to the rule of law, which he defined as a system of formal rules. Formal rules "do not aim at the wants and needs of particular people." Rather, "[t]hey are intended to be merely instrumental in the pursuit of people's various individual ends."[62] A regime of formal rules is the opposite of a regime of collectivist planning, Hayek argued. Government planners "must provide for the actual needs of people as they arise and then choose deliberately between them."[63]

Hayek's argument for reducing to the absolute minimum the amount of discretion—i.e., coercive power—government officials can wield was really an elaboration on the same theme that Stephen J. Field had developed in the Supreme Court's constitutional property cases throughout the late nineteenth century.[64] Like Field, Hayek thought that equality, that is, formally equal treatment of all groups and individuals, was the root of the matter. Government planning decisions inevitably are unequal; they involve choices of one group or another, creating a hierarchy that resembles feudal society:

> [Government planning decisions] depend inevitably on the circumstances of the moment, and, in making such decisions, it will always be necessary to balance one against the other the interests of various persons and groups. In the end somebody's views will have to decide whose interests are more important; and these views will become part of the law of the land, a new distinction of rank which the coercive apparatus of government imposes upon the people.[65]

This phenomenon exists, Hayek argued, not only under socialist planning, strictly so called, but in any political system that attempts to provide for the substantive welfare of the less well-off. Substantive equality as a government policy is fundamentally incompatible with formal equality:

> [F]ormal equality before the law is in conflict, and in fact incompatible, with any activity of government deliberately aiming at material or substantive equality of different people, and . . any policy aiming directly at a substantive ideal of distributive justice must lead to the destruction of the Rule of Law. To produce the same result for different people, it is necessary to treat them differently. To give different people the same objective opportunities is not to give them the same subjective chance.[66]

Respect for the rule of law did not foreclose all regulation of business interests or other forms of property. It required only that regulations meet two conditions: they must be permanent and must be general in application. Permanent and general restrictions are compatible with individual liberty because they provide the necessary information for individuals to plan their affairs around them. But most modern welfare state laws satisfied neither of these requirements. Most were administrative provisions over which state agencies had a great deal of discretion to change, overtly or through interpretation. Generality posed an even greater problem. Both in England and the United States, welfare laws were intended to benefit particular groups. True, by aiding disadvantaged portions of the populations, they would enhance the welfare of the entire community, but Hayek's requirement of generality could not be so easily satisfied. The law itself could not single out particular persons or groups for special treatment, but that is precisely how most welfare laws operated. The unavoidable upshot of Hayek's theory, then, was that the great bulk of government welfare policy on both sides of the Atlantic violated the rule of law and, consequently, deeply encroached on individual liberty.

Hayek was hardly the first to develop the thesis of the inevitable conflict between the rule of law and the welfare state. As he himself acknowledged, he followed a tradition that dated back at least to the late nineteenth century, when the modern welfare state first began to emerge. What Hayek contributed to that tradition was an intellectual coherence and a relevance to the mid-twentieth century that no other work approached. In particular, his argument rejected the Anglo-American conception of the rule of law ideal earlier described and defended by the Oxford political theorist Albert Venn Dicey. In two notable books, *Law and Public Opinion*[67] and *Law of the Constitution,*[68] Dicey, like Hayek, had contended that the rule of law and the administrative welfare state were irreconcilable. Dicey's critics have long attacked his argument as relying on a warped understanding of administrative law in welfare systems like those in France and Germany.[69] What has been less noticed is the provincialism that underlies his identification of the rule of law with the English common law system. The common law, for all of its homage to precedent, is also an intensively particularistic system. Even more telling, perhaps its greatest strength has been its impermanence and malleability, yet that characteristic can easily be viewed as precisely the sort of discretionary power that the classical rule-of-law ideal spurned. Hayek's rejection of Dicey's exposition of the rule of law idea was less a product of his own provincial admiration for the German *Rechtsstaat* than it was a desire to develop a normative theory of the state that repudiates all forms of arbitrary collective power.

Hayek's theory had clear implications for the role of property in a free (as he defined it) society. The market society was the only truly free society. Nothing short of a thoroughly commodified conception of property was consistent with individual liberty. The entire thrust of Hayek's critique was to maximize the individual's power to pursue her own ends. Hayek, along with Ludwig von Mises and others in the Austrian school of economics,[70] stressed that government economic planning was fatally flawed for informational reasons. The argument actually had two dimensions, economic and moral. The economic concern is that government planners simply could never have all of the information necessary to satisfy individual preferences. Only individuals have access to that information, and consequently they must be allowed to plan their own affairs.

The moral argument rests on the familiar classical liberal conception of the subjectivity of ends. Hayek considered that the state should be neutral with respect to ends. Values are inherently subjective, and only each person can define what is best for herself. When the state takes it upon itself to satisfy preferences for members of society, it cannot be neutral; it must takes sides and choose ends for people.[71]

Within the framework of this theory, the function of property is set. Property has only one role to play—to satisfy individual preferences. To fulfill that role, property must be free from collective constraints on use, possession, and, most important of all, transfer. No constraint can be justified on the basis of realizing a substantive, nonconsensual vision of the common good or promoting the virtuous republic. The state's core legitimate function is to facilitate individual attempts to satisfy personal preferences, which will ordinarily occur through market transactions. Property, then, must always (or nearly always) be available as market property, or commodity.

Hayek's critique was widely read and debated by American legal scholars, as well as economists and political theorists. For those on the political Right, Hayek's critique was a compelling tocsin against the dangerous path the federal government had taken since the New Deal. His message was especially welcomed and influential at the University of Chicago, which had already established itself as the center of a free market-oriented approach to legal and economic analysis. Hayek moved to the University of Chicago in 1950, largely through the efforts of Aaron Director, an economist on the Chicago law faculty. As George Stigler and other have acknowledged,[72] Director himself was perhaps the single most influential economist at Chicago at the time, influencing members of both the economics department and the law school. Hayek was appointed to the university's famous Committee on Social Thought rather than its economics department because of some resistance from members of that department.[73] The money for Hayek's appointment came from a private foundation, the Volker Fund, which was active from the late 1940s through the mid-1970s in supporting free market studies at Chicago and elsewhere.[74]

Hayek remained at Chicago for ten years, returning to Europe in 1960. That period saw the first significant growth of law-and-economics studies at Chicago, and Hayek influenced, directly and indirectly, all of the major figures of that movement, including Milton Friedman, George Stigler, Aaron Director, and others. Hayek's anti-interventionist theory was reflected in a variety of channels from the University of Chicago Law School, including its highly influential (and first of its kind) periodical devoted exclusively to legal economics, the *Journal of Law & Economics*. In describing the mission of that journal, Edward H. Levi, president of the University of Chicago, simultaneously described Hayek's outlook: "*The Journal of Law and Economics*," Levi stated, "represents a commitment to the continuing examination of policy questions which concern individual freedom and the protective or coercive force of law."[75] More than anyone else, Hayek provided the foundation for broadening the appeal of the Chicago noninterventionist approach outside the narrow confines of technical economics.

Legal scholars who were not committed to the far Right were unpersuaded by Hayek's attack on the welfare state. Harry W. Jones reflected the reaction of many in stating that "the mature law of any country is not and never has been as heedless of distributive justice—as blind to 'the particular needs of different people'—as Hayek would have it."[76] There was no prospect of dismantling the welfare state to the minimalist state that Hayek's conception of the rule of law required. The serious question that Hayek's unrealistic and unduly narrow understanding of the rule of law failed to resolve for liberals was not *whether,* but *how* to reconcile the rule-of-law ideal, for which private property is the fundamental mechanism for guarding individual autonomy, with the welfare state. It was not the Hayekians but liberals of a very different stripe, whom we can loosely call reformist liberals, who made the most serious effort to resolve that problem. No single piece of scholarship better exemplified that effort or advanced its cause, albeit only briefly, than Charles A. Reich's famous 1964 article, "The New Property."[77]

The Origins and Development of the "New Property"

In a retrospective on his article, Reich summarized its basic objective. "*The New Property,*" Reich stated, "was written twenty-five years ago as a suggestion for the legal effort to build a system of protection for the individual."[78] Reich thought that the nation was experiencing a "crisis of the individual."[79] The crisis that he saw reflected the pivotal, Janus-faced character of the time at which he wrote. Looking in one direction, the memory of McCarthyesque government tyranny of individual liberty was still very fresh. Reich cited a wide array of more recent instances in which the government had taken steps to repress dissident behavior by cutting off government benefits or denying government-granted licenses. It was easy to view those cases as latter-day McCarthyism. But the cases could be viewed from a different perspective, one that required looking to the future. The victims that Reich identified, unlike their McCarthyite predecessors, were all dependent in some direct way on the government for their livelihood. Their personal wealth derived directly from the government, making them insecure even before the government had taken any repressive action against them. That condition—direct personal dependency on the government for the very means of one's existence—has since become a major feature of American life and the overriding problem associated with the welfare state.

The cases that Reich cited as evidence of the crisis all were instances of a continuing, if less conspicuous, threat to individual freedom by direct government repression: a cut-off of Social Security benefits to a recipient who had once been a member of the Communist Party,[80] a denial of welfare benefits to a mother who was living with a man out of wedlock,[81] a refusal to admit to the bar a man who refused to answer questions concerning membership in "subversive" organizations.[82] Joseph McCarthy might be dead, but it was still "scoundrel time."[83]

What connected all these was the growing dependence of Americans of government largess that was subject to substantive conditions. As Robert Rabin has observed, "The major contribution of Reich's article was to pull together the multiple strands of conditional largess apparent in government programs and activities ranging across the spectrum of jobs, welfare benefits, grants-in-aid, license and franchises, and to link these forms of 'new property' to the corresponding insistence that recipients meet appropriate behavioral standards."[84]

No case better illustrated this phenomenon, or provoked Reich's anxiety, than the Supreme Court's 1960 decision in *Flemming v. Nestor.*[85] Nestor, who had immigrated to the United States from Bulgaria in 1913, had been receiving Social Security retirement benefits since 1955, when he was deported to his native country for his membership in the Communist Party between 1933 and 1939. Membership in "subversive organizations" at any time was one of the statutory bases for termination of old-age benefits, and the government terminated his benefits shortly after it deported him. He challenged the action as a deprivation of his property under the due process clause. The Supreme Court held that Nestor's interest in Social Security benefits was not an "accrued property right" protectible against the government's substantive interference. It was a weaker sort of interest that was protectible only against arbitrary government action, which, the Court said, was not involved in the case.

Reich characterized the *Flemming* Court's theory as "the philosophy of feudal tenure."[86] It treated his interest in Social Security benefits as nonvested, subject to conditions designed to compel the performance of certain duties. "Just as the feudal system linked lord and vassal through a system of mutual dependence, obligation, and loyalty," Reich objected, "so government largess binds man to the state."[87] The bond that it creates between recipients and the state, more to the point, was one that deprived individuals of their very freedom, precisely the same objection that Hayek had leveled against the welfare state.

Reich's objection was essentially the same as Hayek's: state welfare officials possessed discretionary power that undermined rule-of-law protections that are the basis of individual liberty. Moreover, like Hayek,

Reich argued that conditional welfare threatens individual freedom unequally:

> Inequalities lie deep in the administrative structure of government largess. The whole process of acquiring it and keeping it favors some applicants and recipients over others. The administrative process is characterized by uncertainty, delay, and inordinate expense; to operate within it requires considerable know-how. All these factors strongly favor larger, richer, more experienced companies or individuals over smaller ones.[88]

Reich's solution to the dilemma of government largess and the rule of law was not to dismantle the welfare state but to add *procedural* protections that would simultaneously strengthen its rule-of-law character and bolster the welfare state. The key was to treat government largess as "property," and not simply as wealth. Reich's argument for bestowing the legal status of property on government-derived wealth was straightforwardly liberal. The central function of property, he argued, is to "draw a boundary between public and private power." Within the private sphere, "the majority has to yield to the owner."[89] Political rights serve the same function, but political rights are dependent on property. Property rights are, as it were, "the guardian of every other right."

Reich's category of government largess was broad and extremely varied. Professional licenses, taxicab medallions, AFDC benefits, Social Security retirement benefits were all treated as one piece. Reich did not distinguish between those interests, like AFDC, that the government granted strictly on the basis of need, and those that represented some form of social insurance, to which the beneficiary had made lifetime contributions, the sort involved in *Flemming v. Nestor*. From the perspective of their "property-ness," the former was the far more troublesome sort of government largess. The latter type of benefit, an example of which Efraim Nestor was deprived, was not truly largesse. Social Security retirement benefits, like other forms of social insurance, are easily squared with the classical liberal theory of the legitimate means of acquiring property rights. They are a benefit acquired through one's labor; they *are* an entitlement precisely because they are *earned*.[90] Much more problematic is the true welfare benefit, that is, the benefit that one receives from the government merely by virtue of one's need. Treating benefits of this sort as property cannot be reconciled with classical liberal theory, as Hayek saw it.

Reich's notable contribution was to revise the liberal theory of property in a way that justified legal recognition of this form of government-derived wealth, the true welfare benefit, as individually owned property.

Due process, procedural and substantive, was Reich's primary tool for transforming largess into property. Procedurally, he called for the familiar due process safeguards—notice, hearing and contest, judicial review— for all government actions affecting largess. Substantively, he suggested that largess should be regulated the same way that traditional property is regulated, and that forfeiture should be used only as a last resort:

> The presumption should be that the professional man will keep his license, and the welfare recipient his pension. These interests should be "vested." If revocation is necessary, not by reason of the fault of the individual holder, but by reason of overriding demands of public policy, perhaps payment of just compensation would be appropriate. The individual should not bear the entire loss for a remedy primarily intended to benefit the community.[91]

Reich's theory bore fruit quickly but only temporarily. Welfare rights lawyers, eager to find a doctrinal basis for securing their clients' vulnerable interests against government threats, drew on Reich's proposals in litigation involving welfare suspensions and terminations.[92]

Reich was not the only legal scholar whose ideas influenced welfare rights lawyers. They drew on ideas developed in articles by Jacobus tenBroek,[93] Joel Handler,[94] and others.[95] One whose influence on advocacy lawyers was as least as great as Reich's, if not more so, was Edward V. Sparer, dubbed by some the "welfare law guru."[96] Sparer, the founder and director of several influential public interest law firms, including Mobilization for Youth Legal Services, the Columbia University Center on Social Welfare Policy and Law, and the Health Law Project at the University of Pennsylvania,[97] was one of the leaders of the welfare rights social movement, first as an activist lawyer and later as an academic.[98] His overriding objective was to gain legal recognition of a constitutional "right to live," which basically translated into a guaranteed minimum income. While many of his ideas were consistent with Reich's approach,[99] his right-to-live theory went substantially beyond the strategy of formalizing the legal protection of entitlements and was far more controversial. The lawyers who argued the case before the Supreme Court compromised the dispute over which theory to press by offering watered-down versions of both.[100]

The basic point they pushed was that welfare benefits were entitlements, a form of property protected by certain mandatory procedural requirements, including a right to a prior hearing.

Measured in terms of doctrinal change, the welfare lawyers' efforts—and the ideas of Reich and Sparer—were rapidly but only temporarily successful. Between 1968 and 1970, the Court decided in their favor in three major decisions.[101] The story in the last of these, *Goldberg v. Kelly*,[102] presented a textbook example of the sort of government abuse that Reich and others had in mind. John Kelly, a twenty-nine-year-old homeless African American, was struck by a hit-and-run driver in New York City and disabled.[103] Qualifying for the state's home relief program, he received a biweekly check of $80.05, his sole source of income. Kelly's caseworker told him to move into the Barbara Hotel, a flophouse that was a hangout for drug addicts and alcoholics. After spending a few nights in the hotel, Kelly moved out, but he continued to use the Barbara as his mailing address. When he went by the hotel to pick up his welfare check a few weeks later, the front desk clerk told him that his benefits had been terminated because he moved out. Kelly tried to contact his caseworker, but she refused to talk to him. He contacted a social worker with Mobilization for Youth (MFY), a poverty law organization operating on the Lower East Side in New York City. MFY's lawyers had been looking for a suitable client to use in test case challenging welfare agency procedures, and John Kelly presented the ideal set of facts they needed.

What welfare rights lawyers wanted for clients like John Kelly was not simply a fair hearing but a hearing *before* benefits were terminated. Reich's theory that welfare benefits were property protected by procedural due process rights—the "formalization of entitlement"[104]—provided the means for getting what the MFY lawyers wanted for their clients, or so they thought.

The Court in *Goldberg* held that the fourteenth amendment due process clause requires that a welfare recipient be given a pretermination evidentiary hearing. Speaking through Justice Brennan, the Court explicitly acknowledged the propertyness of welfare benefits, stating that "[s]uch benefits are a matter of statutory entitlement for persons qualified to receive them."[105] Citing Reich, Justice Brennan endorsed his "new property" thesis: "It may be realistic today to regard welfare entitlements as more like 'property' than a 'gratuity.' Much of the existing wealth in this country takes the form of rights that do not fall within traditional common-law concepts of property."[106] "Public assistance," he stated, "is not charity, but a means to 'promote the general Welfare, and secure the blessings of Liberty to ourselves and our Posterity.'"[107] Brennan's opinion, however, said nothing that indicated that the Court was prepared to recognize a substantive right to welfare.[108]

Any lingering doubts that the Court might recognize such a right were resolved against it later the same term. In *Dandridge v. Williams*,[109] the Court held that there was no constitutional violation when Maryland enacted a law limiting AFDC monthly payments to $250 regardless of family size. Despite the fact that this left many families with less than 60 percent of the state's calculated minimum need, the Court concluded that the rule was constitutionally valid because it was "rationally based and free from invidious discrimination." "The Constitution may impose certain procedural safeguards upon systems of welfare administration," the Court stated, citing *Goldberg v. Kelly*. "But the Constitution does not empower this Court to second-guess state officials charged with the difficult responsibility of allocating limited public welfare funds among the myriad of potential recipients."[110]

Even the victory in *Goldberg* was short-lived. In the early 1970s many states restructured public assistance programs like AFDC in ways that not only tightened eligibility standards but also made the process of determining eligibility vastly more bureaucratic and impersonal.[111] The responsibility for supplying proof to establish initial and continuing eligibility was shifted from caseworkers to recipients, and the character of required proof became more complex and technical. Moreover, the front-line administrative personnel with whom recipients had to deal for financial assistance matters changed from professionally trained social workers to nonprofessional "eligibility technicians."[112] The combined effect of these changes, along with large federal budget cuts, was, as Sparer put it, "to cut welfare grant levels and remove eligibility for major groups of poor people."[113]

The Dilemma of the New Property and the Civic Conception of Property

On the surface, Reich's theory seems to reflect a commodificationist understanding of property rather than a civic outlook. Explicitly individualist in its premises, the theory lends itself to being interpreted in terms of what Frank Michelman has called the "possessive conception" of constitutional property rights.[114] By that, Michelman means the idea that property is a negative claim that the owner has against others, including the state, not to interfere with her use, possession, and enjoyment of her property.

Most immediately, the claim includes the right to be free from redistributive actions by the state that take away any portion of one's interest in her property. The possessive conception captures the core of the classical liberal understanding of property that is often attributed to Locke and that C. B. Macpherson labeled "possessive individualism."[115]

Reich's theory had one foot at least tentatively planted in that tradition. As others have noted,[116] his premises were starkly individualist, and the theory stressed the need to protect the right of possession of assets that fell into the new category of property he had identified. Moreover, as William Simon has pointed out,[117] the new property theory had antiredistributive consequences that posed a dilemma that Reich apparently did not recognize. While the theory was intended to support the redistributive programs of the welfare state, it in fact undermines their legitimacy. By urging that the old and new property be treated alike, both vested and both entitled to just compensation for any government-induced impairment, Reich unintentionally made it impossible for the state to fund the new property. As Simon succinctly puts it, "If all wealth is to be regarded as 'vested,' then there can be no coercive redistribution."[118] Redistributing wealth to provide welfare benefits for some inevitably requires that the state interfere with the putatively vested property rights of others.

However much Reich's rhetoric may have resembled Michelman's possessive conception of constitutional property, the theory's fundamental thrust was in a very different direction, a direction much closer to a noncommodified, civic understanding of property. The fact that Reich's theory *was* intended to legitimate the redistributive activities of the welfare state itself puts considerable distance between it and the classical liberal outlook on property. As we have discussed, the tenets of classical liberalism require, as Hayek saw, not only that property always be available for market exchange but that any transfers of property from one person or group to another occur only through the mechanism of the market. While Reich shared Hayek's concern with the fragile status of individual liberty in the modern state, he clearly did not accept Hayek's commitment to the market as the central mechanism for protecting liberty. More important, Reich's purpose in seeking protection of the new property was not the economic goal of encouraging the accumulation of wealth. His central concern was with politics, not the market.

The new property was the currency of the civic realm for welfare rights advocates. Toward the end of his article, Reich focused on benefits like old-age insurance, unemployment compensation, and public assistance as especially needful of protection. He explained the function of these benefits in overtly civic terms. Their purpose, he stated,

> is to preserve the self-sufficiency of the individual, to rehabilitate him where necessary, and to allow him to be a valuable member of a family and a community; in theory they represent part of the individual's rightful share in the commonwealth. Only by making such benefits into rights can the welfare state achieve its goal of providing a secure minimum basis for individual well-being and dignity in a society where each man cannot be wholly the master of his destiny.[119]

Reich here was restating the familiar American civic argument that good citizenship requires that individuals sometimes sacrifice their private interests for the well-being of the community.[120] A part of that obligation was to provide for the needs of others who were struck by ill-fortune, for the calamities of some were calamities of the entire community.[121] The welfare state is simply a mechanism for fulfilling that collective responsibility.

Within this framework, the role of the new property, as well as the old, is to satisfy individuals' needs—not necessarily their wants—so that they can contribute to the commonwealth as independent citizens.[122] Welfare as property, in this sense, is no different than the "forty acres and a mule" that Thaddeus Stevens proposed be redistributed to the newly freed slaves during the Reconstruction era.[123] Reich's background principle was the same as Stevens's: in the face of a large class of propertyless citizens, the preservation of the social order requires a scheme of wealth redistribution that confers on all citizens the minimum entitlements necessary for individual self-governance.

Recent commentators have renewed this call for a constitutional scheme of minimum entitlements, drawing support from Reich. Akhil Amar, for example, has argued that section two of the thirteenth amendment, properly read, requires such a scheme.[124] That amendment's original intent, he contends, was to guarantee every American citizen a minimum stake in society in order to free all Americans of the economic dependence that corrodes citizenship. For Amar, as for Reich, the objective is not equality but individual freedom. In Amar's words, "a notion of minimal entitlements is not a notion that everyone should have an equal amount of property. . . . It is not an argument that equal protection under the Fourteenth Amendment means equal property, but rather that freedom under the Thirteenth Amendment implies a notion of some minimal entitlement."[125]

While Reich thought that freedom could be secured primarily through procedural means, Amar, with the benefit of twenty-five years' hindsight on the failures of the "new property," realizes that the vision of independence for all citizens requires substantive guarantees. The same dilemma confronts both strategies, however: How is economic independence secured when the source of entitlements, substantive or procedural, is the state? The development of welfare entitlements as a system of civic property seems as perverse as Hayek thought welfare was for market property. Both the market and civic property systems require individual autonomy (though for quite different reasons), yet welfare entitlements create a social subsystem of direct dependency and hierarchy. The very idea of welfare as property, in this sense, seems self-contradictory.

Amar is acutely aware of the dilemma. This is why he takes pains to distinguish the scheme of minimal entitlements he attributes to the thirteenth amendment—forty acres and a mule—from welfare:

> [F]orty acres and a mule is not a dole. It is not welfare. It is much more like workfare. Forty acres and a mule do not yield a harvest without labor, and in the process of laboring, a citizen can gain self-respect and the respect of others. We must remember that our goal is to create *independent* citizens. Ironically, many current welfare programs may have moved us away from that goal by perpetuating cycles of dependency. By contrast, the kind of education and job-training programs I am advocating are designed to promote self-sufficiency and reward hard work.[126]

Perhaps education and job-training are sufficient responses to the problem of dependency for some welfare recipients, but surely not for all. Some classes of dependents *are* dependent for reasons that have nothing to do with lack of job skills. To the extent that citizenship requires self-governance, what form of property, what alternative to the Reichian scheme of welfare-as-property might be adequate?

This is not the appropriate occasion to answer that question. Two points, however, need to be made to clarify what the question involves. First, the modern civic conception of property builds on the Progressive-Realist insight that no legal property regime can create complete individual freedom from state power. Even in the minimal night-watchman state, private property rights derive from the state as delegated sovereignty. The state logically can and historically sometimes has altered its delegation of sovereignty. The upshot is that the personal security that classical property rights in fact create is inevitably contingent. Ultimately, no property system can eliminate the possibility of state intervention. The real issues are determining which exercises of state power against property interests are legitimate and by what criteria is such legitimacy determined.

The second point is that the notion of individual independence has a different meaning from the civic perspective than it has in classical liberal thought. In classical liberalism, the core meaning of independence, signified by property rights, is personal security against unwanted interference by others, most especially the state. From the civic perspective, personal independence means not security against material losses, that is, losses of commodities viewed as instruments for satisfying individual preferences, but against political-ethical loss, that is, loss of the self-respect that is the basis for proper citizenship and, ultimately, the proper social order.

Neither of these points resolves or evades the dilemma of independence in the welfare state for the civic conception. In recent years, a number of legal scholars, attempting to develop an explicitly civic understanding of property, have directly acknowledged that dilemma.[127] Indeed, it is no exaggeration to describe the dilemma of independence as the central predicament facing the civic conception of property in late twentieth-century legal discourse. Whether or not the recent responses have been successful at pointing the way past the dilemma, they have underscored the continuing dialectic of property in American legal thought.

Epilogue

RATHER THAN ATTEMPT a full account of the development of legal thought about property in the recent past—a task that would be presumptuous—I will only sketch the broad outlines of the latest stage, as it appears to me. The major change that occurred in the legal discourse of property within the past quarter-century has been the steady strengthening of the commodificationist outlook. Legal writing, especially scholarly writing and judicial opinions, has increasingly come to reflect the idea that the basic, if not the sole, purpose of property is the satisfaction of individual preferences through market transactions. The commodificationist outlook has become more conspicuous, more explicit, and more systematically developed in legal discourse than at any other time in our nation's history. If I am correct about this phenomenon, then the key questions that must be addressed, however preliminarily and tentatively, are:(1) what are the sources of this shift in legal perceptions? (2) what does the change portend for the dialectic between market and nonmarket roles of property in American society in the future? Does the rise of the commodificationist outlook, in short, suggest that the dialectic that has thus far characterized American legal habits of speaking and thinking about property is at or near its end, to be replaced by a single interpretation of property?

Evidence of the shift in legal perceptions toward a commodity conception of property is not hard to come upon in legal discourse. The dramatic growth of the law-and-economics movement within the past twenty-five years itself strongly reflects the change. Economic reasoning treats property exclusively from a market perspective, in which all resources that have market value (or would if the law permitted a market to exist) are property, or at least potentially are property. The sole function of property rights, in the words of the economist Harold Demsetz, is to "guid[e] incentives to achieve a greater internalization of externalities."[1] Translated, the theory holds that property rights maximize aggregate social wealth by encouraging people to take into account the costs and benefits of how they use their property. To perform their wealth-maximizing function, property rights must be freely transferable. As Judge Richard Posner states in his influential book, *Economic Analysis of Law*, "Value maximization requires a mechanism by which the [current owner] can be induced to transfer rights in the property to someone who can work it more productively; a transferable property right is such a mechanism."[2]

The extraordinary influence of economic analysis on legal thought in the past three decades has changed the rhetoric of property in legal discourse. Drawing on the economic theory of property rights, legal scholars increasingly have come to talk about property in terms of "entitlements" in "goods."[3] The shift is not merely rhetorical. The economic concept of an entitlement is at once broader and narrower than the conventional legal concept of property. The criterion for an entitlement is whether an interest is potentially wealth-creating through market transactions, that is, is a market commodity. As Thomas Grey explains, "[E]conomists . . . adopt . . . a purposive account of property, including among property rights all and only those entitlements whose purpose . . . is to advance allocative efficiency by allowing individuals to bear the costs generated by their activities."[4] Illustrating the different content of the conventional legal concept of property and the economic concept of an entitlement, Grey continues:

> [O]n this account rights to life, liberty, and personal security are included within the field of property. On the other hand, legal entitlements to transfer payments, such as are conferred by welfare and social security laws, are presumably excluded.[5]

Law-and-economics analysis incorporates economists' perceptions that value has only one meaning—exchange value—and that everything that has exchange-value is (or could be) property, including babies,[6] politics,[7] even justice itself.[8] From this perspective, the question is why law prohibits market transactions in certain goods and not others; why, in other words, it limits the range of goods that it permits to be commodified. As this way of formulating the basic issue indicates, the starting presumption for law-and-economics scholars is that all goods are commodities.

If the claim that an instrumental, self-consciously market-oriented conception of property has become more conspicuous in legal writing since the 1960s is correct, what explains this development? Why has the discourse of commodification become more evident in legal writing in the past two decades? What factors caused legal writers to develop a systematic market theory of property at this point in history? The telling of the full causal story must await a later day, for the story is too complex and too nuanced to be fully set out in this brief space. The answer concerns the relationship between the commodity conception of property and perceptions of and attitudes toward the market, both internally in legal thought and externally in broader social consciousness.

Among the endogenous factors influencing the shift to a more thoroughly commodificationist understanding of property is the growing acceptance of the Realists' critique of the old Blackstonian conception of property. As we saw earlier,[9] the Realists demolished what little coherence remained in the idea that ownership is the absolute dominion and control that one person has over a thing. They were responsible for replacing in mainstream legal consciousness that conception with the disaggregated, more explicitly social "bundles of rights" conception. Far more fluid and flexible than the old Blackstonian conception, the bundles-of-rights idea was quite congenial to the economic outlook. From this point of view, it simply makes no sense to think of property as pertaining only to things. Property exists in whatever resources have market value, and increasingly in American society the most valued goods are not the tangible things but the intangible interests, expectations, and promises. The bundles-of-rights idea also reflects the insight that ownership is not absolute and autonomous but relative and relational. No single person has exclusive and absolute ownership of any resource. Many individuals have simultaneously existing legally recognized interests, or "entitlements," in assets, and the "owner" is simply the one whose package of entitlements is larger than that of others.

This disaggregative and social way of thinking about property is essential to an economic analysis of legal property issues. The transition in legal thought from the conception of ownership as autonomous and unified to social and disaggregated facilitated a basic redefinition of legal property issues. Under the old Blackstonian conception, the key questions in any legal dispute over property were, who is the owner and was that person's ownership unlawfully injured in some way. From the economist's perspective, this way of formulating the issues only obscures what is really at stake in any dispute over property. As Bruce Ackerman explains, "[I]t is the Scientist's [i.e, economist's] main point to deny the propriety of a muddled search amongst the diverse bundles of user rights in quest of those that contain 'the' rights of property."[10] Rather, economic analysis of property disputes is a matter of choosing which among competing users should be legally entitled to prevail, using wealth-maximization as the criterion for choosing.[11]

A second endogenous factor contributing to the shift toward a commodificationist understanding of property is the growing acceptance within American legal thought of the view that substantive values, moral, political, and legal, are inherently subjective and nonrational. To some extent, the growth of this view among legal scholars can be attributed to the influence of intellectual developments in other fields, especially the social sciences, with which academic law is most closely related. The dominant intellectual mood in the social sciences generally during the 1950s was one of skepticism about the possibility of rational solutions of substantive value conflicts.[12] Influenced both by the recent traumas of totalitarian movements around the world and the enhanced stature of the "hard" sciences, scholars in economics, political science, history, and sociology produced work that was more positivist, empirical, and technical. Above all, the new mode of scholarship was based on the widely shared syllogism that to be rational was to be scientific, to be scientific was to be value-free, therefore, to be rational was to be value-free.

Law was hardly immune from this value-purging trend. In part, the quest for value-free legal analysis was a continuation of a project that had begun under the Legal Realists in the 1920s and 1930s. One strand of Realism was committed to the idea that facts and values were radically separate and that rational discourse was possible only with respect to facts.[13] Realists of this stripe sought to push legal scholarship in a strongly empirical and behaviorist direction. Law-and-economics scholars explicitly endorsed the value-free, behaviorist methodology of this branch of Realism.[14] Regarding substantive moral values as purely subjective, they welcomed a form of legal-policy analysis that treated values as personal preferences and that rested policy choices on the apparently neutral basis of social wealth maximization.

The conception of property as commodity seemingly advances this goal of value-free legal analysis. So long as property is understood as a commodity there is no occasion for choosing and rationally justifying any particular substantive conception of the proper social order. Treating property as a commodity means that the legal system assigns no substantive role to property other than the satisfaction of individual preferences. The state plays a strictly facilitative role; other than assuring that transactions are free from fraud and that individuals respect each others' property rights, the state has no interest in how property is used. The function of property, from this perspective, is to fulfill, for each owner, that person's vision of what is good, *not* some substantive vision of the good society. The market, not the legal system, is the final arbiter of conflicts over values or what Calabresi and Melamed called "moralisms."[15]

The causal factors that I have identified as endogenous to legal thought and culture are, in fact, not strictly endogenous. They reflect a broader shift in perceptions of and attitudes towards the market and politics as alternative mechanisms of governance that has occurred since the 1960s. Within both the legal academy and American society generally, politics has come to be viewed with far more skepticism than existed prior to 1970. Concomitantly, the private sphere, especially the market, has gained favor as the more effective mechanism for making collective choices. This change bears some resemblance to the phenomenon that the political economist Albert Hirschman calls "shifting involvements."[16] Disillusioned with several decades' experience with governmental approaches to social and economic problems, the American public after 1970 increasingly looked to market-oriented solutions.

Public discontent with government solutions to the nation's domestic problems in the post–Great Society era is by now a too-familiar story. Correctly or incorrectly, most policy analysts concluded by the 1970s that most of the Great Society programs were failures. Expressions of disillusionment with governmental approaches to solving social welfare problems became common, both in the policy literature and the press.[17] This view was trumpeted most loudly by President Reagan and his supporters, but it was not confined solely to the Right. As early as the late 1960s, moderates and even some liberals (in the modern American sense of the term) were disenchanted with government programs dealing with problems from poverty to pollution and had begun looking to market based alternatives.[18] Assuming for the moment that most of the governmental programs actually were failures, the reason for this growing sense of discontent with governmental solutions was not solely the fact that they failed. At least as important is the fact that people had such high expectations of them at the outset. The expectations of the early and mid-1960s sowed the seeds for the destruction of the era of public action as the central mechanism for solving social and economic problems, laying the foundation for the 1980s, in which the pursuit of private happiness was the dominant ideology.[19] Of course, this is not to say that the turn from the public to the private sphere was total and complete. Government welfare programs did continue, some even increased, during the Reagan years. Nor had the market been banished during the Great Society era. But there *was* a turn, and that turn, fueled by a sense of disappointment and disillusionment, is the dominant factor that explains the strengthening of the commodificationist outlook since 1970.

If disappointment and disillusion are the primary causes of the recent predominance of the commodified conception of property, where does that leave us for the future? Should we now declare that the dialectic between the marketized and the political understandings of property has reached its terminus with the triumph of the former? Even more uneasy about peering into the future than I am about describing and explaining the historical developments of the recent past, I will nevertheless hazard a prediction that the dialectic has not ended and that a reversal of the cycle between private and public ideologies lies ahead.

The theory of oscillation between periods of government and market solutions to socioeconomic problems itself suggests that the dialectic between civic and commodified understandings of property will reach no end point. Public sentiments about and perceptions of the efficacy of individual, market-based, and collective regulatory responses to social ills shift as disappointment follows high expectations. Perceptions of the social effects of the market and government imply different understandings regarding the dominant role of property. As shifts in consciousness about the role of the market and government occur, then, we should expect to find correlative shifts in attitudes toward commodified and civic property.

The basis for my prediction that the period of commodification thought as the dominant mode of legal consciousness will give way to a period of a more civically oriented consciousness is not theory alone, however. There is evidence that a shift in perceptions of the market generally and commodified property specifically has already begun to occur, both in popular and legal consciousness. Statements such as President Reagan's that "[w]hat I want to see above all is that this country remains a country where someone can always get rich"[20] are much rarer today in political discourse than they were in 1980. Even after the fall of state socialism in the former Soviet Union and its bloc, public expectations of the benefits of an unregulated market have declined. For all of the talk about markets being on the march around the world, one increasingly encounters expressions of cynicism about the effects of the high-flying activities of Wall Street during the 1980s.

The same shift is perceptible in scholarly discourse. The recent communitarian movement and the renaissance of interest in the civic republican tradition are only the most obvious examples of a broader search for alternatives to possessive individualism as the dominant ideology in American thought. Somewhat less conspicuous but more interesting have been attempts to sketch the outlines of a political economy and conception of property that integrates the political ideal of democracy and the economic ideal of wealth-creation. In economics, this project is represented by works like Michael Piore and Charles Sabel's book *The Second Industrial Divide,*[21] and in sociology, by Robert Bellah and his colleagues' recent book, *The Good Society,* and Fred Block's *Post-Industrial Possibilities.*[22]

In law, a growing body of work exploring various aspects of a civic conception of property has emerged within the past few years. Notable contributors to this effort include Margaret Jane Radin,[23] William H. Simon,[24] Joseph Singer,[25] Frank Michelman,[26] and Duncan Kennedy.[27] Taken together, this work represents an ongoing effort to construct the theoretical and institutional foundations for a mode of private ownership of property that instantiates a civic vision.

Such a shift will, like other shifts in legal consciousness, not be wholesale or exclusive. A central claim of this book has been that throughout the nation's history elements of the opposed conceptions of property have been simultaneously present in legal thought and discourse. This is why I have described the character of American legal thought about property as genuinely dialectical: each conception acquires meaning in relation to the other; neither can exist without the other. This is also why in the Introduction I stated that the story of American legal thought about property can aptly be characterized as one of stability rather than one of transformations. There is no reason to expect that the stability that this dialectic creates will disappear in the foreseeable future, if it ever does.

At the same time, the recent changes described here are entirely consistent with the other side of the story that this book has tried to tell. Change has accompanied stability. This, too, follows from the dialectical character of American property thought. Like any true dialectic, aspects of each property conception interpenetrate the other, generating, together with external social, political, and economic factors, conceptual and discursive changes. The whole is more than the sum of the parts.

This way of putting the story may have disquieting implications for some individuals, especially those whose commitment to one conception or the other is so complete that they cannot accept the existence of the other. For others, including myself, the implications are more positive. The story suggests that since American legal (and, I daresay, popular) consciousness about property is complex and multidimensional it has the capacity constantly to correct itself in ways that improve American society. We can expect no more of the American legal system of property—and no less.

Notes

Introduction

1. See Carol M. Rose, *Property and Persuasion: Essays on the History, Theory, and Rhetoric of Ownership* (Boulder, Colo.: Westview Press, 1994), 58ff.

2. On this maxim and its impact on early nineteenth-century legal regulation, see William J. Novak, "Public Economy and the Well-Ordered Market: Law and Economic Regulation in 19th-Century America," *Law & Social Inquiry* 18 (1993): 1.

3. Michael Kammen, *Spheres of Liberty: Changing Perceptions of Liberty in American Culture* (Madison: University of Wisconsin Press, 1986), 5.

4. See Alan Ryan, *Property* (Milton Keynes, U.K.: Open University Press, 1987), 35–36. For a superb extended analysis of this distinction in relation to property, see C. Edwin Baker, "Property and Its Relation to Constitutionally Protected Liberty," *University of Pennsylvania Law Review* 134 (1986): 741.

5. The best study of this phenomenon with respect to "liberty" is Kammen, *Spheres of Liberty.*

6. See Gordon S. Wood, *The Radicalism of the American Revolution* (New York: Vintage, 1991), 269.

7. Here I part company with Professor Wood, who argues that "the entire Revolution could be summed up by the radical transformation Americans made in their understanding of property." Ibid. Even if this statement is accurate with respect to ordinary Americans (which I very much doubt), it is most assuredly *not* true of American lawyers.

8. For an insightful overview of some of these changes, see Thomas C. Grey, "The Disintegration of Property," *Nomos XXII: Property,* ed. J. Roland Pennock and John W. Chapman (New York: New York University Press, 1980), 69.

9. Louis Hartz, *The Liberal Tradition in America* (New York: Harcourt Brace, 1955).

10. See, e.g., Edward S. Corwin, *The "Higher Law" Background of American Constitutional Law* (Ithaca, N.Y.: Great Seal Books, 1955); Edward S. Corwin, *Liberty against Government: The Rise, Flowering and Decline of a Famous Juridical Concept* (Baton Rouge: Louisiana State University Press, 1948).

11. Jennifer Nedelsky, *Private Property and the Limits of American Constitution-*

alism: The Madisonian Framework and Its Legacy (Chicago: University of Chicago Press, 1990).

More recently, Professor Nedelsky's thesis has been vigorously defended in David Abraham, "Liberty without Equality: The Property-Rights Connection in a 'Negative Citizenship' Regime," *Law & Social Inquiry* 21 (1996): 1. Professor Abraham, like Professor Nedelsky, sees property as having had only one meaning and one role throughout American history.

12. Nedelsky, *Private Property,* 227.

13. For a perceptive critique of Nedelsky's thesis, see William W. Fisher III, "Making Sense of Madison: Nedelsky on Private Property," *Law & Social Inquiry* 18 (1993): 547.

14. I have in mind scholars like Richard Epstein and Bernard Siegan, to name only two legal scholars who hold this view. See Richard A. Epstein, *Takings: Private Property and the Power of Eminent Domain* (Cambridge: Harvard University Press, 1985); Bernard H. Siegan, "One People As to Commercial Objects," in *Liberty, Property, and the Foundations of the American Constitution,* ed. Ellen Frankel Paul and Howard Dickman (Albany: State University of New York Press, 1989), 101.

15. 505 U.S. 1003 (1992).

16. Phinizy Spalding, *Oglethorpe in America* (Chicago: University of Chicago Press, 1977), 156.

17. Ibid.

18. The seminal work identifying the close link between property ownership and municipal governance is Hendrik Hartog, *Public Property and Private Power: The Corporation of the City of New York in American Law, 1730-1870* (Chapel Hill: University of North Carolina Press, 1983).

19. See, e.g., Oscar Handlin and Mary Flug Handlin, *Commonwealth: A Study of the Role of Government in the American Economy—Massachusetts, 1774–1861,* rev. ed. (Cambridge: Harvard University Press, Belknap Press, 1969); Leonard W. Levy, *The Law of the Commonwealth and Chief Justice Shaw* (1957); Harry N. Scheiber, "Public Rights and the Rule of Law in American Legal History," *California Law Review* 72 (1984): 217; Harry N. Scheiber, "The Road to *Munn:* Eminent Domain and the Concept of Public Purpose in the State Courts," *Perspectives in American History* 5 (1971): 327; William J. Novak, "Common Regulation: Legal Origins of State Power in America," *Hastings Law Journal* 45 (1994): 1061.

20. Novak, "Common Regulation," 1083.

21. I cannot improve on Dorothy Ross's definitions of the two terms. She defines "modernism" as "the late-nineteenth-century cognitive move toward subjectivity and its aesthetic ramifications." Dorothy Ross, "Modernism Reconsidered," in *Modernist Impulses in the Human Sciences, 1870–1930,* ed. Dorothy Ross (Baltimore: Johns Hopkins University Press, 1994), 2. By "modernity," she explains, we mean "the actual world brought into existence by democracy, capitalism, social differentiation, and science, a world against which aesthetic modernists rebelled and to which the cognitive

modernists of the Enlightenment tradition continued to attach their hopes for progress." Ibid., 8.

22. Simon Schama, *Citizens: A Chronicle of the French Revolution* (New York: Alfred A. Knopf, 1989).

23. Hendrik Hartog, "Distancing Oneself from the Eighteenth Century: A Commentary on Changing Pictures of American History," in *Law in the American Revolution and the Revolution in the Law,* ed. Hendrik Hartog (New York: New York University Press, 1981), 229, 235.

24. See Christopher Lasch, *The True and Only Heaven: Progress and Its Critics* (New York: W. W. Norton, 1991).

25. Ibid., 46.

26. Ibid., 39.

27. T. J. Jackson Lears, *No Place of Grace: Antimodernism and the Transformation of American Culture, 1880–1920* (Chicago: University of Chicago Press, 1981), 17–18.

28. I examine these reforms and their ideological roots in chapter 1.

29. J. Willard Hurst, *Law and the Conditions of Freedom in the Nineteenth-Century United States* (Madison: University of Wisconsin Press, 1956), 5.

30. Ibid., 27.

31. I discuss this case and the "vested rights doctrine" at length in chapter 7.

32. Ibid., 506.

33. Of these critics, Professor Joyce Appleby has been the most prominent. See, e.g., Joyce Appleby, "What Is Still American in Jefferson's Political Philosophy?" in Joyce Appleby, *Liberalism and Republicanism in the Historical Imagination* (Cambridge: Harvard University Press, 1992), 291.

The most insightful overview and critique of the historiography of republicanism is Daniel T. Rodgers, "Republicanism: The Career of a Concept," *Journal of American History* (June 1992): 11.

34. This is Jefferson's famous theory of political relativism, developed in a letter written to James Madison. I examine the theory in detail in chapter 1.

35. J. G. A. Pocock, *The Machiavellian Moment: Florentine Political Thought and the Atlantic Tradition* (Princeton: Princeton University Press, 1975), 509.

36. This distinction was first drawn in the famous paper by William Gallie, "Essentially Contested Concepts," *Proceedings of the Aristotelian Society* 56 (1965): 167.

37. Alfred S. Konefsky, "Law and Culture in Antebellum Boston," review of *Law and Letters in American Culture,* by Robert A. Ferguson, *Supreme Court Justice Joseph Story: Statesman of the Old Republic,* by R. Kent Newmyer, and *The Web of Progress: Private Values and Public Styles in Boston and Charleston, 1828–1843,* by William H. Pease and Jane H. Pease, *Stanford Law Review* 40 (1988): 1119, 1121.

38. Among the substantial amount of writing on the professionalization of lawyers, one of the most illuminating studies is A. G. Roeber, *Faithful Magistrates and Republican Lawyers: Creators of Virginia Legal Culture, 1680–1810* (Chapel Hill: University of North Carolina Press, 1981).

39. On the relationship between property and storytelling in general, see Carol M. Rose, "Property as Storytelling: Perspectives from Game Theory, Narrative Theory, Feminist Theory," in *Property and Persuasion,* 25.

40. Margaret Jane Radin, *Reinterpreting Property* (Chicago: University of Chicago Press, 1993), 166.

Part One Prologue

1. See generally A. W. B. Simpson, "The Rise and Fall of the Legal Treatise: Legal Principles and the Forms of Legal Literature," *University of Chicago Law Review* 48 (1981): 632.

2. See Charles Fearne, *Essay on the Learning of Contingent Remainders and Executory Devises* (1772; reprint, Dublin: John Rice, 1795). This famous work appeared in an American edition in 1819.

3. See Geoffrey Gilbert, *The Law and Practice of Ejectments* (London: R. and B. Nutt and F. Gosling, for T. Waller, 1741). This monograph was only one of a vast number of technical legal monographs written by Sir Geoffrey Gilbert (1675–1726). All of them were published posthumously, and some appeared without attribution.

4. See Thomas L. Haskell, *The Emergence of Professional Social Science: The American Social Science Association and the Nineteenth-Century Crisis of Authority* (Urbana: University of Illinois Press, 1977), 18–20.

5. Perry Miller, *The Life of the Mind in America from the Revolution to the Civil War* (New York: Harcourt, Brace, 1965), 109.

6. This view has come under attack in recent years. Some historians have argued that the Revolution produced no dramatic change in the bar's social stature or economic clout. See, e.g., Dennis R. Nolan, "The Effect of the Revolution on the Bar: The Maryland Experience," *Virginia Law Review* 62 (1976): 969. For a penetrating critique of the standard narrative chronicling the legal profession's "rise" in socioeconomic power, see Alfred S. Konefsky, "Law and Culture in Antebellum Boston," review of *Law and Letters in American Culture,* by Robert A. Ferguson, *Supreme Court Justice Joseph Story: Statesman of the Old Republic,* by R. Kent Newmyer, and *The Web of Progress: Private Values and Public Styles in Boston and Charleston, 1828–1843,* by William H. Pease and Jane H. Pease, *Stanford Law Review* 40 (1988): 1119.

7. On the importance of republican political ideology to American lawyers on the final quarter of the eighteenth century, see A. G. Roeber, *Faithful Magistrates and Republican Lawyers: Creators of Virginia Legal Culture, 1680–1810* (Chapel Hill: University of North Carolina Press, 1981), 160–202.

8. Charles Nisbet, president of Dickinson College, quoted in Saul Cornell, "Aristocracy Assailed: The Ideology of Backcountry Anti-Federalism," *Journal of American History* 76 (1990): 1162.

9. See Gordon S. Wood, *The Radicalism of the American Revolution* (New York: Vintage Books, 1991), 254.

10. The Federalist No. 35 (New York: Mentor Books, 1961), 215.

11. Ibid., 216.

12. Letter of Thomas Jefferson to Thomas Mann Randolph, Jr., May 30, 1790, in *The Papers of Thomas Jefferson,* ed. Julian R. Boyd (Princeton: Princeton University Press, 1950), 16:449.

13. Daniel Boorstin, *The Americans: The Colonial Experience* (New York: Random House, 1958), 205.

14. See Robert A. Ferguson, *Law and Letters in American Culture* (Cambridge: Harvard University Press, 1984), 9, 17.

15. Robert W. Gordon, "The Independence of Lawyers," *Boston University Law Review* 68 (1988): 1, 15 (footnote omitted).

16. Alexis de Tocqueville, *Democracy in America,* trans. Henry Reeve (New York: Schocken Books, 1961), 1:322.

Chapter One

1. Thomas Jefferson to James Madison, 6 September 1789, *The Papers of Thomas Jefferson,* ed. Julian R. Boyd (Princeton: Princeton University Press, 1950), 15:392.

2. Herbert Sloan, "'The Earth Belongs in Usufruct to the Living,'" in *Jeffersonian Legacies,* ed. Peter S. Onuf (Charlottesville: University Press of Virginia, 1993), 281–82.

3. See, e.g., John Rawls, *A Theory of Justice* (Cambridge: Harvard University Press, Belknap Press, 1971), 284–93 (considering relations between present and future generations rather than present and past generations).

4. Sloan, "'The Earth Belongs in Usufruct to the Living,'" 294.

5. Sloan's essay provides a careful analysis of the linguistic points of originality to Jefferson's letter. See ibid., 296–300.

6. *Jefferson Papers,* 15:392.

7. John Locke's own theory placed the origins of contemporary property rights both in nature and social convention. In this sense, as Richard Schlatter observed, Locke himself was not always "Lockean." See Richard Schlatter, *Private Property: The History of an Idea* (New York: Russell & Russell, 1973), 152, 157–61.

8. See F. H. Lawson and Bernard Rudden, *The Law of Property,* 2d ed. (Oxford: Oxford University Press, 1982), 163–64; Barry Nicholas, *An Introduction to Roman Law* (Oxford: Oxford University Press, 1962), 110–11, 144–47.

9. The ambiguity in Jefferson's conception of dynamic property—land in usufruct for the living—is indicated by the possibility that the same conception could be used to justify actions by the present generation in overexploiting resources, to the detriment of future generations. That is, the doctrine of political relativism provides a paradoxical justification for the living to sell out the future, not just to cast off the shackles of the past. J. Willard Hurst vividly chronicled just such a move in his famous study of the Wisconsin lumber industry in the nineteenth century. J. Willard Hurst, *Law and Economic Growth: The Legal History of the Lumber Industry in Wisconsin, 1836–1915* (Cambridge: Harvard University Press, Belknap Press, 1964). He argued that the enormous

growth of the lumber industry, which wiped out Wisconsin's forests, resulted in part from an ambiguity in the discourse of public land policy in the 1850s. The dynamic land policy in which the prevailing sentiment was "what we do now counts most" obscured a tension between an egalitarian social-political ideal of small independent farm owners and a commitment to increasing productivity. From this point of view, "settlement" of land was an ambiguous symbol. See ibid., 25–26, 40–47. What I am suggesting is that Jefferson's conception of dynamic land ownership can be understood as a progenitor of this ambiguity.

10. In this respect Jefferson's political relativism doctrine prefigured Roberto Unger's political theory of "superliberalism." In particular, Unger's notion of "destabilization rights" echoes the Jeffersonian embrace of political re-creation. See Roberto Unger, *Politics: Social Theory* (New York: Cambridge University Press, 1987), 210–14; Roberto Unger, *Politics: False Necessity* (New York: Cambridge University Press, 1987), 530–35.

11. See note 10 supra.

12. My interpretation of Jefferson and the Jeffersonian meaning of property differs from that developed by Professor Joyce Appleby. See Joyce Appleby, "What Is Still American in Jefferson's Political Philosophy of Thomas Jefferson?" in *Liberalism and Republicanism in the Historical Imagination* (Cambridge: Harvard University Press, 1992), 291. She interprets Jefferson's views as repudiating the civic tradition and identifies a revision in his political thought, leading him, for example, to abandon his early admiration for Montesquieu. Appleby so strongly associates the civic tradition with political elitism, represented by figures like Montesquieu and John Adams, that she interprets any element of egalitarianism as a rejection of the republican ideology. Hence, in her view, Jefferson's political relativism doctrine and his efforts to reform inheritance law make it impossible to characterize him as working within the civic paradigm. I view Jefferson's writing as consistently preoccupied with the same basic dialectic, a dialectic of stability and dynamism. Professor Appleby's commitment to a linear interpretive framework prevents her from seeing it dialectically.

The same interpretive framework has also influenced her interpretation of American political discourse in the 1790s. See Joyce Appleby, *Capitalism and a New Order: The Republican Vision of the 1790s* (New York: New York University Press, 1984). She there argued that the 1790s were the crucial decade in which Jeffersonians led a decisive break from the civic paradigm to create "the first truly American political movement." Ibid., 4. I argue that the same dialectic of temporality, stability versus dynamism, organized American political-legal discourse throughout the 1790s, although there were multiple meanings of the terms of this dialectic.

13. Gordon S. Wood, *The Creation of the American Republic* (New York: W. W. Norton, 1969), 47.

14. See J. G. A. Pocock, *The Machiavellian Moment: Florentine Political Thought and the Atlantic Tradition* (Princeton: Princeton University Press, 1975).

15. Wood, *The Creation of the American Republic,* 54.

16. See Thomas Jefferson, "Autobiography," in *The Works of Thomas Jefferson,* ed. Paul Leicester Ford (New York: Knickerbocker Press, 1904–5), 1:1.

17. On the theory of possessive individualism, see C. B. Macpherson, *The Political Theory of Possessive Individualism: Hobbes to Locke* (Oxford: Oxford University Press, 1962).

18. For a recent statement of this position, see Richard A. Epstein, *Takings: Private Property and the Power of Eminent Domain* (Cambridge: Harvard University Press, 1985).

19. J. G. A. Pocock, "The Mobility of Property and the Rise of Eighteenth-Century Sociology," in *Virtue, Commerce, and History* (Cambridge: Cambridge University Press, 1985), 103.

20. Appleby, *Capitalism and a New Social Order,* 9.

21. John Adams to James Sullivan, 26 April 1776, in *The Works of John Adams,* ed. Charles Francis Adams (Boston: Little, Brown, 1854), 9:376.

22. Thomas Jefferson, *Notes on the State of Virginia* (1785; reprint, New York: Harper Torchbooks, 1964), 157.

23. Jefferson later revised his general hostility toward manufacturing, limiting his earlier critique that manufacture begets dependence on manufacturing to the "great cities in the old countries," because of the abundance of Western land. This was an early example of the theme of what Henry Nash Smith has called "the West as safety valve." See Henry Nash Smith, *Virgin Land: The American West as Symbol and Myth* (Cambridge: Harvard University Press, 1978), 203.

In this passage Jefferson was also contributing to the greatest symbolic role played by land in eighteenth- and nineteenth-century American—the myth of the Garden of Eden. See generally Leo Marx, *The Machine in the Garden: Technology and the Pastoral Ideal in America* (Oxford: Oxford University Press, 1964). Land's symbolic role within this mythology was to mask "poverty and industrial strife with the pleasing suggestion that a beneficent nature stronger than any human agency, the ancient resource of Americans, the power that had made the country rich and great, would solve the new problems of industrialism." Smith, *Virgin Land,* 206.

24. Thomas Jefferson to John Jay, 23 August 1785, *Jefferson Papers,* 8:426.

25. Jefferson, *Notes on the State of Virginia,* 157–58.

26. Ibid., 164–65.

27. It is also bears mention that Jefferson's suggestion, which his fear of dependence prompted, did not remove that threat altogether. Rather it substituted one form of dependence—on other nations to our trading for us—for another.

28. Thomas Jefferson to Rev. James Madison, 28 October 1785, *Jefferson Papers,* 8:681–82.

29. James Sullivan to John Adams, 26 April 1776, *The Works of John Adams,* 376–77.

30. See Stanley N. Katz, "Jefferson and the Right to Property," *Journal of Law & Economics* 19 (1976): 467.

31. Stanley Katz has pointed out that "the regulation of inheritance was viewed as a focal point of scattered, ineffectual statutory efforts to reform the economic structure of society in order to promote egalitarian ideals and to establish the foundation of a republican polity." Stanley N. Katz, "Republicanism and the Law of Inheritance in the American Revolutionary Era," *Michigan Law Review* 76 (1977): 1.

32. Indicative of this strategy was Jefferson's bill to the Virginia legislature in 1778, proposing that every freeborn Virginian who marries and resides in that state for one year receive "seventy five Acres of waste or unappropriated Land." *Jefferson Papers*, 2: 139–40. The proposal, however, was not enacted. Ibid., 147n. 12.

33. See generally Alan Ryan, *Property and Political Theory* (Oxford: Basil Blackwell, 1984).

34. See Pocock, *Machiavellian Moment*, 423–61; Forrest MacDonald, *Novus Ordo Seclorum: The Intellectual Origins of the Constitution* (Lawrence: University Press of Kansas, 1985), 137–45.

35. On the theme of stability in the American civic republican vision, see Appleby, *Capitalism and a New Social Order*, 37–38; on the theme of stability in earlier versions of the republican tradition, see generally Pocock, *The Machiavellian Moment*.

36. See note 26 supra.

37. Pocock, *The Machiavellian Moment*, 535.

38. See, e.g., Harold Demsetz, "Toward a Theory of Property Rights," *American Economic Review* 57 (Papers & Proc. 1967): 347.

39. See Margaret Jane Radin, "Market-Inalienability," *Harvard Law Review* 100 (1987): 1849.

40. The influence of this republican anxiety on nineteenth-century writings about property can be seen in the idea of the evil land speculator, which Henry George effectively developed. See Henry George, *Progress and Poverty* (New York: Appleton, 1879); Henry George, *Our Land and Land Policy* (San Francisco, 1872). He argued that land policy, and in particular, land *monopoly,* had been the downfall of the Roman republic, and it was now the main threat to the survival of the American republic. See generally John L. Thomas, *Alternative America: Henry George, Edward Bellamy, Henry Demarest Lloyd and the Adversary Tradition* (Cambridge: Harvard University Press, Belknap Press, 1983).

41. I do not suggest that eighteenth-century writers were aware of either dilemma. Their discourse of commerce and property must be understood within the context of a culture that was preoccupied with moral personality and that linked the creation of that personality with the ready availability of land, not within a structure of meaning constructed from the concepts of profit and market commodity. My point is that their discourse gains meaning to us within the context of our present-day dilemmas of free alienation of property.

42. See Pocock, *The Machiavellian Moment*, 386–87.

43. James Harrington, "The Prerogative of Popular Government," in *The Political*

Works of James Harrington, ed. J. G. A. Pocock (Cambridge: Cambridge University Press, 1977), 389, 458.

44. "[A]n agrarian [law] is a law fixing the balance of a government, in such manner that it cannot alter." Ibid., 459.

45. John Adams to James Sullivan, 26 April 1776, *The Works of John Adams,* 9: 376–77.

46. See Pocock, "Historical Introduction," in *The Political Works of James Harrington,* 1:60–61.

47. See Katz, "Republicanism and the Law of Inheritance," 11–14.

48. See, e.g., Carol Shammas, Marylynn Salmon, and Michel Dahlin, *Inheritance in America: From Colonial Times to the Present* (New Brunswick, N.J.: Rutgers University Press, 1987), 30–51; Philip Greven, *Four Generations: Population, Land, and Family in Colonial Andover, Massachusetts* (Ithaca: Cornell University Press, 1970), 133–35; Ray Keim, "Primogeniture and Entail in Colonial Virginia," *William & Mary Quarterly,* 3d ser., 25 (1968): 545–46. Keim's paper shows the particularly significant facts that although primogeniture and entail existed in Virginia until 1785, neither was a prevailing custom in colonial Virginia, a colony with just the aristocratic planter class that one would expect to engage in these inheritance practices to maintain land with a family dynasty, following the English practice.

49. Owing to the legal and social disabilities imposed on women at that time, it was men for whom such dispositions of lands were meaningful.

50. See, e.g., David Grayson Allen, *In English Ways: The Movement of Societies and the Transfer of English Local Law and Custom to Massachusetts Bay in the Seventeenth Century* (Chapel Hill: University of North Carolina Press, 1981); Richard B. Morris, *Studies in the History of American Law* (1930; reprint, New York: Columbia University Press, 1958); Julius Goebel, Jr., "King's Law and Local Custom in Seventeenth-Century New England," *Columbia Law Review* 31 (1931): 416–18.

51. On the European debate concerning primogeniture, see Joan Thirsk, "The European Debate on Customs of Inheritance 1500–1700," in *Family and Inheritance: Rural Society in Western Europe, 1200–1800,* ed. Jack Goody, Joan Thirsk, and E. P. Thompson (Cambridge: Cambridge University Press, 1976), 177–91.

52. See J. P. Cooper, "Patterns of Inheritance and Settlement by Great Landowners from the Fifteenth to the Eighteenth Centuries," in Goody et al., *Family and Inheritance,* 193. On the other hand, writers like Sir Matthew Hale developed functional arguments in favor of entails, contending that favoring the eldest son forced younger sons, who otherwise remained idle, to seek socially useful occupations. See Sir Matthew Hale, *The History of the Common Law of England,* ed. Charles M. Gray (Chicago: University of Chicago Press, 1971), 142. The instrumental debates over entail, then, like those over primogeniture, had a stalemated character.

At the risk of restating the obvious, it must be noted that daughters were expected to engage in the only socially useful occupation that the eighteenth-century English legal mentality recognized for them, namely, marriage. The consequence of pursuing that occupation was to end their legal capacity independently to own land.

53. See chapter 2, notes 57–72 infra.

54. On the Harringtonian principle of the balance of property, see text accompanying notes 42–45 supra.

Preambles to late eighteenth-century American statutes repealing primogeniture and entail explicitly drew on the balance of property principle. The preamble to the 1794 Delaware statute, for example, stated: "It is the duty and policy of every republican government to preserve equality amongst its citizens, by maintaining the power of property as far as is consistent with the rights of individuals." 2 Laws of the State of Delaware, ch. 53, Samuel and John Adams publ., 1797.

55. The point that I am making here is that in interpreting the eighteenth-century elite American legal writers' attack on primogeniture and entail we can, indeed must, take into account both Bernard Bailyn's and Gordon Wood's theses regarding the ideological sources of the American Revolution and John Phillip Reid's thesis that the Revolution was a controversy over law and that the revolutionaries' driving force was a constitutional vision framed by the common law. See John Phillip Reid, *Constitutional History of the American Revolution,* vol. 1, *The Authority of Rights* (Madison: University of Wisconsin Press, 1986). The line between republican ideology and the common law mentality of the American revolutionaries was not categorical. Republican politics was not distinct from law. A central challenge (perhaps the central challenge) to the American revolutionaries, both during and after the Revolution, was to reconcile basic retention of the common law of property with the act of Revolution. The republican ideology, recreated by American revolutionaries (most of whose leaders were lawyers, trained in the English common law), was the path they took to effect this reconciliation.

56. In recent years an important strand of early American historiography has interpreted colonial life as characterized by a plurality of customary practices and beliefs among small colonial communities. Important examples of this colonial communities line of social history include work by John Waters, James Henretta, A. G. Roeber, and G. B. Warden. See, e.g., John Waters, "Family, Inheritance, and Migration in Colonial New England: The Evidence from Guilford, Connecticut," *William & Mary Quarterly,* 3d ser., 39 (1982): 64 ; James Henretta, "Families and Farms: *Mentalité* in Pre-Industrial America," *William & Mary Quarterly,* 3d ser., 35 (1978): 3; G. B. Warden, "Law Reform in England and New England, 1620–1660," *William & Mary Quarterly,* 3d ser., 35 (1978): 668; A. G. Roeber, "In German Ways? Problems and Potentials of Eighteenth-Century German Social and Emigration History," *William & Mary Quarterly,* 3d ser., 44 (1987): 750. To some extent these differences were the result of particular customs that colonists brought with them from their European communities. With respect to inheritance practices, the persistence of local customary practices did not always cut against primogeniture. Professor Waters, for example, argues that colonial New Englanders generally believed in and practiced unequal treatment among heirs. His work on Guilford, Connecticut, responds to the Philip Greven's claim that primo-

geniture was quite rare in colonial New England. See Greven, *Four Generations,* 133–35. For a critical assessment of the emphasis on discontinuities among local customary practices, see Ruttman, "Assessing the Little Communities in Early America," *William & Mary Quarterly,* 3d ser., 43 (1986): 163.

57. See, e.g., Reid, *The Authority of Rights;* Jack Greene, *Peripheries and Center: Constitutional Development in the Extended Polities of the British Empire and the United States, 1607–1788* (Athens: University of Georgia Press, 1986).

58. The critique of entailments by linking them with feudal law was certainly a move uniquely made by American republicans. Scottish Enlightenment writers, particularly Lord Kames, pursued the same strategy. Entails followed, Kames argued, from the very nature of feudalism, which he labeled a "violent and unnatural system." Henry Home, Lord Kames, "History of Property," in *Historical Law Tracts,* (Edinburgh, 1758), 1:198. From the perspective of the Scottish writers, what made entails objectionable was the fact that they removed large amounts of land from circulation, thereby frustrating the needs of a commercial society. Paralleling arguments developed by Adam Smith (see Adam Smith, *Lectures on Jurisprudence: Report of 1762–63,* ed. R. L. Meek, D. D. Raphael, and P. G. Stein [Oxford: Clarendon Press, 1978], 1:116–33), Kames contended that "no circumstance tends more to the advancement of commerce than a free circulation of the goods of fortune from hand to hand." Henry Home, Lord Kames, *The Principles of Equity,* 2d ed. (Edinburgh, 1767), 259. This, of course, is quite a different basis from which to attack entails than that provided by republicanism. The Scottish critique of entails, which was well known to American republican elite lawyers like Jefferson, thus was an important instance in which republican ideology and commercial ideology complemented each other. Such instances of overlap were sources of ambiguity and paradox that facilitated the subsequent transformation of civic republican legal thought under the influence of the commercial ideology. See chapter 2, text accompanying notes 57–72 infra. On Kames's role in the Scottish Enlightenment critique of entails, see David Lieberman, "The Legal Needs of a Commercial Society: The Jurisprudence of Lord Kames," in *Wealth and Virtue: The Shaping of Political Economy in the Scottish Enlightenment,* ed. Istvan Hunt and Michael Ignatieff (Cambridge: Cambridge University Press, 1983), 203.

59. I am suggesting here that in the republican dialogue about property we will find the theme of "the release of energy" that J. Willard Hurst has described as characterizing nineteenth-century legal thought and practice. See J. Willard Hurst, *Law and the Conditions of Freedom in the Nineteenth-Century United States* (Madison: University of Wisconsin Press, 1956). I am also pushing forward the origins of the dynamic conception of property in American legal discourse prior to Morton Horwitz's dating. See Morton J. Horwitz, *The Transformation of American Law, 1780–1860* (Cambridge: Harvard University Press, 1977), 31–62.

Hurst and Horwitz correctly point out that the legal developments that most clearly exemplified the dynamic conception of property postdated the conception's discursive origins. The development that perhaps illustrates the Jeffersonian dynamic of property occurred nearly a century after Jefferson mounted his attack on the old feudal vestiges of land inheritance. This was the nineteenth-century homestead legislation that contemplated (but only incompletely achieved) an initial distribution of clear title to relatively small parcels of government-owned land in the West to individuals conditioned merely on their working the land themselves. Its purpose was not to enable homesteaders to trade the land for other forms of property, exchanging in trade in pursuit of personal wealth. It was rather to provide average persons with the means of satisfying their needs so that they would not be dependent on others. In other words, land was not a commodity but a foundation for moral personality. Far more than abolition of entailments and primogeniture, the homestead legislation attempted to fulfill Jefferson's vision of a dynamic of property.

60. See text accompanying notes 43–45 supra.

61. Staughton Lynd has pointed out that the principle that the earth belongs only to the living "approached most nearly the socialist conception that living labor has claims superior to any other property rights." Staughton Lynd, *Intellectual Origins of American Radicalism* (Cambridge: Harvard University Press, 1982), 77.

62. Indeed, unless restricted to changes that were consistent with republican principles, the doctrine permitted the destruction of republican politics itself. Jefferson never addressed the question whether the doctrine was so restricted, but even if such a restriction is implied, there remains the task of explaining how such a denial of self-governance can be reconciled with the republican ideal.

63. Jefferson, *Notes on the State of Virginia,* 157.

64. Thomas Jefferson to John Jay, 23 August 1785, *Jefferson Papers,* 8:426.

65. Ibid.

66. Thomas Jefferson to James Madison, 28 October 1785, *Jefferson Papers,* 8:682.

67. See Albert O. Hirschman, *Exit, Voice, and Loyalty* (Cambridge: Harvard University Press, 1970).

Chapter Two

1. Quoted in James Fallows, *More Like Us: Making America Great Again* (Boston: Houghton Mifflin, 1989), 84.

2. Samuel Williams, The Natural and Civil History of Vermont (1794), xi, quoted in Gordon S. Wood, *Creation of the American Republic* (New York: W. W. Norton, 1969), 5.

3. On the origins of the Whig theory of history, see J. G. A. Pocock, *The Ancient Constitution and the Feudal Law* (Cambridge: Cambridge University Press, 1987).

4. As Gordon Wood points out, however, a few Americans of the revolutionary generation, James Otis in particular, were less Panglossian about the English past, seeing it as at least occasionally in conflict with reason and the law of nature. See Wood, *Creation of the American Republic,* 9–10.

5. Robert A. Ferguson, *Law and Letters in American Culture* (Cambridge: Harvard University Press, 1984), 14.

6. As Pocock points out, Norman storytelling itself aided efforts to get over the stumbling block of the Conquest. Throughout the twelfth and thirteenth centuries, Normans had responded to complaints by dissident barons, assuring them that William the Conqueror had confirmed "the good old law" of Edward the Confessor. By the time Coke wrote his story, the legend of the Norman adoption of Saxon laws as their own was thoroughly established. William, codifying the indigenous law rather than replacing it with his own, was no conqueror after all, eliminating the problem of the Conquest. See Pocock, *The Ancient Constitution,* 42–45.

7. See ibid., 30–55, 232–33.

8. Ibid., 244.

9. See, e.g., William Blackstone, *Commentaries on the Laws of England* (1765–69; reprint, Chicago: University of Chicago Press, 1979), 1:5, 1:17, 4:413.

10. Ibid., 1:5, 1:123.

11. Ibid., 4:400.

12. Ibid., 431.

13. Chapter 33 is entitled "Of the Rise, Progress, and Gradual Improvements, of the Laws of England."

14. Blackstone's contradictory eclecticism, strategically deployed in the interest of rationalizing the existing social and legal order, is also indicated by the fact that while he borrowed the idea of linear social and legal evolution, ending with the commercial order, from Scottish social historians like Hume, Lord Kames, and John Robertson, he perpetuated myths of traditional English legal historiography that the Scottish historians had completely discredited. See David Lieberman, "The Legal Needs of a Commercial Society: The Jurisprudence of Lord Kames," in *Wealth and Virtue: The Shaping of Political Economy in the Scottish Enlightenment,* ed. Istvan Hont and Michael Ignatieff (Cambridge: Cambridge University Press, 1983), 203, 207. The Scottish theory of linear social development is discussed in more detail infra.

15. Blackstone himself became a singular object of the characteristically paradoxical character of the civic republican legal culture: while a symbol of all that was despised about England, he was the source of legal education for that entire generation of American lawyers.

16. John Adams, "A Dissertation on the Canon and Feudal Law," in *Papers of John Adams,* ed. Robert Taylor, M. Kline, and G. Lint (1765; reprint, Cambridge: Harvard University Press, Belknap Press, 1977), 1:111.

17. Ibid., 112.

18. Ibid.

19. Ibid., 113.

20. Ibid., 113–14.

21. As Pocock has noted, there is a sense in which Adams's eighteenth-century Whiggism, depicting America as a nation destined to be liberal, anticipated the twentieth-century whig historiography of Louis Hartz. Both were asserting what Pocock has called "the premise of inescapable liberalism." See J. G. A. Pocock, "Between

Gog and Magog: The Republican Thesis and the *Ideologia Americana*," *Journal of the History of Ideas* 48 (1987): 325, 338.

22. *Adams Papers,* 1:127.

23. This discursive phenomenon with the term "feudal" was neither uniquely American nor uniquely republican. The same linguistic practice was evident in Scottish Enlightenment writing and in English Whig texts as well, as Kames and Blackstone clearly illustrate. On the former, see Lieberman, "The Legal Needs of a Commercial Society."

24. On the use of quitrent in the American land system, see Beverly W. Bond, Jr., *The Quit Rent System in the American Colonies* (New Haven: Yale University Press, 1919).

25. *Adams Papers,* 1:118.

26. See Louis Hartz, *The Liberal Tradition in America: An Interpretation of American Political Thought since the Revolution* (New York: Harcourt, Brace, 1955).

27. Draft of Instructions to the Virginia Delegates in the Continental Congress, in *Jefferson Papers,* 1:121, 1:123. This is the July 1774 manuscript of "A Summary View," which Jefferson's associates later printed without his permission.

28. Ibid., 134. The act doubling the quitrent, to which Jefferson referred, was the Land Ordinance of 1774. See Anthony Marc Lewis, "Jefferson and Virginia's Pioneers, 1774–1781," *Mississippi Valley Historical Law Review* 34 (1948): 551–52.

29. On the federal land policy of placing public land in private hands, see Paul W. Gates, *History of Public Land Law Development* (Washington, D.C.: GPO, 1968), 121–495.

30. See Hendrik Hartog, *Public Property and Private Power: The Corporation of the City of New York in American Law, 1730–1870* (Chapel Hill: University of North Carolina Press, 1983), 108–15.

31. Edmund Pendleton to Thomas Jefferson, 3 August 1776, *Jefferson Papers,* 1:484.

32. Socage, the only tenure encountered in early modern English and American land law that had any real importance, was the residual category of tenure. A socage tenant held land under an obligation either to perform a certain but nonspiritual service for his lord or to pay to him a fixed sum of money. See A. W. Brian Simpson, *An Introduction to the History of the Land Law* (Oxford: Oxford University Press, 1961), 11–13. By the beginning of the modern period the tenant in socage was treated the same as a freeholder. This was certainty the case by Jefferson's time. But while the socage-farmer practically might be the owner in all but name, the fact remained that it was tenure under which he held. For republicans, that fact had enormous symbolic value.

33. *Jefferson Papers,* 1:492.

34. Ibid., 489.

35. One meaning that allodial land unambiguously did not have was liberation of women. Even the most egalitarian versions of land policy simply assumed the dependency of women on the farm.

36. *Adams Papers,* 1:106.

37. *Jefferson Papers,* 1:492. Jefferson specified that settlers would be restricted to appropriating relatively small amounts of land.

38. See text accompanying notes 41–50 infra.

39. For one account of the rarity of primogeniture in colonial America, see Philip Greven, *Four Generations: Population, Land, and Family in Colonial Andover, Massachusetts* (Ithaca: Cornell University Press, 1970), 133–35. John Waters has disputed Greven's findings, arguing that Greven probably asked the wrong questions in analyzing his data. John Waters, "Family, Inheritance, and Migration in Colonial New England: The Evidence from Guilford, Connecticut," *William & Mary Quarterly,* 3d ser., 39 (1982): 64. I do not mean to overlook here the importance of regional variations in the use of primogeniture and entail. Nevertheless, while unequal intestate succession and dynastic estate plans through entailments of land were more commonly found in Southern plantation colonies than in the New England "dissenter" colonies, it is easy to exaggerate the extent of such regional differences. For a survey of the colonial inheritance patterns, discussing testate as well as intestate succession practices, see Carole Shammas, Marylynn Salmon, and Michel Dahlin, *Inheritance in America: From Colonial Times to Present* (New Brunswick, N.J.: Rutgers University Press, 1987), 30–62.

40. On the Financial Revolution, see P. G. M. Dickson, *The Financial Revolution in England: A Study in the Development of Public Credit, 1688–1756* (New York: St. Martin's Press, 1967).

41. Pocock, *The Machiavellian Moment,* 423–61.

42. On the rise of "imaginary" forms of property in the eighteenth century, see chapter 3.

43. One indication of the commodification of land in popular American consciousness at least by the mid-nineteenth century is the failure of the Homestead Act to have its desired effect of using land to anchor populations in the American West. As several supporters of the Act had predicted, failure of impose restrictions upon the land's alienability meant that a large number of "homesteaders" used the land to engage in speculation. See Henry Nash Smith, *Virgin Land: The American West as Symbol and Myth* (Cambridge: Harvard University Press, 1978), 189–94.

44. See generally Kenneth J. Vandevelde, "The New Property of the Nineteenth Century: The Development of the Modern Concept of Property," *Buffalo Law Review* 29 (1980): 325; cf. Morton J. Horwitz, *The Transformation of American Law, 1780–1860* (Cambridge: Harvard University Press, 1977), 31–62.

45. J. G. A. Pocock, "Civic Humanism and Its Role in Anglo-American Thought," in *Politics, Language and Time: Essays on Political Thought and History* (New York: Atheneum, 1973), 80, 100. For Jefferson and Jeffersonians, anxiety about the future stemmed from their recognition that the "safety valve" of Western land—the basis upon which America could escape the fate of Europeans tied to lives of desperation in manufacturing—might eventually close. In this sense the myth of the Garden provided the seeds for its own demise. Signaling the West's demise as a symbol, of course, was the achievement of Frederick Jackson Turner. See Smith, *Virgin Land,* 206.

46. The method of classifying conceptual frameworks, or what I call "public meanings," around contingency and continuity as responses to time in public consciousness is developed by Pocock in his highly suggestive essay, "Modes of Political and Historical Time in Eighteenth-Century England," in *Politics, Language and Time*, 91.

47. On the role of the Christian millenialist conception of time in late eighteenth-century American thought, see Ruth Bloch, *Visionary Republic: Millenialist Themes in American Thought, 1756–1800* (Cambridge: Cambridge University Press, 1985); James Kloppenberg, "The Virtues of Liberalism: Christianity, Republicanism, and Ethics in Early American Political Discourse," *Journal of American History* 74 (1987): 9.

48. See text accompanying notes 45–47 supra.

49. Both the term "fragmented survival" and the meaning to which I am putting it here were originally developed in Alastair MacIntyre, *After Virtue*, 2d ed. (Notre Dame: University of Notre Dame Press, 1984), 110–13, 257.

50. On the English civic humanist theory of history, see J. G. A. Pocock, *The Machiavellian Moment: Florentine Political Thought and the Atlantic Tradition* (Princeton: Princeton University Press, 1975).

51. See Wood, *Creation of the American Republic*, 29.

52. On this cyclical theory of social change, see ibid., 28–30; Stowe Persons, "The Cyclical Theory of History in Eighteenth-Century America," *American Quarterly* 6 (1954): 147.

53. Smith, *Virgin Land*; Leo Marx, *The Machine in the Garden* (Oxford: Oxford University Press, 1964); Ernest Tuveson, *The Redeemer Nation: The Idea of America's Millenial Role* (Berkeley and Los Angeles: University of California Press, 1968).

54. Pocock, *Machiavellian Moment*, 541.

55. The term "public time" is Pocock's. As he explains, history is "time experienced by individuals as public beings, conscious of a framework of public institutions in and through which events, processes, and changes happen to the society of which he perceives himself to be part." Pocock, "Modes of Political and Historical Time in Early Eighteenth-Century England," in *Virtue, Commerce, and History*, 91. This conception of history emphasizes the extent to which "individuals who see themselves as public beings see society as organized into and by a number of frameworks, both institutional and conceptual, in and through which they apprehend things as happening to society and themselves." Ibid.

56. On Kames's contribution to the legal aspects of Scottish historical theory, see David Lieberman, "The Legal Needs of a Commercial Society: The Jurisprudence of Lord Kames," in Hont and Ignatieff, *Wealth and Virtue*, 203; W. C. Lehmann, "The Historical Approach in the Juridical Writings of Lord Kames," *Juridical Review* 64 (1964): 17–38; Peter Stein, "The General Notions of Contract and Property in Eighteenth-Century Scottish Thought," *Juridical Review* 63 (1963): 1–13. As Henry May has noted, it was Kames who had the greatest influence on the legal writers in the American civic republican tradition. See Henry May, *The Enlightenment in America* (New York: Oxford University Press, 1976). Even historians like Ronald Hamowy, who

have expressed skepticism about interpretations of late eighteenth-century American political thought within a Scottish paradigm, have conceded Kames's influence on American writers, particularly those who were trained as lawyers. See Ronald Hamowy, "Jefferson and the Scottish Enlightenment: A Critique of Garry Wills's *Inventing America: Jefferson's Declaration of Independence,*" *William & Mary Quarterly,* 3d ser., 36 (1979): 503, 521.

57. See, e.g., Ronald Meek, *Social Science and the Ignoble Savage* (Cambridge: Cambridge University Press, 1976); Gladys Bryson, *Man and Society: The Scottish Inquiry of the Eighteenth Century* (Princeton: Princeton University Press, 1945); J. G. A. Pocock, "Cambridge Paradigms and Scotch Philosophers: A Study of the Relations between the Civic Humanist and Civil Jurisprudential Interpretation of Eighteenth-Century Social Thought," in Hont and Ignatieff, *Wealth and Virtue,* 235, 240; Paul Bowles, "The Origin of Property and the Development of Scottish Historical Science," *Journal of the History of Ideas* 46 (1985): 197. The project of developing a science of society, comparable to Baconian natural science was the work not only of those contributors to the Scottish Enlightenment whose approach to the study of society was historical and comparative (Ferguson, Millar, Smith, and Kames) but also the branch of the Scottish circle known as the "Common Sense" school, led by Thomas Reid, whose central concern was to repudiate Humean skepticism. See generally Stephen A. Conrad, *Citizenship and Common Sense: The Problem of Authority in the Social Background and Social Philosophy of the Wise Club of Aberdeen* (New York: Garland, 1987).

58. The reasons for the difference between the Scottish and civic humanist interpretations of humanity are the subject of debate. For a sketch of some possibilities, see Pocock, "Cambridge Paradigms and Scotch Philosophers," 246–52.

59. On the development of the four-stages theory, see Meek, *Social Science and the Ignoble Savage.*

60. See generally Pocock, "Cambridge Paradigms and Scotch Philosophers."

61. See Peter Stein, *Legal Evolution* (Cambridge: Cambridge University Press, 1980), 23.

62. The development and role of the four-stages theory in eighteenth-century social thought is fully studied in Meek, *Social Science.* The principal French contributors to this theory were Turgot and Antoine Yves Goguet. See ibid., 68ff., 94ff. The principal Scottish contributors were John Dalrymple, Lord Kames, Adam Smith, and John Millar. See Stein, *Legal Evolution,* 23–46; Bowles, "The Origin of Property."

63. The current version of this story is told, using the metaphor of allocative efficiency, by Chicago school economics like Harold Demsetz. See Harold Demsetz, "Toward a Theory of Property Rights," *American Economics Review* 57 (papers and proceedings, 1967): 347.

64. On the development of the notion of *le doux commerce* in the project of legitimating commercial society, see Albert O. Hirschman, *The Passions and the Interests: Political Arguments for Capitalism before Its Triumph* (Princeton: Princeton University Press, 1977), 56–63.

65. See Albert O. Hirschman, *Rivals Views of Market Society* (Cambridge: Harvard University Press, 1992), 105.

66. Here, of course, we have a source of the thesis, with which Sir Henry Maine's name is so famously associated, that societies evolve from status to contract. Henry Maine, *Ancient Law* (1861; reprint, New York: E. P. Dutton, 1917). Maine, though, moved the thesis identifying individual liberation with commerce from the level of progressive evolution to that of teleology.

67. On the influence of Scottish Enlightenment ideas on Americans in the eighteenth century, see, e.g., Forrest McDonald, *Novus Ordo Seclorum: The Intellectual Origins of the Constitution* (Lawrence: University Press of Kansas, 1985), 119–23, 131–35; Garry Wills, *Explaining America* (Garden City, N.Y.: Doubleday, 1981); Garry Wills, *Inventing America* (New York: Vintage Books, 1978); Henry May, *The Enlightenment in America* (New York: Oxford University Press, 1976); Andrew Hook, *Scotland and America: A Study of Cultural Relations, 1750–1835* (Glasgow: Blackie, 1975); Philip Hamburger, "The Constitution's Accommodation of Social Change," *Michigan Law Review* 88 (1989): 239, 254–58; Stephen A. Conrad, "Metaphor and Imagination in James Wilson's Theory of Federal Union," *Law & Social Inquiry* 13 (1988): 1, 18–19.

68. See generally Drew R. McCoy, *The Elusive Republic: Political Economy in Jeffersonian America* (New York: W. W. Norton, 1980). Within antebellum nineteenth-century legal culture, the most influential articulation of this redefinition was James Kent's discussion of property in his *Commentaries on American Law*, published in the 1830s. See chapter 5 infra.

69. On Adams's pessimism about the American character, see Wood, *Creation of the American Republic*, 567–92. For discussions of Adams as the last great American classical republican, see John R. Howe, Jr., *The Changing Political Thought of John Adams* (Princeton: Princeton University Press, 1966); Zoltan Haraszti, *John Adams and the Prophets of Progress* (New York: Grosset & Dunlap, 1964).

70. Henry Home, Lord Kames, *Sketches of the History of Man* (1774; reprint, 1813), 1:525.

71. See McCoy, *The Elusive Republic*, 32–40. On the theme of cyclical social change in eighteenth-century American thought, see Stowe Persons, "The Cyclical Theory of History in Eighteenth Century America," *American Quarterly* 6 (1954): 147.

72. See Pocock, "The Mobility of Property and the Rise of Eighteenth-Century Sociology," in *Virtue, Commerce, and History*, 121–23.

73. See J. G. A. Pocock, "Civic Humanism and Its Role in Anglo-American Thought," in *Politics, Language and Time*, 80, 100–3.

74. On the theme of functional necessity in legal historiography, see Robert W. Gordon, "Critical Legal Histories," *Stanford Law Review* 36 (1984): 57.

75. The notion of adaptive preferences is developed at length in Jon R. Elster, *Sour Grapes: Studies in the Subversion of Rationality* (Cambridge: Cambridge University Press, 1983).

76. This interpretation is explained and corrected in Lance Banning, "Some Second Thoughts on Virtue and the Course of Revolutionary Thinking," in *Conceptual Change and the Constitution*, ed. Terence Ball and J. G. A. Pocock (Lawrence: University Press of Kansas, 1988), 194–212.

77. Benjamin Rush, "On the Defects of the Confederation," (1787), in *The Selected Writings of Benjamin Rush*, ed. Dagobert D. Runes (1787; New York: Philosophical Library, 1947), 31.

78. Banning, "Second Thoughts on Virtue," 200.

79. See Drew R. McCoy, *The Last of the Fathers: James Madison and the Republican Legacy* (Cambridge: Cambridge University Press, 1989), 41.

80. See generally Hirschman, *The Passions and the Interests*.

81. For a perceptive discussion of Madison's essay, see Laura S. Underkuffler, "On Property: An Essay," *Yale Law Journal* 100 (1990): 127, 135–42. Professor Underkuffler rightly points out that Madison's conception of property was squarely within the tradition of the English Whigs. Ibid., 137.

82. "Property," in *The Papers of James Madison*, ed. William T. Hutchinson and William M. E. Rachel (Chicago: University of Chicago Press, 1983), 14, 266 (originally published in the *National Gazette*, 27 March 1792). Madison added a qualification to this second definition: "and *which leaves to everyone else the like advantage.*" This, of course, echoes the Lockean proviso concerning the extent of each individual's right to appropriate resources from the state of nature.

83. See Jennifer Nedelsky, *Private Property and the Limits of American Constitutionalism* (Chicago: University of Chicago Press, 190), 21–22.

John Phillip Reid has rightly stressed what he calls "the 'propertyness' of rights" in the legal culture of eighteenth-century America. John Phillip Reid, *Constitutional History of the American Revolution*, vol. 1, *The Authority of Rights* (Madison: University of Wisconsin Press, 1986).

The bolstering effect of assimilating the language of property and the language of civil rights was reciprocal. Not only did it enhance the stature of civil rights but, to the extent that those rights were considered natural and sacred it protected property rights as well. Both Federalists and Anti-Federalists were anxious to protect private property in order to encourage prosperity. (See George L. Haskins and Herbert A. Johnson, *Foundations of Power: John Marshall, 1801–1815*, vol. 2 of *History of the Supreme Court of the United States* [New York: Macmillan, 1981], 560.) The Federalists differed from the Anti-Federalists, however, in identifying the tyranny of the masses, resulting from democratic excesses, as the source of the threat to private property. The classic expression of this view is, of course, *The Federalist* no. 10. This diagnosis led them to rely on the judiciary, rather than legislatures, as the appropriate institution to set the boundaries of property rights. In the early nineteenth century, the U.S. Supreme Court, under the leadership of the Federalist John Marshall, eagerly assumed that responsibility, creating a legal meaning of property rights as rooted in the common law, understood as the ancient constitution. The clearest articulation of this understanding is Fletcher v. Peck, 10 U.S. (6 Cranch) 87 (1810). I discuss Fletcher v. Peck at greater length in chapter 7.

84. Blackstone, *Commentaries,* 2:16.

85. Blackstone devoted an entire chapter of the second volume of his treatise to incorporeal hereditaments. See Blackstone, *Commentaries,* 2:20–43. Modern property lawyers, at least in the United States, are scarcely aware of the term.

86. "Advowson" was the right to nominate the rector of a church. On the development of incorporeal hereditaments, see generally A. W. Brian Simpson, *An Introduction to the History of the Land Law* (Oxford: Oxford University Press, 1961), 97–100.

87. Blackstone, *Commentaries,* 2:20.

88. See Horwitz, *Transformation of American Law, 1780–1860,* 212–15.

89. See generally E. James Ferguson, *The Power of the Purse: A History of American Public Finance, 1776–1790* (Chapel Hill: University of North Carolina Press, 1961), 179–286.

90. See McDonald, *Novus Ordo Seclorum,* 97–142.

91. In England the reaction against speculative and liquid forms of property, particularly shares in the public debt, Walpole and his "sinking fund" scheme for managing the large public debt that had been created by protracted foreign wars made him a hated symbol among those who comprised the "Opposition ideology," mainly, neo-Harringtonian agrarian republicans and Tories. See Dickson, *The Financial Revolution in London;* Isaac Kramnick, *Bolingbroke and His Circle* (Cambridge: Harvard University Press, 1968).

92. See, e.g., David Hume, *Treatise of Human Nature,* bk. 3, pt. 2, sec. 3 (1739–40); Adam Smith, *Lectures on Jurisprudence,* ed. R. L. Meek, D. D. Raphael, and P. Stein (Oxford: Clarendon Press, 1978), 17.

93. See John Dawson, "Economic Duress—An Essay in Perspective," *Michigan Law Review* 45 (1947): 253.

94. It is now widely recognized that Hamilton's promotion of the Bank of the United States, his endorsement of a class of fundholding public creditors, and his vision of America as a commercial empire made him the American Walpole, whose name symbolized precisely the modern Whig corruption that consumed the attention of the English descendants of Harrington. On Hamilton's critique of republicanism, see generally Gerald Stourzh, *Alexander Hamilton and the Idea of Republican Government* (1970).

Chapter Three

1. Gerald Stourzh, *Alexander Hamilton and the Idea of Republican Government* (Stanford: Stanford University Press, 1970); Garry Wills, *Explaining America: The Federalist* (Garden City, N.Y.: Doubleday, 1981), 66–71; Stanley Elkins and Eric McKitrick, *The Age of Federalism: The Early American Republic, 1788–1800* (New York: Oxford University Press, 1993), 107–14.

2. John Adams to Mercy Warren, 16 April 1776, in *The Papers of John Adams,* ed. Robert Taylor (Cambridge: Harvard University Press, Belknap Press, 1979), 124, 125.

3. John Adams, "Defence of the Constitutions of the United States," in *The Works of John Adams,* ed. Charles Francis Adams (Boston, 1851), 6:206-7.

4. William Vans Murray, "Virtue," no. 8 of "Political Sketches: By a citizen of the United States," in *The American Museum and Repository* 2 (September 1787): 231.

5. *Memoir of Theophilus Parsons . . . by his son, Theophilus Parsons* (Boston: Ticknor and Fields, 1859), 378.

6. *The Papers of Alexander Hamilton,* ed. Harold C. Syrett (New York: Columbia University Press, 1961), 5:85.

7. Ibid., 43.

8. Baron de Montesquieu, *Spirit of the Laws,* ed. Franz Neumann (New York: Hafner, 1949), bk. 1, ch. 3, p. 41.

9. *The Records of the Federal Convention of 1787,* ed. Max Farrand (New Haven: Yale University Press, 1937), 1:432.

10. *Papers of Hamilton,* 5:42.

11. Elkins and McKitrick, *The Age of Federalism,* 92.

12. See Donald F. Swanson and Andrew P. Trout, "Alexander Hamilton, 'the Celebrated Mr. Neckar,' and Public Credit," *William & Mary Quarterly,* 3d ser., 47 (1990): 422.

13. Elkins and McKitrick, *The Age of Federalism,* 107.

14. *Papers of Hamilton,* 10:255–56.

15. Carol Rose has discussed the relationship between the federal Constitution, which she has felicitously characterized as the "plain vanilla" Constitution, and the constitutional vision of local political authority, the ancient constitution tradition. Rose points out that while 1787 marked the rejection of localism as the dominant constitutional meaning, it did not mark its disappearance. Rather, she identifies a continuous dialectic of politics that parallels the continuous dialectic of property. See Carol M. Rose, "The Ancient Constitution vs. The Federalist Empire: Antifederalism from the Attack on 'Monarchism' to Modern Localism," *Northwestern University Law Review* 84 (1989): 74.

16. See, e.g., Benjamin F. Wright, "Editor's Introduction," in *The Federalist* (Cambridge: Harvard University Press, 1961), 21; John C. Miller, *Alexander Hamilton: Portrait in Paradox* (New York: Harper & Row, 1959), 290.

17. Clinton Rossiter, *Alexander Hamilton and the Constitution* (New York: Harcourt, Brace, 1964), 179.

18. Elkins and McKitrick, *The Age of Federalism,* 116.

19. *Papers of Hamilton,* 6:70–71.

20. Ibid., 10:281–82.

21. See Elkins and McKitrick, *The Age of Federalism,* 258–63.

22. See text accompanying notes 42–45 infra.

23. The *locus classicus* expressing this view is Hamilton's social analysis in *The Federalist* no. 35.

24. Noah Webster, "An Examination of the Leading Principles of the Federal Constitution," in *Pamphlets on the Constitution of the United States,* ed. Paul Leicester Ford (Brooklyn, N.Y., 1888), 25.

25. Robert Ferguson has called Noah Webster "[t]he most important man of letters in the . . . generation [succeeding the Revolutionaries]." Robert A. Ferguson, *Law and Letters in American Culture* (Cambridge: Harvard University Press, 1984), 274.

26. Webster, "An Examination of the Leading Principles," 59–60.

27. Gordon S. Wood, *Creation of the American Republic* (New York: W. W. Norton, 1969), 606–12.

28. Pocock, *Machiavellian Moment,* 534.

29. John Adams unambiguously expressed this understanding of the relationship between property and equality in a letter written a few years after Webster's essay to his son criticizing Chancellor James Kent's contention that many aspects of English law were "utterly subversive of Equality of rights." Adams construed this to refer to doctrines of property law like primogeniture. Adams's response to the assertion is one with which Kent in fact would have found little to disagree:

> I contend that the laws from our own Country, and every other Country where the hereditary Descent of real estates is established, is as utterly subversive of Equality as the Descent of the Whole of real estate to the first born, or of a Lordship in Parliament, or of the Crown itself. All laws which establish Property are inconsistent with Equality in one sense. The very idea of Property is inconsistent with Equality. . . .
>
> It is the establishment of Property . . . which introduce[s] the great Inequalities in fact, but no Inequalities of right.

John Adams to Charles Francis Adams, 15 February 1795, in William Kent, *Memoirs and Letters of James Kent* (Boston: Little, Brown, 1898), 69, 70–71.

30. Webster, "An Examination of the Leading Principles," 60.

31. Ibid., 60–61.

32. William Blackstone, *Commentaries on the Laws of England* (1765–69; reprint, Chicago: University of Chicago Press, 1979), 2:2.

33. John Adams, *A Defence of the Constitutions of Government of the United States,* in *The Works of John Adams, Second President of the United States,* ed. Charles Francis Adams (Boston, 1851), 4:401. The latter work might have been, as historians have evaluated it, otherwise anomalous, but it was consistent with other contemporaneous writing, as well as his own earlier work, in its assertion that the Promise was realized in the American republic: "The people of America have now the best opportunity and the greatest trust in their hands that Providence ever committed to so small a number since the transgression of the first pair; if they betray their trust their guilt will merit even greater punishment than other nations have suffered and the indignation of Heaven." Ibid.

Gordon Wood argues that Adams's understanding of the system of mixed constitutionalism, his conception of sovereignty, and his version of republicanism were thoroughly contrary to mainstream American political thought in 1787. At the same time Wood rightly points out that the *Defence* was a work riddled with contradiction. Affirmations of America's uniqueness were juxtaposed with characterizations of American society as aristocratic. See Wood, *The Creation of American Republic,* 580–87.

34. On the millenialist theme in American writing, see Ruth H. Bloch, *Visionary Republic: Millenial Themes in American Thought, 1756–1800* (New York: Cambridge University Press, 1985); Sacvan Bercovitch, *The American Jeremiad* (Madison: University of Wisconsin Press, 1978); Ernest Tuveson, *The Redeemer Nation: The Idea of America's Millenial Role* (Chicago: University of Chicago Press, 1968).

35. See McCoy, *The Elusive Republic;* Wood, *The Creation of the American Republic.*

Part Two Prologue

1. "Office Duties," *American Law Register* 4 (1856): 193.

2. Maxwell Bloomfield, *American Lawyers in a Changing Society, 1776–1876* (Cambridge: Harvard University Press, 1976), 142.

3. Anon., "Codification," *Monthly Law Reporter* 7 (1844): 350.

4. Reality seldom, if ever, matched rhetoric, even for lawyer-politicians like Webster. His actual experience as a lawyer failed to conform entirely to the old republican ideal. See William W. Fisher III, "Webster's Legal Legacy," *Reviews in American History* 18 (1989): 44.

5. Rufus Choate, "The Position and Functions of the American Bar, as an Element of Conservatism in the State [1845]," *The Works of Rufus Choate* (Boston: Little, Brown, 1862), 1:414.

6. Bloomfield, *American Lawyers in a Changing Society,* 137.

7. See John H. Langbein, "Chancellor Kent and the History of Legal Literature," *Columbia Law Review* 93 (1993): 547, 571–78.

8. Lawrence M. Friedman, *A History of American Law,* 2d ed. (New York: Simon & Schuster, 1985), 324.

9. "Notes on the Early Jurisprudence of Maine," *Monthly Law Reporter* 3 (1840): 126.

10. Joseph Story, *Commentaries on the Law of Bailments* (Cambridge, Mass.: Hilliard & Brown, 1832); *Commentaries on the Constitution of the United States* (Boston: Hilliard, Gray, 1833); *Commentaries on the Conflict of Laws* (Boston: Hilliard, Gray, 1834); *Commentaries on Equity Jurisprudence* (Boston: Hilliard, Gray, 1836); *Commentaries on Equity Pleadings* (Boston: C. C. Little & J. Brown, 1838); *Commentaries on the Law of Agency* (Boston: C. C. Little & J. Brown, 1839); *Commentaries on the Law of Partnership* (Boston: C. C. Little & J. Brown, 1841); *Commentaries on the Law of Bills of Exchange* (Boston: Little, Brown, 1843); *Commentaries on the Law of Promissory Notes* (Boston: Little, Brown, 1845).

11. See, e.g., Roscoe Pound, *The Formative Era of American Law* (Boston: Little, Brown, 1938), 3. More recently, Morton Horwitz has continued this interpretation of

Kent's *Commentaries* as the beginning of the treatise tradition. See Morton J. Horwitz, *The Transformation of American Law, 1780–1860* (Cambridge: Harvard University Press, 1977), 257.

12. Langbein, "Chancellor Kent," 585–94.

13. Ibid., 593.

14. R. Kent Newmyer, *Supreme Court Justice Joseph Story: Statesman of the Old Republic* (Chapel Hill: University of North Carolina Press, 1985), 283.

15. The discussion that follows draws substantially on Bloomfield, *American Lawyers in a Changing Society,* 142–44.

16. Ibid., 143.

17. Quoted in ibid.

18. See Ferguson, *Law and Letters in American Culture,* 200-2; Friedman, *A History of American Law,* 312–14.

19. See Ferguson, *Law and Letters in American Culture,* 230.

Chapter Four

1. This requirement apparently is still in effect in two states (Maine and South Carolina) even today. See Jesse Dukeminier and James E. Krier, *Property,* 3d ed. (Boston: Little, Brown, 1993), 208.

2. Lawrence M. Friedman, *A History of American Law,* 2d ed. (New York: Simon & Schuster, 1985), 238.

3. Reprinted in Paul Ford, ed., *Pamphlets on the Constitution of the United States* (Brooklyn, N.Y., 1888), 25.

4. Time remained a problem within early nineteenth-century political thought generally. See Major Wilson, "The Concept of Time and the Political Dialogue in the United States, 1828–48," *American Quarterly* 19, no. 4 (winter 1967): 619.

5. See, e.g., J. Willard Hurst, *Law and the Conditions of Freedom in the Nineteenth-Century United States* (Madison: University of Wisconsin Press, 1956); Harry Scheiber, "The Road to *Munn:* Eminent Domain and the Concept of Public Purpose in the State Courts," in *Law in American History,* ed. Donald Fleming and Bernard Bailyn (Boston: Little, Brown, 1971).

6. See chapter 5.

7. Peter Laslett, *The World We Have Lost,* 3d ed. (London: Methuen, 1983).

8. On the backward-looking sentiment of Americans in the first half of the nineteenth century, see Fred Somkin, *Unquiet Eagle: Memory and Desire in the Idea of American Freedom, 1815–1860* (Ithaca: Cornell University Press, 1967).

9. The outstanding critique of the concept of Jacksonian Democracy is Lee Benson, *The Concept of Jacksonian Democracy: New York as a Test Case* (Princeton: Princeton University Press, 1961), which has largely laid to rest Dixon Ryan Fox's classic thesis the development of democracy in New York was the consequence of a continuous struggle between conservative, aristocratic forces (Federalist, Clintonian, then Whig) and liberal, democratic forces (Jeffersonian-Jacksonian). See Dixon Ryan Fox, *The De-*

cline of Aristocracy in the Politics of New York (New York: Columbia University Press, 1919).

10. See Alvin Kass, *Politics in New York State, 1800–1830* (Syracuse: Syracuse University Press, 1965).

11. Benson, *The Concept of Jacksonian Democracy.*

12. Webster, "An Examination of the Leading Principles," 59.

13. Charles Sellers, *The Market Revolution: Jacksonian America, 1815–1846* (New York: Oxford University Press, 1991), 19.

14. See Hurst, *Law and the Conditions of Freedom;* Friedman, *A History of American Law;* Morton J. Horwitz, *The Transformation of American Law, 1780–1860* (Cambridge: Harvard University Press, 1977); Harry N. Scheiber, *Ohio Canal Era: A Case Study of Government and the Economy, 1820–1861* (Athens: Ohio University Press, 1969). This is not to say that Hurst, Friedman, Scheiber, and Horwitz all interpret the development of legal doctrine during the first half of the nineteenth century. Among their differences, the most important is that Horwitz, unlike Hurst, Friedman, and Scheiber, emphasizes the extent to which the pro-entrepreneurial attitude of judges was ideological and class-based. My own sense is that Horwitz's interpretation more accurately captures the social and economic forces at work.

15. On the Bank War and its symbolic significance, see Marvin Meyers, *The Jacksonian Persuasion: Politics and Belief* (Stanford: Stanford University Press, 1960), 10–14.

16. In this sense, Jacksonian republicanism resembled eighteenth-century civic republicanism in its backward-looking, nostalgic longing for a lost premodern era.

17. See Maxwell Bloomfield, *Lawyers in a Changing Society, 1776–1876* (Cambridge: Harvard University Press, 1976), 32–58, 136–90.

18. As Lawrence Friedman has stated, "The codification movement is one of the set pieces of American legal history." Friedman, *A History of American Law,* 403.

19. See Charles M. Cook, *The American Codification Movement: A Study of Antebellum Legal Reform* (Westport, Conn.: Greenwood Press, 1981); Robert W. Gordon, review of *The American Codification Movement: A Study in Antebellum Legal Reform,* by Charles Cook, *Vanderbilt Law Review* 36 (1983): 431.

20. See chapter 1, text accompanying notes 30–32 supra.

21. See text accompanying notes 65–67 infra.

22. On law reform and codification in seventeeth-century New England, see George L. Haskins, *Law and Authority in Early Massachusetts: A Study in Tradition and Design* (1960; reprint, Lanham, Md.: University Press of America, 1984), 113–40; G. B. Warden, "Law Reform in England and New England," 1620–1660, *William & Mary Quarterly,* 3d ser., 36 (1978): 668.

23. See Donald Veall, *The Popular Movement for Law Reform, 1640–1660* (Oxford: Clarendon Press, 1970); Warden, "Law Reform in England and New England"; Barbara Shapiro, "Law Reform in Seventeenth Century England," *American Journal of Legal History* 19 (1975): 280. For an earlier dating of the English tradition of criticizing

lawyers, see E. W. Ives, "The Repudiation of the Common Lawyer in English Society, 1450–1550," *University of Birmingham History Journal* 7 (1960): 130.

24. On the development of the idea of legal science, see Michael H. Hoeflich, "Law & Geometry: Legal Science from Leibniz to Langdell," *American Journal of Legal History* 30 (1986): 95.

25. Perry Miller, *The Life of the Mind in America: From the Revolution to the Civil War* (New York: Harcourt, Brace, 1965), 156–64.

26. James Gould, "The Law School at Litchfield," *United States Law Journal* (1822), quoted in Miller, *The Life of the Mind,* 156.

27. See chapter 2, text accompanying notes 55–74.

28. For a representative expression of this view, see "Edward Livingston and His Code," *United States Magazine and Democratic Review* 9 (1841): 12.

29. On Rantoul as a political Progressive, see Meyers, *The Jacksonian Persuasion,* 206–33.

30. *Memoirs, Speeches and Writings of Robert Rantoul, Jr.,* ed. Luther Hamilton (Boston: J. P. Jewett, 1854), 280.

31. Ibid., 278. The leading labor lawyer, Frederick Robinson, expressed similar views. See, e.g., Frederick Robinson, "A Program for Labor," in *Social Theories of Jacksonian Democracy,* ed. Joseph Blau (Indianapolis: Bobbs-Merrill, 1954), 331.

32. See Gordon, review of *The American Codification Movement,* 445–46.

33. See Robert W. Gordon, "Legal Thought and Legal Practice in the Age of American Enterprise," 1870–1920, in *Professions and Professional Ideologies in America,* ed. Gerald L. Geison (Chapel Hill: University of North Carolina Press, 1984), 82–85.

34. The first post-independence revision, completed by Samuel Jones and Richard Varick in 1789, largely assembled all of the statutes that satisfied the 1777 state constitution's description of the law of New York as including nonrepugnant parts of the common law and statutes of England and the colony in force as of April 19, 1775. The 1801 revision was done by Chief Justice Kent and Justice Radcliffe of the New York Supreme Court. The revisers for the 1813 revision were William Van Ness and John Woodworth. See William Allen Butler, *The Revision of the Statutes of the State of New York and the Revisers* (Albany: Banks & Brothers, 1889), 5.

35. Fox, *Decline of Aristocracy,* ch. 8. Indispensable commentaries on the issues and personalities involved in New York politics around the time of the convention are provided in the classic work by Judge Jabez D. Hammond, *The History of Political Parties in the State of New York,* 2 vols. (Albany: C. Van Benthuysen, 1842).

36. Nathaniel H. Carter and William L. Stone (reporters), *Reports of the Proceedings and Debates of the Convention of 1821: Assembled for the Purpose of Amending the Constitution of the State of New York,* 220.

37. Meyers, *Jacksonian Persuasion,* 243–44. At the same time, though, even the Old Federalists were not always anti-democratic in their leanings. On the issue of extending suffrage to free Blacks, for example, the Federalists strongly tended to support calls for greater democracy. See Kass, *Politics in New York State,* 85.

38. A pamphlet that circulated in Albany during the constitutional convention under the obviously ironic pseudonym of "Hamilton," contended that the propertied interests were using the system of equity to undermine republican institutions. See Miller, *The Life of the Mind in America,* 171–72.

39. See text and notes 85–97 infra.

40. See Kass, *Politics in New York State,* 45–47.

41. Ibid., 47–51.

42. Benson, *The Concept of Jacksonian Democracy,* 10.

43. Ibid.

44. Hammond, *History of the Political Parties,* 1:107–8.

45. Hammond observed that the legislature "could never find the time to attend to [the call for statutory revision] until after the election in November." Ibid., 181.

46. Ibid., 182.

47. Kent denied a rumor, circulating at the time, that he was unwilling to be associated with Butler because of comments that Butler had made in oral arguments before the Court of Errors about some of Kent's opinions as Chancellor. See Butler, *The Revision and the Revisors,* 8.

48. See Robert F. Jones, *"The King of the Alley": William Duer—Politician, Entrepreneur, and Speculator, 1768–1799* (Philadelphia: American Philosophical Society, 1992).

49. Kass, *Politics in New York State,* 117.

50. See Revision of the Laws, *Atlantic Magazine* 2 (1825): 459, 460.

51. Ibid., 460.

52. Charles A. Lincoln, ed., *Message from the Governors, Comprising Executive Communications to the Legislature* (Albany: J. B. Lyon, 1909), 2:90.

53. *New York American,* 24 March 1825.

54. Butler, in his inaugural address at the University of the City of New York, specifically cited, with evident approval, Bacon's conception that "the common law should be reduced and systematically digested." See Miller, *The Life of the Mind,* 257.

55. Bernard Rudden, "A Code Too Soon—The 1826 Property Code of James Humphreys: English Rejection, American Reception, English Acceptance," in *Essays in Memory of Professor F. H. Lawson,* ed. Peter Wallington and Robert H. Merkin (London: Butterworth, 1986), 105.

56. In their first report to the legislature, they were anxious to point out that their work "must be carefully distinguished from codification. . . . We have found it necessary in our report to exclude this idea which has got abroad and has exposed us to much prejudice with those who believe every project of that sort visionary and dangerous." Quoted in Butler, *The Revision and the Revisors,* 22.

57. See Avner Offer, *Property and Politics, 1870–1914: Landownership, Law, Ideology and Urban Development in England* (Cambridge: Cambridge University Press, 1981), 23–34.

58. Writing to James Humphreys in 1826, Edward Sugden, later Lord St. Leonards, stated: "It is a singular circumstance, that whilst we complain of our law of property,

and are so anxious for new laws, the infant state of America is daily adopting ours, with scarcely any variation, and particularly those portions of the operation of which we appear to complain most loudly." Edward Sugden, *Letters to James Humphreys,* 3d ed. (London: J. & W. T. Clarke, 1826), 76.

59. N.Y. Rev. Stat. of 1836, vol. 3, appendix, p. 414.

60. Humphreys's influence on the New York statutory revision has not been widely discussed. An unpublished doctoral dissertation argues that the property sections of the Revised States were "largely an attempt to put into effect changes in the law of real property recommended by an Englishman, James Humphreys." W. D. Driscoll, "Benjamin F. Butler: Lawyer and Regency Politician" (Ph.D. diss., Fordham University, 1965), 147. The most careful and insightful discussion of Humphreys's influence on the New York revisers is Rudden, "A Code Too Soon."

61. James Humphreys, *Observations on the Actual State of the English Laws of Real Property* (London: John Murray, 1826), 203.

62. Ibid., 172.

63. Ibid., 172, 202.

64. Bernard Rudden, "A Code Too Soon," 102.

65. N.Y. Rev. Stat. of 1829, pt. 2, ch. 1, tit. 1, art. 1, §3.

66. Act of February 20, 1787.

67. Rhys Isaac, *The Transformation of Virginia, 1740–1790* (Chapel Hill: University of North Carolina Press, 1982), 131.

68. On Brackenridge, see Robert A. Ferguson, *Law and Letters in American Culture* (Cambridge: Harvard University Press, 1984), 119–28.

69. Hugh Henry Brackenridge, *Law Miscellanies* (Philadelphia: Byrne, 1814), 146–47 (emphasis in original).

70. 1 W. Bl. 672 (1769).

71. Reprinted in Francis Hargrave, ed., *A Collection of Tracts Relative to the Laws of England from Manuscripts* (Dublin, 1787), 490–41.

72. Brackenridge, *Law Miscellanies,* 150–52 (emphasis in original).

73. New York State Commission to Revise the Statutory Laws of New York, Report of the Commissioners Made to the Senate, Nov. 2, 1827, pt. 2, ch. 1, tit. 2, art. 1, notes, p. 26 (1827).

74. If no other interest was created that intervenes between A's life estate and his remainder, under the separate doctrine of merger, A's two estates combine to yield a fee simple, which is the common law's equivalent of complete ownership.

75. The rule prevented evasion of feudal incidents during fiscal feudalism in the sixteenth century because those incidents were due only if land passed by descent (i.e., inheritance) rather than by purchaser (i.e., by gift, deed, or will). Since A took a fee simple, unless he subsequently transferred the land to someone else or devised it to his heirs by will, his heirs would receive the land by descent, triggering payment of the relevant feudal incidents.

76. Hargrave, *Collection of Tracts,* 500.

77. Friedman, *History of American Law,* 412.

78. The twenty-one-year period in gross was not authoritatively held to be part of the rule in England until 1833. Cadell v. Palmer, 1 Cl. & F. 372, 6 Eng. Rep. 956 (1832–33). American courts quickly followed the English courts' lead.

79. 11 Ves. Jr. 112, 32 Eng. Rep. 1030 (1805).

80. 39 & 40 Geo. III, c. 98.

81. Humphreys, *Observations,* 282–301.

82. Notes of the Original Revisers, in Robert L. Fowler, *Real Property Law of the State of New York* (New York: Baker, Voorhis, 1909), 762, 769–70.

83. N.Y. Rev. Stat. of 1829, pt. 2, ch. 1, tit. 2, art. 1, §35.

84. N.Y. Rev. Stat. of 1828–35, pt. 2, ch. 1, tit. 2, art. 2, notes, p. 583.

85. Id. at 583.

86. Id. at 585.

87. Fowler, *Real Property Law,* 1293.

88. Ibid., 728–29.

89. Ibid.

90. New York State Commission to Revise the Statutory Laws of New York, Report of the Commissioners Made to the Senate, Nov. 2, 1827, pt. 2, ch. 1, tit. 1, art. 2, notes, p. 35 (1827).

91. Lawrence Friedman, "The Dynastic Trust," *Yale Law Journal* 73 (1964): 547.

92. Ibid., 585.

93. See Edward B. Sugden, *A Practical Treatise of Powers* (Philadelphia: T. & J. W. Johnson, 1847), 105: "By our law one man may create an unalienable personal trust in favour of another, for his support and maintenance."

94. Brandon v. Robinson, 18 Ves. 429, 34 Eng. Rep. 379 (Ch. 1811).

95. Indicative of this consciousness, Blackstone's discussion of the law of husband and wife appears in a category of private rights that includes other relations of social hierarchy, including parent-and-child and master-and-servant. William Blackstone, *Commentary on the Laws of England* (1765; reprint, Chicago: University of Chicago Press, 1979), 1:421–33.

96. See chapter 6.

97. See chapter 7.

98. Thomas Skidmore, *The Rights of Man to Property! Being a Proposition to Make It Equal among the Adults of the Present Generation: and to Provide for Its Equal Transmission to Every Individual of Each Succeeding Generation, on Arriving at the Age of Maturity* (New York, 1829).

99. Ibid., 354.

100. Ibid., 353.

Chapter Five

1. See, e.g., Maurice G. Baxter, *One and Inseparable: Daniel Webster and the Union* (Cambridge: Harvard University Press, 1984), 448; Robert A. Ferguson, *Law and Letters*

in American Culture (Cambridge: Harvard University Press, 1984), 276–78; Marvin Meyers, *The Jacksonian Persuasion: Politics and Belief* (Stanford: Stanford University Press, 1960), 238; John Theodore Horton, *James Kent: A Study in Conservatism, 1763–1847* (New York: D. Appleton-Century, 1939).

More balanced views are found in Lawrence M. Friedman, *A History of American Law,* 2d ed. (New York: Simon & Schuster, 1985), 332; David W. Raack, "'To Preserve the Best Fruits': The Legal Thought of Chancellor James Kent," *American Journal of Legal History* 23 (1989): 320, 325 (arguing that the perception of Kent as an "extreme conservative" is "mistaken").

2. Robert H. Wiebe, *The Opening of American Society: From the Adoption of the Constitution to the Eve of Disunion* (New York: Vintage Books, 1984), 312.

3. Donald Roper, "James Kent and the Emergence of New York's Libel Law," *American Journal of Legal History* 17 (1973): 223, 225.

4. Walter Hamilton, review of *James Kent: A Study in Conservatism, 1763–1847,* by John T. Horton, *Yale Law Journal* 49 (1940): 1507.

5. James W. Ely, Jr., *The Guardian of Every Other Right: A Constitutional History of Property Rights* (New York: Oxford University Press, 1992), 80.

6. The best discussions of Kent's opposition to popular democracy and universal suffrage are Meyers, *The Jacksonian Persuasion,* and Louis Hartz, *The Liberal Tradition in America: An Interpretation of American Political Thought since the Revolution* (New York: Harcourt, Brace, 1955).

7. Meyers, *The Jacksonian Persuasion,* 243.

8. Kent Newmyer has called Kent's *Commentaries* "the most influential treatise on american law to appear in the nineteenth century." R. Kent Newmyer, *Supreme Court Justice Joseph Story: Statesman of the Old Republic* (Chapel Hill: University of North Carolina Press, 1985), 136.

9. See, e.g., Stowell v. Flagg, 11 Mass. 364 (1814); Wolcott Woolen Mfg. Co. v. Upham, 22 Mass. (5 Pick.) 292 (1827); Cogswell v. Essex Mill Corp., 23 Mass. (6 Pick.) 94 (1828). These cases are analyzed in Morton J. Horwitz, *The Transformation of American Law, 1780–1860* (Cambridge: Harvard University Press, 1977), 47–54. As Horwitz observes, the mills acts "were, more than any other legal measure, crucial in dethroning landed property from the supreme position it had occupied in the eighteenth century world view, and, ultimately, in transforming real estate into just another cash-valued commodity." Ibid., 47–48.

10. I have in mind the canon of contract clause cases that extended from Fletcher v. Peck, 10 U.S. (6 Cranch) 87 (1810), in the era of the Federalist Marshall Court to the icon of the Taney Court's Jacksonianism, Proprietors of the Charles River Bridge v. Proprietors of the Warren Bridge, 36 U.S. (11 Pet.) 420 (1837). As G. Edward White has aptly stated, these cases "furnish us with an index of the changes in American economic and political life that took place during the Court's tenure, as a society whose primary economic indicator was speculation in and control of undeveloped land (Fletcher v. Peck) gave way to a society in which the corporate franchise was the pri-

mary unit of economic activity (the *Charles River Bridge* case)." G. Edward White, *The Marshall Court and Cultural Change: 1815–1835* (New York: Oxford University Press, 1991), 597.

11. The phrase is, of course, R. W. B. Lewis's. See R. W. B. Lewis, *The American Adam: Innocence, Tragedy, and Tradition in the Nineteenth Century* (Chicago: University of Chicago Press, 1955).

12. Gordon Wood has offered a reading of Kent's views, expressed in the 1820–21 New York constitutional conventions debates, as unequivocally enthusiastic about the emergence of market society. Gordon S. Wood, *The Radicalism of the American Revolution* (New York: Vintage, 1991), 268–70. While I agree with Wood that Kent rejected a civic conception of property, I think that his enthusiasm for the type of society that commodity property created was mixed with anxiety.

13. A pervasive ambivalence to America's prosperity and change in the antebellum years is sensitively described in Fred Somkin, *Unquiet Eagle: Memory and Desire in the Idea of American Freedom, 1815–1860* (Ithaca: Cornell University Press, 1967).

14. Newmyer, *Supreme Court Justice Joseph Story.*

15. See James Kent to Thomas Washington, New York City, 6 October 1828, reprinted as "An American Law Student of a Hundred Years Ago," in Association of American Law Schools, *Select Essays in Anglo-American Legal History* (Boston, 1907), 837, 838.

16. George Goldberg, "James Kent, The American Blackstone: The Early Years," in *Law-Making and Law-Makers in British History: Papers Presented to the Edinburgh Legal History Conference, 1977,* ed. Alan Harding (1980), 157, 162.

17. See John H. Langbein, "Chancellor Kent and the History of Legal Literature," *Columbia Law Review* 93 (1993): 547, 558; Goldberg, "James Kent, The American Blackstone," 175.

18. Langbein, "Chancellor Kent," 560–62.

19. Ibid., 553.

20. See William Kent, *Memoirs and Letters of James Kent* (Boston: Little, Brown, 1898), 31–32.

21. James Kent to Theodorus Bailey, 27 January 1791, Papers of James Kent, vol. 1, Manuscripts Division, Library of Congress.

22. *Commentaries,* 1:253.

23. See Joseph Dorfman, "Chancellor Kent and the Developing American Economy," *Columbia Law Review* 61 (1961): 1290, 1304.

24. James Kent to Theodorus Bailey, 27 February 1791, in Kent, *Memoirs and Letters,* 42.

25. See ibid., 1290.

26. James Kent to Elizabeth Hamilton, 10 December 1832, in Kent, *Memoirs and Letters,* 315.

27. Kent himself acknowledged that he had "no talents for an attorney." "Memoranda," Papers of James Kent, vol. 3, Manuscripts Division, Library of Congress.

28. See Horton, *Kent: A Study in Conservatism,* 51–52, 101–4.

29. Dorfman, "Chancellor Kent," 1291.

30. The complete text of Kent's lectures during his first professorship at Columbia, between 1794 and 1797, was apparently lost or destroyed, possibly by Kent himself. In a letter written while he was publishing the first edition of the *Commentaries,* Kent dismissed the first set of lectures as "slight and trashy productions." 1828 Letter, in Kent, *Memoirs and Letters,* 841. All that remains of the initial lectures are the texts of the first four and a syllabus of the rest. See James Kent, "An Introductory Lecture to a Course of Law Lectures Delivered Nov. 17, 1794," reprinted in *Columbia Law Review* 3 (1903): 330; James Kent, *Dissertations: Being the Preliminary Part of a Course of Law Lectures* (New York: George Forman, 1795). John Langbein notes that the pamphlets of these lectures "bombed on the marketplace" as much as the lectures did in the classroom. Langbein, "Chancellor Kent," 559n. 58.

31. The 1821 Constitution, continuing a provision of the 1777 Constitution, imposed a mandatory retirement requirement for all judges at age 60. See Butler, *The Revision and the Revisors,* 6. Democrats in the New York legislature had attempted various ploys to get Kent to retire earlier. Failing initially to get his court abolished, they succeeded in severely cutting his salary several times. See Horton, *Kent: Study in Conservatism,* 259–60.

32. In the preface to the *Commentaries* he frankly acknowledged that he took the position for "want of occupation."

33. Ibid., iv.

34. James Kent to Simeon Baldwin, 10 October 1782, in Kent, *Memoirs and Letters,* 16.

35. Some of them did. For the reactions of William Livingstone, Josiah Quincy, and Daniel Webster, substantially similar to Kent's, see *The Papers of Daniel Webster: Legal Papers,* ed. Alfred S. Konefsky and Andrew J. King (Hanover, N.H.: University Press of New England, 1982), 1:3, 1:6–7.

36. See, e.g., Horton, *Kent: Study in Conservatism,* 264. The first reference I have discovered explicitly drawing the comparison is in a letter from Joseph Story to Kent first reacting to the work. The *Commentaries,* Kent stated, "will become an American textbook and range on the same shelf with the classical work of Blackstone in all our libraries." Joseph Story to James Kent, 15 December 1827, quoted in Horton, *Kent: Study in Conservatism,* 302.

37. Langbein, "Chancellor Kent," 591.

38. Ibid.

39. Kent, 1828 Letter, 838. In the same letter, Kent recalled that while studying the law, he read Blackstone "again and again." Ibid.

40. See Newmyer, *Supreme Court Justice Joseph Story,* xiv. On the antebellum conception of legal science, see chapter 4.

41. Kent, *Memoirs and Letters,* 178.

42. One example of the difference in coverage is criminal law. Kent's *Commentaries*

did not cover criminal law, while Blackstone devoted an entire volume to it. Kent explained that although the criminal was "a very important part of our legal system," he omitted it because it was based on "an exact knowledge of local law . . . in each state." His objective was "professedly national, and not local." Kent, *Commentaries*, 4: 1527. Another difference was the treatment of civil procedure. Kent declined to cover procedure for the same reason he gave for omitting criminal law.

43. Kent, *Commentaries*, 2:418. Kent's selective coverage, excluding criminal law, for example, was guided precisely by this objective. See note 41 supra.

44. See G. Edward White, *The American Judicial Tradition* (New York: Oxford University Press, 1976), 46.

45. Langbein, "Chancellor Kent," 585–94.

46. Ibid., 593.

47. Blackstone, *Commentaries*, vol. 2.

48. See Alan Watson, "The Structure of Blackstone's Commentaries," *Yale Law Journal* 97 (1988): 795.

49. Ibid., 798.

50. Kenneth Vandevelde, "The New Property of the Nineteenth Century: The Development of the Modern Concept of Property," *Buffalo Law Review* 29 (1980): 325, 331–32 (quoting Blackstone, *Commentaries*, 2:17).

51. Carol Rose has emphasized how the "properness" of "property"—property as *proprietas*—contrasts with the modern notion of property as wealth. See Carol M. Rose, "'Takings' and the Practices of Property: Property as Wealth, Property as 'Propriety,'" in *Property and Persuasion: Essays on the History, Theory, and Rhetoric of Ownership* (Boulder, Colo.: Westview Press, 1994), 49.

52. Blackstone, *Commentaries*, 1:317.

53. Ibid.

54. Ibid., 316.

55. The "mirroir" to which Blackstone refers is the medieval treatise *Mirror of Justices*, written about 1290, about the same period as Britton and Fleta. Plucknett states that the presumptive author was Andrew Horn, chamberlain of London during the reign of Edward II. An extraordinary and entertaining work, the *Mirror* is filled with wild tales about the law. It was not circulated until the sixteenth century, when it was discovered by antiquarians. Coke, among others, made the mistake of treating it entirely seriously, thereby legitimating many of its fables. See T. F. T. Plucknett, *A Concise History of the Common Law*, 5th ed. (Boston: Little, Brown, 1956), 267.

56. Blackstone, *Commentaries*, 2:385.

57. Ibid.

58. See chapter 2, text and notes 67–74 supra.

59. Kent, *Commentaries*, 2:263.

60. See S. F. C. Milsom, *Historical Foundations of the Common Law*, 2d ed. (Toronto: Butterworth, 1981), 105–12.

61. Ibid., 106.

62. Kent, *Commentaries*, 2:264.

63. Ibid., 264 (emphasis added).

64. Kent, *Commentaries*, 4:436.

65. Ibid.

66. Ibid., 438.

67. See chapter 2, text and notes 9–16 supra.

68. See, e.g., Kent, *Commentaries*, 3:397–401.

69. Ibid.

70. E.g., ibid. 3:513: "Thus, by one of those singular revolutions incident to human affairs, allodial estates once universal in Europe, and then almost universally exchanged for feudal tenures, have now, after the lapse of many centuries, regained their primitive estimation in the minds of freemen."

71. Kent, *Commentaries*, 4:437.

72. Ibid., 3:406.

73. Ibid., 4:435.

74. Ibid.

75. Rather than Prometheus, one is perhaps tempted to draw upon the literary heroes of Kent's time who collectively personified what R. W. B. Lewis called the myth of "the American Adam." R. W. B. Lewis, *The American Adam: Innocence, Tragedy, and Tradition in the Nineteenth Century* (Chicago: University of Chicago Press, 1955). The exemplar of this figure was Natty Bumppo, the hero of James Fenimore Cooper's Leatherstocking novels set in the late eighteenth-century American frontier (although Cooper wrote the Leatherstocking tales during the first half of the nineteenth century). One is tempted to associate Kent's theme of the effects of the new stage of civilization with Cooper's hero, not the least because of Kent's and Fenimore Cooper's proximity to each other in time, place, and politics (Fenimore Cooper shared Kent's staunchly Federalist views). But however much they were alike in other respects, Cooper's views about American society and culture in the antebellum nineteenth century differed sharply from Kent's in important respects. Most obvious among these was Cooper's fear about the effects of a commercialized society and his adherence to the classical theory that a leisured class of large landowners who maintained and lived on their land was the only means for fostering the high values of a society.

76. Kent, *Commentaries*, 3:401.

77. Quoted in Dorfman, "Chancellor Kent," 1292.

78. Kent, *Commentaries*, 4:19.

79. Ibid.

80. Ibid., 19–20.

81. James Kent to Daniel Webster, 21 January 1830, in Kent, *Memoirs and Letters*, 207.

82. Kent, *Commentaries*, 4:20.

83. Ibid., 258.

84. Ibid., 2:265.

85. Ibid., 266n. a.

86. Ibid., 266.

87. Ibid., 267. Shortly after this passage, Kent enlisted Adam Smith in his attack on sumptuary laws as unnecessarily and unreasonably intrusive of the private sphere: "Dr. Adam Smith, in his *Wealth of Nations,* justly considers it to be an act of the highest impertinence and presumption, for kings and rulers to pretend to watch over the economy and expenditure of private persons." Ibid., 268n. a.

88. See chapter 4.

89. James Kent to Moss Kent, Jr., 3 April 1835, in Kent, *Memoirs and Letters,* 218.

90. Ibid., 219.

91. See chapter 2, text and notes 67–74 supra.

92. Kent, *Commentaries,* 3:307.

93. Kent, *Commentaries,* 4:8n. b.

94. See, e.g., Douglas Baird and Thomas Jackson, "Information, Uncertainty, and the Transfer of Property," *Journal of Legal Studies* 13 (1984): 299.

95. N.Y. Rev. Stat. of 1827–28, pt. 2, ch. 1, tit. 2, art. 3 (1829).

96. Kent, *Commentaries,* 4:107n. b.

97. See chapter 4, text and notes 73–75 supra.

98. Kent, *Commentaries,* 4:224.

99. Ibid., 225. This argument still appears today, often dressed up in the economic language of reducing "transaction costs." Judge Richard Posner, for example, recently has explained the rule on the basis of the insight that "[t]he more owners a piece of property has, the more costly it is to sell, improve, or otherwise transact with regard to it." First Nat'l Bank of Chicago v. Comptroller of the Currency of the United States, 956 F.2d 1360 (7th Cir. 1992). The basic insight is correct, but it does not justify the Rule in Shelley's Case. The Rule, as all first-year law students are taught, is easily avoided through any of several techniques. One evasion technique is to use two pieces of paper instead of one: first convey a life estate to A, then by a second deed convey the rest to A's heirs. The second deed does not transfer to the heirs a remainder interest, but a reversion, to which the rule does not apply. For further examples of evasion tactics, see Jesse Dukeminier and James E. Krier, *Property,* 3d ed. (Boston: Little, Brown, 1993), 292–93.

100. Kent, *Commentaries,* 4:221.

101. Ibid., 226.

102. Ibid., 226n. a.

103. James Kent to Joseph Story, 5 October 1842, in Joseph Story Papers, 3 vols., Massachusetts Historical Society.

104. See Ferguson, *Law and Letters,* 277–80.

105. Kent used the law of mortgage, for example, to illustrate equity's superiority: "[T]he case of mortgages is one of the most splendid instances in the history of our

jurisprudence, of the triumph of equitable principles over technical rules, and the homage which those principles have received by their adoption in the courts of law." Ibid., 152.

106. Kent, *Commentaries,* 4:306–7.

107. Ibid., 307–8.

108. Ibid., 306–7.

109. For illustrative data on the use of trusts among elite families in the nineteenth century, see Carole Shammas, Marylynn Salmon and Michel Dahlin, *Inheritance in America: From Colonial Times to Present* (New Brunswick, N.J.: Rutgers University Press, 1987), 107–8.

110. New York State Commission to Revise the Statutory Laws of New York, Report of the Commissioners Made to the Senate, Nov. 2, 1827, pt. 2, ch. 1, tit. 2, art. 1, notes, p. 35 (1827).

Chapter Six

1. See Norma Basch, *In the Eyes of the Law: Women, Marriage, and Property in Nineteenth-Century New York* (Ithaca: Cornell University Press, 1982); Marylynn Salmon, *Women and the Law of Property in Early America* (Chapel Hill: University of North Carolina Press, 1986); Richard H. Chused, "Late Nineteenth Century Married Women's Property Law: Reception of the Early Married Women's Property Acts by Courts and Legislatures," *American Journal of Legal History* 29 (1985): 3; Richard H. Chused, "The Oregon Donation Act of 1850 and the Nineteenth Century Federal Married Women's Property Law," *Law & History Review* 2 (1984): 44; Richard H. Chused, "Married Women's Property Law: 1800–1850," *Georgetown Law Journal* 71 (1983): 1359; Peggy A. Rabkin, *Fathers to Daughters: The Legal Foundations of Female Emancipation* (Westport, Conn.: Greenwood Press, 1980); Peggy A. Rabkin, "The Origins of Law Reform: The Social Significance of the Nineteenth-Century Codification Movement and Its Contribution to the Passage of the Early Married Women's Property Acts," *Buffalo Law Review* 24 (1974): 683; Elizabeth Bowles Warbasse, *The Changing Legal Rights of Married Women, 1800–1861* (New York: Garland, 1987); Reva B. Siegel, "Home as Work: The First Woman's Rights Claims Concerning Wives' Household Labor, 1850–1880," *Yale Law Journal* 103 (1994): 1073; Reva B. Siegel, "The Modernization of Marital Status Law: Adjudicating Wives' Rights to Earnings, 1860–1930," *Georgetown Law Journal* 82 (1994): 2127.

2. Basch, *In the Eyes of the Law,* 38.

3. See Carole Shammas, Marylynn Salmon, and Michel Dahlin, *Inheritance in America: From Colonial Times to the Present* (New Brunswick, N.J.: Rutgers University Press, 1987), 6.

4. For discussions of wives' status as property owners today, see, e.g., Carol M. Rose, "Women and Property: Gaining and Losing Ground," in *Property and Persuasion: Essays on the History, Theory, and Rhetoric of Ownership* (Boulder, Colo.: Westview Press, 1994), 233; Joan C. Williams, "Privatization as a Gender Issue," in *A Fourth Way?*

Privatization, Property, and the Emergence of New Market Democracies, ed. Gregory S. Alexander and Grazyna Skapska (New York: Routledge, 1994), 215; Diane Pearce, "Welfare Is Not for Women," in *Women, the State, and Welfare,* ed. Linda Gordon (Madison: University of Wisconsin Press, 1990), 266.

5. Basch, *In the Eyes of the Law,* 69.

6. Blackstone, *Commentaries,* 1:430.

7. Hendrik Hartog, "Marital Exits and Marital Expectations in Nineteenth Century America," *Georgetown Law Journal* 80 (1991): 95, 128.

8. Ibid., 96–97.

9. Blackstone's purpose was also to stress that marriage was a municipal institution rather than an ecclesiastical one, in the sense that secular legislation and doctrines regulated it, not ecclesiastical institutions. This concern about affirming secular law's regulatory authority over marriage was prompted by the fact that ecclesiastical courts applied civil law, not common law, and the civil law's conception of marriage differed in certain fundamental ways from the common law's.

10. Marriage completely and automatically revoked a woman's, but not a man's, prenuptial will.

11. Blackstone, *Commentaries,* 1:430.

12. See Salmon, *Women and the Law of Property in Early America,* 5–13; Chused, "Married Women's Property Law, 1800–1850," 1389–97.

13. The classic American legal text on marriage and marital property throughout much of the nineteenth century was Tapping Reeve's *The Law of Baron and Feme* (New Haven: Oliver Steele, 1816). The first American book on domestic relations law and one of the first legal treatises written by an American, Reeve's book went through four editions. Reeve's treatise was an attempt to Americanize the English common law of marriage and marital property. Substantively, it largely tracked Blackstone's discussion of married women's property, although Reeve was far more likely to criticize legal rules. Reeve's treatment of marital property law was far more technical and detailed than Blackstone's. Like Blackstone, though, Reeve extolled the contractual character of marriage and seldom acknowledged the paternalistic character of married women's property rules.

14. Hulme v. Tennant, 1 Bro. C.C. 16, S.C. 2 Dick. 560 (Ch. 1778).

15. Pybus v. Smith, 3 Bro. C.C. 339, 1 Ves. Jr. 189 (Ch. 1791).

16. See Walter G. Hart, "The Origin of the Restraint upon Anticipation," *Law Quarterly Review* 40 (1924): 221.

17. Tullet v. Armstrong, 4 My. & Cr. 390, 405–6 (Ch. 1839).

18. There were numerous other examples of equity's continuing protectionist attitude. Two can be cited here. The first was equity's enforcement of the so-called secret trust. Chancery decisions held that a person to whom a decedent had devised money or other personalty had to comply with the oral understanding between the decedent and the devisee to hold the transferred assets in trust for a person whose identity was not disclosed in the will. Oral agreements of this type flew in the face of the Statute

of Wills requirement that wills could be enforced only according to their expressed terms. Equity judges were willing to enforce these oral trusts because the beneficiaries usually were the nonmarital family of the wealthy decedent.

The second example is equity's protection of heirs-to-be. Throughout the eighteenth century the Chancellors very closely scrutinized agreement that the expectant heirs of wealthy family heads made with others for the purpose of capitalizing their expectant interests at a steeply discounted rate, for "brown paper and old ginger," as Shakespeare stated in *Measure for Measure* (act 4, scene 3). On equity's protective tradition in the eighteenth century, see Patrick S. Atiyah, *The Rise and Fall of Freedom of Contract* (Oxford: Oxford University Press, 1979), 172–77.

19. They also enforced, albeit haltingly and reluctantly, separate maintenance agreements.

20. Methodist Episcopal Church v. Jaques, 1 Johns. Ch. 450 (1815).

21. Jaques v. Methodist Episcopal Church, 17 Johns. 548 (1820).

22. See Salmon, *Women and the Law of Property,* 107.

23. 17 Johns. at 453.

24. Id. at 455.

25. The usually given date for the beginning of the married women's property acts is 1839, the year in which Mississippi passed what historians often claim was the first such act. In fact, however, Arkansas passed the first statute in 1835. See Chused, "Married Women's Property Law, 1800–1850," 1398–1400.

26. Here I draw on Warbasse, *The Changing Legal Rights of Married Women, 1800–1861,* and Chused, "Married Women's Property Law, 1880–1850," 1397–1412.

27. See Chused, "Married Women's Property Law, 1800–1850," 1398–99.

28. See Reginald C. McGrane, *The Panic of 1837* (New York: Russell & Russell, 1965).

29. Chused, "Married Women's Property Law, 1880–1850," 1411.

30. Ibid., 1410.

31. See Chused, "Late Nineteenth Century Married Women's Property Law"; Suzanne D. Lebsock, "Radical Reconstruction and the Property Rights of Southern Women," *Journal of Southern History* 43 (1977): 195.

32. *New York Assembly Journal,* 24 April 1837, 121.

33. Thomas Herttell, *Argument in the House of Assembly of the State of New York in the Session of 1837 in Support of the Bill to Restore to Married Women "The Right of Property" as Guaranteed by the Constitution of This State* (New York, 1839).

34. Ibid., 44.

35. Ibid., 22.

36. This is not to say that there was no commonality between Herttell's bill and the 1848 act or that Herttell was isolated from the major law reformers in New York State. To the contrary, Herttell was assisted in drafting his bill by two leading figures in the legal establishment, John C. Spencer, one of the revisers of the 1828 statutory revision, and John Savage, Chief Justice of the New York Supreme Court. See *New*

York Evening Star, 18 January 1838. Herttell's efforts were an important catalyst for the eventual statutory changes.

37. Herttell, *The Right of Property,* 11.

38. Mary Beard, *Women as a Force in History* (New York: Macmillan, 1946).

39. Even prior to the trust law revision, the equitable estate was an entirely inadequate substitute for legal recognition of married women's status as autonomous property owners for two reasons. First, the equitable estate device was not widely available; only the relatively wealthy could afford it. Second and more fundamentally, by creating a separate property interest that was insulated from husbands and others, it reinforced the hierarchical relationship between husbands and wives that was premised on the view that married women were unable to take care of themselves. To the extent that married women's property statutes represented the extension of the commodified conception of property to the realm of marital property—and it did so only incompletely—those statutes represented the repudiation of this view. Beard's thesis totally ignores this dimension of the shift from the equitable estate to legal empowerment.

40. Rabkin, *Fathers to Daughters,* 75.

41. *Constitution of the State of New York, 1846,* art. 6, §§2–4.

42. Criticism of equity's discretionary character appeared in England as early as the sixteenth century. See S. F. C. Milsom, *Historical Foundations of the Common Law,* 2d ed. (Toronto: Butterworth, 1981), 88–96. In America, opposition to Chancery as a separate court came early and was intense. As Stanley Katz has pointed out, "No colonial legal institution was the object of such sustained and intense political opposition as the courts dispensing equity law." Stanley N. Katz, "The Politics of Law in Colonial America and Equity Courts in the Eighteenth Century," *Perspectives in American History* 5 (1971): 257–58. The opposition was not uniform throughout the colonies, however. While Connecticut, Pennsylvania, and Massachusetts, which were heavily influenced by Quaker-Puritan reform ideology, refused to transplant the English institution, other colonies, including New York, Virginia, and South Carolina created them.

43. Basch, *In the Eyes of the Law,* 148.

44. The vote in the Assembly was 93–9; in the Senate, the margin was even more lopsided: 28–1. Basch, *In the Eyes of the Law,* 156.

45. Ibid.

46. Laws of New York, 1848, ch. 200, §1.

47. Id. §2.

48. Westervelt v. Gregg, 12 N.Y. 202 (1854).

49. Elizabeth Cady Stanton, Susan B. Anthony, Matilda Joslyn Gage, and Ida Husted Harper, eds., *History of Woman Suffrage* (New York: Fowlers & Wells, 1889), 1:65.

50. A third traditional disability that the statute retained was that married women could not unilaterally devise their separate estates.

51. Laws of New York, 1849, ch. 375, §3.

52. Id. §3.

53. See Marylynn Salmon, "The Legal Status of Women in Early America," *Law & History Review* 1 (1983): 129, 131.

54. The most that one can plausibly assert is that all formal legal differences in ownership rights between men and women have now been eliminated. Gross substantive inequalities between the genders are still very evident. See, e.g., Martha Albertson Fineman, *The Illusion of Equality: The Rhetoric and Reality of Divorce Reform* (Chicago: University of Chicago Press, 1991); Rose, "Women and Property: Gaining and Losing Ground," 233. Moreover, formal legal differences in property rights for men and women continued to exist well into the twentieth century.

55. See Lawrence M. Friedman, "Law Reform in Historical Perspective," *St. Louis University Law Journal* 13 (1969): 351.

56. The letters, which originally appeared in the *New England Spectator,* were collectively published in 1838 as *Letters on the Quality of the Sexes and the Condition of Women.* See Sarah Grimke, *Letters on the Equality of the Sexes and the Condition of Women* (New York: Source Book Press, 1970).

57. Basch, *In the Eyes of the Law,* 162.

58. Ibid., 119.

59. See Gordon S. Wood, *The Radicalism of the American Revolution* (New York: Vintage Books, 1993), 43–50; Robert H. Wiebe, *The Opening of American Society: From the Adoption of the Constitution to the Eve of Disunion* (New York: Vintage Books, 1984), 265–73; Mary Beth Norton, *Liberty's Daughters: The Revolutionary Experience of American Women, 1750–1800* (Boston: Little, Brown, 1980).

60. Susan Staves, *Married Women's Separate Property in England, 1660–1883* (Cambridge: Harvard University Press, 1990), 4.

61. The best discussion of the separate sphere ideology is Nancy F. Cott, *The Bonds of Womanhood: "Women's Sphere" in New England, 1780–1835* (New Haven: Yale University Press, 1977). See also Barbara Welter, "The Cult of True Womanhood: 1820–1860," in *The American Family in Social-Historical Perspective,* ed. Michael Gordon (New York: St. Martin's Press, 1978), 313.

62. As Barbara Welter has expressed the point, "In a society where values changed frequently, where fortunes rose and fell with frightening rapidity, where social and economic mobility provided instability as well as hope, one thing at least remained the same—a true woman was a true woman, wherever she was found." Ibid., 313.

63. From "Circles," in *The Collected Works of Ralph Waldo Emerson,* ed. Robert E. Spiller and Alfred R. Ferguson (Cambridge: Harvard University Press, 1971), 2:180.

64. Paul Leicester Ford, ed., *The Writings of Thomas Jefferson* (New York: G. P. Putnam's Sons, 1899), 10:86.

65. James Rogers Sharp, *The Jacksonians versus the Banks: Politics in the States after the Panic of 1837* (New York, 1970), 287; Major L. Wilson, *The Presidency of Martin Van Buren* (Lawrence: University Press of Kansas, 1984), 54.

66. The phrase is drawn, of course, from Christopher Lasch, *Haven in a Heartless World: The Family Besieged* (New York: Basic Books, 1977).

67. Quoted in Cott, *The Bonds of Womanhood,* 64.

68. Robert H. Wiebe, *The Opening of American Society: From the Adoption of the Constitution to the Eve of Disunion* (New York: Vintage Books, 1985), 267.

69. Wiebe, *The Opening of American Society,* 265–90.

70. Ralph Waldo Emerson, "Man the Reformer," in *Collected Works,* 1, 147.

71. James Fenimore Cooper, *Home as Found* (New York: Mohawk, 1896), 103.

72. Joel Porte, *Representative Man: Ralph Waldo Emerson in His Time* (New York: Columbia University Press, 1988).

73. The best discussion of Emerson's ambivalence regarding the market is Michael T. Gilmore, *American Romanticism and the Marketplace* (Chicago: University of Chicago Press, 1985), 18–34.

74. Introductory lecture to the series "The Present Age," in *The Early Lectures of Ralph Waldo Emerson,* vol. 3, *1838–1842,* ed. Stephen E. Whicher, Robert E. Spiller, and Wallace E. Williams (Cambridge: Harvard University Press, 1959, 1964, 1972), 191.

75. Quentin Anderson, "Property and Vision in 19th-Century America," *Virginia Quarterly Review* 54 (1978): 385, 394.

76. "Transportation revolution" is drawn, of course, from George Rogers Taylor, *The Transportation Revolution, 1815–1860* (New York: Harper & Row, 1951).

Chapter Seven

1. Exemplars of this interpretation are Kermit L. Hall, *The Magic Mirror: Law in American History* (Oxford: Oxford University Press, 1989), 114–19; Morton J. Horwitz, *The Transformation of American Law, 1780–1860* (Cambridge: Harvard University Press, 1977); J. Willard Hurst, *Law and the Conditions of Freedom in the Nineteenth-Century United States* (Madison: University of Wisconsin Press, 1956).

2. Hurst, *Law and the Conditions of Freedom,* 23.

3. Herbert Hovenkamp, *Enterprise and American Law, 1836–1937* (Cambridge: Harvard University Press, 1991), 17–35, 105–24.

4. This chapter examines the relationship between the judicial vested rights doctrine only in its antebellum incarnation. In a subsequent chapter I examine the post–Civil War vested rights doctrine.

5. See Charles Sellers, *The Market Revolution: Jacksonian America, 1815–1846* (New York: Oxford University Press, 1991), 59.

6. Quoted in Harry L. Watson, *Liberty and Power: The Politics of Jacksonian America* (New York: Hill and Wang, 1990), 133.

7. See ibid., 132–71; Marvin Meyers, *The Jacksonian Persuasion: Politics and Belief* (Stanford: Stanford University Press, 1960), 101–41.

8. Francis Lieber, *The Stranger in America* (London, 1835), 1:68–69, 2:29–30.

9. See, e.g., Adam Smith, *An Inquiry into the Nature and Causes of the Wealth of Nations,* ed. R. H. Campbell, A. S. Skinner, and W. B. Todd (Oxford: Oxford University Press, 1975), 2:43.

10. See Horwitz, *Transformation of American Law, 1780–1860,* 110–11.

11. See Stanley Kutler, *Privilege and Creative Destruction: The Charles River Bridge Case* (New York: W. W. Norton, 1971).

12. 10 U.S. (6 Cranch) 87 (1810).

13. Albert J. Beveridge, *The Life of John Marshall* (Boston: Houghton Mifflin, 1919), 3:551.

14. The story of the Georgia legislature's finagling is told in C. Peter Magrath, *Yazoo: Law and Politics in the New Republic: The Case of Fletcher v. Peck* (Providence, R.I.: Brown University Press, 1966), 4–19, and Beveridge, *Life of John Marshall,* vol. 3, ch. 10.

15. Quoted in Benjamin F. Wright, *The Contract Clause of the Constitution* (Cambridge: Harvard University Press, 1938), 22.

16. On the role of mercantilist theory in the early republic and eventual replacement by classical economics, see Hovenkamp, *Enterprise and American Law,* 11–36.

17. See Magrath, *Yazoo,* 3.

18. 10 U.S. (6 Cranch) at 130.

19. Hurst, *Law and the Conditions of Freedom,* 25.

20. See Wright, *The Contract Clause of the Constitution,* 31n. 13. Marshall's biographer points out that Marshall's interest in stability of contractual obligations and land titles in particular stemmed in no small in part from legal challenges to his own estates. Beveridge, *Life of John Marshall,* 3:582.

21. Quoted in Magrath, *Yazoo,* 13–14.

22. Ibid., 134.

23. Ibid., 135.

24. Ibid.

25. Ibid.

26. 10 U.S. (6 Cranch) at 130.

27. The legal basis for this conclusion is not entirely clear from the text of Marshall's opinion in *Fletcher.* Scholars have disagreed whether Marshall intended that one basis for the decision was natural law. On the one hand, his opinion is replete with references to "certain great principles of justice." See, e.g., 10 U.S. (6 Cranch) at 133. Some scholars have interpreted that language as indicating that natural law was the Court's primary basis for decision. See, e.g., G. Edward White, *The Marshall Court and Cultural Change: 1815–1835* (New York: Oxford University Press, 1991), 604. David Currie has recently pointed out, though, that Marshall's statement that legislative repeal cannot "devest" vested property rights is better read as a statement of fact than of law. David P. Currie, *The Constitution in the Supreme Court: The First Hundred Years, 1789–1888* (Chicago: University of Chicago Press, 1985), 131. Moreover, Currie

persuasively argues, Marshall may have regarded the "general principles" to which he referred as principles as being properly read into the Georgia state constitution's delegation of legislative power. Ibid., 132.

Whether or not Marshall viewed natural law as an independent basis for the decision in *Fletcher,* he clearly did base the decision, at least alternatively, on the contract clause of the federal Constitution. Eager to define a broad scope of applicability for this clause, Marshall dismissed the possible objection, based on the familiar common-law distinction, that the legislative transfer of land was a "conveyance," not a "contract." That distinction might have led the Court to conclude that the legislature's rescission of its earlier conveyance was an uncompensated taking of title, governed by the fifth amendment, and not an impairment of contract. Approaching the case that way, however, would have left the grantee without any constitutional protection since the takings clause applied only to action by the federal government. Citing Blackstone, Marshall reasoned that the term "contract" includes those that are executed as well as executory contracts. 10 U.S. (6 Cranch) at 137. A grant, moreover, includes an implied contract by the grantor not to reassert his rights in the future. Id. Marshall might have pointed out, although, curiously, he did not, that it was well-established in the common law that a conveyance ordinarily implied a warranty of title and that this warranty barred a later action by the grantor against the grantee for the land. See Simpson, *An Introduction to the History of Land Law,* 118–19.

28. Hawkins v. Barney's Lessee, 30 U.S. (5 Pet.) 457 (1831); Jackson v. Lamphire, 28 U.S. (3 Pet.) 280 (1830); Green v. Biddle, 21 U.S. (8 Wheat.) 1 (1823).

29. New Jersey v. Wilson, 11 U.S. (7 Cranch) 164 (1812).

30. Ogden v. Saunders, 25 U.S. (12 Wheat.) 213 (1827); Sturges v. Crowninshield, 17 U.S. (4 Wheat.) 122 (1819).

31. Providence Bank v. Billings, 29 U.S. (4 Pet.) 514 (1830); Trustees of Dartmouth College v. Woodward, 17 U.S. (4 Wheat.) 518 (1819); Terrett v. Taylor, 13 U.S. (9 Cranch) 43 (1815).

32. See Francis N. Stites, *Private Interest and Public Gain: The Dartmouth College Case, 1819* (Amherst: University of Massachusetts Press, 1972), 12.

33. Ibid., 13.

34. Ibid., 16 (emphasis in original).

35. Ibid., 23.

36. Ibid., 25–26.

37. 17 U.S. (4 Wheat.) at 650.

38. Id. at 654.

39. Id. at 666.

40. Trustees of Dartmouth College v. Woodward, 1 N.H. 111, 132–34 (1817). The New Hampshire court relied on Story's earlier concession in Terrett v. Taylor, 13 U.S. (9 Cranch) 43 (1815), that the legislature could modify "public corporations which exist only for public purposes, such as counties, towns, cities, &c. . . ." Id. at 52.

41. 17 U.S. (4 Wheat.) at 630.

42. For trenchant criticisms of this and other aspects of Marshall's opinions, see Currie, *The Constitution in the Supreme Court,* 142–45.

43. 17 U.S. (4 Wheat.) at 645.

44. Id. at 647 ("It is probable, that no man ever was, and that no man ever will be, the founder of a college, believing at the time, that the act of incorporation constitutes no security for the institution").

45. Id. at 648.

46. See, e.g., Providence Bank v. Billings, 29 U.S. (4 Pet.) 514 (1830).

47. 17 U.S. (4 Wheat.) at 636.

48. See Ronald H. Coase, "The Nature of the Firm," *Economica* (n.s.) 4 (1937): 386.

49. Stuart Bruchey, *The Wealth of the Nation: An Economic History of the United States* (New York: Harper & Row, 1988), 43.

50. Ibid.

51. 10 U.S. (6 Cranch) at 137–38.

52. See John Demos, *A Little Commonwealth: Family Life in Plymouth Colony* (Oxford: Oxford University Press, 1970).

53. See, e.g., Mass. Acts 1788, ch. 60.

54. Oscar Handlin and Mary Flug Handlin, *Commonwealth: A Study of the Role of Government in the American Economy—Massachusetts, 1774–1861,* rev. ed. (Cambridge: Harvard University Press, Belknap Press, 1969), 130.

55. See text and notes 64–66 infra.

56. Handlin and Handlin, *Commonwealth,* 139–55.

57. Ibid., 140–47.

58. On the emergence of the distinction between public and private corporations, see Horwitz, *Transformation of American Law, 1780–1860,* 111–14.

59. The corporation's separation from politics existed only to the extent that the original corporate charter did not reserve to the legislature the power to repeal or amend the charter. Many corporate charters in fact included such reservation clauses. See text and notes 67–68 infra.

60. Handlin and Handlin, *Commonwealth,* 154.

61. 17 U.S. (4 Wheat.) at 637.

62. Id. at 631.

63. Id. at 639.

64. Id. at 666.

On Story's contribution to the distinction between public and private corporations, see R. Kent Newmyer, "Justice Joseph Story's Doctrine of 'Public and Private Corporations' and the Rise of the American Business Corporation," *DePaul Law Review* 25 (1976): 825.

65. 17 U.S. (4 Wheat.) at 668–69.

66. Story's theory was rapidly accepted. It was presented as established law in the

major treatises of the time, including Kent's *Commentaries* and Joseph K. Angell and Samuel Ames, *Treatise on the Law of Private Corporations Aggregate* (Boston, 1832), 8–9.

67. See Bruchey, *The Wealth of the Nation*, 45.

68. James Kent, *Commentaries on American Law* (New York, 1830), 2:305.

69. Ibid., 305.

70. Ibid., 305–6.

71. Allen v. McKean, 1 F. Cas. 489, 498 (C.C.D. Me. 1833) (No. 229).

72. Commonwealth v. Essex County, 79 Mass. (13 Gray) 239 (1859); Oldtown & Lincoln R.R. v. Veazie, 39 Me. 571 (1855); Sage v. Dillard, 54 Ky. (15 B. Mon.) 340 (1854); Miller v. New York & Erie R.R., 21 Bard. 513 (N.Y. App. Div. 1856), *limited by* Albany N. R.R. v. Brownell, 24 N.Y. 345 (1862).

For discussion of these cases and the use of reservation clauses generally, see Stephen A. Siegel, "Understanding the Nineteenth Century Contract Clause: The Role of the Property-Privilege Distinction and 'Takings' Clause Jurisprudence," *Southern California Law Review* 60 (1986): 1, 33–35.

73. Commonwealth v. Essex Co., 79 Mass. (13 Gray) at 253.

74. Among the factors contributing to the shift in the Marshall Court's contract clause jurisprudence were changes in the Court's membership. In 1823, Smith Thompson replaced Brockholst Livingstone, who had concurred with Marshall *and* Story in *Dartmouth College*. Thompson's record on the New York Court of Appeals gave every indication that he would be more sympathetic with the exercise of legislative power. See White, *The Marshall Court and Cultural Change*, 648. Moreover, Justice Todd, who had sided with Marshall in every single constitutional case in his tenure on the Court, died in 1823 and was replaced by Robert Trimble. Trimble died in 1828 and was replaced by John McLean, a man whose Presidential aspirations led him to be careful not to offend Jacksonians after 1828. Ibid., 295.

75. Odgen v. Saunders, 25 U.S. (12 Wheat.) 213 (1827) (4–3).

76. Stuges v. Crowninshield, 17 U.S. (4 Wheat.) 122 (1819).

77. *Odgen*, 25 U.S. (12 Wheat.) at 266.

78. Id. at 237.

79. The best telling of the case's story is in Kutler, *Privilege and Creative Destruction*.

80. Horwitz, *Transformation of American Law, 1780–1860*, 130.

81. Kutler, *Privilege and Creative Destruction*, 35.

82. Horwitz, *Transformation of American Law, 1780–1860*, 130.

83. Proprietors of Charles River Bridge v. Proprietors of Warren Bridge, 7 Pick. 344 (Mass. 1830).

84. See R. Kent Newmyer, *Supreme Court Justice Joseph Story: Statesman of the Old Republic* (Chapel Hill: University of North Carolina Press, 1985), 224.

85. See Kutler, *Privilege and Creative Destruction*, 50–53.

86. Ibid., 176–78. Further evidence that Marshall favored upholding the Massa-

chusetts statute comes from Simon Greenleaf's statement that he had been "credibly informed" that Marshall "held the charter of Warren Bridge constitutional." William Cruise, *Digest of the Law of Real Property*, ed. Simon Greenleaf (Boston: Charles C. Little, 1850), 2:68.

87. See, e.g., Morton Keller's characterization of it as the Magna Carta, Morton Keller, "Law, Enterprise, and the Marketplace of Ideas: Hovenkamp's View," *Law & Social Inquiry* 18 (1993): 337, 343. But see Currie, *The Constitution in the Supreme Court*, 150; Wright, *The Contract Clause of the Constitution*, 62–63, 245–46.

88. Currie, *The Constitution in the Supreme Court*, 209.

89. 36 U.S. (11 Pet.) at 545–46.

90. Id. at 548.

91. See chapter 3.

92. 36 U.S. (11 Pet.) at 547.

93. See Bruchey, *The Wealth of the Nation*, 65.

94. Joseph K. Angell and Samuel Ames, *A Treatise on the Law of Private Corporations Aggregate*, 3d ed. (Boston: Little, Brown, 1846), 121.

Chapter Eight

1. Andrew Fede, *People without Rights: An Interpretation of the Fundamentals of the Law of Slavery in the U.S. South* (New York, Garland, 1992), 6.

2. Drew Gilpin Faust, *A Sacred Circle: The Dilemma of the Intellectual in the Old South, 1840–1860* (Baltimore: Johns Hopkins University Press, 1977), x.

3. James Oakes, *The Ruling Race: A History of American Slaveholders* (New York: Vintage Books, 1982).

4. Elizabeth Fox-Genovese and Eugene D. Genovese, *Fruits of Merchant Capital: Slavery and Bourgeois Property in the Rise and Expansion of Capitalism* (Oxford: Oxford University Press, 1983).

5. Robert A. Ferguson, *Law and Letters in American Culture* (Cambridge: Harvard University Press, 1984), 290–97.

6. Eugene D. Genovese and Elizabeth Fox-Genovese, "Slavery Economic Development, and the Law: The Dilemma of the Southern Political Economists, 1800–1860," *Washington & Lee Law Review* 41 (1984): 1, 5–6.

7. Ibid., 10.

8. For an overview of recent historiography on the relationship between proslavery arguments and social visions, see Drew Gilpin Faust, "Introduction," in *The Ideology of Slavery: Proslavery Thought in the Antebellum South, 1830–1860* (Baton Rouge: Louisiana State University Press, 1981).

9. Genovese and Fox-Genovese, "Slavery, Economic Development, and the Law," 2.

10. Thomas Reade Rootes Cobb, *An Inquiry into the Law of Negro Slavery in the United States, to Which is Prefixed an Historical Sketch of Slavery* (1858; reprint, New York: Negro Universities Press, 1968).

11. Little historical scholarship exists concerning Cobb or his writings. The only biography of him, William B. McCash, *Thomas R. R. Cobb: The Making of a Southern Nationalist* (Macon, Georgia: Mercer University Press, 1983), is inadequate in several respects and devotes only a few pages to his scholarship.

12. See William W. Fisher III, "Ideology and Imagery in the Law of Slavery," *Chicago-Kent Law Review* 68 (1993): 1051, 1065.

13. James Henry Hammond, "Letter to an English Abolitionist," in Faust, *Ideology of Slavery*, 177. Hammond's essay was first published in pamphlet form. James Henry Hammond, *Two Letters on Slavery in the United States, Addressed to Thomas Clarkson, Esq.* (Columbia, S.C.: Allen, McCarter, 1845). On Hammond's essay, see Drew Gilpin Faust, *James Henry Hammond and the Old South: A Design for Mastery* (Baton Rouge: Louisiana State University Press, 1982), 278–82.

Southern defenses of slavery were replete with references to slavery as the "cornerstone" or "edifice" of the Southern social order. The origin of that vocabulary is sometimes mistakenly attributed to an 1861 speech by Alexander Stephens, the Confederate Vice-President, but as Hammond's essay demonstrated, it had long since been introduced into Southern slavery discourse. Hammond's own attribution of the origin of the expression is probably more accurate. He attributed it to an 1836 speech by South Carolina Governor George McDuffie. See Faust, *Ideology of Slavery*, 2n. 2.

14. The clearest statement of this line of thought is Hubbard Winslow, *The Means of the Perpetuity and Prosperity of Our Republic, an Oration, Delivered by Request of the Municipal Authorities, of the City of Boston, July 4, 1838* (Boston: Samuel H. Eastburn, 1838).

15. Frank I. Michelman, "Possession vs. Distribution in the Constitutional Idea of Property," *Iowa Law Review* 72 (1987): 1319, 1330.

16. See Frank I. Michelman, "The Supreme Court, 1985 Term—Foreword: Traces of Self-Government," *Harvard Law Review* 100 (1986): 3, 20.

17. Cobb, *Historical Sketch of Slavery*, ccxiii (emphasis in original).

18. Ibid (emphasis in original).

19. For an extensive and penetrating discussion of pro-slavery republicanism, see Larry E. Tise, *Proslavery: A History of the Defense of Slavery in America, 1701–1840* (Athens: University of Georgia Press, 1987), 347–62.

20. Hammond, "Letter to an English Abolitionist," 176.

21. John Codman Hurd, *The Law of Freedom and Bondage in the United States* (Boston: Little, Brown, 1858), 1:468.

22. Cobb, *Historical Sketch of Slavery*, ccxiii.

23. On the importance of the sense of independence among non-elite Southern whites, see Steven Hahn, *The Roots of Southern Populism* (New York: Oxford University Press, 1983), 105–16.

24. As Drew Gilpin Faust has remarked, Fitzhugh has received extravagant attention from slavery historians, particularly Eugene Genovese, in recent years. Drew Gilpin Faust, *A Sacred Circle: The Dilemma of the Intellectual in the Old South, 1840–1860*

(Baltimore: Johns Hopkins University Press, 1977), 127. Still, Genovese seems right in focusing on Fitzhugh's writings as the clearest statements of anti-modernity among all Southern slavery theorists. Genovese's principal analysis of Fitzhugh is in his book *The World the Slaveholders Made* (New York: Pantheon, 1969).

25. George Fitzhugh, "Southern Thought," in Faust, *Ideology of Slavery,* 277, was originally published in *DeBow's Review,* 23 (1857): 338–50.

26. Faust, *Ideology of Slavery,* 282.

27. Ibid.

28. Cobb, *Historical Sketch of Slavery,* lix.

29. On poverty as a threat to republican independence in traditional republican thought, see J. G. A. Pocock, *The Machiavellian Moment: Florentine Political Thought and the Atlantic Republican Tradition* (Princeton: Princeton University Press, 1975).

30. Cobb, *Historical Sketch of Slavery,* lviii.

31. James Oakes has argued that protectionism, or paternalism, as he calls it, was not the mainstream worldview of slaveholders. Most slaveholders, he contends, thoroughly embraced individualism and the market mentality. Oakes, *The Ruling Class,* 192–94. However accurate that claim may be as applied to those slaveholders who were not intellectuals, it was not true of the Southern elite who defended slavery on the basis of a coherent theory of humanity and society.

32. Accord, Peter J. Parish, *Slavery: History and Historians* (New York: Harper & Row, 1989), 143.

33. Cobb, *Historical Sketch of Slavery,* cli–clii.

34. Ibid., clvi–clvii.

35. Ibid., clxx.

36. Ibid., ccii–cciii.

37. Ibid., cxcvvi.

38. Ibid., quoting Robert Baird, *Impressions and Experiences of the West Indies and North America* (Edinburgh: W. Blackwood and Sons, 1850).

39. Ibid., ccv.

40. Cobb, *Law of Negro Slavery,* 49–50 (footnotes omitted).

41. Ibid., 51.

42. See Eugene D. Genovese, *The World the Slaveholders Made: Two Essays in Interpretation* (Middletown, Conn.: Wesleyan University Press, 1988), 124–29.

43. Winslow, *Means of the Perpetuity and Prosperity of Our Republic,* 16.

44. On the influence of the protectionist ideology on judicial decisions, see Mark Tushnet, *The American Law of Slavery, 1810–1860: Considerations of Humanity and Interest* (Princeton: Princeton University Press, 1981).

45. The depiction of the relationship between master and slave as filial was not confined to Southern writers. Frederick Law Olmstead, travelling by horseback through the seaboard South, wrote an account of the master/slave relationships he saw that was virtually identical to Cobb's: "[T]he planters of [Liberty County, Georgia] are as a body remarkably intelligent, liberal, and thoughtful for the moral welfare of the

22

childlike wards Providence has placed under their care and tutorship." Frederick Law Olmstead, *The Cotton Kingdom* (New York, 1861), 2:215.

46. Cobb, *Historical Sketch of Slavery,* ccxvii–ccxviii (footnote omitted).

47. Cobb, *Law of Negro Slavery,* 84.

48. Lewis Hyde, *The Gift: Imagination and the Erotic Life of Property* (New York: Vintage Books, 1979), 60. Hyde is paraphrasing a line from Marx's famous analysis of commodities in *Capital:* "I cannot express the value of linen in terms of linen."

49. John Belton O'Neall, *The Negro Law of South Carolina* (1848). See Linda O. Smiddy, "Judicial Nullification of State Statutes Restricting the Emancipation of Slaves: A Southern Court's Call for Reform," *South Carolina Law Review* 42 (1991): 589, 635–36.

50. See Smiddy, "Judicial Nullification," 634.

51. Karl Marx, *Capital,* trans. Ben Fowkes (1867; reprint, New York: Vintage Books, 1977), 1:125.

52. Eric Foner, *Politics and Ideology in the Age of the Civil War* (New York: Oxford University Press, 1980), 57.

53. Eugene D. Genovese, *The Southern Tradition: The Achievement and Limitations of an American Conservatism* (Cambridge: Harvard University Press, 1994), 79.

54. See Eric Foner, *Free Soil, Free Labor, Free Men: The Ideology of the Republican Party before the Civil War* (New York: Oxford University Press, 1970), 11–72.

55. John C. Calhoun, "Remarks on Receiving Abolition Petitions," 6 February 1837, in *The Papers of John C. Calhoun,* ed. Clyde N. Wilson (Columbia: University of South Carolina Press, 1980), 13:396–97.

56. Once again, it has been left to Eugene Genovese to remind us of what ought not to require reminding. Pro-slavery attacks on wage labor did not constitute some kind of proto-Marxist critique of bourgeois capitalist relations. "[P]oor old John C. Calhoun," Genovese writes, "bears as much intellectual relationship to Marx as to, say, St. Francis of Assisi. . . ." Genovese, *The World the Slaveholders Made,* 182.

57. For more on Trescot, see Eugene D. Genovese, *The Slaveholders' Dilemma: Freedom and Progress in Southern Conservative Thought, 1820–1860* (Columbia: University of South Carolina Press, 1992), 76–85.

58. William Henry Trescot, *The Position and Course of the South* (Charleston, S.C.: Walker and James, 1850), 9–10.

59. Cobb, *Historical Sketch of Slavery,* ccxiv.

60. Trescot, *The Position and Course of the South,* 10–11.

61. Fitzhugh, "Southern Thought," 276–77.

62. See Thomas D. Russell, "South Carolina's Largest Slave Auctioneering Firm," *Chicago-Kent Law Review* 68 (1993): 1241, 1256.

63. Gavin Wright, *The Political Economy of the Cotton South: Households, Markets, and Wealth in the Nineteenth Century* (New York: W. W. Norton, 1978), 41–42.

64. Laurence Shore, *Southern Capitalists: The Ideological Leadership of an Elite, 1832–1885* (Chapel Hill: University of North Carolina Press), 47.

65. Ibid., 48.

66. Roger L. Ransom and Richard Sutch, "Capitalists without Capital: The Burden of Slavery and the Impact of Emancipation," *Agricultural History* 62 (1988): 133, 138–39.

67. For figures on the South Carolina upcountry, see Lacy K. Ford, Jr., *Origins of Southern Radicalism: The South Carolina Upcountry, 1800–1860* (New York: Oxford University Press, 1988), 12; for Georgia's upcountry, see Hahn, *The Roots of Southern Populism.*

68. Hahn, *The Roots of Southern Populism,* 110.

69. Wright, *Political Economy of the Cotton South,* 26–37; Eugene D. Genovese, *The Political Economy of Slavery: Studies in the Economy and Society of the Slave South* (New York: Vintage Books, 1965).

70. See Wright, *Political Economy of the Cotton South,* 143.

71. Shore, *Southern Capitalists,* 51.

72. See Herbert G. Gutman, *The Black Family in Slavery and Freedom, 1750–1925* (New York: Vintage Books, 1976), 145.

73. See Michael Tadman, *Speculators and Slaves: Masters, Traders, and Slaves in the Old South* (Madison: University of Wisconsin Press, 1989), 111–32.

74. Robert William Fogel, *Without Consent or Contract: The Rise and Fall of American Slavery* (New York: W. W. Norton), 68. Fogel doubts that slave trading provided much, if any, of the profits that slaveowners reaped from their slaves. Ibid., 69.

75. See ibid., 248–76.

76. Russell, "South Carolina's Largest Slave Auctioneering Firm," 1241.

77. Ibid., 1252–53.

78. Cobb, *Historical Sketch of Slavery,* clviii.

79. Ibid.

80. Ibid., clix.

81. Ibid. (emphasis in original).

82. Cobb, *Historical Sketch of Slavery,* ccxv.

83. Ibid.

84. On the views of the Southern political economists, see generally Genovese and Fox-Genovese, "Slavery, Economic Development, and the Law," 1.

85. Oakes, *Slavery and Freedom,* 22.

86. See Russell, "South Carolina's Largest Slave Auctioneering Firm," 1227.

87. Genovese and Fox-Genovese, "Slavery, Economic Development, and the Law," 2.

88. The best study of antebellum Southern law's contradictory character and its mediating strategies is Mark Tushnet, *The American Law of Slavery, 1810–1860: Considerations of Humanity and Interest* (Princeton: Princeton University Press, 1981).

89. See Margaret Jane Radin, "Justice and the Market Domain," in *Nomos XXXI: Markets and Justice,* ed. John W. Chapman and J. Roland Pennock (New York: New York University Press, 1989), 165.

90. The notable exception was the work of George Fitzhugh. Concluding that slavery as a noncommodified property system was fundamentally incompatible with a capitalist economy, he called for the abolition of capitalism as the necessary means to preserve slavery. See text accompanying notes 94–95 infra.

91. Cobb, *Historical Sketch of Slavery,* ccxv.

92. Ibid.

93. Ibid., ccxv–ccxvi.

94. See, e.g., George Fitzhugh, *Cannibals All! Or, Slaves without Masters* (1857; reprint, Cambridge: Harvard University Press, 1960), 6. See generally Genovese, *The World the Slaveholders Made,* 165–94.

95. Cobb, *Historical Sketch of Slavery,* ccxxi.

Part Three Prologue

1. For contemporaneous expressions of law as a business, see George F. Shelton, "Law as a Business," *Yale Law Journal* 10 275 (1901); John F. Dillon, "The True Professional Ideal," *American Bar Association Reporter* 17 (1894): 17.

2. On the modern law firm and its practice, see Wayne K. Hobson, "Symbol of the New Profession: Emergence of the Large Law Firm, 1870–1915," in *The New High Priests: Lawyers in Post-Civil War America,* ed. Gerard W. Gawalt (Westport, Conn.: Greenwood Press, 1984), 3; Robert W. Gordon, "'The Ideal and the Actual in the Law': Fantasies and Practices of New York City Lawyers, 1870–1910," in ibid., 51; Gerard W. Gawalt, "The Impact of Industrialization on the Legal Profession in Massachusetts, 1870–1900," in ibid., 97.

3. For the history of the modern American law school, see William P. LaPiana, *Logic and Experience: The Origin of Modern American Legal Education* (New York: Oxford University Press, 1994); Robert Stevens, *Law School: Legal Education in America from the 1850s to the 1980s* (Chapel Hill: University of North Carolina Press, 1983).

4. The story of the modern American law school is by now a familiar one. The best tellings of that story are in the sources cited in note 3 supra.

5. *Harvard Law Review* 1 (1888): 265, 307.

6. See Lawrence M. Friedman, *A History of American Law,* 2d ed. (New York: Simon & Schuster, 1985), 630.

7. *Harvard Law Review* 1 (1887): 35.

8. Thomas C. Grey, "Langdell's Orthodoxy," *University of Pittsburgh Law Review* 45 (1983): 1, 47.

9. Ibid.

10. Austin Wakeman Scott, Notebook on Property Course, Taught by J. C. Gray, 1908–1909 (Manuscripts Collection, Harvard Law School Library), 1; L. A. Burleigh, Notebook on Property Course, Taught by J. C. Gray, 1891–1892 (Manuscripts Collection, Harvard Law School Library), 96.

11. See Burleigh, Notebook, 11. Recently, the idea that for every case there is a single correct answer has been developed, albeit with far more sophistication, by Ron-

ald Dworkin. See, e.g., Ronald Dworkin, *Taking Rights Seriously* (Cambridge: Harvard University Press, 1977), 81–130.

12. For an extremely perceptive discussion of classical legal thought's effect on the bar, see Robert W. Gordon, "The Case for (and against) Harvard," *Michigan Law Review* 93 (1995): 1231.

13. See ibid., 1251–58.

14. See Clyde Jacobs, *Law Writers and the Courts* (Berkeley and Los Angeles: University of California Press, 1954).

15. See Paul D. Carrington, "The Civic Virtue of Populism" (9 February 1994).

16. Quoted in Stevens, *Law School,* 134.

Chapter Nine

1. The classical expressions of this interpretation include Robert G. McCloskey, *American Conservatism in the Age of Enterprise* (Cambridge: Harvard University Press, 1951); Charles Grove Haines, *The Revival of Natural Law Concepts: A Study of the Establishment and of the Interpretation of Limits on Legislatures* (Cambridge: Harvard University Press, 1930); Edward S. Corwin, *Liberty against Government: The Rise, Flowering, and Decline of a Famous Judicial Concept* (Baton Rouge: Louisiana State University Press, 1948). The "laissez-faire constitutionalism" label still persists in recent historical writing. See, e.g., James W. Ely, Jr., *The Guardian of Every Other Right: A Constitutional History of Property Rights* (New York: Oxford University Press, 1992), 100; Arthur S. Miller, "Toward a Definition of 'the' Constitution," *University of Dayton Law Review* 8 (1983): 633, 647.

2. Ely, *The Guardian of Every Other Right,* 82.

3. Progressive history is lucidly explained and analyzed in Ernst A. Breisach, *American Progressive History: An Experiment in Modernization* (Chicago: University of Chicago Press, 1993).

4. For a brief excellent critique of Progressive legal history, see Morton J. Horwitz, "Progressive Legal Historiography," *Oregon Law Review* 63 (1984): 679. As Horwitz explains, while Progressive historiography has now been widely repudiated in virtually all other areas of American history, it continues to exert a strong pull in late nineteenth-century legal history, especially constitutional history. Horwitz's explanation is that constitutional historians continue to focus on "questions that originally arose because of the Supreme Court's attack on and then capitulation to the New Deal." Ibid., 680.

For examples of the general critique of Progressive historiography, which has been ongoing for the past three decades, see Richard Hofstadter, *The Progressive Historians* (New York: Knopf, 1968); Robert E. Brown, *Charles Beard and the Constitution* (Princeton: Princeton University Press, 1956).

5. For examples of this historiography, see Arnold Paul, *Conservative Crisis and the Rule of Law: Attitudes of Bar and Bench, 1887–1895* (Ithaca: Cornell University Press, 1960); Clyde E. Jacobs, *Law Writers and the Courts: The Influence of Thomas M. Cooley, Christopher G. Tiedemann, and John F. Dillon upon American Constitutional*

Law (Berkeley and Los Angeles: University of California Press, 1954); Benjamin R. Twiss, *Lawyers and the Constitution: How Laissez Faire Came to the Supreme Court* (Princeton: Princeton University Press, 1942).

6. See, e.g., Stephen A. Siegel, "Understanding the Nineteenth Century Contract Clause: The Role of the Property-Privilege Distinction and 'Takings' Clause Jurisprudence," *Southern California Law Review* 60 (1986): 1; Stephen A. Siegel, "Understanding the *Lochner* Era: Lessons from the Controversy over Railroad and Utility Rate Regulation," *Virginia Law Review* 70 (1984): 187; Alan Jones, "Thomas Cooley and Laissez-Faire Constitutionalism: A Reconsideration," *Journal of American History* 53 (1967): 751. The works that have contributed most to my understanding of judicial thought during the Gilded Age are Michael Les Benedict, "Laissez-Faire and Liberty: A Reevaluation of the Meaning and Origins of Laissez-Faire Constitutionalism," *Law & History Review* 3 (1985): 293; Charles W. McCurdy, "Stephen J. Field and the American Judicial Tradition," in *The Fields and the Law*, ed. Philip J. Bergan, Owen M. Fiss, and Charles W. McCurdy (San Francisco: United States District Court for the Northern District of California Historical Society, 1986), 5; Charles W. McCurdy, "Justice Field and the Jurisprudence of Government-Business Relations: Some Parameters of Laissez-Faire Constitutionalism, 1863–1897," *Journal of American History* 61 (1975): 970.

7. See Howard Gillman, *The Constitution Besieged: The Rise and Demise of Lochner Era Police Powers Jurisprudence* (Durham: Duke University Press, 1995); Jones, "Thomas Cooley and Laissez-Faire Constitutionalism"; McCurdy, "Justice Field and the Jurisprudence of Government-Business Relations"; Louise A. Halper, "Christopher G. Tiedeman, 'Laissez-Faire Constitutionalism' and the Dilemmas of Small-Scale Property in the Gilded Age," *Ohio State Law Journal* 51 (1990): 1349.

8. See Gillman, *The Constitution Besieged.*

9. See, e.g., Miller, "Toward a Definition of 'the' Constitution."

10. Horwitz, "Progressive Legal Historiography."

11. See, e.g., Morton J. Horwitz, *The Transformation of American Law, 1870–1960: The Crisis of Legal Orthodoxy* (New York: Oxford University Press, 1992), 23.

12. Jones, "Thomas Cooley and Laissez-Faire Constitutionalism," 973.

13. O. W. Holmes, Jr., "The Gas-Stokers' Strike," *American Law Review* 7 (1873): 582, reprinted in *The Collected Works of Justice Holmes*, ed. Sheldon M. Novick (Chicago: University of Chicago Press, 1995), 1:323.

14. Ibid., 325.

15. On Holmes as a Social Darwinist, see the very perceptive essay by J. W. Burrow, "Holmes in His Intellectual Milieu," in *The Legacy of Oliver Wendell Holmes, Jr.*, ed. Robert W. Gordon (Stanford: Stanford University Press, 1992), 17. This side of Holmes was emphasized earlier in a famous article by Yosal Rogat, "Mr. Justice Holmes—The Judge as Spectator," *University of Chicago Law Review* 31 (1964): 213.

16. See Mark DeWolfe Howe, *Justice Oliver Wendell Holmes*, vol. 1, *The Shaping Years, 1841–1870* (Cambridge: Harvard University Press, 1957), and vol. 2, *The Proving Years, 1870–1882* (Cambridge: Harvard University Press, 1963).

17. Vegelahn v. Guntner, 167 Mass. 92, 104 (1896) (Holmes, J., dissenting).

18. O. W. Holmes, Jr., "Economic Elements [1920]," in *Collected Works of Justice Holmes*, 3:432, 3:433.

19. Burrow, "Holmes in His Intellectual Milieu," 29.

20. Lochner v. New York, 198 U.S. 45 (1905) (Holmes, J., dissenting).

21. Stephen Diamond, "Citizenship, Civilization, and Coercion: Justice Holmes on the Tax Power," in Gordon, *The Legacy of Oliver Wendell Holmes, Jr.*, 115.

22. Blackstone v. Miller, 188 U.S. 189, 205 (1903).

23. See William J. Novak, "Public Economy and the Well-Ordered Market: Law and Economic Regulation in 19th-Century America," *Law & Social Inquiry* 18 (1993): 1; Harry N. Scheiber, "The Road to *Munn:* Eminent Domain and the Concept of Public Purpose in the State Courts," in *Law in American History*, ed. Donald Fleming and Bernard Bailyn (Boston: Little, Brown, 1971), 329.

24. *The Education of Henry Adams* (Boston, 1907), 237–38, quoted in Eric Foner, *Reconstruction: America's Unfinished Revolution, 1863–1877* (New York: Harper & Row, 1988), 460.

25. Foner, *Reconstruction*, 461.

26. Ibid.

27. C. Peter Magrath, *Morrison R. Waite: The Triumph of Character* (New York: Macmillan, 1963), 173.

28. Ibid.

29. Stuart Bruchey, *The Wealth of the Nation: An Economic History of the United States* (New York: Harper & Row, 1988), 107.

30. Ibid., 108.

31. Ibid., 104–7.

32. For an overview of the debate in political economy, see Herbert Hovenkamp, *Enterprise and American Law, 1836–1937* (Cambridge: Harvard University Press, 1991), 296–307.

33. A particularly striking expression of this sense of anxiety is Justice Field's essay "The Centenary of the Supreme Court of the United States," *American Law Review* 24 (1890): 351. Field there acknowledged that "the enormous aggregation of wealth possessed by some corporations excites uneasiness lest their power should become dominating in the legislature of the country, and thus encroach upon the rights or crush out the businesses of individuals of small means." Ibid., 366–67. Field argued that constitutional protection of property was the antidote to this imbalance of power.

34. Robert H. Wiebe, *The Search for Order, 1877–1920* (Westport, Conn.: Greenwood Press, 1980).

35. The best single treatment of George, Bellamy, and Lloyd, treating them as the core of the "adversary tradition" in the late nineteenth century, is John L. Thomas, *Alternative America: Henry George, Edward Bellamy, and Henry Demarest Lloyd and the Adversary Tradition* (Cambridge: Harvard University Press, 1983).

36. Henry George, "What the Railroad Will Bring Us," *Overland Monthly* (October 1868), quoted in Thomas, *Alternative America,* 49.

37. Thomas, *Alternative America,* 119–20.

38. Henry George, *Progress and Poverty* (New York: Appleton, 1879), 320.

39. On Ely's and Rauschenbusch's contributions to the social gospel, see James T. Kloppenberg, *Uncertain Victory: Social Democracy and Progressivism in European and American Thought, 1870–1920* (New York: Oxford University Press, 1986), 207–12.

40. Quoted in ibid., 257.

41. Quoted in *American Law Review* 29 (1895): 8–9.

42. As recent scholarship has shown, Tiedeman, contrary to his reputation among Progressive tradition historians, was no unreconstructed apologist for big business. To the contrary, Tiedeman's overriding concern was the decline of the individual entrepreneur, squeezed out of business by large corporations. See especially Halper, "Christopher G. Tiedeman, 'Laissez-Faire Constitutionalism,' and the Dilemmas of Small-Scale Property in the Gilded Age."

43. Christopher G. Tiedeman, *A Treatise on the Limitations of the Police Power in the United States* (St. Louis: F. H. Thomas Law Book Co., 1886), 569.

44. John F. Dillon, *The Law of Municipal Corporations* (New York: James Cockcraft, 1873).

45. John F. Dillon, "Property—Its Rights and Duties in Our Legal and Social Systems," *American Law Review* 29 (1895): 161, 173.

46. Thomas M. Cooley, *A Treatise on the Constitutional Limitations Which Rest upon the Legislative Power of the States of the American Union* (Boston: Little, Brown, 1868). Cooley's treatise went through six editions, and its ideas originated in his lectures as a professor at the newly established law department at the University of Michigan in the early 1860s. Jones, "Thomas Cooley and Laissez-Faire Constitutionalism," 757.

47. Ibid., 759.

48. Cooley, *Constitutional Limitations* (2d ed. 1878), 493.

49. See Hurst, *Law and the Conditions of Freedom,* 17–18.

50. John R. Commons, *Legal Foundations of Capitalism* (New York: Macmillan, 1924). Commons's thesis is followed in Horwitz, *Transformation of American Law, 1870–1960,* 145–67; Martin J. Sklar, *The Corporate Reconstruction of American Capitalism, 1890–1916* (Cambridge: Cambridge University Press, 1988), 49–50; Siegel, "Understanding the *Lochner* Era," 210–21; and Kenneth Vandevelde, "The New Property of the Nineteenth Century: The Development of the Modern Concept of Property," *Buffalo Law Review* 29 (1980): 325.

51. Commons, *Legal Foundations of Capitalism,* 11–21.

52. Chicago, Minneapolis & St. Paul Ry. v. Minnesota, 134 U.S. 418 (1890).

53. Commons, *Legal Foundations of Capitalism,* 14.

54. See George H. Miller, *Railroads and the Granger Laws* (Madison: University of Wisconsin Press, 1971).

55. 94 U.S. 113 (1877). Unlike the other Granger Cases, *Munn* involved a challenge to state regulation of prices on grain warehouses and elevators. The price term was actually not the major focus of the regulation. What prompted the regulation was the Chicago Board of Trade's desire to institute an inspection system of Chicago grain elevators. See Edmund Kitch and Clara Bowler, "The Facts of *Munn v. Illinois,*" *Supreme Court Review* 1978:313, 320.

56. An especially clear example of this rhetoric was the following statement in Justice Field's concurring opinion in Pollock v. Farmers' Loan & Trust Co., 157 U.S. 429, *modified on reh'g,* 158 U.S. 601 (1895), the (in)famous decision holding the federal income tax unconstitutional: "It must be conceded that whatever affects any element that gives an article its value, in the eyes of the law affects the article itself." 157 U.S. at 591.

Pollock is sometimes misrepresented as manifesting a bias on the Court in favor of the rich over the poor. See, e.g., Horwitz, *Transformation of American Law, 1870– 1960,* 25–27. The decision itself did not rest on anti-redistributive grounds. The basis for the Court's decision was that the income tax violated the requirement, imposed by article I, sections 2 and 9 of the Constitution, that direct taxes must be apportioned among the states by population. The Court's opinion virtually ignored the argument that Joseph H. Choate, opposing the tax, made to the effect that the tax was unconstitutional because its progressive rate made it "communistic." It is true that Justice Field, concurring with the majority, additionally attack the statute as "class legislation" that discriminated among different categories of taxpayers. That was, however, not the only basis for his vote. A substantial portion of his opinion was devoted to restating the majority's theory that the tax was a direct, rather than an indirect tax. That theory in no way focused on the tax's redistributive consequences. More to the point, Field's attack on the tax as "class legislation" did not reflect a pro-business or pro-property rights bias as such. Rather, it was a direct outgrowth of his general theory of equality as the central constitutional value and his concern that American society was increasing becoming polarized by class. That concern led him to object to legislation that favored the rich over poor as much as legislation that was, in his view, slanted in favor of the poor. Again, these were views that would have resonated much better with Andrew Jackson than with Jay Gould or other "robber barons" of the late nineteenth century.

57. 80 U.S. (13 Wall.) 166 (1872).

58. Id. at 177 (emphasis added).

59. Scheiber, "The Road to *Munn,*" 383.

60. See ibid., 364; Joseph M. Cormack, "Legal Concepts in Cases of Eminent Domain," *Yale Law Journal* 41 (1931): 221, 223–33.

61. As Harry Scheiber has pointed out, the rule that excluded consequential damages from unconstitutional "takings" resulted from the state courts' desire to subsidize enterprises rather than from a conceptual inability to recognize value as property. Scheiber, "The Road to *Munn,*" 364.

62. 94 U.S. (4 Otto) at 125.

63. Id. at 126.

64. Id. at 133.

65. Id.

66. Kitch and Bowler, "The Facts of *Munn*," 315.

67. 94 U.S. (4 Otto) at 131.

68. Id. at 132. It has been argued that though the elevators did not constitute a true monopoly, there was no price competition among them. Kitch and Bowler, "The Facts of *Munn*," 316.

69. 94 U.S. (4 Otto) at 134.

70. 83 U.S. (16 Wall.) 36 (1873).

71. Id. at 60.

72. See Novak, "Public Economy and the Well-Ordered Market"; Alfred S. Konefsky, "Law and Culture in Antebellum Boston," review of *Law and Letters in American Culture,* by Robert A. Ferguson, *Supreme Court Justice Joseph Story: Statesman of the Old Republic,* by R. Kent Newmyer, and *The Web of Progress: Private Values and Public Styles in Boston and Charleston, 1828–1843,* by William H. Pease and Jane H. Pease, *Stanford Law Review* 40 (1988): 1119, 1132–37.

73. 83 U.S. (16 Wall.) at 64. For an account of the statute's role in a broader plan to secure for New Orleans control of the Texas cattle trade, see Mitchell Franklin, "The Foundation and Meaning of the Slaughterhouse Cases," *Tulane Law Review* 18 (1943): 14.

74. On Sedgwick's views and Field's indebtedness to them, see Charles W. McCurdy, "Stephen J. Field and the American Judicial Tradition," in *The Fields and the Law,* ed. Philip J. Bergan, Owen M. Fiss, and Charles W. McCurdy (New York: Federal Bar Council, 1986), 5.

75. 83 U.S. (16 Wall.) at 83, 88.

76. Id.

77. On the free labor ideology generally, see Eric Foner, *Free Soil, Free Labor, Free Men: The Ideology of the Republican Party before the Civil War* (New York: Oxford University Press, 1970).

78. 83 U.S. (16 Wall.) at 110.

79. 94 U.S. (4 Otto) at 136, 148.

80. Id. at 140.

81. See text accompanying notes 33–43 supra.

82. Chicago, Milwaukee & St. Paul Ry. v. Minnesota, 134 U.S. 418 (1890).

83. Stone v. Farmers Loan & Trust Co., 116 U.S. 307 (1886).

84. Id. at 331.

85. Id. at 458.

86. See Siegel, "Understanding the *Lochner* Era," 200.

87. Ibid., 205–6.

88. Chicago, Milwaukee & St. Paul Ry. v. Minnesota, 134 U.S. at 461.

89. 94 U.S. at 143.

90. McCurdy, "Justice Field and the Jurisprudence of Government-Business Relations," 999.

91. Stone v. Wisconsin, 94 U.S. 181, 184-185 (1877) (Field, J., dissenting).

92. Justices Gray and Lamar joined Bradley's opinion.

93. 134 U.S. at 461, 466.

94. 169 U.S. 466 (1898).

95. For a penetrating discussion of *Smyth,* see Siegel, "Understanding the *Lochner* Era," 224–32.

96. 169 U.S. at 546–47.

97. Novak, "Public Economy and the Well-Ordered Market"; Harry N. Scheiber, "Law and the Imperatives of Progress: Private Rights and Public Values in American Legal History," in *Nomos XXIV: Ethics, Economics, and the Law,* ed. J. Roland Pennock and John W. Chapman (New York: New York University Press, 1982), 303.

98. See generally Gillman, *The Constitution Besieged.*

99. Pumpelly v. Green Bay Canal Co., 80 U.S. (13 Wall.) 166 (1872) (Miller, J.).

100. There is an enormous body of legal scholarship dealing with the public trust doctrine. Among the best contemporary discussions are Joseph Sax, "The Public Trust Doctrine in Natural Resource Law: Effective Judicial Intervention," *Michigan Law Review* 68 (1970): 471; and Richard Lazarus, "Changing Conceptions of Property and Sovereignty in Natural Resources: Questioning the Public Trust Doctrine," *Iowa Law Review* 71 (1986): 631. The best historical treatments are Carol M. Rose, "The Comedy of the Commons: Custom, Commerce, and Inherently Public Property," *University of Chicago Law Review* 53 (1986): 711; Molly Selwin, "The Public Trust Doctrine in American Law and Policy, 1789–1920," *Wisconsin Law Review* 1980:1403; Daniel R. Coquillette, "Mosses from an Old Manse: Another Look at Some Historic Property Cases about the Environment," *Cornell Law Review* 64 (1979): 761; and Harry N. Scheiber, "Public Rights and the Rule of Law in American Legal History," *California Law Review* 72 (1984): 217.

101. See Rose, "The Comedy of the Commons," 727–29.

102. Ibid., 729.

103. 146 U.S. 387 (1892).

104. Chicago, Milwaukee & St. Paul Ry. v. Minnesota, 134 U.S. at 451.

105. As Professor Currie has observed, "[*Illinois Central*] looked for all the world like *Fletcher v. Peck,* where Marshall had held that a state could not rescind its grant." David P. Currie, "The Constitution in the Supreme Court: The Protection of Economic Interests, 1889–1910," *University of Chicago Law Review* 52 (1985): 324, 331 (footnote omitted).

106. 146 U.S. at 452.

107. 6 N.J.L. 1 (1821).

108. Martin v. Waddell, 41 U.S. (16 Pet.) 367, 417 (1842). *Martin* involved circumstances that were quite similar to those in the New Jersey case. The Taney Court discussed but ultimately avoided the New Jersey court's trust theory.

109. 41 U.S. (16 Pet.) at 13. *Arnold* and its public trust theory is lucidly discussed in Rose, "The Comedy of the Commons," 735–39.

110. 101 U.S. 814 (1880).

111. 146 U.S. at 406n. 1.

112. In a very curious attempt to respond to the condition, Field argued that it "placed no impediments upon the action of the railroad company which did not previously exist." Id. at 451. One would have thought that this cut against his position rather than strengthen it. See Currie, "The Constitution in the Supreme Court," 333.

113. *Sic utere tuo ut alienum non laedas.*

114. For a subtle and perceptive discussion of how this might be done, see Rose, "The Comedy of the Commons."

Chapter Ten

1. In discussing the reaction against paternalism as part of the general sentiment against protectionism, I do not mean to imply that the two concepts are today understood as synonymous. Paternalism today is generally understood to refer to efforts by others to act in the welfare of another even though this involves overruling the preferences of the person supposedly benefited. See, e.g., Duncan Kennedy, "Distributive and Paternalist Motives in Contract and Tort Law, with Special Reference to Compulsory Terms and Unequal Bargaining Power," *Maryland Law Review* 41 (1982): 563, 572. By "protectionism," on the other hand, I mean all efforts to prevent harm from occurring to another person, whether the harm is self-induced or externally caused and whether the protected person agrees that the protection benefits her or prefers that the action not be taken. "Protectionism," then, includes the modern notion of paternalism but covers a wider array of actions as well. In late nineteenth-century public discourse, however, this distinction was usually not drawn. "Paternalism" and "protectionism" were often used interchangeably. My usage in this chapter follows that discursive practice. The primary difference between the late nineteenth-century usage of the two terms was that "protectionism" sometimes referred to tariffs and similar governmental measures that interfered with free trade. That is not the usage to which I will refer in this book.

2. The term is borrowed from John Demos's wonderful study of the family as a colonial institution, *A Little Commonwealth: Family Life in Plymouth Colony* (New York: Oxford University Press, 1970).

3. See chapter 5.

4. Roger Cotterrell has drawn a similar distinction between two roles of private trusts, which he terms the "moralistic conception" and the "property-receptacle conception." See Roger Cotterrell, "Some Sociological Aspects of the Controversy Around the Legal Validity of Private Purpose Trusts," in *Equity and Contemporary Legal Developments*, ed. Stephen Goldstein (Jerusalem: Hebrew University Press, 1992), 302, 310–14.

5. Lawrence M. Friedman, "The Dynastic Trust," *Yale Law Journal* 73 (1964): 547.

6. The phrase "crime against self" is drawn from an 1887 essay that vehemently denounced government paternalism as "communism." W. M. Grosvenor, "The Communist and the Railway," *International Review* 4 (1877): 585, 597. Grosvenor, the economics editor of the *New York Times* from 1875 to 1900, was an influential journalist who had substantial political contacts. He was an ardent free-trader and frequently assailed trade tariffs. See W. M. Grosvenor, *Does Protectionism Protect? An Examination of the Effect of Different Forms of Tariff upon American Industry* (New York: D. Appleton, 1871).

7. See Richard Hofstadter, *Social Darwinism in American Thought,* rev. ed. (Boston: Beacon Press, 1955).

8. David A. Hollinger, "Comments on Papers by Sharlin and Wall," in "Symposium on Spencer, Scientism and American Constitutional Law," *Annals of Science* 33 (1976): 476. The leading works reinterpreting Social Darwinism as un-Darwinian are Robert C. Bannister, *Social Darwinism: Science and Myth in Anglo-American Social Thought* (Philadelphia: Temple University Press, 1979); Howard L. Kaye, *The Social Meaning of Modern Biology: From Social Darwinism to Sociobiology* (New Haven: Yale University Press, 1984); Peter J. Bowles, *The Eclipse of Darwinism: Anti-Darwinian Evolution Theories in the Decades around 1900* (Baltimore: Johns Hopkins University Press, 1983).

9. Aviam Soifer, "The Paradox of Paternalism and Laissez-Faire Constitutionalism: United States Supreme Court, 1888–1921," *Law & History Review* 5 (1987): 249, 252.

10. For a recent, and penetrating, expression of the view that it was, see J. W. Burrow, "Holmes in His Intellectual Milieu," in *The Legacy of Oliver Wendell Holmes, Jr.,* ed. Robert W. Gordon (Stanford: Stanford University Press, 1992), 17.

11. Arthur Twining Hadley, president of Yale University from 1899 to 1921, was later to point out the folly of this fear of socialism in America:

> However much public feeling may at times move in the direction of socialistic measures, there is no nation which by its constitution is so far removed from socialism or from a socialistic order. This is partly because the governmental means provided for the control or limitation of private property are weaker in America than elsewhere, but chiefly because the rights of private property are more formally established in the Constitution itself.

Arthur Twining Hadley, "The Constitutional Position of Property in America," *The Independent,* 16 April 1908.

Hadley was one of the principal architects of the new economic theory of the capitalist market that broke with the classical model. Far more rooted in empirical conditions than the classical model was, the new theory tried to explain why modern industrial capitalism did not conform to the classical model of competitive markets. More specifically, it tried to explain the growing trend toward corporate consolidation and other anticompetitive practices in a way that did not embrace the socialist critique of capitalism. The new theory "substituted [for the classical model] a concept of the business cycle as generated by the periodic disequilibrium of production and demand." Martin J. Sklar, *The Corporate Reconstruction of America, 1890–1916* (Cambridge: Cambridge University Press, 1988), 57. The new theory led Hadley to favor government regulation but not government ownership of the means of production.

12. Christopher G. Tiedeman, *A Treatise on the Limitations of Police Power in the United States* (St. Louis: F. H. Thomas, 1886), vi–vii.

13. 157 U.S. 429 (1895).

14. Id. at 532.

15. H. Teichmueller, "Economic Freedom," *American Law Review* 29 (1895): 373, 382.

16. John H. Keyser, "The Problem of Poverty, and How to Deal with It, Through Immediate Colonization," submitted to the Church of the Strangers, New York City, 25 February 1874. Keyser's preferred solution to the problem of increasing poverty in New York was to create agricultural colonies in the South to which the unemployed would be sent, with or without their consent, to work for their food and shelter. (Nothing like working in a turpentine forest in Georgia to build character!) Keyser himself was hardly a practitioner of Social Darwinist messages. The plumbing and heating contractor in Boss Tweed's famed ring, he bilked the City of New York of huge sums of money. It is estimated that in one year alone, he made more than $1 million. See Alexander B. Callow, Jr., *The Tweed Ring* (New York: Oxford University Press, 1966), 202.

17. On the discretionary character of late nineteenth-century anti-paternalism, see Soifer, "Paternalism and Laissez-Faire Constitutionalism."

18. For an example of calls to avoid ostentation (though not necessarily to avoid acquiring great wealth), see John F. Dillon, "Property—Its Rights and Duties in Our Legal and Social System," *American Law Review* 29 (1895): 11, 187.

19. On the moral dimension of this vision, focusing on the work of one of its exponents, see David M. Gold, "John Appleton of Maine and Commercial Law: Freedom, Responsibility, and Law in the Nineteenth Century Marketplace," *Law & History Review* 4 (1986): 55.

20. See Oliver Wendell Holmes, Jr., "Economic Elements," reprinted in *The Collected Works of Justice Holmes*, ed. Sheldon M. Novick (Chicago: University of Chicago Press, 1995), 3:432, 3:433 (originally published in *Cosmopolitan*, February 1906, 397).

21. Ibid., 3:432.

22. Ibid.

23. Ibid. (emphasis added).

24. Oliver Wendell Holmes, Jr., "Law and the Court," in *Collected Legal Papers* (New York: Peter Smith, 1952), 291, 293–94.

25. Ibid., 294.

26. O. W. Holmes, Jr., to R. T. Ely, 25 October 1903, quoted in Stephen Diamond, "Citizenship, Civilization, and Coercion: Justice Holmes on the Tax Power," in Gordon, *The Legacy of Oliver Wendell Holmes, Jr.*, 145.

27. The only occasion on which Holmes addressed the matter of alienability was in *The Common Law*. He there expressed his familiar view that property rights are not absolute, stating, "The absolute protection of property . . . is hardly consistent with the requirements of business. Even when the rules which we have been considering were established, the traffic of the public markets was governed by more liberal principles. On the continent of Europe it was long ago decided that the policy of protecting titles must yield to the policy of protecting trade." Oliver Wendell Holmes, Jr., *The Common Law*, ed. Mark DeWolfe Howe (Boston: Little, Brown, 1963), 80.

28. See, e.g., Richard Posner, *Economic Analysis of Law*, 3d ed. (Boston: Little, Brown, 1986), 9–10.

29. On the Mugwumps, see Richard Hofstadter, *The Age of Reform* (New York: Vintage Books, 1955), 91–93, 141–48. On the theme of personal responsibility and self-reliance throughout American history, see John G. Cawelti, *Apostles of the Self-Made Man* (Chicago: University of Chicago Press, 1965). Holmes's place in Mugwumpery is discussed in a penetrating essay by Stephen Diamond, "Citizenship, Civilization, and Coercion," 115.

30. The best single discussion of this enterprise, focusing on its leader, Langdell, is Thomas Grey, "Langdell's Orthodoxy," *University of Pittsburgh Law Review* 45 (1983): 1.

31. See, e.g., Stewart Chapin, *Suspension of the Power of Alienation and Postponement of Vesting* (New York: Baker, Voorhis, 1891); Albert S. Bolles, *The Law of the Suspension of the Power of Alienation* (New York: Homans, 1891).

32. William Twining has observed that "Gray was considered by both practitioners and scholars to be the leading property lawyer of his time." William Twining, *Karl Llewellyn and the Realist Movement* (Norman: University of Oklahoma Press, 1973), 20.

33. On the close personal and professional relationship between Holmes and Gray, see Mark DeWolfe Howe, *Justice Oliver Wendell Holmes: The Shaping Years, 1841–1870* (Cambridge: Harvard University Press, 1957), 251–52. As Howe notes, part of the basis for the friendship and shared vision of the world between Holmes and Gray was their common experience as combat soldiers in the Civil War.

34. The *American Law Review* has, with cause, been described as "the most significant legal periodical of its generation." Arthur E. Sutherland, *The Law at Harvard* (Cambridge: Harvard University Press, 1967), 140. A few years after establishing the journal, Gray and Ropes turned the editorship over to Holmes.

35. Alfred S. Konefsky, "Law and Culture in Antebellum Boston," review of *Law and Letters in American Culture*, by Robert A. Ferguson, *Supreme Court Justice Joseph Story: Statesman of the Old Republic*, by R. Kent Newmyer, and *The Web of Progress: Private Values and Public Styles in Boston and Charleston, 1828–1843*, by William H. Pease and Jane H. Pease, *Stanford Law Review* 40 (1988): 1119, 1121.

36. Albert Boyden, *Ropes-Gray* (Boston: privately printed, 1942), 38.

37. John Chipman Gray, *The Rule against Perpetuities* (Boston: Little, Brown,

1886). On Gray's influence on the Rule against Perpetuities, see Stephen A. Siegel, "John Chipman Gray, Legal Formalism, and the Transformation of Perpetuities Law," *University of Miami Law Review* 36 (1982): 439.

38. Gray, *The Rule against Perpetuities,* iii.

39. Ibid., 4–5.

40. An example of this problem is as follows. Suppose that an owner of a parcel of land transfers the land by will to his son for the duration of the son's life, and at the son's death possession of the land shifts to the son's children for their respective lives, and upon the death of the last of the son's children to die, full possessory ownership to "those of my great-grandchildren who attain age 21." The problem is that the full legal title to the land cannot be transferred for several generations. In order to transfer full legal title in the land, every person who has an ownership interest in the land must agree to transfer their interest. But here not all of the persons who have an ownership interest in the land are identifiable at the time of the original transfer or even years later. Indeed, since the law recognizes property interests in the unborn, some of these owners may not even have been born yet! Practically, then, the land will remain inalienable until at least the identities of all the beneficiaries is ascertained.

41. John Chipman Gray, *Restraints on the Alienation of Property* (Boston: Soule and Bugbee, 1883).

42. See chapter 4.

43. Gray's legal positivism was clearly evident in his famous work on jurisprudence, *The Nature and Sources of the Law.* The best discussion of Gray's legal theory is Neil MacCormick, "A Political Frontier of Jurisprudence," *Cornell Law Review* 66 (1981): 973.

44. For an example of the repugnancy argument, see James Kent, *Commentaries on American Law* (New York, 1830), 4:131.

45. Gray, *Restraints on Alienation,* 2.

46. For a rich contemporary version of this argument, see Jeremy Waldron, *The Right to Private Property* (Oxford: Oxford University Press, 1988), 310–13.

47. 18 Ves. 429, 34 Eng. Rep. 379 (Ch. 1811).

48. 34 Eng. Rep. at 379.

49. See generally Gregory S. Alexander, "The Transformation of Trusts as a Legal Category," *Law & History Review* 5 (1987): 303, 322–27.

50. See, e.g., Nichols v. Levy, 72 U.S. (5 Wall.) 433 (1866); Smith v. Moore, 37 Ala. 327 (1861); Tillinghast v. Bradford, 5 R.I. 205 (1858); Mebane v. Mebane, 39 N.C. (4 Ire. Eq.) 131 (1845); Hallett v. Thompson, 5 Paige Ch. 583 (N.Y. Ch. 1836).

51. 91 U.S. (1 Otto) 716 (1875).

52. Id. at 727.

53. 133 Mass. 170 (1882).

54. Id. at 171.

55. Id. at 172.

56. Boyden, *Ropes-Gray,* 145.

57. John Chipman Gray, *Restraints on the Alienation of Property,* 2d ed. (Boston: Boston Book Co., 1895), viii–ix.

58. Ibid., 242–43.

59. Ibid., iii.

60. Ibid., 2.

61. Ibid., 246–47.

62. Ibid., 247.

63. Ibid.

64. Ibid., 140.

65. Ibid., x.

66. Ibid.

67. See, e.g., Erwin C. Griswold, *Spendthrift Trusts,* 2d ed. (Albany: Matthew Bender, 1947).

68. On the class bias of Chancery's protection of expectant heirs, see John P. Dawson, "Economic Duress—An Essay in Perspective," *Michigan Law Review* 45 (1947): 253, 267–68.

69. Steib v. Whitehead, 111 Ill. 247 (1884).

70. Guernsey v. Lazear, 41 S.E. 405 (W. Va. 1902).

71. See Soifer, "Paternalism and Laissez-Faire Constitutionalism," 254,

72. Gray, *Restraints on Alienation,* 2d ed., 139.

73. Pybus v. Smith, 3 Bro. C.C. 339 (Ch. 1791).

74. Frederick Maitland, "Trust and Corporation," in *Maitland: Selected Essays,* ed. H. D. Hazeltine, G. Lapsley, and P. H. Winfield (Cambridge: Cambridge University Press, 1936).

75. Mary M. Barthelme, "Spendthrift Trusts," *Albany Law Journal* 50 (1894): 6, 10.

76. Ibid.

77. Nathaniel S. Brown, "Spendthrift Trusts," *Central Law Journal* 54 (1902): 382, 387.

78. Leigh v. Harrison, 11 So. 604, 606 (Miss. 1902).

79. Holdship v. Patterson, 7 Watts 547, 551 (Pa. 1838).

80. George Marcus, *Lives in Trust: The Fortunes of Dynastic Families in Late Twentieth-Century America* (Boulder, Colo.: Westview Press, 1992), 63.

81. Ibid.

82. This reluctance also influenced judicial regulation of how trustees invested trust assets. Under the Prudent Investor Rule, which was first developed in the famous case of Harvard College v. Amory, 26 Mass. (9 Pick.) 446 (1830), trustees were forbidden from using trust property for speculation. Rather, they were to "observe how men of prudence, discretion and intelligence manage their own affairs, not in regard to speculation, but in regard to the permanent disposition of their funds. . . ." Id. at 461. The effect of this rule was to limit the extent to which trust property is commodified. In this respect the underlying trust property was treated somewhat differently from

the beneficiaries' property, which, under the spendthrift trust doctrine, was *completely* decommodified.

Part Four Prologue

1. The best single discussion of this development is Richard A. Posner, "The Decline of Law as an Autonomous Discipline: 1962–1987," *Harvard Law Review* 100 (1987): 761.

2. See, e.g., Oliver Wendell Holmes, Jr., "The Path of the Law," *Harvard Law Review* 10 (1897): 457; Roscoe Pound, "The Scope and the Purpose of Sociological Jurisprudence," *Harvard Law Review* 24 (1911): 591; *Harvard Law Review* 25 (1911): 140; *Harvard Law Review* 25 (1912): 489.

3. See Robert W. Gordon, "The Case for Harvard," review of *Logic and Experience: The Origin of Modern American Legal Education,* by William P. LaPiana, *Michigan Law Review* 93 (1995): 1231, 1255n. 73.

4. William A. Keener, "Quasi-Contract, Its Nature and Scope," *Harvard Law Review* 7 (1893): 57.

5. On this controversy, see Morton J. Horwitz, *The Transformation of American Law, 1870–1960: The Crisis of Legal Orthodoxy* (New York: Oxford University Press, 1992), 169–92.

6. Karl N. Llewellyn and E. Adamson Hoebel, *The Cheyenne Way* (Norman: University of Oklahoma Press, 1941).

7. See Posner, "The Decline of Law," 764–65.

8. The story of these initiatives is told well in John Henry Schlegel, "American Legal Realism and Empirical Social Science: The Singular Case of Underhill Moore," *Buffalo Law Review* 29 (1980): 195, 238–57.

9. See generally Thomas Grey, "Langdell's Orthodoxy," *University of Pittsburgh Law Review* 45 (1983): 1.

10. Schlegel, "American Legal Realism and Empirical Social Science," 256.

11. See generally Peter H. Irons, *The New Deal Lawyers* (Princeton: Princeton University Press, 1982).

12. See G. Edward White, "Recapturing New Deal Lawyers," *Harvard Law Review* 102 (1988): 489, 514 (suggesting that legal Progressivism was not a fully modernist culture).

Recently, Brandeis's image as the independent and virtuous advocate for the people has been reexamined. In a very insightful article, Clyde Spillenger has argued that Brandeis's very independence prevented him from becoming thoroughly engaged, either in lawyer-client relationships or with the public sphere generally. See Clyde Spillenger, "Elusive Advocate: Reconsidering Brandeis as People's Lawyer," *Yale Law Journal* 105 (1996): 1445.

13. See Schlegel, "American Legal Realism and Empirical Social Science," 256.

14. Representative work by these scholars includes Richard A. Posner, *Economic Analysis of Law* (Boston: Little, Brown, 1972); Henry G. Manne, *The Economics of Legal*

Relationships (St. Paul: West, 1975); Guido Calabresi, "Transaction Costs, Resource Allocation and Liability Rules—A Comment," *Journal of Law & Economics* 11 (1968): 67.

15. Harry T. Edwards, "The Growing Disjunction between Legal Education and the Legal Profession," *Michigan Law Review* 91 (1992): 34.

16. Ibid., 35.

Chapter Eleven

1. The following is a much-truncated list of accounts of the Legal Realist movement: Laura Kalman, *Legal Realism at Yale, 1927–1960* (Chapel Hill: University of North Carolina Press, 1986); Wilfred Rumble, *American Legal Realism: Skepticism, Reform, and the Judicial Process* (Ithaca: Cornell University Press, 1968); Robert S. Summers, *Instrumentalism and American Legal Theory* (Ithaca: Cornell University Press, 1982); William Twining, *Karl Llewellyn and the Realist Movement,* 2d ed. (Norman: University of Oklahoma Press, 1985); N. E. H. Hull, "Some Realism about the Llewellyn-Pound Exchange over Realism: The Newly Uncovered Private Correspondence, 1927–1931," *Wisconsin Law Review* 1987:921; Edward Purcell, "American Jurisprudence between the Wars: Legal Realism and the Crisis of Democratic Theory," *American History Review* 75 (1969): 424; John Henry Schlegel, "American Legal Realism and Empirical Social Science: From the Yale Experience," *Buffalo Law Review* 28 (1979): 459; John Henry Schlegel, "American Legal Realism and Empirical Social Science: The Singular Case of Underhill Moore," *Buffalo Law Review* 29 (1980): 195; G. Edward White, "From Sociological Jurisprudence to Realism: Jurisprudence and Social Change in Early Twentieth-Century America," *Virginia Law Review* 58 (1972): 999.

2. Morton J. Horwitz, *The Transformation of American Law, 1870–1960: The Crisis of Legal Orthodoxy* (New York: Oxford University Press, 1992), 169.

3. Ibid., 170–71.

4. For a useful, succinct overview of recent historiography of this period, see Richard L. McCormick, "Public Life in Industrial America, 1877–1917," in *The New American History,* ed. Eric Foner (Philadelphia: Temple University Press, 1990), 93.

5. Alan Dawley, *Struggles for Justice: Social Responsibility and the Liberal State* (Cambridge: Harvard University Press, Belknap Press, 1991), 1.

6. Dorothy Ross, *The Origins of American Social Science* (Cambridge: Cambridge University Press, 1991), 98.

7. See Dawley, *Struggles for Justice,* 98.

8. The main exponent of this view is Gabriel Kolko, *The Triumph of Conservatism: A Reinterpretation of American History, 1900–1916* (New York: Free Press, 1963).

9. Dawley, *Struggles for Justice,* 138.

10. Progressive-era labor reform had its greatest success in the context of child labor. See Robert H. Wiebe, *The Search for Order, 1877–1920* (Westport, Conn.: Greenwood Press, 1980), 169–73.

11. Both the federal income and estate taxes were the products of Progressive re-

form efforts. The first income tax was enacted in 1913, following passage of the Six-teenth Amendment. The first federal death tax was introduced in 1898, but was abol-ished in 1902 with the close of the Spanish-American War. After sustained pressure from a variety of quarters, including President Roosevelt and Andrew Carnegie (whose "Gospel of Wealth" argued that the evils of inherited wealth far outweighed its bene-fits), Congress enacted an estate tax as part of the Revenue Act of 1916.

12. On the antitrust debates of the Progressive era, see generally Martin Sklar, *The Corporate Reconstruction of American Capitalism, 1890–1916* (New York: Cambridge University Press, 1988).

13. Dawley, *Struggles for Justice,* 98–105.

14. The *Encyclopedia of the Social Sciences,* published between 1930 and 1935, was only the most conspicuous (and among the last), signs of intellectual interactions be-tween the Progressive (institutional) economists and Legal Progressives and Realists. Edwin R. A. Seligman, an influential political economist at Columbia, was the editor-in-chief, while Roscoe Pound served as its legal editor. Earlier, Karl Llewellyn identified John R. Commons's book *Legal Foundations of Capitalism* as an exemplary form of interdisciplinary scholarship on law and economics. See Karl N. Llewellyn, "The Effect of Legal Institutions upon Economics," *American Economic Review* 15 (1925): 665. Earlier still, Richard T. Ely's book *Property and Contract in Their Relation to the Distri-bution of Wealth* (1914), was taught at several law schools, including Harvard, where Roscoe Pound required it in his jurisprudence seminar. "There is nothing else on the subject worth talking about," he declared. See Benjamin G. Rader, *The Academic Mind and Reform: The Influence of Richard T. Ely in American Life* (Lexington: University of Kentucky Press, 1966), 199.

15. See Horwitz, *Transformation of American Law, 1870–1960,* 80–81; Herbert Ho-venkamp, "The Sherman Act and the Classical Theory of Competition," *Iowa Law Review* 74 (1989): 1019; Herbert Hovenkamp, "The Antitrust Movement and the Rise of Industrial Organization," *Texas Law Review* 68 (1989): 105.

16. Sklar, *The Corporate Reconstruction of American Capitalism,* 55.

17. See Horwitz, *Transformation of American Law, 1870–1960,* 83 (quoting the president of the American Cotton Oil Trust as asserting that the development of trusts was part of "a steady, wise, and logical evolution, or improvement in the method of conducting industrial affairs.").

18. See generally Sklar, *Corporate Reconstruction,* 57–68; Ross, *Origins of American Social Science,* 145–51, 174–75.

19. Richard T. Ely, *Ground under Our Feet* (New York: Macmillan, 1938), 146.

20. See Ross, *Origins of American Social Science,* 148–51.

21. Ibid., 159.

22. Ibid., 159–61.

23. The close interaction, based on shared aspirations for professionalization and scientism, between legal scholars and social scientists in the late nineteenth century is indicated by the fact that several leading law school teachers involved in the revision

of legal education actively participated in the newly founded American Social Science Association. Yale Law School professor Simeon Baldwin served as its president from 1897 to 1899, while Christopher Columbus Langdell and James Bradley Thayer of Harvard, and T. W. Dwight of Columbia were early and active members. See Thomas L. Haskell, *The Emergence of Professional Social Science: The American Social Science Association and the Nineteenth-Century Crisis of Authority* (Urbana: University of Illinois Press, 1977), 219–21.

24. See text and notes 39–43 infra.

25. Wesley N. Hohfeld, "Some Fundamental Legal Conceptions as Applied to Judicial Reasoning," *Yale Law Journal* 23 (1913): 16. See Thomas C. Grey, "The Disintegration of Property," in *Nomos XXII: Property,* ed. J. Roland Pennock and John W. Chapman (New York: New York University Press, 1980), 85.

26. See, e.g., William Twining, *Karl Llewellyn and the Realist Movement* (Norman: University of Oklahoma Press, 1973); Kalman, *Legal Realism at Yale;* William T. Fisher, "The Development of Modern American Legal Theory and the Judicial Interpretation of the Bill of Rights," in *A Culture of Rights: The Bill of Rights in Philosophy, Politics, and Law, 1791 and 1991,* ed. Michael J. Lacey and Knud Haakonssen (New York: Cambridge University Press, 1991), 266.

Natalie Hull recently revealed that Corbin objected to his inclusion on Karl Llewellyn's famous list of twenty Realists, published in his article, Karl N. Llewellyn, "Some Realism about Realism, A Reply to Dean Pound," *Harvard Law Review* 44 (1931): 1222. See N. E. H. Hull, "Some Realism about the Llewellyn-Pound Exchange: The Newly Uncovered Private Correspondence, 1927–1931," *Wisconsin Law Review* 1987: 921, 956–57. Nevertheless, since, as Hull notes, Corbin objected to any scheme that classified individuals as members of particular "schools," his objection is hardly sufficient grounds for rejecting the now-conventional view that he was a Realist.

27. John Henry Schlegel, "A Tasty Tidbit," review of *Transformation in American Law, 1870–1960,* by Morton Horwitz, *Buffalo Law Review* 41 (1993): 1045, 1067. As Frank Michelman and Duncan Kennedy pithily expressed the disparaging view of Hohfeld, "By today's law students (not to speak of their teachers), Hohfeld is often envisaged as a chap with a scholastic passion for terminological nicety—at worst a carping bore, at best an authentic, if pedantic exemplar of the academic virtue of precision." Duncan Kennedy and Frank Michelman, "Are Property and Contract Efficient?" *Hofstra Law Review* 8 (1980): 711, 752.

28. Wesley N. Hohfeld, "Some Fundamental Legal Conceptions as Applied in Judicial Reasoning," *Yale Law Journal* 23 (1913): 16.

29. Wesley N. Hohfeld, "Fundamental Legal Conceptions as Applied in Judicial Reasoning," *Yale Law Journal* 26 (1917): 710.

30. The best discussion of the implications of Hohfeld's project is Joseph William Singer, "The Legal Rights Debate in Analytical Jurisprudence from Bentham to Hohfeld," *Wisconsin Law Review* 1982:975.

31. See, e.g., Arthur L. Corbin, "Jural Relations and Their Classification," *Yale Law*

Journal 30 (1921): 226; Arthur L. Corbin, "Legal Analysis and Terminology," *Yale Law Journal* 29 (1919): 163; Walter Wheeler Cook, "Privileges of Labor Unions in the Struggle for Life," *Yale Law Journal* 27 (1918): 779.

32. Ibid., 787.

33. Singer, "The Legal Rights Debate," 987.

34. Kennedy and Michelman, "Are Property and Contract Efficient?" 754.

35. Corbin, "Privileges of Labor Unions," 799 (quoting from Justice Holmes's dissenting opinion in Vegelahn v. Guntner, 167 Mass. 92, 107 [1896]).

36. See, e.g., John Austin, *Lectures on Jurisprudence* (London: J. Murray, 1873).

37. Hohfeld was not tilting at windmills here. The person-thing conception of ownership remained widely used in legal treatises as well as judicial opinions. Hohfeld cited a wide range of examples, including Joseph Henry Beale's *Treatise on Conflict of Laws* (1916). See Hohfeld, "Fundamental Legal Conceptions," 725.

38. Ibid., 746.

39. Hohfeld's analysis in this respect influenced not only legal writers but economists as well. Two who conspicuously applied his analysis to property were John R. Commons and Robert L. Hale. See John R. Commons, *Legal Foundations of Capitalism* (New York: Macmillan, 1924), 91–100; Robert L. Hale, "Rate Making and the Revision of the Property Concept," *Columbia Law Review* 22 (1922): 209, 214.

40. Hohfeld seems not to have used the "bundles of rights" metaphor at all. The first use of that metaphor to express the modern conception of property that I have found was in John Lewis, *A Treatise on the Law of Eminent Domain* (Chicago: Callahan, 1888), 43: "The dullest individual among the *people* knows and understands that his *property* in anything is a bundle of rights."

41. An early and influential expression of the nonphysicalist conception is Eaton v. Boston, Concord & Montreal R.R., 51 N.H. 504, 510–12 (1872). For a general discussion of the development of the non-physicalist conception, see Kenneth J. Vandevelde, "The New Property of the Nineteenth Century: The Development of the Modern Conception of Property," *Buffalo Law Review* 29 (1980): 325.

42. See chapter 9.

43. Lewis, *The Law of Eminent Domain*, 45.

44. Hohfeld, "Fundamental Legal Conceptions," 747.

45. James T. Kloppenberg, *Uncertain Victory: Social Democracy and Progressivism in European and American Thought, 1870–1920* (New York: Oxford University Press, 1986), 207.

46. On the German historical approach to economics and its influence on American social science, see Jürgen Herbst, *The German Historical School in American Scholarship: A Study in the Transfer of Culture* (Ithaca: Cornell University Press, 1965).

47. See Rader, *The Academic Mind*, 77–82.

48. Ely was an astonishingly prolific writer. Between 1881 and 1892 alone, he published more than fifty scholarly articles and seven monographs. Kloppenberg, *Uncertain Victory*, 460n. 18.

49. Institutional economics grew out of the German historical school of economics. Its generally acknowledged leader was Thorstein Veblen, who, in the words of George Stigler, "somehow rallied around him a large number of people whose common unifying theme was a great dissatisfaction with neoclassical price theory or indeed formal theory of any sort." Remarks of George Stigler in Edmund W. Kitch, ed., "The Fire of Truth: A Remembrance of Law and Economics at Chicago, 1932–1970," *Journal of Law & Economics* 26 (1983): 163, 169.

50. Ross, *Origins of American Social Science,* 106–22.

51. Rader, *The Academic Mind,* 204–8. Ely moved the Institute to Northwestern when he relocated there after his decision to resign from Wisconsin. Ibid., 212–14.

52. However true this charge may have been, the real basis for the repeated attacks on the Institute was Ely's opposition to Henry George's single tax scheme. The leader of the anti-Institute campaign was a strong single-tax proponent. Ibid., 209.

Ely's opposition to the single-tax theory typified the limited scope of his reformism. "[T]he natural rights doctrine of Henry George," Ely wrote, "was thoroughly unscientific, a belated revival of the social philosophy of the eighteenth century."

> I believed that the economics underlying Henry George's pleas was unsound. My experience had shown me that his idea of unearned increment worked untold injury. Therefore, I was accused of forsaking my earlier faith because I could not attach myself to a movement which I felt was producing harm and retarding social progress.

Ely, *Ground under Our Feet,* 92. For a recent defense of George's single-tax proposal by an economist, see T. Nicolaus Tideman, "Takings, Moral Evolution, and Justice," *Columbia Law Review* 88 (1988): 1714.

53. The story of Ely's trial for economic heresy is told in Rader, *The Academic Mind,* 135–50. For a description of the social and economic conditions in Wisconsin that provided the context for the attack on Ely, see David Thelen, *The New Citizenship: Origins of Progressivism in Wisconsin, 1885–1900* (Columbia: University of Missouri Press, 1972), 67–70.

54. See text and notes 104–34 infra.

55. Richard T. Ely, *Property and Contract in Their Relations to the Distribution of Wealth,* 2 vols. (New York: Macmillan, 1914). The book originated in Ely's lectures at Wisconsin beginning in 1892. The lectures took on a publishable format within a few years, and a manuscript of them circulated not only among his graduate students (several of whom, with Ely's encouragement, used it as the basis for their own teaching) but also among economists and lawyers, including Justice Holmes. Rader, *The Academic Mind,* 196–97.

56. Ely, *Property and Contract,* 1:96 (emphasis in the original).

57. Ibid., 107 (footnote omitted).

58. Ibid., 137.

59. Ibid., 136 (emphasis in the original).

60. Ibid., 137.

61. Ibid., 142–43 (emphasis in the original).

62. Ibid., 136.

63. Ibid., 169–70.

64. Ibid., 206–7 (emphasis in the original).

65. Ibid., 220.

66. Ibid., 226.

67. Ibid., 248.

68. Ibid., 251.

69. Ibid., 253.

70. Ibid., 257.

71. See chapter 9.

72. This was Justice Field's famous test, developed in his dissenting opinion in Munn v. Illinois, 94 U.S. 113, 143 (1876).

73. See, e.g., James C. Bonbright, "Depreciation and Valuation for Rate Control," *Columbia Law Review* 27 (1927): 113; James C. Bonbright, "The Problem of Judicial Valuation," ibid., 493; Robert L. Hale, "Value and Vested Rights," ibid., 523; Edward W. Bemis, "Going Value in Rate Cases in the Supreme Court," ibid., 530; Donald R. Richberg, "Valuation—By Judicial Fiat," *Harvard Law Review* 40 (1927): 567.

74. McCardle v. Indianapolis Water Co., 272 U.S. 400 (1926).

75. See Stephen A. Siegel, "Understanding the *Lochner* Era: Lessons from the Controversy over Railroad and Utility Rate Regulation," *Virginia Law Review* 70 (1984): 187, 233–34.

76. A very incomplete list of the articles discussing this issue includes the following leading contributions: Robert L. Hale, "The Supreme Court's Ambiguous Use of 'Value' in Rate Cases," *Columbia Law Review* 18 (1918): 208; Robert L. Hale, "The Physical Fallacy in Rate Cases," *Yale Law Journal* 30 (1920): 710; Gerard C. Henderson, "Railway Valuation and the Courts," *Harvard Law Review* 33 (1920): 902, 1031; Robert L. Hale, "Rate Making and the Revision of the Property Concept," *Columbia Law Review* 22 (1922): 209.

77. Hale, "Rate Making," 210.

78. Commons had been one of Ely's graduate students at Johns Hopkins and remained close, personally and intellectually, to Ely throughout his career. After bouncing around several schools, all of which let him go after discovering his "dangerous" sympathies for socialism, Commons landed a position on the faculty at the University of Wisconsin, largely due to Ely's efforts. He taught economics at Wisconsin from 1904 until his retirement in 1932. Along with Ely, Thorstein Veblen, and others, Commons was instrumental in developing the so-called institutional school of economics. That school rejected abstract models in favor of a behaviorist approach to economics, focusing particularly on the behavior of institutional actors in markets.

For an expression of Commons's influence on legal writers, especially the Realists, see Llewellyn, "The Effect of Legal Institutions upon Economics."

79. Milton Friedman has pointed out that while Commons's influence within the economics profession was negligible, "he had a tremendous influence on the growth of many legal institutions, principally through his disciples at Wisconsin." Remarks of Milton R. Friedman in Kitch, "The Fire of Truth," 171. Friedman quickly added that during a year that he had spent at Wisconsin, he found the influence of Commons "oppressive." Ibid.

80. Commons, *Legal Foundations of Capitalism*, 18.

81. Ibid., 19.

82. Ibid.

83. Ibid.; see also ibid., 21–28.

84. Ibid., 25. In his autobiography Commons credited a Wisconsin state senator with whom he had worked in drafting public utility regulation for the idea that all legal valuation looks to future behavior: "From this starting point I worked for many years in making Futurity the main principle of economics, distinguished from all the schools of economic thought which based their theories on past labor or present feelings." John R. Commons, *Myself* (Madison: University of Wisconsin Press, 1963), 125.

85. Commons, *Legal Foundations of Capitalism*, 21.

86. Ibid., 53.

87. Ibid.

88. Ibid., 60.

89. Ibid., 62–64.

90. Hale, "Rate Making," 213.

91. Gabriel Kolko, *Main Currents in Modern American History* (New York: Pantheon, 1984), 100.

92. Ibid., 101.

93. Hale, "Rate Making," 196.

94. Kolko, *Main Currents in Modern American History*, 102.

95. Hale, "Rate Making," 197.

96. Ibid.

97. Dawley, *Struggles for Justice*, 297.

98. Louis Galambos and Joseph Pratt, *The Rise of the Corporate Commonwealth: U.S. Business and Public Policy in the Twentieth Century* (New York: Basic Books, 1988), 90.

99. Ibid.

100. Horwitz, *Transformation of American Law, 1870–1960*, 170.

101. An unusually clear expression of the belief in legal and moral rationality by two influential figures from the Progressive generation is John H. Wigmore and Albert Kocourek, "Editorial Preface," in *Rational Basis of Legal Institutions* (New York: Macmillan, 1923).

102. The best treatment of the pre-1920 intellectual project to construct alternative theories of rationality is Kloppenberg, *Uncertain Victory*.

103. See Edward A. Purcell, Jr., *The Crisis of Democratic Theory: Scientific Naturalism and the Problem of Value* (Lexington: University of Kentucky Press, 1973).

104. For biographical information on Hale, see Joseph Dorfman, *The Economic Mind in American Civilization* (New York: Viking Press, 1959), 4:160–63.

105. See, e.g., James C. Bonbright, *Principles of Public Utility Rates* (New York: Columbia University Press, 1961), 33, 164, 183.

106. See FPC v. Natural Gas Pipeline Co., 315 U.S. 575 (1942) (Black and Douglas, JJ., concurring); M. Witmark & Sons v. Fred Fisher Music Co., 125 F.2d 949 (2d Cir. 1949) (Frank, J., dissenting).

Many of Hale's relationships with judges, including Douglas, began as collegial relationships at Columbia Law School, particularly during the 1920s when Columbia was the center of Legal Realism. On Columbia's role in the development of American Legal Realism, see Kalman, *Legal Realism at Yale*, 68–97.

107. *Political Science Quarterly* 38 (1923): 470.

108. Robert L. Hale, "Bargaining, Duress, and Economic Liberty," *Columbia Law Review* 43 (1943): 603.

109. Robert L. Hale, *Freedom through Law* (New York: Columbia University Press, 1952).

110. Hale, "Coercion and Distribution," 472. Hale's attraction to Hohfeldian analysis was especially apparent in his articles on ratemaking, where he cited Hohfeld extensively. See, e.g., "Labor Law: Anglo-American," in *Encyclopedia of the Social Sciences* (1932), 8:669; "Rate Making," 214–15.

111. Warren J. Samuels, "The Economy as a System of Power and Its Legal Bases: The Legal Economics of Robert Lee Hale," *University of Miami Law Review* 27 (1973): 261, 279. By "volitional freedom," Hale meant choices constrained by others. Ibid., 277.

112. Ibid., 279.

113. See ibid., 280.

114. Hale, "Coercion and Distribution," 471.

115. See Frank I. Michelman, "Possession vs. Distribution in the Constitutional Idea of Property," *Iowa Law Review* 72 (1987): 1319, 1329.

116. To avoid the power problem at the stage of initial distribution, we must also assume away pre-political individual claims to ownership, that is, entitlement to land (or whatever) based on natural law. For if one is entitled to ownership as a matter of natural law, prior to the creation of the state, then any state distribution *may* be seen as a power grab.

117. On this aspect of the civic double-bind problem, see Michelman, "Possession vs. Distribution," 1334–37.

118. See J. G. A. Pocock, "Civic Humanism and Its Role in Anglo-American Thought," in *Politics, Language and Time: Essays on Political Thought and History* (New York: Atheneum, 1973), 91.

119. For the early American chapter of this story of exclusion, see Robert J.

Steinfeld, "Property and Suffrage in the Early American Republic," *Stanford Law Review* 41 (1989): 335.

120. See Samuels, "The Economy as a System of Power," 278.

121. Morris R. Cohen, "Property and Sovereignty," *Cornell Law Quarterly* 13 (1927): 8.

122. David A. Hollinger, *Morris R. Cohen and the Scientific Ideal* (Cambridge: MIT Press, 1975), 203.

123. See Morris R. Cohen, *Law and the Social Order* (1933), 198–218; Morris R. Cohen, "Justice Holmes and the Nature of the Law," *Columbia Law Review* 31 (1931): 352.

124. See Walter Wheeler Cook, "Privileges of Labor Unions in the Struggle for Life," *Yale Law Journal* 27 (1918): 779.

125. See M. Witmark & Sons v. Fred Fisher Music Co., 125 F.2d 949 (2d Cir. 1942) (Frank, J., dissenting).

126. 261 U.S. 525 (1923).

127. Cohen, "Property and Sovereignty," 11.

128. Ibid., 13.

129. Ibid., 14.

130. Ibid., 19.

131. Ibid., 17.

132. Ibid., 26.

133. Ibid., 23.

134. Ibid., 19.

135. See generally Alan Brinkley, *The End of Reform: New Deal Liberalism in Recession and War* (New York: Alfred A. Knopf, 1995), 31–47.

136. Adolf A. Berle, Jr. and Gardiner C. Means, *The Modern Corporation and Private Property* (New York: Macmillan, 1932). Recently, the book has been described as "one of the most influential books of the twentieth century." Thomas Gale Moore, "Introduction," *Journal of Law & Economics* 26 (1983): 235 (Hoover Institution conference on "Corporations and Private Property"). Even as vigorous an opponent of the book's political message as George Stigler has acknowledged the book's importance. "If I were asked to name the single most important thing that's ever been done in collaboration by a lawyer with an economist in the United States I think I would pick Berle and Means." Kitch, "The Fire of Truth," 174.

On Berle and the book, see generally Scott R. Bowman, *The Modern Corporation and American Political Thought: Law, Power, and Ideology* (University Park: Penn State Press, 1996), 186–87, 203–17.

137. The story of the Columbia faculty split is told in Kalman, *Legal Realism at Yale*, 72–78.

138. Ibid., 75–78.

139. Berle and Means, *The Modern Corporation and Private Property*, 8–9.

140. Ibid., 338–39.

141. Ibid., 9.

142. William E. Leuchtenburg, *Franklin D. Roosevelt and the New Deal, 1932–1940* (New York: Harper & Row, 1963), 34.

The election of Franklin D. Roosevelt in 1932 allowed Berle to realize his vision by serving one of Roosevelt's "Brain Trust" and principal architects of the New Deal.

143. See Thomas Nixon Carver, *The Present Economic Revolution in the United States* (Boston: Little, Brown, 1925); William Z. Ripley, *Main Street and Wall Street* (Boston: Little, Brown, 1927).

144. Thorstein Veblen, *Absentee Ownership and Business Enterprise in Recent Times* (New York: B. W. Huebsch, Inc., 1923).

145. Alfred Marshall, *Principles of Economics* (New York: Macmillan, 1924), 641.

146. On Means's contribution to the book and his institutionalist economics generally, see Warren J. Samuels and Steven G. Medema, *Gardiner C. Means: Institutionalist and Post Keynesian* (Armonk, N.Y.: M. E. Sharpe, 1990).

147. George Stigler and Claire Friedland, "The Literature of Economics: The Case of Berle and Means," *Journal of Law & Economics* 26 (1983): 237, 258.

148. The impetus for this debate in the United States was the Supreme Court's controversial decision in Santa Clara v. Southern Pac. R.R., 118 U.S. 394 (1886), holding that a corporation is protected as a "person" under the Fourteenth Amendment. The personality theory of the corporation originated in the German legal theorist Otto Gierke's massive work, *Political Theories of the Middle Ages,* published in 1881. Gierke's work set off a debate among German and French legal scholars concerning the true nature of the corporation. Gierke's theory, and indeed the whole question, was brought to the attention of English-speaking lawyers largely through the work of the great English legal historian Frederic Maitland and the German-trained University of Chicago law professor Ernst Freund. For accounts of this story, see Morton J. Horwitz, "*Santa Clara* Revisited: The Development of Corporate Theory," *West Virginia Law Review* 88 (1985): 173; Mark M. Hager, "Bodies Politic: The Progressive History of Organizational 'Real Entity' Theory," *University of Pittsburgh Law Review* 50 (1989): 575.

149. See John Dewey, "The Historical Background of Corporate Legal Personality," *Yale Law Journal* 35 (1926): 655.

150. See text and notes 63–65 supra.

151. 291 U.S. 502 (1934).

152. Walton H. Hamilton, "Affectation with Public Interest," *Yale Law Journal* 39 (1930): 1089–90.

153. An outstanding example of this Realist critique of the affectation doctrine is Hamilton's article. See ibid. For other contemporary critiques, see Dexter M. Keezer, "Some Questions involved in the Application of the 'Public Interest' Doctrine," *Michigan Law Review* 25 (1926): 596; Comment, *Yale Law Journal* 39 (1929): 256.

154. Berle and Means, *The Modern Corporation and Private Property,* 355.

155. Ibid., 356.

156. For a discussion of corporate voluntarism, see David L. Engel, "An Approach to Corporate Social Responsibility," *Stanford Law Review* 32 (1979): 1.

157. E. Merrick Dodd, "For Whom Are Corporate Managers Trustees?" *Harvard Law Review* 45 (1932): 1145, 1157.

158. Berle and Means, *The Modern Corporation and Private Property*, 247–48.

159. Adolf A. Berle, Jr., "For Whom Corporate Managers *Are* Trustees: A Note," *Harvard Law Review* 45 (1932): 1365, 1368.

160. Ibid.

161. Ibid., quoting Dodd, "For Whom Are Corporate Managers Trustees?" 1148.

162. Berle and Means, *The Modern Corporation and Private Property*, 356.

163. Adolf A. Berle, Jr., *The 20th Century Capitalist Revolution* (New York: Harcourt, Brace, 1954), 169.

164. A. A. Berle, Jr., "Foreword," in *The Corporation in Modern Society*, ed. Edward S. Mason (Cambridge: Harvard University Press, 1960), xii.

165. See Wilber G. Katz, "Responsibility and the Modern Corporation," *Journal of Law & Economics* 3 (1960): 75, 77.

166. There was no clearer expression of this insight than Herbert Croly's observation about the significance of Mark Hanna's rise of prominence in the Republican Party: "In one way or another every kind of business was obtaining state aid, and was dependent upon state policy for its prosperity. At the very moment when both business and politics were being modified by specialization and organization, business itself was being fastened to politics." Herbert Croly, *Marcus Alonzo Hanna: His Life and Work* (New York: Macmillan, 1912), 469.

167. On the expertise model of legal regulation, see Gerald R. Frug, "The Ideology of Bureaucracy in American Law," *Harvard Law Review* 97 (1984): 1276, 1318–34.

168. On the Realists and Progressives' contributions to the regulatory state, see Horwitz, *Transformation of American Law, 1870–1960*, 213–46. On the rise of the regulatory state generally, see Thomas K. McCraw, *Prophets of Regulation* (Cambridge: Harvard University Press, 1984).

169. William H. Simon, "Contract versus Politics in Corporate Doctrine," in *The Politics of Law*, rev. ed., edited by David Kairys (New York: Pantheon, 1990), 387, 395.

Chapter Twelve

1. Myres S. McDougal and David Haber, *Property, Wealth, Land: Allocation, Planning and Development* (Charlottesville, Va.: Michie, 1948), 1.

2. See generally Robert S. McElvaine, *The Great Depression: America, 1929–1941* (New York: Times Books, 1993), 224–49.

3. See Nelson Lichtenstein, "From Corporatism to Collective Bargaining: Organized Labor and the Eclipse of Social Democracy in the Postwar Era," in *The Rise and*

Fall of the New Deal Order, 1930–1980, ed. Steve Fraser and Gary Gerstle (Princeton: Princeton University Press, 1989), 12.

4. Ibid., 126.

5. Quoted in Walter I. Trattner, *From Poor Law to Welfare State: A History of Social Welfare in America,* 5th ed. (New York: Free Press, 1994), 68.

6. Ibid., 51.

7. Francis Walker, "The Causes of Poverty," *Century* 55 (1897): 210, 216. On nineteenth-century pseudo-scientific theories of poverty, see John S. Haller, Jr., *Outcasts from Evolution: Scientific Attitudes of Racial Inferiority, 1859–1900* (Urbana: University of Illinois Press, 1971); Mark Haller, *Eugenics: Hereditarian Attitudes in American Thought* (New Brunswick, N.J.: Rutgers University Press, 1963).

8. See Roy Lubove, *The Professional Altruist: The Emergence of Social Work as a Career, 1880–1930* (Cambridge: Harvard University Press, 1965).

9. On the gospel of prevention, see James T. Patterson, *America's Struggle against Poverty, 1900–1980* (Cambridge: Harvard University Press, 1981), 20–34.

10. Ibid., 29.

11. Ibid.

12. Ibid.

13. See Trattner, *From Poor Law to Welfare State,* 223–27.

14. On the limited purposes and effects of the New Deal, see Paul K. Conkin, *FDR and the Origins of the Welfare State* (New York: Thomas Y. Crowell, 1967).

15. Even within the New Deal, the new premise took hold only gradually. In Roosevelt's first term, the reigning assumption remained that the federal government was responsible only for its citizens residual needs. See Patterson, *America's Struggle against Poverty,* 60.

16. Alan Brinkley, "The New Deal and the Idea of the State," in Fraser and Gerstle, *Rise and Fall of the New Deal Order,* 85, 86.

17. See Patterson, *America's Struggle against Poverty,* 56–77.

18. See ibid., 76.

19. See William H. Simon, "The Invention and Reinvention of Welfare Rights," *Maryland Law Review* 44 (1985): 1, 2.

20. Charlotte Towle, *Common Human Needs: An Interpretation for Staff in Public Assistance Agencies* (Washington, D.C., 1945), 56 (emphasis in original). For a lucid discussion of this school of social work thought, see Simon, "The Invention and Reinvention of Welfare Rights," 2–14.

21. Simon, "The Invention and Reinvention of Welfare Rights," 5.

22. Public Law No. 271, §§2(a)(4), 402(a)(4), 49 Stat. 620, 627, 645 (1935).

23. See Trattner, *From Poor Law to Welfare State,* 308; Patterson, *America's Struggle against Poverty,* 78.

24. The federal programs created between 1941 and 1960 included the G.I. Bill of Rights (1944), the National Mental Health Act (1946), the National School Lunch

Program (1946), the Full Employment Act (1946), the Housing Act of 1949, the School Milk Program (1954), and the Vocational Rehabilitation Act (1954). Trattner, *From Poor Laws to Welfare State,* 313.

25. Patterson, *America's Struggle against Poverty,* 85–94.

26. See Trattner, *From Poor Law to Welfare State,* 309–10.

27. John Kenneth Galbraith, *The Affluent Society* (Boston: Houghton Mifflin, 1958).

28. For a discussion of the structuralist analysis of poverty, see Patterson, *America's Struggle against Poverty,* 94–96.

29. See Richard Polenberg, *One Nation Divisible: Class, Race, and Ethnicity in the United States since 1938* (New York: Penguin Books, 1980).

30. Robert Nisbet, "The Decline and Fall of Social Class," *Pacific History Review* 2 (1959): 11.

31. Patterson, *America's Struggle against Poverty,* 84.

32. Ibid., 99–114.

33. On the great northern migration, see Nicholas Lemann, *The Promised Land* (New York: Knopf, 1991).

34. See Trattner, *From Poor Law to Welfare State,* 314–16.

35. Frances F. Piven and Richard A. Cloward, *Regulating the Poor: The Functions of Public Welfare* (New York: Random House, 1971), 196–97.

36. See Frances F. Piven and Richard A. Cloward, "Reaffirming the Regulation of the Poor," *Social Service Review* 48 (1974): 147.

37. The number of people receiving public assistance doubled between 1960 and 1970, and the total expenditures increased from approximately $3 billion to more than $6 billion in the same period. See Trattner, *From Poor Law to Welfare State,* 315.

38. Michael Harrington, *The Other America: Poverty in the United States* (New York: Macmillan, 1962), 3.

39. Patterson, *America's Struggle against Poverty,* 99.

40. The Social Services Amendments increased (from 50 to 75 percent of the cost) federal support to states for direct services to public assistance recipients. See Trattner, *From Poor Law to Welfare State,* 321.

41. Of the $962.5 million in total funding for the first year, $462.5 million came from elsewhere in the budget. Patterson, *America's Struggle against Poverty,* 141.

42. Sar A. Levitan, *The Great Society's Poor Law: A New Approach to Poverty* (Baltimore: Johns Hopkins University Press, 1969), ix.

43. See Patterson, *America's Struggle against Poverty,* 137.

44. Ibid., 164.

45. Ibid., 167.

46. Quoted in ibid.

47. Harry W. Jones, "The Rule of Law and the Welfare State," *Columbia Law Review* 58 (1958): 143, 144.

48. See Gabriel Kolko, *Main Currents in Modern American History* (New York: Pantheon, 1984), 144.

49. Brinkley, "The New Deal," 94.

50. On the Wagner Act and its judicial defanging, see Karl E. Klare, "Judicial Deradicalization of the Wagner Act and the Origins of Modern Legal Consciousness, 1937–1941," *Minnesota Law Review* 62 (1978): 265.

51. For overviews of these changes, see Mary Ann Glendon, "The Transformation of American Landlord-Tenant Law," *Boston College Law Review* 23 (1982): 503; Charles Donahue, "Change in the American Law of Landlord and Tenant," *Modern Law Review* 37 (1974): 242.

52. The current version of the Act is 42 U.S.C. §§3601–3619, 3631 (1988).

53. *Grundgesetz* (BRD) Article 14(2).

54. See Edward H. Rabin, "The Revolution in Residential Landlord-Tenant Law: Causes and Consequences," *Cornell Law Review* 69 (1984): 517.

55. For powerful expressions of the perception of housing as noncommodity, see Margaret Jane Radin, "Residential Rent Control," *Philosophy & Public Affairs* 15 (1986): 350; William H. Simon, "Social-Republican Property," *UCLA Law Review* 38 (1991): 1335, 1356–68.

56. Radin, "Residential Rent Control," 365.

57. Friedrich A. Hayek, *The Road to Serfdom* (1944; reprint, Chicago: University of Chicago Press, 1976), viii.

58. Ibid., iii.

59. Ibid., viii.

60. Ibid., 72.

61. Ibid., 72–73.

62. Ibid., 73.

63. Ibid., 74.

64. See chapter 9.

65. Hayek, *The Road to Serfdom*, 74.

66. Ibid., 79.

67. Albert V. Dicey, *Lectures on the Relation between Law and Public Opinion in England during the Nineteenth Century* (New York: Macmillan, 1905).

68. Albert V. Dicey, *Introduction to the Study of the Law of the Constitution* (New York: Macmillan, 1885).

69. See Richard A. Cosgrove, *The Rule of Law: Albert Venn Dicey, Victorian Jurist* (Chapel Hill: University of North Carolina Press, 1980), 94.

70. On the debate between Austrian economics and socialists regarding central planning, see Don Lavoie, *Rivalry and Central Planning: The Socialist Calculation Debate Reconsidered* (New York: Cambridge University Press, 1985).

71. Hayek, *The Road to Serfdom*, 76–77.

72. See Edmund W. Kitch, ed., "The Fire of Truth: A Remembrance of Law

and Economics at Chicago, 1932–1970," *Journal of Law & Economics* 26 (1983): 163, 185–86.

73. Ibid., 187, 189.

74. See ibid., 180–81.

75. Edward H. Levi, "Aaron Director and the Study of Law and Economics," *Journal of Law & Economics* 9 (1966): 3.

76. Jones, "The Rule of Law," 143, 151.

77. Charles A. Reich, "The New Property," *Yale Law Journal* 73 (1964): 733.

78. Charles A. Reich, "The New Property after 25 Years," *University of San Francisco Law Review* 24 (1990): 223, 224.

79. Ibid., 223.

80. Flemming v. Nestor, 363 U.S. 603 (1960).

81. See Reich, "The New Property," 761–62.

82. In re Anastaplo, 366 U.S. 82 (1961).

83. See Lillian Hellman, *Scoundrel Time* (Boston: Little, Brown, 1976).

84. Robert L. Rabin, "The Administrative State and Its Excesses: Reflections on *The New Property*," *University of San Francisco Law Review* 24 (1990): 273, 277 (footnote omitted).

85. 363 U.S. 603 (1960).

86. Reich, "The New Property," 769.

87. Ibid., 769–70 (footnote omitted).

88. Ibid., 765.

89. Ibid., 771.

90. See Simon, "The Invention and Reinvention of Welfare Rights," 25.

91. Reich, "The New Property," 785.

92. See Martha F. Davis, *Brutal Need: Lawyers and the Welfare Rights Movement, 1960–1973* (New Haven: Yale University Press, 1993), 86.

93. See, e.g., Jacobus tenBroek, "California's Dual System of Family Law: Its Origin, Development, and Present Status," pts. 1 and 2, *Stanford Law Review* 16 (1964): 257, 900; pt. 3, *Stanford Law Review* 17 (1965): 614.

94. See, e.g., Joel Handler, "Controlling Official Behavior in Welfare Administration," *California Law Review* 54 (1966): 479.

95. See, e.g., Daniel Mandelker, "Exclusion and Removal Legislation," *Wisconsin Law Review* 1956:57.

96. Davis, *Brutal Need,* 22.

97. Sparer later became a professor of law at the University of Pennsylvania, where he continued to work and write on behalf of welfare rights issues. His important role in the welfare rights social movement is carefully chronicled in Davis, *Brutal Need.*

98. See Edward V. Sparer, "The New Legal Aid as an Instrument of Social Change," *University of Illinois Law Forum* (1965): 59; "The Role of the Welfare Client's Lawyer," *UCLA Law Review* 12 (1965): 366; "Social Welfare Law Testing," *Practicing Lawyer* 12

(1966): 13; "The Right to Welfare," in *The Rights of Americans,* ed. Norman Dorsen (New York: Pantheon, 1971), 65.

99. In an article published shortly after his untimely death, Sparer stated that while his early writing "might appear to lend credence to [Reich's] approach," he in fact was "trying to build a legal involvement which . . . would follow a different approach." Ed Sparer, "Fundamental Human Rights, Legal Entitlements, and the Social Struggle: A Friendly Critique of the Critical Legal Studies Movement," *Stanford Law Review* 36 (1984): 509.

100. Davis, *Brutal Need,* 104.

101. King v. Smith, 392 U.S. 309 (1968); Shapiro v. Thompson, 394 U.S. 618 (1969); Goldberg v. Kelly, 397 U.S. 254 (1970).

102. 397 U.S. 254 (1970).

103. The facts are drawn from the account in Davis, *Brutal Need,* 87–98.

104. William H. Simon, "Legality, Bureaucracy, and Class in the Welfare System," *Yale Law Journal* 92 (1983): 1198, 1199.

105. 397 U.S. at 262.

106. Id. at 262n. 8.

107. Id. at 265.

108. Indeed, an earlier draft of Brennan's opinion explicitly put that question aside. See Davis, *Brutal Need,* 113.

109. 397 U.S. 471 (1970).

110. Id. at 487.

Further sealing the fate of a need-based welfare jurisprudence was the Court's decision the same term in Rosado v. Wyman, 397 U.S. 397 (1970). That case gave the Court an opportunity to interpret a 1969 amendment to the AFDC title of the Social Security Act as requiring increases in benefits proportionate with increases in the cost of living. The Court chose, however, to interpret the amendment as requiring only an adjustment in the need standard according to cost-of-living increases with states retaining discretion over how much of the increased need to cover. See William H. Simon, "Rights and Redistribution in the Welfare State," *Stanford Law Review* 38 (1986): 1431, 1489–92.

111. See Simon, "Legality, Bureaucracy, and Class in the Welfare System," 1201–6.

112. Ibid., 1215.

113. Sparer, "Fundamental Human Rights, Legal Entitlements, and the Social Struggle," 561–62.

114. Frank I. Michelman, "Possession vs. Distribution in the Constitutional Idea of Property," *Iowa Law Review* 72 (1987): 1319.

115. C. B. Macpherson, *The Political Theory of Possessive Individualism* (New York: Oxford University Press, 1962).

116. See, e.g., Rand E. Rosenblatt, "Social Duties and the Problem of Rights in

the American Welfare State," in *The Politics of Law*, rev. ed., edited by David Kairys (New York: Pantheon, 1990), 90, 103.

117. See Simon, "The Invention and Reinvention of Welfare Rights," 31–33. Simon elsewhere speculates, plausibly enough, that Reich failed to consider the distributive aspects of his theory because the inflationary public finance policies that characterized the time at which he wrote he articles obscured the redistributive consequences of welfare. The redistributive effects became apparent later, in the late 1970s—the "zero sum" society rather than the Great Society—when welfare programs were financed through taxation. Simon, "Rights and Redistribution," 1488.

118. Simon, "The Invention and Reinvention of Welfare Rights," 31.

119. Reich, "The New Property," 785–86 (footnote omitted).

120. See Gordon S. Wood, *The Creation of the American Republic, 1776–1787* (New York: W. W. Norton, 1969), 68.

121. See ibid., 69.

122. See Carol M. Rose, "'Takings' and the Practices of Property: Property as Wealth, Property as 'Propriety,'" in *Property and Persuasion: Essays on the History, Theory, and Rhetoric of Ownership* (Boulder, Colo.: Westview Press, 1994), 238.

123. See Eric Foner, *Politics and Ideology in the Age of the Civil War* (New York: Oxford University Press, 1980), 128–49.

124. See Akhil Amar, "Republicanism and Minimum Entitlements: Of Safety Valves and the Safety Net," *George Mason University Law Review* 11 (1988): 47, 49; "Forty Acres and a Mule: A Republican Theory of Minimal Entitlements," *Harvard Journal of Law & Public Policy* 13 (1990): 37.

125. Amar, "Forty Acres and a Mule," 41.

126. Ibid., 42.

There is, of course, another way of looking at the whole question. A very different cultural outlook on welfare, citizenship, and self-sufficiency is suggested by the following exchange from Barbara Kingsolver's wonderful recent novel, *Pigs in Heaven*. The speaker is Annawake Fourkiller, a Cherokee lawyer living on a reservation in Oklahoma. She is talking about Boma, "the town lunatic":

> "One time in law school we were studying the concept of so-called irresponsible dependents. That a ward of society can't be a true citizen. I wanted to stand up and tell the class about Boma and the bottle tree. That there's another way of looking at it."
> "What's that?"
> "Just that you could love your crazy people, even admire them, instead of resenting that they're not self-sufficient."

Barbara Kingsolver, *Pigs in Heaven* (New York: HarperCollins, 1993), 231.

127. See, e.g., Cass R. Sunstein, "Beyond the Republican Revival," *Yale Law Journal* 97 (1988): 1539; Frank I. Michelman, "Law's Republic," *Yale Law Journal* 97 (1988): 1493; Frank I. Michelman, "Republican Property" (1989); Joel F. Handler, "Dependent

People, the State, and the Modern/Postmodern Search for the Dialogic Community," *UCLA Law Review* 35 (1988): 999.

Epilogue

1. Harold Demsetz, "Toward a Theory of Property Rights," *American Economic Review* 57 (papers and proceedings 1967): 347.

2. Richard A. Posner, *Economic Analysis of Law*, 2d ed. (Boston: Little, Brown, 1977), 29.

3. An early and influential example of this tendency is Guido Calabresi and A. Douglas Melamed, "Property Rules, Liability Rules, and Inalienability: One View of the Cathedral," *Harvard Law Review* 85 (1972): 1089.

4. Thomas C. Grey, "The Disintegration of Property," in *Nomos XXII: Property*, ed. J. Roland Pennock and John W. Chapman (New York: New York University Press, 1979), 69, 71.

5. Ibid (footnote omitted).

6. See, e.g., J. Robert S. Prichard, "A Market for Babies?" *University of Toronto Law Journal* 34 (1984): 341.

7. See, e.g., James Buchanan and Gordon Tullock, *The Calculus of Consent* (Ann Arbor: University of Michigan Press, 1974).

8. See Posner, *Economic Analysis of Law*, 26, 244.

9. See chapter 11.

10. Bruce A. Ackerman, *Private Property and the Constitution* (New Haven: Yale University Press, 1977), 28.

11. See Calabresi and Melamed, "Property Rules, Liability Rules, and Inalienability," 1089–90.

12. See Edward A. Purcell, Jr., *The Crisis of Democratic Theory: Scientific Naturalism and the Problem of Value* (Lexington: University of Kentucky Press, 1973).

13. See ibid., 159–78.

14. See remarks of Milton R. Friedman in Edmund W. Kitch, ed., "The Fire of Truth: A Remembrance of Law and Economics at Chicago, 1932–1970," *Journal of Law & Economics* 26 (1983): 163, 176.

15. Calabresi and Melamed, "Property Rules, Liability Rules, and Inalienability," 1112.

16. Albert O. Hirschman, *Shifting Involvements: Private Interest and Public Action* (Princeton: Princeton University Press, 1982).

17. See, e.g., Charles Murray, *Losing Ground: American Social Policy. 1950–1980* (New York: Basic Books, 1984); George Gilder, *Wealth and Poverty* (New York: Basic Books, 1981); Martin Anderson, *Welfare: The Political Economy of Welfare Reform in the United States* (Stanford: Hoover Institution, 1978).

18. See Walter I. Trattner, *From Poor Law to Welfare State: A History of Social Welfare in America,* 5th ed. (New York: Free Press, 1994), 362.

19. For a somewhat parallel analysis, see Robert N. Bellah, Richard Madsen, Wil-

liam M. Sullivan, Ann Swidler, and Steven M. Tipton, *The Good Society* (New York: Alfred A. Knopf, 1991), 90–91.

20. Ronald Reagan, press conference, 1983, quoted in Jennifer L. Hochschild, "The Double-Edged Sword of Equal Opportunity," in *Power Inequality and Democratic Politics: Essays in Honor of Robert A. Dahl,* ed. Ian Shapiro and Grant Reeher (Boulder, Colo.: Westview Press, 1988), 168.

21. Michael Piore and Charles Sabel, *The Second Industrial Divide: Possibilities for Prosperity* (New York: Basic Books, 1985).

22. Fred Block, *Post-Industrial Possibilities: A Critique of Economic Discourse* (Berkeley and Los Angeles: University of California Press, 1990).

23. See, e.g., Margaret Jane Radin, "Market-Inalienability," *Harvard Law Review* 100 (1987): 1849; "Justice and the Market Domain," in *Nomos XXXI: Markets and Justice,* ed. John W. Chapman and J. Roland Pennock (New York: New York University Press, 1989), 165.

24. See, e.g., William H. Simon, "Social-Republican Property," *UCLA Law Review* 38 (1991): 1335.

25. See, e.g., Joseph Singer, "The Reliance Interest in Property," *Stanford Law Review* 40 (1988): 611.

26. See, e.g., Frank I. Michelman, "Possession vs. Distribution in the Constitutional Idea of Property," *Iowa Law Review* 72 (1987): 1319.

27. See, e.g., Duncan Kennedy, "Neither the Market nor the State: Housing Privatization Issues," in *A Fourth Way? Privatization, Property, and the Emergence of New Market Economies,* ed. Gregory S. Alexander and Grazyna Skapska (New York: Routledge, 1994), 253.

Index

theory of property as coercive power, 335–37
on the unscientific character of rate regula-
tion, 331
See also Economics, institutional
Hale, Sir Matthew, 46, 47, 61
Hamilton, Alexander, 13, 23, 71, 72, 189
as favoring commodified property, 73–78
influence on James Kent, 134–35
plan for funding the public debt, 70–71
Report on Manufactures, 76, 77
Report on the Public Credit, 76, 77
Hamilton, Walton, 347
Hammond, James Henry, 212, 218
Letter to an English Abolitionist, 212, 216
Handler, Joel, 371
Harlan, Justice John M., 269–70
Harper, William, 212
Harrington, James
on the agrarian law, 37
on the balance of power, 36–37, 40–41
on liberty, 3
on primogeniture and entails, 39
Harrington, Michael
The Other America, 358
Hartog, Hendrik, 10, 162
Hartz, Louis, 6, 51
Harvard Law Review, 244, 305
Harvard Law School, 243, 244, 284, 286, 305
Hayek, Friedrich
attack on the welfare state, 363–68
conception of the rule of law, 364–66
influence at the University of Chicago, 367
influence of his work in the United States,
367–68
preference-satisfaction on the sole function
of property, 366–67
rejecting Dicey's views, 365–66
rejection of substantive equality, 364–65
The Road to Serfdom, 363
views as resembling those of Stephen J.
Field, 364
See also Rule of Law; Welfare state
Haymarket Square riot, 267
Herttell, Thomas, 170–72, 177
Hierarchy, social, 4, 36–37
within the family, 159, 160–61, 178, 300
in married women's property law, 161–62,
170, 171, 173–74, 176

in nineteenth-century slavery thought, 214,
215, 217, 219–26, 228
post-1870 changes in, 255–56
spendthrift trust linked with, 294–95
as symbolized by feudalism, 44
See also Privilege; Patriarchy; Technicality
Hirschman, Albert O.
theory of shifting involvements, 383
Historical explanations
idealism vs. materialism, 8
Historicism, in republican thought, 57–60
History
cyclical theory of, 47–48, 55, 58, 63, 144
linear theory of, 47–48, 55, 63–66, 144–45
seen as directional, 11
viewed as a legal problem, 43–46
Whig theory of, 45–48
Hobbes, Thomas, 72, 74
Hoebel, E. Adamson, 307
Hofstadter, Richard, 280
Hohfeld, Wesley N., 312, 313, 319–23, 325,
346
emphasizing nonphysicalist conception of
ownership, 322–23
influence on Arthur L. Corbin, 320–21
as not introducing "bundles of rights" metaphor, 319, 322
rejecting deductive solutions about property, 323
rejection of the Blackstonian conception of
ownership, 321, 325
on the relational aspect of ownership,
321–23
status as a Legal Realist contested, 319
theory of legal rights as jural relations,
320–21
Hollinger, David, 340
Holmes, Justice Oliver Wendell, 286, 305
defense of great wealth, 283–84
dissent in *Lochner*, 252
dissent in *Vegelahn v. Guntner*, 252
essay on the British gas-stokers' strike, 251
regarding consumption as more important
than ownership, 284–85
as a Social Darwinist, 251–52, 284
views on the predicament of power, 251–
52
Horwitz, Morton, 249, 312

Predicament of independence, 359, 368, 373–77. *See also* Welfare state
Predicament of modernity, 8, 14, 59, 131
changes in, 14–15
Predicament of power
in the late nineteenth century, 251–54, 255–56, 257, 263
as not confined to the commodity conception alone, 337–40
in Progressive-Realist legal thought, 312, 333, 335, 337, 350
Predicament of time and property, 55–60
Primogeniture, 37–41, 81, 82, 85
abolition of, 34, 56, 59
Privilege, 186, 206, 207, 294
progress, social
relationship to modernity, 10–11
Progressive era, 5, 306, 308
conventionally defined, 311
rise of the regulatory state, 314–15
reforms during, 314–15
social and economic changes during, 313–15
Progressive historiography, 248, 249
Progressive political economics
differences with classical economics, 317–19
emphasis on empiricism, 317–18
influence of German historical school on, 317
value-neutrality of, 318
Progressives, 248, 249, 259, 308, 319, 325, 340
as laying the foundation for the regulatory state, 334
as liberal reformers, 314
Progressivism
as a liberal ideology, 314
relationship with Legal Realism, 311–12
value-neutrality of, 318
Promethean figure, 11, 145
property
Blackstonian conception of, 68, 69, 87, 138–41, 311, 325, 330
"bundle of rights" conception of: as congenial to economic analysis, 381; origins of, 319, 322

classical conception of attacked in Progressive-Realist thought, 311–13, 325, 340–41, 344, 347
commodity theory of, 1
constitutional meaning of, 253, 259–61
constitutional protection of, 194, 248, 249, 266, 275–76
as a cultural symbol, 16–17, 139
distinguished from "entitlement," 380
economic function of, 379–80
effect of welfare state on idea of, 360–63
exchange-value conception of, 259–61, 329–31
family, 12, 301, 298, 301, 302
imaginary, 69–71
in rem/in personam distinction, 245
Lockean conception of, 27, 41
marital, 160–68, 169–70. *See also* Coverture; Curtesy; Dower; Equitable estate; Married women, status of as owners in nineteenth-century law; Married women's property acts
as market commodity, 1, 5
marketability of, 12, 143–48
mediating role of, 328
nonphysicalist conception of, 322–23
physicalist conception of, 259–60, 322
post–World War II institutional changes in, 359–60
propriety theory of, 1–2. *See also* Propriety conception
real/personal distinction, 141–42
Realist critique of Blackstonian conception accepted, 381
as relational, 320–23, 325–29, 340–42
relationship to power, 312, 330, 335–40
relationship to time in republican thought, 55–60
republican as hierarchical, 5, 36–37
seen as having one purpose, 1, 6–7
social aspect of, 313, 320–22, 323, 325–29, 341–42, 346–50
as sovereignty, 340–42
takings of, 12, 260–61, 322–23
tradition of, 1
welfare benefits as, 353, 359, 370–73
Proprietas, 237, 238